A PRACTICAL GUIDE TO HUMAN RIGHTS LAW IN SCOTLAND

AUSTRALIA
LBC Information Services—Sydney

CANADA and USA
Carswell—Toronto

NEW ZEALAND
Brooker's—Auckland

SINGAPORE and MALAYSIA
Sweet and Maxwell Asia
Singapore and Kuala Lumpur

A PRACTICAL GUIDE TO HUMAN RIGHTS LAW IN SCOTLAND

General Editor

The Honourable Lord Reed

Contributors

Aidan O'Neill, Q.C.
Advocate
Professor Chris Gane,
University of Aberdeen
Dr Alastair Brown,
Solicior and Senior Procurator Fiscal Depute
Morag Wise,
Advocate
Dr Douglas Brodie,
University of Edinburgh
Kay Springham
Advocate
Brian Napier
Advocate and Member of English Bar
Scott Blair
Advocate

EDINBURGH
W. GREEN/Sweet & Maxwell
2001

Published in 2001 by W. Green & Son Ltd
21 Alva Street
Edinburgh EH2 4PS

Typeset by YHT Ltd
Ealing, London

Printed and bound in Great Britain by MPG Books
Bodmin, Cornwall

No natural forests were destroyed to make this product;
only farmed timber was used and replanted

A CIP catalogue record for this book is available from the British
Library

ISBN 0 414 01369 7

Chapter 1 © Aidan O'Neill 2001
Chapters 2–9 © W. Green & Son Ltd 2001

PREFACE

The thinking behind this book was to invite a number of contributors, having particular experience or expertise in different areas of Scots law, to consider the likely impact of the effect given to the European Convention on Human Rights by the Scotland Act 1998 and the Human Rights Act 1998. It was recognised from the outset that the content of the book would inevitably be to some extent speculative. In advance of authoritative guidance from the courts, however, it was felt that it would be helpful to practitioners to have an informed view of some of the possibilities and problems which incorporation of the Convention might create: this is a subject of considerable practical importance on which even preliminary thoughts are to be welcomed. As decisions have flooded out of the courts, particularly since 2 October 2000, it has become difficult to know when to bring the process of revisal of the various contributions to an end and to go to print. Inevitably, fresh decisions of significance are emerging every week, if not every day. The flood of new law has however merely increased the need for a review and analysis of developments to date, and a consideration of possible future developments.

Some important points have already become clear. One is that it is important to pay close attention to the terms of the domestic legislation giving effect to the Convention, as well as to the Convention jurisprudence created by the European Court of Human Rights. It is plainly necessary to be informed of the Strasbourg jurisprudence, and one of the purposes of this book is to relate that material to existing Scots law. It is however equally important to appreciate that some of the most difficult problems to have arisen since the coming into force of the 1998 legislation have concerned the effect of the statutory provisions: for example, the effect of the interpretative obligation created by section 3 of the Human Rights Act, and the consequence of defining the court as a "public authority" within the meaning of section 6.

The Convention itself is an unusual instrument in international law, and its specific features have been reflected in some of the difficulties which have been experienced by the domestic courts when they have tried to apply it. The Convention is, in the first place, precisely what its name would suggest: a European Convention, rather than a national human rights instrument. It created a European Court of Human Rights to interpret its provisions; and the decisions of that court in any individual case are binding upon the state in question. Moreover, that court can hear applications brought by individual citizens. Consequently, it is possible for a litigant who has been unsuccessful before the domestic courts to take his case to Strasbourg, and if he is successful there, the Government will be bound to apply the court's ruling. This unique aspect of the Convention formed the background to its incorporation into domestic law: "bringing rights home", as it was put. The Scotland Act incorporated the Convention so as to make it impossible, generally speaking, for the devolved institutions to contravene the Convention and thereby place the United Kingdom in breach of its international obligations. The Human Rights Act sought to enable domestic courts to apply the Convention, subject to respect for Parliamentary sovereignty, and so in most cases to afford redress for contraventions of the Convention at domestic level, obviating the need for any application to the Strasbourg institutions. Accordingly, although section 2 of the Human Rights Act merely requires the courts to "take into account" the jurisprudence of the European Court of Human Rights, that does not mean that the courts can adopt a "take it or leave it" attitude towards the judgments of the European Court. On the contrary, as Lord Slynn of Hadley observed in the recent *Alconbury*[1] case: "in the absence of some special circumstances it seems to me that the court should follow any clear and constant jurisprudence of the European Court of Human Rights". That has some particular implications. The first is that, because the Strasbourg Court reflects the standards prevailing amongst the Contracting States in interpreting the Convention for the benefit of all those states, it is sometimes necessary to know what the law and practice are in those states, or at least what the prevailing standard may be, in order to decide how the Convention should be interpreted, and whether a particular state of affairs is acceptable under the Convention. Obtaining information about prevailing European standards is however a matter of practical difficulty. The answer may lie partly in making greater use of the resources available in the universities, in particular the available expertise in comparative law: something which would indeed make sense in a much wider context than the Convention, given the growing influence of foreign law more generally, particularly via European Community law.

A related problem is that the Convention binds the state as a whole. Within the domestic context, on the other hand, the domestic legislation may require one to ask whether particular institutions of the state may be bound by a Convention provision to act in a particular way. This point has raised a particular difficulty in Scotland, because the prosecution service is a devolved

---

[1]   *R. v. Secretary of State for the Environment, Transport and the Regions, ex p. Alconbury Developments Limited,* May 9, 2001, House of Lords.

institution whereas the courts are not. Questions whether a devolved institution is acting compatibly with the Convention have to be raised under a procedure which involves the participation of the United Kingdom Government, and in which the final appeal lies, in criminal proceedings, to the Privy Council in London. On the other hand, if the question is whether the court is acting compatibly with the Convention in a criminal context, then the United Kingdom Government is not involved in the proceedings, and the final appeal lies to the High Court of Justiciary in Edinburgh. So if, for example, the prosecution want to lead evidence and it is argued by the defence that the admission of the evidence would contravene the Convention, then the procedure to be followed for deciding that question, and the court with the final jurisdiction to determine it, depend on whether the prosecutor's attempting to lead the evidence is regarded as incompatible with the Convention, or whether it is the court's decision to admit the evidence or not which alone gives rise to an issue under the Convention. Similar questions may arise under the Human Rights Act, in situations in which the court has to apply law which is incompatible with the Convention (for example because it is contained in an Act of the Westminster Parliament which cannot be interpreted compatibly with the Convention, or because the common law is so well settled that it cannot be rendered compatible with the Convention without amending legislation), and in which the question may arise whether a public authority which has invited the court to apply that law has *ipso facto* acted in a way which is incompatible with a Convention right.

One consequence of the incorporation of the Convention is that the citation of foreign judgments and of international law before our courts has ceased to be an exceptional occurrence. The Strasbourg case law, although extensive, is far from comprehensive; and its coverage of the sorts of problems which arise in a common law system is particularly incomplete. On a multitude of issues which arise day in day out in our criminal trials and civil proofs, and on the particular problems that arise from our particular constitutional and institutional arrangements, one will often find that there is no direct guidance available in the Strasbourg case law at all. One still has to look to it as the primary source of guidance, but trying to draw inferences, from a case concerned for example with the position of the *Procureur General* in the Belgian Cour de Cassation, and to apply its reasoning to a case concerned with the position of the clerk to the justices in the District Court, may be far from easy. So it has been natural to see whether assistance can be found in decisions of other courts of high authority dealing with similar problems in an analogous context: to see how the problem has been dealt with, for exwnple, in the Irish system under the Irish Constitution, or in the Canadian system under the Charter of Fundamental Rights and Freedoms, or in the New Zealand system under the Bill of Rights Act. Similarly, recourse has been had in some cases of that kind to a variety of international instruments for such guidance as they might offer as to the existence of any consensus, actual or emerging, as to how a problem ought to be addressed. At the same time, the decisions of our courts on human rights issues have been a matter of interest in other jurisdictions both within the United Kingdom and further afield. If the effect given to the Convention has tended to make Scots lawyers more outward looking, and has equally encouraged external observers to take a greater interest in Scots law, that can only be to the good.

An infinite variety of issues lie ahead for determination. The prospect is not however one which need alarm or dismay practitioners. Scottish lawyers have, on the whole, succeeded in coping with the challenge which the Convention has presented. Mistakes have of course been made: that much is inevitable when an entirely new and unfamiliar body of law suddenly has to be assimilated. Increasing familiarity has however resulted in increasing confidence and skill. Practitioners have become better able to identify issues where the Convention may have a real contribution to make. It has also become clearer, as time has gone on, that in most cases the existing law is likely to be Convention-compliant, and that reference to the Convention is unlikely to add anything of substance. The Convention has however already made a significant difference in a surprisingly wide range of areas of law: mention might be made of the law of privacy[2] the law of consumer credit,[3] mental health law,[4] contempt of court[5] and delay in bringing accused persons to trial.[6]

Unsurprisingly, the incorporation of the Convention has spawned a multitude of books on the subject. It is hoped that this book will make a particular contribution by focusing on different areas of practice and highlighting, in an accessible way, the key issues facing Scots lawyers.

Finally, it should be made clear that the book is a collection of contributed pieces from individual practitioners and academic lawyers. These were prepared individually, and each author should be regarded as responsible only for his or her own contribution.

---

[2] *Douglas v. Hello! Limited* [2001] 2 W.L.R. 992; *Venables v. News Group Newspapers Limited* [2001] 2 W.L.R. 1038.
[3] *Wilson v. First County Trust (No. 2)*, 2 May 2001, unreported, Court of Appeal.
[4] *R. (H) v. Mental Health Review Tribunal, North and East London Region*, 20 March 2001, unreported, Court of Appeal.
[5] *eg. Galbraith v. H.M. Advocate*, 2000 S.C.C.R. 935.
[6] *eg. Kane v. H.M. Advocate*, 4 May 2001, unreported, High Court of Justiciary.

CONTENTS

Page

Preface v
Table of Cases xi
Table of Statutes xxxv
Table of Statutory Instruments xliii
EC Treaties and Conventions xlv

1. The Human Rights Act and the Scotland Act—the
   New Constitutional Matrix 1
     by Aidan O'Neill, Q.C.
2. The Substantive Criminal Law 61
     by Professor Christopher Gane
3. Criminal Evidence and Procedure 93
     by Dr Alastair Brown
4. Sentencing and Prisoners' Rights 133
     by Professor Christopher Gane
5. Human Rights and Family Law 169
     by Morag Wise
6. Negligence and the Convention 213
     by Dr Douglas Brodie
7. Property Law 235
     by Kay Springham
8. Human Rights and Employment Law 277
     by Brian Napier
9. Public Law 313
     by Scott Blair

Index 409

TABLE OF CASES

A v. U.K. [1998] 2 F.L.R. 959; [1998] 3 F.C.R. 597 ...... 2.02, 2.04, 4.39, 5.20, 6.05
A (A Mental Patient) v. Scottish Ministers; D (A Mental Patient) v. Scottish
    Ministers; R (A Mental Patient) v. Scottish Ministers, 2001 S.C. 1;
    2000 S.L.T. 873 .... 1.05, 1.55, 7.30, 9.20, 9.21, 9.55, 9.56, 9.58, 9.67
A (Children) (Conjoined Twins: Medical Treatment) (No.1), Re; *sub nom.* A
    (Children) (Conjoined Twins: Surgical Separation), Re [2001] 2
    W.L.R. 480; [2000] 4 All E.R. 961 .... 5.10, 5.11
ADT v. U.K. [2000] 2 F.L.R. 697; 9 B.H.R.C. 112 .... 2.02, 2.28
Abbas v. Secretary of State for the Home Department, 1993 S.L.T. 502 ....   9.52
Abdadou v. Secretary of State for the Home Department, 1998 S.C. 504; 1999
    S.L.T. 229 ....   1.06
Abdulaziz v. U.K. (A/94); Cabales v. U.K. (9473/81); Balkandali v. U.K.
    (9474/81) (1985) 7 E.H.R.R. 471, ECHR; affirming in part (1984) 6
    E.H.R.R. 28 .... 6.06, 7.14
Adair v. McGarry; Byrne v. Advocate (H.M.), 1933 J.C. 72; 1933 S.L.T. 482   3.20
Adamson v. U.K. (42293/98), unreported, January 23, 1999 .... 4.08, 4.30
Advocate (H.M.) v. Burns, 2001 J.C. 1; 2000 S.L.T. 1242 .... 1.38, 1.45
Advocate (H.M.) v. Campbell, unreported, September 21, 1999 ....   3.09
Advocate (H.M.) v. Conlan, unreported, December, 1983 ....   2.21
Advocate (H.M.) v. Cunningham, 1939 J.C. 61; 1939 S.L.T. 401 ....   3.09
Advocate (H.M.) v. Dickson, 1997 S.C.C.R. 859 ....   9.72
Advocate (H.M.) v. Doherty, 1954 J.C. 1; 1954 S.L.T. 169 ....   2.05
Advocate (H.M.) v. DP and SM, unreported, February 16, 2001 ....   3.30
Advocate (H.M.) v. Duffy, 1983 S.L.T. 7; 1982 S.C.C.R. 182 ....   2.21
Advocate (H.M.) v. Fox, 1947 S.L.T. 52 ....   3.09
Advocate (H.M.) v. K, 1994 S.C.C.R. 499 ....   2.17
Advocate (H.M.) v. Little, 1999 S.L.T. 1145; 1999 S.C.C.R. 625 .... 1.31, 3.30-3.32
Advocate (H.M.) v. Martin, 1956 J.C. 1; 1956 S.L.T. 193 ....   2.21
Advocate (H.M.) v. McCawley (1959) S.C.C.R. (Supp.) 3 ....   2.16
Advocate (H.M.) v. McGlinchey, 2000 S.L.T. 995; 2000 S.C.C.R. 593 ......   3.30
Advocate (H.M.) v. McKenzie, 1969 J.C. 52; 1970 S.L.T. 81 ....   2.21
Advocate (H.M.) v. Montgomery (Amendment of Minute), 2000 J.C. 111;
    2000 S.L.T. 122 ....   8.06
Advocate (H.M.) v. Nulty, 2000 S.L.T. 528; 2000 S.C.C.R. 431 ....   3.40
Advocate (H.M.) v. Paxton, 1985 S.L.T. 96; 1984 S.C.C.R. 311 ....   2.21
Advocate (H.M.) v. RM, 1969 S.C. 52 ....   2.16
Advocate (H.M.) v. Robb, 2000 J.C. 127; 1999 S.C.C.R. 971 1.38, 3.09, 3.32
Advocate (H.M.) v. Scottish Media Newspapers Ltd, 2000 S.L.T. 331; 1999
    S.C.C.R. 599 .... 1.42, 3.34
Advocate (H.M.) v. Stuurman (Pre-trial), 1980 J.C. 111; 1980 S.L.T. 182 ..   1.04
Advocate (H.M.) v. Wilson, 1984 S.L.T. 117; 1983 S.C.C.R. 420 ....   2.21
Aggee v. U.K. (1976) 7 D.R. 164 ....   9.42
Agrotexim v. Greece (A/330) (1996) 21 E.H.R.R. 250 ....   9.21
Ahmad v. U.K. (8160/78) (1982) 4 E.H.R.R. 126 .... 8.01, 8.15
Ahmed v. U.K. [1999] I.R.L.R. 188; (2000) 29 E.H.R.R. 1 ....   8.03
Air Canada v. U.K. (A/316) (1995) 20 E.H.R.R. 150; *The Times*, May 13,
    1995 ....   9.32
Airey v. Ireland (No.1) (A/32) (1979-80) 2 E.H.R.R. 305 .... 9.43, 9.44

Albert v. Belgium (A/58); Le Compte v. Belgium (A/58) (1983) 5 E.H.R.R.
 533 .... 7.11, 9.43
Amministrazione delle Finanze dello Stato v. San Giorgio SpA (C199/82)
 [1983] E.C.R. 3595; [1985] 2 C.M.L.R. 658 .... 9.53
Amuur v. France (1996) 22 E.H.R.R. 533 .... 3.05
Anderson v. Scottish Ministers. *See* A (A Mental Patient) v. Scottish
 Ministers.
Anderson v. U.K., unreported, September 1, 1993 .... 4.40-4.42
Andersson v. Sweden (A/226) (1992) 14 E.H.R.R. 615 .... 5.14
Andrew v. Advocate (H.M.), 2000 S.L.T. 402; 1999 G.W.D. 32-1517 .... 3.01
Anisminic Ltd v. Foreign Compensation Commission (No.2) [1969] 2 A.C.
 147; [1969] 2 W.L.R. 163 .... 9.28, 9.53, 9.61
Anns v. Merton L.B.C.; *sub nom.* Anns v. Walcroft Property Co. Ltd [1978]
 A.C. 728; [1977] 2 W.L.R. 1024 .... 6.08
Antoniades v. Spain, 64 D.R. 232 .... 7.04
Application against Italy (10889/84) (1988) 56 D.R. 40 .... 3.23
Armstrong v. U.K., unreported, September 1, 1993 .... 4.42
Arrondelle v. U.K. (7889/77) (1983) 5 E.H.R.R. 118; [1982] J.P.L. 770 ..... 7.13
Arrowsmith v. U.K. (1981) 3 E.H.R.R. 218 .... 1.28
Arthur JS Hall and Co. v. Simons; Barratt v. Woolf Seddon; Cockbone v.
 Atkinson Dacre and Slack; Harris v. Scholfield Roberts and Hill; *sub
 nom.* Harris v. Scholfield Roberts and Hall; Barratt v. Ansell (t/a as
 Woolf Seddon) [2000] 3 W.L.R. 543; [2000] 3 All E.R. 673 .... 6.10, 6.12
Asch v. Austria (A/203A) (1993) 15 E.H.R.R. 597 .... 3.27, 3.40
Ashbridge Investments Ltd v. Minister of Housing and Local Government
 [1965] 1 W.L.R. 1320; [1965] 3 All E.R. 371 .... 7.25, 9.36
Ashingdane v. U.K. (A/93) (1985) 7 E.H.R.R. 528, ECHR; affirming (1982) 4
 E.H.R.R. 590 .... 4.17, 9.43
Ashley v. Rothesay Magistrates (1874) 1 R. 14; (1873) 11 M. 708 .... 9.70
Associated Newspapers Ltd v. U.K., unreported, November 30, 1994 .... 2.02
Associated Newspapers Ltd v. Wilson; Associated British Ports v. Palmer; *sub
 nom.* Wilson v. Associated Newspapers Ltd [1995] 2 A.C. 454; [1995] 2
 W.L.R. 354 .... 8.08
Associated Provincial Picture Houses Ltd v. Wednesbury Corp. [1948] 1 K.B.
 223; [1947] 2 All E.R. 680 .... 9.25-9.27, 9.31-9.35
Association of Optical Practitioners Ltd v. Secretary of State for Scotland,
 unreported, December 10, 1985 .... 9.20
Association X v. Sweden (1977) 9 D.R. 5 .... 8.08
Att.-Gen. v. Guardian Newspapers Ltd (No.1); Att.-Gen. v. Observer Ltd;
 Att.-Gen. v. Times Newspapers; *sub nom.* Spycatcher: Guardian/
 Observer Discharge [1987] 1 W.L.R. 1248; [1987] 3 All E.R. 316 .... 8.09
Att.-Gen. v. X [1992] 2 C.M.L.R. 277 .... 5.08
Att.-Gen. of Hong Kong v. Lee Kwong-Kut; Att.-Gen. of Hong Kong v. Lo
 Chak Man [1993] A.C. 951; [1993] 3 W.L.R. 329 .... 1.11, 9.55, 9.58
Att.-Gen. of the Gambia v. Momodou Jobe [1984] A.C. 689; [1984] 3 W.L.R.
 174 .... 1.11, 9.55
Aubrey Investments Ltd v. DSC (Realisations) Ltd (In Receivership), 1999
 S.C. 21; 2000 S.L.T. 183 .... 7.32, 7.33
Axen v. Germany (A/72) (1984) 6 E.H.R.R. 195 .... 3.29
Aydin v. Turkey (1998) 25 E.H.R.R. 251; 3 B.H.R.C. 300 .... 3.02, 3.16
Ayr Magistrates v. Secretary of State for Scotland, 1965 S.C. 394; 1966 S.L.T.
 16 .... 9.22
Ayuntamiento de M v. Spain (1991) 68 D.R. 209 .... 9.21
B (A Minor), Re [1990] 3 All E.R. 927 .... 5.09
B v. France (A/232-C) [1992] 2 F.L.R. 249; (1993) 16 E.H.R.R. 1 .... 1.26, 5.37
B v. Netherlands (1985) 43 D.R. 198 .... 9.41
B v. U.K. (A/121) (1988) 10 E.H.R.R. 87 .... 1.27
B v. U.K. [2000] 1 F.L.R. 1; [2000] 1 F.C.R. 289 .... 5.29
BBC, Petrs (No.1), 2000 J.C. 419; 2000 S.L.T. 845 .... 1.25

BBC, Petrs (No.2); *sub nom.* British Broadcasting Corp, Petrs (No.2); Petition
   (No.2) of BBC, 2000 J.C. 521; 2000 S.L.T. 860 ....1.25, 3.29
Bain v. Lady Seafield (1887) 14 R. 939 .... 9.70
Baker v. State of Vermont, unreported, December 20, 1999 .... 1.47
Balfour v. U.K. [1997] E.H.R.L.R. 665 .... 8.01, 8.24
Ballantyne v. U.K., unreported, April 12, 1991 .... 4.40
Balmer-Schafroth v. Switzerland (1998) 25 E.H.R.R. 598 .... 7.30
Banff Magistrates v. Ruthin Castle Ltd, 1944 S.L.T. 373 .... 7.35
Barbera v. Spain (A/146); Messegue v. Spain (A/146); Jabardo v. Spain (A/
   146) (1989) 11 E.H.R.R. 360 .... 3.35
Barrett v. Enfield L.B.C. [1999] 3 W.L.R. 79; [1999] 3 All E.R. 193 .... 6.05,
                                                                     6.07-6.09, 9.23
Barrs v. British Wool Marketing Board, 1957 S.C. 72; 1957 S.L.T. 153 ..... 9.50
Barty v. Hill, 1907 S.C.(J) 36 .... 2.21
Bates v. Lord Hailsham of St Marylebone [1972] 1 W.L.R. 1373; [1972] 3 All
   E.R. 1019 .... 9.63
Beaumartin v. France (A/296-B) (1995) 19 E.H.R.R. 485 .... 9.50
Beedell v. West Ferry Printers Ltd [2000] I.C.R. 1263; [2000] I.R.L.R. 650 . 8.22
Belgian Linguistic Case (No.2) (A/6) (1979-80) 1 E.H.R.R. 252 .... 5.21, 8.21
Belilos v. Switzerland (A/132) (1988) 10 E.H.R.R. 466; *The Times,* June 14,
   1988 .... 9.49
Bell v. Fiddes, 1996 S.L.T. 51 .... 9.17
Bellinger v. Bellinger, *The Times Law Reports,* November 22, 2000 .... 5.39
Benthem v. Netherlands (8848/80) (1986) 8 E.H.R.R. 1, ECHR; reversing
   (1984) 6 E.H.R.R. 283 .... 9.42, 9.49
Berry v. Berry (No.2), 1989 S.L.T. 292 .... 7.34
Bett v. Brown; *sub nom.* Bett v. Hamilton, 1998 J.C. 1; 1997 S.L.T. 1310 .. 2.21
Bett Properties v. Scottish Ministers, 2001 S.C. 238; 2000 G.W.D. 29-1160 1.51
Bett v. Hamilton. *See* Bett v. Brown.
Biggs v. Somerset CC [1996] 2 C.M.L.R. 292; [1996] I.C.R. 364 .... 1.22
Bilodeau v. Att.-Gen. of Manitoba [1986] 1 S.C.R. 449 .... 9.68
Birse v. Advocate (H.M.); *sub nom.* Birse v. MacNeill, 2000 J.C. 503; 2000
   S.L.T. 869 .... 3.13
Bivens v. Unknown Named Agents of Federal Bureaux of Narcotics, 403 U.S.
   388 (U.S.) 9.22
Black v. Carmichael; Carmichael v. Black, 1992 S.L.T. 897; 1992 S.C.C.R.
   709 .... 2.22, 2.23
Blair v. Lochaber D.C., 1995 S.L.T. 407; 1994 S.C.L.R. 1070 .... 9.08
Blythswood Investments (Scotland) Ltd v. Clydesdale Electrical Stores Ltd (in
   Receivership), 1995 S.L.T. 150; *The Times,* October 20, 1994 .... 7.33
Boddaert v. Belgium (1992) A235-D 3.32
Boddington v. British Transport Police [1999] 2 A.C. 143; [1998] 2 W.L.R.
   639 .... 9.18, 9.68
Bollan v. U.K., unreported, May 4, 2000 .... 4.39
Bonnechaux v. Switzerland, 18 D.R. 100 .... 4.36
Booker Aquaculture Ltd (t/a Marine Harvest McConnell) v. Secretary of
   State for Scotland (Judicial Review), 2000 S.C. 9; [2000] U.K.H.R.R.
   1 .... 1.25, 1.45, 7.29, 7.37
Boychuk v. HJ Symons Holdings [1977] I.R.L.R. 395 .... 8.20
Boyle (Peter) v. Advocate (H.M.), 1995 S.L.T. 162; *Scotsman,* January 12,
   1995 .... 3.19
Boyle v. Castlemilk East Housing Cooperative Ltd, 1998 S.L.T. 56; 1997
   Hous. L.R. 58 .... 9.08
Bozano v. France (A/111) (1987) 9 E.H.R.R. 297; *The Times,* January 7, 1987 4.17
Bradford v. McLeod, 1986 S.L.T. 244; 1985 S.C.C.R. 379 .... 3.34, 9.50
Brady v. U.K. (8575/79) (1981) 3 E.H.R.R. 297 .... 3.26
Bramelid v. Sweden (8588/79, 8589/79) (1983) 5 E.H.R.R. 249 .... 7.04
Brennan v. Advocate (H.M.), 1977 J.C. 38; 1977 S.L.T. 151 .... 2.26, 2.27
Brentnall v. Free Presbyterian Church of Scotland, 1986 S.L.T. 471 .... 9.08

Bricmont v. Belgium (A/158) (1990) 12 E.H.R.R. 217 .... 3.21
Brind v. Secretary of State for the Home Department. *See* R. v. Secretary of State for the Home Department, ex p. Brind.
British Railways Board v. Pickin; *sub nom.* Pickin v. British Railways Board [1974] A.C. 765; [1974] 2 W.L.R. 208 .... 9.61
Brock v. Hamilton (1857) 19 D. 701 .... 7.35
Brogan v. U.K. (A/145-B) (1989) 11 E.H.R.R. 117; *The Times*, November 30, 1988 .... 3.07
Bromley L.B.C. v. Greater London Council [1983] 1 A.C. 768; [1982] 2 W.L.R. 92 .... 9.29
Brown v. Executive Committee of the Edinburgh District Labour Party, 1995 S.L.T. 985 .... 9.08
Brown v. Hamilton D.C., 1983 S.C. (H.L.) 1; 1983 S.L.T. 397 .... 9.18
Brown v. Selfridge, 2000 J.C. 9; 2000 S.L.T. 437 .... 3.20
Brown v. Stott; *sub nom.* Stott (Procurator Fiscal) v. Brown; Procurator Fiscal, Dunfermline v. Brown; Brown v. Procurator Fiscal, Dunfermline, 2001 S.L.T. 59; 2000 G.W.D. 40-1513 .... 1.04, 1.05, 1.08, 1.09, 1.13, 1.32, 3.09, 3.10, 7.22, 7.33, 9.73
Brozicek v. Italy (A/167) (1990) 12 E.H.R.R. 371; *The Times*, January 3, 1990 3.24
Bruggemann v. Germany (6959/75); Scheuten v. Germany (1981) 3 E.H.R.R. 244 .... 5.07, 5.08
Bryan v. U.K. (A/335-A) (1996) 21 E.H.R.R. 342; [1996] 1 P.L.R. 47 .... 7.11, 7.17, 7.19, 7.20, 7.45, 9.32, 9.41, 9.43, 9.45, 9.49, 9.50
Buchanan v. McLean; *sub nom.* Procurator Fiscal v. McLean, 2000 S.L.T. 928; 2000 S.C.C.R. 682 .... 1.31, 3.39
Buchholz v. Germany (A/42) (1981) 3 E.H.R.R. 597 .... 9.47
Buckley v. U.K. (1997) 23 E.H.R.R. 101; [1997] 2 P.L.R. 10 .... 1.06, 7.13, 9.55, 9.56
Buitrago Montes and Perez Lopez v. U.K., unreported, December 2, 1992 .... 4.40, 4.42
Bullivant v. U.K., unreported, March 28, 2000 .... 4.25
Bulut v. Austria (1997) 24 E.H.R.R. 84 .... 9.50
Bunkate v. Netherlands (A/248-B) (1995) 19 E.H.R.R. 477 .... 5.27
Burmah Oil Co. (Burma Trading) Ltd v. Advocate (Lord); Burmah Oil Co. (Burma Concessions) v. Advocate (Lord); Burmah Oil Co. (Overseas) v. Advocate (Lord); Burmah Oil Co. (Pipe Lines) v. Advocate (Lord) [1965] A.C. 75; [1964] 2 W.L.R. 1231 .... 7.23, 9.38
Burn, Petr; McQuilken v. Procurator Fiscal; *sub nom.* Burn (Geoffrey Keith) v. Miller, 2000 J.C. 403; 2000 S.L.T. 538 .... 3.19
Burrett v. West Birmingham HA [1994] I.R.L.R. 7 .... 8.20
Burrows v. Burrows, 1996 S.C. 378; 1996 S.L.T. 1313 .... 7.34
Butt v. Secretary of State for the Home Department, unreported, March 15, 1995 .... 9.19
C (A Baby), Re [1996] 2 F.L.R. 43; [1996] 2 F.C.R. 569 .... 5.09
C (A Minor) (Wardship: Medical Treatment) (No.1), Re [1990] Fam. 26; [1989] 3 W.L.R. 240 .... 5.09
C and C v. S; *sub nom.* C, Petr; C v. S, 1996 S.L.T. 1387; 1996 S.C.L.R. 837 .... 5.03, 5.06
CC v. U.K. [1999] Crim. L.R. 228 .... 3.19
CILFIT Srl v. Ministro della Sanita (Minister of Health) (C-283/81) [1982] E.C.R. 3415; [1983] 1 C.M.L.R. 472 .... 1.34
CIN Properties Ltd v. Dollar Land (Cumbernauld) Ltd, 1992 S.L.T. 669; 1992 S.C.L.R. 820 .... 7.33
Cameron v. Normand, 1992 S.C.C.R. 866 .... 2.17
Campbell and Cosans v. U.K. (No.2) (A/48) (1982) 4 E.H.R.R. 293 .... 2.02, 3.17, 5.19, 5.21, 5.22, 9.21
Campbell and Fell v. U.K. (A/80) (1985) 7 E.H.R.R. 165, ECHR; affirming (1983) 5 E.H.R.R. 207 .... 3.29, 4.07, 4.45, 9.49-9.51
Canea Catholic Church v. Greece (1999) 27 E.H.R.R. 521 .... 1.25

Cantoni v. France, R.J.D. 1996-v, P.1682 .... 2.15
Caparo Industries Plc v. Dickman [1990] 2 A.C. 605; [1990] 2 W.L.R. 358 . 6.08-6.10
Carmichael v. Ashrif, 1985 S.C.C.R. 461 .... 2.17
Carr v. U.K. Central Council for Nursing, Midwifery and Health Visiting,
    1989 S.L.T. 580 .... 9.18
Carter v. U.K. (36417/97), unreported, June 29, 1999 .... 4.12
Castells v. Spain (A/236); *sub nom.* Castes v. Spain (1992) 14 E.H.R.R. 445;
    The Guardian, May 20, 1992 .... 2.13
Catamaran Cruisers Ltd v. Williams [1994] I.R.L.R. 386 .... 8.06
Central Canada Potash Co. v. Government of Saskatchewan [1979] 1 S.C.R.
    42 .... 9.68
Chahal v. U.K. (1997) 23 E.H.R.R. 413; 1 B.H.R.C. 405 .... 4.32, 9.49
Chappell v. U.K. (A/152) (1990) 12 E.H.R.R. 1; [1989] 1 F.S.R. 617 .... 2.11,
    2.12, 4.44-4.46
Chare v. France, 71 D.R. 141 .... 8.12
Chartier v. Italy, 33 D.R. 41 .... 4.36
Cheall v. Association of Professional, Executive, Clerical and Computer Staff
    (APEX) [1983] 2 A.C. 180; [1983] 2 W.L.R. 679 .... 8.05
Cheall v. U.K. [1985] 42 D.R. 178 .... 8.08
Chichlian v. France (A/162-B); *sub nom.* Ekindjian v. France (1991) 13
    E.H.R.R. 553 .... 3.22
Chicot County Drainage District v. Baxter State Bank, 308 U.S. 371 (1940) 9.68
Chief Adjudication Officer v. Foster [1993] A.C. 754; [1993] 2 W.L.R. 292 . 9.18
Chief Constable of West Yorkshire v. A [2001] I.C.R. 128; [2000] I.R.L.R. 465 8.24
Chinoy v. U.K. (15199/89), unreported, September 4, 1991 .... 3.11
Christians against Racism and Fascism v. U.K., 21 D.R. 148 ..... 2.02, 8.21
Chung Tak Lam v. Brennan (t/a Namesakes of Torbay); *sub nom.* Lam v.
    Torbay B.C.; R. v. Lam [1998] E.H.L.R. 111; [1997] P.I.Q.R. P488 . 6.06
City of Glasgow District Council v. Secretary of State for Scotland, 1980 S.C.
    150; 1982 S.L.T. 28 .... 9.45
Ciulla v. Italy (A/148) (1991) 13 E.H.R.R. 346 ....3.04, 3.07
Clancy v. Caird (No.1), 2000 S.C. 441; 2000 S.L.T. 546 ...... 1.28, 1.38, 1.42, 8.23,
    9.19/1, 9.50
Clark v. Advocate (H.M.), 1997 S.L.T. 1099; 1997 S.C.C.R. 416 .... 4.18
Clark v. Kelly, 2001 J.C. 16; 2000 S.L.T. 1038 .... 3.34
Clarke v. Bradlaugh (1884) 12 Q.B.D. 271 .... 9.07
Clayton v. Heffron (1960) 105 C.L.R. 214 .... 9.68
Clinton v. U.K., Committee of Ministers Resolution DH (95) 4, January 11,
    1995 .... 3.08
Cockenzie and Port Seton Community Council v. East Lothian D.C., 1997
    S.L.T. 81; 1996 S.C.L.R. 209 .... 9.20
Cocks v. Thanet D.C. [1983] 2 A.C. 286; [1982] 3 W.L.R. 1121 .... 1.17
Colhoun v. Friel, 1996 S.L.T. 1252; 1996 S.C.C.R. 497 .... 2.17
Commission for Local Authority Accounts in Scotland v. Grampian R.C.,
    1994 S.L.T. 1120 .... 9.30
Commission of the European Communities v. BASF (C137/92 P) [1994]
    E.C.R. I-2555; *The Times,* July 9, 1994 .... 9.68
Conway v. Secretary of State for Scotland, 1996 S.L.T. 689 .... 9.19/1
Corbett v. Corbett (otherwise Ashley) (No.1 [1971] P. 83; [1970] 2 W.L.R.
    1306 .... 5.36
Cormack v. Cope (1974) 131 C.L.R. 432 .... 9.63
Cossey v. U.K. (A/184); *sub nom.* C v. U.K. (A/184) [1991] 2 F.L.R. 492;
    [1993] 2 F.C.R. 97 .... 5.37
Costello-Roberts v. U.K. (A/247-C) [1994] 1 F.C.R. 65; (1995) 19 E.H.R.R.
    112 .... 5.20, 6.05, 9.10
Council for Civil Service Unions v. U.K. (1988) 10 E.H.R.R. 269 8.03, 9.21
Council of Civil Service Unions v. Minister for the Civil Service [1985] A.C.
    374; [1984] 1 W.L.R. 1174 .... 9.09, 9.25, 9.31

County Properties Ltd v. Scottish Ministers, 2000 S.L.T. 965; [2000] H.R.L.R.
    677 .... 1.25, 1.33, 1.42, 7.11, 7.17, 7.20, 7.26, 7.45, 9.19/1, 9.36, 9.43, 9.50
Cox Bros. v. Binning (1867) 6 M. 161 .... 9.70
Crake v. Supplementary Benefits Commission; Butterworth v. Supplementary
    Benefits Commission [1982] 1 All E.R. 498 .... 9.40, 9.45
Crawford v. Strathclyde R.C., 1999 Fam. L.R. 119 .... 5.23
Crociani, Palmiotti, Tanassi and Lefebre D'Ovidio v. Italy (1981) 22 D.R. 147   6.27
Croissant v. Germany (A/237B) (1993) 16 E.H.R.R. 135 .... 1.43, 3.39
Crooks v. Haddow, 2000 S.C.L.R. 755; 2000 G.W.D. 10-367 .... 6.07
Crummock (Scotland) Ltd v. Advocate (H.M.), 2000 J.C. 408; 2000 S.L.T.
    677 .... 3.32, 3.34
Cuddy Chicks Ltd v. Ontario Labour Relations Board [1991] 2 S.C.R. 5 ...   9.16
Currie v. McGlennan, 1989 S.L.T. 872; 1989 S.C.C.R. 466 .... 3.20
Cyprus v. Turkey (6780/74 and 6950/75) (1982) 4 E.H.R.R. 482 ....   7.13
D (An Infant) (Adoption: Parent's Consent), Re [1977] A.C. 602; [1977] 2
    W.L.R. 79 .... 5.33
D (Minors) (Adoption Reports: Confidentiality), Re [1996] A.C. 593; [1995] 3
    W.L.R. 483 .... 5.18
D v. U.K. (1997) 24 E.H.R.R. 423; 2 B.H.R.C. 273 .... 4.32, 6.05
D and J Nicol v. Dundee Harbour Trustees; *sub nom.* Dundee Harbour
    Trustees v. D and J Nicol [1915] A.C. 550; 1915 S.C. (H.L.) 7 ....   9.08,
                                                                             9.20
Darnell v. U.K. (A/272) (1994) 18 E.H.R.R. 205; *The Times,* November 24,
    1993 .... 8.04, 8.25
Davy v. Spelthorne B.C. [1984] A.C. 262; [1983] 3 W.L.R. 742 ....   1.17
De Cubber v. Belgium (Investigating Judge) (A/86) (1985) 7 E.H.R.R. 236   9.42
De Freitas v. Permanent Secretary of Ministry of Agriculture, Fisheries,
    Lands and Housing [1999] 1 A.C. 69; [1998] 3 W.L.R. 675 .... 9.34, 9.38
De Geouffre de la Pradelle v. France (A/253B) 7.12, 9.43
De Haan v. Netherlands (1998) 26 E.H.R.R. 417 .... 9.50
De Jong v. Netherlands (A/77) (1986) 8 E.H.R.R. 20 .... 3.07
De Lille v. Speaker of the National Asembly, 1998 S.A. 430 .... 9.61
De Wilde v. Belgium (No.1) (A/12) (1979-80) 1 E.H.R.R. 373 .... 1.28
Delazarus v. U.K., unreported, February 16, 1993 .... 4.35
Delcourt v. Belgium (1867) 10 Y.B. 238 .... 3.08
Delcourt v. Belgium (A/11) (1979-80) 1 E.H.R.R. 355 .... 9.52
Demetriades v. Glasgow Corp. [1951] 1 All E.R. 457; 1951 S.L.T. (Notes) 18   9.30
Deumeland v. Germany (A/120) (1986) 8 E.H.R.R. 448 .... 9.41
Deweer v. Belgium (A/35); *sub nom.* De Weer v. Belgium [1980] E.C.C. 169;
    (1979-80) 2 E.H.R.R. 439 .... 1.28, 4.31
Dhoest v. Belgium, unreported, May 14, 1987 .... 4.25, 4.35
Diennet v. France (A/315-B) (1996) 21 E.H.R.R. 554 .... 9.41, 9.46
Dikme v. Turkey (20869/92), unreported, July 11, 2000 .... 3.08
Dillon v. Secretary of State for the Home Department, 1997 S.L.T. 842; 1996
    G.W.D. 38-2229 .... 9.45
Director General of Fair Trading v. Proprietary Association of Great Britain;
    sub nom. Medicaments and Related Classes of Goods (No.2), Re
    (2001) 98(7) L.S.G. 40; (2001) 151 N.L.J. 17 .... 8.07
DPP v. Hutchinson; DPP v. Smith (Georgina); *sub nom.* R. v. Secretary of
    State for Defence, ex p. Parker; R. v. Secretary of State for Defence, ex
    p. Hayman [1990] 2 A.C. 783; [1990] 3 W.L.R. 196 .... 9.70
DPP v. Majewski; *sub nom.* R. v. Majewski [1977] A.C. 443; [1976] 2 W.L.R.
    623 .... 2.26
DPP v. Marshall; *sub nom.* Mills v. Marshall [1998] I.C.R. 518; [1998]
    I.R.L.R. 494 .... 1.22, 9.19/1
Docherty v. Advocate (H.M.), unreported, January 14, 2000 .... 3.32
Dombo Beheer BV v. Netherlands (A/274-A) (1994) 18 E.H.R.R. 213 ... 3.20, 9.44
Donaldson (James) v. Vannet, 1998 S.L.T. 957; 1998 S.C.C.R. 421 .... 2.17
Doorson v. Netherlands (1996) 22 E.H.R.R. 330 .... 3.27

Dorchester Studios (Glasgow) Ltd v. Stone, 1975 S.C. (H.L.) 56; 1975 S.L.T.
153 .... 7.32
Dosoo v. Dosoo, 1999 S.L.T. (Sh Ct) 86; 1999 S.C.L.R. 905 .... 5.18
Draper v. U.K., 24 D.R. 72 .... 5.24
Dudgeon v. U.K. (No.2) (A/45) (1982) 4 E.H.R.R. 149 .... 1.26, 2.02, 2.28, 5.33
Duff v. Highlands and Islands Fire Board, 1995 S.L.T. 1362; *The Times*,
November 3, 1995 .... 6.03
Dumfries and Galloway Council v. Scottish Ministers, 2000 G.W.D. 27-1019 1.51
Dutton v. Bognor Regis Urban D.C. [1972] 1 Q.B. 373; [1972] 2 W.L.R. 299 6.04
E v. Norway, unreported, March 7, 1988 .... 4.35
EIS, Petrs v. Robert Gordon University, unreported, May 29, 1996 9.20, 9.21
E.L.H. v. U.K. (32586/96), unreported, October 22, 1997 .... 4.13
Early v. Early, 1990 S.L.T. 221, 1 Div; affirming 1989 S.L.T. 114 .... 5.33
Eckle v. Germany (A/45) (1991) 13 E.H.R.R. 556 .... 1.27
Eckle v. Germany (A/51) (1983) 5 E.H.R.R. 1 .... 3.30-3.32, 4.31, 9.21
Edinburgh and Dalkeith Railway v. Wauchope (1842) 8 Cl. and F. 710 .... 9.61
Edinburgh D.C. v. Secretary of State for Scotland, 1985 S.L.T. 551 ...... 9.25, 9.31
Editions Periscope v. France (A/234-B) (1992) 14 E.H.R.R. 597 .... 9.41
Edwards v. U.K. (A/247B) (1993) 15 E.H.R.R. 417; *The Times*, January 21,
1993 .... 3.27, 3.37
Egan v. Willis (1998) 73 A.L.J.R. 75 .... 9.07
Eldridge v. Att.-Gen. of British Columbia, 3 B.H.R.C. 137 .... 9.10
Elsholz v. Germany [2000] 2 F.L.R. 486; [2000] 3 F.C.R. 385 .... 5.31
Elton v. U.K., unreported, September 11, 1997 .... 4.31
Engel v. Netherlands (No.1) (A/22) (1979-80) 1 E.H.R.R. 647 .... 2.03
Eriksson v. Sweden (A/156) (1990) 12 E.H.R.R. 183 .... 5.14
Erkner and Hofauer v. Austria (A/117) (1987) 9 E.H.R.R. 464 .... 7.12, 7.24
Errington v. Wilson, 1995 S.C. 550; 1995 S.L.T. 1193 .... 7.37
Errington v. Wilson, 1995 S.C. 550; 1995 S.L.T. 1193 .... 9.54
Ettl v. Austria (A/117) (1988) 10 E.H.R.R. 255, 9.49
Ezelin v. France (A/202) (1992) 14 E.H.R.R. 362 .... 2.15
F (In Utero), Re [1988] Fam. 122; [1988] 2 W.L.R. 1288 .... 5.08
F v. Switzerland (A/128) (1988) 10 E.H.R.R. 411 .... 5.02, 5.24
Fairmount Investments Ltd v. Secretary of State for the Environment; *sub
nom.* Fairmount Investments Ltd v. Southwark L.B.C. [1976] 1 W.L.R.
1255; [1976] 2 All E.R. 865 .... 7.26
Feldbrugge v. Netherlands (A/99) (1986) 8 E.H.R.R. 425 .... 9.41
Fenning v. Advocate (H.M.); 1985 J.C. 76; 1985 S.L.T. 540 .... 2.05
Ferguson v. Secretary of State for Social Services, 1988 S.C. 418; 1989 S.L.T.
117 .... 9.28
Ferrantelli and Santangelo v. Italy (1997) 23 E.H.R.R. 288 .... 9.50
Ferrier v. Scottish Milk Marketing Board; *sub nom.* Scottish Milk Marketing
Board v. Ferrier [1937] A.C. 126; 1936 S.L.T. 487 .... 9.18
Firma Rheinmuhlen-Dusseldorf v. Einfuhrund Vorratsstelle fur Getreide und
Futtermittel (166/73); *sub nom.* Rheinmuhlen-Dusseldorf v. EVST
(166/73) [1974] E.C.R. 33; [1974] 1 C.M.L.R. 523 .... 1.21
Fischer v. Austria (A/312) (1995) 20 E.H.R.R. 349 .... 9.43
Fitzpatrick v. Sterling Housing Association Ltd [2001] 1 A.C. 27; [1999] 3
W.L.R. 1113 .... 5.02, 5.34, 5.35
Fleming v. Liddlesdale District Committee (1897) 5 S.L.T. 191 .... 9.30
Foley v. Post Office; HSBC Bank Plc (formerly Midland Bank Plc) v.
Madden; *sub nom.* Post Office v. Foley [2001] 1 All E.R. 550; [2000]
I.C.R. 1283 .... 8.22
Forbes v. Dundee D.C., 1997 S.L.T. 1330; 1997 S.C.L.R. 682 .... 6.04, 6.11
Forbes v. Underwood (1886) 13 R. 465 .... 9.08
Foster v. British Gas Plc [1991] 2 A.C. 306; [1991] 2 W.L.R. 1075 .... 9.10
Fox v. U.K. (A/182); Campbell v. U.K.; Hartley v. U.K. (1991) 13 E.H.R.R.
157; *The Times*, October 16, 1990 .... 3.07, 3.08, 3.12, 4.45

Francovich v. Italy (C6/90); Bonifacti v. Italy (C9/90) [1991] E.C.R. I-5357;
   [1993] 2 C.M.L.R. 66 .... 9.22
Fraser (1848) Arkley 280 .... 2.09
Fraser v. Professional Golfers Association; *sub nom.* Fraser, Petr, 1999
   S.C.L.R. 1032; 1999 G.W.D. 22-1025 .... 9.08
Fredin v. Sweden (A/192) (1991) 13 E.H.R.R. 784 .... 7.04, 7.09, 7.14, 7.15
Friedl v. Austria (A/305-B) (1996) 21 E.H.R.R. 83 .... 3.12
Friel v. Initial Contract Services Ltd, 1994 S.L.T. 1216; 1993 S.C.C.R. 675   2.21
Frydlender v. France, unreported, 2000 .... 8.02
Funke v. France (A/256-A) [1993] 1 C.M.L.R. 897; (1993) 16 E.H.R.R.
   297 .... 1.04, 1.05, 3.11, 3.12, 4.31
G v. France (A/325-B) (1996) 21 E.H.R.R. 288 .... 2.10
G v. Netherlands, 16 E.H.R.R. 39 .... 5.04
G and RS v. U.K. (17142/90), unreported, July 10, 1991 .... 4.13
Garland v. British Rail Engineering Ltd (No.2); Roberts v. Cleveland AHA;
   MacGregor Wallcoverings v. Turton [1983] 2 A.C. 751; [1982] 2
   W.L.R. 918 .... 1.12
Gea Catalan v. Spain (A/309) (1995) 20 E.H.R.R. 266 .... 3.22
General Poster and Publicity Co. Ltd v. Secretary of State for Scotland and
   East Lothian CC, 1960 S.C. 266; 1961 S.L.T. 62 .... 7.25
Georgiadis v. Greece (1997) 24 E.H.R.R. 606 .... 9.42, 9.45
Germany v. Council of Ministers (C426/93) [1995] E.C.R. I-3723 .... 9.34
Gibson v. Advocate (H.M.), unreported, December 5, 2000 .... 3.32
Gibson v. British Gas Energy Centres Ltd, unreported, February 20, 2001,
   EAT 8.05
Gibson v. Orr; *sub nom.* Gibson v. Chief Constable of Strathclyde, 1999 S.C.
   420; 1999 S.C.L.R. 661 .... 6.02, 6.03
Gibson v. U.K., unreported, September 1, 1993 .... 4.42
Gillow v. U.K. (1989) 11 E.H.R.R. 335; *The Times*, November 29, 1986 ... 2.12,
                                             2.13, 2.14, 7.13, 7.15
Glasenapp v. Germany (A/104) (1987) 9 E.H.R.R. 25 .... 8.02
Glaser v. U.K., unreported, September 19, 2000 .... 5.31
Glasgow and District Restaurateurs and Hotelkeepers Association v. Dollan,
   1941 S.C. 93 .... 9.20
Glasgow Corp. v. Glasgow Churches Council, 1944 S.L.T. 317 .... 9.25
Glasgow D.C. v. Doyle (Licensing), 1993 S.C. 203; 1995 S.L.T. 327 .... 9.40
Glasgow Rape Crisis Centre, Petrs, unreported, 2000 .... 9.20
Glass v. U.K., unreported, December 3, 1997 .... 7.30
Golder v. U.K. (A/18) (1979-80) 1 E.H.R.R. 524 .... 4.45, 9.43
Gordon v. Kirkcaldy D.C., 1990 S.C. 107; 1990 S.L.T. 644 .... 9.28
Governors of Donaldson's Hospital v. Educational Endowments Commis-
   sioners, 1932 S.L.T. 417 .... 9.31
Grahame v. Kirkcaldy Magistrates (1882) L.R. 7 App. Cas. 547; (1882) 9 R.
   (H.L.) 91 .... 9.69
Grant v. Allen [1981] Q.B. 486; [1980] 3 W.L.R. 422 .... 2.09
Gray v. Kerner, 1996 S.C.L.R. 331 .... 7.34
Greenhuff (1838) 2 Swinton 236 .... 2.09
Grice v. U.K., unreported, April 14, 1994 .... 4.25, 4.27, 4.28
Griffith v. Kentucky, 497 U.S. 314 (1987) 9.68
Groppera Radio AG v. Switzerland (A/173) (1990) 12 E.H.R.R. 321; *The
   Times*, April 16, 1990 .... 2.11
Guenoun v. France (1990) 66 D.R. 181 .... 9.21
Guerra v. Italy (1998) 26 E.H.R.R. 357; 4 B.H.R.C. 63 .... 6.03, 6.06, 7.31
Gustafsson v. Sweden (1996) 22 E.H.R.R. 409 .... 8.08, 9.41
H, Petrs, 1997 S.L.T. 3 .... 9.17
H v. Belgium (A/127 (1988) 10 E.H.R.R. 339; *The Times*, January 6, 1983 .   9.42
H v. Norway, 73 D.R. 155 .... 5.06
H v. U.K., unreported, April 4, 1990 .... 2.03
Hadjianastassiou v. Greece (A/252A) (1993) 16 E.H.R.R. 219 .... 9.45

Hakansson v. Sweden (A/171); *sub nom.* Sturesson v. Sweden (1991) 13
  E.H.R.R. 1 .... 9.21, 9.46
Halford v. U.K. [1997] I.R.L.R. 471; (1997) 24 E.H.R.R. 523 .... 8.01, 8.10
Hallett v. Nicholson, 1979 S.C. 1 .... 9.23
Hamer v. U.K. (7114/75) (1982) 4 E.H.R.R. 139 .... 4.13, 5.24
Hamilton v. Secretary of State for Scotland, 1972 S.C. 72; 1972 S.L.T. 233   9.53
Hands v. Kyle and Carrick D.C., 1988 S.C. 233; 1989 S.L.T. 12 .... 9.19
Handyside v. U.K. (A/24) (1979-80) 1 E.H.R.R. 737 .... 1.06, 2.02, 3.15, 9.34, 9.55
Harper v. Heywood, 1998 S.L.T. 644; 1998 G.W.D. 3-110 .... 3.34
Harris v. Evans [1998] 1 W.L.R. 1285; [1998] 3 All E.R. 522 .... 6.06
Harvey v. Strathclyde R.C., 1989 S.L.T. 612 .... 9.29
Hashman v. U.K. (2000) 30 E.H.R.R. 241; 8 B.H.R.C. 104 .... 2.13
Hauschildt v. Denmark (A/154) (1990) 12 E.H.R.R. 266 .... 3.34, 9.50
Helle v. Finland (1998) 26 E.H.R.R. 159; [1998] H.R.C.D. 186 .... 9.45
Hendriks v. Netherlands (8427/78) (1983) 5 E.H.R.R. 223 .... 5.14
Hendry v. Advocate (H.M.), 2001 G.W.D. 2-88 .... 3.32
Hentrich v. France (A/296-A) (1994) 18 E.H.R.R. 440 .... 7.06
Herczegfalvy v. Austria (A/242B) (1993) 15 E.H.R.R. 437 .... 4.17, 4.37, 4.38
Herron v. Best, 1976 S.L.T. (Sh. Ct.) 80 .... 2.22
Heudens v. Belgium, unreported May 22, 1995 .... 4.25, 4.27
Higson v. Boyle, 2000 G.W.D. 36-1358 .... 3.32
Hill v. Chief Constable of West Yorkshire [1989] A.C. 53; [1988] 2 W.L.R.
  1049 .... 6.02, 6.08
Hiro Balani v. Spain (A/303-B) (1995) 19 E.H.R.R. 566 .... 9.45
Hoekstra v. Advocate (H.M.) (No.1), 2000 S.C.C.R. 263; 2000 G.W.D. 6-
  221 .... 1.48, 3.27, 3.38
Hoekstra v. Advocate (H.M.) (No.2), 2000 J.C. 387; 2000 S.L.T. 602 .... 1.31,
                                                                   1.48, 1.49, 3.34
Hoekstra v. Advocate (H.M.) (No.3); Van Rijs v. Advocate (H.M.); Van Rijs
  v. Advocate (H.M.); Van Rijs v. Advocate (H.M.), 2000 J.C. 391; 2000
  S.L.T. 605 .... 1.48
Hoekstra v. Advocate (H.M.) (No.4), 2000 S.C.C.R. 676; 2000 G.W.D. 22-
  849
Hogefeld v. Germany (35402/97), unreported, January 20, 2000 .... 4.11
Holmes v. U.K., unreported, September 1, 1993 .... 4.42
Holy Monasteries v. Greece (A/301-A) (1995) 20 E.H.R.R. 1 .... 7.07, 7.42
Howard v. U.K., 52 D.R. 198 .... 7.24
Huber v. France (1998) 26 E.H.R.R. 457; [1998] H.R.C.D. 263 .... 9.42
Hunter v. Canary Wharf Ltd; *sub nom.* Hunter v. London Docklands
  Development Corp. [1997] A.C. 655; [1997] 2 W.L.R. 684 .... 7.28
Hunter v. Southam Inc. [1984] 2 S.C.R. 145 .... 9.55
Hurtado v. Switzerland, unreported, July 8, 1993 .... 4.36
Hussain v. U.K.; Singh v. U.K. (1996) 22 E.H.R.R. 1; 1 B.H.R.C. 119 ..... 4.23
Huvig v. France (A/176-B) (1990) 12 E.H.R.R. 528 .... 2.12
Hydro Seafood GSP Ltd v. The Scottish Ministers, 2000 G.W.D. 7-260 .... 7.37
ISKCON v. U.K., 76A D.R. 90 .... 7.11, 7.17
Iatridis v. Greece (2000) 30 E.H.R.R. 97 .... 7.06
Incal v. Turkey (2000) 29 E.H.R.R. 449; 4 B.H.R.C. 476 .... 9.50
Ingram v. Macari (No.2), 1983 S.L.T. 61; 1982 S.C.C.R. 372 .... 2.17
Inverclyde Council v. SM, unreported, September, 2000 .... 5.16
Inze v. Austria (A/126) (1988) 10 E.H.R.R. 394; *The Times,* November 13,
  1987 .... 5.24, 7.15
Ireland v. U.K. (A/25) (1979-80) 2 E.H.R.R. 25 .... 3.16, 4.26
Islay Estates v. McCormick, 1937 S.N. 28 .... 9.70
J (A Minor) (Child in Care) (Medical Treatment), Re [1993] Fam. 15; [1992] 3
  W.L.R. 507 .... 5.09
J (A Minor) (Wardship: Medical Treatment), Re [1991] Fam. 33; [1991] 2
  W.L.R. 140 .... 5.09
J. v. Ireland (1983) 34 D.R. 131 .... 1.26

Jacobsson v. Sweden (A/163) (1990) 12 E.H.R.R. 56 .... 7.10, 7.20
Jacques v. Jacques; *sub nom.* Lightbody v. Jacques, 1997 S.C. (H.L.) 20; 1997
    S.L.T. 459 .... 5.26
James v. Commonwealth (1939) 62 C.L.R. 339 .... 9.68
James v. U.K. (A/98) (1986) 8 E.H.R.R. 123; [1986] R.V.R. 139 .... 5.14, 7.06,
    7.14, 7.40, 7.45
Jamil v. France (A/320) (1996) 21 E.H.R.R. 65 .... 4.08
Jastrzebski v. Poland, unreported, may 19, 1998 .... 4.36
Jespers v. Belgium (1982) 27 D.R. 61 .... 3.37
Jeznach v. Poland, unreported, September 10, 1999 .... 4.36
Johansen v. Norway (1997) 23 E.H.R.R. 33 .... 5.13-5.15, 5.31
Johnston v. Chief Constable of the Royal Ulster Constabulary (C222/84); *sub*
    nom. J v. Chief Constable of the Royal Ulster Constabulary (C222/84)
    [1987] Q.B. 129; [1986] 3 W.L.R. 1038 .... 9.10, 9.53
Joobeen v. University of Stirling, 1995 S.L.T. 120 .... 9.17
Jordan v. U.K., unreported, January 14, 1998 .... 4.36
Just v. Queen in Right of British Columbia [1985] 5 W.W.R. 570 .... 6.03
K v. Finland; T v. Finland [2000] 2 F.L.R. 79; [2000] 3 F.C.R. 248 .... 5.14
K-F v. Germany (1998) 26 E.H.R.R. 390; [1998] H.R.C.D. 117 .... 3.06
KS v. U.K. (45035/98), unreported, March 7, 2000 .... 4.08, 4.30
Kamasinski v. Austria (A/168) (1991) 13 E.H.R.R. 36; *The Times*, January 1,
    1990 .... 3.25
Kaplan v. U.K. (7598/76) [1981] E.C.C. 297; (1982) 4 E.H.R.R. 64 .... 9.43
Katte Klitsche de la Grange v. Italy (A/293-B) (1995) 19 E.H.R.R. 368 .... 7.20
Kaur v. Advocate (Lord), 1980 S.C. 319; 1981 S.L.T. 322 .... 9.59
Kelly v. Kelly, 1997 S.C. 285; 1997 S.L.T. 896 .... 5.02, 5.06
Kemmache v. France (A/218) (1992) 14 E.H.R.R. 520 .... 3.19
Kennan v. U.K., unreported, September 6, 1999 .... 4.39
Kent v. Griffiths (No.3) [2001] Q.B. 36; [2000] 2 W.L.R. 1158 .... 9.23
Kerkhoven , Hinke and Hinke v. Netherlands 5.33
Kerr v. Hill, 1936 J.C. 71; 1936 S.L.T. 320 .... 2.09
Khaliq v. Advocate (H.M.), 1984 J.C. 23; 1984 S.L.T. 137 .... 2.09
Khan v. U.K. (11579/85) 48 D.R. 253 .... 4.13
Khan v. U.K., 8 B.H.R.C. 310; [2000] Crim. L.R. 684 .... 3.11, 3.13, 8.13
Khatun v. U.K., 26 E.H.R.R. CD 212 .... 7.28
Khokhlich v. U.K.raine, unreported, May 25, 1999 .... 4.34
Kidston v. Annan, 1984 S.L.T. 279; 1984 S.C.C.R. 20 .... 2.22
Kincardine and Deeside D.C. v. Forestry Commissioners, 1992 S.L.T. 1180;
    [1991] S.C.L.R. 729 .... 9.20
King v. East Ayrshire Council, 1998 S.C. 182; 1998 S.L.T. 1287 1.51, 9.19/1
Kingston v. U.K. (1995). See R. v. Kingston (Barry).
Kingston v. U.K., unreported, April 9, 1997 .... 2.03
Kinsella v. Chief Constable of Nottinghamshire, *The Times*, August 24, 1999 6.09
Kinsella v. U.K., unreported, September 1, 1993 .... 4.42
Kjeldsen v. Denmark (A/23); Busk Madsen v. Denmark; Pedersen v.
    Denmark (1979-80) 1 E.H.R.R. 711 .... 5.22
Klass v. Germany (A/28) (1979-80) 2 E.H.R.R. 214 .... 3.11, 3.13
Kleinwort Benson Ltd v. Lincoln City Council; Kleinwort Benson Ltd v.
    Birmingham City Council; Kleinwort Benson Ltd v. Southwark
    L.B.C.; Kleinwort Benson Ltd v. Kensington and Chelsea RLBC
    [1999] 2 A.C. 349; [1998] 3 W.L.R. 1095 .... 1.36, 9.68
Kokkinakis v. Greece (A/260-A) (1994) 17 E.H.R.R. 397; *The Times*, June 11,
    1993 .... 2.08, 2.10, 2.14, 2.15
Konig v. Germany (No.1) (A/27) (1979-80) 2 E.H.R.R. 170 .... 3.30, 8.22, 9.41
Konttinen v. Finland (1996) 87 D.R. 68 .... 8.17
Kopp v. Switzerland (1999) 27 E.H.R.R. 91; 4 B.H.R.C. 277 .... 2.11, 2.12, 8.10
Kosiek v. Germany (A/105) (1987) 9 E.H.R.R. 328 .... 3.26, 8.02
Koskinnen v. Finland, unreported, August 30, 1994 .... 4.25, 4.27, 4.35

Kostovski v. Netherlands (A/166) (1990) 12 E.H.R.R. 434; *The Times*, November 22, 1989 .... 9.44
Kremzow v. Austria (A/268-B) (1994) 17 E.H.R.R. 322 .... 3.38
Kriba v. Secretary of State for the Home Department, 1998 S.L.T. 1113; 1997 G.W.D. 20-983 .... 9.31
Kroon v. Netherlands (A/297-C) [1995] 2 F.C.R. 28; (1995) 19 E.H.R.R. 263 5.04
Kruger v. Commonwealth (1997) 109 C.L.R. 1 .... 9.22
Kruslin v. France (A176-A) (1990) 12 E.H.R.R. 547; *The Times*, May 3, 1990 .... 2.12, 3.13
Krzycki v. Germany (1978) 13 D.R. 57 .... 4.17
Kwik Save Stores Ltd v. Secretary of State for Scotland, 1999 S.L.T. 193; 1997 G.W.D. 29-1457 .... 9.19/1
L v. Finland [2000] 2 F.L.R. 118; [2000] 3 F.C.R. 219 .... 5.15
LCB v. U.K. (1999) 27 E.H.R.R. 212; 4 B.H.R.C. 447 .... 6.03
LM and R v. Switzerland (1996) E.H.R.R. CD 130 .... 7.30
Lafarge Redland Aggregates Ltd v. Scottish Ministers, 2000 S.L.T. 1361; [2000] 4 P.L.R. 151 .... 9.47, 9.49
Laker Airways v. Department of Trade [1977] Q.B. 643; [1977] 2 W.L.R. 234 9.49
Lakin Ltd v. Secretary of State for Scotland, 1988 S.L.T. 780 .... 9.54
Lamy v. Belgium (A/151) (1989) 11 E.H.R.R. 529 .... 3.20, 9.44
Langborger v. Sweden (A/155) (1990) 12 E.H.R.R. 416 .... 9.50
Laskey v. U.K.; Jaggard v. U.K.; Brown v. U.K. (1997) 24 E.H.R.R. 39; *The Times*, February 20, 1997 .... 2.28
Latta v. Herron (1967) S.C.C.R. (Supp.) 18 .... 2.16
Law Hospital NHS Trust v. Advocate (Lord), 1996 S.C. 301; 1996 S.L.T. 848 5.09
Lawless v. Ireland (No.3) (A/3) (1979-80) 1 E.H.R.R. 15 .... 2.20
Lawrie (Jeanie) v. Muir, 1950 J.C. 19; 1950 S.L.T. 37 .... 3.11
Le Compte v. Belgium (A/43); Van Leuven v. Belgium (A/43); De Meyere v. Belgium (A/43) [1982] E.C.C. 240; (1982) 4 E.H.R.R. 1 .... 3.34, 9.42
Leander v. Sweden (A/116) (1987) 9 E.H.R.R. 433; *The Times*, April 25, 1987 .... 7.31, 8.12
Leech v. Secretary of State for Scotland, 1992 S.C. 89; 1993 S.L.T. 365 .... 9.14, 9.31, 9.63
Letellier v. France (A/207) (1992) 14 E.H.R.R. 83 .... 3.19
Libman v. Att.-Gen. of Quebec (1998) 3 B.H.R.C. 269 .... 9.57
Lindsay v. U.K. (1986) 49 D.R. 181 .... 8.21
Linkletter v. Walker, 381 U.S. 618 (1965) 9.68
Lithgow v. U.K. (A/102) (1986) 8 E.H.R.R. 329; *The Times*, July 7, 1986 .. 7.07, 7.09, 7.10, 7.12, 7.14, 7.44, 9.40
Litster v. Forth Dry Dock and Engineering Co. Ltd; *sub nom.* Forth Estuary Engineering v. Litster [1990] 1 A.C. 546; [1989] 2 W.L.R. 634 1.10, 1.12
Lloyd v. McMahon [1987] A.C. 625; [1987] 2 W.L.R. 821 .... 9.46
Locabail (U.K.) Ltd v. Bayfield Properties Ltd (Leave to Appeal); Locabail (U.K.) Ltd v. Waldorf Investment Corp. (Leave to Appeal); Timmins v. Gormley; Williams v. Inspector of Taxes; R. v. Bristol Betting and Gaming Licensing Committee, ex p. O'Callaghan [2000] Q.B. 451; [2000] 2 W.L.R. 870 .... 1.49
Lockhart v. Stephen, 1987 S.C.C.R. 642 .... 2.18
Loizidou v. Turkey (1996) (1997) 23 E.H.R.R. 513 .... 7.13
London and Clydeside Estates Ltd v. Secretary of State for Scotland, 1987 S.L.T. 459; 1987 S.C.L.R. 195 .... 9.50, 9.53, 9.68
London and Midland Developments v. Secretary of State for Scotland, 1996 S.C.L.R. 465 .... 9.29
London Joint Stock Bank Ltd v. Macmillan; *sub nom.* Macmillan v. London Joint Stock Bank Ltd [1918] A.C. 777, HL; reversing [1917] 2 K.B. 439 1.33
London Underground Ltd v. National Union of Rail Maritime and Transport Workers; *sub nom.* National Union of Rail Maritime and Transport Workers v. London Underground Ltd [2001] EWCA Civ 211; *The Times*, March 7, 2001 .... 8.03

Loosefoot Entertainment Ltd v. Glasgow District Licensing Board, 1991
S.L.T. 843, 2 Div; affirming 1990 S.C.L.R. 584 .... 9.31
Lopez Ostra v. Spain (A/303-C) (1995) 20 E.H.R.R. 277 .... 6.06, 7.13, 7.15,
7.29, 7.30
Lowry v. Portugal, unreported, July 6, 1999 .... 4.36
Lukanov v. Bulgaria, R.J.D. 1997-II No.34 .... 3.07
Ludi v. Switzerland (A/238) (1993) 15 E.H.R.R. 173; *The Times*, August 13,
1992 .... 3.17, 9.21
Lustig-Prean v. U.K.; Beckett v. U.K. (2000) 29 E.H.R.R. 548; 7 B.H.R.C.
65 .... 1.13, 1.27, 9.31
M v. Home Office; *sub nom.* M, Re [1994] 1 A.C. 377; [1993] 3 W.L.R. 433   9.22
MB (Caesarean Section), Re; *sub nom.* L (Patient: Non-Consensual
Treatment), Re; L (An Adult: Non-Consensual Treatment), Re; MB
(Medical Treatment), Re [1997] 2 F.L.R. 426; [1997] 2 F.C.R. 541 ..   5.08
MM v. U.K., unreported, April 2, 1992 .... 4.25, 4.27
Maan, Petr, 2001 G.W.D. 6-186 .... 3.38
McAllister v. U.K., April 2, 1992 .... 4.25, 4.27, 4.28
McBrearty v. Advocate (H.M.), 1999 S.L.T. 1333; 1999 S.C.C.R. 122 .... 2.05
Mccafferty v. Secretary of State for Scotland, 1998 S.C.L.R. 379; 1998
G.W.D. 3-144 .... 6.03
McCallum v. U.K. (A/183) (1991) 13 E.H.R.R. 597; *The Times*, October 16,
1990 .... 4.44
McCann v. U.K. (A/324) (1996) 21 E.H.R.R. 97; *The Times*, October 9,
1995 .... 2.02, 2.05, 6.11, 9.21
McCartan Turkington Breen v. Times Newspapers Ltd; *sub nom.* Turkington
v. Times Newspapers Ltd [2000] 3 W.L.R. 1670; [2000] 4 All E.R. 913   1.20
McColl v. Strathclyde R.C., 1983 S.L.T. 616; [1984] J.P.L. 351 .... 9.14
McCombe v. U.K., unreported, September 1, 1993 .... 4.42
McCotter v. U.K., unreported, September 1, 1993 .... 4.42
McCutcheon v. Advocate (H.M.), 2001 G.W.D. 1-22 .... 3.41
McDaid v. Clydebank D.C.; *sub nom.* Gill v. Clydebank D.C., 1983 S.C. 76;
1984 S.L.T. 162 .... 9.53
MacDonald v. Burns, 1940 S.C. 376 .... 9.08
McDonald v. Cain [1953] V.L.R. 411 .... 9.63
McDonald v. Council of Saint Andrew's Ambulance Association, 1999
G.W.D. 3-112 .... 9.08
MacDonald v. Ministry of Defence; *sub nom.* McDonald v. Ministry of
Defence [2001] 1 All E.R. 620; [2001] I.C.R. 1 .... 1.13, 8.05
McDonald v. Secretary of State for Scotland, 1994 S.C. 234 .... 9.22
McDonald v. Secretary of State for Scotland (No.2), 1996 S.C. 113; 1996
S.L.T. 575 .... 9.17, 9.18
McDonnell v. U.K., unreported, September 1, 1993 .... 4.42
McDouall's Trustees v. MacLeod, 1949 S.C. 593; 1949 S.L.T. 449 .... 7.33
McDougall v. Dochree, 1992 J.C. 154; 1992 S.L.T. 624 .... 2.17
McFadyen v. Annan, 1992 J.C. 53; 1992 S.L.T. 163 .... 3.30, 3.31
McFeeley v. U.K., 20 D.R. 44 .... 4.35
McGinley v. U.K. (1999) 27 E.H.R.R. 1; 4 B.H.R.C. 421 .... 1.28, 7.31, 9.44
McGinley v. U.K. (No.2), unreported, January 28, 2000, ECtHR 1.28
McGonnell v. U.K. (2000) 30 E.H.R.R. 289; 8 B.H.R.C. 56 .... 1.53, 7.17, 9.50
McGrath v. McGrath, 1999 S.L.T. (Sh Ct) 90; 1999 S.C.L.R. 1121 .... 5.01, 5.18
McIndoe v. Glasgow District Licensing Board, 1989 S.C.L.R. 325 .... 9.46
McIntosh v. Aberdeenshire Council, 1999 S.L.T. 93; 1998 S.C.L.R. 435 . 9.08, 9.12
McIntosh v. Advocate (H.M.), unreported, February 5, 2001 .... 3.36
McIntosh v. Advocate (H.M.), unreported, October 13, 2000   1.31, 1.33, 4.07, 4.31
McKenny v. U.K., unreported, September 1, 1993 .... 4.42
Mackie v. Grampian R.C., 1999 Fam. L.R. 119 .... 5.23
Mackintosh v. Advocate (Lord) (1879) 2 App.Cas. 41 .... 1.31
McKnight v. Clydeside Buses Ltd, 1999 S.L.T. 1167; 1999 S.C.L.R. 272 ... 6.04
McLaughlan v. Boyd, 1934 J.C. 19; 1933 S.L.T. 629 .... 2.17

McLean v. Advocate (H.M.) (Devolution Issue), 2000 J.C. 140; 2000 S.C.C.R. 112 .... 3.24, 3.30

MacLennan v. MacLennan, 1958 S.C. 105; 1958 S.L.T. 12 .... 5.02

McLeod v. Advocate (H.M.) (No.2); *sub nom.* McLeod, Petr, 1998 J.C. 67; 1998 S.L.T. 233 .... 3.38, 9.44

McMichael v. U.K. (A/308) [1995] 2 F.C.R. 718; (1995) 20 E.H.R.R. 205 .... 5.17, 5.18, 5.29, 9.44

McNab v. Advocate (H.M.), 2000 J.C. 80; 2000 S.L.T. 99 .... 3.31, 3.32

McNeil v. Advocate (H.M.), 1968 J.C. 29; 1968 S.L.T. 338 .... 2.16

McNeill v. U.K. (A35373/97), unreported, 1997 .... 9.61

McPhee v. North Lanarkshire Council, 1998 S.L.T. 1317; 1998 G.W.D. 25-1238 .... 9.54

McTear v. Scottish Legal Aid Board, 1997 S.L.T. 108; 1995 S.C.L.R. 611 . 9.31

Magistrates and Town Council of the City of Edinburgh v. Paterson (1880) 8 R. 197 .... 9.18

Maharaj v. Att.-Gen. of Trinidad and Tobago (No.2) [1978] 2 W.L.R. 902; [1978] 2 All E.R. 670 .... 9.22

Maillard v. France (1999) 27 E.H.R.R. 232; [1998] H.R.C.D. 618 .... 9.42

Malloch v. Aberdeen Corp. (No.1) [1971] 1 W.L.R. 1578; [1971] 2 All E.R. 1278 .... 9.18, 9.39, 9.46

Mallon v. Monklands D.C., 1986 S.L.T. 347 .... 9.23

Malone v. U.K. (A/82) (1985) 7 E.H.R.R. 14, ECHR; affirming (1983) 5 E.H.R.R. 385 .... 2.11, 2.12, 2.16, 3.12, 3.13, 8.10, 9.38

Manitoba language Rights, Re [1985] 1 S.C.R. 721 .... 9.68

Marckx v. Belgium (A/31) (1979-80) 2 E.H.R.R. 330 .... 5.24, 7.04

Markt Intern Verlag GmbH and Beermann v. Germany (A/164) (1990) 12 E.H.R.R. 161; *The Times*, November 23, 1989 .... 1.19, 2.12

Martin v. Bearsden and Milngavie D.C., 1987 S.C. 80; 1987 S.L.T. 300 .... 9.53

Martin v. U.K., 1999 S.C.C.R. 941 .... 3.29

Matzwetter v. Austria (A/10) (1979-80) 1 E.H.R.R. 198 .... 3.19

Maynard v. Osmond [1977] Q.B. 240; [1976] 3 W.L.R. 711 .... 9.52

Mellacher v. Austria (A/169) (1990) 12 E.H.R.R. 391; *The Times*, January 3, 1990 .... 7.06

Mercury Communications Ltd v. Director General of Telecommunications [1996] 1 W.L.R. 48; [1996] 1 All E.R. 575 .... 1.17

Mersch v. Luxembourg (1985) 43 D.R. 34 .... 3.13

Michael v. Edinburgh Magistrates (1895) 3 S.L.T. 109 .... 9.30

Micosta SA v. Shetland Islands Council (Reparation), 1985 S.L.T. 193 ..... 9.23

Middlebrook Mushrooms v. Transport and General Workers Union [1993] I.C.R. 612; [1993] I.R.L.R. 232 .... 8.05, 8.09

Miles v. Secretary of State for the Environment, Transport and the Regions [2000] J.P.L. 192 .... 7.26

Millar v. Dickson; Stewart v. Heywood; Payne v. Heywood; Tracey v. Heywood; Marshall v. Ritchie, 2000 S.L.T. 1111; 2000 S.C.C.R. 793 9.19/1

Millar v. Procurator Fiscal, Elgin, unreported, August 3, 2000, HCJ 1.28, 1.36

Millar and Bryce Ltd v. Keeper of the Registers of Scotland, 1997 S.L.T. 1000; 1997 G.W.D. 25-1265 .... 9.22

Miller and Denovan v. Advocate (H.M.), 1960 .... 2.16

Milne v. Milne, 1994 S.L.T. (Sh Ct) 57; 1994 S.C.L.R. 437 .... 7.36

Milne v. Tudhope, 1981 J.C. 53; 1981 S.L.T. (Notes) 42 .... 2.22, 2.23

Ming Pao Newspapers Ltd v. Att.-Gen. of Hong Kong [1996] A.C. 907; [1996] 3 W.L.R. 272 .... 9.34, 9.58

Minister for Immigration and Ethnic Affairs v. Teoh (1995) 183 C.L.R. 273 9.54

Minister of Home Affairs (Bermuda) v. Fisher [1980] A.C. 319; [1979] 2 W.L.R. 889 .... 1.11, 9.55

Ministry of Transport v. Noort [1992] 3 N.Z.L.R. 260 .... 9.55

Mitchell v. Advocate (H.M.), 2001 G.W.D. 2-89 .... 3.32

Modinos v. Cyprus (A/259) (1993) 16 E.H.R.R. 485; *The Times*, May 17, 1993 .... 1.26

Monnell v. U.K. (A/115); Morris v. U.K. (1988) 10 E.H.R.R. 205; *The Times*, March 3, 1987 .... 3.04, 3.29, 3.30
Montgomery v. Advocate (H.M.); Coulter v. Advocate (H.M.); *sub nom.* Advocate (H.M.) v. Montgomery, 2001 S.L.T. 37; 2000 S.C.C.R. 1044 .... 1.04, 1.08, 1.30-1.32, 3.28, 9.73
Montgomery v. McLeod, 1977 S.L.T. (Notes) 77 .... 2.17
Morrison v. Advocate (H.M.), 1990 J.C. 299; 1991 S.L.T. 57 .... 3.41
Morrissens v. Belgium (1988) D.R. 56 .... 8.15
Moss's Empires v. Glasgow Assessor, 1917 S.C. (H.L.) 1 .... 9.53
Motsepe v. IRC (1997) (6) B.C.L.R. 692 .... 9.24
Muller v. Switzerland (A/133) (1991) 13 E.H.R.R. 212 .... 2.02, 9.38
Murphy v. Brentwood D.C. [1991] 1 A.C. 398; [1990] 3 W.L.R. 414 .... 6.04
Murphy v. Murphy, 1992 S.C.L.R. 62 .... 5.26
Murray v. Social Fund Inspector, 1996 S.L.T. 38 .... 9.03
Murray v. United Kingdom (1996) 22 E.H.R.R. 29; *The Times*, February 9, 1996 .... 3.09
N v. U.K., unreported, May 6, 1986 .... 4.25
NATFHE v. U.K. (1998) 25 E.H.R.R. CD 122 .... 8.03
NH v. U.K., unreported, June 30, 1993 .... 4.35
NWL Ltd v. Woods (The Nawala) (No.2); NWL Ltd v. Nelson and Laughton [1979] 1 W.L.R. 1294; [1979] 3 All E.R. 614 .... 8.09
Naik v. University of Stirling, 1994 S.L.T. 449 .... 9.12
National and Provincial Building Society v. U.K.; Leeds Permanent Building Society v. U.K.; Yorkshire Building Society v. U.K. [1997] S.T.C. 1466; (1998) 25 E.H.R.R. 127 .... 9.41, 9.42
National Association of Teachers in Further and Higher Education v. U.K. [1998] E.H.R.R. 773 .... 8.03
National Coalition for Gay and Lesbian Equality v. Minister of Justice, 6 B.H.R.C. 127 .... 2.03, 9.71
National Union of Belgian Police v. Belgium (A/9) (1979-80) 1 E.H.R.R. 578   8.03
National Union of Teachers v. Governing Body of St Mary's Church of England (Aided) Junior School; *sub nom.* Fidge v. Governing Body of St Mary's Church of England (Aided) Junior School [1997] 3 C.M.L.R. 630; [1997] Eu. L.R. 221 .... 9.10
Nationwide News Pty Ltd v. Wills (1992) 177 C.L.R. 1 .... 9.59
Neigel v. France (1997) *Reports* 1997-II, p.410 .... 8.01
Nelson v. U.K. (1986) 49 D.R. 170 .... 8.21
Neumeister v. Austria (No.1) (A/8) (1979-80) 1 E.H.R.R. 91 .... 3.30, 3.32
New Zealand Police v. Beggs, 8 B.H.R.C. 116 .... 9.07, 9.61
Niderost-Huber v. Switzerland (1998) 25 E.H.R.R. 709 .... 1.27
Niemietz v. Germany (A/251B) (1993) 16 E.H.R.R. 97 .... 3.12, 8.10
Nilabati Bahera v. State of Orissa AIR, 1993 S.C. (India) 9.22
Norney v. U.K., unreported, September 1, 1993 .... 4.42
Norris v. Ireland (A/142) (1991) 13 E.H.R.R. 186; *The Times*, October 31, 1988 .... 1.26, 2.28, 3.15, 9.21
Norton v. Shelby County, 118 U.S. 425 (1886) 9.68
Obermeier v. Austria (A/179) (1991) 13 E.H.R.R. 290 .... 8.04, 9.43
Oberschlick v. Austria (No.2) (1998) 25 E.H.R.R. 357 .... 8.17
Observer and Guardian v. U.K. (A/216); Sunday Times v. U.K. (Spycatcher) (A/217) (1992) 14 E.H.R.R. 153; *The Times*, November 27, 1991   2.11, 2.12, 9.21, 9.38
O'Dwyer v. U.K., unreported, September 1, 1993 .... 4.42
Oerlemans v. Netherlands (A/219) (1993) 15 E.H.R.R. 561 .... 7.09
Olsson v. Sweden (A/130) (1989) 11 E.H.R.R. 259; *The Times*, March 28, 1988 .... 3.15, 5.14, 5.31
Omkaranda v. Switzerland (1981) 25 D.R. 105 .... 9.42
O'Neill v. Advocate (H.M.), 1999 S.L.T. 958; 1999 S.C.C.R. 300 .. 1.10, 4.18, 4.22
O'Neill v. Governors of St Thomas More Roman Catholic Voluntary Aided Upper School [1997] I.C.R. 33; [1996] I.R.L.R. 372 .... 8.17

O'Neill v. O'Neill, 1987 S.L.T. (Sh. Ct.) 26 .... 5.26
Open Door Counselling Ltd v. Ireland (A/246); Dublin Well Woman Centre
    v. Ireland (A/246) (1993) 15 E.H.R.R. 244; *The Times*, November 5,
    1992 .... 2.12, 5.08
O'Reilly v. Mackman; Millbanks v. Secretary of State for the Home
    Department; Derbyshire v. Mackman; Dougan v. Mackman; Mill-
    banks v. Home Office [1983] 2 A.C. 237; [1982] 3 W.L.R. 1096 ... 1.17, 9.08
Orru v. Advocate (H.M.), 1998 S.C.C.R. 59; 1998 G.W.D. 5-235 .... 1.34
Osman v. Ferguson [1993] 4 All E.R. 344 .... 6.03
Osman v. U.K. [1999] 1 F.L.R. 193; (2000) 29 E.H.R.R. 245 .... 4.03, 4.39, 5.29,
    6.02, 6.03, 6.06-6.12, 7.30, 9.07, 9.10, 9.12, 9.23
Otto-Preminger Institute v. Austria (A/295-A) (1995) 19 E.H.R.R. 34 .... 2.02
Oyeneyin v. Oyeneyin, 1999 G.W.D. 38-1836 .... 5.18
Ozturk v. Germany (A/73) (1984) 6 E.H.R.R. 409 .... 4.29
P v. U.K. (1987) 54 D.R. 256 .... 9.42
PK, MK and BK v. U.K., unreported, December 9, 1992 .... 4.41
PTOA Ltd v. Renfrew D.C., 1997 S.L.T. 1112 .... 9.20
Padfield v. Minister of Agriculture, Fisheries and Food [1968] A.C. 997;
    [1968] 2 W.L.R. 924 .... 9.30
Pakelli v. Germany (A/64) (1984) 6 E.H.R.R. 1 .... 1.43
Palmer v. Tees HA (2000) 2 L.G.L.R. 69; [2000] P.I.Q.R. P1 .... 6.09
Pammel v. Germany (1998) 26 E.H.R.R. 100 .... 7.12
Panesar v. Nestle Co. Ltd [1980] I.C.R. 144; [1980] I.R.L.R. 64 .... 8.17
Paterson v. Lees; 1999 J.C. 159; 1999 S.C.C.R. 231 .... 2.06
Paton v. British Pregnancy Advisory Service Trustees [1979] Q.B. 276; [1978] 3
    W.L.R. 687 .... 5.06, 5.08
Paton v. Ritchie, 2000 J.C. 271; 2000 S.L.T. 239
Paton v. U.K. (8416/78) (1981) 3 E.H.R.R. 408 .... 5.10
Pauger v. Austria (1998) 25 E.H.R.R. 105 .... 9.46
Pearce v. Governing Body of Mayfield Secondary School; *sub nom.*
    Governing Body of Mayfield Secondary School v. Pearce [2000]
    I.C.R. 920; [2000] I.R.L.R. 548 .... 1.13
Peers v. Greece, unreported, June 4, 1999 .... 4.34
Peggie v. Clark (1868) 7 M. 89 .... 3.07
Pellegrin v. France, unreported, December 8, 1999, ECtHR 1.04, 8.02, 8.24
Perks v. U.K. (2000) 30 E.H.R.R. 33; [2000] R.A. 487 .... 3.04
Perrett v. Collins [1998] 2 Lloyd's Rep. 255; [1999] P.N.L.R. 77 .... 6.04, 6.10, 6.11
Petra v. Romania, 5 B.H.R.C. 497; [1998] H.R.C.D. 886 .... 2.11
Pett v. Greyhound Racing Association (No.2) [1970] 1 Q.B. 67 (Note); [1970]
    2 W.L.R. 256 .... 9.52
Pham Hoang v. France (A/243) (1993) 16 E.H.R.R. 53 .... 2.26, 4.31
Phelps v. Hillingdon L.B.C.; Anderton v. Clwyd CC; Jarvis v. Hampshire CC;
    sub nom. G (A Child) v. Bromley L.B.C. [2000] 3 W.L.R. 776; [2000] 4
    All E.R. 504 .... 6.05
Piddington v. Bates; Robson v. Ribton Turner; *sub nom.* Robson v. Ribton-
    Turner [1961] 1 W.L.R. 162; [1960] 3 All E.R. 660 .... 8.09
Piersack v. Belgium (A/53) (1983) 5 E.H.R.R. 169 .... 1.27, 3.34, 9.50
Pine Valley Developments v. Ireland (A/246-B) (1993) 16 E.H.R.R. 379 7.04, 7.15,
    7.18
Pinnacle Meat Processors Co. v. U.K., 27 E.H.R.R. CD 217 .... 7.38, 7.42
Platform 'Artze fur des Lieben. v. Austria (A/139), unreported, 1988 .... 8.09
Poitrimol v. France (A/277-A) (1994) 18 E.H.R.R. 130 .... 3.39
Pollock v. Secretary of State for Scotland, 1993 S.L.T. 1173; 1992 S.C.L.R.
    972 .... 9.53
Pollok School Co. Ltd v. Glasgow Town Clerk (No.1), 1946 S.L.T. 365, 1
    Div; 1946 S.L.T. 125 .... 9.30
Powell v. U.K. (A/172); Rayner v. U.K. (1990) 12 E.H.R.R. 355; *The Times*,
    February 22, 1990 .... 7.10, 7.30
Prebble v. Television New Zealand Ltd [1995] 1 A.C. 321; [1994] 3 W.L.R. 970 9.07

Pressos Compania Naviera SA v. Belgium (A/332) (1996) 21 E.H.R.R. 301 .... 7.04
Pretto v. Italy (A/71) (1984) 6 E.H.R.R. 182 .... 9.46
Priddle v. Dibble [1978] 1 W.L.R. 895; [1978] 1 All E.R. 1058 .... 8.17
Procola v. Luxembourg (A/326) (1996) 22 E.H.R.R. 193 .... 9.42, 9.50
Procurator Fiscal, Kirkaldy v. Kelly, unreported, August 18, 2000, HCJ ... 1.31
Pullar v. Advocate (H.M.), 1993 J.C. 126; 1993 S.C.C.R. 514 .... 1.04
Pullar v. U.K., 1996 S.C.C.R. 755; (1996) 22 E.H.R.R. 391 .... 1.04, 3.34
Purcell v. Ireland (1991) 70 D.R. 262 .... 9.21
Queensberry v. Officers of State (1807) Mor.App.Juris. 19 .... 9.61
R. v. Admiralty Board of the Defence Council, ex p. Lustig-Prean. *See* R. v.
    Ministry of Defence, ex p. Smith.
R. v. Advocate (H.M.), 1988 S.L.T. 623; 1988 S.C.C.R. 254 .... 2.17
R. v. Army Board of Defence Council, ex p. Anderson [1992] Q.B. 169; [1991]
    3 W.L.R. 42 .... 9.46
R. v. Benjafield (Confiscation Order); R. v. Leal; R. v. Rezvi; R. v. Milford,
    The Times, December 28, 2000; The Independent, January 31, 2001 1.33
R. v. Bow Street Metropolitan Stipendiary Magistrate, ex p. Pinochet Ugarte
    (No.2); *sub nom.* Pinochet Ugarte (No.2), Re; R. v. Evans, ex p.
    Pinochet Ugarte (No.2); R. v. Bartle, ex p. Pinochet Ugarte (No.2)
    [2000] 1 A.C. 119; [1999] 2 W.L.R. 272 .... 1.49
R. v. Chief Constable of North Wales, ex p. AB; *sub nom.* R. v. Chief
    Constable of North Wales, ex p. Thorpe [1999] Q.B. 396; [1998] 3
    W.L.R. 57 .... 8.17
R. v. Chief Constable of Sussex, ex p. International Trader's Ferry Ltd [1999]
    2 A.C. 418; [1998] 3 W.L.R. 1260 .... 1.09, 9.34, 9.55
R. v. Chief Rabbi of the United Hebrew Congregations of Great Britain and
    the Commonwealth, ex p. Wachmann; *sub nom.* R. v. Jacobovits, ex p.
    Wachmann [1992] 1 W.L.R. 1036; [1993] 2 All E.R. 249 .... 9.08
R. v. City of London Corp, ex p. Matson [1997] 1 W.L.R. 765; 94 L.G.R. 443 9.45
R. v. Civil Service Appeal Board, ex p. Cunningham [1991] 4 All E.R. 310;
    [1992] I.C.R. 817 .... 9.45
R. v. Commissioner for Local Administration, ex p. Croydon L.B.C. [1989] 1
    All E.R. 1033; 87 L.G.R. 221
R. v. Commissioner for Local Administration, ex p. H (A Minor) [1999]
    E.L.R. 314, CA; affirming (1999) 1 L.G.L.R. 932 .... 9.03
R. v. Daviault, 1994 3 S.C.R. 63 .... 2.03
R. v. Disciplinary Committee of the Jockey Club, ex p. The Aga Khan [1993]
    1 W.L.R. 909; [1993] 2 All E.R. 853 .... 9.08
R. v. DPP, ex p. Kebilene; R. v. DPP, ex p. Boukemiche (Ferine); R. v. DPP,
    ex p. Souidi (Sofiane); R. v. DPP, ex p. Rechachi; *sub nom.* R. v. DPP,
    ex p. Kebelene [2000] 2 A.C. 326; [1999] 3 W.L.R. 972 ..... 1.11, 1.21, 1.55,
        3.36, 7.30, 8.05, 9.16, 9.54, 9.56, 9.58
R. v. Edwards Books and Art [1986] 2 S.C.R. 713 .... 9.56
R. v. Grayson and Taylor [1997] 1 N.Z.L.R. 399 .... 9.55
R. v. Hertfordshire CC, ex p. Green Environmental Industries Ltd; *sub nom.*
    Green Environmental Industries Ltd, Re; Green Environmental
    Industries Ltd v. Hertfordshire CC [2000] 2 A.C. 412; [2000] 2
    W.L.R. 373 .... 7.22
R. v. Higher Education Funding Council, ex p. Institute of Dental Surgery
    [1994] 1 W.L.R. 242; [1994] 1 All E.R. 651 .... 9.45
R. v. Imam of Bury Park Mosque, Luton, ex p. Ali; *sub nom.* Ali v. Imam of
    Bury Park Mosque, Luton [1994] C.O.D. 142; *The Times*, May 20,
    1993 .... 9.08
R. v. Inland Revenue Commissioners, ex p. Woolwich Equitable Building
    Society [1990] 1 W.L.R. 1400; [1991] 4 All E.R. 92 .... 9.70
R. v. Inner London Education Authority, ex p. Westminster City Council
    [1986] 1 W.L.R. 28; [1986] 1 All E.R. 19 .... 9.30
R. v. Kingston [1995] 2 A.C. 355; [1994] 3 W.L.R. 519 .... 2.27
R. v. Lam. See Chung Tak Lam v. Brennan (t/a Namesakes of Torbay).

R. v. Lemon; Whitehouse v. Gay News Ltd; R. v. Gay News Ltd; *sub nom.*
  Whitehouse v. Lemon [1979] A.C. 617; [1979] 2 W.L.R. 281 .... 2.14
R. v. Lewisham B.C., ex p. Shell U.K. [1988] 1 All E.R. 938; (1988) 152 L.G.
  Rev. 929 .... 9.30
R. v. Local Commissioner for Administration for England, ex p. Eastleigh
  B.C.; *sub nom.* R. v. Local Commissioner for Administration for the
  South, the West, the West Midlands, Leicestershire, Lincolnshire and
  Cambridgeshire, ex p. Eastleigh B.C. [1988] Q.B. 855; [1988] 3 W.L.R.
  113 .... 9.03
R. v. Local Commissioner for Administration in North and North East
  England, ex p. Liverpool City Council; *sub nom.* R. v. Local
  Commissioner for Local Government for North and North East
  England, ex p. Liverpool City Council [2001] 1 All E.R. 462; (2000) 2
  L.G.L.R. 603 .... 9.03
R. v. Lord Chancellor, ex p. Lightfoot; *sub nom.* Lightfoot v. Lord Chancellor
  [2000] Q.B. 597; [2000] 2 W.L.R. 318 .... 1.54
R. v. Lord Chancellor, ex p. Witham [1998] Q.B. 575; [1998] 2 W.L.R.
  849 .... 1.54, 9.31
R. v. Lord President of the Privy Council, ex p. Page; *sub nom.* Page v. Hull
  University Visitor; R. v. Hull University Visitor, ex p. Page [1993] A.C.
  682; [1993] 3 W.L.R. 1112 .... 9.28
R. v. Lord Saville of Newdigate, ex p. B (No.2); *sub nom.* R. v. Lord Saville of
  Newdigate, ex p. A [2000] 1 W.L.R. 1855; [1999] 4 All E.R. 860 ..... 9.31
R. v. Ministry of Agriculture, Fisheries and Food, ex p. First City Trading
  Ltd (1996) [1997] 1 C.M.L.R. 250; [1997] Eu. L.R. 195 .... 9.34, 9.35
R. v. Ministry of Agriculture, Fisheries and Food, ex p. Hamble (Offshore)
  Fisheries Ltd [1995] 2 All E.R. 714; [1995] 1 C.M.L.R. 533 .... 9.54
R. v. Ministry of Defence, ex p. Smith; R. v. Admiralty Board of the Defence
  Council, ex p. Lustig-Prean; R. v. Admiralty Board of the Defence
  Council, ex p. Beckett; R. v. Ministry of Defence, ex p. Grady [1996]
  Q.B. 517; [1996] 2 W.L.R. 305 .... 1.07, 1.13, 8.05, 9.31-9.33
R. v. Monopolies and Mergers Commission, ex p. Argyll Group Plc [1986] 1
  W.L.R. 763; [1986] 2 All E.R. 257 .... 9.69
R. v. North and East Devon HA, ex p. Coughlan [2000] 2 W.L.R. 622; [2000]
  3 All E.R. 850 .... 9.54
R. v. Oakes [1986] 1 S.C.R. 103 .... 9.56
R. v. Panel on Take-overs and Mergers, ex p. Datafin Plc [1987] Q.B. 815;
  [1987] 2 W.L.R. 699 .... 9.10
R. v. Parliamentary Commissioner for Administration, ex p. Balchin [1998] 1
  P.L.R. 1; [1997] J.P.L. 917 .... 9.03
R. v. Parliamentary Commissioner for Administration, ex p. Dyer [1994] 1
  W.L.R. 621; [1994] 1 All E.R. 375 .... 9.03
R. v. Parliamentary Commissioner for Standards, ex p. Fayed [1998] 1
  W.L.R. 669; [1998] 1 All E.R. 93 .... 1.54
R. v. R (Rape: Marital Exemption) [1992] 1 A.C. 599; [1991] 3 W.L.R. 767 2.19
R. v. Secretary of State for Foreign and Commonwealth Affairs, ex p. World
  Development Movement Ltd [1995] 1 W.L.R. 386; [1995] 1 All E.R.
  611 .... 9.30
R. v. Secretary of State for Health, ex p. Eastside Cheese Co. [1999] 3
  C.M.L.R. 123; [1999] Eu. L.R. 968 .... 7.38
R. v. Secretary of State for Health, ex p. Wagstaff; R. v. Secretary of State for
  Health, ex p. Associated Newspapers Ltd; *sub nom.* R. (on the
  application of Wagstaff) v. Secretary of State for Health; R. (on the
  application of Associated Newspapers Ltd) v. Secretary of State for
  Health [2001] 1 W.L.R. 292; [2000] H.R.L.R. 646 .... 9.31
R. v. Secretary of State for the Environment, ex p. Alconbury, unreported 1.33
R. v. Secretary of State for the Environment, ex p. Nottinghamshire CC; City
  of Bradford MBC v. Secretary of State for the Environment; *sub nom.*

Nottinghamshire CC v. Secretary of State for the Environment [1986] A.C. 240; [1986] 2 W.L.R. 1 .... 9.31

R. v. Secretary of State for the Environment, ex p. Ostler; *sub nom.* R. v. Secretary of State for the Home Department, ex p. Ostler [1977] Q.B. 122; [1976] 3 W.L.R. 288 .... 9.53

R. v. Secretary of State for the Environment, Transport and the Regions, ex p. Challenger [2001] Env. L.R. 12; [2000] H.R.L.R. 630 .... 9.44

R. v. Secretary of State for the Environment, Transport and the Regions, ex p. Holdings and Barnes Plc. *See* R. (on the application of Holding and Barnes Plc) v. Secretary of State for the Environment, Transport and the Regions.

R. v. Secretary of State for the Home Department, ex p. Ahmed; R. v. Secretary of State for the Home Department, ex p. Patel [1999] Imm. A.R. 22; [1998] I.N.L.R. 570 .... 9.54

R. v. Secretary of State for the Home Department, ex p. Brind [1991] 1 A.C. 696; [1991] 2 W.L.R. 588 .... 1.07, 9.26, 9.27, 9.32, 9.35, 9.37

R. v. Secretary of State for the Home Department, ex p. Doody; R. v. Secretary of State for the Home Department, ex p. Pierson; R. v. Secretary of State for the Home Department, ex p. Smart; R. v. Secretary of State for the Home Department, ex p. Pegg [1994] 1 A.C. 531; [1993] 3 W.L.R. 154 .... 9.45

R. v. Secretary of State for the Home Department, ex p. Hargreaves; R. v. Secretary of State for the Home Department, ex p. Briggs; R. v. Secretary of State for the Home Department, ex p. Green [1997] 1 W.L.R. 906; [1997] 1 All E.R. 397 .... 9.54

R. v. Secretary of State for the Home Department, ex p. Jeyeanthan; Ravichandran v. Secretary of State for the Home Department; *sub nom.* R. v. Immigration Appeal Tribunal, ex p. Jeyeanthan; Secretary of State for the Home Department v. Ravichandran [2000] 1 W.L.R. 354; [1999] 3 All E.R. 231 .... 9.53

R. v. Secretary of State for the Home Department, ex p. Khan; *sub nom.* Khan v. Immigration Appeal Tribunal [1984] 1 W.L.R. 1337; [1985] 1 All E.R. 40 .... 9.51

R. v. Secretary of State for the Home Department, ex p. Launder (No.2) [1997] 1 W.L.R. 839; [1997] 3 All E.R. 961 .... 1.07

R. v. Secretary of State for the Home Department, ex p. Robb. *See* Secretary of State for the Home Department v. Robb.

R. v. Secretary of State for the Home Department, ex p. Ruddock [1987] 1 W.L.R. 1482; [1987] 2 All E.R. 518 .... 9.54

R. v. Secretary of State for the Home Department, ex p. Venables; R. v. Secretary of State for the Home Department, ex p. Thompson [1998] A.C. 407; [1997] 3 W.L.R. 23 .... 9.59

R. v. Secretary of State for Trade and Industry, ex p. Lonrho [1989] 1 W.L.R. 525; [1989] 2 All E.R. 609 .... 9.45

R. v. Secretary of State for Transport, ex p. Factortame Ltd (C-213/89) [1990] 2 Lloyd's Rep. 351; [1990] E.C.R. I-2433 .... 1.13, 1.52

R. v. Secretary of State for Transport, ex p. Factortame (No.2) [1991] 1 A.C. 603; [1990] 3 W.L.R. 818 .... 9.22

R. v. Secretary of State for Wales, ex p. Emery [1998] 4 All E.R. 367; [1997] E.G.C.S. 114 .... 9.46

R. v. Somerset CC, ex p. Fewings [1995] 1 W.L.R. 1037; [1995] 3 All E.R. 20 9.29

R. v. Uxbridge Magistrates Court, ex p. Adimi; R. v. Crown Prosecution Service, ex p. Sorani; R. v. Secretary of State for the Home Department, ex p. Sorani; R. v. Secretary of State for the Home Department, ex p. Kaziu [2000] 3 W.L.R. 434; [1999] 4 All E.R. 520 9.54

R. (on the application of Holding and Barnes Plc) v. Secretary of State for the Environment, Transport and the Regions; R. (on the application of Premier Leisure U.K. Ltd) v. Secretary of State for the Environment, Transport and the Regions; R. (on the application of Alconbury

Developments Ltd) v. Secretary of State for the Environment,
Transport and the Regions; Secretary of State for the Environment,
Transport and the Regions v. Legal and General Assurance Society
Ltd; *sub nom*. R. v. Secretary of State for the Environment, Transport
and the Regions, ex p. Holdings and Barnes Plc [2001] 05 E.G. 170;
[2001] J.P.L. 291 .... 7.17
Raffaelli v. Heatly, 1949 J.C. 101; 1949 S.L.T. 284 .... 2.17
Raimondo v. Italy (A/281-A) (1994) 18 E.H.R.R. 237 .... 4.31
Rape Crisis Centre v. Brindley, unreported, July 4, 2000, (OH) 1.26
Raymond v. Honey [1983] 1 A.C. 1; [1982] 2 W.L.R. 465 .... 9.63
Rediffusion (Hong Kong) Ltd v. Att.-Gen. of Hong Kong [1970] A.C. 1136;
[1970] 2 W.L.R. 1264 .... 9.63
Rees v. U.K. (A/106) [1987] 2 F.L.R. 111; (1987) 9 E.H.R.R. 56 ... 5.24, 5.36, 5.37
Reid v. Secretary of State for Scotland, 1999 S.C.L.R. 74 .... 9.58
Reilly v. Advocate (H.M.), 2000 S.L.T. 1330; 2000 S.C.C.R. 879 .... 3.32
Rekvény v. Hungary, R.J.D. 1999, para.34 .... 2.15
Ribitsch v. Austria (A/336) (1996) 21 E.H.R.R. 573 .... 3.16
Riera-Blume v. Spain, unreported, October 14, 1999 .... 3.06
Ritchie v. Burns, unreported, June 14, 2000 .... 7.36
Ritchie v. Secretary of State for Scotland, 1999 S.L.T. 55; 1998 G.W.D. 3-102 9.45
Robertson v. Advocate (H.M.), 1997 S.C.C.R. 534; 1997 G.W.D. 24-1188 . 1.10
Robertson v. Smith, 1980 J.C. 1; 1979 S.L.T. (Notes) 51 .... 2.17
Roe v. Ministry of Health; Woolley v. Ministry of Health [1954] 2 Q.B. 66;
[1954] 2 W.L.R. 915 .... 6.09
Rommelfanger v. Germany (1989) 62 D.R. 151 .... 8.15
Rooney v. Chief Constable of Strathclyde, 1997 S.L.T. 1261; 1997 S.C.L.R.
367 .... 9.08, 9.51
Ross v. Advocate (H.M.), 1991 J.C. 210; 1991 S.L.T. 564 .... 2.26
Ross v. Secretary of State for Scotland, 1990 S.L.T. 13 .... 9.23
Rost v. Edwards [1990] 2 Q.B. 460; [1990] 2 W.L.R. 1280 .... 9.07
Rothenthurm Commune v. Switzerland (1989) 59 D.R. 251 .... 1.25, 9.21
Roy v. Kensington and Chelsea and Westminster Family Practitioner
Committee [1992] 1 A.C. 624; [1992] 2 W.L.R. 239 .... 1.17
Royal Society for the Protection of Birds v. Secretary of State for Scotland;
sub nom. RSPB, Petrs2000 S.L.T. 1272; 2000 S.C.L.R. 1045 .... 9.20
Ruiz Torija v. Spain (A/303-A) (1995) 19 E.H.R.R. 553 .... 9.45
Ruiz-Mateos v. Spain (A/262) (1993) 16 E.H.R.R. 505 .... 9.44
Ruotolo v. Italy (1992) A230-D 3.32
Russell v. DU.K.e of Norfolk [1949] 1 All E.R. 109; 65 T.L.R. 225 .... 9.44
Ryrie (Blingery) Wick v. Secretary of State for Scotland, 1988 S.L.T. 806 .. 9.53
S v. Advocate (H.M.), unreported, August, 1982 .... 2.21
S v. Advocate (H.M.); *sub nom*. Stallard v. Advocate (H.M.), 1989 S.L.T. 469;
1989 S.C.C.R. 248 .... 2.21
S v. France, unreported, May, 1990 .... 7.30
S v. Germany, unreported, August 5, 1960 .... 7.30
S v. Gloucestershire CC; L v. Tower Hamlets L.B.C.; *sub nom*. RL v.
Gloucestershire CC; DS v. Gloucestershire CC; RL v. Tower Hamlets
L.B.C. [2000] 3 All E.R. 346; [2000] 1 F.L.R. 825 .... 9.23
S v. Switzerland (1988) 59 D.R. 256 .... 9.42
S v. Switzerland (A/220) (1992) 14 E.H.R.R. 670 .... 4.45
S v. U.K. (1984) 41 D.R. 226 .... 5.33, 7.33
SP v. U.K. (43478/98), unreported, January 18, 2000 .... 4.09
SW v. U.K. (A/355-B); CR v. U.K. [1996] 1 F.L.R. 434; (1996) 21 E.H.R.R.
363 .... 2.02, 2.08, 2.18-2.21, 3.06
Sadik v. Greece (1997) 24 E.H.R.R. 323 .... 2.02
Sadowski v. Poland, unreported, October, 12, 2000 .... 4.36
St Johnstone Football Club Ltd v. Scottish Football Association Ltd, 1965
S.L.T. 171 .... 9.08
Salabiaku v. France (A/141-A) (1991) 13 E.H.R.R. 379 . 2.03, 2.25, 2.26, 3.36, 4.31

Salah Abadou v. Secretary of State for the Home Department, 1998 S.C.
504 .... 9.26, 9.27, 9.31, 9.32, 9.35, 9.56
Salesi v. Italy (A/257-E) (1998) 26 E.H.R.R. 187 .... 9.41
Salgueiro da Silva Mouta v. Portugal, 2001 Fam. L.R. 2 ..... 1.13, 5.33, 5.34, 5.35,
                                                                                    8.05
Sanderson v. MacManus; *sub nom.* S v. M (A Minor: Access Order);
    Sanderson v. McManus, 1997 S.C. (H.L.) 55; 1997 S.L.T. 62 5.01, 5.30
Saunders v. Scottish National Camps Association [1981] I.R.L.R. 277, IH;
    affirming [1980] I.R.L.R. 174 .... 8.19
Saunders v. U.K. [1998] 1 B.C.L.C. 362; [1997] B.C.C. 872 .. 1.04, 1.05, 3.09, 3.10,
                                                                            3.27, 7.22
Scanfuture U.K. Ltd v. Secretary of State for Trade and Industry, unreported,
    March 23, 2001, EAT 8.06, 8.22
Schacter v. canada [1992] 2 S.C.R. 679 .... 9.71
Schenk v. Switzerland (A/140) (1991) 13 E.H.R.R. 242; *The Times*, August 2,
    1988 .... 3.11
Schiesser v. Switzerland (1979-80) 2 E.H.R.R. 417 .... 3.07
Schmautzer v. Austria (A/328-A) (1996) 21 E.H.R.R. 511 .... 4.29
Schmidt v. Sweden (A/21); Dahlstrom v. Sweden [1978] E.C.C. 17; (1979-80) 1
    E.H.R.R. 632 .... 8.03
Schouten v. Netherlands (A/304); Meldrum v. Netherlands (A/304) (1995) 19
    E.H.R.R. 432 .... 9.42
Schuler-Zgraggen v. Switzerland (A/263) [1994] 1 F.C.R. 453; (1993) 16
    E.H.R.R. 405 .... 9.46
Scollo v. Italy (A/315-C) (1996) 22 E.H.R.R. 514 .... 7.12
Scott v. Smith, 1981 J.C. 46; 1981 S.L.T. (Notes) 22 .... 2.17
Scott v. U.K. [2000] 1 F.L.R. 958; [2000] 2 F.C.R. 560 .... 5.15
Scottish Old People's Welfare Council, Petrs, 1987 S.L.T. 179 ...... 1.26, 9.20, 9.51
Scrimgeour v. Scrimgeour, 1988 S.L.T. 590 .... 7.34
Secretary of State for Employment v. ASLEF (No.2) [1972] 2 Q.B. 455; [1972]
    2 W.L.R. 1370 .... 8.08
Secretary of State for the Home Department v. Robb [1995] Fam. 127; [1995]
    2 W.L.R. 722 .... 4.37
Sheffield v. U.K.; Horsham v. U.K. [1998] 2 F.L.R. 928; [1998] 3 F.C.R. 141   5.38
Shetland Line (1984) Ltd v. Secretary of State for Scotland, 1996 S.L.T.
    653 .... 9.17, 9.23, 9.54
Sibson v. U.K. (A/258-A) (1994) 17 E.H.R.R. 193; *The Times*, May 17,
    1993 .... 8.08, 8.15
Silva Pontes v. Portugal (A/286-A) (1994) 18 E.H.R.R. 156 .... 9.47
Silver v. U.K. (A/161) (1983) 5 E.H.R.R. 347, ECHR; affirming (1981) 3
    E.H.R.R. 475 .... 2.11, 2.12, 4.44, 9.38
Simmons v. Hoover [1977] Q.B. 284; [1976] 3 W.L.R. 901 .... 8.08
Simpson v. Att.-Gen. of New Zealand [1994] 3 N.Z.L.R. 667 .... 9.16, 9.22
Simpson v. U.K., 47 D.R. 274 .... 7.04, 7.13, 9.42
Singh, Petr (1988) G.W.D. 32-1377 .... 9.31
Singh v. Secretary of State for Scotland, 2000 S.L.T. 533 .... 1.51
Skilton v. T and K Home Improvements Ltd; *sub nom.* T and K Home
    Improvements v. Skilton [2000] I.C.R. 1162; [2000] I.R.L.R. 595 ....   8.14
Sleigh v. Edinburgh D.C., 1987 S.C. 70; 1988 S.L.T. 253 .... 9.17
Sloan, Petr, 1991 S.L.T. 527 .... 9.17
Smith v. Advocate (H.M.), 2000 S.C.C.R. 926; 2000 G.W.D. 30-1168 .... 3.32
Smith v. East Elloe Rural D.C.; *sub nom.* Smith v. East Rural D.C. [1956]
    A.C. 736; [1956] 2 W.L.R. 888 .... 9.53
Smith v. Gardner Merchant Ltd [1998] 3 All E.R. 852; [1999] I.C.R. 134 ...   1.13
Smith v. Safeway Plc [1996] I.C.R. 868; [1996] I.R.L.R. 456 .... 8.20, 8.21
Smith v. U.K.; Grady v. U.K.; Beckett v. U.K.; Lustig-Prean v. U.K. [1999]
    I.R.L.R. 734; (2000) 29 E.H.R.R. 493 .... 1.13, 5.34, 8.01, 8.05, 8.12, 8.20
Smith Kline and French Laboratories v. Netherlands, 66 D.R. 70 .... 7.04
Societe Levage Presentations v. France (1997) 24 E.H.R.R. 351 .... 9.43

Soderback v. Sweden [1999] 1 F.L.R. 250; (2000) 29 E.H.R.R. 95 .... 5.15
Soering v. U.K. (A/161) (1989) 11 E.H.R.R. 439; *The Times*, July 8, 1989 .... 3.28, 4.04, 4.15, 4.26, 4.32, 4.34, 8.10, 9.21
South of Scotland Electricity Board v. Elder, 1978 S.C. 132; 1980 S.L.T. (Notes) 83 .... 9.18
Sporrong and Lonnroth v. Sweden (A/52) (1983) 5 E.H.R.R. 35 .. 7.05, 7.15, 9.41, 9.47
Sramek v. Austria (A/84) (1985) 7 E.H.R.R. 351 .... 9.50
Stallard v. Advocate (H.M.). See S v. Advocate (H.M.); *sub nom.* Stallard v. Advocate (H.M.).
Starrs v. Ruxton; *sub nom.* Ruxton v. Starrs; Starrs v. Procurator Fiscal (Linlithgow), 2000 J.C. 208; 2000 S.L.T. 42 .... 1.31, 1.36. 3.34, 8.23, 9.50
Stedman v. U.K. (1997) 23 E.H.R.R. 168 CD 8.01, 8.17
Steel v. U.K. (1999) 28 E.H.R.R. 603; 5 B.H.R.C. 339 .... 2.02, 2.03, 2.13, 8.09
Stefan v. General Medical Council [1999] 1 W.L.R. 1293; [2000] H.R.L.R. 1   9.45
Stefan v. U.K. (1998) 25 E.H.R.R. CD 130 .... 8.22
Stevens v. U.K. (1986) 46 D.R. 245 .... 8.20
Stockdale v. Hansard (1839) 9 Ad. and El. 1 .... 9.07
Stogmuller v. Austria (A/9) (1979-80) 1 E.H.R.R. 155 .... 3.30, 3.32
Stornoway Magistrates v. Macdonald, 1971 S.C. 78; 1971 S.L.T. 154 .... 9.18
Stott v. Minogue, 2000 G.W.D. 37-1386 .... 3.34
Stovin v. Wise and Norfolk CC [1996] A.C. 923; [1996] 3 W.L.R. 388 .. 6.04, 6.12, 9.23
Stran Greek Refineries and Stratis Andreadis v. Greece (A/301-B) (1995) 19 E.H.R.R. 293 .... 7.04, 7.15, 9.41
Strathern v. Seaforth, 1926 J.C. 100; 1926 S.L.T. 445 .... 2.09
Stubbings v. U.K. [1997] 1 F.L.R. 105; [1997] 3 F.C.R. 157 .... 9.19/1
Sunday Times v. U.K. (No.1) (A/30) (1979-80) 2 E.H.R.R. 245; (1979) 76 L.S.G. 328 .... 2.08, 2.11, 2.12, 2.16, 3.06
Sussmann v. Germany (1998) 25 E.H.R.R. 64 .... 9.47
Sutherland v. U.K., unreported, May 21, 1996, ECommHR 2.02, 2.28
Swan v. Secretary of State for Scotland (No.1); *sub nom.* Swan, Petr, 1998 S.C. 479; 1998 S.C.L.R. 763 .... 1.51, 9.19/1
Swanson v. The Queen, 80 D.L.R. (4th) 741 .... 6.04
Swedish Engine Drivers Union v. Sweden (A/20); *sub nom.* Svenska Lokmannaforbundet v. Sweden (A/20) [1978] E.C.C. 1; (1979-80) 1 E.H.R.R. 617 .... 8.03
Sweenie (1858) 3 Ivine 109 .... 2.09
Swinney v. Chief Constable of Northumbria (No.1) [1997] Q.B. 464; [1996] 3 W.L.R. 968 .... 6.09
T, Petr; *sub nom.* AMT, Petrs; AMT (Known as A) (Petrs for Authority to Adopt SR), 1997 S.L.T. 724; 1996 S.C.L.R. 897 . 1.10, 5.33, 8.05, 9.21, 9.59
T. v. U.K.; V. v. U.K., unreported, December 16, 1999 .... 2.02, 2.24, 3.29, 4.19
TI v. U.K. [2000] I.N.L.R. 211 .... 9.32
TM v. U.K., unreported, October 18, 1995 .... 4.26
TP v. U.K. (2000) 2 L.G.L.R. 181 .... 9.23
Tait v. Central Radio Taxis (Tollcross) Ltd , 1989 S.C. 4; 1989 S.L.T. 217 .... 9.17, 9.52
Tanko v. Finland, D.R. 77-A 133 .... 6.05
Taylor, unreported, October 19, 1808 .... 2.09
Tehrani, Petr, unreported, January 25, 2001 .... 8.04, 8.07, 8.22
Tehrani v. Argyll and Clyde Health Board (No.2), 1989 S.C. 342; 1990 S.L.T. 118 .... 9.08, 9.12
Teixeira de Castro v. Portugal (1999) 28 E.H.R.R. 101; 4 B.H.R.C. 533 .... 3.17
Tennant v. Houston, 1987 S.L.T. 317; 1986 S.C.C.R. 556 .... 3.34
Tetreault-Gadoury v. Canada Employment and Immigration Commission [1991] 2 S.C.R. 22 .... 9.16
Thomann v. Switzerland (1997) 24 E.H.R.R. 553 .... 9.50
Thomas v. Baptiste [2000] 2 A.C. 1; [1999] 3 W.L.R. 249 .... 9.54

Thomson Newspapers Co. Ltd v. Att.-Gen. of Canada, 5 B.H.R.C. 567 .... 9.34
Thorgeirson v. Iceland (A/239) (1992) 14 E.H.R.R. 843; *The Guardian*, July
    15, 1992 .... 2.12
Thynne v. U.K. (A/190); Wilson v. U.K.; Gunnell v. U.K. (1991) 13 E.H.R.R.
    666; *The Times*, December 10, 1990 .... 1.10, 4.22, 4.24
Tinnelly and Sons Ltd v. U.K.; McElduff v. U.K. (1999) 27 E.H.R.R. 249; 4
    B.H.R.C. 393 .... 9.53
Togher v. U.K., unreported, April 16, 1998 .... 4.42
Tolstoy Miloslavsky v. U.K. (A/323) [1996] E.M.L.R. 152; (1995) 20
    E.H.R.R. 442 .... 1.19, 2.12
Tomasi v. France (A/241-A) (1993) 15 E.H.R.R. 1 .... 3.19
Torquay Hotel Co. Ltd v. Cousins [1969] 2 Ch. 106; [1969] 2 W.L.R. 289 .. 8.08
Toth v. Austria (A/224) (1992) 14 E.H.R.R. 551 .... 3.19
Tre Traktorer AB v. Sweden (A/159) (1991) 13 E.H.R.R. 309 ...... 7.04, 7.09, 9.41
Treholt v. Norway, 71 D.R. 191 .... 4.25, 4.26
Tsirilis v. Greece (1998) 25 E.H.R.R. 198 .... 4.17
Tudhope v. Barlow, 1981 S.L.T. (Sh. Ct.) 94 .... 2.17
Tyrer v. U.K. (A/26) (1979-80) 2 E.H.R.R. 1 .... 3.17, 4.04, 4.19, 4.26, 4.29, 5.19
U.K. Association of Professional Engineers (U.K.APE) v. Advisory,
    Conciliation and Arbitration Service (ACAS); *sub nom.* Advisory,
    Conciliation and Arbitration Service v. U.K. Association of Profes-
    sional Engineers and Butchart; U.K.APE v. ACAS [1981] A.C. 424;
    [1980] 2 W.L.R. 254 .... 8.08
Umlauft v. Austria (A/328B) (1996) 22 E.H.R.R. 76 .... 4.29
Unterpertinger v. Austria (A/110) (1991) 13 E.H.R.R. 175; *The Times*,
    December 10, 1986 .... 3.40, 9.44
Upper Crathes Fishings Ltd v. Bailey's Executors; *sub nom.* Upper Crathes
    Fishings Ltd v. Barclay, 1991 S.L.T. 747, 1 Div; affirming 1990 S.L.T.
    46 .... 7.34, 7.35
Uprichard v. Fife Council, 2000 S.C.L.R. 949; [2001] Env. L.R. 8 .... 1.51
Valsamis v. Greece (1997) 24 E.H.R.R. 294; [1998] E.L.R. 430 .... 5.22
Van de Hurk v. Netherlands (A/288) (1994) 18 E.H.R.R. 481 .... 7.12, 9.45, 9.49
Van Droogenbroeck v. Belgium (A/50) (1982) 4 E.H.R.R. 443 .... 4.17, 4.22
Van Oosterwijck v. Belgium (A/40) (1981) 3 E.H.R.R. 557 .... 5.36
Vella v. U.K., unreported, September 1, 1993 .... 4.42
Velosa Bareto v. Portugal (A/334) 7.33
Vereinigung Demokratischer Soldaten Osterreichs and Gubi v. Austria (A/
    302) (1995) 20 E.H.R.R. 56 .... 2.12
Vereniging Rechtwinkel Utrecht v. Netherlands (1986) 46 D.R. 200 ...... 8.01, 8.15
Victoria v. Commonwealth (1975) 134 C.L.R. 81 .... 9.63
Vilvarajah v. U.K. (A/215) (1992) 14 E.H.R.R. 248; *The Times*, November 12,
    1991 .... 9.32
Vogt v. Germany (A/323) (1996) 21 E.H.R.R. 205; [1996] E.L.R. 232 ... 2.13, 8.02
Vriend v. Alberta (1994) 152 A.R. 1, QBD 1.47
Vriend v. Alberta, 4 B.H.R.C. 140; [1998] S.C.R. 493 .... 1.47, 9.71
W v. U.K. (A/121) (1988) 10 E.H.R.R. 29 .... 5.14, 7.11, 7.45, 9.43
W and DM v. U.K.; M and IH v. U.K., 7 E.H.R.R. 135 .... 5.22
Wachauf v. Germany (5/88); *sub nom.* Wachauf v. Bundesamt fur Ernahrung
    und Forstwirtschaft [1989] E.C.R. 2609; [1991] 1 C.M.L.R. 328 ...... 1.08
Walker v. Strathclyde R.C. (No.2), 1987 S.L.T. 81 .... 9.19
Walsh v. Secretary of State for Scotland, 1990 S.L.T. 526; 1990 S.C.L.R. 350   9.54
Wang v. Inland Revenue Commissioner [1994] 1 W.L.R. 1286; [1995] 1 All
    E.R. 637 .... 9.53
Ward v. Bradford Corp., 115 S.J. 606 .... 9.52
Watt v. Advocate (Lord), 1979 S.C. 120; 1979 S.L.T. 137 .... 9.28
Watt v. Annan, 1978 J.C. 84; 1978 S.L.T. 198 .... 2.17
Watt v. Jamieson, 1954 S.C. 56; 1954 S.L.T. 56 .... 7.28
Weeks v. U.K. (A/114) (1988) 10 E.H.R.R. 293; *The Times*, March 5,
    1987 .... 1.27, 4.17, 4.19, 4.22, 4.24, 4.26

Welch v. U.K. (A/307-A) (1995) 20 E.H.R.R. 247; *The Times*, February 15,
  1995 .... 2.08, 4.08, 4.31
Wemhoff v. Germany (A/7) (1979-80) 1 E.H.R.R. 55 .... 3.30, 3.32
Wenn v. Att.-Gen. of Victoria (1948) 77 C.L.R. 84 .... 9.71
West v. Scottish Prison Service; *sub nom.* West v. Secretary of State for
  Scotland, 1992 S.C. 385; 1992 S.L.T. 636 . 1.17, 9.08, 9.09, 9.12, 9.35
West v. Secretary of State for Scotland. See West v. Scottish Prison Service.
Western Australia v. Commonwealth (1995) 183 C.L.R. 373 .... 9.68
Western Isles Islands Council v. Caledonian MacBrayne Ltd, 1990 S.L.T. (Sh.
  Ct.) 97 .... 9.18
Westminster City Council v. Great Portland Estates Plc; *sub nom.* Great
  Portland Estates Plc v. Westminster City Council [1985] A.C. 661;
  [1984] 3 W.L.R. 1035 .... 7.21
Whaley v. Lord Watson of Invergowrie; *sub nom.* Whalley v. Lord Watson of
  Invergowrie, 2000 S.C. 340; 2000 S.L.T. 475 1.29, 9.12, 9.61, 9.63, 9.67
White v. White, 1999 S.L.T. (Sh Ct) 106; 1999 G.W.D. 28-1308 .. 5.30, 5.31
Whitehouse v. Gay News and Lemon. See R. v. Lemon (Denis).
Wickramasinghe v. U.K. [1998] E.H.R.L.R. 338 .... 8.22, 9.45
Wiggins v. U.K., 13 D.R. 40 .... 7.13
Wildridge v. Anderson (1897) 25 R. (J.) 27 .... 9.50
Wille v. Liechtenstein (2000) 30 E.H.R.R. 558; 8 B.H.R.C. 69 .... 1.49, 1.53
Wilson v. Brown, 1982 S.L.T. 361; 1982 S.C.C.R. 49 .... 8.09
Wilson v. Independent Broadcasting Authority, 1979 S.C. 351; 1979 S.L.T.
  279 .... 9.20
Wilson v. United Counties Bank Ltd [1920] A.C. 102 .... 8.08
Windisch v. Austria (A/186) (1991) 13 E.H.R.R. 281 .... 1.27
Windsor v. U.K., unreported, December 12, 1991 .... 4.44
Wingrove v. U.K. (1997) 24 E.H.R.R. 1; 1 B.H.R.C. 509 .... 2.02
Winterwerp v. Netherlands (A/33) (1979-80) 2 E.H.R.R. 387 .... 3.06, 4.17
Woningen v. Netherlands (1997) 24 E.H.R.R. 456 .... 9.49
Wordie Property Co. Ltd v. Secretary of State for Scotland, 1984 S.L.T.
  345 .... 9.29, 9.36, 9.45
Worm v. Austria (1998) 25 E.H.R.R. 454; 3 B.H.R.C. 180 .... 2.02
Wynne v. U.K. (A/294-A (1995) 19 E.H.R.R. 333; *The Times*, July 27,
  1994 .... 4.19, 4.21
X (Minors) v. Bedfordshire CC; M (A Minor) v. Newham L.B.C.; E (A
  Minor) v. Dorset CC; Christmas v. Hampshire CC (Duty of Care);
  Keating v. Bromley L.B.C. [1995] 2 A.C. 633; [1995] 3 W.L.R. 152
  .... 6.05-6.08, 6.12, 9.23
X, Petr, 1957 S.L.T. (Sh. Ct.) 61; (1957) 73 Sh. Ct. Rep. 203 .... 5.36
X v. Austria (1963) 11 C.D. 31 .... 3.28, 3.29
X v. Austria (1989) 11 E.H.R.R. 112 .... 3.07
X v. Austria (4161/69) (1970) 13 Y.B. 798 .... 2.13
X v. Belgium (8249/78); *sub nom.* Belgian Advocate, Re [1981] E.C.C. 214 . 2.08
X v. Germany (6541/74) (1974) 1 D.R. 82 .... 3.26
X v. Iceland (1976) 5 D.R. 86 .... 3.12
X v. Ireland (1971) 14 Y.B. 198 .... 9.10
X v. Netherlands (A/91); Y v. Netherlands (1986) 8 E.H.R.R. 235 ...... 2.02, 2.04,
                                                            3.02, 3.12, 5.29, 6.11, 8.10
X v. Switzerland (1978) 12 D. and R. 241 .... 5.02
X v. U.K. (1978) 2 Digest 688 .... 3.28
X v. U.K. (1984) 6 E.H.R.R. 583 .... 8.22
X v. U.K. (1998) 25 E.H.R.R. CD 88 .... 9.43
X v. U.K., 2 D.R. 105 .... 5.02
X v. U.K., 28 D.R. 177 .... 7.24
X v. U.K., unreported, July 18, 1974 .... 4.42
X and Y v. U.K. 5.33
X Association v. Sweden (1982) 28 D.R. 204 .... 1.26
X, Y and Z v. U.K. [1997] 2 F.L.R. 892; [1997] 3 F.C.R. 341 1.26, 5.04, 5.34, 5.37

Y v. U.K. (A/247-A) (1994) 17 E.H.R.R. 238 .... 5.20
Yasa v. Turkey (1999) 28 E.H.R.R. 408; [1998] H.R.C.D. 828 .... 3.02
Young v. Criminal Injuries Compensation Board, 1997 S.L.T. 297 .... 9.46
Young v. Heatly, 1959 J.C. 66; 1959 S.L.T. 250 .... 2.17
Young, James and Webster v. U.K. (A/55) (Art.50) [1983] I.R.L.R. 35; (1983)
    5 E.H.R.R. 201 .... 1.27, 8.03, 8.08, 9.10
Yuen Kun Yeu v. Att.-Gen. of Hong Kong [1988] A.C. 175; [1987] 3 W.L.R.
    776 .... 6.09
Z v. U.K. [2000] 2 F.C.R. 245; (2000) 2 L.G.L.R. 212 .. 6.05, 6.07, 6.08, 6.11, 9.23
Zand v. Austria [1981] E.C.C. 50 .... 9.50, 9.51
Zander v. Sweden (A/279-B) (1994) 18 E.H.R.R. 175 .... 1.27
Zimmerman and Steiner v. Switzerland (1984) 6 E.H.R.R. 17 .... 9.47
Zumtobel v. Austria (A/268-A) (1994) 17 E.H.R.R. 116 .... 9.46

TABLE OF STATUTES

1567 Incest Act (9 Eliz. 1) 2.16
1845 Lands Clauses Consoli-
        dation   (Scotland)
        Act (8 & 9 Vict.,
        c.19)
        s.61 .... 7.26
1861 Offences Against the Per-
        son Act (24 & 25
        Vict., c.100)
        s.47 .... 2.04
1876 Appellate   Jurisdiction
        Act (39 & 40 Vict,
        c.59)
        s.25 .... 1.30
1880 Married Women's Policy
        of Assurance (Scot-
        land) Act (43 & 44
        Vict., c.26) 5.25
1947 Acquisition of Land
        (Authorisation Pro-
        cedure) (Scotland)
        Act (10 & 11 Geo.6,
        c.42) 7.25
        s.5(1) 7.25
        Sched.1, para.15 .. 7.25, 9.15
                     (1) ... 9.36
               para.16 .. 7.25, 9.15
        Crown Proceedings Act
        (10 & 11 Geo.6, c.44)
        s.21 .... 9.63
        (1)(a) 9.22
1959 Building (Scotland) Act
        (c.24)
        s.16 .... 9.15
1963 Land   Compensation
        (Scotland) Act (c.51) 7.26
1964 Succession   (Scotland)
        Act (c.41)
        s.8 .... 5.24
        s.9 .... 5.24
1965 Registration of Births,
        Deaths and Mar-
        riages   (Scotland)
        Act (c.49) 5.36
        Murder (Abolition of the
        Death penalty) Act
        (c.71) 4.15

1967 Parliamentary Commis-
        sioner Act (c.13) ... 9.03
        Abortion Act (c.87) . 5.05, 5.06
        s.1 .... 5.04
        (1)(a)-(d) 5.05
        s.5(2) 5.04
        Leashold Reform Act
        (c.88) 7.45
1970 Conveyancing and Feu-
        dal Reform (Scot-
        land) Act (c.35)
        s.1(4)(ii) 7.41
1971 Misuse of Drugs Act
        (c.38)
        s.23(3) 3.13
        Civil Aviation Act (c.75)
        s.3(2) 9.49
        Immigration Act (c.77)
        s.3(6) 4.30
        s.20 .... 9.43
1972 National Health Service
        (Scotland) Act (c.58) 9.03
        European Communities
        Act (c.68) 1.52
        s.3(1) 1.04
1973 Local Government (Scot-
        land) Act (c.65) 7.26
        s.71 .... 7.23
1974 Land Tenure Reform
        (Scotland) Act (c.38) 7.40
1975 Local Government (Scot-
        land) Act (c.30)
        Pt II 9.03
        Inheritance (Provisions
        for Family and De-
        pendents) Act (c.63)
        s.1A 5.24
        Sex Discrimination Act
        (c.65) 1.13, 1.22,
                         8.05, 8.20, 8.21
        s.76(5) 1.22, 9.19/1
1976 Damages (Scotland) Act
        (c.13)
        s.10 .... 5.25
        s.13(1)(b) 5.25
        Sched.1 .... 5.25
        Licensing (Scotland) Act
        (c.66) 9.36

1976	Licensing (Scotland) Act—*cont.*	
	s.16(1)(f)	9.50
	s.18	9.45
	s.31(1)	9.50
	s.39	9.15
	(4) . 9.25, 9.36, 9.39,	9.40
	(d)	9.36
	Race Relations Act (c.74)	
	s.68(6)	9.19/1
1977	Marriage (Scotland) Act (c.15)	
	s.1	5.24
	s.2	5.24
	s.5(4)(e)	5.35
	Sched.1	5.24
	Rent Act (c.42)	5.34
	Sched.1, para.2(2)	5.34
	para.3	5.34
1978	Northern Ireland (Emergency Provisions) Act (c.5)	4.27
	Adoption (Scotland) Act (c.28)	5.13, 5.33
	s.6	5.33
1980	Licensed Premises (Exclusion of Certain Persons) Act (c.32) .	4.12
	Education (Scotland) Act (c.44)	5.22
	s.28A	5.22
	(3)(a)(i)	5.22
	(ii)	5.22
	(vi)	5.22
	s.28F	9.15
	s.28H	5.23
	(1)	5.23
	(6)	5.23
	s.38	9.15
	s.48A	2.02, 5.20
	s.65	9.15
	Married Women's Policy of Assurance (Scotland) (Amendment) Act (c.56)	5.26
	Local Government Planning and Land Act (c.65)	7.26
1981	Animal Health Act (c.22)	7.37
	s.32	7.37
	Matrimonial Homes (Family Protection) (Scotland) Act (c.59)	5.24, 5.26, 5.28, 7.36
	ss.1-5	5.26
	s.4(2)	5.28
	s.5	5.28
	(2)	5.28
	s.14	5.26

1918	Matrimonial Homes (Family Protection) (Scotland) Act—*cont.*	
	s.15	5.26
	(1)(a)	5.28
	(b)	5.28
	s.19	7.36
	Wildlife and Countryside Act (c.69)	9.46
1982	Civil Aviation Act (c.16)	6.04
	Civil Jurisdiction and Judgments Act (c.27)	1.04
	Civic Government (Scotland) Act (c.45)	9.36
	s.4	9.25, 9.36, 9.39, 9.40
	s.76	9.15
	s.84	9.15
	s.106	9.15
	s.116	9.15
	Sched.1, para.11	9.50
	para.17	9.45
	para.18(7)	9.25, 9.36, 9.39, 9.40
	Administration of Justice Act (c.53)	
	s.8	5.25
	s.9	5.25
1984	Mental health (Scotland) Act (c.36)	
	s.17	9.58
	s.64	9.58
	Police and Criminal Evidence Act (c.60)	
	s.78	3.11
1985	Companies Act (c.6)	
	s.432	3.09
	s.442	3.09
	Family Law (Scotland) Act (c.37) .	5.24, 5.26, 5.27
	s.1	5.24
	(1)(a)	5.25
	(b)	5.25
	s.8(1)(aa)	5.27
	(bc)	5.27
	s.9(1)(a)	5.26
	(a)-(e)	5.26
	s.10	5.26
	s.14	5.27
	(1)	5.27
	(2)(a)	5.27
	(b)	5.27
	(c)	5.27
	s.18	5.24
	Bankruptcy (Scotland) Act (c.66)	7.36
	s.40	7.36
	Housing Act (c.68)	5.34

Law Reform (Miscella-
neous Provisions)
(Scotland) Act (c.73)   7.32,
                        7.33
s.4 ....   7.32
s.5 ....   7.32
1986 Drug Trafficking Of-
fences Act (c.32) ...   4.08,
                        4.31
s.2 ....   4.31
Legal Aid (Scotland) Act
(c.47) 8.06
Building Societies Act
(c.53) 9.03
Family Law Act (c.56) .   5.31
ss.25–33 ....   5.31
Education (No.2) Act
(c.61)
s.47 ....   5.20
s.48 ....   2.02
1987 Housing (Scotland) Act
(c.26)
s.52 ....   5.25
1988 Merchant Shipping Act
(c.12) 1.52
Court of Session Act
(c.36)
s.45(b) 9.22
Finance Act (c.39)
s.32 ....   5.25
Housing (Scotland) Act
(c.43)
s.31 ....   5.25
Road Traffic Act (c.52)   7.22
s.5(1)(a) 3.10
s.172 ....   1.13, 3.10
1989 Prevention of Terrorism
(Temporary Provi-
sions) Act (c.4)
s.22 ....   4.27
Children Act (c.41) ..   5.15, 5.29
1990 Town and Country planning Act (c.8) 9.43
Food Safety Act (c.16) .   7.37
s.9 ....   7.37
s.13 ....   7.38
1990 Contracts (Applicable
Law) Act (c.36)
s.3 ....   1.04
Human Fertilisation and
Embryology Act
(c.37) 5.02–5.05
s.3(1) 5.04
ss.5-26 ....   5.02
s.27(2) 5.03
s.28 ....   5.03
(1) 5.03, 5.37
(2) 5.03, 5.37
s.29(1) 5.03, 5.37

1990 Matrimonial Homes (Family Protection)
(Scotland) Act—
cont.
s.30 ....   5.03
s.37 ....   5.04
s.49(3) 5.03, 5.37
Sched.2, para.3 ....   5.04
Environmental Protec-
tion Act (c.43) ..   7.22, 7.28
s.71(2) 7.22
ss.79–80 ....   7.29
1991 Age of Legal Capacity
(Scotland) Act (c.50)
s.1(f) 5.17
s.2(4A) 5.17
(4B) 5.17
1992 Social Security Administration Act (c.5)
Pt II (ss.17–70) 9.45
s.12 ....   9.03
ss.64–66 ....   9.03
s.78 ....   5.25, 9.03
ss.167-168 ....   9.03
Local Government Fi-
nance Act (c.14)
s.75 ....   5.25
Trade Union and Labour
Relations (Consoli-
dation) Act (c.52) ..   8.03
s.15 ....   8.08
s.146 ....   8.08
s.220 ....   8.21
Tribunals and Inquiries
Act (c.53) 7.25
s.11 ....   9.15, 9.25, 9.43
1993 Prisoners and Criminal
Proceedings (Scot-
land) Act (c.9) ..   4.22, 4.24
s.2 ....   4.22, 4.23
(2) 4.22
(4) 4.22
(6) 1.10, 4.22
s.3 ....   4.22
Sched.2 ....   4.24
Asylum and Immigration
Appeals Act (c.23) .   9.16
Education Act (c.35)
s.293 ....   5.20
s.294 ....   5.20
1995 Environment Act (c.25)   7.29
Children (Scotland) Act
(c.36) 4.01, 5.17, 5.18,
                5.20, 5.29, 5.30
s.1(1) 5.30
s.3(1) 5.29
s.4 ....   5.29
s.6 ....   5.01, 5.17
s.11 ....   5.15, 5.29

1995 Children (Scotland)
Act—*cont.*
(7) 5.01, 5.17
s.16(2) 5.17
ss.32–85 .... 5.13
Criminal Law (Consoli-
dation) (Scotland)
Act (c.39)
s.24 .... 3.06
Proceeds of Crime (Scot-
land) Act (c.43) 4.30
s.3(2) ... 1.31, 3.36, 4.07, 4.31
s.249 .... 4.30
Criminal Procedure
(Scotland) Act (c.46) 4.01
s.14 .... 3.06
(6) 3.08
s.22A 3.19
s.23A 3.19
s.24 .... 3.19
s.26 .... 3.19
s.32 .... 3.19
s.41 .... 2.24
s.54(1)(c) 4.16
(6) 4.16
s.55(3) 4.16
s.57(1) 4.16
(2) 4.16
(3) 4.16
s.124(2) 1.31, 1.48
s.204(2) 4.16
(5) 4.16
s.205(1) 4.18
(2) 4.18, 4.23
(3) 4.18, 4.21
s.207(1) 4.16
(2) 4.16
(3) 4.16
s.228 .... 4.09
s.238 .... 4.09
(2) 4.29
ss.245A-245I 4.09
s.259 .... 3.40
(4) 3.40
1996 Employment Rights Act
(c.18) 8.11
Pt 10 .... 8.14
s.21 .... 9.43
s.96(2)(b) 8.11
s.98(1) 8.11
(b) 8.17
(4) . 8.11, 8.14, 8.18, 8.20
s.108(1) 8.22
s.111 .... 1.22
s.123(6) 8.12
1997 Town and Country Planning (Scotland) Act
(c.8) 7.20, 7.23,
7.24, 9.18, 9.36, 9.50

1997 Town and Country Planning (Scotland)
Act—*cont.*
Pt VI 7.22
Pt VIII 7.24
s.8(9) 9.45
s.10 .... 7.20
s.17 .... 7.20
s.18 .... 7.20
s.19 .... 7.20
s.90(1)(c) 9.45
s.125 .... 7.22
s.126 .... 7.22
s.179 .... 7.26
ss.188-201 .... 7.23, 7.24
s.189 .... 7.24
s.200 .... 7.25
s.238 .... 7.21, 9.15, 9.36
ss.238-239 .... 9.18, 9.19/1
s.239 .... 9.15, 9.36
s.272 .... 7.22
(4) 7.22
Planning (Listed Build-
ings and Conserva-
tion Areas)
(Scotland) Act (c.9)
s.58 .... 7.18
Nurses, Midwives and
Health Visitors Act
(c.24)
s.12 .... 8.07
Scottish Legal Services
Ombudsman and
Commissioner for
Local Administra-
tion in Scotland Act
(c.35) 9.03
Crime and Punishment
(Scotland) Act (c.48)
s.5 .... 4.09
s.16 .... 4.23
Police Act (c.50) 3.13
Sex Offenders Act (c.51) 4.08
Pt S.I. 4.30
Sched.1 .... 4.30
1998 Social Security Act (c.14)
s.10(1) 9.49
s.14 .... 9.43
s.26 .... 9.50
ss.36–38 .... 9.03
Crime and Disorder Act
(c.37)
s.36 .... 4.15
Government of Wales
Act (c.38) 1.01,
1.29, 1.50, 1.52
s.107 .... 1.01, 1.39
(4)(a) 1.18, 1.41
(b) 1.40

1998 Government of Wales
  Act—*cont.*
    s.110 .... 1.36
    Sched.8 .... 1.29, 1.52
      para.1 .... 1.29
      para.2 .... 1.29
      para.6 .... 1.34
      para.7 .... 1.34
      para.8 .... 1.34
      para.10 ...... 1.34
      para.11 ...... 1.34
      para.15 ...... 1.34
      para.16 ...... 1.34
      para.17 ...... 1.34
      para.18 ...... 1.34
      para.19 ...... 1.34
      para.20 ...... 1.34
      para.21 ...... 1.34
      para.25 ...... 1.34
      para.26 ...... 1.34
      para.27 ...... 1.34
      para.28 ...... 1.34
      para.29 ...... 1.34
      paras 30-31 . 1.35
      para.32 ...... 1.33
  Human Rights Act (c.42) 1.01–
    1.04, 1.06, 1.07, 1.09–1.11,
    1.13, 1.17–1.26, 1.28, 1.31,
    1.33, 1.37, 1.42, 1.44, 1.45,
    1.50–1.53, 1.55, 1.56, 2.02,
    2.03, 3.01, 4.15, 5.09–5.11,
    5.21, 5.26, 5.34, 6.01, 7.01,
    7.15, 7.28, 7.29, 7.32, 7.34,
    7.37, 7.40, 8.01, 8.05–8.07,
    8.10, 8.11, 8.16, 8.17, 8.19,
    8.20, 8.27, 9.01–9.06, 9.09,
    9.12, 9.13, 9.19, 9.20–9.22,
    9.24, 9.31, 9.35, 9.45, 9.54,
    9.56, 9.59, 9.61, 9.63, 9.65,
                    9.72–9.74
    s.1 .... 2.02
      (1) 1.02
    s.2 ...... 1.04, 9.10, 9.22, 9.35
      (1) 9.27
      (a) 9.27
    s.3 .... 1.10, 1.11, 1.13,
    1.20, 1.21, 1.50, 7.33, 8.06,
    8.07, 8.16, 9.01, 9.02, 9.07,
    9.21, 9.28, 9.35, 9.53, 9.61,
                9.65, 9.71, 9.73
      (1) 1.16, 1.21, 1.22,
            1.44, 7.33, 8.11, 9.65
      (2) 1.14, 8.16
    s.4 .... 1.14, 1.45, 1.50,
    1.53, 7.33, 8.22, 9.01,
                9.07, 9.28, 9.65
      (2) 1.14
      (6)(a) 1.14
      (b) 1.14

1998 Human Rights Act—
  cont.
    s.5 .... 1.14
      (2) 1.14
    s.6 ...... 1.17, 1.20, 1.21, 1.48,
    3.13, 7.28, 8.07, 8.22, 9.02,
    9.03, 9.07–9.10, 9.27–9.29
      (1) ... 1.07, 1.17, 6.01, 8.07,
    8.11, 8.20, 8.22, 9.06, 9.08,
        9.10, 9.16, 9.63, 9.72
      (2) ... 1.18, 1.41, 1.42, 8.07,
                  9.53, 9.72
        (a) 9.06
        (b) 1.13, 1.18, 9.06,
                        9.16
      (3) ... 1.17, 6.01, 8.19, 9.48
        (a) 1.19, 1.44, 7.34,
                        9.06
        (b) 1.50, 9.06, 9.08–9.10
      (5) ... 1.17, 1.38, 9.06, 9.08,
                        9.09
      (6) ... 1.16, 1.17, 1.38, 1.45,
        9.06, 9.07, 9.61, 9.63
    s.7 ...... 8.06, 8.07, 8.12, 8.19,
        9.16, 9.18, 9.74
      (1) ... 1.22, 1.25, 8.19, 9.06,
            9.09, 9.14, 9.74
        (a) 1.22, 9.16, 9.18,
                        9.19/1
        (b) 1.50, 1.52, 9.16,
                        9.18
      (3) 9.09, 9.16, 9.20
      (4) 9.16, 9.20
      (5) 9.09
        (a) 1.22
        (b) 1.22, 9.19/1
      (6) 9.16
      (7) 1.25
      (9) 1.23, 1.50
        (b) 9.16
      (11) 9.16
        (a) 9.22
        (b) 9.22
    s.8 ...... 1.27, 6.01, 7.15, 8.19,
        9.17, 9.22, 9.23, 9.74
      (1) 6.01
      (3) ... 1.40, 8.06, 9.66, 9.74
      (4) ... 1.27, 1.40, 9.66, 9.74
    s.9(1) 1.23
      (b) 9.09
      (3) 1.27
    s.10 .... 1.16, 9.07
    ss.10–12 .... 1.44
    s.11 .... 9.14
      (a) 1.03
      (b) 1.22
    s.12 .... 1.23, 9.57
      (2) 8.09
      (b) 1.23

1998 Human   Rights   Act—
      cont.
      (4) 9.57
      s.13 .... 1.25, 9.57
      (1) 9.57
      s.15 .... 5.21
      s.17 .... 5.21
      s.19 .... 1.01, 1.22, 9.07
      s.20(1) 9.16
      (4) 9.15
      s.21 .... 1.16
      (1) 9.48, 9.65, 9.73
      s.22(4) 1.22, 9.16
      s.23(a) 9.22
      Sched.1 2.02, 4.15, 9.22, 9.54
      Sched.2 .... 1.16
      Sched.4, para.7(2) 1.43
      Scotland Act (c.46) 1.01,
          1.28–1.30, 1.32, 1.38, 1.42,
          1.45, 1.47, 1.50–1.53, 1.55,
          1.56, 2.02, 7.29, 7.37, 7.40,
          9.01, 9.02, 9.04, 9.05, 9.13,
          9.18, 9.19/1-9.21, 9.24, 9.27–
          9.29, 9.35, 9.59, 9.61, 9.63,
              9.65, 9.66, 9.72, 9.74
      s.19 .... 9.61
      s.20 .... 9.61
      s.21 .... 9.61
      s.22 .... 9.61
      ss.23–27 .... 9.61
      s.28(5) 9.61
      s.29 .... 2.03, 7.40, 9.28
      (1) . 4.15, 9.60, 9.64, 9.68
      (2) 9.60, 9.67
      (d) 1.16, 1.42, 4.15,
              9.58, 9.60, 9.64
      s.31 .... 9.61, 9.62, 9.63
      (1) 9.62
      (2) 9.62, 9.63
      s.33 .... 9.62, 9.63, 9.74
      (1) ....
      s.35 .... 9.62
      (1)(a) 9.14
      s.40 .... 9.61, 9.63, 9.67
      (3) 9.67
      (4) 9.67
      s.41 .... 9.61
      (1)(a) 9.61
      (b) 9.61
      s.44(2) 9.72
      s.47 .... 9.72
      s.49 .... 9.72
      s.52(2) 9.63
      (7) 9.63
      s.53 .... 1.01
      (1) 9.72
      (2) 9.72
      s.54 .... 9.28
      (1) 9.72

1998 Scotland Act—*cont.*
      (2)(a) 9.72
      (b) 9.72
      (3) 9.72
      s.57 .... 3.31, 9.28
      (2) 1.16, 1.36, 1.38,
              1.42, 1.45, 3.01,
              3.30, 7.18, 9.72
      (3) 1.18, 1.42, 9.72
      s.58 .... 1.46, 9.62
      (1) 9.14
      (3) 1.46
      s.91 .... 9.03
      s.98 .... 9.65, 9.74
      s.100 .... 1.39, 1.45, 9.20
      (1) 1.25, 9.74
      (3) 1.27, 1.40, 9.23,
              9.66, 9.74
      (4) 1.45, 9.23, 9.63, 9.72
      (b) 1.38
      s.101 ... 1.16, 9.01, 9.02, 9.21,
              9.28, 9.35, 9.53,
              9.64, 9.65, 9.71
      (3)(a) 9.65
      (b) 9.65
      s.102 ... 1.36, 1.44, 9.38, 9.67,
              9.69
      (2) 9.69
      (a) 9.69
      (b) 9.69
      (3) 9.69
      (7) 9.69
      s.103 .... 1.33, 9.62
      s.107 .... 9.69
      (a) 9.69
      (b) 9.69
      s.126(1) 1.46, 2.02,
              9.61–9.63
      Sched.2 .... 9.61
      Sched.3 .... 9.61
      Sched.4, para.1(2)(f) .. 4.15
      Sched.5, Pt 1, para.7(2) 9.59
      Pt III, para.1 9.72
      Sched.6 .... 1.01, 1.29, 1.36,
              1.52, 1.53, 9.67, 9.74
      para.1 .... 1.29
      (e) ..1.38, 1.45
      para.2 .... 1.29
      para.7 .... 1.34
      para.8 .... 1.34
      para.9 .... 1.34
      para.10 ..... 1.34
      para.11 ..... 1.34
      para.12 ..... 1.34
      para.13 ..... 1.34
      para.18 ..... 1.34
      para.19 ..... 1.34
      para.20 ..... 1.34
      para.21 ..... 1.34

1998	Scotland Act—*cont.*	
	para.22	1.34
	para.23	1.34
	para.28	1.34
	para.29	1.34
	para.30	1.34
	para.31	1.34
	para.32	1.34
	paras 33-35	1.35
	Northern Ireland Act (c.47)	1.01, 1.29, 1.50, 1.52
	s.6(2)(c)	1.01
	s.24(1)(a)	1.01
	s.71	1.39
	(3)(a)	1.18, 1.40
	(b)	1.40
	(4)(a)	1.18, 1.40
	(b)	1.40
	s.81	1.36
	s.82	1.33
	Sched.10	1.29, 1.52
	para.1	1.29
	para.2	1.29
	para.7	1.34
	para.8	1.34
	para.9	1.34
	para.10	1.34
	para.15	1.34
	para.16	1.34
	para.17	1.34
	para.18	1.34
	para.19	1.34
	para.20	1.34
	para.25	1.34
	para.26	1.34
	para.27	1.34
	para.28	1.34
	para.29	1.34
	para.30	1.34
	para.31	1.34
	para.32	1.34
	paras 33-35	1.35
1999	Youth Justice and Criminal Evidence Act (c.23)	
	s.34	1.43
	Employment Relations Act (c.26)	8.08
	s.3	8.12
	s.16	8.08
	Sched.15	8.08
	Welfare Reform and Pensions Act (c.30)	
	s.20	5.27
2000	Regulation of Investigatory Powers Act (c.23)	3.13
	s.65(2)(a)	1.22

Acts of the Scottish Parliament

1999	Mental Health (Public Safety and Appeals) (Scotland) Act (asp 1)	1.55, 9.58
2000	Abolition of Feudal Tenure etc. (Scotland) Act (asp 5)	7.32, 7.40
	ss.7-12	7.40
	s.8(1)	7.40
	s.9	7.40
	s.16	7.40
	s.17	7.40
	s.18	7.40
	s.19	7.40
	s.32	7.41
	ss.32–38	7.41
	s.34(2)	7.41
	s.36	7.41
	s.42	7.41
	s.53	7.32
	Standards in Scotland's Schools etc. (Scotland) Act (asp 6)	
	s.1	5.21
	s.41	5.23
	Bail, Judicial Appointments etc. (Scotland) Act (asp 9)	3.19, 3.34
	Regulation of Investigatory Powers (Scotland) Act (asp 11)	3.13

TABLE OF STATUTORY INSTRUMENTS

1975	Schools General (Scotland) Regulations (S.I. 1975 No.1135)	5.23
1981	Pensions Appeal Tribunals (Scotland) Rules (S.I. 1981 No.500) .	1.28
	r.6	1.28
1982	Schools General (Amendment) (Scotland) Regulations (S.I. 1982 No.56) ...	5.23
	Schools General (Amendment) (Scotland) Regulations (S.I. 1982 No.1735)	5.23
1986	Children's Hearing (Scotland) Rules (S.I. 1986 No.2291)	5.17
1987	Social Security Commissioner Procedure Regulations (S.I. 1987 No.214)	9.46
1992	Town and Country Planning (General Development Procedure) (Scotland) Order (S.I. 1992 No.224)	
	Art.22	9.45
1993	Act of Sederunt (Sheriff Court Ordinary Cause Rules) (S.I. 1993 No.1956)	
	Ch.33	5.27
	r.33.7(1)(h)	5.19
	r.33.49	5.27
	Parole Board (Scotland) Rules (S.I. 1993 No.2225)	4.24
1994	Act of Sederunt (Rules of the Court of Session) (S.I. 1994 No.1443)	
	r.14.3(d)	9.17
	Ch.25A	1.50
	r.41.18	9.17
	Ch.49	5.27
	r.49.8(1)(h)	5.19
	(7)	5.19
	r.49.47	5.27

1994	Act of Sederunt (Rules of the Court of Session) —cont.	
	Ch.58	9.17
	r.58.3(2)	9.19
	r.58.4	9.17, 9.22
	r.58.7	9.19
	Diseases of Fish (Control) Regulations (S.I. 1994 No. 1447)	7.37
	Prisons and Young Offenders Institutions (Scotland) Rules (S.I. 1994 No.1931 (s.85))	4.37
	Pt 5	4.10
	r.116	4.42
	Parental Orders (Human Fertilisation and Embryology) (Scotland) Regulations (S.I. 1994 Nos 2767, 2804 and 3345)	5.03
1997	Town and Country planning (Inquiries Procedure) (Scotland) Rules (S.I. 1997 No.796)	9.53
1998	Compulsory Purchase by Public Authorities (Inquiries Procedure) (Scotland) Rules (S.I. 1998 No.2313)	
	r.17(2)	7.25
	r.18(4)	7.25
	r.21	7.25
	Human Rights Act 1998 (Commencement No.1) Order (S.I. 1998 No.2882)	1.01, 1.22
	Scotland Act 1998 (Commencement) Order (S.I. 1998 No.3179)	
	Art.2(1)	1.01
	Art.2(2)	1.01
	Sched.3	1.01
	Sched.4	1.01

1999 Judicial Committee (Devolution Issues) Rules Order (S.I. 1999 No.665) 1.50

Sex Discrimination (Gender Reassignment) Regulations (S.I. 1999 No.1102) 8.20

Act of Sederunt (Devolution Issue Rules) (S.I. 1999 No.1345) 1.50

Act of Adjournal (Devolution Issue Rules) (S.I. 1999 No.1346) 1.50

Act of Sederunt (Proceedings for Determination of Devolution Issue Rules) (S.I. 1999 No.1347) 1.50

Scotland Act 1998 (Transitory and Transitional Provisions) (Complaints of Maladministration) Order (S.I. 1999 No.1351) 9.03

2000 Human Rights Act 1998 (Commencement No.2) Order (S.I. 2000 No.1851) .. 1.01, 1.22

Scottish Statutory Instruments
2000 Human Rights Act 1998 (Jurisdiction) (Scotland) Rules (S.S.I. 2000 No.301) 1.22, 1.50, 9.16
    reg.3 .... 1.22
    reg.4 .... 1.23

Act of Sederunt (Rules of the Court of Session Amendment (No.5) Public Interest Intervention in Judicial Review) (S.S.I. 2000 No.317) 9.20

2001 Advice and Assistance (Assistance by Way of Representation) (Scotland) Regulations (S.S.I. 2001 No.2) 8.06

EC TREATIES AND CONVENTIONS

1950 European Convention on
      Human Rights and
      Fundamental Free-
      doms 1.01–1.05,
      1.07, 1.08, 1.10–1.21, 1.25–
      1.28, 1.36, 1.42, 1.48, 1.54,
      2.01, 2.02, 2.06, 2.08–2.10,
      2.12, 2.16, 2.18, 2.20, 2.25,
      2.28, 3.08, 3.21, 3.27, 3.34,
      3.38–3.40, 4.14, 4.15, 4.18,
      4.19, 4.25, 4.29, 4.32, 4.34,
      4.39, 4.41, 4.44, 4.45, 4.47,
      5.01–5.04, 5.06, 5.08, 5.10,
      5.11, 5.15, 5.17, 5.19–5.25,
      5.30, 5.33, 5.34, 5.37, 5.38,
      6.01, 6.06, 7.01, 7.03, 7.04,
      7.13, 7.14, 7.16, 7.19, 7.23,
      7.26–7.28, 7.32–7.35, 7.37–
      7.45, 8.01, 8.02, 8.06, 8.08,
      8.10, 8.21, 9.21, 9.27, 9.28,
      9.33, 9.37, 9.55, 9.59, 9.62,
      9.63
      Pt III 4.14
      Art.1 ... 1.19, 2.04, 5.26, 9.10
      Art.2 ... 1.02, 2.02, 2.05, 3.02,
      3.14, 4.03, 4.39, 5.06–5.10,
      5.21, 6.02–6.04, 6.11, 7.30,
      7.31
          (1) 2.05, 4.15, 5.06,
          5.10, 5.11
          (2) 2.02, 2.05
      Art.3 ... 1.02, 1.03, 2.04, 2.24,
      3.02, 3.16, 3.28, 4.04, 4.15,
      4.17, 4.19, 4.25, 4.26, 4.29,
      4.34–4.40, 5.06, 5.19, 5.20,
      6.03, 6.05, 6.11, 9.32, 9.57
          (2) 4.31
      Art.4 ... 1.02, 1.03, 4.05, 4.29
          (1) 4.29
          (2) 4.05, 4.29
      Art.5 .. 1.02, 1.03, 1.55, 3.03–
      3.05, 3.26, 4.05, 4.06, 4.17,
      4.18, 4.20, 4.27, 4.28, 5.28
          (1) 2.10, 2.13, 3.04,
          3.06, 3.08, 4.17, 4.19,
          4.22, 4.26
          (a) 4.06, 4.17
          (b) 4.06

1950 European Convention on
      Human Rights and
      Fundamental Free-
      doms—cont.
          (c) ... 3.04, 3.06, 3.07
          (d) 4.06
          (e) ... 1.56, 4.06, 4.17,
          9.58
          (2) 3.08, 3.08
          (3) 3.08, 3.18–3.20
          (4) 1.56, 3.18, 3.20,
          4.06, 4.19–4.22, 4.24
          (5) 1.27, 4.06
      Art.6 .. 1.02–1.04, 1.08, 1.30–
      1.33, 1.36, 2.26, 3.01, 3.09,
      3.11, 3.17, 3.26, 3.27, 3.29,
      3.31, 3.32, 3.38, 3.40, 3.41,
      4.06, 4.07, 4.31, 4.45, 5.16,
      5.18, 5.26, 6.07–6.10, 7.02,
      7.08–7.10, 7.19, 7.26, 7.30,
      7.39, 7.45, 8.01, 8.02, 8.04,
      8.06–8.08, 8.22, 8.24–8.26,
      9.19, 9.24, 9.36, 9.38, 9.40–
      9.43, 9.45, 9.48, 9.49, 9.52,
      9.53
          (1) 1.04, 1.08, 1.13,
          1.25, 1.28, 1.36, 1.45, 1.53,
          3.11, 3.17, 3.27–3.31, 3.33,
          3.34, 3.36, 3.40, 4.07, 4.45,
          5.17, 5.18, 5.27, 6.07, 7.09–
          7.12, 7.15, 7.17, 7.19, 7.22,
          7.25, 7.26, 7.45, 8.02, 8.04,
          8.06, 8.07, 8.22, 8.24, 9.07,
          9.19/1, 9.39, 9.40,
          9.42–9.48, 9.51, 9.53,
          9.61
          (2) 1.30, 2.26,
          2.27, 3.09, 3.35,
          3.36, 4.07, 4.31,
          8.07, 9.39
          (3) 3.21, 9.39
          (a) ... 3.21, 3.22, 3.24,
          3.25
          (b) 3.37, 3.38
          (c) ... 1.43, 3.09, 3.29,
          3.39
          (d) ... 3.27, 3.40, 3.41
          (e) 3.25

1950 European Convention on
         Human Rights and
         Fundamental Free-
         doms—*cont.*
         Art.7 ... 1.02, 1.03, 2.06, 2.08,
             2.10, 2.15, 2.19, 2.20,
                 3.21, 4.08
             (1) 2.08, 2.09, 2.19, 2.21
             (2) 2.08, 2.09, 4.08, 4.31
         Art.8 ... 1.02, 1.03, 1.08, 1.13,
             2.04, 2.20, 2.28, 3.02, 3.07,
             3.11–3.13, 3.16, 3.17, 3.27,
             4.09, 4.40–4.42, 4.44, 4.45,
             5.04, 5.07, 5.08, 5.13–5.16,
             5.20, 5.24, 5.26, 5.28, 5.29–
             5.31, 5.33, 5.34, 5.36–5.38,
             6.03, 6.06, 6.11, 7.02, 7.13,
             7.18, 7.24, 7.25, 7.28, 7.30–
             7.32, 7.36, 8.01, 8.05, 8.10–
             8.12, 8.20, 9.27, 9.31, 9.32,
                 9.40, 9.54, 9.61
             (1) 3.11, 3.12, 5.03,
             5.04, 5.07, 5.13, 5.14, 9.54
             (2) 1.15, 2.10, 2.11, 3.11,
             3.13, 4.09, 4.44, 5.13–5.15,
             5.29, 8.10, 8.11, 8.17, 8.20,
                 9.32, 9.54, 9.57
         Arts 8–11 .... 1.08, 9.38, 9.57
         Arts 8–12 .... 9.30
         Art.9 ... 1.02, 1.03, 4.10, 7.17,
                 8.01, 8.15, 8.17
             (1) 8.15, 8.17
             (2) 1.15, 2.10, 4.10,
                 8.15, 8.17
         Art.10 . 1.02, 1.03, 1.08, 1.15,
             1.19, 1.25, 1.49, 3.29, 3.34,
             4.11, 7.31, 8.02, 8.03, 8.05,
             8.09, 8.10, 8.15, 8.17, 8.19,
                 8.20, 9.31
             (1) 5.08
             (2) 2.10, 8.15, 8.20,
                 9.32
         Art.11 . 1.02, 1.03, 1.15, 4.12,
             8.03, 8.08, 8.09, 8.15, 8.21
             (1) 8.03, 8.05
             (2) 2.10, 4.12, 8.08,
                 8.09
         Art.12 . 1.02, 1.03, 4.13, 5.02,
                 5.03, 5.24, 5.25,
                 5.35–5.39
         Art.13 . 1.03, 1.19, 1.45, 1.52,
                 7.30, 9.10, 9.22
         Art.14 . 1.02, 1.13, 4.27, 4.28,
             5.02, 5.03, 5.18, 5.21, 5.24,
             5.25, 5.29, 5.33, 5.38, 7.02,
             7.14, 7.17, 7.18, 7.25, 7.26,
                 7.39, 8.05, 8.21, 9.69
         Art.15 .... 2.08
             (1) 1.03

1950 European Convention on
         Human Rights and
         Fundamental Free-
         doms—*cont.*
             (2) 1.03
         Art.17 .... 2.20
         Art.25 .... 1.25
         Art.34 .... 1.25, 1.39
         Art.35 .... 1.28
         Art.40(3)(a) 2.24
         Art.41 .... 1.27, 1.40, 7.02,
                 7.15
         Art.50 .... 1.27, 5.20
         Protocol 1 .... 4.31
             Art.1 .. 1.02, 1.03,
             1.15, 1.25, 3.02, 3.14, 4.29,
             4.31, 5.26, 5.27, 7.02–7.05,
             7.07, 7.14, 7.17, 7.18, 7.24,
             7.25, 7.28, 7.33, 7.35, 7.38,
                 9.32, 9.57
             r.1 ... 7.05,
                 7.07
             r.2 ... 7.05,
                 7.06, 7.33
             r.3 .. 7.05–
                 7.07
             Art.2 .. 1.02, 1.03,
                 5.19, 5.21
             Art.3 .... 1.02
         Protocol 6 .... 4.15
             Art.1 .. 1.02, 4.15
             Art.2 .. 1.02, 4.15
         Protocol 7 .... 5.26
             Art.5 .... 5.26
         Protocol 11 . 1.05, 1.25, 1.27,
                 1.28, 4.03
1957 Treaty of Rome 1.04
         Art.29 (ex Art.34) 7.38
         Art.30 (ex Art.36) 7.38
         Art.230 .... 9.68
         Art.231 .... 9.68
             (2) 9.68
         Art.234 (ex Art.177) 1.34
1961 European Social Char-
         ter 1.46
1966 International Covenant
         on Civil and Political
         Rights (UN) 1.46, 9.14,
                 9.59
         Art.15(1) 2.06
1966 International Covenant
         on Economic, Social
         and Cultural Rights
         (UN) 1.46, 9.14
1979 Convention on the Elim-
         ination of all Forms
         of Discrimination
         Against Women
         (UN) 9.14

1989 Convention on the
        Rights of the Child
        (UN) 5.01, 5.17, 9.14, 9.59
1997 Treaty of Amster-
        dam 7.38
     African Convention on
        Human Rights
        Art.9 .... 2.06
     African Charter on Hu-
        man and Peoples'
        Rights
        Art.7(2) 2.06
        Art.9 .... 2.06

Beijing Rules
     r.4 .... 2.24
     Art.12 .... 5.17
     Art.19(1) 5.20
Convention 98 of the
     International La-
     bour Organisa-
     tion 8.08

THE HUMAN RIGHTS ACT AND THE SCOTLAND ACT—THE NEW CONSTITUTIONAL MATRIX

The European Convention was formally brought into force in   1.01
domesti'c Scots law in the same way as it was incorporated into the
laws of England and Wales and of Northern Ireland, namely by the
Human Rights Act 1998. Human rights considerations accordingly
impact on individual substantive issues of law in Scotland, for
example in areas such as family law, prisoners' rights, privacy
claims and delict, protection of property, employment law and
criminal law and procedure, in a similar manner to their effect in the
rest of the United Kingdom.

With the creation of a Scottish Parliament and the setting up of a
Scottish Executive answerable thereto, however, the European
Convention on Human Rights was given a different constitutional
status in Scotland from the rest of the United Kingdom. Under the
Scotland Act 1998, the rights guaranteed under the Convention
effectively have the status of a higher law as against any legislation
passed by the Scottish Parliament or any act of a member of the
Scottish Executive. Given this different constitutional character, the
domestication of the European Convention rights has a more
immediate and significant impact in Scotland than in the rest of the
United Kingdom.

The Scottish Ministers (other than the law officers) took up office
with effect from May 6, 1999,[1] but only began to exercise the
functions encompassed in section 53 of the Scotland Act on July 1,
1999, being the "principal appointed day".[2] The Lord Advocate's
actions have, however, been subject to direct Convention rights
scrutiny with effect from May 20, 1999, "Law Officer day", when
the offices of Lord Advocate and Solicitor General for Scotland
were devolved and they became members, *ex officio*, of the Scottish
Executive.[3] Since that date decisions made by the Lord Advocate as
head of the Crown Office, and as such responsible for criminal
prosecutions and the investigation of fatal accidents in Scotland,

---

[1]   See Art. 2(2) and Sched. 3 to the Scotland Act 1998 (Commencement) Order 1998
      (S.I.1998 No.3179)
[2]   See Art. 2(1) of the Scotland Act 1998 (Commencement) Order 1998 (S.I.1998
      No.3179)
[3]   See Art. 2(2) and Sched. 4 to the Scotland Act 1998 (Commencement) Order 1998
      (S.I.1998 No.3179)

became subject to review by the courts under the provisions of Schedule 6 to the Scotland Act 1998 insofar as raising "devolution issues". Similarly, the devolved assembly and executive committee created under the Government of Wales Act 1998 have been made subject to Convention rights from the outset of their operations.[4] Specific provision has also been made in Northern Ireland for the devolved institutions created by the Northern Ireland Act 1998 to work within the framework of respect for Convention rights.[5]

Such partial implementation of the Human Rights Act in the Celtic fringes of the United Kingdom has meant that prior to October 2, 2000, when the Human Rights Act was finally fully brought into force throughout the United Kingdom,[6] there had already been a number of important decisions from the courts in Scotland as to the proper interpretation and application of the Convention rights. Courts and practitioners in Scotland were given a head start over those of the rest of the United Kingdom in these matters. Judgments from the Scottish courts on the Convention thus could provide a model for the other jurisdictions of the United Kingdom's proper understanding and application of Convention rights in domestic law.

It must always be borne in mind in comparing Convention rights decisions across the United Kingdom jurisdictions, however, that in Scotland human rights have to be looked at and understood within the context of the dual framework of the Scotland Act and the Human Rights Act. This chapter will look at some of the issues raised by the inter-relationship between the Scotland Act and the Human Rights Act. It is the inter-relationship between these two constitutional statutes, and the new place that they give to the Scottish Judiciary, the Scottish Parliament and the Scottish Executive which will make the Scottish outlook on incorporation quite different from the rest of the United Kingdom.

THE HUMAN RIGHTS ACT 1998

The enumerated Convention Rights

1.02   The Human Rights Act 1998 incorporates into the domestic law of the United Kingdom a number of the rights set out in the European Convention on Human Rights and its associated protocols. Section 1(1) of the Act specifies that the following

---

[4]   s.107 of the Government of Wales Act 1998
[5]   See ss. 6(2)(c) and 24(1)(a) of the Northern Ireland Act 1998.
[6]   See The Human Rights Act 1998 (Commencement No. 2) Order 2000 (S.I.2000 No.1851) bringing the remaining provisions of the Act wholly into force with effect from October 2, 2000. The Human Rights Act 1998 (Commencement No. 1) Order 1998 (S.I.1998 No.2882) had already brought s.19 of the Act on Ministerial Statements to Parliament regarding the compatibility of a Bill within the requirements of the Convention into force with effect from November 24, 1998

rights, termed "Convention Rights", have been translated from the Convention into domestic law:

- Article 2 guaranteeing the right to life;
- Article 3 prohibiting torture;
- Article 4 prohibiting slavery or forced labour;
- Article 5 guaranteeing a right to liberty and security of the person;
- Article 6 giving a right to a fair trial both in the determination of civil rights and obligations and in relation to criminal charges;
- Article 7 which incorporates the principle that there should be no punishment without law and in particular no retrospectivity in the definition of criminal offences;
- Article 8 guaranteeing a right to respect for private and family life;
- Article 9 upholding the right to freedom of thought, conscience and religion;
- Article 10 protecting the right to freedom of expression;
- Article 11 setting out the right to freedom of peaceful assembly and freedom of association including the right to form and join trade unions;
- Article 12 giving men and women of marriageable age the right to marry and found a family;
- Article 14 prohibiting discrimination in the enjoyment of the rights set out in the Convention "on any ground such as sex, race, colour, language, religion, political or other opinion, national or social origin, association with a national minority, property, birth or other status";
- Article 1 Protocol 1 guaranteeing the protection of property and the peaceful enjoyment of possessions;
- Article 2 Protocol 1 guaranteeing the right to education by the State in accordance with the philosophical and religious beliefs of parents, insofar as this is compatible with the provision of efficient instruction and training and the avoidance of unreasonable public expenditure;
- Article 3 Protocol 1 setting out the right to free elections in the choice of legislature; and
- Article 1 and 2 of Protocol 6 prohibiting the use of the death penalty except in respect of acts committed in time of war or of imminent threat of war.

Articles 3 (prohibition against torture), 4 (prohibition on slavery and forced labour) and 7 (no retrospective criminal offences) are absolute unqualified rights and by virtue of Article 15(2) they may not be derogated from by the Contracting States. The liberty and due process provisions of Articles 5 and 6 may only be derogated from by the Contracting State in time of war or public emergency by virtue of Article 15(1). Articles 8 (privacy), 9 (freedom of religion), 10 (freedom of expression) and 11 (freedom of assembly), Protocol 1 Article 1 (right to property) and Protocol 1 Article 2 1.03

(right to education) are not absolute rights, but rather rights the exercise of which may lawfully be qualified or restricted by the Contracting States provided that these qualification or restrictions are justified in the sense of being proportionate responses which are "necessary in a democratic society". Article 12 (right to marry) may be exercised "according to the national laws governing the exercise of this right".

It should be noted that Article 13 of the Convention, which gives the right to an effective remedy before a national authority to everyone whose rights and freedoms, as set forth in the Convention, have been violated, notwithstanding that the violation has been committed by persons acting in an official capacity, has not been included among the Convention Rights which have been incorporated by the Human Rights Act 1998 into domestic law. The explanation given for this omission by the promoters of the Bill which became the Human Rights Act was that the Act itself is intended to give effect to Article 13 and that there is accordingly no need for the courts to look outwith the parameters of the Act in order to provide appropriate remedies against possible violations of Convention rights.

The incorporation of certain rights taken from the European Convention is intended to supplement the existing body of individual rights guaranteed under the law. This is made clear by section 11(a) of the Human Rights Act 1998 which provides that a person's reliance on a Convention right does not restrict either his claim to the protection of any other right or freedom conferred on him by or under any other law in the United Kingdom.

The relevance of the Strasbourg jurisprudence

1.04   In coming to their decisions on the compatibility of acts or omissions of public authorities with any of the defined "Convention rights", the courts are enjoined by section 2 of the Human Rights Act to "take into account" all and any relevant decisions of the institutions established under the Council of Europe, namely the Court of Human Rights, the Commission on Human Rights and the Committee of Ministers. The Human Rights Act 1998 does not, then, incorporate into United Kingdom law and bind the United Kingdom courts to the jurisprudence of the Strasbourg institutions. The apparently non-binding nature of the decisions of the Strasbourg Court on national courts is to be contrasted with the position of the European Court of Justice in matters concerning European Community law. National courts are *obliged* to decide cases involving matters of substantive Community law under the Treaty of Rome and associated treaties, or involving jurisdictional or conflict of laws question arising between the Member States under the Brussels and/or Rome Conventions, "*in accordance with* the principles laid down by and any relevant decision of the

European Court of Justice".[7] It may be that the non-binding nature of the general Strasbourg jurisprudence is intended simply to reflect the position under public international law under which a contracting state to the European Convention is bound only by judgments addressed to that State. Alternatively, it may be thought that since the European Court of Human Rights itself treats the Convention as a "living instrument" meaning that its interpretation of its provisions may change over time,[8] it would not be appropriate to bind national courts to Strasbourg judgments which are not binding on the Council of Europe institutions themselves. The fact that domestic courts would appear not to be formally bound to apply the decisions of the European Court of Human Rights to the facts of the case before them, arguably leaves the way open for a national human rights jurisprudence to be pursued and for a native human rights culture to be developed.

In the decision of the Judicial Committee of the Privy Council in *Montgomery and Coulter*[9] Lord Hope's judgment on the substantive issue (as to whether or not the pre-trial publicity precluded the possibility of a fair trial) contains, in addition to references to numerous Scottish and English domestic authority, an impressive citation and analysis of New Zealand legal research and Strasbourg, Canadian, Australian and Irish case law, leading him ultimately to uphold the compatibility of the existing common law approach on the matter of possible prejudice[10] with the fair trial requirements of the Convention.[11]

In the subsequent Privy Council decision in *Brown v. Stott*,[12] however, it would appear that the Judicial Committee took a decision *not* to follow a developing Strasbourg jurisprudence as to the *absolute nature* of the privilege against enforced self-incrimination implicit in Article 6 seen, most notably, in the following decisions of the European Court of Human Rights, *Funke v. France*,[13] where the Strasbourg Court found that the imposition of fines by the French customs authorities against an individual in

---

[7] See s.3(1) of the European Communities Act 1972, s.3 of the Civil Jurisdiction and Judgments Act 1982 and s.3 of the Contract (Applicable Law) Act 1990.

[8] See, for example, *Pellegrin v. France*, unreported decision of the EctHR, December 8, 1999, accessible at www.dhcour.coe.fr/hudoc in which the Strasbourg Court explicitly reversed its earlier case law and found that Art. 6(1) fair trial rights might be prayed in aid in certain categories of public sector employment.

[9] *Montgomery v. H.M.Advocate and the Advocate General for Scotland* and *Coulter v. H.M.Advocate and the Advocate General for Scotland*, 2001 P.C.1; 2001 S.L.T. 37.

[10] As laid down in *Stuurman v. H.M.Advocate*, 1980 J.C. 111 at 122, namely whether or not there was a substantial risk of prejudice so grave that no direction of the trial judge, however careful, could reasonably remove it.

[11] See, in particular *Pullar v. U.K.* (1996) 22 E.H.H.R. 391, a Strasbourg case arising from the Scottish proceedings in *Pullar v. H.M.Advocate*, 1993 J.C. 135

[12] *Brown v. Stott*, 2001 P.C.; 2001 S.L.T. 59.

[13] *Funke v. France*, A/256-A (1993) 16 E.H.R.R. 297

respect of his failure to disclose documents concerning financial transactions violated Article 6(1) ECHR; and *Saunders v. United Kingdom*[14] in which the use at a subsequent fraud trial of transcripts of even non-self incriminating evidence taken from the accused by DTI inspectors acting in relation to the investigation of company take-overs under compulsory powers was found to contravene Article 6(1) ECHR.

1.05   The Privy Council decision in *Brown v. Stott* makes one thing clear, at least, past case law, whether from the Strasbourg institutions, from other constitutional or human rights courts or from their domestic courts, should therefore not be applied mechanistically or with an undue emphasis on the rules of precedent. Previous cases should not be seen as establishing the extent of a Convention right—they simply provide examples of its application in particular circumstances. When faced with a Convention argument it may be argued that the courts have always to seek to ensure "a fair balance between the general interests of the community and the requirements of the protection of individuals' fundamental rights",[15] having regard to the particular circumstances before them and the consequences which might flow from their particular decision. In the early days of wrestling with human rights arguments there will clearly be a temptation for practitioners and the courts to elevate *dicta* of the European Court of Human Rights into binding pronouncements on the law, in a manner which may perhaps be criticised in the light of *Brown v. Stott* as overly deferential to that court. At the same time, however, it would appear that the Judicial Committee also wish proper account should be taken of the effect and import of, for example, admissibility decisions of the Commission (and post-Protocol 11 Court) of Human Rights and they should not be summarily dismissed as of little or no account because considered to be "obscurely reasoned". The question that remains is whether an approach to the case law of the Strasbourg Court which, on apparently the basis of the considerations derived from the "margin of appreciation" of the national institutions, seems to allow for a lower standard of protection for the Convention right against self-incrimination than that set out by the European Court of Human Rights in *Funke* and *Saunders*, is itself compatible with the requirements of the Convention. This question can ultimately only be answered by a decision of the Strasbourg court.[15a]

---

[14] *Saunders v. U.K.*, A/702 (1997) 23 E.H.R.R. 313
[15] See *A. v. The Scottish Ministers*, 2000 S.L.T. 873, (IH) *per* L-P Rodger at para. 48
[15a] In *Alconbury* [2001] U.K.H.L. 23, Lord Slynn of Hadley observed at para. 26 of his judgment that "in the absence of some special circumstances it seems to me that the court should follow any clear and constant jurisprudence of the European Court of Human Rights. If it does not do so there is at least a possibility that the case will go to that court which is likely in the ordinary case to follow its own constant jurisprudence."

Margin of appreciation in Strasbourg case law

Another reason for treating the case law emanating from the   1.06
Strasbourg institutions with some degree of care, and in order to
guard against the ready assumption that Strasbourg decisions
should be followed automatically and applied uncritically by the
United Kingdom courts considering Convention points, is the
influence of the doctrine of the Contracting States' "margin of
appreciation" on some of these decisions.[16] This doctrine was
explained in one case before the Court of Human Rights as follows:

> "By reason of their direct and continuous contact with the vital
> forces of their countries, the national authorities are in
> principle better placed than an international court to evaluate
> local needs and conditions."[17]

It might be thought that the decisions of domestic courts
considering human rights points should be less trammelled by the
Strasbourg institutions' deference to the contracting states' "margin
of appreciation" since they are in contact with the vital forces in
their countries.[18] David Pannick Q.C. has, however, suggested that
it might be appropriate for there to be a local translation of this
doctrine as follows:

> "Although the doctrine of margin of appreciation will not
> apply (being concerned with the circumstances in which an
> international court should substitute its judgment for that of a
> national court), the courts applying the Human Rights Act
> should recognise an analogous doctrine which will accord a
> discretionary area of judgment in relation to policy decisions
> which the legislature, executive and public bodies are better
> placed than the judiciary to decide."[19]

---

[16] See N. Lavender, "The Problem of the Margin of Appreciation" [1997]
E.H.R.L.R. 380

[17] *Buckley v. U.K.* (1996) E.H.R.R. 101 at 129 para. 75. See to like effect *Handyside
v. U.K.*, A/24 (1979-80) 1 E.H.R.R. 737 at 754 para. 48

[18] For an example of a more robust approach taken by national courts to the
decisions of the national administration where human rights issues are raised see
Salah Abdadou v. Secretary of State for the Home Office, 1998 S.C. 504, 1999
S.L.T. 229, (OH) *per* Lord Eassie in which he displays an apparently more
sceptical approach than that in the Strasbourg Court's case law, to the States'
"margin of appreciation" in immigration and asylum cases

[19] D. Pannick Q.C., "Comment: Principles of interpretation of Convention Rights
under the Human Rights Act and the discretionary area of judgment" [1998] P.L.
545.

Intensity of Review in Convention rights cases

1.07   Prior to the "bringing home" of the Convention rights there was a
growing awareness among practitioners and judges that the stark
choice between either high "*Wednesbury* unreasonableness" as
traditionally defined, and the standards of ordinary reasonableness
with judges substituting their views for those of the administrators
was insufficient if judicial review was to be properly responsive to
the requirements of the changing constitution. In fundamental
rights cases, the phrase a "most anxious scrutiny" came to be used
in relation to the courts reviewing the administration's actions and
a recognition that "the more substantial the interference with
human rights the more the court will require by way of justification
before it is satisfied that the decision is reasonable"[20] in the sense of
it actually falling within the range of responses open to a reasonable
decision maker.[21] With the coming into force of the Human Rights
Act, however, things have changed. By virtue of section 6(1) of the
Human Rights Act (discussed below) the actings and omissions of a
public body in breach of a Convention right are no longer to be
characterised in judicial review terms as a species of "irrationality"
and thus subject to the high hurdle of *Wednesbury* unreasonableness,[22] but rather have to be regarded as a form of illegality and
thereby made subject to a stricter scrutiny by the courts examining
whether or not the decision maker has, in fact, acted in a manner
which is compatible with Convention rights. This means that the
Strasbourg doctrine of proportionality rather than "irrationality" is
directly imported into domestic consideration of challenges to
public authorities on Convention grounds.[22a]

1.08   It is, however, implicit within the doctrines of proportionality
and the "margin of appreciation" that a weighing of individual

---

[20]   *R v. Admiralty Board of the Defence Council, ex p. Lustig-Prean and Beckett* [1996]
I.R.L.R. 100, C.A. *per* Thorpe L.J. at 106-7

[21]   See, for example, *R. v Secretary of State for the Home Department ex p. Launder*
[1997] 1 W.L.R. 839 *per* Lord Hope of Craighead at 867 in which he observed
that: "If the applicant is to have an effective remedy against a decision which is
flawed because the decision-maker has misdirected himself on the Convention
which he himself says he took into account, it must surely be right to examine the
substance of the argument. The ordinary principles of judicial review permit this
approach because it was to the rationality and legality of the decision, and not to
some independent remedy, that [counsel for Launder] directed his argument."

[22]   As in *Brind v. Secretary of State for the Home Department* [1991] A.C. 696, H.L.
and *R v. Ministry of Defence, ex p. Smith* [1996] Q.B. 517, C.A. *per* Lord Bingham
M.R. at 558-9

[22a] In *R. v. Secretary of State for the Home Department, ex p Daly* [2001] U.K.H.L.
26, Lord Steyn observed at para. 28 of his judgment that "the differences in
approach between the traditional grounds of review and the proportionality
approach may therefore yield different results. It is therefore important that cases
involving Convention rights must be analysed in the correct way. This does not
mean that there has been a shift to merits review ... [T]he respective roles of judges
and administrators are fundamentally distinct and will remain so...in law, context
is everything."

rights against considerations of the common good is followed.[23]
But the adoption of the proportionality test should not mean the
simple substitution of the court's views for that of the decision
maker, as this would be to replace judicial review by a substantive
appeal. Although there is no explicit hierarchy of rights within the
Convention, in practice, it may be that the national courts, guided
by some of the Strasbourg Court's own jurisprudence, will develop
an informal weighting of the relative importance of these
fundamental rights in the event of a possible clash between
them—for example as between the fair trial rights of property
developers under Article 6(1) and the rights of neighbours to an
acceptable environment implicit in Article 8, or between the press's
free expression rights under Article 10 and an individual's right to
privacy under Article 8. In coming to his decision in *Montgomery
and Coulter*, however, Lord Hope noted (at pages 40-41):

"Article 6, unlike Articles 8 to 11 of the Convention, is not
subject to any words of limitation. It does not require **nor
indeed does it permit** a balance to be struck between the rights
which it sets out and other considerations such as the public
interest."

By contrast, in *Brown v. Stott*, a different approach to Article 6 is
evident. Lord Bingham states (at page 31) that:

"The jurisprudence of the European Court [of Human Rights]
very clearly establishes that while the overall fairness of a
criminal trial cannot be compromised, the constituent rights
comprised, whether expressly or implicitly, within Article 6 are
not themselves absolute. Limited qualification of these rights is
acceptable if reasonably directed by national authorities
towards a clear and proper public objective and if representing
no greater qualification than the situation calls for."

Lord Steyn states (at 37):

"[A] single minded concentration on the pursuit of fundamental rights of individuals to the exclusion of the interests of
the wider public might be subversive of the ideal of tolerant

---

[23] Thus the (Luxembourg based) Court of Justice of the European Communities
commonly uses a variation on the following formula (in this instance found in
Case 5/88 *Wachauf v. Germany* [1989] E.C.R. 2609 at para. 18) when discussing
fundamental rights: "The fundamental rights recognised by the Court are not
absolute however, but must be considered in relation to their social function.
Consequently, restrictions may be imposed on the exercise of those rights ...
provided that those restrictions in fact correspond to objectives of general interest
pursed by the Community and do not constitute, with regard to the aim pursued,
a disproportionate and intolerable interference, impairing the very substance of
those rights."

European democracies. The fundamental rights of individuals are of supreme importance but those rights are not unlimited: we live in communities of individuals who also have rights".

And Lord Hope notes (at 55):

"[T]he European Court [of Human Rights] and the European Commission [of Human Rights] have interpreted...Article [6] broadly by reading into it a variety of other rights to which the accused is entitled in the criminal context. Their purpose is to give effect, in a practical way, to the fundamental and absolute right to a fair trial. They include the right to silence and the right against self-incrimination with which this case is concerned. As these other rights are not set out in absolute terms in...Article [6] they are open, in principle, to modification or restriction so long as this is not incompatible with the absolute right to a fair trial."

1.09   The approach of the Judicial Committee in *Brown* was therefore directed at the question as to whether the provision in question represented a "disproportionate response to a serious social problem" given that (*per* Lord Bingham at 34) "the possession and use of cars (like for example, shotguns, the possession of which is very closely regulated) are recognised to have the potential to cause grave injury". None of the five judges had any difficulty in finding, in the light of the statistics presented to them for death and injury on the roads, that requiring the registered keeper of a vehicle to advise as to the identity of the driver of his or her car was not disproportionate measure, even if it meant the keeper being compelled to incriminate herself. This apparent readiness of the Privy Council in *Brown v. Stott* to find in favour of the Crown's claims as to the proportionate nature of the legislative measure under challenge, and to hold that the individual's privilege against self-incrimination could properly be limited by the State highlights the fact that the importation of the European test of proportionality, long advocated by civil libertarian lawyers, may be something of a double-edged sword. The traditional black letter law approach to judicial review was concerned not with the merits of the particular decision as such, but with the decision making process; accordingly a strict and formal approach in favour of those affected by the decision, which emphasised the legal limits on the jurisdiction of the decision maker and the need for procedural fairness could properly be taken by the courts, concerned as they were to police decisions rather than to make them. With the new doctrine of proportionality, however, the courts are concerned with the merits of the decision in question and, in particular, with whether or not, (i) the decision or measure in question is in fact aimed at a legitimate end; (ii) the decision or measure is effective in achieving that end; and (iii) the decision or measure shows a proper regard for, and balance, of the rights of the individual against the interests of society. Given the balancing exercise required in this last aspect of the proportionality, the procedural and substantive rights of the individual can no longer be regarded as the trump cards they were under the older model of judicial review. Accordingly, the doctrine of proportionality may, in fact, lead to greater rather than less deference by the courts to administrative and legislative decisions, than might have been expected under the older constitutional model, under which individual's substantive and procedural rights in effect ring-fenced against the whims of the decision maker.

A similar balancing exercise, treating the individual fundamental rights protected under Community law as "non-absolute" but important factors in coming to their decision, was adopted by the House of Lords in *R v. Chief Constable of Sussex, ex parte International Traders' Ferry*.[24] Domestic courts dealing with arguments concerning at least the non-absolute Convention rights will have to develop new doctrines of due deference in the interests of continued good government following the coming into force of the Human Rights Act.

The interpretative obligation and the <u>indirect</u> effect of Convention rights

In Scots law it is accepted that there is now a presumption in the common law that Parliament intends to legislate in conformity with its international commitments, including the Convention, and that where a statutory provision is susceptible of more than one interpretation the court should give it the construction which complies most closely with those commitments. As Lord President Hope stated in *T, Petitioner*:

1.10

> "[W]hen legislation is found to be ambiguous in the sense that it is **capable** of a meaning which either conforms to or conflicts with the [European] Convention, Parliament is to be **presumed** to have legislated in conformity with the Convention, not in conflict with it."[25]

Thus in *O'Neill v. H.M.Advocate* the criminal appeal court made reference to and relied upon certain of the case-law of the European Court of Human Rights[26] in the context of the proper interpretation of the requirements of section 2(6) of the Prisoners' and Criminal Proceedings (Scotland) Act 1993. In its judgment in the appeal, substituting a period of three years for the seven years

---

[24] *R v. Chief Constable of Sussex, ex p. International Traders' Ferry* [1999] 1 All E.R. 129, H.L.
[25] *T, Petitioner*, 1997 S.L.T. 724, (IH) at 733-4.
[26] Notably *Thynne, Wilson and Gunnell v. U.K.*, A/190-A (1991) 13 E.H.R.R. 666.

imposed by the trial judge, the court observed that an earlier decision in the matter in *Robertson v. H.M.Advocate*[27] in which the purpose of the statutory provisions in question had been discussed without reference to this Strasbourg case law and had been made *per incuriam.*

The decision of the High Court in *O'Neill* illustrates the importance of the Convention even prior to its incorporation, where failure to make reference to it and its associated case law has actually led to a misunderstanding and misapplication of a provision of national law. The point about the decision in *O'Neill* is that the court finds to be the correct meaning of the legislation as a purposive one which ensure convention compatibility, *rather than* literal or plain meaning of the wording provision without reference to Convention considerations, such as appears to have been favoured in the decision in *Robertson.*

This common law doctrine of purposive construction of national legislation in line with the requirements of the Convention and decisions of the European Court of Human Rights has now been given statutory backing by section 3 of the Human Rights Act 1998. This provision, echoing the language of Lord Hope in *T, Petitioner,* restates the duty on *all* domestic courts and tribunals, so far as it is *possible* to do so, to read and give effect to *all* primary and subordinate legislation in a way which is compatible with the Convention rights which have been incorporated into United Kingdom domestic law by the Human Rights Act.

The Lord Chancellor, Lord Irvine of Lairg, has made a parallel with the interpretative obligation already imposed under Community law,[28] and has emphasised the strength of the interpretative obligation placed on the courts by the Human Rights Act as follows:

> "The [Human Rights] Act will require the courts to read and give effect to the legislation in a way which is compatible with Convention rights 'so far as it is possible to do so'. This...goes far beyond the present rule. **It will not be necessary to find an ambiguity**. On the contrary the courts will be required to interpret legislation so as to uphold the Convention rights unless the legislation itself is so clearly incompatible with the Convention that it is **impossible** to do so....
>
> The court will interpret as consistent with the Convention

---

[27]   *Robertson v. H.M.Advocate,* 1997 S.C.C.R. 534 at 541C-D
[28]   See *Litster v. Forth Dry Dock Co. Ltd,* 1990 S.C. (H.L.) 1, *per* Lord Oliver of Aylmerton at 30: "[T]he greater flexibility available to the court in applying a **purposive construction** to legislation designed to give effect to the United Kingdom's Treaty obligations to the Community enables the court, where necessary, **to supply by implication words appropriate to comply with those obligations**....Having regard to the manifest purpose of the regulations I do not for my part feel inhibited from making such an implication in the instant case."

not only those provisions which are ambiguous in the sense that the language used is capable of two different meanings but also those provisions where there is no ambiguity in that sense unless a clear limitation is expressed. In the latter category of cases it will be 'possible' (to use the statutory language) to read the legislation in a conforming sense because there will be no clear indication that a limitation on the protected right was intended so as to make it 'impossible' to read it as conforming."[29]

There is of course an ambiguity about the word ambiguity. Strictly the word means something *capable* of bearing two or more meanings. It is often used by the courts as if it meant that two possible meanings were in the context of ordinary language use *equally* possible or convincing. This is, however, arguably to confuse the ambiguous with the equivocal. Aside from the interpretative obligation imposed by section 3 of the 1998 Act the meaning of the provision might be said to be clear or obvious, and in that sense unequivocal. This interpretative provision of the 1998 Act requires the courts to attempt, *so far as possible*, to interpret the national provision in accordance with Convention rights. The interpretative provision, however, requires the courts to attempt, *so far as possible*, to interpret the national provision in accordance with Convention rights. As Lord Hope noted in *R v. Director of Public Prosecutions, ex parte Kebeline*:

> "In *Attorney General of Hong Kong v. Lee Kwong Kut* [1993] AC 951 at 966, Lord Woolf referred to the general approach to the interpretations of constitutions and bills of rights in the previous decisions [of the Judicial Committee of the Privy Council] which he said were equally applicable to the Hong Kong Bill of Rights Ordinance 1991.[30] He mentioned Lord Wilberforce's observation in *Minister of Home Affairs v. Fisher* [1980] AC 319 at 328 that **instruments of this nature call for a generous interpretation suitable to give individuals the full measure of the fundamental rights and freedoms referred to**, and Lord Diplock's comments in *Attorney General of the Gambia v. Momodou* Jobe [1984] AC 696 at 700 that **a generous and purposive construction is to be given to that part of the constitution which protects and entrenches fundamental rights and freedoms to which all persons in the State are to be entitled. The same approach will now have to be applied in this country where issues are raised under the Human Rights Act 1998 about the compatibility of domestic legislation and of the acts of public**

1.11

---

[29] Lord Irvine of Lairg "The Development of Human Rights in Britain under an Incorporated Convention on Human Rights" [1998] Public Law 221 at 228-9

[30] See, now, Nicholas Roberts "The Law Lords and Human Rights: the experience of the Privy Council in interpreting Bills of Rights" 2000 E.H.R.L.R. 147-180.

authorities with the fundamental rights and freedoms which are enshrined in the Convention."[31]

1.12   The provision in question, then, has to be at least *capable* (but not necessarily reasonably capable) of bearing such a Convention compatible meaning as well as (but not more obviously than) another *prima facie* meaning.[32] In that sense a possible reading in accordance with the Convention may be said to render the provision ambiguous. The resolution of the matter seems to be as follows;

- in the absence of any Convention rights element, then the ordinary language canons of statutory construction should be applied to elucidate Parliamentary intention;

- where there is a Convention right element, however, a construction of the provision in question which accords with the requirements of the Convention should be favoured over even the ordinary language "obvious" or *prima facie* construction, however strained or artificial this may seem;

- it is only where the statutory language is so phrased as to make it *impossible* to construe the provision in accordance with the requirements of the protection of the Convention right, that the statute may be construed as in contravention of the Convention.[33]

1.13   In summary, in contrast to clear and precise provisions of Community law, the rights incorporated from the European Convention by the Human Rights Act do not have "direct effect" against contrary Westminster legislation in the way that that term is understood in Community law as allowing the suspension or disapplication of contrary provisions of national law.[34] Direct effect involves the assertion of rights which have been conferred by

---

[31] *R v. Director of Public Prosecutions, ex p. Kebeline* [1999] 4 All E.R. 801 at 838-839.

[32] Compare with the position under Community law as seen in *Garland v. British Rail Engineering* [1983] 2 A.C. 751 in which Lord Diplock observed (at 770-1) that unless an Act of Parliament passed after the U.K.'s accession to the European Community expressly stated that it was passed with the intention of breaching Community obligations, then U.K. legislation should be construed in a manner consistent with Community law "however wide the departure from the *prima facie* meaning of the language of the provision might be needed to achieve consistency."

[33] See, again in the context of Community law, *Litster v. Forth Dry Dock Co. Ltd*, 1990 S.C. (H.L.) 1, *per* Lord Oliver of Aylmerton at 27: "If your Lordships are in fact compelled to the conclusion [that the regulations are gravely defective and the Government of the United Kingdom has failed to comply with its mandatory obligations under the Directive], so be it; but it is not, I venture to think, a conclusion which any of your Lordships would willingly embrace in the absence of the most compulsive context rendering any other conclusion **impossible**."

[34] See, for example, Case C-213/89 *R v. Secretary of State for Transport, ex p. Factortame Ltd. (No. 2)* [1991] A.C. 603, H.L., [1990] E.C.R. 2433, ECJ.

Community law but which, by definition, national law does not adequately reflect. It requires the national court to displace, rather than to uphold, the terms of national law. Sympathetic interpretation or indirect effect, on the other hand, is available, in the case of both Community law and Convention rights. The argument for sympathetic interpretation asserts that national legislation does indeed fully reflect the demands of the incorporated Convention rights if only the national court would interpret it in the manner required by section 3 of the Human Rights Act.[34a]

Thus, in the decision of the High Court of Justiciary sitting as a court of criminal appeal of three judges in *Brown v. Stott*,[35] Rodger L.J.-G expressed the view (which was not reversed in the successful Crown appeal to the Privy Council) that the appropriate manner of proceeding in such cases where Convention rights were prayed in aid against provisions of primary Westminster legislation (*in casu* the privilege against self-incrimination implicit in Article 6(1) against section 172 of the Road Traffic Act 1988 authorising the police to require information of the registered keeper as to the identity of the driver of his or her vehicle), was for the following steps to be followed;

(i)   first, the court was to "identify the scope" of the Convention right or rights relied upon in the circumstances of the case;

(ii) secondly, the court should consider whether the statutory provision at issue was, on its "established construction", compatible with that Convention right. If it is then the established construction may be applied.

(iii) If, however, the established construction is found to be incompatible with the Convention right relied upon in the case, the court should then turn to consider whether or not the statutory provision could nevertheless be "read down" so as to make it compatible with the Convention right (see section 3 of the Human Rights Act 1998);

(iv) it is only where the statutory provision of (or made under) primary Westminster legislation cannot be read or given effect to in a way which is compatible with the Convention rights that a public authority could rely on section 6(2)(b) of the Human Rights Act (discussed below) and give effect to or enforce the national provisions, notwithstanding their incompatibility with the Convention.

The decision of the Employment Appeal Tribunal in *MacDonald v.*

[34a] See *R. v. A* [2001] U.K.H.L. 25 for an example of the House of Lords straining to give a Convention compatible interpretation of statutory provisions (s.41 of the Youth Justice and Criminal Evidence Act 1999) which seek severely to restrict the possibility of a complainant in a rape trial from giving evidence or being cross-examined as to any past sexual behaviour, including the existence of a sexual relationship with the defendant.

[35] *Brown v. Stott*, 2000 S.L.T. 379, HCJ.

MOD,[36] provides a recent example of the impact that human rights considerations might have on traditional methods of statutory construction. In the light of decisions from the European Court of Human Rights to the effect that dismissal of service personnel from the Armed Forces on grounds of their homosexuality contravened their Article 8 rights[37] and that the Article 14 prohibition on discrimination covered discrimination on grounds purely of sexual orientation,[38] the Employment Appeal Tribunal in Scotland was persuaded to re-read the Sex Discrimination Act 1975 contrary to established English authority[39] so that the statutory phrase "discrimination on grounds of her sex" was held to cover not only discrimination on grounds of an individual's gender but also on grounds of his or her sexual orientation.[39a]

Declarations of incompatibility of primary Westminster legislation

1.14   Where it is not possible to read Westminster primary legislation in a manner which is compatible with Convention rights, section 3(2) provides that the legislative provisions in question remain fully valid, operative and enforceable. In contrast to the situation where there is an incompatibility with Community law, national courts are not empowered, even after incorporation of the Convention, to "disapply" or suspend primary statutory provisions emanating from the Westminster Parliament which contravene Convention rights.

If the court is satisfied that the provision cannot be "read down" so as to make it compatible with the relevant Convention right, it may then make, effectively as a last resort, a "declaration of incompatibility" under section 4(2) of the Human Rights Act 1998. Section 4 of the Act gives only the higher domestic courts (in Scotland, that is the Court of Session or the High Court of Justiciary sitting as a court of criminal appeal) the power to make a declaration as to the incompatibility of the national provision with the Convention rights as incorporated.[40]

---

[36] *MacDonald v. Ministry of Defence* [2000] I.R.L.R. 748, EAT

[37] *Duncan Lustig-Prean and John Beckett v. U.K.* (2000) 29 E.H.R.R. 493 and *Jeanette Smith and Graeme Grady v. U.K.* [1999] I.R.L.R. 734, ECtHR

[38] *Salgueiro da Silva Mouta v. Portugal*, ECtHR unreported decision of December 29, 1999, accessible at www.dhcour.coe.fr/hudoc

[39] See, for example: *R v. Ministry of Defence, ex p. Smith and Grady*, *R v. Admiralty Board of the Defence Council, ex p. Lustig-Prean and Beckett* [1996] Q.B. 517, [1996] I.R.L.R. 100, CA; *Smith v. Gardner Merchant Ltd* [1998] 3 All E.R. 853; [1999] I.C.R. 134, [1998] I.R.L.R. 510, CA; and *Pearce v. Governing Body of Mayfield School* [2000] I.C.R. 920, EAT.

[39a] The E.A.T. decision was subsequently overturned by a 2–1 majority decision on appeal to the Inner House: see *Advocate General for Scotland v. Macdonald*, June 1, 2001, unreported decision of Lords Prosser, Kirkwood and Caplan accessible at www.scotcourts.gov.uk/

[40] The other "higher courts" for the purposes of the power to make "declarations of incompatibility" are the House of Lords, the Judicial Committee of the Privy Council, the Courts-Martial Appeal Court and in England and Wales or Northern Ireland, the High Court and the Court of Appeal

In the case of a provision of secondary legislation, such a declaration of incompatibility is appropriate only where this provision is itself protected from amendment by primary legislation of the Westminster Parliament. The principle of ultimate Westminster Parliamentary sovereignty is said thereby to be maintained. As Lord Irvine of Lairg has stated:

"This innovative technique will provide the right balance between the judiciary and [the Westminster] Parliament. [The Westminster] Parliament is the democratically elected representative of the people and must remain sovereign. The judiciary will be able to exercise to the full the power to scrutinise legislation rigorously against the fundamental freedoms guaranteed by the Convention but without becoming politicised. The ultimate decision to amend [primary Westminster] legislation to bring it into line with the Convention, however, will rest with [the Westminster] Parliament. The ultimate responsibility for compliance with the Convention must be [the Westminster] Parliament's alone."[41]

Where a higher court is considering whether or not to make a declaration of incompatibility, section 5 of the Act gives the Crown the right to be notified of this and under section 5(2) allows a Minister of the Crown or his nominee, as well as a member of the Scottish Executive, a Northern Ireland Minister or a Northern Ireland Department to intervene in any such case as parties to the proceedings after giving due notice to the court.[41a]

Such a declaration of incompatibility by the courts will, by virtue of section 4(6)(a) of the Act, have no effect on the validity, continuing operation or enforceability of the offending legislative provision. Further, section 4(6)(b) provides that any declaration of incompatibility is not binding on the parties to the proceedings in which it is made. The obtaining of a declaration of incompatibility will therefore be a Pyrrhic victory for the party in whose favour it is granted unless the applicable law is changed with retrospective effect in his case.[42] It is therefore of no immediate assistance to the person challenging the national provision, although pressure group led litigation may present such a result as a political or moral victory. As the Lord Justice General put it in *Brown v. Stott*, "irremediable incompatibility assists the Crown".

---

[41] Lord Irvine of Lairg "The Development of Human Rights in Britain under an incorporated Convention on Human Rights" [1998] Public Law 221-236 at 225
[41a] In *Wilson v. First County Trust (No.2)*, May 2, 2001, CA, unreported decision of Sir A. Morritt V.C., Chadwick and Rix L.JJ., the Court of Appeal of England and Wales made a s.4 declaration of incompatibility in relation to provisions of the Consumer Credit Act 1974 which gave undue protection to consumers.
[42] See generally N. Bamforth "Parliamentary Sovereignty and the Human Rights Act 1998" [1998] P.L. 572-582

1.15   Questions as to the compatibility or otherwise of national legislation with the requirements of the Convention raise new problems of interpretation for the courts, notably in the case where the court is required to determine the justifiability of a national provision as a lawful and proportionate restriction ("necessary in a democratic society") in relation to such non-absolute Convention rights as those set out in Article 8(2) (privacy and respect for family life), Article 9(2) (manifestation of religious beliefs), Article 10 (freedom of expression) and Article 11 (freedom of peaceful assembly and association including the right to form trade unions) and Protocol 1 Article 1 (right to property). As has been noted:

> "The determination of whether a legislative provision is compatible with a Convention right will require a court to interpret the allegedly incompatible provision as well as determining the meaning of the right that gives rise to the allegation of incompatibility. Moreover a court may be required to determine whether the interests served by an allegedly incompatible piece of legislation justify the restriction or interference with the Convention right, thus rendering the piece of legislation compatible. Where a court is required to determine the interests served or protected by the allegedly incompatible legislative instrument, thereby determining whether the purpose of the instrument is compatible with the values protected and upheld by the Convention, it will be required to grapple with what are known as 'legislative facts'."[43]

1.16   Any *final* declaration of incompatibility, that is one against which no right of appeal exists or is being exercised, gives Ministers of the Crown the power to order under section 10 such amendment to, or repeal of, the primary or secondary legislation in question as they think is appropriate to remove the incompatibility. A remedial order may also be pronounced by a Minister of the Crown if it appears to him or her that a finding of the European Court of Human Rights produces an incompatibility with the United Kingdom's Convention obligations. Any such remedial order will require the approval of Parliament under the affirmative resolution procedure, all as set out in Schedule 2 to the Act. In cases of urgency, however, such approval may be made *ex post facto* up to 40 days later.

It is to be assumed that the decision as to whether or not to make any such remedial orders, and whether or not to make any such order, with or without retrospective effect, will itself be subject to judicial review by the courts. The effect of section 6(6) of the Act

---

[43]   See A. Henderson "*Brandeis* briefs and the proof of legislative facts in proceedings under the Human Rights Act 1998" [1998] P.L. 563-571 at 563 for a discussion of the issues raised thereby.

(discussed below) may simply be to prevent a review of any such omission being made on human rights grounds, and on that point at least avoid the possibility of a unending spiral of litigation.

It should be noted that in contrast to the position in relation to primary Westminster legislation, a provision of subordinate legislation relied upon by a public authority which is found to be incompatible with the Convention (whether emanating from Westminster, Holyrood or Cardiff) would seem, by contrast, to be impliedly repealed to the extent of its incompatibility, except where there is a provision of primary Westminster legislation which *prevents* such a reading of the secondary provision in question.

Section 101 of the Scotland Act 1998, however, seeks to give specific guidance to the courts in their approach to the interpretation of provisions of both Bills and Acts of the Scottish Parliament as well as of any subordinate legislation emanating from a member of the Scottish Executive. On the face of it, the effect of section 29(2)(d) and section 57(2) of the Scotland Act is that all and any legislation emanating from the Scottish Parliament or the Scottish Executive will be void because *ultra vires* insofar as it is incompatible with any of the Convention Rights. Section 101 of the Scotland Act however requires the courts to seek to avoid a finding that any such provision is *ultra vires*, by interpreting any provision which could be read in such a way as to put it outside either the legislative competence of the Parliament or the powers conferred on members of the Scottish Executive under the Act "as narrowly as is required for it to be within competence, if such a reading is possible" and to give effect to it accordingly. Further, standing the inclusion both of Acts of the Scottish Parliament and of any "order, rule, regulations, scheme, warrant, bye-law or other instrument made by a member of the Scottish Executive" in the definition of "subordinate legislation" set out in Section 21 of the Human Rights Act 1998, the courts will *also* be required by section 3(1) of that Act to interpret and apply Scottish legislation so far as it is *possible* to do so "in a way which is compatible with the Convention rights."

Public/Private Distinction under the Human Rights Act

Section 6(1) of the Human Rights Act 1998 makes it unlawful for a *public authority* to *act* (or, by virtue of section 6(6), *to fail to act*) in a manner which is incompatible with a Convention right. Section 6(3) defines a "public authority" as including "any person certain of whose functions are functions of a public nature". Section 6(5) provides, however, that in relation to a particular act or omission, a person will *not be regarded as a public authority* if the nature of the act or omission is *private*.[44] This would seem to mean, on the face of

1.17

---

[44] See A. Sherlock "The Applicability of the United Kingdom's Human Rights Bill: identifying public functions" [1998] 4 E.P.L. 593-612

it, that the Convention rights incorporated by the Human Rights Act 1998 will *not* be able to used *directly* against private parties and will not provide a whole new list of additional rights which might directly be prayed in aid in private litigation. As the Lord Chancellor noted in the Second Reading of the Human Rights Bill before the House of Lords:

> "[Section 6 of the Human Rights Act] should apply only to public authorities, however defined, and not to private individuals. That reflects the arrangement for taking cases to the Convention institutions in Strasbourg. The Convention had its origins in a desire to protect people from the misuse of power by the State, rather than by actions of private individuals."[45]

The distinction between "public bodies" and "private acts" is not always an easy one to draw and indeed, has generated a considerable amount of case law, particularly in English law where, in contrast to the position in Scotland post-*West v. Secretary of State for Scotland*,[46] this distinction is used to de-limit the availability of judicial review. In effect, this statutory definition of reviewability under the Human Rights Act seems to be extending throughout the United Kingdom the public/private law test developed by the House of Lords as the basis for general judicial review in England and Wales.[47]

"Public authority" as defined in the Act specifically excludes both Houses of the Westminster Parliament, as well as persons "exercising functions in connection with proceedings" in that Parliament. Section 6(6) provides that the failure to introduce or lay before the Westminster Parliament a proposal for legislation to make any primary legislation or remedial order will not constitute an act which, for the purposes of the Human Rights Act at least, requires to be compatible with a Convention right.

Justified breach of the Convention

1.18 Section 6(2) of the Act allows for the possibility of justified breach

---

[45] House of Lords Debates, November 3, 1997, vol. 582 columns 1231–1232

[46] *West v. Secretary of State for Scotland*, 1992 S.C. 385, (IH)

[47] See the following cases: *O'Reilly v. Mackman* [1983] 2 A.C. 237; *Cocks v. Thanet D.C.* [1983] 2 A.C. 286; *Davy v. Spelthorne B.C.* [1984] A.C. 262; *Roy v. Kensington, Chelsea and Westminster Family Practitioners Association* [1992] 1 A.C. 624; and *Mercury Communications Ltd. v. Director General of Telecommunications* [1996] 1 All E.R. 575. See, however, the discussion of the issue in *Wallbank v. Parochial Council of the Parish of Aston Cantlow*, May 17, 2001, CA, unreported *per* Sir A. Morritt V.C., Walker and Sedley L.JJ., where the Court of Appeal held that a Church of England parochial council constituted a "public authority for the purposes of the Human Rights Act 1998".

of the Convention where, as a result of a provision of primary Westminster legislation the authority in question could not have acted differently or where it was acting to give effect to or to enforce a provision of or made under primary legislation which cannot be read in a manner compatible with Convention rights. In such a case the court cannot make a finding that the authority has acted illegally in breach of the requirements of the Convention.

Section 107(4)(a) of the Government of Wales Act and sections 71(3)(a) and 71(4)(a) of the Northern Ireland Act effectively place the Welsh Assembly and the Northern Ireland Assembly and Northern Ireland Ministers and Department in the same position as any other public authority under section 6(2) of the Human Rights Act 1998. Significantly, however, there is no such general tie in to section 6(2)(b) of the Human Rights Act in the case of the Scottish Parliament or Scottish Executive, although section 57(3) of the Scotland Act allows the Lord Advocate when prosecuting any offence or in his capacity as head of the systems of criminal prosecution and investigation of deaths in Scotland to rely upon this provision of the Human Rights Act allowing for justifiable breach of Convention rights. The implications of this will be considered below.

Courts as "public authorities"—the effect on the common law

Under the European Convention, national courts are regarded by the Strasbourg court as organs or emanations of the Contracting States. The national courts themselves, then, have a *duty*, under Article 1 ECHR, to secure to everyone within their jurisdiction the rights and freedoms set out in the Convention. They are also *required*, under Article 13 ECHR, to ensure that there exists an effective remedy against what the European Court of Human Rights consider to be violations of the Convention rights and freedoms. Thus, in *Markt Intern v. Germany*[48] the Strasbourg court found that the granting of an injunction by a German court on an application by a commercial competitor constituted an interference by a public authority with the applicant's free expression rights. Similarly, in *Tolstoy v. United Kingdom*,[49] the non-review by the judges of the excessively high level of a jury award of damages in a defamation case in England was held to constitute a disproportionate interference by the courts with the applicant's Convention rights, notably his right to freedom of expression under Article 10.

Section 6(3)(a) of the Human Rights Act 1998 follows this line of jurisprudence by providing that a court or tribunal is a public authority for the purposes of the Human Rights Act. In defining

1.19

---

[48] *Markt Intern v. Germany* (1989) 12 E.H.R.R. 161
[49] *Tolstoy v. U.K.* (1995) 20 E.H.R.R. 442.

"public authority" to include courts and tribunals, the 1998 Act requires them to act and come to their decision in a manner which is compatible with a Convention Rights. In the discharge of their functions, then, the courts are themselves directly forbidden by the Human Rights Act 1998 from acting in any manner which is incompatible with the Convention Rights. The implications of this statutory definition are potentially revolutionary—arguably the Human Rights Act now requires courts to act in a manner compatible with the rights guaranteed under the Convention, regardless of the public or private nature of the parties appearing before it. In effect, the courts are arguably themselves required to act in a manner which is compatible with the Convention rights of (each of) the parties appearing before them. As the Lord Chancellor also noted when the Human Rights Bill was under consideration by the House of Lords:

> "We...believe that it is right as a matter of principle for the courts to have the duty of acting compatibly with the Convention not only in cases involving other public authorities but also in developing the common law in deciding cases between individuals. Why should they not? In preparing this Bill, we have taken the view that it is the other course, that of excluding Convention considerations altogether from case between individuals, which would have to be justified. We do not think that it would be justifiable; nor indeed do we think it would be practicable."[50]

1.20   What this may mean is that the Human Rights Act is not simply incorporating the European Convention in the sense that it is making the existing international obligations of the State directly enforceable in the domestic courts (what in a Community law context is know as "vertical direct effect") but is in fact transposing, by virtue of an interpretative obligation, what were the international obligations of the State into obligations owed by every individual within the State to one another (what Community law writers refer to as "horizontal indirect effect") and, in effect, making what were constitutional public law norms applicable and enforceable within the purely private sphere.[51]

---

[50] House of Lords Debates, November 24, 1997, vol. 583 column 783.
[51] The House of Lords in *Turkington v. Times Newspapers Ltd (NI)*, unreported decision of November 2, 2000 has effectively approved the notion of horizontal effect of the HRA rights in developing common law rights (notably of privacy and free expression)—see in particular the speeches of Lord Steyn and Lord Cooke of Thorndon. For academic discussion on the point, see: A. Bowen, "Fundamental Rights in Private Law" (2000) S.L.T. 157; J. Cooper, "Horizontality: The Application of Human Rights Standards in Private Disputes" in *An Introduction to Human Rights and the Common Law* (R. English and P. Havers Q.C. eds., Oxford, Hart Publishing, 2000), p.53; M. Hunt "The Horizontal Effect of the Human Rights Act" (1998) Public Law 423; I. Leigh "Horizontal Rights, the

An alternative view is that the effect of section 3 and 6 of the Human Rights Act is to require the courts to develop the common law in conformity with the requirements of the Convention. Thus, while it will not be possible to say that an act or omission of a private party is unlawful purely and simply because it violates a Convention right ("horizontal direct effect"), it may be possible for the first time to say that an act or omission of a private party is unlawful because it is contrary to legislation (or is unauthorised by legislation) construed in accordance with section 3, or is contrary to the common law developed in accordance with section 6 ("indirect effect").[51a]

Further, existing doctrines of precedent and the binding nature of past judgment of higher courts may themselves require to be subordinated to the requirements of the Convention. In other words, the courts may have to adapt their past law (reversing or distinguishing contrary precedents where necessary) to ensure that the law they apply is compatible with the full and proper protection of the Convention rights.[52] By imposing a new rule of statutory interpretation, section 3 of the Human Rights Act renders pre-Human Rights Act decisions (insofar as based upon a different rule of statutory interpretation) *ipso facto* distinguishable. The statutory duty under section 3 requires all courts to interpret legislation in a new way, and they cannot be prevented from so doing by precedent. An even more radical interpretation of section 6 is that any court before which the protection of a Convention right is properly and relevantly raised will have the *duty*, if it considers the complaint to be well-founded, to "disapply" any contrary prior authority which might otherwise be binding upon it, in similar manner to the power already available under Community law wholly to subordinate existing doctrines of precedent and the binding nature of the past judgments of higher courts to the requirements of the Convention.[53]

1.21

Human Rights Act and Privacy: Lessons from the Commonwealth?" (1999) 48 I.C.L.Q. 57; B. Markesenis "Privacy, Freedom of Expression and the Horizontal Effect of the Human Rights Bill: Lessons from the Germany" (1999) 115 L.Q.R. 47; G. Phillipson "The Human Rights Act, 'Horizontal Effect' and the Common Law: a bang or a whimper?" 62 M.L.R. 824-849; Sir William Wade "The United Kingdom's Bill of Rights" in *Constitutional Reform in the United Kingdom: Practice and Principles* (Hare and Forsyth eds., Oxford, Hart, 1998); and Sir William Wade Q.C. "Opinion: Human Rights and the Judiciary" [1998] E.H.R.L.R. 520-533

[51a] For arguments to this effect see *J.A.Pye (Oxford) Ltd v. Graham*, February 5, 2001, CA, unreported decision of Mummery L.J., Keen L.J.

[52] Compare however with the views expressed by Lord Justice Buxton "The Human Rights Act and Private Law" (2000) 116 L.Q.R. 48-65

[53] Compare within the field of Community law the rejection of national doctrines of the binding nature of past precedent and of the judgments of higher courts in the national hierarchy implicit in the decision of the Court of Justice in Case 146/73 *Rheinmühlen Düsseldorf v. Einfuhr- und Vorratsstelle für Getreide und Futtermittel* [1974] E.H.R.R. 33. See, too, *Tehrani v. U.K.C.C.* [2001] I.R.L.R. 208, (OH) at 218 §62, for an example of an Outer House judge considering that he is no longer bound to follow pre-Human Rights Act, Inner House authority.

As Francis Bennion has noted:

> "No pre-1998 Act court decision on the legal meaning of an
> enactment to which a Convention right is relevant can now
> stand unexamined. Even though it truly reflected the intention
> Parliament had when passing the enactment, the decision needs
> to be looked at again in the light of [the interpretative
> obligation set out in] Section 3(1). Parliament's original
> intention is no longer the sole deciding factor. While it retains
> its importance, it must now be reassessed in the light of the new
> rule. For pre-1998 Act enactment the interpretative criteria can
> therefore be ultimately reduced to legislative intention plus
> [Convention] compatible construction rule, to which must now
> be added the fundamental rights criterion [set out by Lord
> Hope in *R v. Director of Public Prosecutions, ex parte Kebeline
> and others* [1999] 4 All ER 801 at 838-839]."[54]

Procedure for raising Convention points in domestic courts

1.22   Section 7(1) of the Human Rights Act provides that a person who
claims that a public authority has acted or proposes to act in a way
which is incompatible with a Convention right may (a) either rely
on the Convention as a sword by bringing proceedings (including a
counter-claim) against the authority under the Act in the
appropriate court or tribunal or (b) may use the Convention as a
shield or defence by relying on it in any legal proceedings, including
appeals, against a decision of a court or tribunal. Regulation 3 of
the Human Rights Act 1998 (Jurisdiction)(Scotland) Rules 2000
provides that

> "insofar as ~~not~~ determined by any enactment [for example
> section 65(2)(a) of the Regulation of Investigatory Powers Act
> 2000] the appropriate court or tribunal for the purposes of
> Section 7(1)(a) of the Act [bringing proceedings against a
> public authority] is any **civil** court or tribunal which has
> jurisdiction to grant the remedy sought."[55]

Section 22(4) provides that the Convention rights may be used
defensively in any proceedings brought by or at the instigation of a
public authority whenever the act in question took place, but that
otherwise they cannot be so used as regards any act or omission
prior to October 2, 2000, when the Act came fully into force.[56] And

---

[54] Francis Bennion "What interpretation is 'possible' under Section 3(1) of the
Human Rights Act 1998"[2000] P.L. 77 at 91

[55] The Human Rights Act 1998 (Jurisdiction)(Scotland) Rules 2000 (S.I.2000 No.
301)

[56] See The Human Rights Act 1998 (Commencement No. 2) Order 2000 (S.I.2000
No.1851). The Human Rights Act 1998 (Commencement No. 1) Order 1998
(S.I.1998 No.2882) had brought s.19 of the Act on Ministerial Statements to
Parliament regarding the compatibility of a Bill within the requirements of the
Convention into force with effect from November 24, 1998.

section 11(b) provides that a person's reliance on a Convention right does not restrict his right to make any claim or bring any proceedings which he could make apart from the provisions of the 1998 Act.

In the absence of any rule imposing a stricter time limit in relation to the procedure in question (for example, the three months from the effective date of termination in relation to complaints of unfair dismissal claims brought before Employment Tribunals which is fixed by section 111 of the Employment Rights Act 1996) section 7(5)(a) sets a time limit for the bringing of proceedings against a public authority alleging action or inaction incompatible with a Convention right.

Section 7(5)(b), however, gives the court a discretion or power to extend this period for "such longer period as the court or tribunal consider equitable having regard to all the circumstances." This time bar extension provision has a parallel in section 76(5) of the Sex Discrimination Act 1975 which provides that, in relation to an individual's claims to have suffered sex discrimination, "a court or tribunal may nevertheless consider any such complaint, claim or application which is out of time if, in all the circumstances of the case, it considers that it is **just and equitable** to do so". In *Mills v. Marshall* the Employment Appeal Tribunal held that the Employment Tribunal properly exercised its discretion in allowing an application of sex discrimination on the basis of a transsexuality to proceed to a hearing on the merits notwithstanding a delay of over three years from the alleged act of discrimination. It was unsuccessfully argued by the respondents, under reference to the European administrative principle of "legal certainty"[57] and the general public interest in there being a finality of claims, that the fixed statutory time limits, such as the three month limit in sex discrimination cases, should not be waived except in the most exceptional circumstances. Morison J. made the following observation:

"In this legislation, the Sex Discrimination Act 1975, the court's power to extend time is on the basis of what is just and equitable. These words could not be wider or more general. The question is whether it would be just and equitable to deny a person the right to bring proceedings when they were reasonably unaware of the fact that they had the right to bring them until shortly before the complaint was filed. That unawareness might stem from a failure of the lawyers to appreciate that such a claim lay, or because the law 'changed' or was differently perceived after a particular decision of another court. The answer is that in some cases it will be fair to extend time and in others it will not. **The industrial tribunal**

---

[57] See *Biggs v. Somerset C.C.* [1996] I.C.R. 364, C.A., [1995] I.C.R. 811, EAT at 828.

must balance all the factors which are relevant, including importantly, and perhaps crucially, whether it is now possible to have a fair trial of the issue raised by the complaint. Reasonable awareness of the right to sue is but one factor....If a fair trial is possible despite delay, on what basis can it be said that it would be unjust or inequitable to extend time to permit such a trial?"[58]

1.23   The Human Rights Act makes provision in section 7(9) for rules to be made as regards the procedure to be followed in proceedings brought under the Act against a public authority alleging breach of Convention rights, having regard to section 9(1) which provides as a general rule that any complaint that a *judicial act* has been in breach of a Convention right may *only* be brought by way of appeal against the judicial decision or, if the court in question is otherwise subject to judicial review, by way of judicial review. Otherwise any Convention rights challenge to a judicial act *must* be brought before the Court of Session, regardless of the financial value of the claim.[59]

Section 12 of the Act makes particular provision in respect of remedies in relation to the right to freedom of expression under the Convention. The courts should not grant any relief which might affect this Convention right in the absence of the respondent against whom the relief is sought unless the court is satisfied either that all practicable steps have been taken to notify the respondent or that there are compelling reasons that no such notification should be made. In effect this provision provides for something like a deemed statutory *caveat* in the case of challenges to free expression, although section 12(2)(b) allows the court to grant appropriate relief in the absence of the respondent where it is satisfied that there exist compelling reasons as to why the respondent should not receive prior notification.[59a] Interim relief might only be granted where "the court is satisfied that the applicant is likely to establish that publication should not be allowed, having particular regard in the case of journalistic, literary or artistic material to, public availability or public interest and any relevant privacy code".

No prospective over-ruling

1.24   Where a human rights challenge is made under the Human Rights Act 1998 there is no statutory basis to allow the courts to limit or

---

[58]   *Mills v. Marshall* [1998] I.C.R. 518, EAT
[59]   See Reg. 4 of the Human Rights Act 1998 (Jurisdiction)(Scotland) Rules 2000 (S.I.2000 No.301)
[59a]   See *BBC, petr*, May 2, 2001, HCJ, unreported, *per* Lord Justice General Rodger and Lords Kirkwood and Abernethy for a discussion of the effect of the Convention right of free expression on the courts' past practice of granting orders *ex parte* under s.4(2) of the Contempt of Court Act to restrict contemporaneous reporting of trials.

suspend the retrospective effect of their decisions. Any such power awarded for the sake of the preservation of good administration, would require specific amendment to the Human Rights Act 1998, in a manner which might be justified as simply a more general extension to the United Kingdom courts of the powers already granted to (though not yet exercised by) the courts considering devolution issues under the Devolution Statutes (on which see below).

"Victims" and title and interest to sue

Sections 7(1) and 7(7), read together, restrict the class of those who might either bring proceedings alleging breach of a Convention right or who might rely upon the Convention in legal proceedings to those who would be defined by the European Court of Human Rights (under reference to Article 34 of the Convention) as "victims".[60] Article 34 of the post Protocol 11 Convention[61] (previously Article 25) is in the following terms:

> "The Court [of Human Rights] may receive applications from any person, non-governmental organisation or group of individuals claiming to be the victim of a violation by one of the High Contracting Parties of the rights set forth in the Convention and the Protocols thereto. The High Contracting Parties undertake not to hinder the effective exercise of this right."

The effect of section 7(7) of the 1998 Act is that a party can only complain before the national courts of a breach of the rights incorporated within the Convention, if s/he or it would be recognised by the Court of Human Rights as having sufficient locus, title and interest, or standing as to permit him to take a case before the Strasbourg court alleging breach of the Convention.[62]

Legal persons or corporate bodies may bring applications insofar as they claim that there has been a violation of the rights actually granted them under the Convention, for example the right to a fair

1.25

---

[60] See, too, the parallel provision s.100(1) in the Scotland Act 1998 which similarly restricts the class of those whom might complain about a breach of Convention rights by the Scottish Parliament of Executive to "victims" for the purposes of Art. 34 of the Convention.

[61] See H. G. Schermers "Human Rights after the Reform of 1 November 1998" (1998) 4 E.P.L. 335-343 for an overview of the changes in the structure of the Strasbourg Institutions brought about by the coming into force of Protocol 11.

[62] For a survey of the Commission's decisions on admissibility in this area see Rogge "The 'victim' requirement in Article 25 of the European Convention on Human Rights" in *Protecting Human Rights: the European Dimension. Essays in honour of Gérard Wiarda* (F Matscher and H. Petschold eds., Cologne, 1990), p.539.

trial under Article 6(1)[63] or the right to free expression under Article 10,[64] or their right to property (Article 1, Protocol 1).[65]

It is clear from the Strasbourg jurisprudence that governmental bodies governed by and acting under public law cannot bring an application to the Court.[66] Unincorporated associations who can point to specific individuals within their membership who, they claim, have suffered violation of their Convention rights have been permitted by the Commission to bring applications to the Court.

The standing of churches to bring actions in their own right alleging breach of their Convention rights has also been accepted by the Strasbourg institutions, and indeed it has been held to constitute a violation of the Convention for a State to refuse to recognise the separate legal personality of churches established within it.[67] Interestingly, the Human Rights Act 1998 itself makes specific provision for formal recognition of the particular interests of religious organisations. By virtue of section 13 of the 1998 Act where a court's determination of any question arising under the Act might affect the exercise by a religious organisation and/or its collective membership of the Convention right to freedom of thought, conscience and religion, the court is required to have particular regard to the importance of that right.

1.26   "Victim" in the context of the Convention has also been held to encompass potential victims in that the Commission on Human Rights has recognised the right of persons who can show that they run the risk in the future of being directly affected by the legal situation complained of to bring applications before the court: for example, married persons denied the possibility of divorce.[68] Indeed in certain circumstances individuals have been held by the Strasbourg Court to constitute "victims" simply by virtue of aspects of national legal systems which, for example, stigmatise certain behaviour or ways of life, even if the national laws in question are not enforced or have no actual effect on the individuals in question, for example, homosexuals in contracting states which continue to outlaw homosexuality,[69] or transsexuals in countries which do not allow for any official recognition of an individual's

---

[63] See, for example, *County Properties Ltd v. The Scottish Ministers*, 2000 S.L.T. 965, (OH)

[64] See, for example, *British Broadcasting Corporation, Petitioners (No. 1)*, 2000 S.L.T. 845, (HCJ) and *British Broadcasting Corporation, Petitioners (No. 2)*, 2000 S.L.T. 860, (HCJ)

[65] See, for example, *Booker Aquaculture Ltd v. The Secretary of State for Scotland* [1999] Eu.L.R. 54, [1999] 1 C.M.L.R. 35, (OH); on appeal *Booker Aquaculture Ltd v. The Scottish Ministers*, 2000 S.C. 9, (IH).

[66] See Appl. 13252/87 *Rothenthurm Commune v. Switzerland*, December 14, 1988, (1989) 59 D.R. 251.

[67] See, for example, *The Catholic Church of Canea v. Greece*, Judgment of December 16, 1997, (1997) RJD VIII

[68] See Appl. 9697/82 *J v. Ireland*, October 7, 1983, (1983) 34 D.R. 131.

[69] See, for example, *Dudgeon v. U.K.* A/45 (1982) 4 E.H.R.R. 149; *Norris v. Ireland* A/142 (1991) 13 E.H.R.R. 186; and *Modinos v. Cyprus* (1994) 16 E.H.R.R. 485

change of gender.[70]

Representative actions seeking to challenge the law in the abstract will not, however, be accepted from associations or campaigning groups by way of an *actio popularis*, as the Commission has stated:

> "[T]he applicant cannot complain as a representative for people in general, because the Convention does not permit such an *actio popularis*. The Commission is only required to examine the applicant's complaints that he himself is a victim of a violation."[71]

Concern has been expressed that the imposition of the "victim test" in relation to challenges made under the Human Rights Act will in effect restrict the class of individuals or other bodies who currently have been permitted to bring general judicial review challenges before the courts in England and Wales.[72] Standing the Scottish courts' continued insistence that an applicant for judicial review must be able to show both title and interest to sue,[73] it is unlikely that the statutory importation of the Strasbourg victim test as this is presently understood by the courts will make much difference to Scottish practice on standing in judicial review, since the Scottish and Strasbourg tests appear to be similar in their impact.

Compensation for damages for breach of a Convention right

Section 8 of the 1998 Act allows the court to grant such relief or remedy against an act, including a proposed act, which is contrary to the incorporated Convention rights as it consider just and appropriate including, if such is already within its jurisdiction, making an award of damages or compensation.[73a]   1.27

By virtue of section 9(3) no damages will be awarded in respect of a judicial act done in good faith except as required by Article 5(5) of the Convention which provides that "everyone who has been the victim of arrest or detention in contravention of the provisions of this Article shall have an enforceable right to compensation". Any such damages award falls to be made against the Crown, but may

---

[70] See, for example, *B. v. France* A/232-C (1994) 16 EHRR 1. Compare with *X, Y and Z v. U.K.* A/573 (1997) 24 E.H.R.R. 143

[71] Appl. 9297/81 *X Association v. Sweden,* March 1, 1982, (1982) 28 D.R. 204 at 206.

[72] See J. Marriott and D. Nicol "The Human Rights Act, Representative Standing and the Victim Culture" [1998] E.H.R.L.R. 730.

[73] See, for example, *Scottish Old People Welfare Council ("Age Concern"), Petitioners,* 1987 S.L.T. 179, (OH) and, more recently, *The Rape Crisis Centre v. Brindley,* (OH) unreported decision of Lord Clarke, July 4, 2000 concerning a challenge by way of judicial review of a decision of the Secretary of State for the Home Department to allow Mike Tyson to enter the United Kingdom.

[73a] See, generally *Damages under the Human Rights Act 1998,* Law Com. No. 266/ Scot.Law.Com. No.180 (October 2000) for a survey and discussion by the Law Commissions of the Strasbourg caselaw on damages.

only be pronounced if the Minister responsible for the Court concerned has been conjoined as a party in the proceedings.

In court actions concerning claims that a Convention right has been unlawfully breached, damages should only be awarded if the court is satisfied that in all the circumstances of the case such an award is necessary in order to afford "just satisfaction" to the injured person. In deciding whether and how much to award by way of damages, the national courts are required by section 8(4) to take into account the principles applied by the Strasbourg court in relation to the award of compensation under Article 41 of the Convention as amended by Protocol 11 (previously Article 50),[74] which provides that:

> "If the Court finds that there has been a violation of the Convention or the protocols thereto, and if the internal law of the High Contracting Party concerned allows only partial reparation to be made, the Court shall, if necessary, afford just satisfaction to the injured party."

The purpose of a just satisfaction award is compensatory rather than punitive,[75] so that "the applicant should as far as possible be put in the position he would have been in had the requirements [of the Convention] not been disregarded."[76] and the Court has refused to award aggravated or exemplary damages.[77] The just satisfaction award will normally include a sum to cover legal costs and expenses in bringing the case both in domestic and Convention proceedings.[78] Such legal expenses must be found by the Strasbourg court to have been actually and necessarily incurred and must be considered by them to be reasonable as to quantum.[79] If equitable in all the circumstances of the case, including questions as to the severity of the breach and the ready quantifiability of the loss, an award should be made covering pecuniary and non-pecuniary loss to achieve "a situation as close to *restitutio in integrum* as was possible in the nature of things".[80]

Under the head of pecuniary damage, loss of past and future

---

[74] See s.100(3) of the Scotland Act 1998 which similarly restricts the national courts to Strasbourg damages in relation to claims of breaches of Convention rights by the Scottish Parliament or Scottish Executive

[75] See, generally, A. Mowbray "The European Court of Human Rights' Approach to Just Satisfaction" [1997] P.L. 647

[76] *Piersack v. Belgium (Article 50)* A/54, (1983) 5 E.H.R.R. 251

[77] See, for example, *B v. U.K.* A/121 and *Article 50* A/136D (1988) 10 E.H.R.R. 87 and *Zander v. Sweden,* A/279-B (1994) 18 E.H.R.R. at paras 30–35.

[78] See, for example, *Duncan Lustig-Prean v. U.K. (Article 41)*, unreported decision of July 25, 2000, ECtHR accessible at www.dhcour.coe.fr/hudoc) at para. 32.

[79] *Eckle v. Germany (Article 50)* A/65, (1991) 13 E.H.R.R. 556.

[80] *Windisch v. Austria(Article 50)* Judgment of 28 June 1993, A/255-D at paragraph 14

earnings,[81] reduction in the value of property[82] and loss of opportunity[83] have been compensated. Awards in respect of non-pecuniary or moral damage have been made by the court to cover such non-quantifiable matters as "anxiety, distress, loss of employment prospects, feelings of injustice, deterioration of way of life and other varieties of harm and suffering".[84] Since October 1991 the Strasbourg Court has set out in the operative provisions of the judgment, a period of three months from the date of the decision within which the applicant must be paid. Since January 1996 the Strasbourg Court has provided for interest to be paid in the event of failure to comply with this time-limit.

Application to the Strasbourg Court

It should be borne in mind that insofar as the domestic courts have, despite incorporation, failed to give full and adequate protection of the right or rights protected and guaranteed under the Convention, this may form the basis for an application to the Strasbourg court, once all domestic remedies have been exhausted. Incorporation does not, then, remove the possibility or need of ultimately obtaining a final authoritative judgment from the European Court of Human Rights on the proper interpretation and application of the European Convention.

1.28

It is a basic principle of the Convention, set out in Article 35 of the post-Protocol 11 Convention, that direct recourse to the Strasbourg court is only possible once all domestic judicial remedies have been exhausted, otherwise it will not be possible to show that the State is in violation of the Convention. An application to the Court of Human Rights in Strasbourg must be made within a period of six months from the date upon which the final decision complained of was made, that is when all available domestic remedies have been exhausted.

The State must have been given the opportunity of remedying the alleged violation or redressing the damage by domestic measures. Accordingly the substance of the matter on which an alleged breach of the Convention is based should, if possible, be raised in the course of the domestic proceedings. By way of example, in *McGinley and Egan v. United Kingdom*[85] the Ministry of Defence successfully thwarted an application by former servicemen to the Strasbourg court relative to the non-recovery of their Army medical

---

[81] *Young, James and Webster v. U.K.* A/44 and *(Article 50)* A/55 (1982) 4 E.H.R.R. 38

[82] *Huber v. Switzerland* A/188 Judgment of October 23, 1990.

[83] *Weeks v. U.K.,* Judgment of March 2, 1987, (1988) 10 E.H.R.R. 293, Series A No. 114 and *(Article 50)* Series A No. 145 (1988) at para. 13.

[84] See Sharpe "Just Satisfaction under Article 50" in *La Convention Européene des droits de l'homme* (Imbert and Pettiti eds., 1995) at paras 34-35.

[85] *McGinley and Egan v. U.K.,* ECtHR Judgment of June 9, 1998, *Reports of Judgments and Decisions* 1998-III

records, as well as contemporaneous records of general environmental radiation level records, relating to nuclear weapons tests which had carried out by the United Kingdom at Christmas Island in 1958. The applicants sought such recovery in order to substantiate their claims for severe disability pension in respect of alleged radiation linked illnesses and cancers resulting from their participation in and exposure to the United Kingdom's nuclear tests programme. The applicants were found to have failed to exhaust their statutory remedies since they had made no formal application to the President of the Pensions Appeal Tribunal for recovery of these documents as was apparently open to them under Rule 6 of the Pensions Appeal Tribunals (Scotland) Rules 1981. Consequently their claim before the European Court of Human Rights that their Article 6(1) fair trial rights had been violated failed, notwithstanding doubts as to the effectiveness of the procedure for recovery of documents under the 1981 Rules.[86]

Prior to incorporation, the failure to cite the provisions of the Convention by way of defence to a criminal trial in the United Kingdom did not bar the applicant from subsequently making an application to Strasbourg.[87] With the coming into force of the Scotland Act and the Human Rights Act, it is clear that the Convention rights may now be relied upon directly as a defence in criminal trials in Scotland. Accordingly if a relevant Convention point is not timeously raised in domestic criminal proceedings, the Strasbourg court might be persuaded that there had been a failure to exhaust available domestic remedies and/or a waiver of the relevant Convention rights[88] such as to bar an application to the Council of Europe institutions.

In cases where the applicant has been reliably and properly advised by counsel there is no prospect of an appeal or other judicial procedure being successful or effective in remedying the alleged breach, the Commission may deem the domestic remedies to have been exhausted.[89] The onus is on the contracting state, if it wishes to take the point, to show that that there was an effective domestic remedy which the applicant had failed to pursue.[90]

---

[86] *McGinley and Egan v. U.K. (No. 2)—revision request*, ECtHR Judgment of January 28, 2000, accessible at www.dhcour.coe.fr/hudoc

[87] Appl. 7050/75 *Arrowsmith v. U.K.*, 19 D.R. 8/123, (1980) 3 E.H.R.R. 218.

[88] See *Clancy v. Caird*, 2000 S.L.T. 546, IH; 2000 J.C. 441 and *Millar v. Procurator Fiscal, Elgin*, HCJ, 2000 S.C.C.R. 793 for discussion of the possibility of waiver of Convention rights.

[89] See *De Wilde, Ooms and Versypo v. Belgium* A/12 June 18, 1971 (1979-80) 1 E.H.R.R. 432.

[90] *Deweer v. Belgium* A/35 (1979-80) 2 E.H.R.R. 39.

THE SCOTLAND ACT 1998

Devolution Issues

The Scotland Act 1998, the Government of Wales Act 1988 and the Northern Ireland Act 1998, all make reference to and define a new category of legal questions, "devolution issues", arising out of the creation of devolved governments for the non-English parts of the United Kingdom.[91] Devolution issues are boundary markers. They are concerned with questions as to whether or not the devolved assemblies and administrations have transgressed the limits of the powers granted them under their founding acts—for example, by entering into areas reserved to the Westminster Parliament, or by being in breach of Community law, or in being incompatible with any Convention rights or by otherwise being outwith the legislative competence of the devolved institutions.

Since the limits of the new devolved legislative bodies and administrations are set out in statute, the task of ensuring that the devolved institutions stay within the limits of the powers granted to it is one for the courts. What has been created by the Devolution Statutes then are democratic institutions whose acts are, however, subject to control by the judiciary. As Lord President Rodger robustly observed in the first case to reach the courts concerning the rights and duties of the devolved Holyrood Parliament:

> "[T]he [Scottish] Parliament [i]s a body which—however important its role—has been created by statute and derives its powers from statute. As such, it is a body which, like any other statutory body, must work within the scope of those powers. If it does not do so, then in an appropriate case the court may be asked to intervene and will require to do so, in a manner permitted by the legislation. **In principle, therefore, the Parliament like any other body set up by law is subject to the law and to the courts which exist to uphold that law.**"[92]

Questions as to the "constitutionality" of the acts or omissions of the devolved institutions and administrations (in the sense of whether or not these conform to the limits set out in their founding statutes) may, if relevant to the matter at hand, competently be raised in any proceedings before any courts in the United Kingdom. Such matters are not reserved for decision by the higher courts. In principle, devolution issues may arise within any of the legal jurisdictions of the United Kingdom, thus, questions as to the *vires*

1.29

---

[91] For the various definitions of "devolution issues" see para. 1 of each of: Sched. 6 to the Scotland Act 1998; Sched. 8 to the Government of Wales Act 1998; and Sched. 10 to the Northern Ireland Act 1998

[92] In *Whaley v. Lord Watson of Invergowrie*, 2000 S.L.T. 475, (IH) *per* Lord President Rodger at 481B.

of a Welsh measure might be raised before a Scottish Court; while Scottish legislation may be challenged in Northern Ireland or in England. Schedules 6, 8 and 10 of the Scotland Act, Government of Wales Act and Northern Ireland Act respectively set out the procedures to be followed when devolution issues are raised before courts in the United Kingdom. All provide that frivolous or vexatious challenges to the competency of devolved legislation or administrative action or omissions need not, however, be taken up by the courts.[93]

The Privy Council as the constitutional court in devolution issues

1.30   While the Devolution Statutes have put it within the power of all United Kingdom Courts to review and strike down on grounds of competency both primary and subordinate legislation emanating from the devolved institutions, the three Devolution Statutes have also created a new role for the Judicial Committee of the Privy Council in that they have given it, rather than the House of Lords, jurisdiction on the question of the final domestic resolution of any "devolution issues".[94] But it is only those Privy Councillors who hold or have held the office of a Lord of Appeal in Ordinary, or high judicial office as defined in section 25 of the Appellate Jurisdiction Act 1876 (that is to say English and Northern Ireland High Court and Court of Appeal Judges and, in Scotland, Senators of the College of Justice) may sit and act as a member of the Committee in proceedings under the Act. In effect, what this means is that, first, Privy Councillors who are Commonwealth judges (for example Lord Cooke of Thorndon) are excluded from sitting in devolution issue proceedings, and secondly, unless new Privy Councillors are created who do not sit in Parliament are specifically called to sit on a particular hearing of the Judicial Committee—as Lord Kirkwood was in *Brown v. Stott*, there will be high degree of overlap between those who are active House of Lords judges and the Privy Council judges.[95]

In *Montgomery and Coulter v. H.M.Advocate and the Advocate General for Scotland*,[96] the first devolution issue case to come before

---

[93]   See para. 2 of each of Sched. 6 to the Scotland Act 1998, Sched. 8 to the Government of Wales Act 1998 and Sched. 10 to the Northern Ireland Act 1998.

[94]   For extra-judicial reservations about the appropriateness of using the Judicial Committee of the Privy Council in this way, rather than the House of Lords, see Rt. Hon Lord Steyn "Incorporation and Devolution—a few reflection on the changing scene" [1998] E.H.R.L.R. 153-156.

[95]   Lord Hope of Craighead "Edinburgh v. Westminster & Others: resolving constitutional disputes – inside the crystal ball again?" (1997) 42 J.L.S.S. 140-143 for a discussion of the differences between the House of Lords and the Judicial Committee of the Privy Council.

[96]   *Montgomery v. H.M.Advocate and the Advocate General for Scotland* and *Coulter v. H.M.Advocate and the Advocate General for Scotland*, 2000 P.C. 1.

the Privy Council acting under its Scotland Act jurisdiction, the Judicial Committee was composed in the traditional manner one now expects of Scottish appeals to the House of Lords, namely by two Scottish judges (Lord Hope and Lord Clyde) together with three non-Scots (Lord Slynn of Hadley, Lord Nicholls of Birkenhead and Lord Hoffmann). However, a clear division of opinion arose among these judges as to whether or not a decision of the Lord Advocate to initiate criminal proceedings on indictment against the accused could properly be said to raise a devolution issue at all. The non-Scots judges, led by Lord Hoffman, clearly tended to the view that the matter of respect for and enforcement of an individual's Article 6 rights to a fair trial was *not* a matter for a prosecutor, but lay *wholly* with the court before which the trial was to be conducted. Accordingly, they tended to the view that one could not take Article 6 fair trial point against the prosecutor before the trial has actually started.

The Scottish judges, by contrast, emphasised the peculiar role and history of the Lord Advocate, noting his status as "master of the instance" in criminal trials[97] and insisting that the approach which the Scotland Act had taken was to make the right of the accused to receive a fair trial a responsibility of the Lord Advocate as well as of the court. In what appears to be an implicit rebuke to Lord Hoffman, Lord Hope noted (at pages 15-16) that this case was the first time in which an appeal on a matter of Scots criminal law and procedure had ever come before a court situated outside Scotland; he therefore stressed the need for all the judges of that court to think themselves into the history and modes of understanding of Scots criminal lawyers, rather than simply for the judges to assume that the Scottish criminal system mirrored English criminal and the English derived criminal legal systems.

The matter at stake was clearly one of the highest general constitutional importance. If Lord Hoffman's view were to prevail and questions regarding the proper protection of Article 6 did not raise devolution issues (since they concerned only the acts of the courts rather than the devolved Lord Advocate) then two consequences followed, first, it would appear that all of the Scottish jurisprudence on the Lord Advocate's duties under Article 6[98]

1.31

---

[97] Lord Hope relied in part on the following passage from Hume's *Commentaries on the Law of Scotland Respecting Crimes* (1844) vol. II 134: "The Lord Advocate is master of his instance in this other sense, that even after he has brought his libel into court, it is a matter of his discretion, to what extent he will insist against the pannel; and he may freely, at any period of the process, before return of the verdict, nay after it has been returned, restrict his libel to an arbitrary punishment, in the clearest case, even of a capital crime."

[98] Notably, *H.M.Advocate v. Little,* 1999 S.L.T. 1145 on the Lord Advocate's delays in bringing a case to trial; *Starrs v. Ruxton (Procurator Fiscal, Linlithgow),* 2000 J.C. 208 on temporary sheriffs; *Hoekstra v. H.M.Advocate (No.2),* 2000 S.L.T. 605 on the requirements of an impartial judiciary; *Buchanan (Procurator Fiscal, Fort William) v. McLean,* 2000 S.L.T. 928, HCJ (decision of Lord Prosser, Lord

which had developed since the coming into force of the Scotland Act and prior to the implementation of the Human Rights Act had been decided on the wrong statutory basis;[98a] secondly, and perhaps more importantly, there would effectively be no role for the Judicial Committee in deciding on the proper interpretation and application of Convention fair trial rights within the context of Scottish criminal procedure. There would be no space for the Judicial Committee to carry out its envisaged function of ensuring a uniform United Kingdom wide interpretation for Convention rights in matters of both criminal and civil law. The result of this could well be the development of a peculiarly Scottish Convention rights jurisprudence in criminal matters, since there remains no appeal from the High Court of Justiciary to the House of Lords on "pure" human rights challenges which might be brought in the Scottish criminal courts under the Human Rights Act.[99]

In the event, since all the judges in *Montgomery and Coulter* were agreed that the appeal should be dismissed on the basis that the facts did not show any potential breach of the accuseds' fair trial rights, the non-Scots did not find it was not necessary for them to reach any final decision to be reached on the point as to whether a devolution issue had properly been raised as regards the applicability of Article 6 to the acts and omissions of the Lord Advocate, leaving the point to be argued and resolved on another occasion.

1.32   In *Hoekstra (No.4)*[1] the three judge screening committee of the Privy Council, comprising Lord Slynn, Lord Hope and Lord Clyde, had little difficulty in rejecting the accuseds' application for special leave to appeal to with, with Lord Hope, delivering the Judgment of the Board, noting that the Judicial Committee was *not* a constitutional court of general jurisdiction and re-affirming that it could only hear appeals from Scotland which raised a devolution issue as defined under the Scotland Act; which had been determined

---

Milligan and Lord Morison) on fixed fees criminal legal aid and the equality of arms; *Procurator Fiscal, Kirkcaldy v. Kelly*, HCJ, unreported decision of Lord Milligan, Lord Cameron of Lochbroom and Lord Allanbridge, August 18, 2000, accessible at www.scotcourts.gov.uk on District Courts and the appearance of independence; and *McIntosh v. H.M.Advocate*, 2000 S.L.T. 1280, in which a majority of the court (Lord Kirkwood dissenting) found that the assumptions set out in s.3(2) of the of the Proceeds of Crime (Scotland) Act 1995 relating to the recovery of the proceeds of trafficking were incompatible with the presumption of innocence set out in Art. 6(2) ECHR.

[98a] See Angus Stewart Q.C. "Devolution Issues and Human Rights" 2000 S.L.T. (News) 239,for a detailed argument to the effect that the legislation has indeed been misunderstood and misapplied by the Scottish judges and that the Scotland Act was not intended to allow Convention points to be raised in ordinary criminal proceedings.

[99] The non-availability of appeals from the Scottish Criminal Courts to the House of Lords was confirmed by the House of Lords in *Mackintosh v. Lord Advocate* (1876) 2 App. Cas. 41 and most recently statutorily re-affirmed by s.124(2) of the Criminal Procedure (Scotland) Act 1995.

[1] *Hoekstra v. H.M.Advocate (No.4)*, JCPC, unreported decision of October 26, 2000, accessible at www.privy-council.org.uk

by the court appealed against.[1a] In all other issues every interlocutor of the High Court of Justiciary is final and conclusive and is not subject to review by any court whatsoever. Thus, where it was alleged that the judges of the High Court of Justiciary had acted unlawfully, this did not give rise to an issue which the Judicial Committee could adjudicate on, since such an allegation, although raising a constitutional point, did *not* raise a Scotland Act point. The limits within which the powers of the High Court of Justiciary may be exercised were said by Lord Hope to be for determination by that court and had nothing to do with the functions of the Scottish Ministers, the First Minister or the Lord Advocate.

The composition of the Judicial Committee in *Brown v. Stott*[2] is of particular interest in the context of the split in approach between the Scots and non-Scots judges which was revealed in *Montgomery and Coulter*. Again the two Scottish Law Lords, Lord Hope and Lord Clyde were included on the Committee, but they were joined by a third Scottish judge, Lord Kirkwood, who was eligible to sit on the Judicial Committee by virtue of the recent appointment of Inner House judges to the rank of Privy Councillor. Thus, for the first time, Scottish judges made up a majority of the Judicial Committee, being joined in *Brown and Stott* by Lord Bingham and Lord Steyn. This time, the Committee were unanimous in deciding that the proposed acts of the Lord Advocate properly raised a devolution issue under reference to Article 6 fair trial rights. The disputed analysis of this issue by Lords Hope and Clyde in *Montgomery and Coulter* would seem to have prevailed over the approach of Lord Hoffmann, and the doubts expressed by Lord Slynn and Lord Nicholls. Had the Scots judges' analysis of what constitutes a devolution not been followed, and the Hoffmann approach preferred, the likely result would have been that Lord Rodger's finding, backed as it was by an impressive citation and detailed critique of many Commonwealth and US authorities, as to the central and (almost) absolute nature of the right against enforced self-incrimination implicit in Article 6 of the Convention would have prevailed in the context of the Scots criminal law and procedure. By contrast, it seems likely that the House of Lords in any criminal appeal in England would have followed the approach favoured by the pressure group JUSTICE (who were permitted to intervene in the Judicial Committee proceedings in *Brown v. Stott*) and allowed the right to be limited in a proportionate manner for legitimate reasons. One suspects that it was precisely the possibility of such a major disparity of approach between the two jurisdiction which drove Lord Hope's insistence (in the face of Lord

---

[1a] See, on this point, Lord Hope in *Follen v. H.M.Advocate*, March 8, 2001, JCPC, unreported, (accessible at www.privy-council.org.uk) at para.49 of his judgment.

[2] *Brown v. Stott*, JCPC, unreported decision of December 5, 2000, accessible at www.privy-council.org.uk/

Hoffmann's scepticism) as to the fair trial responsibilities of the Lord Advocate.

The Privy Council as the final court of appeal in human rights issues

1.33   Section 103 of the Scotland Act, section 82 of the Northern Ireland Act and paragraph 32 of Schedule 8 to the Government of Wales Act all assert the binding nature of decisions of the Judicial Committee of the Privy Council in proceedings under the Act in all other courts and legal proceedings, apart from later cases brought before the Committee. This alters the general rule that the House of Lords in its judicial capacity is not bound by decisions of the Judicial Committee of the Privy Council.[3] It would appear that the purpose of this provision was to ensure uniformity of approach across the United Kingdom on matters of Convention rights, among others. It is a provision the significance of which has apparently been little understood, because in effect it means that on questions of the effect and scope of Convention rights (which have been duly raised under the Devolution Statutes) the House of Lords has been superseded as the final court of appeal in the United Kingdom. This will come as a great shock to many English lawyers, who have been engaged in litigation over Convention rights issues since the coming into force of the Human Rights Act in England at the beginning of October 2000. The English final court of appeal in civil and criminal matters, the House of Lords, has itself been placed at level lower in the judicial hierarchy by another court, the Judicial Committee, which a developing constitutional convention seems to indicate will be a court composed substantially, (and at times by a majority) of Scots lawyers deciding cases brought primarily from Scotland.

The somewhat surprising (and surely unintended) result of this is an effective Scottish take-over of English law when matters of Convention rights are raised, and the exclusion of the majority of English lawyers and English judges effectively to reach final and binding decisions on Convention points. Thus, while the English Court of Appeal[4] has considered the compatibility with Convention rights of the procedure for property confiscation orders to be made in drug trafficking cases, the final decision on this matter has effectively been taken not on any appeal by the parties to the House of Lords, but by the decision of the Judicial Committee in the Scottish case of *McIntosh*.[5] Similarly, in a series of conjoined judicial review application the English High Court in December

---

[3] See *London Joint Stock Bank v. MacMillan and Arthur* [1918] A.C. 777 at 807

[4] In *R v. Karl Benjafield*, December 21, 2000, CA, unreported decision of Woolf L.C.J. and Collins J., at para. 69; digested in [2000] Times Law Reports 902.

[5] *McIntosh v. H.M.Advocate*, unreported decision of Lord Prosser, Lord Kirkwood and Lord Allanbridge, October 13, 2000 (accessible at www.scotcourts.gov.uk)

2000 considered the applicability of Article 6 to the call-in procedure to the Secretary of State in planning matters.[6] But again, as a matter of strict law, the final decision on this point cannot be made by the judges in this case whether at first instance or on appeal to the House of Lords.[6a] Instead all of these judges will have to defer on the Convention point issue to a decision of the Judicial Committee should Lord MacFadyen's decision in *County Properties v. Scottish Ministers*[7] be taken to the Privy Council.

One cannot but feel that this kind of *ad hoc* constitutional structure will not prove to be an inherently stable one. Ultimately, it is suggested, the logic of the on-going constitutional change will require the setting up a properly established constitutional court for the United Kingdom, with properly identified, tenured and independent judges, perhaps along the lines of the United States Supreme Court or the European Court of Justice. The genie of constitutional reform is out of the bottle and has acquired its own dynamic. It would appear that our legislators have not yet completed the task of writing the constitution.

Preliminary reference procedure to the Privy Council in devolution issues

The Devolution Statutes all provide for the possibility of preliminary references on a devolution issue from the lower courts to higher courts; a procedure modelled, in part, on Article 234 (formerly Article 177) of the Treaty of Rome. Under this procedure, 1.34

- courts and tribunals lower than the Court of Appeal (or, in Scotland, the Inner House or the High Court sitting as an appellate court) have a discretion to refer any devolution issue arising in proceedings before them to the relevant appellate court;[8]
- lower courts against whose decisions there is no right of appeal have a duty to refer any devolution issue arising in proceedings before them to the relevant appellate court;[9]
- the decision of the appellate court on the devolution reference

---

[6] *R v. Secretary of State for the Environment, ex p. Alconbury*, December 12, 2000, unreported.

[6a] See *Alconbury*, May 9, 2001, (HL), unreported decision of Lords Slynn of Hadley, Nolan, Hoffman, Hutton and Clyde.

[7] *County Properties Ltd v. The Scottish Ministers*, 2000 S.L.T. 965, OH

[8] See, paras 7, 9, 18, 19, 21 and 28 of Sched. 6 to the Scotland Act 1998; paras 6, 7, 15, 17, 18, 19 and 25 of Sched. 8 to the Government of Wales Act 1998; and paras 7, 15, 16, 18, 25, 27 of Sched. 10 to the Northern Ireland Act 1998

[9] See, paras 8, 20, 29 of Sched. 6 to the Scotland Act 1998; paras 8, 16 and 26 to Sched. 8 to the Government of Wales Act 1998; and paras 8, 17, 26 of Sched. 10 to the Northern Ireland Act 1998

may itself be appealed to the Judicial Committee of the Privy Council,[10] but normally only with leave;[11]

- higher and appellate courts may themselves refer devolution issues which have been raised directly before them (rather than referred to them by lower courts) to the Judicial Committee of the Privy Council;[12]
- provision is made for the House of Lords to refer any devolution issues arising in judicial proceedings before it to the Judicial Committee of the Privy Council "unless the House considers it more appropriate, having regard to all the circumstances, that it should determine the issue".[13] This provision is perhaps intended to parallel the "*acte clair*" doctrine in the ECJ case law[14] under which national courts against whose decisions there is no further right of appeal[15] are relieved of their duty to make a preliminary reference to the European Court of Justice where the answer to the question at issue is so obvious as to leave no room for any reasonable doubt.

The role of the law officers in devolution issues

1.35   The United Kingdom Attorney General, the Attorney General for Northern Ireland, the Westminster based Advocate-General for Scotland, and the Lord Advocate (*ex officio* a member of the Scottish Executive) are given a variety of powers and rights relative to the institution, defending and receiving of intimation of proceedings concerning the determination of any devolution issue. Mandatory references directly to the Judicial Committee of the Privy Council may be made of devolution issues in proceedings in which any of the Law Officers are parties, on their application.[16]

---

[10] See, paras 12, 23 and 31 of Sched. 6 to the Scotland Act 1998; paras 11, 20, 28 of Sched. 8 to the Government of Wales Act 1998 and paras 10, 20, 30 of Sched. 10 to the Northern Ireland Act 1998

[11] See, paras 13, 23, 31 of Sched. 6 to the Scotland Act 1998; paras 11, 20, 21 and 28 of Sched. 8 to the Government of Wales Act 1998 and paras 31 of Sched. 10 to the Northern Ireland Act 1998

[12] See, paras 10, 11, 22, 30 of Sched. 6 to the Scotland Act 1998; paras 10, 18, 19, and 27 of Sched. 8 to the Government of Wales Act 1998 and paras 9, 19, 28, 29 of Sched. 10 to the Northern Ireland Act 1998

[13] See, para. 32 of Sched. 6 to the Scotland Act 1998; para. 29 of Sched. 8 to the Government of Wales Act 1998 and para. 32 of Sched. 10 to the Northern Ireland Act 1998

[14] See, Case 283/81 *CILFIT Srl v. Italian Ministry of Health* [1982] E.C.R. 3415.

[15] See, *H.M.Advocate v. Orru and Stewart*, 1998 S.C.C.R. 59 for an example of the application of this doctrine by the Scottish Criminal Appeal Court.

[16] See paras 33–35 of Sched. 6 to the Scotland Act 1998; paras 30–31 of Sched. 8 to the Government of Wales Act 1998 and paras 33–35 of Sched. 10 to the Northern Ireland Act 1998.

Prospective over-ruling in devolution issues

When considering any devolution issue, the courts are given the express power under section 102 of the Scotland Act 1998, section 110 of the Government of Wales Act, and section 81 of the Northern Ireland Act to remove or limit the retrospective effect of any decision which they might make to the effect that the devolved legislature or administration has acted outwith their respective *legislative* competences. It is no longer the case that, as Lord Goff noted in another context, "[a] system [of prospective over-ruling...has no place in our legal system."[17] Under the Devolution Statutes, the courts may also suspend the effect of their decision as to incompetency "for any period and on any conditions to allow the defect to be corrected". If considering whether to make any such limitation or suspensory order, the courts are required to intimate this to the appropriate law officer. Such intimation allows the law officers not already parties to the action to take part in the proceedings so far as they relate to the making of such an order. In deciding whether to make any order in relation to temporal limitation or suspension of their decision the courts are enjoined to have regard to, among other things, "**the extent to which persons who are not parties to the proceedings would be otherwise adversely affected**".

1.36

While the courts have power to suspend or to limit the retrospective effect of their rulings in relation to successful challenges to the *vires* of the *legislative activity* of the devolved legislature or administration, the courts are given no such power to limit the retrospective effect of their decisions in relation to the *non-legislative activity* of members of the devolved administration. Thus, the finding by the High Court in *Starrs v. Ruxton*[18] that the bringing of criminal prosecutions before temporary sheriffs contravened the accused's Article 6(1) Convention rights could *not* be made wholly or partly prospective or otherwise suspended by the court to allow the Scottish Executive time to remedy the situation. The challenge was made against an administrative act of the Lord Advocate, the decision to bring a prosecution, rather than against a legislative act of the Scottish Executive or Parliament.

It is a matter for the Westminster legislature to decide whether or not for the sake of consistency of approach the Devolution Statutes should be amended to give the courts the power to pronounce prospective judgments where devolution issues are raised against decisions or omissions of the members of the Devolved Executives acting in an administrative capacity. If such a power had already existed and been exercised, then the administrative uncertainty and lengthy delays to all business before the sheriff courts which

---

[17] *Kleinwort Benson v. Leicester C.C.* [1998] 4 All E.R. 513 at 536a–b.
[18] *Starrs v. Ruxton (Procurator Fiscal, Linlithgow)*, 2000 J.C. 208, 2000 S.L.T. 42, HCJ

resulted from the *Starrs v. Ruxton* decision might have been avoided. Alternatively, if a power of prospective over-ruling is seen as a good thing for judges to have in the new constitutional dispensation, it is not clear why it should be limited to cases which raise devolution issues under the Devolution Statutes.

The counter-argument to this is that the very power to limit the retrospective effect of judgments may not be consistent with the court's duty to ensure the full protection of Convention rights in cases before it. Thus, following the decision in *Starrs v. Ruxton* it seems clear that the Lord Advocate in bringing criminal proceedings against individuals to be tried before temporary sheriffs had been acting contrary to section 57(2) of the Scotland Act and hence acting *ultra vires* from at least May 20, 1999, the date when he became directly subject to the provisions of the Convention. Such action on the part of the Lord Advocate contravened the accuseds' Article 6 rights, insofar as they had not waived these.[19] Any attempt by the courts to limit the retrospective effect of this judgment, assuming that they had such power under national law, might itself contravene the Convention.

DEVOLUTION ISSUES AND HUMAN RIGHTS

1.37   Given that the question as to the compatibility of Convention rights with devolved legislation and administrative (in)action is also designated a "devolution issue" under the relevant Schedules to the Devolution Statutes, it is necessary to consider how the provisions of the Devolution Statutes interact with the Human Rights Act 1998.

Acts and omissions equally reviewable

1.38   Section 57(2) of the Scotland Act 1998 provides that "a member of the Scottish Executive has no power to make any subordinate legislation or to do any other act so far as the legislation or act is incompatible with any of the Convention rights." It seems clear, at least from the case law to date, that it is not only the positive acts of the Scottish Ministers which are subject to review under the Scotland Act for their compatibility with individuals' Convention rights, but also their omissions.[20]

---

[19]   On waiver of Art. 6(1) rights prior to the decision in *Starrs v. Ruxton* see *Millar v. Procurator Fiscal, Elgin*, HCJ, [2000] S.C.C.R. 793.

[20]   See *H.M.Advocate v. Robb*, 2000 J.C. 127 *per* Lord Penrose at 130D-E: "Section 6(6) of the Human Rights Act 1998 defines 'act' as including a failure to act, subject to certain exceptions. There is no express provision to that effect in the Scotland Act, but it is plain that, while the express qualifications are necessarily different in the context of the two Acts, the expressions must have the same

This interpretation of section 57(2) of the Scotland Act to include, in line with section 6(5) of the Human Rights Act, omissions or failure to act is also consonant with section 100(4)(b) of the Scotland Act which, in the context of making provision for damages to be awarded by the court in respect of an act which is incompatible with any of the Convention rights, specifically defines act as meaning (a) making any legislation or (b) any other act or failure to act, if it is an act or failure of a member of the Scottish Executive". Similarly, paragraph 1(e) of Schedule 6 to the Scotland Act includes within the definition of devolution issue "a question whether a failure to act by a member of the Scottish Executive is incompatible with any of the Convention rights or with Community law".

Common *"Victim test" for breach of Convention rights*

Section 100 of the Scotland Act 1998, section 107 of the Government of Wales Act 1998 and section 71 of the Northern Ireland Act 1998 provide that, apart from the relevant law officers, only those who would be regarded by the European Court of Human Rights as "victims" under and in terms of Article 34 of the European Convention on Human Rights are able to bring proceedings before the courts under the statute on the ground that an Act of the devolved legislature or an act or omission of the devolved executive or administration is incompatible with the Convention, or otherwise to rely on any of the Convention rights in any such proceedings.   1.39

Common *"Just satisfaction" rule for damages for breach of Convention rights*

Section 100(3) of the Scotland Act, Section 107(4)(b) of the   1.40

---

general scope, and the word 'act' in Section 57(2) [of the Scotland Act] must include failure to act." See for similar observations, *Clancy v. Caird*, 2000 S.L.T. 546, (IH) *per* Lord Penrose at 567F para. 12 of his judgment: "In my opinion it is preferable to read Section 57(2) [of the Scotland Act] as encompassing both acts and failures to act, and in that way give content to the whole provisions of Schedule 6 [to the Act]." And in *H.M.Advocate v. Burns*, HCJ, unreported decision of August 4, 2000, accessible at www.scotcourts.gov.uk, Lord Penrose observed as follows: "The implement of any executive or administrative decision must involve an 'act', in my opinion, having regard to the unqualified use of that broad expression in the Scotland Act. I regard the repeated assertion that what had been done or omitted in pursuance of such decisions did not constitute an act to be wholly sterile. ... If there were a case in which a convention right had been infringed in some obvious way by the implement of an executive decision it might be less than clear that it reflected well on the department involved to seek to avoid responsibility by denying that it had acted, on the basis of a purported narrow interpretation of the Scotland Act."

Government of Wales Act and sections 71(3)(b) and 71(4)(b) of the Northern Ireland Assembly all seem to be intended to parallel section 8(3) and (4) of the Human Rights Act 1998 and limit any damages which might be awarded by a national court for breach of Convention rights by the devolved legislatures and administrations to the measure and approach adopted by the Strasbourg Court in relation to the "just satisfaction" of an applicant's claim under reference to Article 41 of the European Convention.

Justification for breach of Convention rights

1.41   As we have seen the effect of section 107(4)(a) of the Government of Wales Act and sections 71(3)(a) and 71(4)(a) of the Northern Ireland Act is to place the Welsh Assembly and the Northern Ireland Assembly and Northern Ireland Ministers and Department in the same position as any other public authority under section 6(2) of the Human Rights Act 1998. These sections make provision for the possibility of a lawful breach of Convention rights if, as a result of one or more provisions of primary Westminster legislation, the devolved Welsh or Northern Ireland institutions could not have acted differently or if the devolved Welsh or Northern Ireland authority was acting so as to give effect to or enforce Convention incompatible Westminster provisions.

The position of the Scottish devolved institutions in relation to justification

1.42   As we noted above there is no such general tie-in provision in the Scotland Act allowing the Scottish Parliament or Scottish Executive to similarly rely upon section 6(2) of the Human Rights Act to justify possible breaches of the Convention under reference to the requirements of Westminster legislation. The only reference to this provision of the Human Rights Act comes in section 57(3) of the Scotland Act which provides that *only* the Lord Advocate when prosecuting any offence or acting in his capacity as head of the systems of criminal prosecution and investigation of deaths in Scotland may rely upon section 6(2) of the Human Rights Act to justify a breach by him of a Convention right on the grounds of the requirements of a contrary and incompatible provision of Westminster legislation. Without such specific Westminster derived authorisation, the Lord Advocate no longer has power to "move the court to grant any remedy which would be incompatible with the European Convention on Human Rights".[21]

---

[21]   *Lord Advocate v. Scottish Media Newspapers Ltd*, 1999 S.C.C.R. 599, IH *per* the Lord President, Lord Rodger of Earlsferry at 561.

In relation to other Members of the Scottish Executive (and other acts of the Lord Advocate), section 57(2) of the Scotland Act simply provides that they have no power to do any act so far as "incompatible with any of the Convention rights or with Community law". As has been noted judicially:

> "Section 57(2) is concerned with a **further** specific limitation on the powers of the [Scottish] Executive expressed by reference to the Convention and Community law. **It is not a temporary or transitional provision. It will continue to apply after the Human Rights Act comes fully into force.**"[22]

Similarly, section 29(2)(d) of the Scotland Act puts an *absolute and unqualified limit* on the power of the Scottish Parliament to legislate in a manner which is incompatible with any of the Convention rights or with Community law. The effect of this failure to tie in Scottish legislative activity to section 6(2) of the Human Rights Act is that, as we stated at the outset, although the European Convention is formally being incorporated into domestic Scots law by the same statute as it is incorporated into the laws of England and Wales and of Northern Ireland, the European Convention on Human Rights will be given a different constitutional status in Scotland from the rest of the United Kingdom.

Under the Scotland Act 1998, the rights guaranteed under the Convention have the status of a higher law as against all and any legislation passed by the Scottish Parliament or any act or omission of a member of the Scottish Executive. Breach of these rights cannot be justified in law. Thus whereas the English planning system may continue even if the Westminster statute on which it is based is found by the courts to be incompatible with the Convention, a judgment such as that of Lord MacFadyen in *County Properties*[23] effectively bars the Scottish Executive and the Holyrood Parliament from operating, authorising or relying upon a similar system of planning controls in Scotland.

Given that there appears to be *no* possibility for justified breach of Convention rights for the devolved Scottish institutions, it is clear that the judges in Scotland have to take particular care in understanding and applying Convention rights, if the business of Government is to be possible (and popularly responsive) in Scotland. The judges have the last word on these issues in Scotland and in contrast to the position in relation to the powers of Westminster, there is no possibility within the devolved Scottish political system for their decisions on the law to be over-ruled. Under the devolved Scottish constitution, the judges have been placed at the apex, in a position similar to that of the United States

---

[22] In *Clancy v. Caird*, 2000 S.L.T. 546, IH *per* Lord Penrose at 566K, para. 9 of his judgment
[23] *County Properties Ltd v. The Scottish Ministers*, 2000 S.L.T. 965, OH

Supreme Court, to questions the definition, extent and requirements for the proper protection of fundamental rights. This is an exposed position for judges to be in, given that in many cases the constitutional purpose of fundamental rights is to set limits on the popular responsiveness of government and to protect unpopular minorities from the tyranny of the majority.

1.43　One example of how this different constitutional status makes for radically different practical results is in relation to cases in which complainers of rape and sexual assault have been subjected to detailed cross-examination by those accused of carrying out those crimes who have decided not to be represented, but rather to defend themselves, in court. The Westminster response to the alleged abuses by such accused of their defence rights has been to see to take away the right of any person charged with a sexual offence to cross-examine *in person* the complainant in connection with that offence or any other offence with which he is also charged in the same criminal proceedings.[24] The *immediate* reported response of the Scottish Executive and Scottish Parliament, by contrast, was to the effect that no changes could be made to the existing law in Scotland on the view that any attempt to increase the protection of complainers and further regulate defence rights might contravene the accused's Convention rights under Article 6(3)(c) "to defend himself in person". Hence any devolved legislation to this effect would be *ultra vires* both the Scottish Ministers and the Holyrood Parliament.[25] Due to public outcry, however, the Scottish Ministers have announced that they will look again at the question. The ultimate resolution of this matter is, however, one for the judges, regardless of public feelings as to the requirements of popular justice.

An Act of the Scottish Parliament may also consolidate, update

---

[24] See s.34 of the Youth Justice and Criminal Evidence Act 1999. See now, on the question of the Convention compatibility of s.41 of this Act, the decision of the House of Lords in *R. v. A*, May 17, 2001, unreported decision of Lords Slynn, Steyn, Hope, Clyde and Hutton; [2001] U.K.H.L. 25.

[25] Compare, however, the decision in *Croissant v. Germany* A/237-B, (1993) 16 E.H.R.R. 135, where the Strasbourg Court made the following observations (at para. 29 of the judgment) in relation to the applicant's objection to being represented by a third court appointed counsel in addition to the two counsel already retained by himself; "It is true that Article 6 para. 3 (c) (art. 6-3-c) entitles 'everyone charged with a criminal offence' to be defended by counsel of his own choosing (see the *Pakelli v. Germany* judgment of 25 April 1983, Series A no. 64, p.15, para.31). Nevertheless, and notwithstanding the importance of a relationship of confidence between lawyer and client, this right cannot be considered to be absolute. It is necessarily subject to certain limitations where free legal aid is concerned and also where, as in the present case, it is for the courts to decide whether the interests of justice require that the accused be defended by counsel appointed by them. When appointing defence counsel the national courts must certainly have regard to the defendant's wishes; indeed, German law contemplates such a course (Article 142 of the Code of Criminal Procedure; see para.20 above). However, they can override those wishes when there are relevant and sufficient grounds for holding that this is necessary in the interests of justice."

and re-state the law, whether at common law or as comprised in an Act of the Westminster Parliament or subordinate legislation thereunder, even within the area of reserved matters, although if there is such restatement of the law in reserved matters by an Act of the Scottish Parliament, it remains outwith the legislative competence of the Scottish Parliament to make any substantive modification to that law.[26] The Scottish Parliament has also been accorded full legislative competence in a broad range of domestic issues. These include; health, education, local government, social work, housing, economic development, judicial appointments, civil and criminal law and procedure, the criminal justice and prosecution system, legal aid; prisons; police and fire services, the environment, agriculture, forestry and fishing.

In England, all of the above areas remain wholly within the competence of the Westminster Parliament, thus;   1.44

- primary Westminster legislation in these areas will therefore be subject only to the "interpretative obligation" placed on the courts by section 3(1) of the Human Rights Act 1998, to read and give effect to that legislation so far as possible in a way which is compatible with the Convention rights;
- where the courts finds that the legislative provision in question cannot be interpreted in accordance with the requirements of the Human Rights Convention, the Westminster provision (and any Welsh or Northern Ireland devolved legislation based on it) nonetheless remains valid, operative and enforceable;
- and under sections 10 to 12 of the Human Rights Act 1998, it is a matter for the Minister of the Crown, answerable to the Westminster Parliament, to decide whether and how to amend the offending provision, and whether or not to give it retrospective effect.

The contrast with the situation in relation to Scottish legislation is stark:

- the courts will be required to strike down primary Scottish legislation which is found to contravene the incorporated Convention rights;
- further, it will be for the courts, and *not* the Scottish Parliament, to consider whether to limit the retrospective effect of any such ruling of invalidity under section 102 of the Scotland Act 1998;
- however, since the courts are themselves defined as public authorities by section 6(3)(a) of the Human Rights Act 1998, any decision limiting retrospectivity will itself have to be

---

[26] Para. 7(2) of Sched. 4 to the Act provides as follows: "7(2) For the purposes of paragraph 2 [the prohibition on the modification of the law on reserved matters] the law on reserved matters includes any restatement in an Act of the Scottish Parliament, or subordinate legislation under such an Act, of the law on reserved matters if the subject-matter of the restatement is a reserved matter."

compatible with the rights guaranteed under the European Convention.

In relation to primary Westminster legislation, then, the manner of remedying any incompatibility between the law and Convention rights is under the Human Rights Act 1998 a decision for the Westminster Parliament and United Kingdom Executive. In relation to Scottish legislation, however, the manner of remedying an incompatibility between the law and the Convention rights rests with the courts before which the matter is raised.

Remedies for breach of a Convention right

1.45   The general principle *ubi ius, ibi remedium* remains a part of the civilian heritage of the Scots courts and Scots common law. This may affect the court's interpretation and application of the human rights provisions of the Scotland Act as regards the provision of new remedies to ensure that Convention rights are respected by the devolved institutions in Scotland.

As has been stated, the Human Rights Act 1998 excludes from among the incorporated Convention rights, Article 13, which specifies that there should be an "effective remedy" available to individuals complaining of a breach of Convention rights by State authorities. The United Kingdom Government's expressed reason for excluding Article 13 was that the effective remedies point was answered by the procedure set out in the Human Rights Act itself and so there was no need for the courts to venture outwith the four corners of the statute to invent new remedies and procedures, as they might otherwise be tempted to do were Article 13 to be made directly effective. Further, while section 6(6) of the Human Rights Act specifies that an act of a public authority includes a failure to act, it also provides that does *not* encompass a failure to introduce in or lay before Parliament a proposal for legislation or a failure to make any primary legislation or remedial order.

While there is no definition of "act" in the terms of section 57(2) of the Scotland Act, as we noted at the outset of this chapter, the courts have held that the word is to be construed broadly such as to include "failure to act".[27] Such an interpretation of section 57(2) is

---

[27]   In *H.M.Advocate v. Burns*, HCJ, unreported decision of August 4, 2000, accessible at www.scotcourts.gov.uk, Lord Penrose observed as follows: "The implement of any executive or administrative decision must involve an 'act', in my opinion, having regard to the unqualified use of that broad expression in the Scotland Act. I regard the repeated assertion that what had been done or omitted in pursuance of such decisions did not constitute an act to be wholly sterile. ... If there were a case in which a convention right had been infringed in some obvious way by the implement of an executive decision it might be less than clear that it reflected well on the department involved to seek to avoid responsibility by denying that it had acted, on the basis of a purported narrow interpretation of the Scotland Act."

also in line with the express terms of section 100 of the Scotland Act which allows the Law Officers and victims to seek judicial review of acts incompatible with Convention rights and which, in section 100(4), defines "act" as meaning "(a) making any legislation or (b) any other act or **failure to act**, if it is the act or failure of a member of the Scottish Executive". In similar terms, paragraph 1(e) of Schedule 6 to the Scotland Act includes within the definition of devolution issue "a question whether **a failure to act** by a member of the Scottish Executive is incompatible with any of the Convention rights or with Community law". Since there is no limitation in the definition of "act", such failure to act would include a failure on the part of the Scottish Ministers to introduce to introduce in or lay before the Holyrood Parliament a proposal for legislation or, indeed, a failure on the part of the Scottish Parliament to make any primary Scottish legislation or remedial order.

So, for example, where a statutory provision within devolved competence fails to make adequate provision in respect of Article 6(1) rights, it may therefore be argued that the *absence* of a specific appeal procedure to the courts or other independent tribunal under the national provision justifies a finding of incompatibility of the statute with the Convention, under section 4 of the Human Rights Act 1998. More usefully and more radically, however, it could also be argued that the failure on the part of the Scottish Ministers to introduce an appropriate appeal procedure constitutes a breach of the Convention, and that therefore a positive declaratory or specific implement order might be sought from the court for such an appeal procedure to be introduced.[28] Such procedure, although unusual, is justified on the broader reading of section 57(2) of the Scotland Act which makes *ultra vires* any act or omission on the part of the Scottish Ministers which is contrary to the rights conferred under the Convention.

In any event, such a positive declaratory order by the courts effectively ordaining the Scottish Ministers to introduce a particular legislative provision in order to comply with the requirements of the Convention would seem to be compatible with the whole scheme of the Scotland Act and, in particular, with section 58 thereof. Under section 58 the Secretary of State has the power to direct a member of the Scottish Executive either, (1) to *refrain* from proposed action where he has reasonable grounds to believe that such action would be incompatible with the *international obligations* of the United Kingdom; or (2) to *order* otherwise competent action from any member of the Scottish Executive where he has reasonable grounds to believe that such action is required for the purpose of giving effect to any such international obligations. Such positive action which may be

1.46

---

[28] A positive declaratory remedy regarding an obligation to introduce a particular legislative provisions was pronounced by Lord Cameron of Lochbroom in *Booker Aquaculture Limited v. The Secretary of State for Scotland* [1999] Eu.L.R. 54, [1999] 1 C.M.L.R. 35, OH

required of the Scottish Executive by the Secretary of State is stated in section 58(3) to include their "making, confirming or approving subordinate legislation" or indeed introducing a Bill to the Scottish Parliament. While the Secretary of State may order a Scottish Minister to introduce a Bill before the Edinburgh Parliament, the Secretary of State is given no power to order that Parliament to enact any such Bill: such power would, perhaps, be seen as too blatant a disregard for the democratic principle. The Secretary of State is required to state his reason in making any such order, and his or her decisions will therefore be subject to judicial scrutiny review on the usual grounds for review of administrative action.

"International obligations" is defined under section 126(1) of the Act as meaning "any international obligations of the United Kingdom *other than* obligations to observe and implement Community law or the Convention rights." This reference to the international obligations of the United Kingdom is potentially a provision of particular significance in that it effectively binds the Scottish Parliament to respect the whole range of international treaties which have been ratified by the Crown even where they have not been incorporated into the domestic law of the United Kingdom. Thus the Scottish Parliament will be bound by, among other treaties, the UN International Covenant on Civil and Political Rights, the International Covenant on Economic, Social and Cultural Rights, and the European Social Charter concluded under the auspices of the Council of Europe in 1961.

1.47   Thus, while the Secretary of State has the power to seek positive action of the Scottish Ministers so that they comply with international obligations other than Community law and Convention rights, in matters of the effective protection of Community law and the Convention rights, it would appear that the Scotland Act leaves it up to the *courts* to develop and grant the appropriate remedies. Accordingly we may anticipate the possibility of court orders along the lines pronounced recently by the Canadian Supreme Court in *Vriend v. Alberta*[29] and by the Supreme Court of Vermont in *Baker v. State of Vermont*.[30] In *Vriend v. Alberta* the judge at first instance, Madame Justice Russell, holding that apparent omission of protection against discrimination on grounds of sexual orientation in the Alberta anti-discrimination statute constituted an unjustified violation of the equal protection provision of the Canadian Charter of Rights.[31] She accordingly

---

[29] *Vriend v. Alberta* [1998] 1 S.C.R. 493
[30] Vermont Supreme Court Docket (98-032) *Baker v. State of Vermont*, unreported decision, filed December 20, 1999
[31] This provision is set out in Section (S) 15(1) of the Canadian Charter and is in the following terms: "[E]very individual is equal before and under the law and has the right to equal protection and equal benefit of the law without discrimination and, in particular, without discrimination based on race, national or ethnic origin, colour, religion, **sex**, age or mental or physical disability.

ordered that the relevant sections of the Alberta statute be **"interpreted, applied and administered as though they contained the words 'sexual orientation'".**[32] This first instance decision was reversed on appeal to the Court of Appeal of Alberta but was reinstated in a successful appeal by the plaintiff to the Supreme Court of Canada which found that sexual orientation discrimination must be included in the grounds of discrimination in both federal and provincial rights legislation because its exclusion violates section 15(1) of the Charter. The Supreme Court therefore ordered that "sexual orientation" be "read in" as one of the prohibited grounds of discrimination in the otherwise "under-inclusive" Alberta statute in the manner suggested by the judge at first instance. In *Baker v. State of Vermont* the Vermont Supreme Court ordered the Vermont legislature to amend the Vermont marriage statutes and enact legislation consistent with their mandate under the 1777 Constitution of the State of Vermont so as to provide for the establishment of same sex civil unions comparable to marriage.

Judges as legislators?

It may be that the apparent constitutional shift of power in favour of the judiciary will be regarded, in time, as a mixed blessing. It would certainly be somewhat ironic if, in upholding individuals' rights to a hearing from an independent and impartial tribunal, the political independence and impartiality of the judges themselves was itself called into question. It would be unfortunate indeed if a result giving the Convention rights "direct effect" made what have previously been treated as purely political conflicts, effectively, a question of jurisdiction. Such a result could conceivably lead, in its turn, to demands for, or complaints of, the explicit politicisation of the national judiciary.[33]   1.48

The alternative might be that of the return to ivory tower or cloister with the effective imposition of a monastic rule of silence on (both actual and potential?) members of the judiciary to prevent them from speaking out or commenting in the public arena (including, arguably, as legislators in the House of Lords) on matters deemed to be publicly or politically controversial for fear of compromising the perception of their independence and imparti-

---

[32] *Vriend v. Alberta* (1994) 152 A.R. 1, QBD

[33] On April 20, 2000 the Scottish Executive initiated a consultation procedure relative to the creation of an independent Judicial Appointment Board intended to make the appointment of sheriffs and judges in Scotland "more open and transparent". The Scottish Minister for Justice, Jim Wallace MSP stated: "The judiciary serve the whole community. They must be people who understand and are in touch with that community. And just as importantly – they must be *seen* to understand that community. **That is why I now want to introduce a lay contribution to the appointment process for the first time.**"

ality. Thus in *Hoekstra (No. 2)*[34] the criminal appeal court, chaired by Lord Justice General Rodger, held that certain extra-judicial comments made in a series of newspaper columns by another serving judge, Lord McCluskey in which he expressed strong misgivings as to the wisdom of the policy decision to make the ECHR directly effective and allow judges "**in effect [to] overrule the elected [Scottish] Parliament**" and where he suggested that the incorporation of the ECHR was "**a revolutionary instrument for change, a Trojan Horse**" which would provide "**a field day for crackpots, a pain in the neck for judges and legislators, and a goldmine for lawyers**" were such as to cast doubt on the appearance of impartiality both of the individual judge and of any court in which he was sitting, when called upon to decide on Convention arguments.

Subsequently, in *Hoekstra (No.3)*[35] the same appellants sought to impugn this decision of the High Court in *Hoekstra (No. 2)*, albeit that it was apparently in their favour, and have a reference made to the Judicial Committee of the Privy Council. Their argument was that the effect of the decision of the court in *Hoekstra (No.2)* to order that the interlocutor of the court in *Hoesktra (No.1)*[36] be set aside on the grounds that it had been pronounced by a court which was not properly constituted by three impartial judges itself constituted an *ultra vires* act because it contravened section 124(2) of the Criminal (Procedure (Scotland) Act. This argument was rejected by the High Court (constituted by Lord Justice General Rodger, Lord Philip and Lord Carloway) as resting on "a gross distortion of the reasoning of the court" in *Hoekstra (No.2)*. Leave to appeal to the Privy Council was refused and the Privy Council itself subsequently refused the accuseds' applications for special leave to appeal to it.[37]

Since section 6 of the Human Rights Act 1998 imposes a general duty on judges, as public authorities, to act compatibly with Convention rights, it is, on one view, difficult to see what judicial function the judge censured in *Hoekstra (No.2)* could carry out after the coming into force of the Act without compromising the appearance of impartiality. No reference was made, however, in the decision in *Hoekstra (No.2)* to the judge's own rights to free expression protected under Article 10.

In *Wille v. Liechtenstein* the European Court of Human Rights affirmed that sitting judges have rights to free expression under Article 10 to allow them to comment on constitutional matters,

---

[34] *Hoekstra v. H.M.Advocate (No. 2)*, 2000 S.L.T. 605, HCJ, the criminal appeal court consisting in Lord Rodger of Earlsferry, Lord Sutherland and Lady Cosgrove

[35] *Hoekstra v. H.M.Advocate (No.3)*, HCJ, 2000 S.C.C.R. 676

[36] *Hoekstra v. H.M.Advocate (No.1)*, 2000 S.L.T. 602, HCJ, the criminal appeal court consisting of Lord McCluskey, Lord Kirkwood and Lord Hamilton.

[37] *Hoekstra v. H.M.Advocate (No.4)*, [2000] 3 W.L.R. 1817; 2001 S.L.T. 28.

noting at paragraphs 65–66 as follows:

> "In the applicant's view this statement [that the Prince of   1.49
> Liechtenstein was subject to the constitutional review and
> fundamental rights jurisdiction of the Liechtenstein courts] was
> an academic comment on the interpretation of Article 112 of
> the Constitution. The [Liechtenstein] Government, on the
> other hand, maintained that although it was being made in the
> guise of a legally aseptic statement, it constituted, in essence, a
> highly political statement involving an attack on the existing
> constitutional order and not reconcilable with the public office
> [of President of the Liechtenstein Administrative Court] held
> by the applicant at the time.
>
> The Court accepts that the applicant's lecture, since it dealt
> with matters of constitutional law and more specifically with
> the issue of whether one of the sovereigns of the State was
> subject to the jurisdiction of a constitutional court, inevitably
> had political implications. It holds that **questions of constitu-
> tional law, by their very nature, have political implications. It
> cannot find, however, that this element alone should have
> prevented the applicant from making any statement on this
> matter.**"[38]

Questions as to the appearance of impartiality of judges hearing
particular cases are being increasingly raised before the courts in the
light of the second *Pinochet* decision of the House of Lords[39] which
overturned their Lordships first decision (on the question of the
lawfulness of the Spanish authorities' application for extradition of
the former Chilean Head of State to face charges on Spanish
territory) in the light of the disclosure of Lord Hoffman's links with
Amnesty International, one of the parties who had been permitted
by the Appellate Committee of the House of Lords as then
constituted (of which he was a member) to intervene in their
Lordships first consideration of the matter. The courts are now
being required to make explicit specific rules when the courts are
faced with claims of apparent judicial partiality.[40] The decision in
Wille v. Liechtenstein, makes it clear that in the formulation of these
rules the judges' own free expression rights under Article 10 will
also require to be taken into account.

---

[38] *Wille v. Liechtenstein,* unreported decision of October 28, 1999 of the European
Court of Human Rights, accessible at www.dhcour.coe.fr/hudoc

[39] *R v. Bow Street Metropolitan Stipendiary Magistrates ex p. Pinochet* [1999] 1 All
E.R. 577, HL

[40] See, for example, *Locabail (U.K.) Ltd v. Bayfield Properties Ltd* [2000] 1 All E.R.
65 in which the Court of Appeal had said that if, before a hearing had begun, the
judge was alerted to some matter which might, depending on the full facts, throw
doubts on his fitness to sit, he should enquire into the full facts, so far as they were
ascertainable, 'in order to make disclosure in the light of them'.

PROCEDURAL EXCLUSIVITY AND THE DEVOLUTION STATUTES

1.50   The Human Rights Act and the three Devolution Statutes of 1998, namely the Scotland Act, the Government of Wales Act and the Northern Ireland Act, were all separately drafted by different government departments. The result of this has been that on certain issues the question as to how the these various constitutional measures inter-relate is sometimes quite obscure. In particular it is not entirely clear under which statute or rules of procedure a court should be acting in considering a claim that an act or omission of a devolved executive or legislature contravenes a Convention right. There are particular rules to be followed in raising and pursuing Convention rights issues under the Scotland Act.[41] But on the face of it, section 7(1)(b) of the Human Rights Act 1998 allows a person who claims that a public authority (defined in section 6(3)(b) as "any person certain of whose functions is of a public nature") has acted or proposes to act in a way which is incompatible with a Convention right to "rely on the Convention right or rights concerned in **any** legal proceedings" before any court in the United Kingdom and section 7(9) envisages rules of court to cover this procedure.[42]

Since both the Acts of the Scottish Parliament and Northern Ireland Assembly and any secondary legislation issued by members of the Scottish Executive, Northern Ireland Minister or Northern Ireland Department or Welsh Assembly are defined as "subordinate legislation" for the purposes of the Human Rights Act 1998, it would seem to follow that any provision of such devolved legislation which appears to any court before which the matter is raised to contravene a Convention right may be treated as invalid and unenforceable under and in terms of section 3 of the Human Rights Act. And if a provision of devolved legislation is challenged under the Human Rights Act the courts will not make a declaration of incompatibility under section 4 since there is nothing in the Devolution Statutes, the primary Westminster legislation, which prevents the removal by the court of incompatible provisions of the devolved legislation.

In contrast to the position under the Devolution Statutes, however:

---

[41] See the following: the Act of Sederunt (Devolution Issue Rules) 1999, (S.I.1999 No.1345) (now forming Chapter 25A of the Rules of Court) in relation to civil proceedings before the Court of Session; the Act of Adjournal (Devolution Issue Rules) 1999, (S.I.1999 No.1346) in relation to criminal proceedings before the High Court of Justiciary; the Act of Sederunt (Proceedings for Determination of Devolution Issue Rules) 1999, (S.I.1999 No.1347) in relation to proceedings before the sheriff court; and the Judicial Committee (Devolution Issues) Rules Order 1999 (S.I.1999 No.665) in relation to procedure before the Privy Council

[42] See, now the Human Rights Act 1998 (Jurisdiction) (Scotland) Rules 2000 (S.I.2000 No.301)

- there is a general one year time limit from the date of the act or   1.51
  omission complained of within which court proceedings alleging
  breach of Convention rights must be brought;
- there is no provision under the Human Rights Act for filtering
  out frivolous or vexatious arguments;
- there is no provision in the Human Rights Act for any variation
  by the court of the retrospective effect of the court's decision on
  incompatibility;
- there is no possibility for a fast track reference on the issue
  raised to higher courts;
- final appeal against any decision on compatibility of devolved
  legislation with the Human Rights Act 1998 would lie either
  with the House of Lords or, if the question were raised in
  Scotland in the course of criminal proceedings, with the High
  Court of Justiciary acting as a criminal appeals court.

If, however, the incompatibility of the devolved legislation with the
Convention right as raised in the course of legal proceedings is
characterised by the courts as a "devolution issue", then:

- the question of the time within which an action raising a
  devolution issue is left unspecified in the Scotland Act,
  presumably allowing the mater to be regulated simply by the
  existing principles of *mora*, taciturnity and acquiescence as
  applied in judicial review in Scotland.[43] In this regard it has been
  judicially observed on a number of occasions in the Outer House
  that there is no Scottish authority in which a petition for Judicial
  Review has been refused on the ground of delay alone, in the
  absence of acquiescence or prejudice.[44]
- the matter has to be intimated to the relevant law officer(s) for
  the jurisdiction of the United Kingdom in which the proceedings
  in question take place;
- the courts are enjoined to consider whether and to what extent
  any decision on incompatibility should be made retrospective;
- the court may also suspend its judgment to allow the identified
  defect to be corrected; and
- the final decision on the question of the compatibility of

---

[43] See, for example, *King v. East Ayrshire Council,* 1998 S.C. 182, IH *per* Lord
President at 196C-D: "It is recognised that the public interest in good
administration requires that public authorities and third parties should not be
kept in suspense as to the legal validity of a decision for any longer than is
necessary in fairness to the person affected by it". See, too, *Swan v. Secretary of
State for Scotland* 1998 SC 479, IH.

[44] See, for example: *Singh v. Secretary of State for Scotland,* 2000 S.L.T. 533, OH *per*
Lord Nimmo Smith at 536, para. (8); *Uprichard v. Fife Council,* OH unreported
decision March 31, 2000 *per* Lord Bonomy at para.(16), accessible at
www.scotcourts.gov.uk; *Dumfries and Galloway Council v. The Scottish Ministers,*
OH unreported decision August 2, 2000 *per* Lord Mackay of Drumadoon at
para.(35), accessible at www.scotcourts.gov.uk; and *Bett Properties v. The
Scottish Ministers,* OH unreported decision September 6, 2000 *per* Lord
MacFadyen at para.(10), accessible at www.scotcourts.gov.uk

devolved legislation with the Convention rights, when this matter is raised as a "devolution issue" would lie with the Judicial Committee of the Privy Council.

1.52   It seems inherently unlikely that the Westminster Parliament would have intended that the complex systems of check, references and balances that has been put in place in relation to the resolution by the courts of "devolution issues" could simply be over-ridden in the case where it is alleged in the course of any legal proceedings that a provision of devolved legislation is incompatible with the rights incorporated by the Human Rights Act, but that is what appears, on one view, to have been done by omission.

It has been argued by some commentators that since the Scotland Act and the Northern Ireland Act both post-dates the Human Rights Act by some 10 days (the first two statutes having received Royal Assent on November 19, the last on November 9, 1998), then the provisions of these acts should be taken as impliedly repealing those of the Human Rights Act, insofar as there is any conflict between them: thus, anything which falls within the scope of the term "devolution issue" must be dealt with under the relevant Schedules of the Scotland Act. Such a line of argument, based on the traditional English constitutional claim that the Westminster Parliament cannot bind itself or its successors, seems to under-play the fundamental constitutional change wrought by the Human Rights Act and its domestication of the Convention rights. It also fails to take into account the fact that the third devolution statutes, the Government of Wales Act was passed on July 31, 1998. It also may be thought to require a somewhat mechanistic view of the hierarchy to be accorded Westminster statutes, with the later always displacing the earlier in a manner which is difficult to reconcile with the general acceptance of the claims of Community law, as mediated through the European Communities Act 1972, to over-rule and require the disapplication of provisions of Westminster statutes (for example the Merchant Shipping Act 1988) passed subsequent to the entry of the United Kingdom into the European Union.[45]

In any event, if the scheme of Schedule 6 to the Scotland Act, Schedule 8 of the Government of Wales Act and Schedule 10 of the Northern Ireland Act are to be preserved in the case of challenges based on incompatibility with Convention rights, either the Westminster Parliament or the courts will have to stipulate that for the purposes of section 7(1)(b) of the Human Rights Act, the *only* reliance that can in law be placed on Convention rights in relation to provisions of devolved legislation is in the context of the matter raising a "devolution issue" for the purposes of the Devolution Statutes. No direct challenge could be made to any

---

[45]   See Case C-213/89 *R v. Secretary of State for Transport, ex p. Factortame Ltd (No.2)* [1991] A.C. 603, HL [1990] E.C.R 2433, ECJ.

such ruling as not providing an effective remedy for the protection of Convention since this provision of the Convention, Article 13,[46] has not been incorporated into the Human Rights Act 1998. One paradoxical result of any such approach would be that secondary legislation passed by members of the devolved Executives would receive more procedural protection from being set-aside by the courts than would subordinate Westminster legislation made by Ministers of the Crown.

The underlying logic and tenor of the approach of, in particular,   1.53 Lord Hope, in the three Privy Council cases decided in the course of the year 2000, all of which emphasise the role of the Judicial Committee of the Privy Council in maintaining a uniformity of approach across the United Kingdom to, in particular, matters of Convention rights in criminal trials, would seems to point to such a ruling in favour of procedural exclusivity, that is to say if a question concerning compatibility of (in)action with a Convention right can be analysed as a raising devolution issue then it must be raised by way of the devolution procedure set out in the relevant statute, rather than by means of direct reliance on the Human Rights Act's procedures. If such an approach to procedural exclusivity is not taken by the Judicial Committee of the Privy Council then the possibility arises of Scotland and England developing separate human rights jurisprudence since, unless a devolution issue is properly raised under and in terms of the Scotland Act, there is no appeal from the decisions of the High Court of Justiciary acting as a court of criminal appeal and decisions of this court while binding in Scots criminal law are, at best, only of persuasive authority in the rest of the United Kingdom.

Finally, if the Convention rights are acknowledged to have a fundamental constitutional status, then, of course, provisions of the Scotland Act may themselves be subject to human rights challenge under the Human Rights Act. For example, the question must arise as to whether the Judicial Committee of the Privy Council, whose members *qua* Privy Councillors are appointed solely at the pleasure of the Crown without formal grant or letters patents and who may be removed or dismissed from the Privy Council at the pleasure of the monarch (albeit on advice from the Prime Minister) simply by striking their names from the Privy Council book, themselves satisfy the Article 6(1) requirements as understood by the European Court of Human Rights of the appearance of an independent and impartial tribunal established by law, see, among others, the decisions of the European Court of Human Rights in *McGonnell v.*

---

[46] Art. 13 of the European Convention is in the following terms: "Everyone whose rights and freedoms as set forth in this Convention are violated shall have an effective remedy before a national authority notwithstanding that the violation has been committed by a person acting in an official capacity."

United Kingdom[47] and *Wille v. Liechtenstein*.[48] The answer may of course be simply that since all the members of the Judicial Committee are tenured judges then no questions as to their independence and impartiality may arise, but it remains at least a theoretical possibility that these appeal provisions of Schedule 6 to the Scotland Act could be declared to be incompatible with the Convention under reference to Section 4 of the Human Rights Act.

CONCLUSION

1.54   Lord Justice Sedley has asserted that:

> "[W]e have today...a new and still emerging constitutional paradigm, no longer Dicey's supreme Parliament...but a bi-polar sovereignty of the Crown in Parliament and the Crown in the courts, to each of which the Crown Ministers are answerable—politically to Parliament and legally to the courts."[49]

And Lord Justice Laws has also observed that "the doctrine of Parliamentary sovereignty cannot be vouched by Parliamentary legislation; a higher law confers it and must of necessity **limit it**"[50] and has claimed that:

> "There remains the possibility that the sovereign Parliament may pass a law which unquestionably denies a fundamental freedom and authorises a public body to give effect to that denial....[I]f the courts develop with sufficient energy a jurisprudence which sets firmly in place a set of norms which chime with those of the European Convention, and elaborate principles of statutory construction which will precisely facilitate that task, **the sovereignty of Parliament will rest in its proper place**, which is to scrutinise and, as it sees fit, to vouchsafe the policies of the government which the people

---

[47] *McGonnell v. U.K.*, unreported decision February 8, 2000 of the European Court of Human Rights, accessible at www.dhcour.coe.fr/hudoc

[48] *Wille v. Liechtenstein*, unreported decision of October 28, 1999 of the European Court of Human Rights, accessible at www.dhcour.coe.fr/hudoc

[49] Sir Stephen Sedley "Human Rights: a twenty-first century agenda" [1995] P.L. 386 at 389.   See, too, the judgment of Sedley J. in *R v. Parliamentary Commissioner for Standards, ex p. Al-Fayed* [1998] 1 W.L.R. 669 at 670 where he describes the relationship between the courts and Parliament as "a mutuality of respect between two constitutional sovereignties". For criticism of Sedley L.J.'s views see Griffith "The Common Law and the Political Constitution" (2001) 117 L.Q.R. 42–67.

[50] Sir John Laws "Law and Democracy" [1995] P.L. 72 at 87. For criticism of Laws L.J.'s views see Griffith "The Brave New World of Sir John Laws" (2000) 63 M.L.R. 159.

have elected **without infringing their inalienable rights.**"[51]

The introduction of a new fundamental rights jurisdiction for the   1.55
courts which has been effected by the Human Rights Act and the
Scotland Act clearly will have a profound effect on our understanding of the constitutional structure of the United Kingdom
and, in particular, of the proper role of judges within this new
dispensation. The United Kingdom is finally falling into line with
many other Western democracies in finally giving the judges a clear
constitutional role in reviewing legislation and appointing them as
guardians of fundamental values even against the legislature, as well
as against the executive. Arguably part of that constitutional role
involves the judges openly articulating their constitutional vision
and giving due recognition to the democratic legitimacy of the
legislature and executive. Others may differ on this point and seek
to maintain the distance of the judges from the general political
process.

Some support for this position can be seen in some recent
Scottish court decisions on human rights matters. In the course of
his judgment in *A v. The Scottish Ministers*[52] (the challenge to the
compatibility of the provisions of the first Act of the Holyrood
Parliament, the Mental Health (Public Safety and Appeals)
(Scotland) Act 1999 with the requirements of Article 5 regarding
the conditions for lawful detention) Lord President Rodger quoted
with approval the remarks of Lord Hope in *R v. DPP ex parte
Kebeline*[53] to the effect that

> "difficult choices may have to be made by the executive or the
> legislature between the rights of the individual and the needs of
> society. In some circumstances it will be appropriate for the
> courts to recognise that there is **an area of judgment within
> which the judiciary will defer, on democratic grounds, to the
> considered opinion of the elected body or person whose act or
> decision is said to be incompatible with the Convention.**"

Significantly, the Lord President made specific reference (at   1.56
paragraphs 31 and 52) to speeches made in the Holyrood
Parliament not only by the proposer of the Bill, but also by other
MSPs including spokespersons from all four of the main parties
represented there, to illustrate the concerns of the legislators in
passing the Act and their awareness of the need to consider, too, the
Convention rights of individuals affected by the legislation. And at

---

[51] "Judicial Remedies and the Constitution" [1994] M.L.R. 213 at 227. See *R v. Lord
Chancellor, ex p. Witham* [1998] Q.B. 575, QBD for an apparent application of
these principles by Laws J. sitting in a judicial capacity in finding that access to
justice is a fundamental constitutional right protected at common law, a position
subsequently approved of by the Court of Appeal in *R v. Lord Chancellor, ex p.
Lightfoot* [1999] 4 All E.R. 583, CA

[52] See *A. v. The Scottish Ministers*, 2000 S.L.T. 873, IH

[53] *R v. DPP ex p. Kebeline* [1999] 3 W.L.R. 972 at 994A (emphasis added)

paragraph 53 he identified the central question for the court as follows:

> "What we must therefore decide is whether, even though the members were conscious of the need to have regard to the human rights of the patients, the Parliament none the less failed to maintain the necessary fair balance by giving too much weight to the perceived danger to members of the public and, thereby, giving too little weight to the requirements of the protection of the patients' right to freedom and in particular their rights under Article 5(1)(e) and (4). In determining that issue, as the authorities show, **it is right that the court should give** due deference to the assessment which the democratically elected legislature has made of the policy issues involved."

There is no doubt that the Scotland Act and the Human Rights Act will have a profound effect on the culture and practice of Scots law. Despite the much vaunted European and Civilian roots to Scots law, Scots lawyers have tendencies toward the insular, the conservative and the antiquarian, harking back to the glories of a system whose authoritative golden age is placed in the seventeenth and eighteenth centuries. The Human Rights Act and the Scotland Act will, it is hoped, shake us out of that elegiac complacency. By reason of the interaction of these two Acts Scottish courts and tribunals have been placed at the vanguard of the development of human rights protection in these islands. It is a challenging and potentially perilous position for them. One challenge is to maintain public confidence in their impartiality. The peril is always that in their emphasis on the rule of law they may be dragged them into the political arena, with their decisions being presented not as the upholding of individual rights but as the thwarting of the democratic will embodied in the acts of the new legislature and executive. Lord Hope has put things more positively, identifying the main challenge to the judiciary in the new dispensation as follows:

> "[T]o maintain the devolution process, so that in the hands of the judges it will be a living instrument capable of adjusting to the demands of changing circumstances as the Parliament develops its expertise and authority in a creative process which will promote the interests of democracy."[54]

However one sees it, it is clear that all involved in the processes of legislation and adjudication in the new Scotland, whether as Members of the Scottish Parliament or Scottish Ministers, judges or lawyers, prosecutors or defenders, litigants or journalists, will have to be alive to the requirements of human rights and work together to develop a culture imbued with their principles.

---

[54] Lord Hope of Craighead, "Judicial Review and Acts of the Scottish Parliament", 1999 *SCOLAG* Journal 107 at 113.

CHAPTER 2

THE SUBSTANTIVE CRIMINAL LAW

INTRODUCTION

This chapter explores the impact of the Convention on the 2.01
substantive criminal law and highlights areas of difficulty and
possible challenge to the present law. It is divided into two parts.
The first deals with the general question of the interaction between
the Convention and the substantive criminal law. The second deals
with general principles of the criminal law, and principles of
criminal responsibility. It also discusses a small number of offences
in order to illustrate how the Convention rights may be relevant as
a defence to a criminal charge.

PART I

1. The impact of the Convention rights on the substantive law

The impact of the European Convention on Human Rights[1] on 2.02
the substantive criminal law of Scotland prior to the implementation of the Scotland Act was slight. None of the cases before the
European Court of Human Rights which originated in Scotland
directly concerned the substantive criminal law.[2] Nor have
decisions originating from other jurisdictions (including other parts
of the United Kingdom) required changes to be made in the
substantive criminal law. The vast majority of cases before the
Strasbourg institutions which have emanated from Scotland have
concerned issues of criminal procedure, or other aspects of the

---

[1] Hereafter, unless otherwise indicated, "the Convention".
[2] The decision of the Court in *Campbell and Cosans v. U.K.* Series A, No. 48, (1983)
13 E.H.R.R. 293, had an indirect effect on the criminal law although it did not
directly address a criminal law issue. The decision led to the abolition of corporal
punishment in state schools. The decision did not affect the common law rule that
a teacher could rely on the defence of reasonable chastisement when inflicting
corporal punishment on a child, nor did the legislation which forbade the use of
such punishment. (See s.48A of the Education (Scotland) Act 1980, as inserted by
s.48 of the Education (No. 2) Act 1986.) However, the abolition of corporal
punishment in state schools greatly reduced the number of occasions on which a
teacher who had used force against a child could legitimately rely upon the
defence.

criminal justice system, such as prisoners' rights.[3]

The experience of the Scottish courts since the implementation of the Scotland Act is very similar. None of the reported decisions on the Convention rights[4] has concerned matters of the substantive law. And while it is too early yet to judge, there is a view that the Human Rights Act will, (and, apparently, should) have an equally limited impact upon the substantive criminal law.[5]

It is certainly the case that the Convention makes few direct references to the criminal law. But the criminal law is one of the principal means by which states restrict individual liberty, and it is not difficult to identify areas of the substantive law which give rise to questions of compatibility with Convention rights. Where, for example, a rule of the criminal law imposes limitations on freedom of expression or freedom of assembly and association, such limitations are now open to challenge on human rights grounds, and must be justified in terms of the Convention. Offences which infringe the privacy of individuals must likewise be justified.

The criminal law, moreover, is an area in which the applicability of Convention rights is more easily demonstrated. Issues of "vertical" and "horizontal" effect of the Convention rights are less troublesome, since for the most part the criminal law concerns the enforcement of sanctions by an obvious public authority against the individual. There are exceptions. The applicability of the provisions

---

[3] For a summary of the case law, see Lord Reed, "Scotland" in *Human Rights Law and Practice*, (Lester and Pannick ed., Butterworths, 1999), pp. 267 *et seq.*

[4] As defined by s.1 and Sched. 1 to the Human Rights Act 1998, and s.126(1) of the Scotland Act 1998.

[5] Buxton, L. J., "The Human Rights Act and the Substantive Criminal Law" [2000] Crim.L.R. 331–340. For contrary views, see Ashworth, "The Human Rights Act and the Substantive Criminal Law: A Non-Minimalist View" [2000] Crim.L.R. 564–567; Ashworth, "The European Convention and the Criminal Law", in *The Human Rights Act and the Criminal Justice and Regulatory Process* (Hart Publishing for the Cambridge Centre for Public Law 1999), at pp. 39–42. The "minimalist" approach, it must be said, is somewhat surprising, given the actual and potential significance of some of the Strasbourg institutions' decisions in the field of substantive criminal law. See, for examples, *Dudgeon v. U.K.* Series A, No. 45 (1981) 4 E.H.R.R. 149, (and see also *ADT v. U.K.* July 31, 2000), *Sutherland v. U.K.* Appl. No. 25186/94, May 21, 1996 (Commission), privacy and sexual relations between men; *McCann v. U.K.* Series A, No. 324 (1996) 21 E.H.R.R. 97, legality of taking human life under article 2; *A v. U.K.* 1998 RJD-VI, 000 (1998) 5 B.H.R.C. 137, "reasonable chastisement" as a defence to a criminal assault; *T v. U.K., V v. U.K.* December 16, 1999, age of criminal responsibility; *Handyside v. U.K.* Series A, No. 24 (1976) 1 E.H.R.R. 737, *Müller v. Switzerland* (1988) 13 E.H.R.R. 212, obscene publications; *SW and CR v. U.K., CR v. U.K.* Series A, No. 335-C and Series A, No. 335-B (1995) 21 E.H.R.R. 363, retrospective use of the criminal law; *Ahmed Sadik v. Greece* (1995) 24 E.H.R.R. 323, *Otto Preminger Institut v. Austria* (1994) 19 E.H.R.R. 34, *Wingrove v. U.K.* (1996) 24 E.H.R.R. 1; *Worm v. Austria* (1997) 25 E.H.R.R. 454, Appl. No. 24770/94; *Associated Newspapers Ltd v. U.K.* November 30, 1994 (Commission), freedom of expression; *Christians against Racism and Fascism v. U.K.* Appl. No. 8440/78, 21 D.R. 148 (Commission); *Steel v. U.K.* (1999) 28 E.H.R.R. 603, freedom of expression and freedom of assembly.

of Article 2(2) to self-defence where the accused is not a member of a public authority is unclear.[6] The issue also arises where it is alleged that the criminal law does not adequately protect one individual from interference with her Convention rights by another individual.[7] But for the most part the question of whether the enforcement of a rule of the criminal law involves the act or omission of a public authority is not problematic.

2. Future use of Convention rights in criminal cases

Leaving aside procedural questions, the Convention rights provide an accused with a "defence" to a criminal charge wherever the basis of the charge is conduct in which, in terms of the Convention rights, the accused has the right to engage.[8] So, for example, an accused who is arrested and prosecuted for breach of the peace while exercising freedom of expression in a peaceful demonstration may claim that his or her prosecution, or conviction, for that offence is unlawful.[9] The Strasbourg court has considerable experience of dealing with challenges to domestic prosecutions on the ground that these constitute an interference with the exercise of a Convention right. In such matters, however, they have shown considerable unwillingness to interfere with the "margin of appreciation" enjoyed by parties to the Convention. The Strasbourg institutions have likewise shown little inclination to engage with cases which have touched upon basic questions of criminal responsibility,[10] preferring to leave such matters to be determined by domestic legal rules. In this respect the international court stands in marked contrast to its domestic equivalents such as the Canadian Supreme Court which has not flinched from applying constitutional provisions in developing the substantive criminal code.[11]

An important question which will have to be faced, sooner rather than later, is how the courts should respond when faced with a rule of the common law which is incompatible with a Convention right. It has been argued that when faced with a conflict between the common law and the Convention rights, the Human Rights Act gives no power to a criminal court to refuse to apply a rule of the common law, since no such power is afforded in relation to a

2.03

---

[6] See below, p. 000.
[7] See, for example, *X and Y v. Netherlands* (1986) 8 E.H.R.R. 235; *A v. U.K.* (1999) 27 E.H.R.R. 611.
[8] *Engel v. Netherlands* (1976) 1 E.H.R.R. 647 at para. 81 and *Salabiaku v. France* (1991) 13 E.H.R.R. 379, at para. 27.
[9] *Steel v. U.K.* (1999) 28 E.H.R.R. 603.
[10] See, for example, *H v. U.K.* Appl. No. 15023/89, Commission Decision, April 4, 1990, defence of insanity and *Kingston v. U.K.* Appl. No. 27837/95, Commission Decision, April 9, 1997, exclusion of defence of involuntary intoxication in English law.
[11] See, for example, *R v. Daviault,* 1994 3 S.C.R. 63.

statutory rule.[12] This, it is submitted, is wrong as a matter of interpretation of the Human Rights Act. It is also an argument which is especially weak in the Scottish context, since it assumes that all statutory rules have the same "status" when the issue of incompatibility with Convention rights arises—an assumption which plainly fails to recognise the limitations placed on the legislative capacity of the Scottish Parliament.[13]

A more robust approach can be found in the judgment of the South African Constitutional Court in *National Coalition for Gay and Lesbian Equality v. Minister of Justice*.[14] In that case the Constitutional Court declared that various offences, including the common law offence of sodomy to be inconsistent with the Constitutional protection of equality and the right to dignity. It was accepted by the State that the common law offence could no longer be applied to consensual sexual acts, but it was argued that the offence should be retained in order to ensure that non-consensual sodomy could still be criminalised. This argument too was rejected by the Court which pointed out that to retain the offence even under this guise would be to perpetuate an offence which, if not originating in discrimination against homosexuals certainly contributed to that discrimination. If the state considered it necessary to have an offence to deal with non-consensual homosexual acts, the appropriate way to achieve this was through legislation tailored to meet that end.

3. Issues of horizontal effect

2.04   As suggested above, consideration of the possible "horizontal" effect of the Convention rights presents fewer problems than in other contexts, simply because the criminal law is enforced by the state. Where the enforcement of the criminal law infringes a Convention right there will rarely be any question about whether the infringement results from the act of a public authority.

In certain cases, however, the issue of horizontality can arise where the victim of an offence claims that the rules of the criminal law do not provide sufficient protection from harm caused by other individuals. Two examples are worth considering here.

In *A v. United Kingdom*[15] the applicant was severely beaten by his stepfather. The latter was prosecuted on a charge of assault occasioning actual bodily harm, contrary to section 47 of the Offences Against the Person Act 1861. The jury accepted a defence of "reasonable chastisement" and acquitted the accused. The applicant complained, *inter alia*, of a violation of Article 3 of the

---

[12]   Buxton, L. J., "The Human Rights Act and the Substantive Criminal Law" [2000] Crim.L.R. 331 at p.335.
[13]   Scotland Act, s.29.
[14]   Constitutional Court, Case CCT 11/98, October 9, 1998.
[15]   (1998) 2 F.L.R. 959.

Convention in that he had been subjected to inhumane and degrading treatment. The Court held that the punishment reached the degree of severity required for a violation of Article 3, and further held that the United Kingdom had a positive obligation, under Article 1 of the Convention, to ensure that the criminal law afforded effective protection from treatment which violated Article 3.

In *X and Y v. Netherlands*[16] the second applicant, a young woman with learning difficulties, was subjected to sexual abuse. Under Dutch law, the offence committed against her could only be prosecuted if the victim made a personal complaint. However, she could not do so since, because of her disability, the authorities would not accept a complaint lodged by her personally. Nor would they accept a complaint lodged on her behalf. The Court held that the second applicant's right to private life under Article 8 had been infringed. That article imposed upon the state the positive duty to protect private life, which duty extended to protecting one individual from a violation of her rights by another.

Although the legal obstacles to effective protection differed in these two cases—in *A*'s case the breach arose from the application of a rule of substantive law, whereas in *X and Y* the problem arose from a combination of substantive rules and procedural flaws— both cases held that in certain circumstances the state has an obligation to ensure that the criminal law provides effective protection for victims of acts which violate their Convention rights.

It is therefore possible to argue that the failure of effective criminal law sanctions can amount to a violation of Convention rights. Such failure may arise because the conduct in question is placed outside the reach of the criminal law altogether, as in the case of the former "marital rape exemption" enjoyed by husbands, or because of over-broad defences which allow conduct which is incompatible with Convention rights to go unpunished, as in the case of *A v. United Kingdom.*

The question of horizontal effect, and the compatibility of a defence with Convention rights, both arise in relation to Article 2(2) of the Convention. Article 2 provides that everyone's right to life shall be protected by law. It further provides that, subject to certain exceptions, no one shall be deprived of his life intentionally. Article 2(2) provides that deprivation of life shall not be regarded as inflicted in contravention of this Article when it results from the use of force "which is no more than absolutely necessary: (a) in defence of any person from unlawful violence; (b) in order to effect a lawful arrest or to prevent the escape of a person lawfully detained; and (c) in actions lawfully taken for the purpose of quelling a riot or insurrection."?

Two questions arise in connection with Article 2(2). The first of these is the extent to which Article 2(2) applies "horizontally", the

2.05

---

[16] (1986) 8 E.H.R.R. 235.

second is the relationship between the phrase "use of force which is not more than absolutely necessary" and the current Scots law test for the application of a plea of private defence or lawful authority.

As to the first question, it is clear that Article 2(2) has potential application where a public authority is accused of a violation of Article 2(1). Typically, this has arisen in the case of deaths at the hands of the military,[17] and, less frequently, the police or other public authorities. What is rather less clear is whether this provision has any application where a private individual seeks to rely on a plea of private defence, or lawful authority when charged with a criminal homicide. This question is best answered along with the second issue, namely the compatibility of our domestic legal rules with Article 2(2).

A person who kills in self-defence is entitled to an acquittal if the following conditions are satisfied: there must have been imminent danger to life or limb (of the accused or a third party)[18]; the force used must have been necessary for the safety of the accused or another person[19]; an exact proportion of injury and retaliation is not required, but there must not have been "cruel excess" on the part of the accused[20]; there must have been no reasonable means of retreat.[21] There are differences between the language of Article 2(2) and the accepted formulation of the plea of self-defence. In particular, Article 2(2) refers to the use of force which is "no more than absolutely necessary" whereas the common law test may in its application be closer to a test of "reasonably necessary" and the "cruel excess" approach certainly allows a greater degree of force and retaliation than would be permitted by the "no more than absolutely necessary" test.

If there is a difference, then Article 2(2) would require a *narrowing* of the plea of self-defence. But if this is the case, then it would give rise to the following anomaly, namely that the scope of self-defence would be narrower when invoked by a member of a public authority such as the armed forces or the police than when invoked by a private citizen. This is because the terms of Article 2(2) do not apply to the acts of private individuals, unless, of course, Article 2(2) is read as having "horizontal" effect.

It could, of course, be argued that a higher standard of care and restraint should be expected of the police and the military, who are trained in the use of force.[22] But the development of a different test for the lawful use of force would be a surprising consequence of the domestication of Article 2(2).

---

[17] See, for example, *McCann v. U.K.* (1996) 21 E.H.R.R. 97.

[18] *H.M. Advocate v. Doherty*, 1954 J.C. 169; *Fenning v. H.M. Advocate*, 1985 S.L.T. 540.

[19] *Fenning v. H.M. Advocate*, ibid.

[20] *Fenning v H.M. Advocate*, ibid.

[21] *McBrearty v H.M. Advocate*, 1999 S.L.T. 1333.

[22] Ashworth, *Principles of Criminal Law* (3rd ed., 1999), p. 242.

PART II: GENERAL PRINCIPLES OF CRIMINAL LIABILITY

1. The Principle of Legality

The principle of legality[23] deserves particular consideration, for two reasons. First, it is one of the few principles of the criminal law to be elevated to the status of a fundamental human right,[24] and secondly because of the particular characteristics of Scottish criminal law, namely its "open texture" and flexibility.   2.06

There is at least a superficial attraction to the argument that the Convention, founded as it is on the rule of law, and imbued with principles of legality, is likely to have a significant effect on this aspect of our system of criminal justice.[25] On closer examination, however, the commitment of the Strasbourg institutions to the principle of legality seems much less definite. Indeed, in many instances, those institutions have proved to be quite willing to embrace and endorse arguments in favour of "flexible" and "responsive" criminal laws—arguments which are wearisomely familiar in the context of the criminal law of Scotland.

The Principle of Legality in Principle

Although we talk of "the" principle of legality, that principle appears to embrace four inter-related propositions: (a) the retrospective imposition of criminal liability is unjust; (b) criminal laws should be accessible; (c) criminal laws should be expressed in as precise terms as possible; and (d) criminal laws should not be   2.07

---

[23] The principle of legality has two heads: the rule that criminal responsibility should not be imposed in the absence of a criminal law (*nullum crimen sine lege*) and the rule that criminal sanctions should not be imposed without a lawful foundation (*nulla poena sine lege*). This chapter is concerned with the first dimension of the principle. The second is discussed in Chapter 00 on Sentencing and Prisoners' Rights. It is important to note that the principle applies also in the context of criminal procedure, where it requires reasonable certainty in the scope of such mattes as powers of arrest, search and seizure. In *Coème et autres c la Belgique*, the European Court of Human Rights observed, judgment of June 22, 2000, para. 102: "La Cour rappelle que le principe de la légalité du droit de la procédure pénale est un principe général de droit. Il fait pendant à la légalité du droit pénal et est consacré par l'adage '*nullum judicium sine lege*'." The discussion of the principle in this chapter relates only to the substantive law.

[24] See, in addition to Art. 7 of the Convention, Art. 15(1) of the International Covenant on Civil and Political Rights, Art. 9 of the American Convention on Human Rights, Art. 9 and Art. 7(2) of the African Charter on Human and Peoples' Rights.

[25] A view which the present writer is happy to confess to having at one time espoused. See, for example, Gane and Stoddart, *A Casebook on Scottish Criminal Law* (2nd ed., W. Green & Son Ltd, Edinburgh, 1988), pp. 7 *et seq.* *Cf.* the observation by Sheriff Gordon in his commentary on *Paterson v. Lees*, 1999 S.C.C.R. 231 at 238.

unreasonably or unforeseeably extended.[26] The following section examines how the elements of the principle are reflected in the European Convention.

2.08   (a) The retrospective imposition of criminal liability

(i) Retrospectivity under the Convention: Article 7(1) of the Convention explicitly prohibits the retrospective application of the criminal law in the following terms:

> "No one shall be held guilty of any criminal offence on account of any act or omission which did not constitute a criminal offence under national or international law at the time when it was committed. Nor shall a heavier penalty be imposed than the one that was applicable at the time the criminal offence was committed."

The object and purpose of Article 7 is to "provide effective safeguards against arbitrary prosecution, conviction and punishment."[27] It follows from this basic proposition that "only the law can define a crime and prescribe a penalty".[28] Practices or procedures by which criminal sanctions may be imposed without a foundation in law will therefore violate Article 7.

The prohibition on the retrospective creation of crimes contained in Article 7(1) is absolute, in the sense that there are no exceptions for "ordinary" criminal offences, nor are states permitted to derogate from Article 7 under the procedures provided for in Article 15 of the Convention. Article 7(2), however, provides that 7(1) "shall not prejudice the trial and punishment of any person for any act or omission which, at the time when it was committed, was criminal according to the general principles of law recognised by civilised nations." The generally accepted view is that the purpose of this provision was to allow the application of legislation relating to war crimes enacted during and after the Second World War to be applied to acts committed during the war,[29] a view apparently supported by the Commission.[30] It would also support the retrospective application of such laws to other conflicts.[31] It has,

---

[26] Andrew Ashworth, *Principles of Criminal Law* (3rd ed.,(1999) who identifies three elements—"the principle of non-retroactivity", "the principle of maximum certainty", and "the principle of strict construction of penal statutes".

[27] *S.W. v. U.K.* ECtHR, Series A, No. 335-B, para. 34.

[28] *Kokkinakis v. Greece*, ECtHR, Series A, No. 260-A, para.52.

[29] See Lester and Pannick, *Human Rights Law and Practice*, para. 4.7.6, Stephen Groscz, *et al*, *Human Rights: The 1998 Act and the European Convention*, para. C7-08. This interpretation of the purpose of Article 7(2) is supported by the *travaux préparatoires* of the Convention: see D. J. Harris, *et al*, *Law of the European Convention on Human Rights* (Butterworths, 1995), p. 282.

[30] Appl. No. 1038/61, *X v. Belgium*, 4 Yearbook 324.

[31] Some countries have, for example, adopted legislation which would, *ex post facto*, apply to the conflicts in the former Yugoslavia, and to the genocide carried out in Rwanda.

however, been pointed out that Article 7(2) "does not relate exclusively to war crimes, but to all acts and omissions which are criminal 'according to the general principles of law recognised by civilised nations.'"[32] It would, therefore, extend to the retrospective application of the criminal law to genocide and other crimes against humanity. Whether it can be applied to other crimes depends entirely on the existence of an international consensus that the conduct in question was recognised as criminal at the time of commission.

Within the Convention States criminal laws will typically be embodied in legislative provisions, but the Convention institutions necessarily recognise that "[i]n a common law system, not only written statutes but also rules of the common or other customary law may provide sufficient basis for the criminal convictions envisaged by Article 7".[33] If this were not the case, then individuals in common law states would be deprived of the protection of the principle of legality[34] (or, alternatively, all common law offences would be incompatible with the Convention).

Although Article 7 "occupies a prominent place in the Convention system of protection",[35] the rule against retrospective imposition of criminal liability has not figured significantly in the case law of the Strasbourg institutions.[36] The reason for this is not hard to discern. The majority of states which are party to the Convention operate codified, or otherwise legislatively-based, systems of criminal law, and developed democracies generally refrain from overtly retrospective criminal legislation.

Judicial development of the criminal law in a common law system such as the Scottish one presents a much greater potential for arguments concerning the retrospective imposition of criminal liability, but again, very few claims to that effect have been made under Article 7. Such claims as have been brought under Article 7 have focused not on simple retrospectivity—since true judicial *creation* of a new offence is a very unusual event—but rather on arguments relating to the vagueness of the law, or have argued that the law has been developed in an unforeseeable way.[37]

---

[32] van Dijk and van Hoof, *Theory and Practice of the European Convention on Human Rights* (3rd ed, 1998, Kluwer), p. 487.

[33] *S. W. v. U.K.* Report of the European Commission of Human Rights, para. 46; *C.R. v. U.K.* Report of the Commission, para. 47.

[34] *Sunday Times v. U.K.* ECtHR, Series A, No. 30, para. 47.

[35] *S.W. v. U.K.* (above), para. 34.

[36] This aspect of Art. 7 appears to have been discussed only twice by the Court in *S.W. v. U.K.*, above, and *C.R. v. U.K.*, above, both of which concerned the judicial removal of the "marital rape exemption" in English law. In *Welch v. U.K.* ECtHR, Series A, No. 307-A, the European Court held that the United Kingdom had violated the prohibition contained in the last sentence of Art. 7(1).

[37] See *S.W. and C.R. v. U.K.*, *C.R. v. U.K.* Series A, No. 335-C and Series A, No. 335-B (1995) 21 E.H.R.R. 363, *post*, p.000.

2.09   *(ii) The rule against retrospective criminal law and the "Declaratory Power" of the High Court*: No clearer example of a conflict with this aspect of the principle of legality could be found than the so-called "Declaratory Power" of the High Court of Justiciary. According to Hume, the High Court

> "have an inherent power as such competently to punish (with the exception of life and limb) every act which is obviously of a criminal nature; though it be such which in time past has never been the subject of prosecution."[38]

The existence of such a power was accepted (without debate) by a majority of the court in *Taylor*[39] in 1808, and was expressly relied upon by the Court in the leading case of *Bernard Greenhuff*.[40] In practice, the Court has not, since the decision in *Greenhuff*, explicitly relied upon this power. It is, however, possible to point to cases in which the Court appears to have used this power to extend the criminal law, albeit without expressly invoking it.[41] Given that the United Kingdom has been bound by the Convention since 1953, one might have expected that the declaratory power would have been allowed quietly to fade into legal history. But its continued existence was asserted by the Crown, and accepted by the High Court in 1983 in the case of *Khaliq v. H.M. Advocate*[42] and again in 1986 in *Grant v. Allan*.[43]

There can be no doubt that the use of the declaratory power as envisaged by Hume and applied in *Greenhuff* would be incompatible with Article 7(1), and presumably the Crown will not now seek to invoke that power.

It has been suggested[44] that Article 7(2) might be invoked to justify the exercise of the declaratory power. This envisages criminalising conduct which is not already criminal according to

---

[38] Hume, i, 12.

[39] October 19, 1808, Burnett, *A Treatise on Various Branches of the Criminal Law of Scotland*, 1811, Appendix X. The case concerned an alleged criminal combination by workers in the paper industry to raise wages. A majority of the court held that the indictment did not disclose an offence—even allowing for the possibility of the court declaring such a combination to be criminal.

[40] (1838) 2 Swinton 236.

[41] See, for example, *William Fraser* (1848) Arkley 280, having intercourse with a woman by pretending to be her husband, *Charles Sweenie* (1858) 3 Irvine 109, having intercourse with a sleeping woman, *Strathern v. Seaforth*, 1926 J.C. 100, 1926 S.L.T. 445 "clandestine taking and using" the property of another, *Kerr v. Hill*, 1936 J.C. 71, wasting the time of the police.

[42] 1983 S.C.C.R. 483, 1984 S.C.C.R. 212.

[43] 1987 S.C.C.R. 402.

[44] Styles, "Something to Declare: A Defence of the Declaratory Power of the High Court of Justiciary" in *Justice and Crime: Essays in Honour of the Right Honourable, the Lord Emslie*, (Hunter ed., 1993, T & T Clark, pp. 211–231 at p. 224. See also Harris, *et al*, *Law of the European Convention on Human Rights*, p.282.

the law of Scotland, but which, at the time the accused engaged in that conduct, was "criminal according to the general principles of law recognised by civilised nations". It is unlikely that such an expansive interpretation of Article 7(2) would be accepted. It is certainly not in line with the accepted purpose of the exception to Article 7(1) which it creates.[45] It is difficult to see how it could be invoked to rescue the application of the criminal law in those cases where it has been openly applied—as in *Greehuff*, or more covertly applied, as in *Strathern v. Seaforth* and *Kerr v. Hill*. It would certainly be difficult to argue that running a public gaming house, vehicular joy-riding or making a false report to the police[46] were examples of conduct which was criminal "according to the general principles of law recognised by civilised nations". Similarly, in those cases where the Crown was prepared to invoked the declaratory power—*Khaliq* and *Grant v. Allan*—it would be difficult to establish that supplying glue sniffing kits to children and young persons and the "theft" of information were so generally recognised as criminal. At the very least, any attempt to invoke the declaratory power would put the Crown to the task of demonstrating that the conduct, not hitherto visited by criminal sanctions in Scotland, satisfied this requirement.

(b) Accessibility and precision

(i) Accessibility and precision under the Convention: As we have noted, Article 7 explicitly forbids the retrospective creation of criminal liability. The principle of legality is not, however, confined to the proscription of retrospective criminal laws, nor is it confined to the provisions of Article 7.

2.10

The principle of legality is embodied in several other Articles of the Convention. Where the Convention imposes restrictions on the exercise of rights and freedoms, it does so subject to certain limitations. Amongst these is the condition that any such interference with the rights of the individual must be "in accordance with (the) law"[47] or according to measures which are "prescribed by law".[48]

These provisions are linked to, and influence the interpretation of, Article 7. The connection between these provisions and Article 7 has been explained by the court in the following way: Article 7, which expressly prohibits the retrospective application of the criminal law, also embodies the principle that crimes must be

---

[45] See above, p. 000.
[46] See *Kerr v. Hill*, 1936 J.C. 71.
[47] Art. 8(2), interference with privacy.
[48] Art. 5(1), deprivation of liberty; Art. 9(2), interference with freedom of religion; Art. 10(2), interference with freedom of expression; Art. 11(2), interference with freedom of assembly and association.

clearly defined in the law.[49] When using the term "law" in this context, the Court is alluding to "the very same concept as that to which the Convention refers elsewhere when using that term, a concept which comprises written as well as unwritten law and implies qualitative requirements, notably those of accessibility and foreseeability."[50] Thus the qualitative conditions which the Court has developed when determining whether or not a measure which interferes with a substantive right is "in accordance with the law" or "prescribed by law" have been imported into Article 7.[51]

2.11   **Accessibility:** The requirement of "accessibility" demands that "the citizen must be able to have an indication that is adequate in the circumstances of the legal rules applicable to a given case".[52] In most instances it has not proved difficult for respondent states to demonstrate that an impugned legal provision is "accessible". Where the law takes the form of a legislative provision, or is embodied in a judicial opinion, there is generally little doubt about its accessibility.[53] The Court has also held that "accessibility" may depend upon "the content of the instrument in issue, the field it is designed to cover and the number and status of those to whom it is addressed".[54] So, for example, where national regulations governing telecommunications had not been published in the appropriate official collection of legislation, they were nevertheless "accessible" to those most directly affected by them (who can be expected to inform themselves fully of the relevant rules[55]), since official information had been given as to how they could be consulted or obtained.[56]

Where, however, a rule having the force of law has not been published, or published in a form which does not make it reasonably accessible to those to whom it is directed, it ought not to be regarded as satisfying the "accessibility" test. In *Petra v. Romania*,[57] for example, the domestic law governing the monitoring of prisoners' correspondence was contained in legislation and in implementing regulations. While the legislation had been duly published, the regulations had not, so that the applicant, a prisoner, was unable to acquaint himself with their contents. The Court held

---

[49]   *C.R. v. U.K.* above, para. 33.
[50]   *ibid.*
[51]   *ibid.*, See also, *Kokkinakis v. Greece*, above; *G. v. France*, European Court of Human Rights, Series A, No. 325-B.
[52]   *Sunday Times v. U.K.* above, para. 31, *Malone v. U.K.* ECtHR, Series A, No. 82, para. 66.
[53]   See, for example, *Kopp v. Switzerland*, ECtHR, R.J.D. 1998–II, paras 54 *et seq.*
[54]   *Groppera Radio AG v. Switzerland*, ECtHR, Series A, No. 173, paras 67-68; *Observer and Guardian v. U.K.* ECtHR, Series A, No. 216, para. 52; *Chappell v. U.K.* ECtHR, Series A, No. 152-A, para. 56.
[55]   *Groppera Radio AG v. Switzerland, ibid.*, para. 68.
[56]   *ibid.*, para. 67.
[57]   ECtHR, R.J.D. 1998–VII, paras 37-39.

that the regulations "did not satisfy the requirement of accessibility entailed by Article 8(2) of the Convention."[58]

Precision: The Convention institutions do not use the term "precision", but "foreseeability" which they appear to use as a test of precision. "Foreseeability" requires the law to be

> "formulated with sufficient precision to enable the citizen to regulate his conduct: he must be able—if need be with appropriate advice—to foresee, to a degree that is reasonable in the circumstances, the consequences which a given action may entail."[59]

2.12

As the language of this test suggests, the Strasbourg institutions do not insist upon a high degree of certainty or precision in the criminal law.

The principal reason why it has not been difficult for states to satisfy the requirement of "foreseeability" is because the Strasbourg institutions have demonstrated an extreme reluctance to challenge the interpretation of national laws by national institutions. It has frequently been emphasised that in determining whether the application of a law to a given set of circumstances was foreseeable it is necessary to have regard to guidance given by national institutions such as courts[60] (even in legal systems which do not treat judicial decisions as a formal source of law[61]) and even to academic opinion.[62]

Other factors may also be relevant in determining whether or not the application of a particular law was "foreseeable". The availability to the individual of legal advice is clearly relevant,[63] as is the fact that the accused have received legal advice that their activities may be subject to legal regulation.[64] The experience of the individual in the legal field under consideration may also be relevant.[65] The fact that a legal provision is capable of more than one interpretation does not mean that it fails to meet the

---

[58] RJD 1998-VII, para. 37. *Cf Silver v. U.K.*, European Court of Human Rights, Series A, No. 61, at paras 85 *et seq.*

[59] See, amongst many judgments to this effect, *Sunday Times v. U.K.* above, para 49, *Silver v. U.K.* above, paras 87–88, *Tolstoy Miloslavsky v. U.K.* ECtHR, Series A, No. 316-B, para. 37, *Malone v. U.K.* above, para. 66.

[60] See, for examples, *Chappell v. U.K.* above, at para. 56; *Observer and Guardian v. U.K.* above, at paras 51–53; *Thorgeir Thorgeirson v. Iceland,* ECtHR, Series A, No. 239, at paras 57–58.

[61] *Kruslin v. France,* ECtHR, Series A, No. 176-A, paras 27 *et seq, Huvig v. France,* ECtHR, Series A, No. 176-B, paras 27 *et seq.*

[62] *Kopp v. Switzerland,* above, para. 60.

[63] *Gillow v. U.K.* above, para. 39.

[64] *Open Door and Dublin Well Woman v. Ireland,* ECtHR, Series A, No. 246-A, at para 57.

[65] *Markt Internand Beermann v. Germany,* ECtHR, Series A, No. 165, at para. 29.

requirement of "foreseeability."[66] As with accessibility, the context of the regulations in question may be relevant. In the case of *Vereinigung demokratischer Soldaten Österreichs and Gubi v. Austria*[67] the Court observed:

> "As far as military discipline is concerned, it would scarcely be possible to draw up rules describing different types of conduct in detail. It may therefore be necessary for the authorities to formulate such rules more broadly."

Similarly, albeit in a different context, the Court in *Markt Intern and Beermann v. Germany*[68] noting that "frequently laws are framed in a manner that is not absolutely precise" observed that

> "[t]his is so in spheres such as that of competition, in which the situation is constantly changing in accordance with developments in the marked and in the field of competition". In such areas, the interpretation and application of the law "are frequently questions of practice."

2.13   The effect of this approach has been to establish substantial obstacles to arguments based on the proposition that a given rule is inherently too vague to be regarded as a "law", and offences containing terms of considerable vagueness have been held to satisfy the "foreseeability" test. In *X v. Austria*[69] for example, the applicant was convicted under an Austrian law which prohibited "unnatural indecency" for engaging in mutual masturbation with another man. The Commission confined itself to considering whether or not the case law of the Austrian courts, as applied at the time of the alleged offence, covered the applicant's conduct. Similarly, in *Steel v. United Kingdom*[70] the Court held that the notoriously flexible concept of "breach of the peace" had been sufficiently clarified in English law for their arrests to be "lawful" under Article 5(1) of the Convention.[71] In *Castells v. Spain*[72] the European Court held that the conviction of the applicant for criminal insult of the Government on the basis of a text which "covered in a general fashion several possible types of insult" was not incompatible with the Convention.

Most troublingly of all, the Court appears to accept the

---

[66] *Vogt v. Germany*, ECtHR, Series A, No. 323, para. 48.
[67] ECtHR, Series A, No. 302, para. 31.
[68] *Markt Intern and Beermann, supra* no. 55, at para. 30.
[69] European Commission on Human Rights, Appl. No. 4161/69, 13 Yearbook p. 798 (1970).
[70] ECtHR, R.J.D. 1998–VI, paras 51 *et seq.*
[71] It may be, however, that certain features of binding-over orders are objectionable on the ground of vagueness: *Hashman and Harrup v. U.K.* ECtHR, November 25, 1999, R.J.D. 1999.
[72] ECtHR, Series A, No. 236.

inevitability of imprecision in the criminal law. In *Gillow v. United Kingdom*, which concerned a prosecution for blasphemous libel under English law, the Court stated:

> "The Court recognises that the offence of blasphemy cannot by its very nature lend itself to precise legal definition. National authorities must therefore be afforded a degree of flexibility in assessing whether the facts of a particular case fall within the accepted definition of the offence."[73]

There is, of course, nothing whatsoever about the offence of blasphemy that makes it incapable of precise legal definition. The legislature could pass legislation defining blasphemy in as precise terms as it wished. In doing so it might exclude categories of behaviour which others might wish to have included in the definition. But that does not mean that it is incapable of precise legal definition, but merely that the desire for an offence of blasphemy that will satisfy those whose religious opinions may be offended in a variety of ways, is incompatible with an offence whose definition satisfies reasonable standards of predictability.   2.14

In practice what appears to matter is a degree of certainty of *definition*, rather than certainty with regard to the scope of a given offence. As the Court noted in *Gillow v. United Kingdom*,

> "[t]here appears to be no general uncertainty or disagreement between those appearing before the Court as to the definition in English law of the offence of blasphemy, as formulated by the House of Lords in the case of *Whitehouse v Gay News and Lemon.*"

This is probably true, but this is not, with respect, the critical issue. If the issue is whether or not the "definition" of an offence permits individuals to know, with a reasonable degree of certainty whether or not their conduct is likely to violate the law, then expansively expressed offences are more, rather than less, likely to satisfy the foreseeability test. The more vaguely and broadly expressed the law, the easier it is to predict that a given course of conduct runs a significant risk of violating that law. At least as interpreted by the Court, foreseeability does not limit the potential scope of crimes, but leaves it open to states to establish broadly defined crimes. Their breadth is unimportant, provided they are "defined" in the sense of having a known definition.

Entirely in line with its approach to "foreseeability" is the Court's attitude towards flexibility of the criminal law. In *Kokkinakis v. Greece*[74] the applicant was convicted of "proselytism". The relevant

---

[73] *Gillow v. U.K.*, above, at para. 41.
[74] Above.

Greek legislation[75] defined "proselytism" as meaning

2.15   "in particular, any direct or indirect attempt to intrude on the
          religious beliefs of a person of a different religious persuasion,
          with the aim of undermining those beliefs, either by any kind of
          inducement or promise of an inducement or moral support or
          material assistance, or by fraudulent means or by taking
          advantage of his inexperience, trust, low intellect or naïvety."

The applicant challenged his conviction on the ground, *inter alia*,
that the application of this provision violated Article 7. He claimed
that the offence was too vaguely worded, that it was capable of
criminalising any attempt at religious conversion, and that the use
of such terms as "in particular" and "indirect attempt" gave too
much latitude for extension of the by the police and by the courts.
The Court rejected this argument:

> "The Court has already noted that the wording of many
> statutes is not absolutely precise. The need to avoid excessive
> rigidity and to keep pace with changing circumstances means
> that many laws are inevitably couched in terms which, to a
> greater or lesser extent, are vague."[76]

Flexibility has been accepted as especially important "in fields in
which the situation changes according to the prevailing views of
society."[77] Again, this has meant that the use by states of
notoriously flexible terms, such as "indecency" and "obscenity"
remains unregulated by the Strasbourg institutions. It is the role of
the national courts to resolve doubts about the interpretation of
domestic law,[78] in the exercise of which they are subject to little
effective control by the Strasbourg organs.

(ii) Accessibility and precision in Scots law: We have noted how the
European Convention requires that a rule can only be termed a
"law" if it is both accessible, and expressed with sufficient precision
to permit the individual to know, in advance, with reasonable
certainty, whether or not his or her conduct might be contrary to
the criminal law.

2.16   **Accessibility**: The formal sources of Scots criminal law are
       legislation, case law and the opinions of the "institutional" writers.
       To the extent that the first two sources are published, it could be
       argued that they do not present problems of accessibility. Reliance

[75] Law No. 1363/1938, s.4, as amended by Law No. 1672/1939.
[76] *Kokkinakis v. Greece*, above, para. 40.
[77] *Ezelin v. France*, ECtHR, Series A, No. 202, at para. 45.
[78] *Cantoni v. France*, ECtHR, R.J.D. 1996–V, p. 1682; *Rekvény v. Hungary*, ECtHR,
      R.J.D. 1999, para. 34.

upon unpublished decisions of the court as a source of criminal law would, however, be difficult to reconcile with this aspect of the principle of legality.[79] Where interpretation of a legislative text requires access to other texts, presumably those texts also must be accessible.[80]

Can it be said that the texts of the Institutional writers, upon whom there is substantial and frequent reliance is compatible with the requirements of the Convention? In so far as the Convention institutions appear to recognise, in the context of a "common law" system both case law and "customary" law, it would appear that judicial acceptance of an Institutional writer's views would be sufficient to characterise these as law. But is this "law" sufficiently accessible at the time prior to its identification by the courts as the appropriate rule of application in a given case? It is true that texts such as Hume's *Commentaries* are published, and in that sense they are "accessible". It should, however, be recalled that the require-ment of "accessibility" demands that "the citizen must be able to have an indication that is adequate in the circumstances of the legal rules applicable to a given case".[81] There is at least a case for arguing that the opinions of a late-eighteenth century commentator on the law, much of it derived from unpublished accounts of proceedings in sixteenth and seventeenth century criminal courts is not an "accessible" source of law. If this is correct, then reliance upon the opinions of institutional writers such as Hume for the development of the law is incompatible with the Convention.[82]

Precision: Judicial rejection of this aspect of the rule has at times been emphatic. In *McLaughlan v. Boyd*[83] Lord Clyde stated: 2.17

> "It would be a mistake to imagine that the criminal common law of Scotland countenances any precise and exact categorisation

---

[79] Not all decisions of the Court of Criminal Appeal are published, even where these contain a discussion of legal principle. For examples of significant unreported cases, see *H.M. Advocate v. McCawley* (1959) S.C.C.R. (Supp.) 3, which was unreported at the time it was discussed in *McNeil v. H.M. Advocate*, 1968 J.C. 29, *Latta v. Herron* (1967) S.C.C.R. (Supp.) 18 which remained unreported for more than ten years, and *Miller and Denovan v. H.M. Advocate*, which was decided in 1960 but not fully reported until 1991.

[80] The case of *H.M. Advocate v. R.M.*, 1969 J.C. 52, in which it was pointed out that in order correctly to construe the terms of the Incest Act of 1567 it was necessary to rely upon the text of Chapter 18 of the Book of Leviticus as set out in the Geneva Bible. It appears that at the time the case was decided only one copy of the Geneva Bible was available in Scotland, and that was held in the National Library. Whether the relevant text of the law was "accessible" in any meaningful sense is questionable (leaving aside the language of the legislation itself).

[81] *Sunday Times v. U.K.* ECtHR, Series A, No. 30, para. 31, *Malone v. U.K.* ECtHR, Series A, No. 82, para. 66.

[82] Even if this is not the case, however, in many instances reliance upon the opinions of Institutional writers will fall foul of the requirement of precision.

[83] 1934 J.C. 19.

of the forms of conduct which amount to crime. It has been pointed out many times in this Court that such is not the nature or quality of the criminal law of Scotland."[84]

This attitude is also reflected in the opinion of Lord Cameron in the case of *Watt v. Annan*,[85] another case of shameless indecency. According to his Lordship:

> "It would be impracticable as well as undesirable to attempt to define precisely the limits and ambit of this particular offence...If it were considered desirable or necessary that this was a chapter of the criminal law in which precise boundaries or limits were to be set then it might be thought that the task is one which is more appropriate for the hand of the legislator."

Like Lord Clyde in *McLaughlan v. Boyd*, Lord Cameron seems to stand the principle of legality on its head. The presumption is not against broad, vaguely defined crimes, but against the *limitation* of crime by means of precise definition. As a general approach to the development of the criminal law, it is submitted that the views of Lord Clyde and Lord Cameron are inconsistent with the requirement of reasonable precision. However weakly this principle is applied by the Strasbourg institutions, it must at least require a national legal system to seek to achieve reasonable certainty, rather than uphold deliberate vagueness as a virtue.

Two Scottish offences in particular can be singled out on account of their vagueness: breach of the peace and shameless indecency.

Breach of the peace requires proof of an actual disturbance of the peace or, in the absence of such proof, "something done in breach of public order or decorum which might reasonably be expected to lead to the lieges being alarmed or upset."[86] The test is an objective one, so that mere evidence of alarm on the part of an individual will not necessarily lead to the conclusion that there has been a breach of the peace.[87]

In practice, the offence has come to be so widely applied[88] that there is virtually no limit to what may constitute breach of the peace, provided a court is prepared to accept that a reasonable person could apprehend alarm as a result of the accused's conduct.[89] The breadth of the offence only really becomes apparent when one considers the vast variety of circumstances to which the

---

[84] 1934 J.C. 19, at p.00.

[85] 1978 S.L.T. 198.

[86] *Raffaeli v. Heatly*, 1949 J.C. 101, 1949 S.L.T. 284; *Young v. Heatly*, 1959 J.C. 66, 1959 S.L.T. 250. *Donaldson v. Vannet*, 1998 S.C.C.R. 422. Just how many of the "lieges" know that they are "lieges" is an interesting question of accessibility.

[87] *Donaldson v. Vannet, ibid.*

[88] For a general discussion of the offence of breach of the peace, see M. Christie, *Breach of the Peace*, (Butterworths 1989).

[89] *Montgomery v. McLeod* (1977) S.C.C.R. (Supplement) 164.

offence has been applied—from "peeping" into houses at night[90] to cross-dressing in the red-light district of Aberdeen, by way of sitting on a felled tree as a protest at its destruction and obstructing its being cut up[91] and playing football in the street at night.[92]

The crime of conducting one's self in a "shamelessly indecent manner" has likewise proved to be open ended.[93] It has been held to include an indecent assault by an adult male on other men,[94] showing an obscene film in private to a paying audience,[95] quasi-incestuous conduct between a man and his 16-year-old daughter,[96] consensual sexual intercourse between a man and his foster daughter,[97] selling, exposing for sale and keeping for sale indecent magazines, books and sex gadgets,[98] showing an obscene video-recording to two teenage girls in private,[99] and presenting (although apparently not performing) an indecent display in a public house.[1]

The question which arises is whether these offences, by their very nature, offend against the requirement of reasonable precision. At first sight this argument appears persuasive, particularly in the case of breach of the peace. An offence which extends from attempted suicide to male cross-dressing appears by any reasonable standard to lack precision. The argument is less striking in the case of shameless indecency, but nevertheless, the offence is one of considerable breadth.   2.18

But as is suggested above,[2] the requirement of precision in the Convention case law is not especially demanding. In particular, the Convention jurisprudence does not require offence to be precisely defined in the sense of being narrowly defined. Broadly described

---

[90] *Raffaeli v. Heatly, supra* no. 86. See also *MacDougall v. Dochree*, 1992 S.C.C.R. 531, watching women using a sunbed by peeping through a hole in a partition separating a toilet cubicle and the solarium where the sunbed was located.

[91] *Colhoun v. Friel*, 1996 S.C.C.R. 497. The complaint in this case read: "in the area known as Patterton Woods, Newton Mearns...you did conduct yourself in a disorderly manner, sit on a felled tree then being cut, refuse to move when requested to do so and did commit a breach of the peace."

[92] *Cameron v. Normand*, 1992 S.C.C.R. 866.

[93] For a general discussion of shameless indecency, see Gane, *Sexual Offences* (Butterworths, 1992).

[94] *McLaughlan v. Boyd*, 1934 J.C. 19.

[95] *Watt v. Annan*, 1978 J.C. 84, 1978 S.L.T. 443.

[96] *R v. H.M. Advocate*, 1988 S.C.C.R. 254.

[97] *H.M. Advocate v. K.*, 1994 S.C.C.R. 499.

[98] *Robertson v. Smith*, 1979 S.L.T. (Notes) 51, *Scott v. Smith*, 1981 J.C. 46, *Ingram v. Macari*, 1982 S.C.C.R. 372, *Tudhope v. Barlow*, 1981 S.L.T. (Sh.Ct) 94. In the latter case it was held that it was not a crime to "warehouse" such articles since the premises concerned were not premises to which the public resorted, and there was therefore no affront to public decency involved in storing the material in question.

[99] *Carmichael v. Ashrif*, 1985 S.C.C.R. 461.

[1] *Lockhart v. Stephen*, 1987 S.C.C.R. 642 (Sh.Ct). In this particular case the sheriff ruled that the conduct (some highly indecent performances by strip-tease artists), although vulgar and in bad taste, was not criminal in that it did not encourage "perverted" conduct.

[2] p. 000.

offences are not incompatible with the Convention in this sense, and everything turns on the extent to which the conduct in question falls within a known definition.

What this suggests, then, is that a charge of breach of the peace or, *mutatis mutandis*, a charge of shameless indecency[3] is within the recognised boundaries of these offences, it will not be open to challenge on the ground that the offence is too broadly drawn. Provided the Crown remain within limits that have been established by the existing case law, then this aspect of the principle of legality presents no obstacle to charges of breach of the peace, or shameless indecency or, indeed, any other criminal offence. Offences of such open-ended potential thus illustrate the shortcomings of the approach adopted by the Strasbourg institutions to the principle of legality, and in particular the Court's reliance on "foreseeability" as a limiting criterion.

(c) No unreasonable or unforeseeable extension of the law

2.19   *(i) The Convention case law*: Although it is legitimate, in the view of the Court and Commission, for the criminal law to be flexible and responsive, development of the criminal law must be kept within reasonable bounds. It is especially important that where the criminal law is developed "by application and interpretation of courts in a common law system" that their law-making function remains "within reasonable limits."[4] Article 7(1) is intended to ensure that acts which were not previously punishable should not be held by the courts to involve criminal liability, and that existing offences should not be extended to cover facts which previously "did not clearly constitute a criminal offence".[5] Similarly, the constituent elements of an offence may not be "essentially changed to the detriment of an accused" and any "progressive development by way of interpretation" must satisfy the test of reasonable foreseeability.[6] Judicial development of the criminal law is permissible only provided that such developments can reasonably be brought under the original concept of the offence.[7] The resultant development must be "consistent with the essence of the offence" (and could reasonably be foreseen).[8]

In *S.W. and C.R. v. United Kingdom*, the issue before the Court was whether or not the judicial abolition of the husband's "marital rape exemption" in English law violated Article 7. Both the

---

[3]   Or, to give another example, a charge of attempting to pervert the course of justice.

[4]   *S.W. and C.R. v. U.K.* Commission Report, at paras 47 and 48.

[5]   Appl. No. 8710/79, DR 28, at p. 77; *S.W. and C.R. v. U.K.* Commission Report at paras 47 and 48.

[6]   8710/79; 10505/83; 13079; *SW and CR v. U.K.* Commission Report at paras. 48 and 49.

[7]   *ibid.*

[8]   *S.W. v. U.K.* (Court) above, at para. 36; *C.R. v. U.K.* (Court) above, at para. 34.

Commission and the Court held that it did not. In reaching this conclusion both bodies noted that although the rule had been in existence for at least 300 years before the decision in the case of *R v. R*[9] that rule had been subjected to a progressive interpretation by the Courts. Consequently, as the Court observed, by the time the decision complained of was handed down, "there was significant doubt as to the validity of the alleged marital immunity for rape".[10] The English courts had subjected the rule to a number of exceptions and there were, furthermore, "strong indications that   that still wider interpretation by the courts of the inroads on the immunity was probable."[11] In concluding that the marital rape exemption should no longer form part of the criminal law,

> "[t]he decisions of the [English Courts] did no more than continue a perceptible line of case law development dismantling the immunity of a husband from prosecution for rape upon his wife. There was no doubt under the law as it stood on 18 September 1990 that a husband who forcibly had sexual intercourse with his wife could, in various circumstances, be found guilty of rape. Moreover, there was an evident evolution, which was consistent with the very essence of the offence, of the criminal law through judicial interpretation towards treating such conduct generally as within the scope of the offence of rape. This evolution had reached a stage where judicial recognition of the absence of immunity had become a reasonably foreseeable development of the law."[12]

Both the Commission and the Court appear to have justified their decisions not only on the basis of the "progressive development" from which the complete abolition of the immunity could have been predicted, but also on the "core" purpose of Article 7 and the nature of the immunity claimed by the accused. According to the Court, the "object and purpose" of Article 7 is to "ensure that no-one should be subjected to arbitrary prosecution, conviction or punishment".[13] In the view of the Court, "the essentially debasing character of rape is so manifest that the result of the decisions of the Court of Appeal and the House of Lords...cannot be said to be at variance with the object and purpose of Article 7."[14] What this seems to suggest, then, is that the appeal to Article 7 is less likely to be successful where the conduct forming the basis of the criminal charge is in some way "manifestly" criminal. The Commission

2.20

---

[9] [1992] 1 A.C. 599; [1991] 4 All E.R. 481. This is the case which led to the application by CR in the instant case.
[10] *S.W. v. U.K.* above, Court, at para. 40; *C.R. v. U.K.* above, Court at para. 38.
[11] *ibid.*
[12] *ibid.*, paras 43 and 41.
[13] *ibid.*, paras 44 and 42.
[14] *ibid.*

seems to have taken a similar view: "The Commission is also of the opinion that it is inconceivable that the applicant when he embarked on the course of conduct in question could have held any genuine belief that it was lawful."[15]

The decision was also made easier by the very nature of the conduct of the applicants when viewed in the light of the purpose of the Convention. As was pointed out in the concurring opinion of one of the Commission members,[16] the marital rape exemption, to the extent that it removed from the ambit of normal criminal sanctions certain categories of forcible rape, violated the victims' right to privacy under Article 8. In invoking Article 7 to justify the sexual assault on their wives, the applicants claimed the right to engage in conduct which destroyed their wives' right to bodily integrity as protected by Article 8. To invoke Article 7 in this way was incompatible with the provisions of Article 17 of the Convention, which precludes an applicant from deriving from the Convention a right to engage in any activity or perform any act aimed at destroying any of the rights or freedoms set forth in the Convention.[17]

The Court was perhaps less forthright in its approach to this argument, but did point out that "the abandonment of the unacceptable idea of a husband being immune against prosecution for rape of his wife was in conformity not only with a civilised concept of marriage but also, and above all, with the fundamental objectives of the Convention, the very essence of which is respect for human dignity and human freedom."[18]

2.21   *(ii) The rule against unreasonable or unforeseeable extension of existing offences—Scots law:* The principle of legality is intended to restrain the unreasonable or unpredictable extension of recognised criminal laws. In terms of statutory crimes, the principle finds its expression in the rule that penal statutes must be strictly construed, a rule which, somewhat paradoxically perhaps, is accepted and applied by the Scottish courts.[19] In relation to the common law, we have seen that the Strasbourg bodies have laid down certain guidelines for the judicial development of the criminal law. How far have these guidelines been followed by the Scottish courts?

The guidelines centre round two key elements—the foreseeability of the development in question, and the extent to which it marks an extension of existing criminal liability.

A development may be foreseeable and may not effect a

---

[15] *S.W. v. U.K.* Commission Report, para. 61.
[16] Mrs Liddy.
[17] Mrs Liddy, para. 12, referring to *Lawless v. Ireland,* Series A, No. 3; (1979-80) 1 E.H.R.R. 15, at para. 7.
[18] Para. 44/42.
[19] *Mackenzie v. H.M. Advocate,* 1969 S.L.T. 81, *Friel v. Initial Contract Services Ltd,* 1994 S.L.T. 1216, *Barty v. Hill,* 1907 S.C. (J) 36.

fundamental change in the nature of the offence. In that case, it appears that there is no violation of the principle of legality as that is understood within the Convention. That, indeed, was the view accepted by the Commission and the Court in *S.W. v. United Kingdom* and *C.R. v. United Kingdom* in which it was held that the judicial abolition of the husband's exemption from liability for rape of his wife did not violate Article 7(1).[20] As the Strasbourg Court pointed out, the husband's exemption had been restricted over time by a sequence of decisions, to the point where it was not unforeseeable that the Courts would take the further step of removing it altogether. And on one view the removal of the exemption did not fundamentally alter the nature of the crime of rape; the decisions of the House of Lords and the Court of Appeal merely removed an anomalous restriction on liability to prosecution for that offence.

The extinction of the husband's marital rape exemption in Scots law would seem to fall into this category of case. It will be recalled that the decision of the High Court in *Stallard v. H.M. Advocate*[21] was preceded by at least two reported first instance decisions[22] which substantially modified the rule as laid down in the institutional writers.[23]

Equally, a development in the law may be wholly unforeseeable, and bring about a fundamental change in the law. A clear example of this, it is suggested, was the decision of the High Court in *H.M. Advocate v. Wilson*.[24] In that case the High Court held that the common law offence of malicious mischief included an act of interference with the property of another which resulted in patrimonial loss. Prior to this decision it had generally been accepted that malicious mischief required destruction of, or at least damage to, the corporeal property of another.[25] The decision is a very clear example of an extension of an existing offence, whose definition had been settled for more than 200 years,[26] in a way which was not "foreseeable", which "essentially changed" the constituent elements of the offence, and which extended the concept of malicious mischief to cover facts "which previously did not clearly constitute a criminal offence".[27]

---

[20] See above, p. 000.
[21] 1989 S.C.C.R. 248.
[22] *H.M. Advocate v. Duffy*, 1984 S.C.C.R. 182, *H.M. Advocate v. Paxton*, 1985 S.L.T. 96. See also the unreported decisions in *S v. H.M. Advocate*, High Court, August 1982; *H.M. Advocate v. Conlan*, High Court, December 1983.
[23] Hume, i, 306. See also Burnett, 103, Macdonald 119.
[24] 1984 S.L.T. 117; 1983 S.C.C.R. 420.
[25] For a detailed critique of this decision see Gane and Stoddart, *A Casebook on Scottish Criminal Law* (2nd ed.) pp.633–638.
[26] *Bett v. Hamilton*, 1997 S.C.C.R. 621. A similar approach can be found in many other areas of the criminal law. See, for examples, *H.M. Advocate v. Martin*, 1956 J.C. 1, where the crime of hindering or frustrating the ends of justice was extended to escaping from prison while working outside the prison.
[27] See above.

2.22   What, however, would be the case where the development was
foreseeable *and* fundamentally altered the nature of the crime?
Cases of this kind may not be frequently encountered. Apart from
any other consideration, developments which are foreseeable will
tend to form part of a sequence of decisions, which will in
themselves have begun the process of change, so that it may be
difficult to argue that there has been a "fundamental" change at any
given point.

An example of this process of change may be found in the judicial
extinction of an intention permanently to deprive as part of the
mens rea of theft. Prior to the case of *Milne v. Tudhope*[28] it had been
accepted thathe modern law of theft required proof of an intention
permanently to deprive.[29] In that case, however, the High Court
held that in "exceptional circumstances" an intention temporarily
to deprive the owner of his property might be sufficient for a theft
conviction. In *Milne v. Tudhope* the alleged thief was a builder, who
had carried out renovation work on a cottage for a client. A dispute
arose as to payment for work which the customer claimed was
needed in order to remedy certain defects in the work done to the
cottage. The accused removed doors, radiators, windows and other
items which he had installed in the cottage, and informed the owner
that he would get them back if the accused was allowed to complete
the work and was paid for the additional work. The High Court
held that the accused was guilty of theft.

That decision was followed in *Kidston v. Annan*.[30] In that case the
accused carried out unauthorised repairs on a television set which
had been left with him by the owner, who had asked the accused to
provide an estimate of the cost of repairing the set. The accused told
the owner that his property would be returned on payment of the
cost of carrying out the repairs. Again it was held that the accused
was guilty of theft.

Finally, in *Black v. Carmichael, Penrice v. Carmichael*[31] it was
held that to apply a wheel clamp to a car thus immobilising it,
without statutory authority, and to refuse to release it until such
time as a release fee was paid, amounted to theft of the car. Again,
there was no intention permanently to deprive.

The important point about *Black v. Carmichael, Penrice v.
Carmichael*, is that although in the earlier cases the court had
qualified its statements on the mental element for theft, by
suggesting that temporary deprivation could be theft where there
were "exceptional circumstances" or where the taking was for a

---

[28] 1981 J.C. 53.
[29] See, for example, Gordon, *The Criminal Law of Scotland* (2d ed.), para. 14-65, at
p. 500: "it is clear that Scots law requires an intention to deprive the owner
permanently of his goods. In the absence of this intent there can be no theft." See
also the opinion of Sheriff MacPhail in *Herron v. Best*, 1976 S.L.T. (Sh.Ct) 80.
[30] 1984 S.L.T. 279; 1984 S.C.C.R. 20.
[31] 1992 S.L.T. 897, 1992 S.C.C.R. 709.

"nefarious purpose", no such qualification was insisted upon.

In just over 10 years a fundamental change was wrought in the   2.23
nature of the crime of theft. All three cases discussed are linked in
the sense that they can all be seen as cases in which, as it were, the
alleged thief held the owner's property to ransom, while making a
demand for payment which he may, or may not, have been entitled
to receive. The third case, however, marks a culmination in that
development in that it appears entirely to abandon any notion of
permanent deprivation, while the first two are more qualified in this
respect. The development in *Black and Penrice*, could not, however,
be said to have been "unforeseeable". This was, therefore, a
development which brought about a fundamental change in the
law, but one which, over the 10-year period, was reasonably
foreseeable. What was not foreseeable, probably, was the decision
in *Milne v. Tudhope*. But it did not effect a fundamental change in
the law, merely, it might be argued, a qualification of it. The
situation would, however, have been different if in that single
decision the requirement of an intention permanently to deprive
had been abandoned without qualification. Then there would have
been a change in the law which was both fundamental and
unforeseeable.

2. The age of criminal responsibility

The age of criminal responsibility is eight.[32] At that it is one of   2.24
the lowest in Europe. Only Cyprus, Switzerland and Liechtenstein
have a lower age of criminal responsibility (at seven). The age of
criminal responsibility is 13 in France, 14 in Germany, Austria, and
Italy, 15 in the Scandinavian countries, 16 in Portugal, Poland and
Andorra and 18 in Spain, Belgium and Luxembourg.[33]

Whether this is compatible with the Convention is very
questionable. In *T v. United Kingdom* and *V v. United Kingdom*[34]
the applicants were convicted in the Crown Court in England of
murdering a two-year-old child. At the time of the offence both
were aged 10, which is the age of criminal responsibility under
English law. They were 11 at the time of the trial. Both argued, *inter
alia*, that the attribution of criminal responsibility at an age as low
as 10 amounted to a violation of Article 3 of the European
Convention on Human Rights (especially when linked to their
public trial in an adult court). The majority of the Court, noting
that there was not, as yet, a prevailing consensus amongst
European States with respect to the age of criminal responsibility,
rejected this argument:

> "70. The Court has considered first whether the attribution to
> the applicant of criminal responsibility in respect of acts

---

[32] Criminal Procedure (Scotland) Act 1995, s. 41.
[33] See *T v. U.K.* ECtHR, December 16, 1999, at para. 48.
[34] Above, n. xx.

committed when he was ten years old could, in itself, give rise to a violation of Article 3. In doing so, it has regard to the principle, well established in its case-law that, since the Convention is a living instrument, it is legitimate when deciding whether a certain measure is acceptable under one of its provisions to take account of the standards prevailing amongst the member States of the Council of Europe ...

71. In this connection, the Court observes that, at the present time there is not yet a commonly accepted minimum age for the imposition of criminal responsibility in Europe. While most of the Contracting States have adopted an age-limit which is higher than that in force in England and Wales, other States, such as Cyprus, Ireland, Liechtenstein and Switzerland, attribute criminal responsibility from a younger age. Moreover, no clear tendency can be ascertained from examination of the relevant international texts and instruments .... Rule 4 of the Beijing Rules which, although not legally binding, might provide some indication of the existence of an international consensus, does not specify the age at which criminal responsibility should be fixed but merely invites States not to fix it too low, and Article 40(3)(a) of the UN Convention requires States Parties to establish a minimum age below which children shall be presumed not to have the capacity to infringe the criminal law, but contains no provision as to what that age should be.

72. The Court does not consider that there is at this stage any clear common standard amongst the member States of the Council of Europe as to the minimum age of criminal responsibility. Even if England and Wales is among the few European jurisdictions to retain a low age of criminal responsibility, the age of ten cannot be said to be so young as to differ disproportionately from the age-limit followed by other European States. The Court concludes that the attribution of criminal responsibility to the applicant does not in itself give rise to a breach of Article 3 of the Convention."

Five members of the Court, however, dissented on the question of the age of responsibility, in part because it was difficult to accept that there was no clear European tendency in relation to the age of responsibility when only four out of the 41 states parties to the Convention were prepared to find criminal responsibility at an age as low as, or lower than England and Wales. There was, in the view of the dissenters, a clear tendency towards setting the age of full criminal responsibility at 18 and above, with special provision in some cases for modified responsibility starting from 13 or 14.[35]

---

[35] Joint partly dissenting opinions of Judges Pastor Ridruejo, Ress, Makarczyk, Tulkens and Butkevych.

In this context it is perhaps also worth noting that the United Nations Committee on the Rights of the Child, in its Report on the United Kingdom[36] dated February 15, 1995 stated, *inter alia*:

"35. The Committee recommends that law reform be pursued to ensure that the system of the administration of juvenile justice is child-oriented ...
36. More specifically, the Committee recommends that serious consideration be given to raising the age of criminal responsibility throughout the areas of the United Kingdom ..."

The Scottish Executive has undertaken a review of the age of criminal responsibility in Scotland, and has referred the question to the Scottish Law Commission. It is extremely unlikely that the age of responsibility will continue at eight.

3. The Mental Element

There is nothing in the Convention which requires general adherence to the principle *actus non facit reum nisi mens sit rea*. In *Salabiaku v. France,* the Court made this observation: 2.25

"In principle the Contracting States remain free to apply the criminal law to an act where it is not carried out in the normal exercise of one of the rights protected under the Convention...and, accordingly, to define the constituent elements of the resulting offence. In particular, and again in principle, the Contracting States may, under certain conditions, penalise a simple or objective fact as such, irrespective of whether it results from criminal intent or from negligence. Examples of such offences may be found in the laws of the Contracting States."[37]

4. Article 6(2) and positive defences

Article 6(2)—which enshrines the presumption of innocence in criminal proceedings—is generally discussed in relation to provisions which place an onus on the accused. In practice, the Court has not found it difficult to uphold "reverse" onus provisions.[38] It may be, however, that Article 6(2) is capable of providing a vehicle to challenge other rules of the substantive criminal law.   2.26

It may, for example, provide a basis for challenging the rule that voluntary intoxication is not a defence to a criminal charge in Scotland. As a result of the decision of the Full Bench in *Brennan v.*

---

[36] CRC/C/15/add.34.
[37] (1991) 13 E.H.R.R. 379, at para. 27.
[38] See, for example, *Salabiaku v. France* (1991) 13 E.H.R.R. 379 and *Pham Hoang v. France*, Series A, No. 243.

H.M. Advocate[39] it is legally possible to convict a person of an offence even though at the time the accused was incapable through voluntary intoxication of forming the *mens rea* for the offence, and even where his intoxication is such that he could not be said to be "acting" consciously.[40] Does this give rise to a human rights question? An argument to that effect can be constructed, by reference to Article 6(2) and the presumption of innocence.

Article 6(2) states that a person charged with an offence "shall be presumed innocent until proved guilty according to law". It may be argued that a person who is convicted of an offence, the definition of which requires proof of *mens rea*, and voluntary conduct, cannot be found guilty "according to law" if the proof of these basic elements of criminal responsibility are absent.

Two objections may be made to this argument. The first is that the reference to "law" in Article 6(2) does not embrace the substantive law, but refers only to the evidential and procedural requirements for a lawful conviction. But it is difficult to see how a conviction could be "according to law" without proof of the elements of the offence. The case law of the Court dealing with reverse or transferred onus provisions all proceed on the assumption that Article 6(2) has a substantive as well as a procedural dimension.

The second objection is that conviction of an acutely intoxicated accused is in accordance with law because the substantive law rule is that in the case of extreme voluntary intoxication the proof of the necessary criminal intent is either dispensed with, or supplied by evidence of the accused's intoxication.

Leaving aside the argument that the true nature of the legal rule is unclear in Scotland, there would appear to be very real difficulties with this rejoinder, which can best be illustrated by reference to the example of the crime of murder. If the first argument is the true explanation, then what we are faced with, when an acutely intoxicated person commits murder is in reality offence of strict liability (since proof of the mental element is dispensed with) or at the very least one in which certain presumptions arise from the combination of the accused's act of killing and his intoxicated condition. This raises very considerable questions of proportionality. It is true that offences of strict liability are not incompatible with Article 6, nor are presumptions.[41] But, to adapt the language used by the court in relation to presumptions in the criminal law, presumptions of fact or of law provided for in the criminal law are not viewed with indifference. Article 6(2) requires States to confine them within reasonable limits which take into account the

---

[39] 1977 J.C. 38.
[40] A person in such a condition as a result of *involuntary* intoxication cannot, however, be convicted, at least where the offence requires proof of *mens rea*: *Ross v. H.M. Advocate*, 1991 J.C. 210.
[41] *Salabiaku v. France*, para. 27.

importance of what is at stake and maintain the rights of the defence.[42] It is also true that the Court has not shown any particular enthusiasm for regulating presumptions of this kind, but it would surely be surprising if the Court were to hold that a presumption of criminal intent could be relied upon to convict of murder. It would be equally surprising if it were to hold that dispensing with any criminal intent in the most serious of offences was compatible with Article 6(2).

An alternative way of explaining why convicting the acutely intoxicated offender is not incompatible with Article 6(2) would be to argue that the accused's conduct in becoming so intoxicated displays the necessary criminal blameworthiness. This is an argument which has, of course, been put forward to justify the exclusion of the defence of intoxication from offences of reckless-ness[43] (which includes the crime of murder). But this is simply a different or disguised presumption, since it involves substituting for the actual state of mind of the accused an assumed state of mind—the person who gets so drunk that he conducts himself in a recklessly violent manner is presumed to have the *actual* state of mind required for conviction. The further problem with this argument is that it cannot be applied in crimes which require proof of intention.

It appears, then, that there is at least an arguable case for saying that the current exclusion of the defence of intoxication is contrary to Article 6(2) of the Convention. This argument may derive some slight additional support from the "procedural" dimension of Article 6(2). It might be argued that when Article 6(2) refers to proof of guilt "according to law" it invokes whatever standard of proof is required under the relevant national legal system. Proof of guilt in Scotland requires proof "beyond reasonable doubt". The current rules on the defence of intoxication are capable of producing the following result: the Crown are able to prove that the accused did the acts required by the definition of the offence. The evidence also shows that the accused was extremely drunk at the time, so that the jury are left with a reasonable doubt as to whether he knew what he was doing. But because the doubt is based on the accused's voluntary intoxication, they must convict. Can it not be argued that, in our system of criminal law, the accused has not been convicted "according to law" where the jury are left in a reasonable doubt about guilt, but are not, at least formally, entitled to give effect to that doubt?

The Court has never been called upon to consider issues of this kind. Such indications as there are from the case law of the Commission are inconclusive. In *Kingston v. United Kingdom*[44] the

2.27

---

[42] *Salabiaku v. France*, para. 28.
[43] See *Brennan v. H.M. Advocate*, above, n. 000 and *DPP v. Majewski* [1977] A.C. 443.
[44] Above, n. 000.

applicant claimed that he had not received a fair trial because the English courts had refused to give effect to his plea of *involuntary* intoxication.[45] The applicant was charged with indecently assaulting a boy. His defence was that without his knowledge he had been drugged by a third party—who intended to place him in a compromising position with the boy and photograph him for the purposes of blackmail. He acknowledged that at the time of the offence he had acted with intent, but argued that he would not have given way to his paedophilic inclinations had he not been drugged. The trial judge refused to rule that such an intent would exclude criminal responsibility, and while he allowed the jury to consider whether, in view of the evidence of intoxication, the accused intended to assault the boy, he directed them that if they found such an intent, it was no defence for the accused to say that it was drug-induced. He was convicted. His conviction was quashed by the Court of Appeal but reinstated by the House of Lords.

Before the Commission the applicant's arguments were mainly directed to a claim that certain rules of evidence had been changed in a manner adverse to his case, and to the suggestion that a defence of involuntary intoxication which had previously been available in English law had been retrospectively removed by the decision of the House of Lords. On the first argument the Commission, in line with its established case law held that the admissibility of evidence was a matter for national law, and on the second held that the House of Lords had not removed a defence but rather demonstrated that it had not existed. The applicant did not seek to persuade the Commission that the absence of the defence impacted on the presumption of innocence. In any case, since the applicant conceded that he acted with intent, the case is quite different from one in which the accused claims that he did not act with intent, albeit because he was intoxicated through his own actions.

The conclusion must therefore be that the matter remains at large, and that the provisions of Article 6(2) may provide grounds for challenging the decision of the High Court in *Brennan*.

5. Privacy, consent and sexual relations

2.28   As indicated above, the Convention has had a profound impact in relation to homosexual offences. The cases of *Dudgeon v. United Kingdom*[46] and *Norris v. Ireland*,[47] confirmed the Court's willingness to protect sexual choice and privacy when faced with State claims to regulate the private sexual behaviour of adults on the grounds of public morality, the prevention of crime and even the paternalistic suggestion that criminalising homosexual acts was a way of protecting young men from later social isolation. In

---

[45] See *Kingston v. U.K.* [1995] 2 A.C. 355.
[46] (1981) 4 E.H.R.R. 149.
[47] (1988) 13 E.H.R.R. 186.

Sutherland v. United Kingdom,[48] the Commission took the opportunity to address the question of discrimination in the criminal law, as a result of which decision—although not without difficulty—Parliament reduced the "age of consent" for homosexual offences from 18 to 16.[49] In *A.D.T. v. United Kingdom,*[50] the Court addressed a different aspect of the law regulating homosexual acts, the restrictive definition of "private" acts, which excluded sexual acts between men when more than two were present.[51]

These decisions are, of course, significant in themselves and for those most directly affected by them. They do, however, raise some broader questions. How far is the principle of non-discrimination respected in the criminal law generally? Does respect for privacy protect sexual acts and relationships which have received less social acceptance even than homosexual acts? The Court itself has drawn a line at sadomasochistic acts[52] arguing that the state is entitled to restrict such conduct, even in private, in the interests of health and morals. One member of the Court indeed was prepared to go so far as to say that such conduct was not even embraced by the concept of "private life" so that there was no need even to consider possible justifications for criminal sanctions.[53]

Is it possible to argue from the above cases that, for example, consensual incest between adults is protected by Article 8? Could it be argued, on the basis of non-discrimination, that it is unlawful to prosecute a 17-year-old youth for having sexual intercourse with his 15-year-old girlfriend, when it is not a criminal offence for a 17-year-old girl to have sexual intercourse with her 15-year-old boyfriend? Indeed, does privacy extend, for example, to consensual sexual relations between parties below the current age of consent when there is no element of corruption or exploitation? Unlikely as such propositions may sound, are they any more unconventional than the suggestion made from the 1960s onwards that sexual relations between adult men are protected by Article 8?

---

[48] Appl. 25186/94, Commission Decision, May 21, 1996.
[49] REF
[50] Judgment, July 31, 2000.
[51] It is understood that the Scottish Executive intends to introduce legislation to give effect to this decision.
[52] *Laskey, Jaggard and Brown v. U.K.* (1997) 24 E.H.R.R. 39.
[53] Judge Petiti.

CHAPTER 3

CRIMINAL EVIDENCE AND PROCEDURE

INTRODUCTION

Aspects of criminal evidence and procedure have been the matters   3.01
with which a very large part of the jurisprudence of the Strasbourg
institutions has been concerned. Scottish experience, since the entry
into force of section 57(2) of the Scotland Act 1998, tends to
confirm that preoccupation. All but a few of the devolution issues
which have been pursued have related to acts of the Lord Advocate
or Procurators Fiscal in pursuit of prosecutions and most of those
have related to the law of evidence and procedure. Much the same
has been true of points taken under reference to the Human Rights
Act 1998 alone. The Strasbourg case law has, however, scarcely
addressed Scottish rules, and the embryonic Convention rights case
law of the High Court of Justiciary has hardly got beyond aspects
of Article 6. This means that, in relation to most issues, one cannot
say with certainty how Scots law will look once the Convention
rights have "bedded in". For what it is worth, it appears to the
writer that there is reason to think that we will see existing Scots law
rules developed in light of the Convention rights but not, for the
most part, rejected as incompatible with those rights. There will be
a new conceptual framework within which it will be necessary to
reason and some additional rights (such as the right to trial within a
reasonable time irrespective of prejudice[1]) but we are unlikely to see
the High Court rewriting Scottish criminal evidence and procedure
law from scratch. So, for example, the High Court in *Andrew v.
H.M. Advocate*[2] gave short shrift to an argument that an
unexpected reference by a witness to the accused's previous
convictions breached Article 6 ECHR so as to justify quashing
the conviction, where it would not have had that effect in existing
Scots law.[3]

---

[1]   See page 119 below.
[2]   2000 S.L.T. 402.
[3]   In fact, although the issue was not explored in *Andrew*, it is most unlikely that the
      Strasbourg organs would even have regarded an application on this basis as
      admissible. In very many other European jurisdictions, reference to the previous
      convictions of accused persons is commonplace and the principle of interpretation
      of the Convention according to widespread European practice must surely have
      led the Court to the conclusion that the prohibition of reference to previous
      convictions is a U.K. peculiarity and not a Convention principle.

It seems best, in this chapter, to avoid speculation and stick to certainties. What is certain is that there is, in relation to criminal evidence and procedure, a substantial body of case law from the European Court of Human Rights ("the European Court") and the European Commission of Human Rights ("the Commission") and a developing body of case law from the High Court of Justiciary and the Judicial Committee of the Privy Council. In this chapter we shall look in turn at each of the main stages through which a criminal case goes and call attention to the European rules and developing High Court jurisprudence which is relevant. A familiarity with the domestic rules of criminal evidence and procedure is, for the most part, assumed.

The material is, accordingly, organised in four broad sections:

(1) the investigation of crime;
(2) bail;
(3) the charge; and
(4) trial.

INVESTIGATION OF CRIME

Introduction

3.02   It may be said that the proper investigation of crime is itself required in order that the United Kingdom may discharge its treaty obligation to guarantee at least the right to life,[4] the right not to be subjected to torture or inhuman or degrading treatment[5] and the right to respect for private life.[6] This principle might well also apply to other Convention rights, including in particular that to peaceful enjoyment of possessions.[7] Space does not permit fuller analysis of the principle here but it is mentioned because it means that the investigator and prosecutor will often be subject to two Convention rights imperatives. The Convention rights of victims of crime will demand an investigation and might militate strongly in favour of a prosecution; and the Convention rights of suspects and accused persons will place limits on what investigative techniques may properly be employed and make certain clear demands on the trial process.

It is with the constraints on investigators that the remainder of this first substantive part of this chapter is chiefly concerned. They may be dealt with under three broad headings: (1). arrest and detention; (2). questioning; and (3). surveillance and search.

---

[4]   Art. 2; *Yaca v. Turkey* (1999) 28 E.H.R.R. 408.
[5]   Art. 3; *Aydin v. Turkey* (1998) 25 E.H.R.R. 251.
[6]   Art. 8; *X and Y v. The Netherlands* (1985) 8 E.H.R.R. 235.
[7]   Protocol 1, Art. 1.

1. Arrest and detention

Introduction

It is frequently possible to find multiple Convention Articles 3.03
relevant to a particular issue, though the European Court tends to
decide cases on the basis of the Article which has most direct
relevance and to treat consideration of other Articles as unnecessary. There can be no doubt that issues relating to the arrest and
detention of persons as part of the investigation of crime will
usually be resolved under reference to aspects of Article 5.

The scheme of Article 5(1)

Article 5(1) begins by stating the general right: "Everyone has the 3.04
right to liberty and security of person". It then states the permitted
exceptions to the right: "No one shall be deprived of his liberty *save
in the following cases* and *in accordance with a procedure prescribed
by law*".[8] Six subparagraphs then set out the cases in which
deprivation of liberty is permitted. They are exhaustive and fall to
be construed narrowly.[9] If a deprivation of liberty cannot be
brought within one of these six cases, it necessarily involves a
breach of Article 5(1).[10] Given a deprivation of liberty for the
purposes of Article 5, the authority responsible for that deprivation
must, if it is to avoid a finding of breach, bring the case within one
of the permitted exceptions to the right. It should be noted,
however, that the mere fact that the decision to deprive a person of
his or her liberty is overturned on appeal will not by itself establish
a breach of Article 5(1).[11]

For the investigation of crime, Article 5(1)(c) is especially
relevant. That permits

> "the lawful arrest or detention of a person effected for the
> purpose of bringing him before the competent legal authority
> on reasonable suspicion of having committed an offence or
> when it is reasonably considered necessary to prevent his
> committing an offence or fleeing having done so".

Following the practice of the European Court, this should be
analysed in the following way:

(a) Is there a deprivation of liberty?
(b) Is it in accordance with a procedure prescribed by law (and
lawful)?

---

[8] Emphasis added.
[9] *Monnell and Morris v. U.K.* (1987) 10 E.H.R.R. 205.
[10] *Ciulla v. Italy* (1991) 13 E.H.R.R. 346.
[11] *Perks v. U.K.*, (2000) 30 E.H.R.R. 33.

(c) Is it within subparagraph (c)?

(a) Deprivation of liberty

3.05   It is not necessary that the person concerned should have been arrested or detained formally for there to be a deprivation of liberty. The concept includes any element of compulsion restricting a person to a particular location. So the confinement of asylum seekers "air-side" at an airport[12] and the confinement to an hotel of sect members undergoing deprogramming[13] have both constituted deprivation of liberty for the purposes of Article 5.

(b) Procedure prescribed by law

3.06   Granted that there has been a deprivation of liberty, it must be in accordance with a procedure prescribed by law. This and the requirement of lawfulness desiderated by Article 5(1)(c) are in practice conflated by the European Court.

It seems clear that, in Scots law, before a deprivation of liberty in the course of an investigation can be regarded as in accordance with a procedure prescribed by law, and lawful, it will have to proceed either by arrest or in terms of section 14 of the Criminal Procedure (Scotland) Act 1995 ("the 1995 Act") (or section 24 of the Criminal Law (Consolidation) (Scotland) Act 1995).

Section 14 of the 1995 Act provides a detailed legislative code for detention. Assuming compliance, it should suffice to constitute a procedure prescribed by law for the purposes of Article 5(1). It is, however, worth noting that section 14 imposes a strict time limit on such detention. Should that time limit not be complied with, the deprivation of liberty will no longer be in accordance with law and will constitute a breach of Article 5(1).[14]

Arrest is less thoroughly regulated by statute but it is thought that it is nevertheless sufficiently regulated by law to satisfy the demands of Article 5(1). The extent to which common law satisfies Convention requirements for "law" has been canvassed in a number of cases in the European Court.[15] The test which emerges is that the law should be reasonably certain and accessible and such as to enable the citizen (with such advice as appropriate) to regulate his or her conduct; and that it should not operate in an arbitrary way.[16] In principle, the European Court has been prepared to accept that common law rules satisfy this requirement and it is thought that arrest in Scots law is a procedure sufficiently regulated by law to pass muster.

---

12   *Amuur v. France*, RJD 1996–III No. 10.
13   *Riera-Blume v. Spain*, October 14, 1999.
14   *KF v. FRG* (1998) 26 E.H.R.R. 390.
15   See, for example, *Sunday Times v. U.K.* (1980) 2 E.H.R.R. 245; *C.R. v. U.K.; S.W. v.U.K.* (1995) 21 E.H.R.R. 363.
16   *Winterwerp v. Netherlands* (1980) 2 E.H.R.R. 387.

(c) The purpose of the deprivation of liberty

The final criterion is that the deprivation of liberty is effected for the   3.07
purpose of bringing the person concerned before the competent
legal authority (*i.e.* the court) on reasonable suspicion of having
committed an offence or when it is reasonably necessary to prevent
his committing an offence or fleeing having done so. The
preventative arrest which this contemplates and the possibility of
arrest to prevent flight have hardly been addressed by the
Strasbourg institutions (though in *Lukanov v. Bulgaria*[17] the
Commission held that the state's right to arrest to prevent flight
depends on the existence of reasonable suspicion that the person
concerned has in fact committed an offence). Deprivation of liberty
to prevent the commission of an offence (without any offence
having been committed) is not a feature of existing Scots law and
has greater application in those jurisdictions with a less developed
law of inchoate offences and attempts. Deprivation of liberty to
prevent flight following the commission of an offence is, however,
well recognised in the law of arrest in Scotland.[18] The concept of
proportionality is, perhaps, implicit in domestic law since there is
said to be a "general principle that arrest is more easily justified the
more serious the offence"[19] and it is possible that this principle will
be given greater clarity under reference to the Convention rights;
though it must be said that the concept of proportionality has
received scant attention in Strasbourg in relation to deprivation of
liberty. The fact that arrest must constitute an interference with the
Article 8 right to respect for private life might provide more fertile
ground for an argument founded on proportionality. In relation to
that Article, the concept of proportionality has been very
thoroughly developed.[20]

The first part of Article 5(1)(c) deals with arrest or detention for
the purpose of bringing a person before the competent legal
authority on reasonable suspicion of having committed an offence.
In the Scottish context, the expression "competent legal authority"
(which denotes an authority authorised to exercise judicial power[21])
can only refer to the court.

Taken literally, the requirement that deprivation of liberty should
have the purpose of placing the person detained before the court
would mean that deprivation of liberty would breach the
Convention unless that person was both kept in custody and
presented to the court. In other words, the police and the
prosecutor could not safely decide to liberate the accused having
once arrested him. In *Brogan v. United Kingdom,*[22] however, the

---

[17] RJD 1997-II No 34.
[18] *Alison* ii, 116-7; *Peggie v. Clark* (1868) 7M 89.
[19] G.H. Gordon, *Renton and Brown's Criminal Procedure* (6th ed, 1996), p.69.
[20] See page 107 below.
[21] *Schiesser v. Switzerland* (1980) 2 E.H.R.R. 417.
[22] (1989) 11 E.H.R.R. 117.

European Court declined to take that approach. It said that Article 5(1)(c) "does not presuppose that the police should have obtained sufficient evidence to bring charges" and proceeded on the basis that it is legitimate to detain so as to further an investigation and that, if sufficient evidence was obtained during that investigation, no doubt the person detained would be put before the court. In *Brogan* the persons detained were not in fact placed before the court (because there was insufficient evidence after investigation). The European Court did not find a breach of the Convention in that regard.[23]

Reasonable suspicion refers to the existence of facts or information that would satisfy an independent observer that the person concerned might have committed the offence[24] but full proof is not necessary[25] (otherwise *Brogan* could not have been decided as it was).

The word "offence" in Article 5(1)(c) refers to a *criminal* offence.[26] Military criminal offences are also included[27] but Article 5(1)(c) would not authorise deprivation of liberty for a mere breach of military discipline.

The rights of the person deprived of liberty

3.08   Article 5(1) is concerned with the legitimacy of depriving a person of his or her liberty. Articles 5(2), 5(3) and 5(4) provide for certain minimum rights for a person who is in that position. Articles 5(3) and 5(4) are dealt with more appropriately below in the context of bail; but it is desirable to deal here with Article 5(2), which requires that such a person should be informed "promptly" (which means as soon as possible unless the person is in such a condition that he cannot understand what he is being told[28]) in a language which he understands (fluency is not necessary) of the reasons for his arrest and of any charge against him. There are obvious similarities between this and section 14(6) of the 1995 Act.

In *Fox, Campbell and Hartley*[29] it was held that the Article 5(2) guarantee means that the detained person must be told in simple, non-technical language that he can understand the essential legal and factual grounds for his arrest so as to be able, if he sees fit, to challenge its lawfulness under Article 5(4). This formula suggests that a high degree of legal precision is not required; and, indeed, it

---

[23] There was held to have been a breach in *Brogan* but that was on the separate basis that detention had lasted for over four days, which was too long.

[24] *Fox, Campbell and Hartley v. U.K.* (1990) 13 E.H.R.R. 157.

[25] *X v. Austria* (1989) 11 E.H.R.R. 112.

[26] *Ciulla v. Italy, above.*

[27] *De Jong, Baljet and Van Den Brink v. Netherlands* (1984) 8 E.H.R.R. 20.

[28] *Clinton v. U.K.* Committee of Ministers Resolution DH (95) 4, January 11, 1995.

[29] *Above.*

has been held in that case and others[30] that if the process of questioning itself makes the charge clear, Article 5(2) will be satisfied.

Perhaps the most extreme example to date is *Dikme v. Turkey*.[31] In that case, the Court held that when a police officer said to a suspect: "You belong to *Devrimci Sol* [a left wing terrorist group] and if you don't give us the information we need the only way for you to get out of here will be as a corpse!" these words were sufficient to satisfy the requirements of Article 5(2). The Court considered that this most reprehensible statement gave a fairly precise indication of the nature of the suspicions entertained about the applicant. Having regard to that, to the fact that the organisation mentioned was illegal and to the reasons which might have prompted the applicant to hide his identity and to fear the police, the Court considered that the applicant should or could have realised at that stage that he was suspected of being involved in prohibited activities such as those of *Dev-Sol*, so that there had been no violation of Article 5(2).

2. Questioning of suspects

The Convention does not in terms address the questioning of persons suspected of crime. However, the European Court has derived a right to silence from the presumption of innocence stipulated by Article 6(2) and this has consequences for such questioning,[32] but it held in *Murray v. United Kingdom*[33] that the right is not absolute. In that case the evidence against the applicant had been formidable. The Court said that

> "on the one hand it is self evident that it is incompatible with the immunities under consideration to base a conviction solely or mainly on the accused's silence or on a refusal to answer questions or to give evidence himself. On the other hand, the Court deems it equally obvious that these immunities cannot and should not prevent that the accused's silence, in situations which clearly call for an explanation from him, be taken into account in assessing the persuasiveness of evidence adduced by the prosecution."

3.09

It has been argued that Article 6(2), in combination with the Article 6(3)(c) right to defend oneself in person or through legal assistance of one's own choosing, entitles the accused to have his solicitor present whenever he is interviewed by the police. In this bald form, however, the argument does not seem to be sustainable. No case

---

[30] For example, *Delcourt v. Belgium* 10 Y.B. 238 (1967).
[31] Appl. 20869/92 (July 11, 2000).
[32] *Saunders v. U.K.* (1997) 23 E.H.R.R. 313.
[33] (1996) 22 E.H.R.R. 29.

decided by the European Court provides authority for the proposition and Lord Penrose noted in *H.M. Advocate v. Robb*[34] that *Murray* does not support that general proposition because that case depended on the particular legal regime applying in Northern Ireland which has no counterpart in Scotland.[35] It might, of course, be possible to argue that the general right to a fair hearing means that a person who asks for legal assistance should get it; but this scarcely takes us beyond what was said rather a long time ago by Lord Moncrieff in *H.M. Advocate v. Cunningham*[36] and *H.M. Advocate v. Fox.*[37] In *Robb*, Lord Penrose took the view that the matter of the fairness of the interview could be raised at the trial and Lord Cameron adopted a similar approach in *H.M. Advocate v. Campbell*[38] in which an unsuccessful attempt was made before trial to secure an order that the evidence of an identification parade, at which the accused had not been assisted by a solicitor, could not competently be led at trial.

Different considerations apply to compulsory powers to require answers to questions. In *Saunders v. United Kingdom*[39] a breach of Article 6(2) was found where the prosecution made extensive use at trial of answers obtained from the accused under compulsory powers in sections 432 and 442 of the Companies Act 1985. However, in *Brown v. Stott*[40] the Judicial Committee of the Privy Council held that Article 6(2) is not absolute. Lord Hope of Craighead explained that

"the jurisprudence of the European Court tells us that the questions that should be addressed when issues are raised about an alleged incompatibility with a right under Article 6 of the Convention are the following: (1) is the right which is in question an absolute right, or is it a right which is open to modification or restriction because it is not absolute? (2) if it is not absolute, does the modification or restriction which is contended for have a legitimate aim in the public interest? (3) if so, is there a reasonable relationship of proportionality between the means employed and the aim sought to be realised? The answer to the question whether the right is or is not absolute is to be found by examining the terms of the Article in the light of the judgments of the Court. The question whether a legitimate aim is being pursued enables account to be taken of the public interest in the rule of law. The principle of proportionality directs attention to the question whether a

---

[34] 1999 S.C.C.R. 971.
[35] See also *Paton v. Ritchie*, 2000 S.L.T. 151.
[36] 1939 J.C. 61.
[37] 1947 J.C. 30.
[38] 1999 S.C.C.R. 980.
[39] (1996) 23 E.H.R.R. 313.
[40] 2000 S.L.T. 59.

fair balance has been struck between the general interest of the community in the realisation of that aim and the protection of the fundamental rights of the individual."

In *Brown v. Stott*, the Board was concerned with section 172 of the 3.10 Road Traffic Act 1988. It was noted that the "means employed" was a question requiring a simple answer and that the aim pursued was the investigation of serious offences (section 172 does not apply to less serious and regulatory offences). The Board considered that the use in evidence of a reply to a section 172 requirement was proportionate where the offence being prosecuted was a contravention of section 5(1)(a) of the Road Traffic Act 1988.

It should be noted that, in *Saunders*, the Court pointed out that, as commonly understood in the legal systems of the Contracting Parties to the Convention and elsewhere, the right to silence does not extend to the use in criminal proceedings of material which may be obtained from the accused through the use of compulsory powers but which has an existence independent of the will of the suspect such as, *inter alia*, documents acquired pursuant to a warrant, breath, blood and urine samples and bodily tissue for the purpose of DNA testing.

3. Surveillance and search

Article 8

Article 8(1) provides that "Everyone has the right to respect for his 3.11 private and family life, his home and his correspondence". This has been one of the most dynamically interpreted provisions of the Convention and it has an extremely wide application. It is clear from a number of cases[41] that it will cover aspects of surveillance and search. If there is a breach of Article 8, it will make the obtaining of the evidence irregular; but that does not make the evidence inevitably inadmissible. In *Chinoy v. United Kingdom*,[42] the Commission was prepared to accept that there might well be occasions when irregularly (or, in that case, unlawfully) obtained evidence might be admitted. The European Court took a similar view in *Schenk v. Switzerland*[43] and, more recently, in *Khan v. United Kingdom*.[44]

The facts in *Khan* were that police officers investigating an allegation of drug trafficking against certain persons, including the applicant, had installed a listening device in a house occupied by one of those persons in circumstances which amounted to a breach

---

[41] For example, *Klass v. Germany* (1980) 2 E.H.R.R. 214 and *Funke v. France* (1994) 16 E.H.R.R. 297.
[42] Appl. 15199/89, September 4, 1991.
[43] (1991) 13 E.H.R.R. 242.
[44] [2000] Crim. L.R. 684.

of Article 8. We shall examine those circumstances in more detail below.[45] Tape recorded conversations obtained by using that listening device constituted the totality of the prosecution case against the applicant (who was prosecuted in an English court). He objected to the admissibility of the evidence of the tape recordings but the trial judge declined to exclude the evidence under section 78 of the Police and Criminal Evidence Act 1984 and the applicant thereafter pled guilty, whereupon he was sentenced to a period of imprisonment.

The applicant complained of, *inter alia*, a breach of Article 6(1) on the ground that the use as the sole evidence in his case of the material which had been obtained in breach of Article 8 of the Convention was not compatible with the fair hearing requirements of Article 6. The Court said, however, that

> "while Article 6 guarantees the right to a fair hearing, it does not lay down any rules on the admissibility of evidence as such, which is therefore primarily a matter for regulation under national law...It is not the role of the court to determine, as a matter of principle, whether particular types of evidence—for example, unlawfully obtained evidence—may be admissible or, indeed, whether the applicant was guilty or not. The question which must be answered is whether the proceedings as a whole, including the way in which the evidence was obtained, were fair. This involves an examination of the "unlawfulness" in question and, where violation of another convention right is concerned, the nature of the violation found."

The Court was much influenced by the fact that the trial court had the discretion to exclude the evidence as unfair and had decided not to do so. The Court held that the use at the applicant's trial of the secretly taped material did not conflict with the requirements of fairness guaranteed by Article 6(1) of the Convention.

Ashworth has maintained that *Schenk* "confirms that there is no automatic rule of exclusion to be deduced from Article 6(1), but it leaves open the question whether the exclusory discretion is exercised properly in a given case"[46] and it appears that *Khan* supports his position. Existing domestic law tells us that irregularities may be excused.[47] *Chinoy*, *Schenk* and *Khan* tell us that Convention law contemplates that possibility as well.

Article 8 follows a pattern common to many of the Convention rights in that it states a right and then states the circumstances in which interference with the right may be permitted. Under Article 8(2), before interference with the right is permitted it must, first, be

---

[45] See page 104.
[46] Andrew Ashworth, "Article 6 and the Fairness of Trials" [1999] Crim L.R. 261, 270.
[47] *Lawrie v. Muir*, 1950 J.C. 19.

in accordance with the law, secondly, it must be necessary, and thirdly, it must be in pursuit of one of the specified objectives. Those objectives include the prevention of disorder or crime and the protection of the rights and freedoms of others. In *Funke v. France*,[48] the European Court said that the exceptions provided for by Article 8(2) are to be interpreted narrowly and the need for them in a given case must be convincingly established and that the relevant legislation and practice must afford adequate and effective safeguards against abuse. On reading the cases, it becomes very clear that the European Court analyses Article 8 issues within a well established framework and we therefore follow that same framework in consideration here. That framework is:

(a)   Is there an interference with an Article 8 right?
(b)   Is the interference in accordance with the law?
(c)   Does the interference pursue one of the permitted objectives?
(d)   Is the interference necessary?

Is there an interference with an Article 8 right?

Depending on its nature, it is very possible that surveillance or search might constitute a failure to respect aspects of the right guaranteed by Article 8(1). "Private" life has been said to encompass "the right to *be* oneself, to *live* as oneself and to *keep* to oneself".[49] Certainly, it goes wider than privacy in the sense of protection from publicity. According to the Commission, in *X v. Iceland*,[50] it comprises also "the right to establish and develop relationships with other human beings especially in the emotional field, for the development and fulfilment of one's own personality". In *X and Y v. Netherlands*,[51] the Court said that the concept covers the physical and moral integrity of the person.   3.12

The concept of the home also receives a somewhat extended application. It includes, for example, a lawyer's office.[52]

Surveillance might, therefore, easily engage consideration of Article 8, subject to the qualification that the right is not entirely unlimited, and does not arise where there is no reasonable expectation of privacy. In *Friedl v. Austria*[53] there was no breach when the applicant was photographed by police officers during a demonstration in the street. Search of the home was found to

---

[48]   *Above.*
[49]   Nuala Mole, Mark Shaw and Tom de la Mare in Lord Lester of Herne Hill and David Pannick (eds), *Human Rights Law and Practice* (London, 1999), p.168.
[50]   5 DR 86 (1976).
[51]   *Above.*
[52]   *Niemitz v. Germany* (1992) 16 E.H.R.R. 97.
[53]   (1995) 21 E.H.R.R. 83.

engage Article 8 in *Funke v. France*[54] and it seems self evident that search of the person would engage that aspect of Article 8 which is concerned with private life. Interception of communications has also been found to engage Article 8.[55]

Is the interference in accordance with law?

3.13   The expression "in accordance with law" carries similar meaning to the word "lawful" in Article 5(1). What is clear from the case law is that a positive legal framework is required, though the law need not be statutory. The essential criterion is that it should be sufficiently precise and expressed with sufficient clarity to enable the citizen to know (with appropriate advice) when it is likely to apply to him, and to regulate his conduct accordingly.[56] It is, however, clear that administrative arrangements are inadequate[57] and in *Khan* the European Court rejected the United Kingdom's submission that the existence of Home Office Guidelines to govern surveillance by planting a listening device in someone's home constituted the necessary "law" for the purposes of Article 8(2). The Court noted that, since such guidelines were neither legally binding nor directly publicly accessible, there was no domestic law regulating the use of covert listening devices at the relevant time and held that the interference could not, therefore, be considered to be "in accordance with law" as required by Article 8(2).

Scots law has a large and well-developed body of law on search with and without warrant.[58] One aspect of that law was considered in light of Article 8 in *Birse v. H.M. Advocate*[59] in which the accused sought suspension of a search warrant under s.23(3) of the Misuse of Drugs Act 1971, on the grounds that it was unlawful and that the granting and enforcing of the warrant violated his Convention right. He argued that as no record had been kept of the proceedings and the justice himself had admitted that he could not recall the particular case or how he handled it and could only provide a statement of his invariable practice, he had been deprived of a proper basis for ensuring that the application had been considered properly. The accused also argued that the information placed before the justice, of recurring strange smells coming from windows on Fridays and Saturdays, was not a proper basis for suspecting under section 23(3) of the 1971 Act that someone was in possession

---

[54] (1994) 16 E.H.R.R. 297.

[55] See, for example, *Malone v. U.K.* (1984) 7 E.H.R.R. 14; *Campbell v. U.K.* (1992) 15 E.H.R.R. 157.

[56] *Kruslin v. France* (1990) 12 E.H.R.R. 528; *Mersch v. Luxembourg* 43 D.R. 34 (1985).

[57] *Malone.*

[58] See generally Alastair N Brown, *Criminal Evidence and Procedure: An Introduction,* (Edinburgh, 1996), p.35.

[59] 2000 S.L.T. 869.

of controlled drugs. He was, however, unsuccessful. It was held that the warrant was *ex facie* valid and the information given was sufficient for the granting of a warrant under section 23(3) and that the justice's statement of his invariable practice, taken with information from the Crown as to what, according to the police officer concerned, had happened on the occasion in question, was sufficient to establish that the justice had acted as an effective safeguard against any possible abuse by the police of their power of search.

As regards surveillance, the United Kingdom and Scottish Parliaments have passed the Regulation of Investigatory Powers Act 2000 and the Regulation of Investigatory Powers (Scotland) Act 2000 respectively, with a view to putting in place the necessary legal framework.

The legislation is complex and detailed analysis is not possible in the space available here.[60] In general, however, it may be said that the legislation is concerned with the interception of communications and with covert investigation techniques and seeks to ensure that the law clearly covers the purposes for which such techniques may be used, which authorities can use the powers and who should authorise each use of the powers. It also provides for independent judicial oversight and a means of dealing with complaints and redress for the individual. Covert surveillance is that which is undertaken in a manner calculated to ensure that the person subjected to it is not aware that it is taking place. The Acts do not seek to regulate less intrusive forms of surveillance of which the public is in any event generally aware. CCTV in town centres is the most obvious example.

In dealing with surveillance, the two Acts are concerned primarily with three sorts of activity. In practice, they will often overlap. The approach which the legislation takes is to provide for the development of statutory codes of practice (which will be capable of being updated quickly to take account of technological developments) and to put in place a framework of authorisations.

The first of the legislative concerns is "directed surveillance", which is surveillance undertaken in relation to a specific investigation in order to obtain information about a particular person. The second is the use of "covert human intelligence sources". In essence, this unattractive mouthful denotes undercover officers and participating informants. The use of either of these techniques will require authorisation from a police superintendent for the purpose of preventing or detecting crime or preventing disorder; in the interests of public safety; or for the purpose of protecting public health. This language clearly reflects aspects of Article 8(2) ECHR.

The third sort of surveillance is "intrusive surveillance" which is

---

[60] See, however, the annotated versions of the Acts in *Renton and Brown's Criminal Procedure Legislation* (looseleaf, W. Green).

surveillance carried out into things which are happening on residential premises or in any private vehicle. Authorisation for such surveillance will have to be given by a Chief Constable and only where necessary for the prevention or detection of serious crime. Serious crime is defined as that which might reasonably be expected to result in imprisonment for a first offence of three years or more, or involves the use of violence, or results in substantial financial gain, or involves a large number of persons in pursuit of a common purpose. These are, of course, intrinsically subjective judgements but it should not be thought that they are incapable of being reviewed. Article 8(2) ECHR goes on to require that any interference with the rights which Article 8 protects should be "necessary" and that includes the concept of proportionality. Chief Constables will be public authorities for the purposes of section 6 of the Human Rights Act and, even in a case of serious crime, a Chief Constable who authorises disproportionate surveillance will act unlawfully.

It is clear from *Klass v. Germany*[61] that the rule of law implies, *inter alia*, that an interference by the executive authorities with an individual's rights should be subject to an effective control which should normally be assured by the judiciary, at least in the last resort, judicial control offering the best guarantees of independence, impartiality and a proper procedure. The Acts therefore take advantage of the creation of Surveillance Commissioners by the Police Act 1997. Except in case of urgency, no intrusive surveillance will become effective until approved by a Commissioner. Moreover, the Chief Surveillance Commissioner will review the use of directed surveillance and of human resources. For the individual, redress will be available before a tribunal established by the United Kingdom Act.

Does the interference pursue one of the permitted objectives?

3.14   The permitted objectives are the interests of national security, public safety or the economic well-being of the country, the prevention of disorder or crime, the protection of health or morals, or the protection of the rights and freedoms of others. Generally it will be possible to see search or surveillance by law enforcement agencies as being in pursuit of the prevention of crime or for the protection of the rights and freedoms of others. Those rights and freedoms may include the Article 2 right to life (*e.g.* where it is drugs which are sought) and the Article 1 Protocol 1 right to property (*e.g.* where the police are attempting to recover stolen property).

---

[61] (1980) 2 E.H.R.R. 214.

Is the interference necessary?

In *Olsson v. Sweden*,[62] the European Court explained that the   3.15
notion of necessity "implies that an interference corresponds to a
pressing social need and in particular that it is proportionate to the
legitimate aim pursued". It is not synonymous with "indispensable"
but neither does it have the flexibility of "reasonable" or
"desirable".[63] The issue of pressing social need assumes particular
significance in the context of attempts by the state to regulate
aspects of a person's private life, such as his or her sexuality.[64] In a
criminal investigation context, the need to prevent crime is likely by
itself to amount to a pressing social need. This is not, however, to
say that the action taken will thereby also be proportionate. A
search of a suspect's home carried out in the small hours of the
morning might well be regarded as proportionate where a serious
firearms or drug trafficking offence is under investigation; but not
where the offence is a minor shoplifting.

Article 3

Article 3 provides that no-one shall be subjected to torture or to   3.16
inhuman or degrading treatment or punishment. The cases on
Article 3 in relation to the investigation of crime have all dealt with
rather extreme conduct[65] but it is clear that treatment which
produces humiliation or debasement above a certain threshold will
constitute degrading treatment.[66] It might be that in some
circumstances particularly intrusive search of the person will
constitute a breach of Article 3; though if it does so it is likely
that it will also breach Article 8 as disproportionate.

Article 6

Article 6 is concerned with the right to a fair hearing and will be   3.17
considered in more detail below, especially in relation to trial.[67]
Under the heading of surveillance and search, however, it is
important to note the case of *Teixeira de Castro v. Portugal*[68] in
which police officers hoped that through a drug addict and small

---

[62] (1988) 11 E.H.R.R. 259.
[63] *Handyside v. U.K.* (1979-80) 1 E.H.R.R. 737.
[64] *e.g. Norris v. Ireland* (1991) 13 E.H.R.R. 186.
[65] *Ireland v. U.K.* (1980) 2 E.H.R.R. 25; *Ribbitsch v. Austria* (1996) 21 E.H.R.R. 573;
    Aydin v. Turkey (1998) 25 E.H.R.R. 251; *Selmouni v. France* (2000) 29 E.H.H.R.
    403.
[66] *Tyrer v. U.K.* (1980) 2 E.H.R.R. 1; *Campbell and Cosans v. U.K.* (1982) 4
    E.H.R.R. 293.
[67] See page 115.
[68] (1998) 28 E.H.R.R. 101.

time dealer they would be able to identify a more significant drug supplier. They strayed into incitement. The European Court held that the use of undercover agents must be restricted and safeguards put in place even in cases concerning the fight against drug trafficking and that the public interest cannot justify the use of evidence obtained as a result of police incitement. The Court concluded that the two police officers' actions went beyond those of undercover agents because they instigated the offence and there was nothing to suggest that without their intervention it would have been committed. That intervention and its use in the impugned criminal proceedings meant that, from the outset, the applicant was deprived of a fair trial. Consequently, there had been a violation of Article 6(1).

3.18   This case should be contrasted with *Lüdi v. Switzerland*[69] in which the Court held that the mere fact that an undercover agent is used does not of itself represent a breach of Article 8 (this point was not analysed in relation to Article 6) and that a person who agrees to deal in drugs must be aware that he runs the risk of encountering such an agent—the implication being that he has no reasonable expectation of privacy. In *Teixeira de Castro*, the European Court distinguished *Lüdi* primarily on the basis that, in *Lüdi* an investigating judge had been aware of what was being done and that the police officer's role had been confined to acting as an undercover agent (by which the Court seems to have meant that there was no element of incitement).

BAIL

Introduction

Articles 5(3) and 5(4) make provision as to the restoration of liberty to a person who has been arrested.

Article 5(3)

3.19   Article 5(3) entitles the accused to trial within a reasonable time or to release pending trial. It is clear that, in Convention terms, if the accused is to be kept in custody there must be relevant and sufficient grounds for doing so. Reid suggests that, for a short period (by which she means a "matter of months"), suspicion itself suffices for keeping the accused in custody,[70] though in *Tomasi v. France*[71] it was held that suspicion alone was not enough to justify a remand in custody which lasted over five years. No exhaustive list of other reasons justifying the remand of the accused in custody

---

[69] (1993) 15 E.H.R.R. 173.
[70] Karen Reid, *A Practitioner's Guide to the European Convention on Human* Rights, (London, 1998), p.307.
[71] (1993) 15 E.H.R.R. 1.

exists. The principle was stated by the European Court in *Letellier v. France*[72] to be that the court before which the accused is brought must consider "all the facts arguing for and against the existence of a genuine requirement of public interest" for the remanding of the accused in custody. In *CC v. United Kingdom*,[73] the Commission said that "the judge must examine all the facts arguing for and against the existence of a genuine requirement of public interest justifying, with due regard to the presumption of innocence, a departure from the rule of respect for the accused's liberty".

It follows from this that it is no longer enough for the Crown simply to tell the sheriff at committal for further examination on petition that there are further enquiries.[74] Applying Article 5(3), the Lord Justice-General (Roger) said, in *Burn, Petitioner*,[75] that

> "the Crown must provide sufficient general information relating to the particular case to allow the sheriff to consider the merits of their motion that the accused should be committed to prison and detained there for further examination. What will be required will depend on the facts of the particular case and for that reason we cannot lay down any hard-and-fast rule. We are satisfied, however, that it will not be necessary for the Crown to disclose operational details. On the other hand, where, for example, the Crown oppose bail on the ground of the risk that the accused would interfere with witnesses, the procurator fiscal depute should be in a position to explain the basis for that fear. The same would be apply where the opposition is based on a fear that the accused would interfere with a possible search of premises which the police wished to carry out."

It is possible to classify the Strasbourg cases in four categories —prevention of crime, danger of flight, risk of interference with the course of justice and prevention of public disorder. This categorisation is, of course, no more than an analytical tool. As to the prevention of crime, it was held in *Toth v. Austria*[76] that previous convictions could be relied on as giving reasonable grounds to fear that further offences would be committed. The danger of flight will vary according to the strength of the accused's ties with the jurisdiction and the court should consider financial guarantees (which include, but are not limited to, money bail) as a means of offsetting the risk.[77] The risk of interference with the course of justice requires to be kept under review and, if it disappears,

---

[72] (1992) 14 E.H.R.R. 83.
[73] [1999] Crim.L.R. 228.
[74] See *Boyle v. Normand*, 1995 S.L.T. 162.
[75] 2000 S.C.C.R. 384 (over-ruling *Boyle v. Normand*).
[76] (1992) 14 E.H.R.R. 551.
[77] *Letellier*; *Matznetter v. Austria* (1979-80) 1 E.H.R.R. 198.

liberation should follow unless there are other grounds for keeping the accused in custody.[78] Finally, the cases on prevention of public disorder have related to terrorist offences[79] or the exceptional circumstances of a high profile, premeditated murder.[80]

Scots law on bail was revised in the Bail, Judicial Appointments etc. (Scotland) Act 2000 with a view to bringing the law fully into compliance with the requirements of the Convention. A new section 22A was inserted into the 1995 Act. It requires a decision on bail to be taken within 24 hours of the first appearance of an accused person on petition or complaint. If no decision is taken by the end of that period the accused must be liberated forthwith.

The Convention obligation to consider bail applies even where the accused is already in custody on some other ground and a new section 23A is inserted into the 1995 Act to deal with precisely this situation. In terms of that section, a person may be admitted to bail even though he or she has been refused bail in respect of another crime or offence or is serving a sentence of imprisonment. However, a decision to admit a person to bail in that situation does not operate so as to liberate the person from custody (because he or she is held on the warrant relating to the other matter(s)).

The principle that a person arrested must be able to seek bail from a very early stage has also led to the amendment of section 32 of the 1995 Act so as to make it possible for the accused to appeal against the refusal of bail between Committal for Further Examination and Full Committal.

There is no room in Convention law for any distinction in treatment based on the nature of the offence charged and so section 24 of the 1995 Act was amended so that it provides that all crimes and offences are bailable. The old exception in the case of murder and treason is removed. Section 26 of the 1995 Act, which made bail unavailable in certain cases of attempted murder, culpable homicide, rape or attempted rape, was repealed in whole.

Article 5(4)

3.20   Article 5(4) provides that a person who has been deprived of his liberty must be able to take proceedings whereby the lawfulness of his detention is decided speedily by a court. This is a different issue from the *appropriateness* of a remand in custody, which is dealt with under Article 5(3). Under Article 5(4) it is the *lawfulness* of the detention which is in issue. It seems clear that, while Scots law contemplates committal for further examination on petition on the basis of something less than a sufficiency of evidence[81] (which must mean reasonable suspicion), full committal on petition will only be

---

[78] *Kemmache (No. 1) v. France* (1992) 14 E.H.R.R. 520.
[79] *e.g. Tomasi.*
[80] *Letellier.*
[81] *Alison, ii*, 134; *Macdonald,* (5th ed.), p.203.

lawful if there is a sufficiency of evidence.[82] It is accepted by the Crown that the same test applies where an accused is detained in custody pending trial on a summary complaint. It follows from Article 5(4) that the accused must be placed in a position to dispute the lawfulness of the detention and that means that he must be placed in a position to dispute the Crown's (hitherto implied) contention that it has a sufficiency of evidence.

If the accused is given no information about the evidence which the Crown has, he cannot meaningfully bring under review the lawfulness of the detention and Article 5(4) cannot be satisfied. In *Lamy v. Belgium*[83] it was held that the principle of equality of arms applies to Article 5(4) so that the accused must be afforded the opportunity to present his case under conditions which do not place him at a substantial disadvantage *vis-à-vis* the Crown.[84]

The Crown has taken the view that the option of doing nothing about this is not open and that the accused should be placed in a position to debate the sufficiency of the Crown case on paper at full committal. In order to place him in a position to do so, the Crown has begun to provide the custody statement—a written summary of the evidential basis of its case. It is therefore open to the accused to debate the Crown's contention that the summary discloses a paper sufficiency but not to attempt to open up the issue of the reliability of the information in the Crown's possession, since that is a matter for trial.[85] In *Brown v. Selfridge*,[86] the defence had persuaded a sheriff that the inclusion of a custody statement on a petition was prejudicial to the accused and rendered the petition incompetent. The argument was that a sheriff, appraised of the nature and strength of the evidence, might take that into account in deciding whether or not to grant bail. The High Court regarded this fear as illusory and passed the Bill.

THE CHARGE

The Convention rights do not deal in terms with the content of the charges (except to prohibit, in Article 7, retrospective criminalisation of conduct). However, Article 6(3) gives everyone charged with a criminal offence certain minimum rights. They include in particular the Article 6(3)(a) right of the person charged to be

3.21

---

[82] *Macdonald,* (5th ed), p.204; *Alison, ii,* 137; *Adair v. McGarry,* 1933 S.L.T. 482 at 487 *per* L.J.-C. (Alness); *Currie v. McGlennan,* 1989 S.L.T. 872 at 873 *per* L.J.-C. (Ross).

[83] (1989) 11 E.H.R.R. 529.

[84] *Dombo Deheer BV v. Netherlands* (1994) 18 E.H.R.R. 213.

[85] It is understood that there is in currency the belief that the Lord Advocate has given an "undertaking" to provide a custody statement. This belief is mistaken. The production of the statement is a tactic adopted by the Crown to meet what it perceived as a risk that persons would be liberated on Art. 5(4) grounds.

[86] 1999 S.C.C.R. 809.

informed promptly, in a language which he understands and in detail of the nature and cause of the accusation against him. This matter is dealt with in Scottish practice by the information provided on the indictment or complaint.

Article 6(3)(a) has on its face the following elements:

(a) the accused must be informed of the nature and cause of the accusation;
(b) that information must be given promptly;
(c) that information must be detailed; and
(d) that information must be given in a language which the accused understands.

It is worth noting that, in *Bricmont v. Belgium*[87] the Commission said that the general purpose of this is to give the accused person the information he needs to prepare his defence.

The nature and cause of the accusation

3.22   In *Gea Catalan v. Spain*[88] the Court approved of the Commission's interpretation of Article 6(3)(a). What the Commission said was that "the accused is entitled to be informed not only of the cause of the accusation, *i.e.* the material facts alleged against him which form the basis of the accusation, but also of the nature of the accusation, *i.e.* the legal classification of those material facts". The circumstances in that case were that the applicant had taken advantage of his position as an employee of the Bank of Fomento to cause the bank to discount in his favour a number of bills of exchange which he had himself drawn, using false names. He was charged with obtaining property by deception as provided for in the Spanish Criminal Code. In pre-trial submissions the public prosecutor referred to a statutory aggravation of the offence but as a result of a typing error the reference given was to Article 529(1) of the Criminal Code; it should have been to Article 529(7). The applicant complained that he had not been informed of a component of the charge against him. The Court, however, held that the discrepancy complained of was clearly the result of a mere clerical error. It could not see how the applicant could complain that he had not been informed of all of the components of the charge since the prosecution case must have been obvious from its pre-trial submissions and since it should have been obvious that the aggravation provided for in Article 529(1) had no application to the facts alleged but that Article 529(7) did. It therefore held that there was no breach.

---

[87]   48 D.R. 106 (1986).
[88]   (1995) 20 E.H.R.R. 266.

In an earlier case,[89] the Commission had said that "in criminal matters the provision of full, detailed information concerning the charges against a defendant and consequently the legal classification that the court might adopt in the matter is a prerequisite for ensuring that the proceedings are fair".[90]

Giving the information promptly

Next, the accused is entitled to be given the information "promptly". In *Application against Italy*,[91] the Commission held that the principal underlying purpose of the requirement for promptness, by which compliance will be judged, is to afford the accused time for the preparation of his defence.   3.23

Detailed information

In *Broziek v. Italy*,[92] the European Court was satisfied with an indictment which specified date and place, listed the offences charged, referred to the relevant Article of the Criminal Code and identified the victim. In *H.M. Advocate v. McLean*,[93] the High Court held that a charge of attempted murder which took a latitude of 27 days was sufficiently detailed to meet the requirements of Article 6(3)(a), the Crown having explained that it knew only that the actual date of the offence was "a few days" prior to the last date specified in the charge and that the latitude taken was less than that implied by the law where a single date is specified. The Lord Justice General said that the contention that the charge did not meet the requirements set out in *Broziek* was "too extreme a proposition" and that the amount of detail required would vary with the nature of the allegation. The High Court held that a four week latitude informed the appellant in detail of the nature and cause of the charge against him.   3.24

Language

The ability of the accused to understand the proceedings is an important component in the fairness of the trial, and so Article 6(3)(e) contains a specific guarantee of the free assistance of an interpreter if the accused cannot understand or speak the language   3.25

---

[89] *Chichlian and Ekindjian v. France* (1991) 13 E.H.R.R. 553 (reported on another point).
[90] Quoted by the Commission itself in *Gea Catalan*.
[91] *Appl. 10889/84* 56 D.R. 40 (1988).
[92] (1990) 12 E.H.R.R. 371.
[93] 2000 S.C.C.R. 112.

used in court. In *Kamasinski v. Austria,*[94] the European Court, whilst holding that the inadequacy of translation in the particular case did not in fact result in an unfair trial, did express clear views on the question of the translation of documents, including the indictment. So far as the general right to interpretation of documents is concerned, what they said was as follows:

> "The right, stated in paragraph 3(e) of Article 6, to the free assistance of an interpreter applies not only to oral statements made at the trial hearing but also to documentary material and the pre-trial proceedings. Paragraph 3(e) signifies that a person 'charged with a criminal offence' who cannot understand or speak the language used in court has the right to the free assistance of an interpreter for the translation or interpretation of all those documents or statements in the proceedings instituted against him which it is necessary for him to understand or to have rendered into the court's language in order to have the benefit of a fair trial. However, paragraph 3(e) does not go so far as to require a written translation of all items of written evidence or official documents in the procedure. The interpretative assistance provided should be such as to enable the defendant to understand the case against him and to defend himself, notably by being able to put before the court his version of events."

As regards the indictment in particular, the Court said that, whilst Article 6(3)(a)

> "does not specify that the relevant information should be given in writing or translated in written form for a foreign defendant, it does point to the need for special attention to be paid to the notification of the 'accusation' to the defendant. An indictment plays a crucial role in the criminal process, in that it is from the moment of its service that the defendant is formally put on written notice of the factual and legal basis of the charges against him. A defendant not conversant with the court's language may in fact be put at a disadvantage if he is not also provided with a written translation of the indictment in a language he understands."

The Court did not hold, and has not held, that the provision of a written translation of the indictment will always be necessary to the fairness of the trial. In the *Kamasinski* case itself, the Court held that there was no unfairness despite the lack of such a translation. In so holding, they were influenced by a number of factors:

(1) the indictment was not complex;

---

[94] (1991) 13 E.H.R.R. 36.

(2) the applicant had been questioned at length by the police and investigating judges and must have been aware of the accusations levelled against him;

(3) notwithstanding the absence of a translation, the applicant had challenged the indictment on the ground of insufficiency of evidence;

(4) at no time did the applicant request that the indictment be translated; and

(5) when asked at the start of the trial, the applicant had told the trial court that he understood the charges.

THE TRIAL

Introduction; the ambit of, and proper approach to, Article 6(1)

Proceedings to which Article 6 applies

Article 6 of the European Convention on Human Rights makes provision as to the fairness of trials. It provides that, in the determination of any criminal charge against him, everyone is entitled to a fair and public hearing within a reasonable time by an independent and impartial tribunal established by law.   3.26

It should be noted, first, that Article 6 applies to the *determination* of civil rights and obligations and of criminal charges. Several cases concerning civil rights and obligations have emphasised that Article 6 does not apply to proceedings which do not determine civil rights or criminal charges.[95] There have been fewer cases on the point arising out of criminal matters but it appears that Article 6 does not apply to those parts of proceedings which do not bear upon the determination of the charge. In particular, it does not apply to proceedings relating to deprivation of liberty which do not bear on the ultimate determination of the charge because they are dealt with by Article 5.[96]

The Court's approach to Article 6

Article 6(1) contains an over-riding requirement that the hearing should be "fair", and a number of specific requirements. The requirement for fairness has been said to have an "open-ended, residual quality"[97] but one of its aspects is that there must be equality of arms between the parties, which means that each party   3.27

---

[95] These include *Brady v. U.K.* (1981) 3 E.H.R.R. 297 and *Kosiek v. Germany* (1987) 9 E.H.R.R. 328.

[96] *X v. Federal Republic of Germany*, Appl. 6541/74 1 DR 82 (1974).

[97] DJ Harris, M O'Boyle and C Warbrick, *Law of the European Convention on Human Rights* (London, 1995), p.202.

must be afforded a reasonable opportunity to present his case, including his evidence, under conditions which do not place him at a substantial disadvantage *vis à vis* his opponent.[98]

Other commentators have noted that "compliance with specific rights set out in Article 6 will not alone guarantee that there has been a fair trial. It is not possible to state in the abstract the content of the requirement of a fair hearing: this can only be considered in the context of the trial as a whole".[99] The concept of the "trial as a whole" includes any appeal proceedings[1] and even where there has been unfairness in the trial itself, the European Court has been prepared to hold that such unfairness has been cured by what has happened on appeal.[2] The focus of the European Court may therefore be said to be on the overall process of *determination* of the criminal charge rather than on the set-piece hearing itself. But by the same token, the focus is on the *process*. The case law of the European Court does not comment on what the *outcome* of the trial should have been and even where it finds that there has been unfairness in the trial proceedings it refrains, sometimes explicitly,[3] from saying that the accused should have been acquitted.

The emphasis placed by the European Court on over-riding fairness may be illustrated by *Asch v. Austria*,[4] in which the Court held that there was no breach, even where there was a *lack* of compliance with one of the specific guarantees construed narrowly (Article 6(3)(d)), provided there was fairness over the procedure as a whole. It is important to note that the European Court said, in *Doorson v. The Netherlands*[5]:

> "It is true that Article 6 does not explicitly require the interests of witnesses in general, and of those of victims called upon to testify in particular, to be taken into consideration. However, their life, liberty or security of person may be at stake, as may interests coming generally within the ambit of Article 8 of the Convention. Such interests of witnesses and victims are in principle protected by other, substantive provisions of the Convention, which imply that Contracting States should organise their criminal proceedings in such a way that those

---

[98] See generally Reid, *op cit*, 81.

[99] Francis G Jacobs and Robin CA White, *The European Convention on Human Rights* (2nd ed., Oxford, 1996), p.124.

[1]   *Edwards v. U. K.* (1992) 15 E.H.R.R. 417; *Crociani, Palmiotti, Tanassi and Lefebre D'Ovidio v. Italy* (1981) 22 D.R. 147.

[2]   By contrast, in *Hoekstra v. H.M. Advocate (No. 1)*, 2000 S.C.C.R. 263, the High Court did not accept that any unfairness in the hearing arose when an Advocate Depute who had formerly advised one of the appellants proposed (until he discovered the identity of the appellants) to represent the Crown at a procedural hearing in the appeal; he passed the papers on as soon as he became aware of the position.

[3]   *e.g. Saunders v. U.K. above.*

[4]   (1993) 15 E.H.R.R. 597.

[5]   (1996) 22 E.H.R.R. 330.

interests are not unjustifiably imperilled. Against this background, principles of fair trial also require that in appropriate cases the interests of the defence are balanced against those of witnesses and victims called upon to testify."

This may be seen in the context of the European Court's earlier remark in *Soering v. United Kingdom*[6] that "inherent in the whole of the Convention is a search for a fair balance between the demands of the general interest of the community and the requirements of the protection of the individual's fundamental rights" (a remark made in the context of Article 3 ECHR, which might well be the most absolute of the Convention rights).   3.28

The High Court has, in *Montgomery and Coulter v. H.M. Advocate*[7] noted the importance of over-riding fairness. In that case, the Lord Justice-General said that

"the only right which Article 6(1) protects is the right to a fair trial and so, in considering a case founded upon that Article, the Court is concerned only with whether the appellants will receive a fair trial...The appellants' rights under the Human Rights Convention exist not to punish the Crown for what may or may not have been unwise decisions, but to ensure that any trial which the appellants face is fair. In this respect, the protection afforded to accused persons under the Convention is similar to the protection afforded by the plea of oppression."

Notice should be taken of *X v. Austria*[8] in which it was said that a virulent press campaign against the accused might violate the right to fair trial, though the case law recognises that much may depend on the way in which the trial judge deals with possible prejudice in directing the jury.[9] Attempts in Scotland to challenge the *vires* of a prosecution on this ground have not so far met with significant success.[10]

Trial in public

The first specific requirement of Article 6(1) is for a hearing in public. In *Axen v. Germany*,[11] the Court said that the purpose of the guarantee of a public hearing is to protect litigants[12] "against the administration of justice in secret with no public scrutiny; it is also one of the means whereby confidence in the courts, superior and inferior, can be maintained. By rendering the administration of   3.29

---

[6] (1989) 11 E.H.R.R. 439, Judgement, para. 89.
[7] 2000 S.C.C.R. 1044 at 1069.
[8] 11 C.D. 31 (1963).
[9] *X v. U.K.* 2 Digest 688 (1978).
[10] See *Montgomery v. H.M. Advocate*, 2001 S.L.T. 37.
[11] (1984) 6 E.H.R.R. 195.
[12] *Axen* concerned a question of civil right.

justice visible, publicity contributes to the achievement of the aim of Article 6(1), namely a fair trial". The Article goes on, however, to authorise the exclusion of the public and even of the press "in the interest of morals, public order or national security in a democratic society, where the interests of juveniles or the protection of the private life of the parties so require, or to the extent strictly necessary in the opinion of the court in special circumstances where publicity would prejudice the interests of justice".

In *British Broadcasting Corporation, Petitioners*,[13] the High Court rejected an argument that Article 10 ECHR entitled the petitioners to broadcast a particular trial.

This part of Article 6 has been the subject of relatively limited consideration by the Strasbourg organs. There was comment in *Campbell and Fell v. United Kingdom*[14] that ordinary criminal proceedings nearly always take place in public, notwithstanding security problems; but this passage[15] was descriptive and not normative. Moreover, the reference was made simply to draw a distinction between an ordinary trial and prison disciplinary proceedings (with which that case was concerned). In *X v. Austria*[16] the Commission approved the exclusion of the public from a trial for sexual offences against children, without identifying the reasoning which led to that conclusion; so the case scarcely goes beyond what is said in the plain words of the Convention. In *Monnell and Morris v. United Kingdom*[17] the European Court held that a decision to grant or refuse of leave to appeal, the question being whether the appellant has demonstrated the existence of arguable grounds, was of such a limited nature as not to call for oral argument at a public hearing or the personal appearance of the prospective appellant. In *Martin v. United Kingdom*[18] the Court applied *Monnell and Morris* and held that an application which attacked the sifting of appeals by the High Court of Justiciary was manifestly ill founded.[19]

Most recently, the Court has dealt with the issue of a public hearing in *V v. United Kingdom* (and *T v. United Kingdom*).[20] The facts of the crime committed by Thomson and Venables, the two applicants, were described by Lord Reed, the British Judge, as "appalling". When they were 10 years old, the applicants had played truant from school and abducted a two-year-old boy from a shopping precinct, taken him on a journey of over two miles, battered him to death and left him on a railway line to be run

---

[13] 2000 S.C.C.R. 533.
[14] (1985) 7 E.H.R.R. 165.
[15] Para. 87.
[16] 2 Digest 438 (1965).
[17] *Above.*
[18] 1999 S.C.C.R. 941.
[19] The application was founded on Article 6(3)(c).
[20] (2000) 30 E.H.R.R. 121.

over. They were tried over three weeks in public, before a judge and jury. Throughout the proceedings, the arrival of the defendants was greeted by a hostile crowd. On occasions, attempts were made to attack the vehicles bringing them to court. In the courtroom, the press benches and public gallery were full. Many aspects of the arrangements for the trial were criticised by those acting for the boys and those criticisms were in some respects upheld by the European Court. It is of particular relevance here that the Court said that, in respect of a young child charged with a grave offence attracting high levels of media and public interest, it will be necessary to conduct the hearing in such a way as to reduce as far as possible his or her feelings of intimidation and inhibition. The Court regarded it as noteworthy that in England and Wales children charged with less serious crimes are dealt with in special Youth Courts, from which the general public is excluded and in relation to which there are imposed automatic reporting restrictions on the media. Whilst public trials might (as the Government had argued) serve the general interest in the open administration of justice, where appropriate in view of the age and other characteristics of the child and the circumstances surrounding the criminal proceedings, this general interest could be satisfied by a modified procedure providing for selected attendance rights and judicious reporting.[21]

Trial within a reasonable time

Article 6(1) requires that, in the determination of a criminal charge against him, everyone is entitled to a hearing within a reasonable time. The development of Scots law on this aspect of Article 6 began with *Little v. H.M.Advocate*,[22] in which the indictment charged a number of sexual offences, up to and including the rape of children. The offences were alleged to have been committed during the 1980s and the accused had been charged by the police in January 1988. Thereafter, the case had been reported to the procurator fiscal. The Crown decided, by April 1988, that the case should be marked "no proceedings". However, as a result of the destruction of old papers, the reasons for that decision were no longer known when, in September 1997, further allegations were made against the same man. On this occasion the Crown chose to proceed in respect both of the "new" allegations and those which had been reported in 1988.[23] Understandably enough, the defence wished to challenge the procedure on the basis of delay. The indictment had been served before the entry into force

3.30

---

[21] At the time of writing it was understood that the age of criminal responsibility in Scotland was under review.

[22] 1999 S.C.C.R. 625.

[23] This pattern suggests that the decision in 1988 was based on insufficiency of evidence but that the combination of the older and newer charges amounted to an arguable sufficiency as regards the older charges; but this is speculation.

of section 57 of the Scotland Act and accordingly the remedies available to the defence did not include the Article 6 guarantee. What was available was a plea in bar of trial, in which the defence was unsuccessful. The Court considered that it could not be said, prior to evidence being led, that there existed a risk of prejudice so grave that no direction by the trial judge could be expected to remove it. It was observed, however, that it remained open to the trial judge to discontinue the proceedings if, in the course of evidence, it became clear that there was such prejudice.

After that decision but before the trial, section 57 of the Scotland Act 1998 entered into force and Mr Little relied on that section to challenge as *ultra vires* the Lord Advocate's intention to proceed to trial against him on the older charges. This argument could only be sustained if the test to be applied was different from that set out in *McFadyen*. If the point resolved itself into whether or not the delay resulted in prejudice, then the issue was already the subject of a judicial decision as regards Mr Little.

The argument was heard by Lord Kingarth. He considered in particular what was said in *Eckle v. Germany*[24] and took the view that Article 6 of the Convention requires the prosecution, in a case in which delay might be said to be inordinate, to provide a satisfactory explanation. In *Little*, the reason for the 1988 decision was unknown. The Crown was therefore unable to offer an explanation and so Lord Kingarth held that to proceed to trial on the older charges would be *ultra vires*. The Crown did not appeal but shortly afterwards, there was a defence appeal in another case, *McNab v. H.M.Advocate*.[25] At first instance in that case, Lord Nimmo-Smith had agreed with the opinion of Lord Kingarth in *Little* that it is not necessary, in a case which turns on Article 6 ECHR, that the accused should be able to demonstrate that he has suffered prejudice by the delay. He did not, however, consider that the delay in *McNab* was unreasonable. On appeal, this approach was confirmed. It is, the Appeal Court said,

> "important to note that there is a clear distinction between a plea based on oppression in the ordinary sense and a plea based on a right under Article 6(1). The former is concerned with the question whether, by reason of delay or some other cause, the prospects of the accused receiving a fair trial have been gravely prejudiced...The latter, on the other hand, is concerned with the alleged failure to bring a case to trial within a reasonable time. It follows that, in order to demonstrate that it is incompatible with his or her right for the prosecutor to insist on the trial, the accused does not require to show that prejudice has been or is likely to be suffered thereby."

---

[24] (1983) 5 E.H.R.R. 1
[25] 2000 S.L.T. 99.

The reasoning in *Little*, which was confirmed in *McNab*, represents 3.31
a clear development in the law, with the High Court of Justiciary
saying explicitly that existing Scots law and Convention law were
not the same. It is now possible for the defence to argue that it is
ultra vires for the Crown to proceed to trial after a long and
unexplained delay even though it cannot be shown that there has
been prejudice. There is no reason to suppose that this development
would have occurred had it not been for the incorporation of the
Convention rights; though the significance which prejudice might
now have seems not to be finally settled yet and that is a matter of
great importance to which we shall return.

Here, however, we need to note that there is an irony in all of
this. In the practice of the Strasbourg organs, some breaches
constituted by not holding the hearing within a reasonable time
may be "cured" by mitigating the sentence.[26] By making the matter
one of *vires* so that the prosecution cannot proceed at all, the
Scotland Act—presumably unintentionally—brings about a more
extreme result than does the Convention itself. (It remains possible
that the High Court will address this anomaly in one of several
cases outstanding at the time of writing.)

Since *Little* and *McNab*, there has been a series of cases in which
aspects of this new law have been considered and refined. We
may—somewhat tentatively—extract the following principles;

- The period to be taken into consideration does not necessarily
  commence on the first occasion on which the suspect (and
  eventual accused) learns that he is under investigation. In
  Convention law, the period commences when the accused has
  been charged, which means, for Convention purposes, the date
  when official notification is given to him by a competent
  authority that it is alleged that he has committed an offence, or
  the date from which his situation is substantially affected as a
  result of the suspicion against him.[27] The High Court of
  Justiciary has drawn a distinction between investigation and
  notification.[28] In a police complaint case, the taking by the
  investigator of the notebook of the police officer under
  investigation does not amount to "notification".[29] In a case
  involving child abuse the taking of steps by those responsible for
  the welfare of the victim, without reference to the police or to the
  procurator fiscal, does not start the clock.[30]

---

[26] *Neubeck v. Germany*, 41 D.R. 13 (1985); *H v. Germany*, 41 D.R. 252 41 (1985).

[27] *Eckle v. Germany*, above.

[28] *Robb v. H.M.Advocate*, 2000 J.C. 368 at 374 and 377; *Reilly v. H.M.Advocate*, 2000 S.C.C.R. 879.

[29] *Procurator Fiscal, Linlithgow v. Watson and Burrows*, April 27, 2001, unreported.

[30] *McLean v. H.M.Advocate*, 2000 J.C. 140.

- The correct approach is for the court to consider whether the period involved is *prima facie* unreasonable. Only if it so considers does the *onus* pass to the prosecutor to explain the delay.[31]

- There is no generally "appropriate" time required, either for the police to report a matter to the Procurator Fiscal, or thereafter for any of the stages which lead to eventual indictment. Every case has to be examined on its own facts.[32] It is, however, the period as a whole that is important[33] and it is not correct to adopt a piecemeal approach either by the defence criticising individual periods of inactivity in a case which as a whole proceeds within a reasonable time[34] or by the Crown seeking to justify each individual chapter of the time taken in a case which, overall, has taken too long.[35] The period to be taken into account lasts until the determination of the charge and that includes any appeal.[36]

- What will amount to a reasonable time will be determined in light of existing Scots law standards and not by reference to the particular periods of time which the Strasbourg Court has in the past regarded as unreasonable.[37] Notwithstanding the Lord Justice-General's recognition in *H.M.Advocate v. McGlinchey and Renicks*[38] that the Convention applies an international standard and that exclusive concentration on national standards would result in the application of Article 6(1) differing as between the States Parties to ECHR, this has meant in practice that the threshold of unreasonableness has been set rather lower in Scotland than elsewhere.

3.32
- An assertion that there has been, even *prima facie*, some unreasonableness will be justified only if some factual basis for inferring such unreasonableness can be identified and averred.[39]

- "It will be easy, but...quite wrong, to describe the timescales achieved by, say, a busy Procurator Fiscal's department as demonstrating some kind of 'failure', merely because greater resources would have made it possible to deal with more cases faster. Correspondingly, it is inappropriate to describe the improvements which could thus theoretically be achieved with greater resources as a 'remedy' for such a 'failure', which it is somehow the duty of the funding authorities to fulfil."[40]

---

[31] *McNab v. H.M.Advocate.*
[32] *Gibson v. H.M.Advocate,* 2001 S.C.C.R. 51.
[33] *Smith v. H.M.Advocate,* 2000 S.C.C.R. 926; *Procurator Fiscal, Linlithgow v. Watson and Burrows.*
[34] *H.M.Advocate v. McGlinchey and Renicks,* 2000 S.C.C.R. 593.
[35] *Kane v. H.M.Advocate,* May 4, 2001, unreported.
[36] *Neumeister v. Austria* (1979-80) 1 E.H.R.R. 91; *Monnell and Morris.*
[37] *McNab*; *McGlinchey and Renicks.*
[38] Above.
[39] *Gibson.*
[40] *Gibson, per* Lord Prosser.

- The right to a hearing within a reasonable time does not, in a case in which there is an insufficiency of evidence, preclude the prosecution authorities from keeping a file open against the possibility of a change in circumstances making it possible to proceed. In *Robb v. H.M.Advocate*,[41] Lord Prosser said that:

> "If at the beginning of the relevant period there is a clear insufficiency of evidence, or if the competent authorities reasonably consider that to be the position, the passage of time thereafter, with no further proceedings being taken will be unsurprising. In some cases, it will be possible to say that further investigations should have been undertaken or that arrangements should be made to review the case. A failure to take proper investigative steps may well constitute unreasonable conduct...[but]...it does not seem to us to be unreasonable to keep the file open for review, when serious allegations have been made. A lapse of time in unchanging circumstances may not be attributable to the State or entail unreasonable delay on the part of the State."

- It is legitimate for the prosecutor to prioritise cases and that process is recognised to be imprecise. In deciding upon priorities, a wide discretion is inevitable.[42] However, particular characteristics of the individual affected by the delay can be a relevant factor, insofar as they render the delay particularly prejudicial. This is especially true of cases involving child accused.[43]

Two matters remain for consideration. The first is the relevance (if any) of the fact that a case is particularly simple. In line with the Strasbourg case law, complexity will be a relevant explanation for a longer period of preparation, as it was in *Crummock (Scotland) Ltd v. H.M.Advocate*[44] in which careful investigation had to be made into matters of scientific complexity. It does not, however, necessarily follow that simplicity will require greater expedition. In *Procurator Fiscal Linlithgow v. Watson and Burrows*,[45] the accused persons were police officers who were charged with perjury. At the conclusion of the trial out of which that charge arose, the trial judge had said that he considered that the officers had lied about whether or not they had taken a person, charged with vandalism, back to the scene of the crime to have him identified by witnesses (without any of the protections appropriate to an identification). There were only four potential witnesses. On any   3.33

---

[41] 2000 S.C.C.R. 354.
[42] *Gibson.*
[43] *H.M.Advocate v. DP and SM,* February 16, 2001, unreported.
[44] 2000 J.C. 408.
[45] Above.

view, the case was a simple one. The person in the prosecutor's office to whom it fell to prepare the case did almost nothing with it for seven months because she was dealing with other, more serious, cases. That contributed to an overall delay of about 25 months which the majority of the Court regarded as unreasonable. However, Lord Hamilton, dissenting, noted the importance of dealing very thoroughly with complaints against the police (as indeed did the majority) but then went on to say that

> "simplicity is not of itself a reason for giving a case priority over other cases. To do so would amount, within the scope of defined resources, to postponing more complex cases. But a wide discretion must inevitably be accorded to the prosecuting authority in relation to the ordering of cases, including their preparation. Unless it is demonstrated that in the circumstances of a particular case that discretion was unreasonably exercised (or not exercised at all) no unreasonableness can in that respect be implied".

The majority did not directly address the significance that simplicity should have in prioritisation and accordingly the weight which should be given to Lord Hamilton's comments in dissent is uncertain. There is, however, clearly an issue there to be resolved in due course.

The second matter is the issue of prejudice. It was established in *Little* and *McNab* that prejudice does not have to be established before the defence can get the benefit of the right to a hearing within a reasonable time. At first, that was regarded as indicating that prejudice had become irrelevant. That, however, is clearly not the case. Rather, its significance has altered. In *Gibson*, Lord Prosser said that

> "While prejudice is not an essential element in breach of Article 6(1), it is in our opinion obvious that if the passage of time is likely to be prejudicial to the accused in a given case, that will weigh heavily in favour of giving that case priority over others where such prejudice is not regarded as likely. In this respect absence of prejudice is very relevant to the issue of reasonableness".

This echoed Lord Nimmo Smith's remark in *McGlinchey and Renicks*, that

> "While it is not necessary for the present respondents to be able to demonstrate that they have been prejudiced by such delay as there has been, *the absence of any prejudice appears to me to be a factor which may legitimately be taken into account* in considering whether the proceedings have taken place within a reasonable time".[46]

---

[46] Emphasis added.

And prejudice to the child accused was a matter on which Lord Reed placed considerable significance in *H.M.Advocate v. DP and SM*.[47] Looking at the cases overall, it appears, it can be said that, while it is clear that it is no longer necessary for the defence to establish prejudice before a plea in bar of trial can succeed, it is equally clear that prejudice will be a significant factor—and sometimes a very significant factor—in determining the reasonableness of any delay. Prejudice, therefore, has moved from being a prerequisite of a successful plea in bar to being a material consideration.

Trial by an independent court

The next element particularly specified by Article 6(1) is that the tribunal which determines the charge should be independent and impartial and established by law. Notwithstanding the publicity it received, it is not necessary here to consider the detail of *Starrs v. Ruxton*[48] because it was concerned with a category of judge—the temporary sheriff—which does not now exist in practice. The issue on which the case was decided related to the security of tenure of such judges. The Bail, Judicial Appointments etc (Scotland) Act 2000 seeks to ensure that the same difficulty does not arise as regards other categories of judge.[49] We turn, therefore, to the other aspect of the guarantee, which relates to the particular judge in the case; and here, we have the advantage of a Scottish criminal case before the European Court—*Pullar v. United Kingdom*.[50]

3.34

The applicant was an elected member of Tayside Regional Council who was indicted for corruption. One of those called and selected for jury service was a man called Forsyth, who was an employee of a key prosecution witness. Both the witness and the juror told the sheriff clerk about this but no action was taken. When the accused (who was convicted) discovered, he appealed unsuccessfully to the High Court[51] and then applied to the Commission.

The European Court held that the view taken by the accused with regard to the impartiality of the tribunal could not be conclusive. What mattered was whether his doubts could be held to be objectively justified.[52] Although the principle of impartiality is an important element in support of the confidence which the courts must inspire in a democratic society, the Court said that "it does not necessarily follow from the fact that a member of a tribunal has

---

[47] Above.
[48] 2000 S.L.T. 42.
[49] We should also note *Clark v. Kelly*, 2000 G.W.D. 27–1041, which establishes that the Clerk and Legal Assessor to the District Court is not part of the tribunal for Art. 6(1) purposes.
[50] 1996 S.C.C.R. 755.
[51] 1993 J.C. 126.
[52] The same line had been taken in *Hauschildt v. Denmark* (1989) 12 E.H.R.R. 266.

some personal knowledge of one of the witnesses in a case that he will be prejudiced in favour of that person's testimony. In each individual case it must be decided whether the familiarity in question is of such a nature and degree as to indicate a lack of impartiality on the part of the tribunal". This accords well with the approach which the High Court took in *Pullar*. The European Court took note of the fact that Forsyth was only one of 15 jurors, that the jury was directed to dispassionately assess the credibility of all the witnesses before them and that all of the jurors took an oath to similar effect. It held that there was no breach of Article 6(1).

It is worth noting here that the High Court was, in *Crummock (Scotland) Ltd v. H.M. Advocate*[53] unimpressed with the argument that a company charged with contaminating the Edinburgh water supply could not get a fair trial from an Edinburgh jury. On a related issue, the High Court held in *H.M. Advocate v. Scottish Media Newspapers*[54] that the test for contempt of court, alleged to have been committed by the publication of material which might prejudice a jury, has to be understood in light of Article 10.

Pullar concerned the jury but contains material which is helpful in considering the position of the judge. The European Court said in *Pullar* that "the principal that a tribunal shall be presumed to be free of prejudice or partiality is long established in the case-law of the court".[55] Reid points out that this presumption is extremely strong and that in the European jurisprudence no claim of bias by a judge has ever been successful notwithstanding frequent complaints.[56] In *Piersack v. Belgium*,[57] however, the European Court did comment that a judge in respect of whom there was a legitimate reason to fear partiality must withdraw. We may compare with this the remarks of the High Court in *Bradford v. McLeod*[58] in which a sheriff had been invited to decline jurisdiction in relation to the trials of mineworkers charged with offences arising out of picketing. He had said, on a social occasion, that he would not grant legal aid to miners. He refused to decline jurisdiction, remarking that he did not propose to disregard his judicial oath (to deal with matters impartially). The High Court held, nevertheless, that "the interests of justice required not merely that he should not display bias but that the circumstances should not be such as to create in the mind of the reasonable man a suspicion of the sheriff's partiality" and quashed the conviction. In *Hoekstra v. H.M. Advocate (No. 2)*[59] the publication by an appellate judge of a newspaper article critical

---

[53] 2000, S.C.C.R. 453

[54] 1999 S.C.C.R. 599.

[55] Citing *Le Compte, Van Leuven and De Meyere v. Belgium* (1982) 4 E.H.R.R. 1.

[56] Reid, *op. cit.* 91.

[57] (1982) 5 E.H.R.R. 169.

[58] 1985 S.C.C.R. 379; but see also *Tennant v. Houston*, 1986 S.C.C.R. 556 and *Harper v. Heywood*, 1998 G.W.D. 3–110.

[59] 2000 S.C.C.R. 367.

of the incorporation of ECHR into Scots law, at a time when the appellant's appeal, based on ECHR, was current before an appellate Bench which he chaired was enough to justify the discharge of the Bench. In *Stott v. Minogue*,[60] by contrast, a sheriff held that Article 6(1) does not create a right for the accused to require the trial judge to make a declaration as to whether or not he (or, in that case, she) was a Freemason.

Article 6(2)

The presumption of innocence.

The classic statement of the primary meaning of Article 6(2) is to   3.35
be found in *Barberà, Messegué and Jabardo v. Spain*[61]: "Paragraph 2 embodies the principle of the presumption of innocence. It requires, *inter alia*, that when carrying out their duties the members of a court should not start with the preconceived idea that the accused has committed the offence charged, and any doubt should benefit the accused."

Presumptions

The European Court has also addressed presumptions under the   3.36
heading of Article 6(2). In *Salabiaku v. France*[62] it said that: "presumptions of fact or of law operate in every legal system. Clearly the Convention does not prohibit such presumptions in principle. It does, however, require the Contracting States to remain within certain limits in this respect as regards criminal law...It requires States to confine them within reasonable limits which take into account the importance of what is at stake and maintain the rights of the defence". The critical issue is whether there is a facility for rebutting the presumption in question.[63]

In *McIntosh, Petitioner*[64] the Judicial Committee of the Privy Council considered the assumptions which the section 3(2) of the Proceeds of Crime Scotland Act 1995 permits the court to make about the provenance of property held, and the source of expenditure made, by a person convicted of a drug trafficking offence to which that section applies. The Board held that the assumptions do not offend against Article 6(2). In part, this was on the basis that Article 6(2) has no application after conviction. The Board also considered, however, what the position would have been if Article 6(2) had applied. Lord Bingham of Cornhill said that:

---

[60] 2000 G.W.D. 37–1386. See also *Salaman v. U.K.* (Appl.43505/98, 15 June, 2000)
[61] (1989) 11 E.H.R.R. 360.
[62] (1991) 13 E.H.R.R. 379.
[63] See also the speech of Lord Hope of Craighead in *R. v. DPP ex p. Kebilene* [2000] 2 A.C. 326.
[64] 2001 S.L.T. 304.

"In weighing the balance between the general interest of the community and the rights of the individual, it will be relevant to ask (as Lord Hope suggested in *Ex parte Kebilene*[65] at page 386) what public threat the provision is directed to address, what the prosecutor must prove to transfer the onus to the defendant and what difficulty the defendant may have in discharging the onus laid upon him. In some cases the acceptability of a reverse onus provision will turn not on consideration of the provision in the abstract but on its application in a particular case...The right to a fair trial, guaranteed by article 6(1), will ensure that any reverse onus provision is fairly applied in the given case."

Later, in *McIntosh*, Lord Hope of Craighead applied these principles to the assumptions at issue. He said that they

"serve the legitimate aim in the public interest of combating that activity [drug trafficking]. They do so in a way that is proportionate. They relate to matters that ought to be within the accused's knowledge, and they are rebuttable by him at a hearing before a judge on the balance of probabilities. In my opinion a fair balance is struck between the legitimate aim and the rights of the accused."

Article 6(3)

Preparation for trial

3.37   Article 6(3)(b) entitles the accused to adequate time and facilities for the preparation of his defence. In *Edwards v. United Kingdom*, the European Court said that it is a requirement of fairness that the prosecution authorities disclose to the defence all material evidence for or against the accused. That followed *Jespers v. Belgium*[66] in which the Commission said:

"... in any criminal proceedings brought by a state authority, the prosecution has at its disposal, to back the accusation, facilities deriving from its powers of investigation, supported by judicial and police machinery with considerable technical resources and means of coercion. It is in order to establish equality, as far as possible, between the prosecution and the defence that national legislation in most countries entrusts the preliminary investigation to a member of the judiciary or, if it entrusts the investigation to the Public Prosecutor's Department, instructs the latter to gather evidence in favour of the accused as well as evidence against him."

---

[65]   [2000] 2 A.C. 326.
[66]   27 D.R. 61 (1982).

The Commission further took the view that the facilities to be
provided should:

> "include the opportunity to acquaint himself, for the purposes   3.38
> of preparing his defence, with the results of investigation
> carried out throughout the proceedings...In short, Article 6,
> paragraph 3(b) recognises the right of the accused to have at
> his disposal, for the purposes of exonerating himself or of
> obtaining a reduction in his sentence, all relevant elements that
> have been or could be collected by the competent authorities.
> The Commission considers that, if the element in question is a
> document, access to that document is a necessary "facility"...if,
> as in the present case, it concerns acts of which the defendant is
> accused, the credibility of testimony, etc."

The European Court said in *Kremzow v. Austria*[67] that restriction of
the right to inspect the court file to an accused's lawyer is not
incompatible with the rights of the defence under Article 6.

In Scotland, the whole issue was considered in light of ECHR by
the High Court in *McLeod v. H.M. Advocate.*[68] The Court
considered that the Crown has a duty at any time to disclose to
the defence information in its possession which would tend to
exculpate the accused. It must respond to specific requests from the
defence for information or the production of statements or other
items where the defence can explain why they would be material to
the defence. This involves the defence making the Crown "aware of
the possible significance of these items for the defence of the
accused". Where this system fails there is available the petition
procedure for the recovery of documents. However, the appellant
failed in his contention that the defence should have substantially
unfettered access to all of the material held by the Crown. *McLeod*
was followed in *Hoekstra (No. 1).*[69] *Maan, Petitioner,*[70] however,
provides an example of the principles set out in *McLeod* being
applied to the benefit of the accused. In that case, an accused who
was charged with assault and who intended to plead self defence
was successful in an application to recover parts of the criminal
records of certain Crown witnesses whom he intended to cross-
examine as to specific acts of violence.

The right to legal assistance

Article 6(3)(c) entitles the accused to defend himself in person or   3.39
through legal assistance of his own choosing. Trial in absence was

---

[67] (1994) 17 E.H.R.R. 322.
[68] 1998 S.L.T. 233.
[69] 2000 S.C.C.R. 263.
[70] 2001 G.W.D. 6–186.

said in *Poitrimol v. France*[71] not to be incompatible with the Convention in principle if the person concerned can subsequently obtain from a court which has heard him a fresh determination of the merits of the charge, in respect of both law and fact. The Court went on to say that it is open to question whether this latter requirement applies when the accused has waived his right to appear and to defend himself, but that at all events such a waiver must, if it is to be effective for Convention purposes, be established in an unequivocal manner and be attended by minimum safeguards commensurate with its importance. As to legal assistance of his own choosing, in *Croissant v. Germany*,[72] the European Court said that

> "Notwithstanding the importance of a relationship of confidence between lawyer and client, this right cannot be considered to be absolute. It is necessarily subject to certain limitations where legal aid is concerned and also where, as in the present case, it is for the courts to decide whether the interests of justice require that the accused be defended by counsel appointed by them. When appointing defence counsel the national courts must certainly have regard to the defendant's wishes...However, they can over-ride those wishes when there are relevant and sufficient grounds for holding that this is necessary in the interests of justice."

The effect of the constraints of the legal aid scheme was considered in *Buchanan v. McLean*.[73] The test identified was whether the constraint in question would necessarily lead to an ineffective defence.

Hearsay

3.40   Hearsay evidence in criminal proceedings in Scotland is dealt with under section 259 of the Criminal Procedure (Scotland) Act 1995, which owes its origins to the Scottish Law Commission Report, *Evidence: Report on Hearsay Evidence in Criminal Proceedings*.[74] It is not intended to describe that law in detail here: it is assumed that it is familiar. What is important is the fact that the Law Commission consciously and deliberately set out to ensure that what they recommended was compatible with ECHR. The Convention law is as follows.

Article 6(3)(d) provides, so far as relevant, that the accused is entitled to "have examined the witnesses against him". The United Kingdom lawyer would read that and tend to take the view that

---

[71] (1994) 18 E.H.R.R. 130.
[72] (1993) 16 E.H.R.R. 135.
[73] 2000 G.W.D. 22–850.
[74] Scot Law Com No. 149, 1995.

hearsay is absolutely excluded. Support for that position would be derived from a superficial reading of *Unterpertinger v. Austria,*[75] in which the applicant had been accused of assault upon his wife and step-daughter. They had made statements to the police but declined to give evidence. He was convicted on the basis of the statements given to the police. The European Court delivered a short judgement. The starting point was that:

> "the reading out of statements in this way cannot be regarded as being inconsistent with Article 6(1) and (3)(d) of the Convention, but the use made of them as evidence must nevertheless comply with the rights of the defence, which it is the object and purpose of Article 6 to protect. This is especially so where the person 'charged with a criminal offence', who has the right under Article 6(3)(d) to 'examine or have examined' witnesses against him, has not had an opportunity at any stage in the earlier proceedings to question the persons whose statements are read out at the hearing."

The conviction had been based "mainly" on the statements made by the wife and stepdaughter, which the Austrian court had treated as proof of the truth of the accusations rather than merely as what the European Court referred to as "information". In these circumstances, it was held, the applicant's defence rights had been "appreciably restricted" so that he had not had a fair trial. The Court held that there had been a breach of Article 6(1) taken with "the principles inherent in paragraph 3(d)"; but it is significant that the European Court said that the reading out of statements was not in itself inconsistent with the Convention.

In *H.M. Advocate v. Nulty,*[76] Lord Abernethy said that in Scots law the safeguards for the accused include the requirement for corroboration, the particular provisions of section 259(4) of the 1995 Act and such directions as the judge might give to the jury.

The European Court went further in *Asch v. Austria*[77] holding that there had been no breach where the conviction was based in part upon the statement given to the police by the complainer in the case, who was the applicant's cohabittee and who had refused to give evidence at trial. However, it was of importance in that case that the evidence of the cohabittee was not the only evidence in the case. The police had observed injuries to the complainer and there was, in addition, medical evidence (though it does not seem to have addressed the identity of the assailant). It was also of importance that the applicant, when interviewed, had given several conflicting accounts of how the complainer came by her injuries which,

---

[75] (1991) 13 E.H.R.R. 175.
[76] 2000 S.C.C.R. 431.
[77] (1993) 15 E.H.R.R. 597.

European Court of Human Rights said, "tended to undermine his credibility".

3.41   Obviously, one could not base a decision about the admissibility of Crown evidence on the credibility or otherwise of the accused. The fact that this was a relevant consideration for the European Court simply emphasises that cases such as *Asch* are not about admissibility at all. The question is whether the trial was fair and that question has been answered with the benefit of 20/20 hindsight. If the Article 6 jurisprudence is to be used to argue that evidence should not be admitted, the argument will have to be not only that the particular evidence involves such incompatibility with a Convention right that it should not be excused but also that the breach is so gross that it is possible to say, even before the trial is completed, that the trial could not possibly be fair if the evidence was admitted.[78]

---

[78]   At the time of writing, the effect of Article 6(3)(d) on the rule in *Morrison v. H.M. Advocate*, 1991 S.L.T. 57 had been remitted for consideration by a Full Bench of nine judges (*McCutcheon v. H.M. Advocate*, 2001 G.W.D. 1–22).

CHAPTER 4

SENTENCING AND PRISONERS' RIGHTS

This chapter discusses sentencing and prisoners' rights.[1] It is, therefore, primarily concerned with post-conviction disposals, although some attention is given to their analogues in cases where the accused's case is disposed of without conviction.[2] It also touches upon the rights of prisoners awaiting trial, since their situation is one which can give rise to acute human rights problems.

"Sentencing" and "prisoners' rights" are of course intimately connected, and what are regarded by the Strasbourg institutions as matters relating to sentence—for example the conditions under which a sentence is served—can equally give rise to issues of prisoners' rights. This chapter divides the topics considered as follows: the section on "sentencing" considers matters which affect the imposition of the sentence, the duration of the sentence (where relevant) and the completion of the sentence; the section on "prisoners' rights" considers those matters which affect the prisoner while in detention, including the conditions of detention and contact with the outside world.

Virtually all of the Convention rights have some relevance to sentencing and prisoners' rights. It is not possible within the scope of this Chapter to give a detailed account of all of the Convention rights, and in any case, it is probably more helpful in a work such as this to identify the domestic issue and then to move to a consideration of the relevant convention provisions and case law.

However, by way of introduction, and as an indicator of how the Convention as a whole relates to sentencing and prisoners' rights, the first part of this Chapter provides an overview of how the various articles relate to the subject matter of this Chapter.

PART I: GENERAL OVERVIEW

A number of Convention provisions are explicitly relevant to

4.01

4.02

---

[1] The chapter is concerned only with adults and does not discuss the special rules relating to children who require measures of care under the Children (Scotland) Act 1995.

[2] E.g. where there the accused has been found insane so that his trial cannot proceed. See Criminal Procedure (Scotland) Act 1995 (hereafter, unless otherwise indicated, "the 1995 Act"), ss. 54 et seq.

questions of sentencing and prisoners' rights.

Article 2: Right to Life[3]

4.03   This article expressly recognises the legality of the death penalty, notwithstanding that it also protects the right to life. Article 2 is also relevant where the state fails in its positive obligation to protect life.[4] It is thus directly relevant to the issue of deaths in prison, including prison suicide.[5]

Article 3: Prohibition of torture

4.04   Article 3 prohibits absolutely "torture and inhuman or degrading treatment or punishment". This article has frequently been invoked (although rarely with success) to challenge the conditions of detention in prison and other institutions.[6] It has also been invoked (successfully) to challenge judicial corporal punishment,[7] and, indirectly, the death penalty.[8]

Article 4: Prohibition of slavery and forced labour

4.05   Article 4(2) prohibits "forced or compulsory labour", but at the same time exempts from that category of work "any work required to be done in the ordinary course of detention imposed according to the provisions of Article 5...or during conditional release from such detention."

Article 5: Right to liberty and security

4.06   Article 5 sets out the right to liberty and security of person, while also setting out the conditions under which a person may be deprived of their liberty. These contemplate a range of measures, some of which relate to pre-trial detention, some of which relate to detention following conviction, and some of which need have nothing whatever to do with the criminal process.[9] The provisions of Article 5 which are directly relevant to this Chapter are:

Article 5(1)(a): This permits the "lawful detention of a person after conviction by a competent court". Compliance with this provision is a necessary condition for the legality of any custodial sentence imposed by a Scottish court. (It is not, however, a sufficient condition, since a sentence lawfully imposed may fall foul

---

3   The headings follow those in the Convention, as amended by Protocol 11.
4   *Cf Osman v. U.K.* (2000) 29 E.H.R.R. 245.
5   Below, p. 162.
6   Below, p. 158.
7   *Tyrer v. U.K* .(1978) 2 E.H.R.R. 1.
8   *Soering v. U.K.* (1989) 11 E.H.R.R. 439.
9   Art. 5(1)(d) provides for, *inter alia*, the "detention of a minor by lawful order for the purpose of educational supervision".

of other Convention provisions.)

Article 5(1)(b): This permits the detention of a person for non-compliance with the lawful order of a court or in order to secure fulfilment of any obligation prescribed by law. This provision is directly relevant to the legality of imprisonment for failing to pay a fine or comply with other orders of the court imposed following conviction.

Article 5(1)(e): This permits the detention of persons for the prevention of the spreading of infectious diseases, of persons of unsound mind, alcoholics or drug addicts or vagrants. Some of these grounds, such as the detention of "vagrants" or those whose only offence against society is that they are ill, sit uneasily in a Human Rights Convention, at least by contemporary standards. But of particular importance is the provision relating to the detention of "persons of unsound mind" since without this provision the detention of those found not guilty by reason of insanity, or found unfit to stand trial would not be lawful.

Article 5(4): This provides that everyone deprived[10] of their liberty by arrest or detention shall be entitled to take proceedings by which the lawfulness of their detention shall be decided speedily by a court and their release ordered if the detention is not lawful. This provision has proved to be of particular importance for those who have received a discretionary life sentence, since it is this provision which ensures that, once the "punishment" element of that sentence has been served, there is proper review of the legality of their continued detention.[11] Bodies which are charged with deciding the legality of a prisoner's detention under Article 5(4), such as the Parole Board, must provide the accused with the guarantees required by Article 6, in particular the guarantee of independence from the executive.[12]

Article 5(5): This provides that everyone who has been the victim of arrest or detention in contravention of the provisions of this Article shall have an enforceable right to compensation.

Article 6: Right to a fair trial

Article 6 has also been invoked to challenge the legality of financial measures imposed following conviction. In *McIntosh v. H.M. Advocate*[13] the High Court held that the "assumptions"   4.07

---

[10] What, in this context, is the position of a person who surrenders their liberty? Are they entitled to rely on Art. 5(4)?

[11] See below, p. 142.

[12] See below, p. 136.

[13] High Court, October 13, 2000, *unreported*.

which the court may make under section 3(2) of the Proceeds of Crime (Scotland) Act 1995 in relation to the origins of the assets of a person convicted of a drug-trafficking offence were incompatible with the presumption of innocence contained in Article 6(2), at least to the extend that those "assumptions" were based on an allegation of criminal offending. Article 6(1) is also relevant to disciplinary proceedings within prisons where the prisoner risks losing remission.[14]

Article 7: No punishment without law

4.08   Article 7(2) prohibits the retrospective increasing of penalties by providing that a person shall not be subjected to a penalty heavier than that which was applicable to the offence in question at the time when it was committed. This provision was successfully invoked to challenge the application of the asset seizure provisions of the Drug Trafficking Offences Act 1986 following conviction for an offence committed before that Act came into force.[15] It has also been relied upon (unsuccessfully) to challenge the requirement to register under the Sex Offenders Act 1997.[16]

All of the above provisions have a more or less explicit relevance to sentencing. But other provisions of the Convention, although they do not expressly refer to sentencing matters, have been held to be relevant, or potentially relevant, to sentencing matters and the rights of sentenced persons:

Article 8: Right to respect for private and family life

4.09   It is obvious that all forms of custodial sentence will, to a greater or lesser degree, interfere with the convicted person's private and family life. They will also interfere with the rights of the sentenced person's family. Article 8 has, therefore, frequently been invoked (but with little success) in order to improve access by a prisoner to his family, and vice-versa.[17] Non-custodial measure may also give rise to questions under Article 8, since these are capable of significant impact on a person's private life. Restriction of liberty orders,[18] probation conditions[19] and community service[20] are all

---

[14]   *Campbell and Fell v United Kingdom* (1985) 7 EHRR 165.

[15]   *Welch v. U.K.* (1995) 20 E.H.R.R. 247. See also *Jamil v. France* (1996) 21 E.H.R.R. 65 (accused ordered to serve a longer period of imprisonment in default of payment of fine, where the law permitting the increased period was passed after the offence was committed).

[16]   See *Adamson v. U.K.* Appl. No. 42293/98, Admissibility decision (Third Section) January 23, 1999, *KS v. U.K.* Appl. No. 45035/98, Admissibility decision (Third Section) March 7, 2000.

[17]   See below, p. 000.

[18]   1995 Act, ss. 245A–245I (as inserted by section 5 of the Crime and Punishment (Scotland) Act 1997).

[19]   See 1995 Act, ss. 228 *et seq* for the statutory framework.

[20]   See 1995 Act, ss. 238 *et seq.*

capable of having such an impact and may call for justification under Article 8(2). Where a person is released on licence the conditions attached to the licence may also raise questions of respect for private and family life.[21]

Article 9: Freedom of thought, conscience and religion

Deprivation of liberty will also have an impact on the freedom of the detained person to engage in religious services or to manifest his religion in other ways.[22] The same could arise in relation to certain non-custodial orders. Care would have to be taken in making such orders that they did interfere with religious freedom in a manner that is not justified by article 9(2).   **4.10**

Article 10: Freedom of expression

Article 10 has been invoked by prisoners seeking access to the news media, or wishing to respond to approaches from the news media.[23] Refusal of such access is potentially an interference with the rights guaranteed under Article 10, although in practice it has not proved difficult for the state of justify the denial of such access.[24]   **4.11**

Article 11: Freedom of assembly and association

Clearly a custodial sentence will interfere with freedom of association, but it is unlikely that any significant difficulty would be encountered in justifying such interference terms of Article 11(2).   **4.12**

More substantial questions might, however, arise in relation to non-custodial disposals which have the effect of restricting freedom of association. Freedom of association, in this context, is not freedom to engage in social intercourse. Freedom of association "is concerned with the right to form or be affiliated to a group or organisation pursuing particular aims."[25] It does not extend to the right to share the company of third parties or to "associate" with them in this sense.[26] The convicted person who complains that a court order excluding him from licensed premises[27] has ruined his social life is unlikely to succeed with a claim under Article 11. But greater weight may have to be given to claims that restriction of

---

[21] See *S.P. v. U.K.* Appl. No. 43478/98, Admissibility decision (Third Section) January 18, 2000.

[22] See, in this respect, the Prisons and Young Offenders Institutions (Scotland) Rules, 1994 (S.I. 1994 No. 1931 (s.85)) (hereafter, unless otherwise indicated, "the Prison Rules"), Part 5.

[23] *Hogefeld v. Germany*, Appl. No. 35402/97, Admissibility decision (Fourth Section) January 20, 2000.

[24] *Ibid.*

[25] See, for example, *Carter v. U.K.* Appl. No. 36417/97, Admissibility decision (Third section), June 29, 1999.

[26] *Ibid.*

[27] Licensed Premises (Exclusion of Certain Persons) Act 1980.

liberty orders, or conditions of probation or other non-custodial measures unjustifiably interfere with a person's freedom, for example, to attend political or trade union meetings.

Article 12: Right to marry

4.13   Custodial measures will almost inevitably interfere with freedom to marry and found a family, and decisions by the responsible authorities not to allow persons the facilities to enter into marriage have been successfully challenged on this ground.[28] The denial of conjugal visits, on the other hand, is not incompatible with Article 12.[29]

PART II: SENTENCING

4.14   In relation to both non-custodial and custodial disposals two questions arise. The first is whether the sentence *as such* is compatible with the Convention. Is corporal punishment compatible with the Convention? Are long determinate sentences, or indeterminate sentences, or preventative detention by their nature incompatible with the Convention rights? The second question is whether the manner in which the sentence is *executed* is compatible with the Convention. The following section discusses the first of these questions. The second, which is closely linked to the question of prisoners' rights is discussed in Part III.

1. The death penalty

4.15   The death penalty as such is not contrary to the Convention. Article 2(1) provides that a person may be deprived of his or her life "in the execution of a sentence of a court following his conviction of a crime for which this penalty is provided by law". The argument that the death penalty as such is contrary to Article 3 was expressly rejected by the Court in *Soering v. United Kingdom*.[30]

The death penalty is unlikely to raise any practical issues at the purely domestic level. It is no longer available as the penalty for an offence in Scotland. The death penalty for murder was abolished by the Murder (Abolition of the Death Penalty) Act 1965 and for treason and piracy by section 36 of the Crime and Disorder Act 1998. The United Kingdom's ratification of the Sixth Protocol to the Convention,[31] and the inclusion of Articles 1 and 2 of that

[28]   *Hamer v. U.K.* (1979) 4 E.H.R.R. 139, Commission Report. See also the Resolution of the Committee of Ministers in this case.
[29]   See *Hamer v. U.K.*, *ibid*; *Khan v. U.K.* Appl. No. 11579/85, 48 DR 253; *E.L.H. v. U.K.* Appl. No. 32586/96, Commission Decision, October 22, 1997; *G. and R.S v. U.K.* Appl. No. 17142/90, Commission Decision, July 10, 1991
[30]   (1989) 11 E.H.R.R. 439, at paras 100–104.
[31]   The United Kingdom ratified the Sixth Protocol on January 27, 1999.

Protocol in Schedule 1 to the Human Rights Act mean that, at least for offences in peacetime,[32] the death penalty cannot be reintroduced into the United Kingdom without denunciation of the Convention.[33]

The death penalty may, however, be significant in relation to criminal cases having an international dimension. In particular, it may not be lawful for the United Kingdom authorities to extradite or deport a person to a country where there is a real risk that she or he will face the death penalty.[34]

2. Custodial sentences

(A) The range of custodial sentences

Custodial sentences take various forms, depending upon the nature of the offence and the age and other characteristics of the offender. Thus imprisonment is only available in respect of persons aged 21 or over.[35] The appropriate form of custodial disposal for offenders aged 16 to 21 is one of detention.[36] Neither imprisonment nor detention may be imposed on an offender who has not previously been sentenced to imprisonment or detention anywhere in the United Kingdom, unless the court considers that no other disposal is appropriate.[37]

4.16

A custodial disposal is also possible even though the accused has not been convicted of an offence or even tried for that offence. So, for example, where a person is acquitted on the ground of insanity,[38] the court may, despite the acquittal, make an order for that person's detention in a hospital, with or without restrictions.[39] Where the crime charged is murder, the court must make a hospital order with restrictions.[40] Similarly, where a court finds that an accused person is insane and cannot be tried, it may remand that

---

[32] Article 2 of the Sixth Protocol provides that a State "may make provision in its law for the death penalty in respect of acts committed in time of war or of imminent threat of war".

[33] The U.K. Parliament could, in theory, re-introduce the death penalty. The Scottish Parliament could not. Any provision to that effect in a Scottish enactment would be outwith the legislative competence of the Parliament in terms of s.29(1) and s.29(2)(d), nor can the Scottish Parliament amend any part of the Human Rights Act: Scotland Act 1998, Sched. 4, para. 1(2)(f).

[34] See below, p. 000.

[35] Criminal Procedure (Scotland) Act 1995 (hereafter, unless otherwise indicated, "the 1995 Act"), s.207(1). There is an exception in the case of a person convicted of murder, for which life imprisonment is the mandatory sentence: 1995 Act, s.204(5).

[36] 1995 Act, s.207(2)..

[37] 1995 Act, ss. 204(2) and 207(3).

[38] 1995 Act, s.54(6) or s.55(3).

[39] 1995 Act, s.57(1) and (2).

[40] 1995 Act, s.57(3).

person in custody or make a temporary hospital order committing him to hospital.[41]

(B) Legality of the detention in terms of article 5

4.17   Whatever the basis of detention in domestic law, it must be lawful in terms of Article 5. In the context of criminal proceedings the deprivation of liberty is most frequently justified in terms of Article 5(1)(a), that is, the lawful detention of a person after conviction by a competent court. But given that a court may order the detention of a person who is insane and cannot be tried, or who has been acquitted on the ground of insanity, it is necessary also to have regard to Article 5(1)(e), which provides, *inter alia*, for the lawful detention of persons of unsound mind.

In order to be "lawful", in either case, such detention "must essentially comply with national law and the substantive and procedural rules thereof."[42] If, therefore, detention is unlawful in terms of Scots law, it is also unlawful in terms of Article 5(1).

The term "lawful" detention in this context refers also to the grounds of detention laid out in Article 5. Where the detention results from a lawful sentence or order of the court, this requirement is satisfied in terms of Article 5(1)(a). The fact, however, that a person's conviction and sentence have been quashed on appeal does not mean that she or he was not initially "lawfully" detained in terms of Article 5(1).[43] The emphasis in this provision is on the lawfulness of the detention rather than the lawfulness of the conviction which preceded it.

The requirement in Article 5(1)(a) that the detention be "after" conviction is of particular significance. In *Weeks v. United Kingdom*[44] the Court explained that,

"the word 'after' in sub-paragraph (a) does not simply mean that the detention must follow the 'conviction' in point of time: in addition, the detention must result from, 'follow and depend upon' or occur 'by virtue of' the 'conviction'. In short, there must be a sufficient causal connection between the conviction and the deprivation of liberty at issue."[45]

This causal connection is of importance, for example, where a decision has been taken to recall to custody a life prisoner released

---

[41]   1995 Act, s.54(1)(c).
[42]   *Herczegfalvy v. Austria* (1993) 15 E.H.R.R. 432, para. 63.
[43]   See, for example, *Krzycki v. Gemany* (1978) 13 D.R. 57. *Cf Tsirlis and Kouloumpas v. Greece* (1998) 25 E.H.R.R. 198.
[44]   (1998) 10 E.H.R.R. 293
[45]   *Ibid.*, para. 42, referring to *Bozano v. France* (1987) 9 E.H.R.R. 297 and *Van Droogenbroeck v. Belgium* (1982) 4 E.H.R.R. 443.

on licence, especially where the indeterminate sentence was discretionary rather mandatory.[46] The original justification for the deprivation of liberty may not be sufficient to justify the recall.[47]

So far as concerns the detention of persons of "unsound mind", the Strasbourg institutions have been remarkably reticent in elaborating what this ground of detention might embrace. The Court has refused to indicate what kinds of mental disorder justify detention, and has confined itself to broad statements about the "quality" of disorder that is required. There must be objective medical evidence to the effect that the individual concerned is of unsound mind to this degree.[48] The individual's disorder must be of such a nature or degree as warrants compulsory detention,[49] (a requirement which seems to border on circularity). Finally, the disorder must be present to this degree throughout the period of detention.[50]

Article 5(1) does not appear to govern conditions of detention, except that in the case of the detention of a person of "unsound mind" under article 5(1)(e), the Court has stated,

> "there must be some relationship between the ground of permitted deprivation of liberty relied on and the place and conditions of detention. In principle, the "detention" of a person as a mental health patient will only be "lawful" for the purposes of sub-paragraph (e) of paragraph 1 (art. 5-1-e) if effected in a hospital, clinic or other appropriate institution authorised for that purpose."[51]

If this were to be applied beyond the limited context of Article 5(1)(e) then it would have implications for the legality of detention of all prisoners in conditions which are inappropriate having regard to the purpose of the detention. This may be relevant, for example, where police cells are used to hold prisoners other than for the purely temporary purposes for which cells are designed. In general, however, conditions of detention have been attacked under Article 3.[52]

(C) Compatibility with other Convention rights

Even if deprivation of liberty is lawful in terms of Article 5, it may nevertheless be objectionable in terms of some other Convention   4.18

---

[46] See, for example, *Weeks v. U.K.* (1988) 10 E.H.R.R. 293, discussed below, p. 000.
[47] *Cf Weeks v. U.K. ibid..*
[48] *Winterwerp v. Netherlands* (1979) 2 E.H.R.R. 387.
[49] *Winterwerp v. Netherlands, ibid.*
[50] *ibid.*
[51] *Ashingdane v. U.K.* (1985) 7 E.H.R.R. 528, para. 44.
[52] As to which, see below, pp. 158 – 163.

provision. The question here is whether a custodial measure, lawfully imposed in terms of domestic law, can be challenged on the ground that it is incompatible with the Convention. It is proposed to consider this question under the following headings: (a) indeterminate sentences; (b) review of indeterminate sentences; (c) length of determinate sentence; (d) discrimination in sentencing.

(a) Indeterminate sentences

The term "indeterminate sentence" is a more accurate description of what are known in Scots law as "life" sentences. It is generally accepted that, as a rule, a sentence of "life" imprisonment is not intended to incarcerate the offender for the remainder of his or her natural life. "Life" sentences are, however, "life" sentences in that they endure for the life of the offender. Thus a person sentenced to life imprisonment for murder may be released. However, such release is not unconditional but on licence. Such a person may, subject to certain conditions, be recalled to custody without the necessity of proving that he or she has committed a further offence warranting imprisonment.

Indeterminate sentences are either mandatory or discretionary. They are mandatory only where the offender has been convicted of murder. In the case of a person aged 21 the sentence is life imprisonment.[53] In the case of a person aged 18 to 21 the sentence is detention, and the accused is liable to be detained for life.[54] A person aged under 18 who is convicted of murder is to be detained without limit of time and in such place and under such conditions as may be directed by the Scottish Ministers.[55]

A court may impose a discretionary indeterminate sentence for any offence for which that sentence is available (all common law offences and some statutory offences). In deciding whether or not to impose a discretionary life sentence the court may have regard to the nature of the offence, the accused's antecedents and the demands of public safety.[56]

4.19   The justifications for these disposals differ. In general, the mandatory life sentence is justified on "punitive" or "deserts" grounds. The sentence reflects the gravity of the offence. The same may be said of the mandatory detention of a person aged 18 to 21 who is convicted of murder. Discretionary life sentences, on the other hand, are generally justified by reference to a combination of punishment, and protection of the public. According to this view, a person may be sentenced to life imprisonment even though the offence for which he has been convicted does not, in terms purely of punishment, warrant such a severe sentence. The severity of the

---

[53] 1995 Act, s.205(1).
[54] 1995 Act, s.205(3).
[55] 1995 Act, s.205(2).
[56] See *Clark v. H.M. Advocate*, 1997 S.C.C.R. 416, *O'Neill v. H.M. Advocate*, 1999 S.C.C.R. 300.

sentence is justified by reference to the need to protect the public (as well as the demands of punishment).

But not all discretionary life sentences are of this kind. It is possible to envisage a case in which the court would be justified in imposing a discretionary life sentence to mark the gravity of the offence, without reference to the need to protect the public.

Indeterminate sentences as such are not incompatible with the Convention, provided that, having regard to the circumstances of the offence and the offender, they do not fall to be regarded as inhumane or degrading within the meaning of Article 3.

In the case of *Weeks v. United Kingdom*[57] the applicant was sentenced to life imprisonment at the age of 17. He had pleaded guilty to the robbery of 35 pence from a pet shop, while armed with a starting pistol loaded with blank shot. The sentence of life imprisonment was not, therefore, based upon the gravity of the offence. The trial judge selected the sentence because he believed that, having regard to the applicant's previous history and his mental condition, the applicant presented a particular danger to the public. The applicant was eventually released from prison, but was subsequently recalled.

The applicant's complaint was based upon alleged violations of Article 5(1) and 5(4) in relation to his recall. However, in relation to the sentence imposed by the trial judge (and upheld by the Court of Appeal) the Court observed:

> "Having regard to Mr Weeks' age at the time and to the particular facts of the offence he committed ... if it had not been for the specific reasons advanced for the sentence imposed, one could have serious doubts as to its compatibility with Article 3 of the Convention, which prohibits, *inter alia*, inhuman punishment."

Given that lengthy *determinate* sentences are not, generally, regarded as being likely to raise an issue under Article 3,[58] the objectionable feature of the sentence imposed in this case would appear to be its *indeterminate* nature, at least when applied to a youthful offender. Without the additional consideration of risk, therefore, a discretionary indeterminate sentence may, be incompatible with the Convention. As suggested above, a discretionary life sentence may be imposed to mark the gravity of the offence, rather than the risk which the accused presents to public safety. But it seems clear from *Weeks* that indeterminate sentences must be justified either in terms of risk or be proportionate to the offence. Where the sentence is seriously disproportionate to the offence, the sentence may be open to challenge, and the age of the offender is

---

[57] (1988) 10 E.H.R.R. 293.
[58] See below, pp. 144–148.

certainly relevant in determining whether or not the sentence is inhumane.[59]

The situation is different, however, in the case of the mandatory indeterminate (life) sentence for murder. Here the gravity of the offence is by itself sufficient to justify an indeterminate sentence, and that is probably true irrespective of the age or circumstances of the accused.[60]

(b) Review of indeterminate sentences

4.20 It is accepted that a person detained under an indeterminate sentence may change and develop over time. A person who initially presented grave risks to the public may, over the years, become less of a risk and his release back to the community may be acceptable. It is also accepted that, in the case of a mandatory life sentence, the offender will, in most cases, be released after he or she has served a sufficient time to reflect the gravity of the offence of murder.

These considerations give rise to complex questions under Article 5. If, for example, a person no longer presents a risk to the public, is his or her continued detention compatible with Article 5? Is a person sentenced to life imprisonment for murder entitled to have his or her continued detention reviewed by a court in terms of Article 5(4)?

The vehicle for review in all cases is Article 5(4), for this is the only provision under which the lawfulness of detention under Article 5 can be determined. The different justifications for mandatory and discretionary life sentences mean, however, that they are treated differently by the Strasbourg institutions.

(i) Mandatory indeterminate (life) sentences

4.21 Adults sentenced to life imprisonment for murder, and persons liable to detention for life for murder under section 205(3) of the 1995 Act are not entitled to invoke Article 5(4) with a view to demanding access to a "court" to determine the continuing legality of their detention. The legality of that detention, and judicial involvement in the determination of that legality, is to be found in the fact that their detention derives from the sentence imposed by the court.

In *Wynne v. United Kingdom*,[61] the applicant was sentenced to life imprisonment for murder in 1964. He was released on licence in 1980, and the following year he was convicted again when he pleaded guilty to the manslaughter of an elderly woman. On this occasion a discretionary life sentence was imposed. In June 1992 he was informed that the "tariff" period fixed in respect of his 1964 conviction had expired, and that his continued detention was based

---

[59] *Cf Tyrer v. U.K.* (1978) 2 E.H.R.R. 1.
[60] *Cf Wynne v. U.K.* (1995) 19 E.H.R.R. 333 and *T v. U.K., V v. U.K.* (2000) 30 E.H.R.R. 121.
[61] (1995) 19 E.H.R.R. 333.

on the risk he represented. (The tariff fixed by the trial judge in respect of his second offence had expired in 1991).

The applicant complained that he was unable to have the continued lawfulness of his detention reviewed by a court, and that there was therefore a violation of Article 5(4). This argument was rejected by the Court. The life licence granted in 1980 was revoked by his conviction for manslaughter. The fact that he had committed a further offence (and that he was suffering from a mental disorder) did not affect the continuing validity of his original sentence. Although the applicant attempted to argue that the two types of life sentence were converging, there remained significant differences between them, and the case law of the Court which insisted that discretionary life sentence prisoners should have access to a court under Article 5(4) did not apply to persons serving a mandatory sentence of life imprisonment for murder.

(ii) Discretionary life sentences
The Court has held that persons serving a discretionary life   4.22
sentence must have access to a court to determine the continuing legality of their detention, once the punitive element of their sentence has been served.[62] In *Weeks v. United Kingdom*, the Court held that where the stated purpose of detention was the protection of the pubic, based upon the perceived risks which the offender posed, it was necessary for the accused to have access to a court in order to determine whether or not the grounds for his continued detention remained operative:

> "The grounds expressly relied upon by the sentencing courts for ordering this form of deprivation of liberty...are by their very nature susceptible of change with the passage of time, whereas the measure will remain in force for the whole of his life. In this, his sentence difference from a life sentence imposed on a person because of the gravity of the offence."[63]

If the decision not to release were to be based on grounds inconsistent with the objective of the sentencing court, the applicant's continuing detention would no longer be "lawful" for the purposes of Article 5(1), and he would therefore be entitled to apply to a "court" having jurisdiction to decide speedily whether or not his deprivation of liberty had become unlawful in this sense. This right is exercisable on the expiry of the punitive element of the sentence, and at reasonable intervals thereafter.[64]

The reasoning in *Weeks* applies, however, only to the case of a

---

[62] *Weeks v. U.K.* (1988) 10 E.H.R.R. 293; *Thynne, Wilson and Gunnell v. U.K.* (1990) 13 E.H.R.R. 666.
[63] *Weeks v. U.K. ibid.*.
[64] *Ibid.*, para. 58. See also, *Van Droogenbroeck v. Belgium* (1982) 4 E.H.R.R. 443, *Thynne, Wilson and Gunnell v. U.K.* (1990) 13 E.H.R.R. 666.

person serving a discretionary life sentence based upon the perceived risks which he or she presents to the public, and it was noted above that it is at least possible to conceive of a discretionary life sentence being imposed purely to mark the gravity of the offence.

As the law presently stands in Scotland, a court when imposing a discretionary life sentence may, under section 2 of the Prisoners and Criminal Proceedings (Scotland) act 1993, fix a part of the sentence at the end of which the prisoner is entitled to require his case to be referred to the Parole Board, which has the power to direct his release.[65] The judge is not required to make such a designation, but if this is not done, then the reasons for not doing so must be stated.[66] Where such an order is made, the prisoner is known as a "designated life prisoner".[67]

A "designated life prisoner" is thus entitled to have the legality of his continued detention reviewed by a "court".[68] But a "non-designated life prisoner" is not so entitled under the 1993 Act, nor, it would seem, in terms of Article 5(4).

(iii) Young persons detained without limit of time and in such place and under such conditions as may be directed by the Scottish Ministers.

4.23   Although such detention is mandatory, it is accepted that such cases have much in common with discretionary life sentences. In *Hussain v. United Kingdom*[69] the Court held that persons "detained during her Majesty's Pleasure"[70] were entitled to have the legality of their continuing detention reviewed by a court in terms of Article 5(4). Section 2 of the Prisoners and Criminal Proceedings (Scotland) Act 1993 (as amended by section 16 of the Crime and Punishment (Scotland) Act 1997) now provides for the inclusion of persons detained under section 205(2) within the category of "designated life prisoner".

(iv) Any body which has the responsibility of reviewing the legality of continuing detention must satisfy the requirements of a "court".

4.24   It must therefore be independent of the executive and impartial, it must have more than merely advisory functions, and must have the competence to "decide" the lawfulness of detention, and to order release if the detention is unlawful.[71]

---

[65] Prisoners and Criminal Proceedings (Scotland) Act 1993, s.2(4). On the procedure and criteria to be adopted by the court in fixing the designated part of a discretionary sentence, see *O'Neill v. H.M. Advocate*, 1999 S.C.C.R. 300.
[66] Prisoners and Criminal Proceedings (Scotland) Act 1993, s.3.
[67] Prisoners and Criminal Proceedings (Scotland) Act 1993.
[68] Prisoners and Criminal Proceedings (Scotland) Act 1993, ss.2(2), 2(4) and 2(6).
[69] (1996) 22 E.H.R.R. 1.
[70] The English equivalent of detention under s.205(2) of the 1995 Act.
[71] *Weeks v. U.K.* (1988) 10 E.H.R.R. 293; *Thynne, Wilson and Gunnell v. U.K.* (1990) 13 E.H.R.R. 666.

In the Scottish context, the body which reviews the detention of designated life prisoners is the Parole Board, sitting as a "Designated Life Tribunal", chaired by a judicial member of the Parole Board.[72] The Tribunal has the power to order release of the prisoner, and therefore satisfies this aspect of Article 5(4). Whether the Designated Life Tribunal satisfies the requirements of independence and impartiality depends upon whether or not the parent body, the Parole Board, satisfies these requirements.

In *Weeks v. United* Kingdom, the applicant argued that the Parole Board for England and Wales was not independent of the Home Secretary, primarily because the Home Secretary appoints members of the Board, staffs the Board and makes the rules under which its procedures are conducted.[73] The Court's view was that the manner of appointment of the Board did not mean that the Board was not independent of the Home Secretary. The Court was also satisfied that in the exercise of their duties the Board remained independent of the Home Secretary. It also concluded that, even from the perspective of the life prisoner, the Board did present an appearance of independence.[74] There was not, however, in these cases, any detailed consideration of the manner of appointment, terms of office or manner of removal of Parole Board members.

In Scotland the Chairman and members of the Parole Board are all appointed by the executive.[75] Scottish Ministers are also responsible for deciding upon the period that individuals should serve, and their remuneration. Remuneration is on a fee basis, and members also receive travel and subsistence at civil service rates. Members of the Board are subject to standard terms and conditions which provide, *inter alia*, that their appointment may be terminated by Scottish Ministers at any time prior to the expiry of their term of office, on the grounds of ill health, failure to attend regularly to the business of the Board or that the are otherwise unable or unfit to discharge the functions of a member of the Board. Board members may, on expiry of their original term of appointment, be appointed for a further term. There have been occasions when members have not been offered a second term.

It may be possible to argue that the Parole Board is not sufficiently independent of the Scottish Executive to satisfy the requirements of Article 5(4). The matter is under consideration by the Scottish Executive, and may be subject to legislative amendment in the near future.

(c) Length of determinate sentences

The general position adopted by the Strasbourg institutions is that   4.25

---

[72] Prisoners and Criminal Proceedings (Scotland) Act 1993, Parole Board (Scotland) Rules 1993 (S.I. 1993 No. 2225).
[73] *Weeks v. United Kingdom, supra* no. 71.
[74] *Ibid.*
[75] Prisoners and Criminal Proceedings (Scotland) Act 1993, Sched. 2.

matters relating to the length of a determinate sentence lawfully imposed are generally outwith the scope of the Convention.[76] It has, however, been argued that the length of a given sentence, whether in absolute terms, or relative to the circumstances of the accused, is incompatible with the Convention, and in particular Article 3. Such arguments are consistently rejected.

In *Treholt v. Norway*[77] a high-ranking civil servant in the Norwegian Ministry of Foreign Affairs was convicted of espionage and sentenced to 20 years' imprisonment. He complained to the Commission that "the total duration of the confinement and the way in which he has been treated should be considered as a continuing violation of Article 3, aggravated by the time passing."[78] The Commission, however, rejected his complaints. Noting that a "right to be released on parole or to leaves of absence does not exist under the Convention," the Commission observed that "should the applicant serve the total of his 20 year term this would not in itself raise an issue under Article 3 (Art. 3) of the Convention" unless the conditions of his detention as such would amount to inhuman or degrading treatment."[79]

In *Bullivant v. United Kingdom*[80] the applicant was convicted of armed robbery and possession of firearms and sentenced to a total of 18 years' imprisonment. He was 50 years old when the sentenced was handed down. In his application to the Court he claimed, *inter alia*, that his 18 year prison sentence, at the age of 50, was degrading in that it aroused fear and anguish capable of humiliating the applicant, and that its intention is to break his moral and physical resistance. The Court was unimpressed:

> "Further, the imposition of a long sentence of imprisonment is generally not sufficient in itself to raise issues under [article 3]. Though the applicant refers to his age, the Court does not find that this constitutes a factor which renders the sentence imposed in this case either inhuman or degrading within the meaning of Article 3 of the Convention."[81]

The same conclusion has been reached where a lengthy period of incarceration has followed from a succession of offences.[82] In

---

[76] See, in addition to the cases discussed below, *Heudens v. Belgium*, Appl. No. 24630/94, May 22, 1995; *M.M. v. U.K.* Appl. No. 19000/91, April 2, 1992; *McAllister v. U.K.* Appl. No. 18943/91, April 2, 1992; *Grice v. U.K.* Appl. No. 22564/93, April 14, 1994.

[77] Appl. No. 14610/89, July 9, 1991, 71 D.R. 191.

[78] *Ibid.*

[79] 71 D.R. 191, at p. 000.

[80] Appl. No. 45738/99, Admissibility decision (First section), March 28, 2000.

[81] *Ibid*, p. 8.

[82] *Koskinnen v. Finland*, Appl. No. 20560/92, August 30, 1994. See also, *Treholt v. Norway, supra*, no. 77.

Dhoest v. Belgium[83] it was argued that the detainee had no prospect of being released from custody and that that amounted to a violation of Article 3. This argument was rejected on the ground that the applicant was not without prospect of release. His case was subject to periodic review, and provided he satisfied the conditions laid down by the relevant legislation he could be released from detention. The Commission did, however appear to cast doubt on whether such an argument could even raise an issue under Article 3.[84]

These decisions virtually adopt the position that a lengthy determinate sentence could never, *per se*, be regarded as inhuman. That is difficult to accept, especially given that the determination of whether or not punishment is to be regarded as "inhuman" or "degrading" is a relative matter, depending upon the circumstances.[85] This gives rise, at least in principle, to issues of proportionality. An extremely long sentence, imposed upon a very young or otherwise vulnerable prisoner might be open to challenge[86] although it would seem unlikely in the current sentencing climate that such a sentence would or could lawfully be imposed by a court in Scotland.

4.26

The possibility that the length of the sentence imposed might give rise to questions of proportionality does seem to have been recognised, at least in passing, by the Commission in *T.M. v. United Kingdom*.[87] The applicants complaints related, *inter alia*, to the tariff fixed in relation to a discretionary life sentence imposed on him following his conviction for manslaughter arising out of the killing of two women. The Commission, in line with its general practice, noted that matters of the fixing of an appropriate sentence for particular offences "generally fall outside the scope of the Convention." However, the Commission then went on to say: "Even assuming an issue could arise as regards the imposition of a sentence excessively disproportionate to the crime charged" the conditions required for a violation of Article 3 were not present in this case.

The reluctance of the Strasbourg institutions to consider the possibility of a determinate sentence being disproportionate to the offence, or the circumstances of the offender is curious, especially given the observations of the Court in *Weeks*[88] in relation to discretionary life sentences. It may well be worth considering the possibility of such an argument in relation to a fixed sentence, not in the context of Article 3 (where the required standard will always be high) but in the context of Article 5(1). In other words, the

---

[83] Appl. No. 10448/83, Commission Report, May 14, 1987.
[84] *Cf N v. U.K.* Appl. No. 1161/85, May 6, 1986.
[85] *Tyrer v. U.K.* (1978) 2 E.H.R.R. 1; *Ireland v. U.K.* (1978) 2 E.H.R.R. 25.
[86] *Cf Soering v. U.K.* (1989) 11 E.H.R.R. 439.
[87] Appl. No. 21848/93, October 18, 1995.
[88] *Weeks v. U.K.* (1988) 10 E.H.R.R. 293.

argument may be put that a sentence which is "excessively disproportionate" having regard to the crime charged is not a "lawful" sentence and that the accused has therefore been deprived of his liberty in violation of Article 5(1).

Closely linked to the question of length of sentence is the absence of parole or remission. It has been argued that the failure to provide for parole or remission may result in a violation of Article 3. The reactions of the Strasbourg institutions to such arguments is very similar to those based on the length of sentence. In *Trehold v. Norway* the Commission stated that "A right to be released on parole or to leaves of absence does not exist under the Convention".[89]

(d) Discrimination in sentencing

4.27   The one exception which is consistently recognised to the rule that sentencing matters are generally outside the Convention is in relation to discrimination. "Where a settled sentencing policy appears to affect individuals in a discriminatory fashion, the Commission has taken the view that this may raise issues under Article 14 read in conjunction with Article 5".[90] Discrimination in sentencing policy relates not only to the initial determination of the sentence, but may also arise in relation to release policy.[91]

It is important, however, to understand what is meant by discrimination in this context. In the first place, mere variations in sentence as between individuals will not give rise to a claim under Articles 14 and 5 together. What is objectionable is, apparently, a "settled sentencing policy" which affects individuals in a discriminatory fashion.

Secondly, an accused cannot establish a claim of discrimination based on comparisons between different offences, albeit that these are perhaps closely linked. In *McCallister v United Kingdom*[92] the applicant was convicted of aggravated burglary and sentenced to six years' imprisonment. In terms of the Northern Ireland (Emergency Provisions) Act 1978, this was a "scheduled offence". Consequently, under section 22 of the Prevention of Terrorism (Temporary Provisions) Act 1998, the remission granted in respect of this offence could not exceed one third of the sentence, whereas remission granted in respect of a non-scheduled offence could be up to half the sentence imposed. If the offence had not been "scheduled" the applicant's release date would have been June 28,

---

[89]   Appl. No. 14610/89, July 9, 1991, 71 D.R. 191. See also, *Koskinen v. Finland*, Appl. No. 20560/92, Commission Decision, August 30, 1994.

[90]   *McAllister v. U.K.* Appl. No. 18943/91, April 2, 1992. See also: Appl. No. 11077/84, December 13, 1986, 49 D.R. 170; *Grice v. U.K.* Appl. No. 22564/93, April 14, 1994; *M.M. v. U.K.* Appl. No. 19000/91, April 2, 1992; *Heudens v. Belgium*, Appl. No. 24630/94, May 22, 1995.

[91]   *Grice v. United Kingdom, supra,* no. 76.

[92]   *Supra,* no. 76.

1993, whereas in fact it was one year later. A person convicted of burglary without aggravation would, therefore, have benefited from the longer remission entitlement.

The applicant complained that he was required to serve a longer period of imprisonment because of the perceived political character of his offence. He invoked Article 14 in conjunction with Article 5. The argument that he had suffered discrimination was rejected by the Commission. The applicant was seeking to compare himself with persons convicted of different offences. As the Commission pointed out, "a person convicted of one offence is, however, not in a comparable position to that of a person convicted of another offence in relation to the question of sentencing and the possibility of early release."

As in other cases of discrimination, the accused must show that he shares the same characteristics of the individuals or individual with whom he compares himself, and that he has been the subject of an arbitrary difference of treatment. In *Grice v. United Kingdom*[93] the applicant was sentenced to four years'; imprisonment for offence of buggery and indecent assault on a seven year old boy. Four months later he was diagnosed as suffering from AIDS. Shortly thereafter he applied for early release on compassionate grounds. This was refused and the refusal was subsequently renewed. The applicant was released on licence 16 months after he was sentenced. His life expectancy at the time of release was 9–12 months.   4.28

The applicant complained to the Commission that he had been refused early release from prison on compassionate grounds. Although he was released on licence having served a third of his sentence, he argued that he should have been released earlier and that he had suffered discrimination in the operation of the provisions for early release. He claimed that he had suffered discrimination because of his AIDS status since he was refused early release, notwithstanding the terminal nature of his illness. He claimed, in support of this argument, that prisoners suffering from other terminal illness had been granted early release. He also submitted evidence to the effect that no prisoner suffering from AIDS had at that time been granted early compassionate release.

This complaint was rejected by the Commission. But whereas the complaint in *McAllister* was rejected because the applicant was not in the same position as those to whom he compared himself, the complaint in this case was rejected because the applicant was unable to show that he had been treated differently in the exercise of the Secretary of State's discretion to order release on compassionate grounds. The Commission noted, in this connection, that the Secretary of State applied the same criteria in all cases of

---

[93] *Supra*, no. 76.

application for early release,[94] and referred to cases of equally, or even more gravely, ill prisoners who had been released with a life expectancy of only a few weeks.

Systematic discrimination in sentencing is likely to prove difficult to establish, not least because of the absence of clear sentencing policies of any kind. It will not, however, avail an accused to argue, for example, that an apparent policy of imposing custodial sentences for certain types of drug-offending, but not for other offences of equivalent seriousness, constitutes discrimination. If, however, it can be shown, for example, that sentencing for comparable offences is determined by reference to gender, or race, this would give rise to defensible complaint under Articles 5 and 14.

3. Non-custodial disposals

4.29   The Scottish courts have a wide range of non-custodial disposals available to them, ranging from an absolute discharge to community service. In practice very few challenges have been mounted under the Convention to non-custodial disposals, other than to challenge the fairness of the procedures by which these disposals have been determined.[95] The one signal exception to this was the case of *Tyrer v. United Kingdom*[96] in which it was held that judicial corporal punishment was necessarily incompatible with Article 3 as being degrading.

It is most unlikely that any of the non-custodial disposals available to the courts could be challenged on the ground that the are incompatible *per se* with the Convention rights. Since the Convention accepts as compatible with the Convention not only the deprivation of liberty but even the deprivation of life, it is unlikely that it harbours a fundamental objection to fines,[97] probation and similar disposals.

It might be argued that since forced labour is prohibited by Article 4(1) of the Convention, and that community service is not among the practices exempted from forced labour by Article 4(2), that there are doubts about the compatibility of community service with the Convention. It is most unlikely that community service could be challenged on the ground of incompatibility with Article 4. In the first place, Article 4 prohibits "forced or compulsory" labour, whereas section 238(2) makes it clear that a community service order may not be made without the consent of the offender. It might be argued that the offender has little choice—the alternative to community service being imprisonment or detention. But the

---

[94] The government submitted that the Secretary of State has regard, in all such cases, to the risk of re-offending, and the imminence of death.

[95] See, for examples, *Özturk v. Germany* (1984) 6 E.H.R.R. 409; *Umlauft v. Austria* (1996) 22 E.H.R.R. 76; *Schmautzer v. Austria* (1996) 21 E.H.R.R. 511.

[96] (1978) 2 E.H.R.R. 1.

[97] Article 1 of the First Protocol clearly accepts that the enforcement of laws designed to secure the payment of "penalties" is acceptable.

convicted person nevertheless has enough of a choice for it to be held that she or he was not "forced" or "compelled" to do the work. Secondly, it is unlikely that a method of disposal so widely used throughout the Convention states would be regarded by the Court as being incompatible with the Convention on other grounds, especially since it is offered to the accused as an alternative to disposal—loss of liberty—which, although much more restrictive of his rights is itself compatible with the Convention.

Although it is unlikely that any non-custodial disposals would be regarded as incompatible *per se*, it may be that the manner in which such disposals are enforced could give rise to questions of Convention right. This matter is discussed above, in Part I.[98]

4. Ancillary orders

In addition to a penalty, whether custodial or non-custodial, a convicted person may be subject to various ancillary requirements or orders. These include such matters as the registration of certain sex offenders,[99] the confiscation of property used in the commission of a crime,[1] the seizure of the proceeds of crime[2] and the payment of compensation to the victim of an offence.[3] In certain cases a court may also recommend that the convicted person be deported from the United Kingdom.[4] Of these, the confiscation of the proceeds of crime and recommendations for deportation give rise to particular difficulties.

(A) Confiscation of criminal proceeds

The confiscation of the proceeds of crime is not especially frowned upon by the Court. The need to combat crime, and particularly organised crime is recognised, as is the role that asset seizure may play in this. In *Raimondo v. Italy*[5] the applicant complained that the seizure of 16 items of heritable property and six vehicles, and their subsequent infringed his property rights under Article 1 of the First Protocol. The applicant was suspected of being a member of a Mafia-type organisation, and the property was seized in connection with criminal proceedings instituted against him. In rejecting his claim under the First Protocol, the Court observed:

4.30

4.31

---

[98] See above, p. 135
[99] Sex Offenders Act 1997, Pt I and Sched. 1. See *Adamson v. U.K.* Appl. No. 42293/98, Admissibility decision (Third Section) January 23, 1999 and *K.S. v. U.K.* Appl. No. 45035/98, Admissibility decision (Third Section) March 7, 2000.
[1] Proceeds of Crime (Scotland) Act 1995.
[2] *Ibid.*
[3] *Ibid*, ss. 249 *et seq.*
[4] Immigration Act 1971, s.3(6).
[5] (1994) 18 E.H.R.R. 237.

"Like the Government and the Commission, the Court observes that the confiscation...pursued an aim that was in the general interest, namely it sought to ensure that the use of the property in question did not procure for the applicant, or the criminal organisation to which he was suspected of belonging, advantages to the detriment of the community. The Court is fully aware of the difficulties encountered by the Italian State in the fight against the Mafia. As a result of its unlawful activities, in particular drug-trafficking, and its international connections, this "organisation" has an enormous turnover that is subsequently invested, *inter alia*, in the real property sector. Confiscation, which is designed to block these movements of suspect capital, is an effective and necessary weapon in the combat against this cancer. It therefore appears proportionate to the aim pursued, all the more so because it in fact entails no additional restriction in relation to seizure."[6]

Similarly, in *Welch v. United Kingdom*,[7] the Court, while holding that the Drug Trafficking Offences Act 1986 had been applied to the case of the applicant in breach of Article 7(2) commented:

"The Court would stress, however, that this conclusion concerns only the retrospective application of the relevant legislation and does not call into question in any respect the powers of confiscation conferred on the courts as a weapon in the fight against the scourge of drug trafficking."[8]

Despite the Court's acceptance of the need for a robust policy in the face of organised crime, doubts have been cast upon the compatibility of specific aspects of the United Kingdom's asset-seizure legislation, and in particular the powers of the Courts in relation to the seizure of the proceeds of drug-trafficking. Attention has focused on the assumption that the court may make under section 3(2) of the Proceeds of Crime (Scotland) Act 1995 when assessing the value of the proceeds of a convicted person's drug-trafficking. Under that section the court may "assume", *inter alia*, that property held by the convicted person is derived from drug-trafficking.

In *Elton v. United Kingdom*[9] it was argued that the equivalent provisions in section 2 of the Drug Trafficking Offences Act 1986 were incompatible with the presumption of innocence in Article 6(2) of the Convention. This argument was rejected by the Commission on the ground that such assumptions of fact were not inconsistent

---

[6]   (1994) 18 E.H.R.R. 237, at para. 30.
[7]   (1995) 20 E.H.R.R. 247.
[8]   *Ibid*, at para. 36.
[9]   Appl. No. 32344/96, Commission Decision, September 11, 1997.

with Article 6(2), relying on the decisions of the Court in *Salabiaku v. France*[10] and *Pham Hoang v. France.*[11]

In *McIntosh v. H.M. Advocate*[12] the High Court held that the assumptions permitted by section 3(2) were not compatible with Article 6(2). It did so on the basis that at least in part such assumptions related to the proceeds of conduct (drug trafficking) which would be a crime in Scotland. That being so, the invitation to the Court to make the assumptions involved an allegation of crime against the individual concerned, and from that point he or she was entitled to the benefit of the presumption of innocence in Article 6(2) as a person charged with a criminal offence.

The correctness of this conclusion is open to doubt. It is true that Article 6(2) may be applied to persons against whom criminal proceedings have in some degree been initiated, but well before the point at which they are formally charged according to the requirements of the legal system in question. Provided he is "substantially affected" by the proceedings he may be regarded as having been "charged".[13] It is also the case that persons may be regarded as "charged" for the purpose of Article 6 when they are not yet facing criminal proceedings, but are under investigation in other types of proceedings, such as administrative proceedings.[14] It seems, however, that these cases all concern the situation where original criminal proceedings are at least in contemplation. It could be argued that the assumptions which the court is empowered to make under section 3(2) do not form part of a preparation for prosecution, but rather the application of penalties following prosecution. If that is so, then Article 6(2) would seem to have no bearing on the question.

(B) Deportation

A court cannot order deportation of a convicted person, but may in terms of section 3(6) of the Immigration Act 1971 recommend deportation. In certain circumstances deportation may expose the individual to the risk of violation of his human rights in the country to which he is deported. It is well-established that to expel someone, whether by extradition, deportation or other means to a country where there is a real risk of a violation of at least certain of the Convention rights, is incompatible with the state's obligations under the Convention.[15] This would be the case, for example, where

4.32

---

[10] (1988) 13 E.H.R.R. 379.
[11] Series A, No. 243.
[12] High Court, October 13, 2000, *unreported.*
[13] *Deweer v. Belgium* (1980) 2 E.H.R.R. 439; *Eckle v. Germany* (1982) 5 E.H.R.R. 1.
[14] *Deweer v. Belgium, ibid; Funke v. France* (1993) 16 E.H.R.R. 297.
[15] See, for example, *Soering v. U.K.* (1989) 11 E.H.R.R. 439; *D v. U.K.* **(19??)** 24 E.H.R.R. 423; *Chahal v. U.K.* (1996) 2 E.H.R.R. 413.

there was a real risk that the deportee would suffer torture or inhumane or degrading treatment, or where his life would be put at risk.

While deportation is, ultimately, an executive act, it is at least arguable given the terms of section 6 of the Human Rights Act, that a court, as a public authority should not act in a manner that is incompatible with an offender's rights by recommending him for deportation in such circumstances.

PART III: PRISONERS' RIGHTS

4.33   This section considers a number of matters which relate to the situation of persons in detention, which do not arise out of the process by which the duration of detention is determined, but out of the conditions under which they are held, and in particular the restrictions which are imposed upon their freedom to communicate with those outside the prison.

1. Conditions of detention

(a) Conditions of detention—general

4.34   A great many cases have been brought before the Strasbourg institutions claiming that the conditions of detention are incompatible with the Convention – principally Article 3. Complaints have also been brought on the ground that the location of the prisoner's detention is such that it is not possible to sustain links with his or her family, and that there is therefore an interference with family life. As with claims that the nature of the sentence itself is incompatible with the Convention (for example because of its length), claims that the conditions of detention (including location) are incompatible with the Convention are rarely successful.

Although claims based on the conditions of detention are rarely successful, it is clear that in principle the conditions under which a person is detained may be so adverse that they amount to inhuman or degrading treatment. This was confirmed by the Court in *Soering v. United Kingdom*[16] in which it was held that detention on death row in Virginia could amount to inhuman treatment. That case is, however, exceptional. The court's conclusion in that case is based in part on the stress suffered by a person under sentence of death, in part on the physical and social conditions on death row, on the length of time which a person under sentence of death could expect to remain on death row, and the personal characteristics of the complainer, including his age and mental condition.

In one other case, *Peers v. Greece*, the Commission held that certain features of the applicant's detention in a Greek prison

---

[16]   (1989) 11 E.H.R.R. 439.

constituted degrading treatment within the meaning of Article 3. In that case the Commission described the conditions:

> "Given that for at least two months the applicant had to spend a considerable part of each 24-hour period practically confined to his bed in a cell with no ventilation and no window which would at times become unbearably hot and given, in particular, that he had to use the toilet in the presence of another inmate and be present while the toilet was being used by his cellmate, the Commission considers that he was subjected to degrading treatment in the sense of article 3 of the Convention."[17]

The lack of adequate sanitary facilities has, of course, been a source of criticism of conditions in various prisons in the United Kingdom for many years. It is especially significant, then, that the Commission singled out in particular the absence of such facilities as of particular importance in their determination in the *Peers* case.

It is clear, however, that the conditions of detention do have to be very poor before an argument based on Article 3 will be upheld. That said, the Court has recently declared admissible a case in which the applicant claimed that the conditions of his detention on death row in the Ukraine amounted to a violation of Article 3. In *Khokhlich v. Ukraine*[18] the applicant complained, *inter alia*, that he had been placed in a cell with another prisoner who was suffering from tuberculosis, and from whom he contracted the disease. Such a claim, if made out, and if it could be shown that the authorities were aware of the other prisoner's condition, would certainly suggest a violation of Article 3.

(b) Special conditions of detention – solitary confinement, segregation etc

Many cases relating to conditions of detention relate not to the general conditions under which the accused was detained, but to the use of special forms of detention in his case. Claims based on solitary confinement or other forms of segregation from the general prison body are frequent.   4.35

It has repeatedly been stated that "solitary confinement is undesirable, especially where the person is detained on remand."[19] However, the segregation of a prisoner from the rest of the prison community does not in itself constitute inhuman and degrading treatment.[20] Whether prolonged removal from association with

---

[17] Appl. No. 28524/95, Commission Report, June 4, 1999.
[18] Appl. No. 41707/98, Admissibility decision (Fourth Section), May 25, 1999.
[19] *Dhoest v. Belgium*, para. 116 and case law there cited.
[20] *Delazarus v. U.K.* Appl. No. 17525/90, Commission Decision, February 16, 1993; *N.H. v. U.K.* Appl. No. 21447/93, Commission Decision, June 30, 1993; *Koksinen v. Finland*, *supra*, no. 82.

others falls within the ambit of article 3 "depends upon the particular conditions of its application, including its stringency, duration and purpose, as well as its effects on the person concerned."[21]

Extreme forms of social isolation can, however, amount to a violation of Article 3. In *Dhoest v. Belgium*[22] the Commission observed:

> "[The Commission] has on other occasions stated that complete sensory isolation, coupled with total social isolation, can destroy the personality and constitutes a form of treatment which cannot be justified by the requirements of security or for any other reason."

What is often significant in cases involving segregation is, of course, the fact that the prisoner has been subjected to such special measures because of his dangerous or anti-social behaviour. In *Dhoest v. Belgium* the Commission noted that the segregation of the prisoner, and the special conditions under which he was held, were "mainly the result of his uncooperative and disruptive behaviour. It was also clear that the applicant represented a special security risk, given his constant obsession to escape from the institution."

It is important to note, however, that the conduct of the detainee does not excuse a departure from the state's obligations under Article 3.[23] Where faced with a challenge to their authority, the authorities must "maintain a continuous review of the detention arrangements employed with a view to ensuring the health and well-being of all prisoners with due regard to the ordinary and reasonable requirements of imprisonment."[24]

The words of the Commission in *E v. Norway*[25] are also important in this context:

> "The question is not whether the prison...authorities have done enough, or whether they can be criticised. The long-lasting isolation of the applicant could be considered inhuman or degrading irrespective of whether any individual or any single institution can be criticised. It is rather a question of a weakness of the system that allows this kind of treatment to occur. The system lacks adequate remedial actions to meet the needs of the applicant. This may be due to lack of resources, inefficient central organisation, or other conditions. But this is irrelevant regarding article 3, which does not allow any such reason as exception."

---

[21] *Delazarus v. United Kingdom, ibid,* and cases there cited.
[22] Appl. No. 10448/83, Commission Report, May 14, 1987.
[23] *Dhoest v. Belgium, supra,* no. 000, para 121.
[24] *McFeeley v. U.K.* Appl. No. 8317/78, Commission Decision, May 15, 1980, 20 D.R. 44, at para. 46.
[25] Appl. No. 11701/85, Commission Decision (Partial), March 7, 1988.

(c) The provision of medical treatment

Failure to provide appropriate medical treatment can give rise to an 4.36
issue under Article 3. "Illness does not exclude detention, but there
is an obligation to provide adequate medical treatment for persons
in detention".[26] The factors to be taken into account in determining
whether or not there has been a violation are the seriousness of the
prisoner's condition, the quality of the medical care received in
prison and whether the prisoner's condition is compatible with
detention.[27]

The Convention does not require a state to release a person from
custody, or to transfer him to a civil hospital, in order to receive
treatment, and this is so even if his condition is particularly difficult
to treat.[28] In determining the appropriate treatment measures,
however, the state is "obliged to maintain a continuous review of
the detention arrangements employed with a view to ensuring the
health and well-being of all prisoners, having regard to the ordinary
and reasonable requirements of imprisonment."[29]

(d) Forcible medical treatment

Except in cases of emergency, or without other lawful authority, it 4.37
is unlawful medically to treat a person without their consent. Even
in an emergency a person—including a prisoner—is entitled to
refuse to accept medical treatment. There is nothing in the Prison
Rules which permits treatment without the prisoner's consent, and
such treatment would, therefore be unlawful. The one exception to
this would be where treatment is required as a matter of emergency
and the prisoner is not capable of giving or withholding consent.

In *Herczegfalvy v. Austria*[30] the Court decided that the forcible
treatment of a detainee cannot be regarded as inhuman or
degrading where such treatment was therapeutically necessary. It
is important to note, however, that that case concerned treatment
necessary "to preserve the physical and mental health of patients
who are entirely incapable of deciding for themselves."[31] Moreover,

---

[26] *Jordan v. U.K.* Appl. No. 30280/96, Commission Decision, January 14, 1998,
referring to *Hurtado v. Switzerland*, Series A, No. 280-A, Commission Report,
July 8, 1993, p. 10.
[27] *Jastrzebski v. Poland*, Appl. No. 25669/94, Report of Commission, May 19, 1998,
para. 61.
[28] *Chartier v. Italy*, Commission Decision, December 8, 1982, 33 D.R. 41;
Jastrzebski v. Poland, supra, no. 000.
[29] *Jastrzebski v. Poland, supra,* no. 000; *Bonnechaux v. Switzerland*, Commission
Report, December 5, 1979, 18 D.R. 100. See also, *Jeznach v. Poland*, Appl. No.
27580/95, Commission Report, September 10, 1999; *Sadowski v. Poland*, Appl.
No. 32726/96, Admissibility decision (Fourth section) October 12, 2000; *Lowry v.
Portugal*, Appl. No. 42296/98, Admissibility decision (Fourth section), July 6,
1999.
[30] (1992) 15 E.H.R.R. 437.
[31] *Herczegfalvy v. Austria* (1992) 15 E.H.R.R. 437, at para. 82.

such patients "remain under the protection of Article 3", and to continue treatment beyond what is in the circumstances justified by the therapeutic needs of the detainee will be contrary to Article 3.

(e) Forcible feeding

4.38   Although the legality of forcible feeding of prisoners does not appear to have been the subject of any judicial opinion in Scotland, the position in England is that the Governor of a prison has neither the right nor the duty to force feed a prisoner who knowingly refuses food.[32] A similar view would presumably be taken in Scotland.

In *Herczegfalvy v. Austria* the applicant complained not only of forcible medication, but of force-feeding as well. The Court's opinions on forcible treatment are probably equally applicable to force-feeding, so that where this is necessary to preserve the life of the detainee, it will not be regarded as inhuman or degrading. However, this must also be read in the context of the case, and it is possible to argue that the forcible feeding of a detainee who is physically and mentally capable of deciding whether or not to accept nutrition would be a violation of Article 3.

(f) Vulnerable prisoners

4.39   Both Articles 2 and 3 impose positive obligations on the state to ensure that persons within their jurisdiction do not suffer infringement of the rights which they enshrine. This obligation extends to ensuring that an individual's rights are not infringed by the acts of another individual.[33] It follows, therefore, that where a prisoner suffers inhuman or degrading treatment at the hands of other prisoners, there may be a violation of Article 3. Similarly, if, in an extreme case, a prisoner is killed by another prisoner, there may be a breach of Article 2. Such a conclusion would, however, involve demonstrating that the state, or the prison authorities deliberately refrained from intervening to prevent such occurrences, or at least failed to take reasonable steps to prevent them, knowing that they were likely to happen.[34]

The Convention obligations may be engaged even where the prisoner has harmed himself or herself.[35]

---

[32]   *R v. Home Secretary ex parte Robb* [1995] Fam. L.R. 127, [1995] 1 All E.R. 677.
[33]   *Osman v. U.K.* (2000) 29 E.H.R.R. 245 (Art. 2); *A v. U.K.* (1999) 27 E.H.R.R. 611.
[34]   *Cf Osman v. U.K.*, *supra*, no. 4; *Keenan v. U.K.* Appl. No. 27229/95, Commission Report, September 6, 1999; *Cf Bollan v. U.K.* Appl. No. 42117/98, Admissibility decision, May 4 ,2000.
[35]   *Keenan v. United Kingdom, ibid.*

2. Access to family members

Although restrictions on access to family members have on occasions been challenged as infringing Article 3,[36] the most frequently invoked provision in this regard is Article 8.   4.40

The Commission has frequently been faced with claims that right to family life of a prisoner, and the prisoner's family, is interfered with on account of the place where the prisoner is detained. A prisoner from the south of England who is detained in Peterhead will in all probability encounter considerably greater difficulties in receiving visits from his family and friends than a prisoner whose family lives in Aberdeen and Dundee.[37]

The Commission has recognised the importance to prisoners of maintaining contact with their families, and the particular problems that they face in this respect:

"[The Commission] recalls that it has held that in the context of prisoners or other persons who are detained the concept of 'family life' must be given a wider scope than in other situations. It has held...that: 'Prisoners generally have limited means of contact with the outside community and of maintaining relationships with family members. 'Family life' for prisoners is inevitably restricted to visits, correspondence and possibly other forms of communication such as telephone calls. Emotional dependency between, for example, parents and adult children, or siblings is even enhanced in these circumstances."[38]

However, the Commission has repeatedly held that "a prisoner has no right as such under the Convention to choose the place of his confinement and that a separation of a detained person from his family and the hardship resulting from it are the inevitable consequences of detention".[39] In general, therefore, the fact that a prisoner's family are unable to visit, or only able to do so with great difficulty, will not result in a violation of the right to family life. This conclusion has been reached in the face of Commission's own opinion that "article 8 requires the State to assist prisoners as far as possible to create and sustain ties with people outside prison in   4.41

---

[36] See *Buitrago Montes and Perez Lopez v. U.K., supra*, no. 000.

[37] *Cf Ballantyne v. U.K.* Appl. No. 14462/88, Commission Decision, April 12, 1991 (prisoner detained in special units in Inverness and Peterhead, while family all lived in the central belt.)

[38] *Anderson v. U.K.* Appl. No. 20478/92, Commission Decision, September 1, 1993.

[39] See, for example, Appl. No 5229/71, Commission Decision, October 5, 1972, 42 Collection, p. 14; Appl. No. 5712/72, Commission Decision, July 15, 1974, 46 Collection p. 112; *P.K., M.K. and B.K. v. U.K.* Appl. No. 19085/91, Commission Decision, December 9, 1992.

order to facilitate prisoners' social rehabilitation."[40]

The basis on which this conclusion is reached appears to vary. In some cases, typically where the ground of complaint is that the state has refused to transfer a prisoner to a location nearer to his family, the Commission has concluded that there has been no interference with the right to respect for family life.[41] In others it has held that there is an interference, but that the circumstances of the case justify that interference.[42]

4.42   The Commission has suggested that there might be exceptional circumstances in which the detention of a prisoner a long way from his home or family might infringe the requirements of Article 8,[43] but it seems extremely reluctant to recognise any such exceptional circumstances. In what would appear to be a wholly exceptional case[44] the Commission accepted that it would in fact be impossible for the detainee's family to visit him. The applicant was convicted in the Bahamas and sentenced to a period of imprisonment. While in prison he attacked and killed a prison officer, and was then sentenced for that offence. Since there was no appropriate prison in the Bahamas for the applicant—who was clearly a violent person who required a high security prison for his safe confinement—the United Kingdom agreed to provide accommodation for him. He complained that his right to family life was interfered with, in that it was impossible for his family to visit him. The Commission accepted that this was the case, but pointed out that his place of confinement was due to his own past record of violence (and the prognosis for the future) and that there was therefore no interference with his right to family life.

---

[40] *P.K., M.K. and B.K. v. United Kingdom*, ibid. Cf Prison Rules, r.33: "The Governor shall ensure that every prisoner is given reasonable assistance and facilities to maintain and develop relationships with his family and friends and with such other persons and agencies outwith the prison as may best offer him assistance during his sentence or period of committal, and in preparation for and after his release."

[41] See, for example, *Anderson v. U.K.* Appl. No. 20478/92, Commission Decision, September 1, 1993.

[42] See, for example, *X v. U.K.* Commission Decision, July 18, 1974, 46 Collection, pp 112-117.

[43] See, for example, the sequence of cases brought by prisoners from Ireland serving their sentences in England and Wales. In none of these cases was it held that there were "exceptional circumstances": *Kinsella v. U.K.* Appl. No. 19200/91, Commission Decision, September 1, 1993; *McCombe v. U.K.* Appl. No.19785/92, Commission Decision, September 1, 1993; *Holmes v. U.K.* Appl. No. 19786/92, Commission Decision, September 1, 1993; *Anderson v. U.K. supra*, no. ???; *McCotter v. U.K.* Appl. No. 20479/92, Commission Decision, September 1, 1993; *McDonnell v. U.K.* Appl. No.20480/92, Commission Decision, September 1, 1993; *Norney v. U.K.* Appl. No. 20481/92, Commission Decision, September 1, 1993; *Vella v. U.K.* Appl. No. 20482/92, Commission Decision, September 1, 1993 ; *Armstrong v. U.K.* Appl. No. 20483/92, Commission Decision, September 1, 1993; *McKenny v. U.K.* Appl. No. 20485/92, Commission Decision, September 1, 1993; *Gibson v. U.K.* Appl. No. 20486/92, Commission Decision, September 1, 1993; *O'Dwyer v. U.K.* Appl. No. 20487/92, Commission Decision, September 1, 1993.

[44] *X v. U.K.* Commission Decision, July 18, 1974, 46 Collection, pp 112-117.

In an analogous case, *Buitrago Montes and Perez Lopez v. United Kingdom*,[45] the applicants were two Colombian nationals convicted of drug trafficking offences and each sentenced to consecutive periods of 12 and eight years' imprisonment. They were classified as Category A prisoners, which classification requires the highest measures of security. They complained, *inter alia,* that they were denied access to a telephone, which was their only means of direct communication with their families. This, they argued, was contrary to Article 8. The Commission noted that "the possibility of remaining in contact with one's family constitutes one of the elements of the right to respect for family life". However, the fact that the applicants could not avail themselves of this means of communication flowed directly from their classification as Category A prisoners, and the fact that they were in detention in the first place was because they had been convicted of serious offences in the United Kingdom. Moreover, the telephone was not the only means by which they could communicate with their families. There was no evidence to suggests that they had been prevented from sending letters or receiving visits from them. In the circumstances, therefore, there was no violation of Article 8.

In *Togher v. United Kingdom*[46] the applicant was arrested and remanded in custody on charges relating to trafficking in cocaine. She had given birth 10 days before her arrest. Because of the seriousness of the charges, and also because of her alleged connections with a well-organised, well-funded criminal enterprise, she was given a provisional Category A status in prison. One consequence of this was that she could not be located in the mother and baby unit in the prison (which had very low security) and she was therefore separated from her infant child. The child was placed with foster parents. She claimed, *inter alia*, that this separation was a violation of Article 8. The government argued in this case that there were no special circumstances which would justify the conclusion that there Article 8 had been infringed.

Clearly even the complete absence of face-to-face contact between a prisoner and his family can be justified by his or her conduct, as, for example, in the case of *X v. United Kingdom*. But given the great weight to be attached to the interests of the child, and taking into consideration the fact that the applicant in *Togher v. United Kingdom* was a remand prisoner, rather than a convicted prisoner, there would seem to be a good case for saying that the circumstances of that case were exceptional. The child was very young. It was being breast-fed by its mother. No practical arrangements were possible for her to feed the child by expressed breast milk. The government's argument was that the provisional classification of the prisoner was necessary because of a high risk of

---

[45] Appl. No. 18077/91, Commission Decision, December 2, 1992.
[46] Appl. No. 28555/95, Commission Decision, April 16, 1998.

escape. But given that the applicant was recognised to have been, at the time of her arrest at least, in a weak and vulnerable condition from the recent birth, the risk of escape must have been low. In circumstances such as these it would seem right to argue that removing the child from her mother infringed the article eight rights of both.[47]

The case was resolved by a friendly settlement in which the United Kingdom government paid £10,000 in non-pecuniary damages, plus reasonable legal costs in connection with the application to the Commission.[48]

3. Interference with correspondence

4.43   It is important to distinguish between general correspondence, and correspondence between the prisoner and his legal advisors or a court. The Strasbourg institutions have placed an especial premium on the latter, and afford it greater protection from scrutiny by the prison authorities.

(a) Correspondence in general

4.44   Article 8 provides that everyone has the right to respect for his "correspondence", but it also provides that this right may be subject to interference by a public authority. The Court has expressed the view that "censorship" of prisoners' correspondence by prison authorities is an interference with the right to respect for the privacy of their correspondence.[49] Such censorship may take the form of stopping letters[50] or delaying letters[51] as well as opening them. Opening correspondence is an interference, even if it is not read by the prison authorities.[52] However, "short periods of delay while letters are checked for conformity with prison regulations are in

---

[47] *Cf* Rule 116 of the Prison Rules: 116(1)—Subject to paragraph (2), the Governor may permit a female prisoner to have her baby with her in prison, and everything necessary for the baby's maintenance and care, including a suitable cot, shall be provided by the Governor.

    (2) Subject to any direction by the Secretary of State for the purposes of this rule, the Governor may in granting permission under paragraph (1) impose such conditions as he thinks fit.

    (3) A female prisoner who is permitted to have her baby with her in prison may, with the consent of the Governor, arrange, at her expense or at the expense of some other person, for the provision of additional articles or food for the baby's maintenance or care.

[48] Appl. No. 28555/95, Commission Report, October 25, 1999.

[49] *Windsor v. U.K.* Appl. No. 16244/90, Commission Decision (Partial), December 12, 1991.

[50] *Silver v. U.K.* (1983) 5 E.H.R.R. 347.

[51] *McCallum v. U.K.* (1990) 13 E.H.R.R. 596; *Silver v. U.K. ibid.*

[52] *Silver v. U.K. ibid.*

general compatible with the provisions of the Convention".[53]

Such interference can, however, be justified in terms of Article 8(2). The Court has recognised that "some measure of control over prisoners' correspondence is called for and is not of itself incompatible with the Convention, regard being paid to the ordinary and reasonable requirements of imprisonment."[54] But in assessing the permissible extent of the control exercised over prisoners' correspondence, it is important not to overlook the fact that "the opportunity to write and receive letters is sometimes the prisoner's only link with the outside world".[55]

In *Windsor v. United Kingdom*, the applicant complained about the interception of a large number of letters sent by him to various people. One of the letters was addressed to a prisoner in another prison and included the sentence "I won't forget this spell Russ and will repay all debts in full regardless of consequences". Another letter was addressed to the Chief Constable of Strathclyde, and contained allegations of theft against a prison officer.

Of these, the Commission held that the interception of the letter addressed to the other prisoner was justified. It contained veiled threats of retribution, and in the view of the Commission the stopping of this letter was "necessary in a democratic society" for the aim of preventing disorder or crime. So far as concerns the letter to the Chief Constable, the Commission's view that this might not be justified. The Government offered the explanation that, following a request by police, the prison authorities accompanied each letter from a prisoner with their comments on the prisoner's allegations. In the view of the Commission "this in effect entails the prison authorities investigating a complaint before passing on a letter to the police and appears to impose a 'de facto' prior ventilation rule."[56] The Commission believed that it was not possible to reject the complaint as ill-founded.

Correspondence raising matters of legitimate concern would seem, rightly, to receive a higher degree of protection. At the other extreme, correspondence which comes close in itself to evidencing an offence will not be protected.

(b) Correspondence with legal advisors

Correspondence with legal advisors is given special protection. As   4.45
the Court stated in *Campbell v. United Kingdom*:[57]

---

[53] *Windsor v. U.K. supra*, 49. But see below for the case of a delay in sending a letter to the prisoner's legal advisor.

[54] *Silver v. U.K. supra*, no. 50, para. 98.

[55] *Campbell v. U.K.* (1990) 12 E.H.R.R. 1, at para. 45.

[56] *Windsor v. U.K. supra*, no. 49.

[57] (1990) 12 E.H.R.R. 1, at para. 46.

"46. It is clearly in the general interest that any person who wishes to consult a lawyer should be free to do so under conditions which favour full and uninhibited discussion. It is for this reason that the lawyer-client relationship is, in principle, privileged. Indeed, in its *S. v. Switzerland*[58] judgment of 28 November 1991 the Court stressed the importance of a prisoner's right to communicate with counsel out of earshot of the prison authorities. It was considered, in the context of Article 6 (art. 6), that if a lawyer were unable to confer with his client without such surveillance and receive confidential instructions from him his assistance would lose much of its usefulness, whereas the Convention is intended to guarantee rights that are practical and effective.

47. In the Court's view, similar considerations apply to a prisoner's correspondence with a lawyer concerning contemplated or pending proceedings where the need for confidentiality is equally pressing, particularly where such correspondence relates, as in the present case, to claims and complaints against the prison authorities. That such correspondence be susceptible to routine scrutiny, particularly by individuals or authorities who may have a direct interest in the subject matter contained therein, is not in keeping with the principles of confidentiality and professional privilege attaching to relations between a lawyer and his client.

48. Admittedly, as the Government pointed out, the borderline between mail concerning contemplated litigation and that of a general nature is especially difficult to draw and correspondence with a lawyer may concern matters which have little or nothing to do with litigation. Nevertheless, the Court sees no reason to distinguish between the different categories of correspondence with lawyers which, whatever their purpose, concern matters of a private and confidential character. In principle, such letters are privileged under Article 8 (art. 8)."

The Court then went on to set out the criteria under which correspondence between a prisoner and his legal advisors may be controlled:

"This means that the prison authorities may open a letter from a lawyer to a prisoner when they have reasonable cause to believe that it contains an illicit enclosure which the normal means of detection have failed to disclose. The letter should, however, only be opened and should not be read. Suitable guarantees preventing the reading of the letter should be provided, e.g. opening the letter in the presence of the prisoner.

---

[58] (1992) 14 E.H.R.R. 670, para. 48. See also, in this context, *Campbell and Fell v. U.K.* (1984) 7 E.H.R.R. 165, paras. 111-113.

The reading of a prisoner's mail to and from a lawyer, on the other hand, should only be permitted in exceptional circumstances when the authorities have reasonable cause to believe that the privilege is being abused in that the contents of the letter endanger prison security or the safety of others or are otherwise of a criminal nature. What may be regarded as 'reasonable cause' will depend on all the circumstances but it presupposes the existence of facts or information which would satisfy an objective observer that the privileged channel of communication was being abused."[59]

The right of an accused person to communicate with his legal advisors, in addition to being protected by Article 8, may also form an aspect of the right of access to a court protected by Article 6(1) where the correspondence relates to actual or potential litigation.[60]

(c) Correspondence with the Strasbourg Court

In *Campbell v. United Kingdom*[61] the applicant complained that   4.46
correspondence between himself and the European Commission on Human Rights had been subject to control by the prison authorities. In fact it appeared that his outgoing mail to the Commission was not subject to scrutiny. The Government accepted, however, that letters addressed to him from the Commission were opened (but not read), and that, in the view of the Court amounted to an interference with the applicant's right to respect for his correspondence, whether or not they were read. The Government claimed that the prison authorities were entitled to open letters which purported to come from the Commission "to confirm that they were what they purported to be."[62] There was, in the view of the Government a risk that letters which appeared to come from the Commission could be used for "illicit materials."[63] This highly implausible explanation was rejected by the Court:

> "there is no compelling reason why such letters from the Commission should be opened. The risk, adverted to by the Government, of Commission stationery being forged in order to smuggle prohibited material or messages into prison, is so negligible that it must be discounted."

There were, on the other hand, good reasons for preventing the

---

[59] (1990) 12 E.H.R.R. 1, at para. 48, referring to *Fox, Campbell and Hartley v. U.K.* (1991) 13 E.H.R.R. 157, para. 32.
[60] *Golder v. U.K.* (1975) 1 E.H.R.R. 524.
[61] (1990) 12 E.H.R.R. 1.
[62] (1990) 12 E.H.R.R. 1, at para. 61.
[63] (1990) 12 E.H.R.R. 1, at para. 62

opening of letters from the Commission:

> "The opening of letters from the Commission undoubtedly gives rise to the possibility that they will be read and may also conceivably, on occasions, create the risk of reprisals by the prison staff against the prisoner concerned."[64]

CONCLUSION

4.47   A review of the approach of the Convention institutions to matters of sentencing and prisoners' rights is to a large extent a dispiriting exercise. This is particularly so in relation to the rights of prisoners. Only the most extreme circumstances will persuade the Strasbourg institutions to conclude that a prisoner has been held in inhumane or degrading conditions. The inconsistency in what is said about the importance of maintaining links between the prisoner and his family and what is actually done is manifest.

   In general terms, the approach of the Strasbourg institutions to most issues relating to sentencing and prisoner's rights means that the Convention rights will add little to the range of remedies available already under Scots or United Kingdom law.

---

[64] *Ibid.*

CHAPTER 5

HUMAN RIGHTS AND FAMILY LAW

PART I: INTRODUCTION

Scots lawyers are already familiar with considering a citizen's rights   5.01
in the context of issues relating to children and families. The
arguments for and against the right of a natural father to have a
relationship with his child against a background of the welfare
principle giving paramountcy to the child's interests has been
argued at the highest domestic level.[1] Children's rights have been
given legal recognition[2] and the balancing exercise between their
right to participate in litigation and to protection from harm
considered.[3] The inclusion of a homosexual partner within the
definition of "family" in the context of succession to a tenancy has
illustrated that there is scope within domestic law, albeit limited, for
the recognition of the rights of those in same sex partnerships.[4] The
notion of a husband's right to protect the life of his unborn child
has been discussed, albeit firmly rejected.[5] This chapter attempts to
consider the impact of the incorporation into our domestic law of
the European Convention on Human Rights ("ECHR") on these
and other issues affecting the family. What emerges is a general
impression that, notwithstanding the previous reluctance to frame
domestic legislation or express judicial decisions using the language
of "rights", there are few substantive areas of Scots Family Law
which the existing European jurisprudence suggests require to be
"rewritten".

---

[1] *Sanderson v. McManus,* 1997 S.L.T. 629
[2] ss. 6 and 11(7) of the Children (Scotland) Act 1995 were enacted primarily to
comply with the U.N. Convention on the Rights of the Child, although there is
little doubt that the relationship between the rights of children and the adults
responsible for them, both ostensibly protected in equal measure by the European
Convention, will require to be developed. See below, in the Childhood section (Pt
III).
[3] See, *e.g. McGrath v. McGrath,* 1999 S.L.T. (Sh.Ct.) 90.
[4] *Fitzpatrick v. Sterling Housing Assoc. Ltd* [1999] 3 W.L.R. 1113.
[5] *Kelly v. Kelly,* 1997 S.L.T. 896

PART II: THE BEGINNING OF LIFE

(a) Assisted Reproduction

5.02   During the last decades of the 20th century, the development of artificially assisted reproduction challenged some of the most fundamental values underlying the legal systems of the western world.[6] While techniques of artificial insemination have a much longer history,[7] it has been the highly sophisticated processes of *in vitro* conception and related techniques that have caused most controversy. We have required to examine whether we regard infertility as a recognised illness or disease for which a cure should be readily available or as a problem resulting in emotional rather than physical or psychiatric needs. In the language of human rights, then, we must consider whether there can be said to be a "right to reproduce". To what extent does ECHR assist those claiming such a right? The primary Convention Article that may apply to any right to reproduce is Article 12, which provides,

> " Men and women of marriageable age have the right to marry and to found a family, according to the national laws governing the exercise of this right. "

The basic rights appear to be qualified to some extent by the words "...according to the national laws", suggesting that, as a general rule, limitations imposed by domestic law may be acceptable. The European Court of Human Rights has confirmed, however, that interference with Article 12 rights which seeks to impair the essence of the right itself will not be justified.[8]

The right to found a family is in principle unqualified,[9] although the terms of the Article seem to extend only to married couples. Can there at least be said, then, to be a right of a married person to reproduce? It seems to the writer that the distinction between upholding non-interference by the state and enlisting its positive assistance is most important. Interference with the right of a married couple to found a family by attempting to restrict, by law, the number of children each couple was "entitled" to produce would surely strike at the root of the Article 12 right and amount to

---

[6]   It is not possible in this general discussion of the human rights issues to include even an overview of the range of assisted reproduction practices which have been developed or advanced during this period. For a detailed, if now dated, discussion of the medical and legal issues see Mason, *Medico Legal Aspects of Reproduction and Parenthood* (Dartmouth Publishing Co. Ltd, 1990); for an updated overview see Mason and McCall Smith, *Law and Medical Ethics* (5th ed., Butterworths, 1999), Chapter 3.

[7]   The Court of Session decided in 1958 that artificial insemination by donor did not constitute adultery in Scots Law. See *MacLennan v. MacLennan*, 1958 S.C. 105.

[8]   *F v. Switzerland* (1987) 10 E.H.R.R. 411, also referred to in "Marriage and Cohabitation" at page 192.

[9]   See *X v. U.K.* Appl. No. 6564/74, 2 D.R. 105.

a violation thereof. A state's refusal to act positively to assist a couple's right to found a family may not interfere with their Convention rights, however. In considering an application in 1978, the Commission found that the Swiss authorities were not obliged to ensure conjugal visits for those serving prison sentences so that they continued to have the opportunity to procreate.[10] However, the age of the case and its particular circumstances render it of very limited assistance in addressing the issue of a right to found a family in the context of reproductive technologies.

A problem more likely to arise at the present time in this country, is the refusal by the state to assist reproduction artificially in a particular situation, or in a certain part of the country, due to decisions related either to social policy or allocation of National Health Service resources. The primary legislation concerning artificial reproduction in the United Kingdom is the Human Fertilisation and Embryology Act 1990.[11] Provision is there made for the legal status and treatment of children born after the use of reproductive technology, but **access** to assisted reproduction is not governed by statute. Instead, it is regulated by a "body corporate", established by the 1990 Act and known as the Human Fertilisation and Embryology Authority ("HFEA"). The Authority is empowered to grant, attach conditions to, refuse, vary, suspend and revoke licences for infertility treatment and associated research.[12] As a result, it has substantial power effectively to refuse treatment to an individual or class of individuals. In this context, the prohibition against discrimination enshrined in Article 14 merits its first consideration in this chapter. Article 14 provides:

> "The enjoyment of the rights and freedoms set forth in this Convention shall be secured without discrimination on any ground such as sex, race, colour, language, religion, political or other opinion, national or social origin, association with a national minority, property, birth or other status."

Article 14 confers no rights independent of the other provisions of the Convention. Accordingly, it must be read in conjunction with Article 12 in this context. The effect would appear to be that impeding the right to found a family by refusing infertility treatment on grounds of, for example, race or sex alone would breach Convention rights. The term "...or other status" in Article 14 is of interest, but would, it is suggested, be unlikely to justify a position that refusal to provide infertility treatment available to married persons to the unmarried is an unlawful interference with Convention rights.

The issue of whether there can be said to be a right to infertility

5.03

---

[10] *X and Y v. Switzerland*, Appl. No. 8166/78, 13 D.R. 241.
[11] c.37
[12] ss. 5–26, 1990 Act.

treatment, reasonable resources permitting, has yet to be directly tested. The most recent and highly publicised potential litigation involved a couple from Fife, who had lost the youngest of their five children, their only daughter, in a bonfire tragedy. They decided to apply for fertility treatment in planning to conceive another child, but only in order to select the sex of the embryo before implantation (they wanted another daughter). While the sex selection issue attracted considerable media and academic discussion, the situation also highlighted the notion of the individual right to reproduce and to be actively assisted in the pursuance of that right. Ultimately, the couple were refused treatment and decided not to challenge the decision by Judicial Review.[13]

In relation to the family relationships created by artificial reproductive practices, the Human Fertilisation and Embryology Act 1990 sets out clear rules as to parentage. For example, a sperm donor is not treated as the father of a child genetically his where a couple, married or unmarried, have sought licensed infertility treatment of artificial insemination by donor.[14] And a surrogate mother, one who carries a foetus to term for another couple, is treated in the first instance as the child's mother, whether or not she has any genetic link with it—the tie of birth governs.[15] Where one of them has a genetic link with the child, a couple who have commissioned the surrogate can then apply for a "parental order" which entitles them to be treated in law as the child's parents for all purposes.[16]

In the absence of the consent of the surrogate, the commissioning parents will be unable to obtain a parental order. In *C v. S*,[17] the Inner House considered the merits of an adoption petition at the instance of a couple who had entered into a surrogacy arrangement with a woman who later refused to consent to a parental order replacing her as legal mother. Much of the controversy in the case surrounded the issue of payment to the surrogate, but an adoption order in favour of the commissioning couple was ultimately made. The decision was undoubtedly consistent with the promotion of the child's welfare, which was said to outweigh the policy considerations against payment.[18] It is doubtful, in the writer's view, whether a similar set of facts would result in a different decision now that legislation must be interpreted in a way compatible with ECHR. The requirement to obtain the consent of the surrogate to a parental order in favour of the couple for whom she bore the child

---

[13] "IVF couple set to lose fight", The Scotsman, 18 October 2000
[14] 1990 Act, ss. 28(1) and (2), s.29(1) and s.49(3).
[15] 1990 Act, s.27(2). The surrogate's husband will, in the first instance, be treated as the baby's father, unless it can be shown that he did not consent to the arrangement. See s.28(2).
[16] 1990 Act, s.30. See also Parental Orders (Human Fertilisation and Embryology) (Scotland) Regulations (S.I. 1994 Nos 2767, 2804 and 3345)
[17] 1996 S.L.T. 1387
[18] *Ibid*, at 1398

must now be regarded as giving recognition to the birth mother's right to family life[19] with her child, unless waived. But the competing interests of the couple, one of whom will also be a parent, will neutralise any perceived advantage it gives the surrogate. In a contest between the birth mother and the couple, then, the governing factor would continue to be the best interests of the child born as a result of the arrangement. Further consideration is given to the relationship between parental rights and welfare considerations below, in the comments on Care Proceedings and Adoption and in the Parenthood section.

While neither the Commission nor the Court has required to address human rights issues arising from surrogacy arrangements to date, there have been applications concerning the rights of sperm donors to family life with their progeny where this is denied to them.[20] The Commission's approach was to regard the donor's role in AID as insufficient *per se* to create a family tie that required protection in terms of Article 8. The 1990 Act seems to be entirely compatible with that approach. The issue of the creation of *de facto* rather than genetic relationships falling within the ambit of Article 8 in the context of artificial reproduction was addressed by the Court in the more recent case of *X, Y and Z v. United Kingdom*.[21] The application concerned a transsexual who, after gender reassignment surgery to become a man, had wanted to create a family with his female partner. She bore a child after AID. The refusal to permit the transsexual partner to be registered as the father of the child led to a complaint by him of a violation of Article 8. The Court's decision on the issue of the alleged violation of Article 8 is dealt with below in looking particularly at transsexuality.[22] What is significant in terms of the approach to families created by artificial reproductive methods, however, is that both the Commission and the Court found that "family life" within the meaning of Article 8(1) existed between the transsexual, his partner and the child, notwithstanding the lack of genetic link between two of them.

5.04

The continued development of scientific advances in this area may lead to a variety of unorthodox family ties falling within the scope of Article 8 protection in the future. And what of the artificially created embryo? How should it be regarded in law? Domestic law gives little protection to it, permitting the creation (and inevitable destruction) of embryos for research, if licensed,[23] and the termination of one or more embryos after implantation to

---

[19] See Art. 8(1) ECHR
[20] *G v. The Netherlands*, 16 E.H.R.R. 39; *Kroon v. The Netherlands*, 19 E.H.R.R. 263
[21] 20 E.H.R.R. 143
[22] see page 209.
[23] ss.3(1) and 15 and Sched. 2, para. 3 of the Human Fertilisation and Embryology Act 1990.

reduce the risk of multiple birth.[24] Does ECHR not apply to that earliest form of life? The issue has not been judicially considered, either in a domestic court or in the European forum. If it is to be addressed in the future, it seems likely that regard will be had to the position taken on the developing embryo *in utero*, which will now be discussed.

(b) Abortion.

5.05   Scots Law on termination of pregnancy is contained in the Abortion Act 1967,[25] as significantly amended by the Human Fertilisation and Embryology Act 1990. The legislation conscientiously avoids the language of rights, focusing as it does on the circumstances in which abortion will not be deemed unlawful.[26] The ongoing debate over the morality of abortion and the legal regulation thereof has proved to be intractable. In considering the role of human rights law in that debate, two distinct interests emerge—the unborn child at one end of life's spectrum and the mother who carries him at the other. It is appropriate to consider each in turn.

(i) The unborn child

5.06   As human fertilisation is a process rather than a single event, it may be impossible to pinpoint a precise definition of when "life" begins. It is essential, however, to formulate a view on when the life created should be afforded legal protection, given the terms of Article 2(1) of the Convention. It provides,

> "Everyone's right to life shall be protected by law. No one shall be deprived of his life intentionally save in the execution of a sentence of a court following his conviction of a crime for which this penalty is provided by law."

It has been over 20 years since the European Commission of Human Rights was first asked to consider whether Article 2 bestowed an absolute right to life on the unborn foetus. In *Paton v. United Kingdom*[27] a married man complained to the Commission that his 10-week-old foetus' right to life had been violated when his wife had terminated the pregnancy, despite his objections and

---

[24] The practice of implanting more embryos than the number of live births desired with a view to destroying some thereafter, is known as "selective reduction." Section 37 of the 1990 Act amends s.5(2) of the Abortion Act 1967 to make clear that the practice is lawful if authorised under s.1 of the 1967 Act.
[25] c.87
[26] s.1(1)(a)–(d)
[27] (1980) 3 E.H.R.R.408.

attempts in the domestic courts to challenge her actions.[28] The Commission was of the view that the term "everyone" in Article 2 did not include the unborn. To recognise a right to life in the unborn, it was thought, would place a higher value on unborn life than on the life of the pregnant woman, effectively limiting her own right to life, contrary to the intention of the drafters of the Convention.[29] This position was adopted both in a later English decision[30] and during a more recent Scottish attempt by a husband to prevent his wife terminating a pregnancy, in *Kelly v. Kelly*.[31] There, the court, in referring to *Paton,* agreed that to recognise the right to life of the foetus would create conflict between the existing legal interests of the mother and those of the unborn child.[32] In a straightforward conflict of rights, then, domestic law falls short of recognising that the life of a foetus should be preserved. But there may yet be scope to develop the argument that the foetus has some rights under the Convention in the absence of a clear general ruling from the European Court that it does not. In *H v. Norway*[33] the father of a 14-week-old foetus claimed that a proposed termination would cause severe pain and would therefore amount to inhuman treatment in terms of Article 3, which provides,

> "No one shall be subjected to torture or to inhuman or degrading treatment or punishment."

While the Commission rejected the application, it did so as a result of the applicant's failure to substantiate his claim by appropriate scientific material. A future claim supported by clear information that a foetus, say of 23 weeks gestation, will suffer considerable pain during a proposed termination could meet with more success. Further, the requirement to give effect to primary legislation in a way which is compatible with Convention rights may raise questions about the use of the 1967 Act to perform abortions on so called "social" grounds, particularly close to the twenty four week limit. This suggestion leads to contemplation of the mother's rights in the context of abortion.

(ii) The mother

While domestic legislation on abortion is consistent with the protection of the mother's right to life in terms of Article 2 of the Convention, it does not, as indicated, encapsulate any right of a   5.07

---

28 see *Paton v. British Pregnancy Advisory Service Trustees* [1979] 1 Q.B. 276
29 3 E.H.R.R 408 at 412.
30 *C v. S* [1987] 2 W.L.R. 1108
31 1997 S.L.T. 896.
32 *ibid.,* at 901.
33 17004/90, 73 D.R. 155

woman to termination of pregnancy. As there is a wide variation in the approach of the States to the regulation of abortion, it seems unlikely that a claim for an unrestricted right to a termination will be any more successful than the argument that any termination breaches the foetus' right to life. Thus in *Bruggeman and Scheuten v. FRG*[34] a challenge to (West) German legislation was made on the basis that it limited abortion, even during the first 12 weeks of pregnancy, to particular grounds. This, claimed the applicants, constituted an interference with their Article 8 rights. Article 8(1) is in the following terms,

"Everyone has the right to respect for his private and family life, his home and his correspondence".

5.08   The restricted availability of abortion was said to interfere with the right to respect for the applicants' private life. However, the Commission rejected that argument on the basis that there was no blanket prohibition on abortion, that the health and distress of the mother were given due weight in a decision whether to permit termination and there were no punitive criminal sanctions attached to it. A similar ruling on a challenge to the United Kingdom legislation could be expected. It may follow from *Bruggeman and Scheuten,* however, that a blanket prohibition on abortion would constitute an interference with the mother's Article 8 rights. In Ireland, the spectre of a challenge under the Convention to the provisions of the Irish Constitution rendering abortion illegal was avoided by a decision of the Supreme Court there. A young woman was permitted by the court to travel abroad in order to terminate the pregnancy where it was probable that to deny her an abortion would involve a substantial risk to her life.[35] This coincided with an important decision of the European Court of Human Rights upholding the claims of individuals and counselling organisations that an injunction restraining the distribution of information to women in Ireland about the availability of lawful abortion in other states was incompatible with Article 10. The decision in *Open Door Counselling and Dublin Well Women v. Ireland,*[36] while significant insofar as it related to support for the right to freedom of expression under Article 10(1) and condemnation of disproportionate restrictions on the exercise of that right, lends no support to an argument that a woman has an enforceable right under the Convention to terminate pregnancy. The Court explicitly clarified that the case did not require an examination of that argument, or indeed of the right to life issue under Article 2.[37]

It would appear, then, that there is little scope for further

---

[34] 3 E.H.R.R 244
[35] *A-G v. X* [1992] 2 C.M.L.R. 277
[36] 15 E.H.R.R. 244
[37] *Ibid.,* at p.264 (para.66).

development of the rights of the mother to abortion using the Convention. Such rights as she has, however, are likely to continue to take precedence over the claim of the foetus to protection of its life. For example, in 1988 the English Court of Appeal in *Re F (in utero)*[38] refused to accept jurisdiction to protect the life of a foetus from the risks associated with the mother's erratic mental condition and lifestyle. The court cited *Paton* and the conflict between the welfare of the foetus and the rights of the mother that the application engendered in justifying its refusal. Some years later, the same court in *Re MB (an adult: medical treatment)*[39] confirmed it had no jurisdiction to order a competent woman to undergo a caesarian section notwithstanding that the consequence of her refusal to consent to the procedure might be the death or serious handicap of her unborn child.

In summary, while one may instinctively be attracted to the application of Convention rights to the foetus, the irreconcilable conflict between those rights and the rights of the carrying mother, is not likely to be resolved in the future by dilution of the adult's Convention protected rights and freedoms. Indeed, at the time of writing, a further most recent attempt by a man to prevent a pregnant woman carrying his child from terminating the pregnancy has just failed.[40]

(c) The neonate

After birth, the conflict between the rights of the foetus and the competing rights of the mother would appear to be resolved. Each has a full complement of human rights, including the all-important Article 2 right to life. But it has never been entirely clear, in relation to the neonate, whether domestic law requires only that no steps are taken to terminate life, or whether there is an obligation to take active steps to preserve life for as long as possible.

A series of English cases decided prior to the passing of the 1998 Act considered this matter insofar as it affected the treatment of new-born infants with profound physical and/or neurological problems. In *Re B (a minor)*[41] a Down's syndrome baby had an intestinal obstruction which would be fatal without surgery. The parents felt it would be better if she was allowed to die. She was duly made a ward of court to protect her interests while the matter was considered by the Court of Appeal, which determined that she must undergo surgery so that she could live. A different result was reached in *Re C (a minor)(wardship: medical treatment)*,[42] but the child there was already dying and those treating her were simply

5.09

---

[38] [1988] 2 All E.R. 193
[39] [1997] 2 F.L.R. 426
[40] See "The rights of man—or just the same old misogyny" and "Ex-boyfriend will ask court for foetus remains" The Independent, March 27, 2001.
[41] The case was decided in 1981 ,but is reported at [1990] 3 All E.R. 927
[42] [1989] 2 All E.R. 782

given authority by the court to treat only to alleviate her pain and suffering and not to take additional invasive measures to prolong her short life. This approach was adopted in the more sensitive case of *Re J (a minor)(wardship: medical treatment)*,[43] in which a severely brain damaged young boy suffered from fits and breathing problems. The respiratory failure would require him to be artificially reventilated in order to survive. The Court of Appeal sanctioned a decision to withhold treatment on the basis that it was not in the boy's interests to prolong his life and thus his suffering. But, it confirmed,

> " There is no question of approving, even in a case of the most horrendous disability, a course aimed at terminating life or accelerating death. The court is concerned only with the circumstances in which steps should not be taken to prolong life."[44]

This dictum summarised the limits to the very particular circumstances in which the English courts felt able to condone the withholding of treatment of young infants where to do otherwise seemed contrary to their interests and the approach was adopted in other cases.[45] The issue did not require to be addressed in the Scottish courts, though it was thought that a similar attitude would prevail here.[46] There seems little doubt, following the decision in *Law Hospital NHS Trust v. Lord Advocate*[47] that the Court of Session could use the *parens patriae* jurisdiction to make whatever order was deemed to be in the patient's best interests, even if that was the withdrawal of treatment.[48]

5.10   Against that background, the English Court of Appeal came to decide, almost on the eve of the coming into force of the 1998 Act, a tragic and unique case that required a review of the accepted position that the courts would not approve the active termination of the life of a young infant. The case, *Re A (children)(conjoined twins: surgical separation)*,[49] involved twins, known for the

---

[43] [1990] 3 All E.R. 930
[44] *Ibid.*, at p.943
[45] See *e.g. Re J (a minor)(medical treatment)* [1992] 4 All E.R. 614 and *Re C (a baby)* [1996] 2 F.L.R. 43
[46] Mason and McCall Smith, at p.373, fn.12 cite the determination of a fatal accident enquiry supporting a medical decision to withhold treatment from a very low birth-weight premature baby in 1997.
[47] 1996 S.L.T. 848
[48] The discontinuance of feeding of an incurable adult in a persistent vegetative state for which court approval was sought in the Law Hospital case raised some different issues than those under discussion here, although, as an authoritative five judge bench decision it would undoubtedly be considered in any application involving a proposal to withhold treatment from a defective new-born. For a discussion of the law relating to the non-treatment of incurable adults see Mason and McCall Smith, Chapter 16
[49] [2000] 4 All E.R. 961

purposes of the action as Jodie and Mary, conjoined at the lower abdomen. While Jodie was capable of an independent existence, Mary was not. Her lungs and heart were not capable of pumping blood through her body. A common artery with her sister enabled Jodie to circulate blood for both of them. Medical opinion was to the effect that the twins could be successfully separated, but that surgery would involve the severing of the common artery, which would inevitably kill Mary. It was common ground that if surgery was not performed both would die, perhaps after only about three to six months. The twins' parents were firmly opposed to surgery, primarily on religious grounds. The Court of Appeal ultimately decided that it's duty was to permit the "least detrimental alternative", which was the certain death of Mary, as opposed to the later, but equally certain death of both infants. In three comprehensive analyses of the medical law, family law and criminal law problems raised by the proceedings, Lord Justices Ward, Brooke and Robert Walker justified their decision according to English law. The surgery would clearly be in the best interests of Jodie and, where her interests were in conflict with those of Mary, her ability to survive in the longer term alone, in contrast with Mary, was a decisive factor.[50]   In the present context, it is the relatively brief, though important references to the Convention and its Article 2 requirements that are of interest.

Lord Justice Ward, in commenting that the 1998 Act was due to come into force 10 days after his decision, felt it would be idle to pretend it should not apply, particularly as the surgery would be performed after October 2, 2000. In referring to the written submissions that, quite exceptionally the court had permitted be lodged by the Pro-Life Alliance, he summarised the Article 2(1) argument as being that "...the negative obligation to refrain from the intentional deprivation of life in effect trumps the positive obligation to take steps to protect the enjoyment of the right to life."[51] He then rejected that argument, on the basis that the Commission in *Paton v. United Kingdom* had construed Article 2 to be subject to an implied limitation that would justify the balancing act undertaken in respect of Jodie and Mary. Many will feel uncomfortable that the balancing act between the mother and the unborn child that has dogged the abortion debate has now been used to justify an act which will terminate the life of a child, who would normally be protected by the rights of the Convention. It could be said, however, that the particular dependence of Mary on Jodie was in some respects an apposite analogy to the foetus incapable of independent viable life.

The second focus of the Article 2(1) argument is best outlined in the opinion of Lord Justice Robert Walker. In describing the right

---

[50]   see in particular the opinion of Ward LJ at 1009–1010

[51]   *Ibid.*, at 1016

as one of the most fundamental provisions of the Convention, he again recorded the submission of the Pro-Life Alliance, this time in relation to the use of the word "intentionally" in the prohibition against the deprivation of life in Article 2(1). The position of the Alliance was that the word "intentionally" should be given its natural and ordinary meaning, and that the Strasbourg jurisprudence had not recognised the doctrine of double effect, or the defence of necessity. Lord Justice Robert Walker accepted that the word should be given its natural and ordinary meaning. He agreed with Counsel representing Jodie, however, that the ordinary meaning of "intentionally" was limited to the purpose of an action. He concluded that,

5.11   "... the word, construed in that way, applies only to cases where the purpose of the prohibited action is to cause death. It does not import any prohibition of the proposed operation other than those which are to be found in the common law of England. The coming into force of the Human Rights Act 1998...does not therefore alter my view of the case. The incorporation of the Convention is a very important event but in this case its effect is to confirm, and not to alter, pre-existing law."[52]

This was a clear statement that the court regarded the conclusion reached in domestic law as compatible with the Convention, though there was no European jurisprudence directly in point. The parents did not appeal against the decision to the House of Lords, and this construction of Article 2(1) was not challenged further. But the views expressed in *Re A* will no doubt be considered important should the Scottish Courts require to deal with applications to withhold treatment from the seriously ill new-born, or even to take action that will result in their death. The dicta on the construction of "intentionally" as limited to the purpose of the act may also have a bearing on the way in which future challenges to abortion, particularly on " social" grounds, are decided.

PART III: CHILDHOOD

5.12   There is no distinction between children's rights and adult's rights in the Convention. While adults have litigated most of the contentious childhood issues, this section attempts to summarise the areas in which the interests of children are most likely to be discussed.

---

[52] *Ibid.*, at 1067

(a) Care Proceedings and Adoption

Scots Law provides separate legislative frameworks for the regulation of care proceedings for children in need of compulsory measures of care or supervision[53] and for adoption.[54] In the context of human rights law, however, it is appropriate to consider these issues together. In very general terms, care proceedings will impose restrictions on the family life between a child and his natural parent, whereas adoption will sever that family life permanently. Both types of proceedings usually involve interference with the right to respect for family life protected by Article 8(1).

5.13

The Court laid down the correct approach to the interpretation of Article 8 insofar as it seeks to respect family life in this context in the leading case of *Johansen v. Norway*.[55] A child was first received into the temporary care of the state against a background of the mother's unsolved mental problems. These affected her ability to parent the child effectively. Decisions were subsequently taken by a local court committee to take the child into care permanently; to deprive the mother of her parental responsibilities; to place the child in a foster home with a view to adoption; to refuse the mother access to the child from the time of the child's placement in the foster home and to withhold the child's address from her.[56] These decisions were challenged by the mother who claimed they gave rise to violations of Article 8 of the Convention. The restrictions on interference with Article 8(1) rights are governed by Article 8(2), which provides as follows,

" There shall be no interference by a public authority with the exercise of this right except such as is in accordance with the law and is necessary in a democratic society in the interests of national security, public safety or the economic well being of the country, for the prevention of disorder or crime, for the protection of health or morals, or for the protection of the rights and freedoms of others."

In considering the mother's application, the Court adopted a well established approach to an allegation of a breach of Article 8. First, it is asked whether there has been an interference with an Article 8(1) right. Secondly, it must be established whether the interference was in accordance with the law. Thirdly, any interference would require to be made in pursuit of one of the legitimate aims enunciated in Article 8(2). Finally, the interference must be justified as "necessary in a democratic society". This last element includes consideration of the principle of proportionality, which demands a

5.14

---

[53] Children (Scotland) Act 1995, ss.32–85
[54] Adoption (Scotland) Act 1978 (as amended)
[55] 23 E.H.R.R. 33
[56] *Ibid.*, at 41

reasonable balance between the legitimate aim and the measures adopted to achieve it.[57]

Applying that approach, the Court ultimately found that there had been a breach of Article 8. The deprivation of the mother's parental rights and access had a permanent character and would thus require particularly strong reasons before it could be considered "necessary".[58] It was recognised that a balance required to be struck between the interests of the child in remaining in public care and those of the parent in being reunited with the child.[59] However, the margin of appreciation given to states in such matters was seen to have been overstepped by the Norwegian authorities. The permanent deprivation of the mother's right to family life with her child was a disproportionate measure as it had not been shown to correspond to any overriding requirement in the child's best interests.[60]

The decision in *Johansen* followed earlier statements by the Court in *Olsson v. Sweden*[61] and *Eriksson v. Sweden*[62] that a parent's Article 8 rights in the context of care proceedings required the state authorities to impose measures consistent with the aim of reuniting parent and child. The margin of appreciation has thus been shown to be narrower where something other than the rehabilitation of the parenting relationship is contemplated. In a recent decision, *K and T v. Finland*,[63] the Court, while reiterating the wide margin of appreciation enjoyed by state authorities at the stage of deciding to take a child into care, confirmed that a decision which would limit or restrict the family relationship more permanently was subject to stricter scrutiny. In *K and T*, a violation of Article 8 was found to have taken place where the reasons adduced to justify care orders, particularly in relation to a new-born child, were "insufficient". The margin of appreciation had thus been exceeded and therefore the measures could not be regarded as "necessary" in a democratic society. The decision is also consistent with the trend of previous cases supportive of a parental right to contact where a child is in care.[64] The rationale is that an attempt by state authorities to restrict parental rights of access may permanently curtail the family relations protected by the Convention.

5.15   It is that trend which has led to a perceived incompatibility between the rights afforded to parents under Article 8 and domestic legislation which treats as paramount the interests of the child when orders relating to his care, short or long term, are being

---

[57] See, *e.g. James v. U.K.*, 8 E.H.R.R. 123
[58] *Johansen*, cited *supra* no.55 at p.71.
[59] *Ibid.*, at 72
[60] *Ibid.*, at 74
[61] (No.1) 11 E.H.R.R. 259
[62] 12 E.H.R.R. 183
[63] [2000] 2 F.L.R. 79
[64] See, *e.g. Hendriks v. Netherlands*, 5 E.H.R.R. 233; *W v. U.K.* 10 E.H.R.R. 29; *Andersson v. Sweden*, 14 E.H.R.R. 615 and *Johansen v. Norway*, cited *supra*, no.55

contemplated.[65] It seems to the writer, however, that while there is certainly a difference in emphasis between the relative interests to be taken into account, the Court has not shied from upholding decisions to restrict parental rights where the welfare of the child so demands. For example, a decision to continue a care order and reduce a natural father's contact with his child against a background of suspicion of sexual abuse was recently held to satisfy the necessity test in Article 8(2), in *L v. Finland*.[66] In adoption proceedings, including applications by local authorities to free children for adoption, the Convention has not been interpreted as providing a charter for inadequate parents to assert their parental rights where this would be contrary to the welfare of the child. For example, the case of *Söderbäck v. Sweden*[67] saw the Court rejecting an unmarried father's contention that a decision to grant permission to the cohabitee of his child's mother to adopt the child, without his consent, violated his Article 8 rights. The Court distinguished the *Johansen* situation of the potential severance of links between a child and a parent who has had care of him from Mr Söderbäck's background of infrequent and limited contact with a child who had lived in family with her prospective adoptive father for some years. The domestic court's assessment of the child's best interests was an important factor in the Court's ultimate view that the adverse effects the adoption would have on the applicant's relations with the child could not be said to be disproportionate.[68] Similarly, an English court's decision to free for adoption the child of an alcoholic mother was held by the court to be proportionate to the aim of protecting the rights of the child to a permanent placement, in *Scott v. United Kingdom*.[69] The detrimental effect on the young girl's welfare of remaining in temporary care was central to the Court's support for the decision.

In the writer's opinion, the scope for future argument in this area may not lie in the perceived conflict between the rights of natural parents and the welfare of the child. It may be better focused in insisting on an examination of the alternatives to compulsory measures of care and adoption where these would not be detrimental to the child's interests. The requirement that a measure which restricts parental rights be necessary and proportionate could lead to successful challenges where the authorities are seen to have rejected options less disruptive of family life than their chosen

5.16

---

[65] Children (Scotland) Act 1995, ss.11 and 16, Adoption (Scotland) Act 1978, s.6.
[66] [2000] 2 F.L.R. 118
[67] [1999] 1 F.L.R. 250; 1999 Fam. L.R. 104; 3 E.H.R.L.R. 342
[68] 1999 Fam.L.R. 104 at 107. The relationship between considerations of welfare of the child and the parent's Art.8 rights was also considered in the recent case of *Elsholz v. Germany* (cited in the Parenthood section at no.62).
[69] [2000] 1 F.L.R. 958

solution. Support for such challenges can be found in the court's decision in *Olsson*.[70] There have been suggestions[71] that several aspects of the Scottish children's hearing system may fail to protect individuals' Convention rights, particularly where the grounds for referral include allegations of criminal offences. However, in the first test to the system since the 1998 Act came into force, the initial opinion of the Inner House is that only the lack of legal aid for representation before children's hearings may be incompatible with the Convention. The decision in *S v. The Principal Reporter and the Lord Advocate*,[72] has confirmed that the children's hearing must be regarded as involving determination of the civil rights and obligations of the children sought to be protected, and that it constitutes an independent tribunal, all in keeping with Article 6(1).[73] However, the absence of a right to apply for legal aid in the form of legal representation in the proceedings before the children's hearing could result in the legislative scheme being declared to be incompatible with the right to a fair hearing protected by Article 6(1).[74] One aspect of that Article will now be considered in the context of children's involvement in litigation.

(b) Children in Litigation

5.17   In recent years, children in Scotland have become more involved in litigation both as witnesses and as parties to proceedings concerning them. All those who have attained the age of 12 years are presumed to have the legal capacity to instruct a solicitor, to sue and to be sued.[75] This has largely been due to attempts in domestic legislation to comply with the UN Convention on the Rights of the Child, which emphasises children's rights to be involved in decisions affecting them.[76] In the context of children's views being sought in

---

[70] Cited *supra* no.61. However, the writer's first attempt to argue that a freeing for adoption order was not necessary in terms of Article 8 as alternatives were available which would serve the interests of the child while preserving the rights of the mother found no favour in the case of *Inverclyde Council v. SM* (Sheriff Herald, Greenock Sheriff Court, November 9, 2000, unreported)

[71] See, *e.g.* the commentary in Butterworths Family Law Service at C1155

[72] A decision of the First Division of the Inner House on March 30, 2001 (unreported).

[73] see below, in the discussion about Children in Litigation.

[74] The First Division directed that notice should be given to the Advocate General that a declaration of incompatibility in relation to this point is being considered. By Order Hearing to consider the matter further has taken place and a decision is awaited.

[75] See ss. 1(f) and 2(4A) and (4B) of the Age of Legal Capacity (Scotland) Act 1991 (as amended by the Children (Scotland) Act 1995). Children under 12 *may* have such capacity but this will depend on the particular understanding and maturity of the individual.

[76] Ss. 6, 11(7) and 16(2) of the Children (Scotland) Act 1995 attempt to give effect to Article 12 of the UN Convention by giving the child a statutory opportunity to express his views in both formal and informal decision making.

the course of court proceedings concerned with their interests, the Scottish courts have begun to address the vexed question of reconciling a parent's right to full disclosure of information relevant to the decision making process with the potential upset and even harm to a child if confidentiality is not preserved.

Article 6(1) of the Convention would appear to support the case for full disclosure by providing, *inter alia*,

"In the determination of his civil rights and obligations...everyone is entitled to a fair and public hearing...by an independent and impartial tribunal established by law".

The European Court had, prior to the coming into force of the Children (Scotland) Act 1995, considered this Article in the context of disclosing material concerning children, in the Scottish application, *McMichael v. United Kingdom*.[77] The applicants were the parents of a son born in 1987. The mother had a history of mental illness. In 1988 the Reporter initiated grounds for referral to the children's hearing. The basis was the mother's condition. The sheriff found the grounds established and the matter went before the children's hearing to consider the appropriate compulsory measures of care. A number of documents were placed before the hearing, including a comprehensive Social Work Department report which recommended that the child remain in foster care. The Children's Hearings' Rules in force at the time did not permit access to such reports by the parents, requiring only that they be advised orally of their substance. The hearing decided that the boy should remain in care. He was ultimately freed for adoption. The parents made an application raising various alleged breaches of the Convention. In relation to Article 6(1), they alleged that the failure to disclose the Social Work Department's reports deprived them of a fair hearing. Mrs McMichael's claim was upheld. The Court first noted the special nature of the children's hearing as an adjudicatory body with special characteristics but nonetheless subject to the requirements of Article 6.[78] It then held that as a matter of principle the right to a fair trial "means the opportunity to have knowledge of and comment on the observations filed or evidence adduced by the other party." Accordingly, the court determined, the withholding of the contents of reports concerning their child from parents involved in care proceedings at the instance of the Children's Reporter contravened the right to a fair hearing required by Article 6.

Following the decision in *McMichael*, the relevant procedural rules were altered to require disclosure of reports before the   5.18

---

[77] 20 E.H.R.R. 205. The case is also referred to in the context of parental rights below, at p. 200.
[78] An attack on the independence of the children's hearing in *S v. the Principal Reporter, supra* no.72, failed under reference to the *McMichael* decision.

children's hearing to parents, as "relevant persons".[79] No provision was made, however, entitling the child to access documents and information. Since the Children (Scotland) Act 1995 was passed, enshrining the child's right to state views in judicial proceedings affecting them, conflicting decisions have been reached on the general applicability of the decision in *McMichael* to the issue of the confidentiality of those expressed views.

In the sheriff court case of *Dosoo v. Dosoo*[80] a motion was made to open confidential envelopes containing views expressed by two boys to a solicitor appointed by the sheriff to report on the question of contact between them and their father. The motion was refused on the basis that the privacy of the children should be respected "except in very compelling circumstances". The view was expressed that the law had moved on from the principle enunciated in *McMichael* as a result of the provisions of the 1995 Act and that the European Court's decision was not relevant to disputes over contact or residence. In contrast, the Sheriff Principal in Glasgow allowed an appeal in the case of *McGrath v. McGrath*[81] against a sheriff's refusal to disclose to a father his daughter's views on increased contact given through a curator ad litem. The correct approach was, it is suggested, there set out, namely that the starting point must be the principle of full disclosure of all material in a case to each party, in accordance with *McMichael*. Thereafter, where a question is raised as to the effect of disclosure of particularly sensitive material, the consideration is whether that disclosure would, in the particular circumstances of the case, involve a real possibility of significant harm to the child. This coincides with the English approach to disclosure of confidential material to parents in adoption cases, set out by the House of Lords in *Re D (minors) (adoption reports: confidentiality)*.[82]

It seems, therefore, that where a child chooses to exercise his right to become involved in litigation generally, his ability to withhold material from others involved in the proceedings, including his parents, will be seen as severely limited by Article 6(1).[83] Where the litigation is at the instance of his parents, it is likely that they will be unable to withhold any material used in the litigation from him.[84]

As a party to the proceedings, of course, the child can insist on compliance with his own Article 6 rights. In the forum of the children's hearing, the child's right to disclosure of information is

---

[79] See r.5(3) of the Children's Hearings (Scotland) Rules 1996. The definition of "relevant person" is that given by s.93(2)(b) of the Children (Scotland) Act 1995.

[80] 1999 S.L.T. (Sh.Ct.) 86

[81] 1999 S.L.T. (Sh.Ct.) 90

[82] [1995] 4 All E.R. 385

[83] The approach of the Sheriff Principal in *McGrath* has generally been followed. See, *e.g. Oyeneyin v. Oyeneyin*, 1999 G.W.D. 38–1836

[84] While the full initiating summons or writ in a family action is not intimated to a child who may be affected by the action at the outset he can access it should he choose to become involved. See R.C.S., r.49.8, (1)(h) and (7); O.C.R., r.33.7(1)(h).

now to be complied with. Notwithstanding the lack of provision for such disclosure in the procedural rules, the Principal Reporter advised the court in *S v. the Principal Reporter and the Lord Advocate*[85] that all reporters would be given guidance that reports made available to "relevant persons" must also be given to the child, subject only to the type of exceptions recommended in *Re D*, referred to above.

In civil cases generally, the child litigant must also be able to insist on the suitable legal representation that is available to adults as anything less may amount to discrimination against him in terms of Article 14, due to his status as a child. The continued availability of civil legal aid to child litigants in this country in appropriate circumstances should meet this requirement.

(c) Corporal Punishment

It is perhaps the issue of corporal punishment that has best focused the ability of the Convention to protect the interests and rights of children, even where this potentially conflicts with the rights and freedoms of those charged with their care.   5.19

The infliction of pain on a child by physical chastisement seems, *prima facie* to violate that child's Article 3 protection against inhuman or degrading treatment or punishment. The first successful challenge against the United Kingdom on this issue arose out of the anachronistic practice of judicially imposed birching on the Isle of Man. The case of *Tyrer v. United Kingdom*[86] resulted in a finding by the Court that a sentence by a juvenile court there of three lashes of the birch on a 15-year-old boy's bare buttocks was degrading punishment and violated his Article 3 rights. The local law was duly changed. However, the subsequent famous Scottish challenge to the previously common regime of corporal punishment in schools succeeded not in terms of Article 3, but on a violation of Article 2 of Protocol 1 of the Convention. That provision imposes a duty on the state to respect the rights of parents to ensure education and teaching in conformity with their own religious and philosophical convictions. In *Campbell and Cosans v. United Kingdom*,[87] two boys had been withdrawn from school by their parents on the basis that if they continued to attend they were at risk of corporal punishment. The Campbell boy's parents had sought an assurance from the local authority that their son would not be subjected to the tawse when disciplined and withdrew him when no such assurance was given. The Cosans' child had been caught taking a prohibited short cut through a cemetery and was to report to the school's headmaster for corporal punishment the following day. When he refused, on the advice of his parents, to accept the punishment, he

---

[85] *Supra*, no. 72.
[86] 2 E.H.R.R. 1.
[87] 4 E.H.R.R. 293.

was suspended. While the European Court ultimately held that the threat alone of corporal punishment did not, in the circumstances, constitute a violation of Article 3, it determined that the United Kingdom had failed to comply with Article 2 of Protocol 1 which requires the parents' philosophical convictions to be respected.[88] Significantly, the Court expressed the view that the parents' views on the issue of corporal punishment concerned,

> "a weighty and substantial aspect of human life and behaviour, namely the integrity of the person, the propriety or otherwise of the infliction of corporal punishment and the exclusion of the distress which the risk of such punishment entails."[89]

5.20   There could thereafter be no doubt that the actual infliction of corporal punishment (or even the very real and immediate threat of it) might well give rise to a successful Article 3 application and such punishment was subsequently effectively prohibited, at least in state schools. In 1988, the Commission did decide that a forceful caning on the buttocks of a 15-year-old private school boy, which caused him significant physical injury and humiliation, violated Article3, in *Y v. United Kingdom*.[90] But a settlement between the applicant and the government was then agreed, and a full Court hearing avoided. The continued use of corporal punishment by some institutions in the private school sector led to a further application, *Costello-Roberts v. United Kingdom*.[91] The headmaster of the preparatory boarding school he attended struck a 7-year-old boy three times on the buttocks. By a slim majority the Court held that the punishment was not severe enough to violate Article 3. The case caused such concern however, that measures were taken, in both England and Scotland, to clarify that, insofar as corporal punishment might still be used in the independent sector, it must not amount to inhuman or degrading treatment.[92]

The use of corporal punishment in schools having been effectively abolished following such decisions, the issue of the scope of more general, legitimate physical chastisement of children in the United Kingdom remained to be tested. In 1992 the Scottish Law Commission, recommended that Scots Law should be reformed, to limit the use of "reasonable chastisement" of children as a defence to assault, though not to abolish it completely.[93] The

---

[88]   See below, at (d) Education, where that provision is set out.
[89]   *Ibid.*, at para. 36
[90]   17 E.H.R.R. 238
[91]   19 E.H.R.R. 112
[92]   The current position in England can now be found in s.47 of the Education (No. 2) Act 1986 (as amended by s.293, Education Act 1993). The equivalent Scottish provision is s.48A of the Education (Scotland) Act 1980 (as amended by s.294 of the Education Act 1993)
[93]   Report on Family Law (Scot Law Comm; 1992), paras 2.67-2.105, recommendation 11 and draft Bill, clause 4.

international instrument that concerned the Commission most at that time was the UN Convention on the Rights of the Child.[94] The opportunity to follow that recommendation was ignored when the Children (Scotland) Act 1995 was enacted and the extent to which those with parental authority could physically discipline the children in their care remained unclear. The challenge eventually came in an application by an English boy, in the determinant case of *A v. United Kingdom*.[95] The applicant was 9-years-old when he was discovered to have been hit with a stick on several occasions by his stepfather. There was medical evidence to the effect that the beatings had been delivered with considerable force. The step father was charged with assault occasioning actual bodily harm and was tried by jury. The defence he presented was that, while the factual allegations were accepted, the beatings amounted to "reasonable chastisement" of a child he was parenting. He was acquitted by a majority verdict. When the boy made an application under the Convention, the United Kingdom Government accepted the Commission's finding that there had been a breach of Article 3. Notwithstanding that acknowledgement, the Court conducted a full examination of the claim and found that the treatment of the boy by his stepfather had been sufficiently severe to reach the level prohibited by Article 3. Under reference to previous decisions, the Court confirmed that,

"Children and other vulnerable individuals, in particular, are entitled to state protection in the form of effective deterrence against such serious breaches of personal integrity...the law did not provide adequate protection to the applicant against treatment or punishment contrary to Article 3."

The government accepted before the Court that a change to the domestic law was required and the boy was awarded substantial compensation of £10,000 in terms of Article 50. Following the European Court's decision, consultation documents have been published on both sides of the border,[96] with a view to a relatively imminent legal reform to restrict physical punishment of children.

On one view the decision of the Court that those exercising parental authority are not the arbiters of what constitutes reasonable punishment of those in their care might be said to be an interference with the parent's right to respect for privacy in terms of Article 8. However, the emphasis on a "minimum level of severity" being required before Article 3 will be breached, again illustrates a

---

[94] Art. 19(1) of which imposes an obligation to "protect the child from all forms of physical or mental violence."
[95] 27 E.H.R.R. 611
[96] The Scottish Executive paper, *"The physical punishment of Children in Scotland"* was published in February 2000, following the English consultation document *"Protecting Children, Supporting Parents"* in January 2000.

sensible balance being struck in Europe between the need to protect the interests and welfare of children and the rights of their parents, where these are perceived to conflict.

(d) Education

5.21   The Convention, as has been shown, has already had an impact on domestic law in relation to the use of corporal punishment in schools. The general right to education is contained in Article 2 of the First Protocol, which is in the following terms,

> " No person shall be denied the right to education. In the exercise of any functions which it assumes in relation to education and to teaching, the State shall respect the rights of parents to ensure such education and teaching in conformity with their own religious and philosophical convictions."

The first sentence thereof is now enshrined as a positive right for children in Scottish legislation, which states that,

> " It shall be the right of every child of school age to be provided with school education by...an education authority."[97]

However, in a reservation entered by the United Kingdom, the second sentence of Article 2 is accepted only insofar as it is "...compatible with the provision of efficient instruction and training and the avoidance of unreasonable public expenditure". While the 1998 Act preserves the reservation, it will require to be reviewed every five years.[98] The scope open to the United Kingdom in invoking the reservation seems to be limited, as it has been held not to apply if it is **possible** to comply with Article 2 while meeting the reservation's conditions.[99] Accordingly, the decisions on interpretation of the second sentence, as well as the first, require consideration in looking at the impact of the Convention on domestic education.

In an early application by French speaking parents living in a Flemish area of Belgium, whose children were effectively denied access to French speaking schools, the *Belgian Linguistics Case*,[1] the European Court upheld the right of individuals to invoke the Convention to protect their children's right to education. However, on the specific complaints made, it was found that Article 2 of Protocol 1 had been violated only to the extent that there was discrimination against the French children as compared with their Flemish counterparts, contrary to Article 14. It was made clear that

---

[97] s.1, Standards in Scotland's Schools etc (Scotland) Act 2000
[98] ss..15 and 17, Human Rights Act 1998.
[99] See *Campbell and Cosans v. U.K.* cited *supra*, no.87, at pp.305–6.
[1]   1 E.H.R.R. 252

the Convention does not guarantee any general right to be educated by the state in the language of one's parents,[2] an important and necessary qualification now, in light of the larger numbers of individuals whose mother tongue is something other than the national language of the state in which they live.

The second right, that of parents to have religious and philosophical convictions respected, has been said by the Court to be aimed at safeguarding the possibility of pluralism in education, an objective which is essential for the preservation of the democratic society envisaged by the Convention's drafters.[3] Thus, the Jehovah's Witness parents in *Valsamis v. Greece*[4] were held to be entitled to rely on respect for their religious convictions in this context, when they complained that their daughter had been punished for refusing to participate in her school's Greek National Day celebrations on the grounds that it conflicted with their faith. Nonetheless, the application ultimately failed on the basis that the celebrations said to offend were found to fall short of being unduly indoctrinating. In addition to attitudes to corporal punishment,[5] philosophical convictions have been held, at least by the Commission in the case of *W and DM, M and IH v. United Kingdom*,[6] to include a view that one's children should be educated in a single sex environment. On the substantive complaint in that case, however, the Commission rejected the applications as inadmissible. Parents could not demand their choice of school where a limited number of places were available for a particular type of education.

The notion of parental rights in education, both in relation to choice of mainstream school, and to a lesser extent in the provision of special needs education, is already given respect in Scots Law. Parents wishing their child to attend a particular school are entitled, in terms of the Education (Scotland) Act 1980[7] to make a written placing request to their local education authority in respect of a specified school. The legislation then sets out various grounds on which an education authority may refuse to grant a placing request. Of particular note in this context are those grounds that can be used to restrict parental choice of school on the basis that additional resources, such as additional teachers or substantial expenditure on accommodation would be required.[8] These provisions are regularly

5.22

---

[2] *Ibid.*, at para. 7.
[3] *Kjeldsen, Busk Madsen and Pederson v. Denmark*, 1 E.H.R.R. 711 at 730.
[4] 24 E.H.R.R. 294
[5] *Campbell and Cosans*, cited *supra*, no.87.
[6] 7 E.H.R.R. 135
[7] s.28A, Education (Scotland) Act 1980, as amended.
[8] s.28A(3)(a)(i) gives the necessity of taking an additional teacher into employment as a ground for refusal and s.28A(3)(a)(ii) permits refusal if the placement would give rise to significant expenditure on extending or otherwise altering the accommodation or facilities at the school. A future requirement to create an additional class if the request is granted is also now a ground for refusal — s.28A(3)(a) (vi).

used to limit parental choice. However, any claim that the present legislation on parental choice does not go far enough in terms of the Convention, is likely, it is submitted, to run into difficulties and would probably require a direct challenge to the United Kingdom reservation mentioned above.

5.23   One aspect of education law in Scotland which, it has been suggested,[9] might fail to comply with the Convention is the procedural content of the regime for excluding a disruptive child from school and the relative appeal system.[10] An appeal committee of the education authority has power to confirm or annul a school's decision to exclude a pupil where the parent or pupil refers the matter to it.[11] The committee's decision can in turn be appealed to the sheriff.[12] However, there has been no consistent approach to such appeals[13] and it may be that challenges could be taken, particularly in respect of the Article 6 right to a fair and public hearing, where no uniform statutory test for considering an appeal is provided.

Further, the provisions of the Education (Scotland) Act 1980 that allow criminal charges to be brought against parents whose children fail to attend school without reasonable excuse[14] have now been the subject of a claim of incompatibility with Article 6(2), which enshrines the presumption of innocence.[15] The claim failed only on the basis that a broad interpretation of "reasonable excuse" in relation to non-attendance could cover circumstances relating to the parent, thus avoiding the apparent lack of an available defence to the charge on the ground of practical innocence.

PART IV: ADULTHOOD

(a) Marriage and Cohabitation.

5.24   The Convention's Article 12 protection of the right to marry and to found a family has been referred to already in the context of assisted reproduction.[16] In *F v. Switzerland*,[17] the Court considered a complaint against the decision of a Swiss Court, prohibiting a

---

[9]   See Butterworths Scottish Family Law Service at C1665-1668
[10]   The basis for such exclusion and the procedure are contained in the Education (Scotland) Act 1980, s.28H and the Schools General (Scotland) Regulations 1975 (as amended by S.I. 1982 No.56 and No. 1735)
[11]   1980 Act, s.28H(1). The Standards in Scotland's Schools etc. (Scotland) Act 2000, s.41 gives pupils who have legal capacity the same rights to appeal as their parents.
[12]   1980 Act, s.28H(6)
[13]   compare *Crawford v. Strathclyde R.C.,* 1999 Fam. L.R. 120 with *Mackie v. Grampian R.C.,* 1999 Fam. L.R. 122.
[14]   See ss. 35 and 42 of the 1980 Act.
[15]   *O'Hagan v. Rea,* 2001 G.W.D. 2-94.
[16]   See pages 170-174.
[17]   10 E.H.R.R. 411

man from marrying within three years when granting decree in his third divorce. The applicant had been found to be solely to blame for the breakdown of the third marriage and the relevant Swiss Law contained provision for restricting his future right to marry in such circumstances. The restriction was held to violate the citizen's Article 12 right. While the promotion of stable marriage was found to be a legitimate policy, the consequence of the time restriction was to strike at the very essence of the right to marry.[18]

In *Rees v. United Kingdom*,[19] the Court confirmed that Article 12 was designed to protect heterosexual marriage as the basis of the family. This was consistent with the *Hamer v. United Kingdom*[20] and *Draper v. United Kingdom*[21] applications where the Commission had found that the Article 12 rights of serving prisoners had been violated by the refusal of the authorities to permit them to marry during the period of their sentences. The general right to marry is of course qualified by the reference to national laws. Statutory restrictions on marriage in this country between those under the age of legal capacity and those with certain relationships of consanguinity,[22] for example, would seem to be unlikely to be open to successful challenge, given the terms of the qualification.

The references in Article 8 to "private and family life" and "home" are not of course restricted to protect only traditional marriage based families. Thus, the development of heterosexual cohabitation as an increasingly common *modus vivendi* for those creating family life could give rise to claims that different, less favourable treatment in domestic law for those who cohabit outside marriage amounts to discrimination of the type prohibited by Article 14.[23]

The Court has consistently expressed the opinion that a difference in treatment between one group of citizens and another is discriminatory if,

" it has no objective and reasonable justification...if it does not pursue a legitimate aim or if there is not a reasonable relationship of proportionality between the means employed

---

[18] *Ibid.*, at p.422 (para.40). Interestingly, the case was decided by a bare majority of the judges (9:8), the dissenting opinion being to the effect that a temporary restriction on remarriage based on legitimate reasons **was** within the state's margin of appreciation.

[19] 9 E.H.R.R. 56. The case concerned the application of Articles 8 and 12 to a transsexual and is referred to again below, at page 000.

[20] Appl. No. 7114/75, 24 D.R. 5

[21] Appl. No. 8186/78, 24 D.R. 72

[22] see ss. 1 and 2 and Sched. 1 of the Marriage (Scotland) Act 1977

[23] Cohabitation in this context refers only to those who are openly unmarried, as distinct from those cohabiting as man and wife and reputed to be such. The latter form of cohabitation can still constitute marriage in Scots Law and no discrimination argument could apply given the ability to have the marriage declared. For the requirements of this remaining form of irregular marriage, see Clive, *Husband and Wife* (4th ed.) at pp. 48–65.

and the aim sought to be realised." [24]

As the Convention is also said by the Court to be a living instrument to be interpreted in the light of existing conditions,[25] the less favourable treatment of cohabitants, particularly those in long term partnerships, in certain areas of Scots Law may now be open to question as disproportionate to the aim sought to be achieved. There are several areas in which differential treatment can be identified. For example, the lack of any obligation to aliment a cohabitant contrasts not only with the previous common law position between spouses, but also the statutory codification of alimentary obligations in the Family Law (Scotland) Act 1985.[26] There is also a two-tier regime of protection for married and unmarried couples under the Matrimonial Homes (Family Protection) (Scotland) Act 1981. While cohabiting partners who are not co-owners or tenants can apply to the court for occupancy rights and many of the ancillary remedies and protections available to spouses, there is no equivalent of the automatic right of a spouse to occupy the family home. Further, the duration of the order available to cohabitants is limited and no provision is made for the grant of interim occupancy rights.[27] The lack of any rights on intestacy for a widowed cohabitant is another aspect of Scots domestic law that could be open to challenge as discriminatory.[28]

5.25   It may be argued that the promotion of traditional marriage is a legitimate aim that some states may consider merits promotion over other personal relationships. Against that could be cited the growing number of statutory provisions that specifically apply equally to those cohabiting " as man and wife" as to spouses, which could present difficulties for any such statement of policy. Cohabitants can claim damages for their loss on the death of their partners as a result of personal injuries in much the same way as those who are widowed.[29] They are entitled to succeed to secure

---

[24] *Marckx v. Belgium*, 2 E.H.R.R. 330; *Inze v. Austria*, 10 E.H.R.R. 394 at 406 (para.41).

[25] e.g. in *Airey v. Ireland*, 2 E.H.R.R. 305 at para.26 and in *Inze v. Austria*, *supra*, at 406 (para. 41) referring to *Johnston v. Ireland*, 9 E.H.R.R.

[26] Obligations to aliment members of one's family are codified in the Family Law (Scotland) Act 1985. Section 1 refers to spouses, parents and children, but cohabitation is not recognised as creating any alimentary obligation and certainly none existed at common law.

[27] Compare s.18 of the 1981 Act, which sets out the occupancy rights of cohabiting couples, with section1, which provides the "automatic" rights of the non entitled spouse.

[28] The regime of ss. 8 and 9 of the Succession (Scotland) Act 1964 applies only to spouses. In England, cohabitants do now have rights on intestacy if they can show they were living "as the husband or wife" of the deceased. See s.1A, Inheritance (Provisions for Family and Dependents) Act 1975 (as amended)

[29] see s.10, Sched. 1, Damages (Scotland) Act 1976 (as amended). In personal injuries actions generally, cohabitants are specifically included as "relatives" for the purpose of services claims in terms of ss.8 and 9 of the Administration of Justice Act 1982—see s.13(1)(b)

tenancies[30] and assured tenancies[31] and are regarded as having rights and obligations towards their partners in some tax and Social Security legislation.[32] Differential treatment in other legislative provisions may thus be said to be more difficult to justify by reference to the pursuit of policies promoting marriage over cohabitation. However, the modern tendency of Scots Law has been to minimise the legal consequences of marriage, at least during its subsistence. That, coupled with the general, but clear, statements of the Court of Human Rights in support of the promotion of traditional marriage may lead to a reluctance to encourage claims of discrimination by cohabitants.

It is important to note again that the purpose of Article 14 is to secure the enjoyment of the Convention's rights and freedoms. It cannot be relied on without reference to a Convention right. Therefore, if traditional marriage is likely to be legitimately promoted over cohabitation by Article 12, discrimination against cohabitants due to their unmarried status could probably only be demonstrated if it interfered with other rights, such as their Article 8 rights to respect for their family life, home or correspondence.

The Convention is also concerned with equality of treatment of spouses *inter se*. Scots Law requires a wife to aliment her husband as much as it is his obligation to aliment her[33] and for some years there has been provision for separate taxation of spouses.[34] Amending legislation has also removed distinctions on grounds of sex from measures originally designed to benefit women when they were unlikely to be providers of financial security to their family, such as the Married Women's Policies of Assurance (Scotland) Act 1880.[35] However, it is in looking at the breakdown of marriage and family relationships that conflict, and therefore concern with rights, is more likely to occur. This aspect of family life therefore merits separate consideration.

(b) Breakdown of the Family

There is no Convention protected right to divorce one's spouse.[36]   5.26
Where divorce is available, it will inevitably affect the property rights of the couple, sometimes including their right to live in a

---

[30] s.52, Housing (Scotland) Act 1987
[31] s.31, Housing (Scotland) Act 1988
[32] *e.g.* Social Security Administration Act 1992 (see s.78); Local Government Finance Act 1992 (see s.75)
[33] s.1(1)(a) and (b), Family Law (Scotland) Act 1985
[34] s.32 of the Finance Act 1988 finally abolished the rule that the income of a wife was deemed to be the income of her husband, with effect from tax year 1990–91.
[35] The advantages of taking out a policy of assurance for the benefit of a wife and/or children was extended to policies taken out by a woman for the benefit of her husband and/or children by amendments made in terms of the Married Women's Policies of Assurance (Scotland) (Amendment) Act 1980
[36] *Johnston v. Ireland*, cited *supra*, no.25.

particular home, and their relative responsibilities to any children of the relationship. An attempt to protect a basic measure of equality of treatment in such situations is made by Article 5 of the Seventh Protocol, which is in the following terms,

> "Spouses shall enjoy equality of rights and responsibilities of a private law character between them, and in their relations with their children, as to marriage, and in the event of its dissolution. This Article shall not prevent states from taking such measures as are necessary in the interests of children."

This Article has not been incorporated into domestic law by the Human Rights Act 1998. It would appear that the United Kingdom Government perceived a difficulty in that certain provisions of existing (English) legislation relative to marriage breakdown and the property rights of spouses were not presently compatible with the Seventh Protocol. In framing the 1998 Act the Government expressed a commitment to the later inclusion of this Article of the Protocol, when the perceived difficulties with existing legislation have been resolved.[37] While there is understandable concern about this matter among family law practitioners in England,[38] it is submitted that the discussion about reform should have little, if any impact on the development of Scots Law.

The reason for this lack of concern is that existing Scots Family Law already carefully promotes the equality of spouses in legislation applicable to family breakdown. For example, the Family Law (Scotland) Act 1985, which sets out five principles governing awards of financial provision on divorce,[39] enshrines a presumption of equal sharing between husband and wife of all property acquired during the marriage where it is classified as "matrimonial property".[40] The discretion that exists to depart from the equal sharing rule tends to be applied, for example, where the interests of children are involved so that a family home can be maintained, or to protect property rights by reflecting input into the family finances by one party through inheritance.[41] All of the principles are designed to apply equally to both sexes and with a

---

[37] "Rights Brought Home: the Human Rights Bill" cm.3782 (1997), the White Paper introducing the Bill both acknowledged the perceived difficulty and expressed the intention to legislate before signing and ratifying the Protocol. (see para. 4.15)

[38] English Family Law continues to include measures designed to protect financially vulnerable wives, both during marriage and on divorce and thus appears to promote the type of inequality Art. 5 of the Seventh Protocol seeks to avoid. For a useful summary of the relevant provisions that may fall foul of the Protocol and the areas in which change is likely in that jurisdiction, see H Swindells et al, *Family Law and the Human Rights Act 1998*, Chapter 12, esp. pages 241–244.

[39] s.9(a)–(e)

[40] s.9(1)(a), read with s.10, as interpreted by the House of Lords in *Jacques v. Jacques*, 1997 S.L.T. 459.

[41] The application of the principles of the Act since 1986 is a major area of Family Law that cannot be considered here. See Clive, (4ᵗʰ edition), Chapter 24.

view to minimising financial dependence after divorce. Similarly, the Matrimonial Homes (Family Protection)(Scotland) Act 1981, insofar as it deals with occupancy rights and protective measures to allow peaceful occupation of the family home by a spouse who has suffered domestic violence, is non-sexist both in its terminology and its application.[42] While the original policy behind the relevant provisions may have been the protection of female victims of domestic violence,[43] there is no question but that the remedies in the Act are equally available to men.[44]

In light of this existing equality of treatment, the issues for practitioners north of the border are more likely to relate to whether legislation relative to family breakdown is consistent with the now incorporated relevant Articles of the Convention, such as Articles 6 and 8 and Article 1 of the First Protocol.

Under the heading "Protection of Property", Article 1 of the First Protocol provides, *inter alia*, the following, 5.27

" Every natural or legal person is entitled to the peaceful enjoyment of his possessions. No one shall be deprived of his possessions except in the public interest and subject to the conditions provided for by law and by the general principles of international law."

The term "possessions" in Article 1 has been interpreted by the Court as including property, including heritable interests.[45] Decisions are made frequently by the Scottish courts to deprive individuals of their property in divorce proceedings, such as orders for transfer of both heritable and moveable property from one spouse to the other.[46] Further, in terms of a recent amendment to the Family Law (Scotland) Act 1985, a spouse's pension can be the subject of an order requiring it to be "split", a percentage of it being hived off to form pension provision for the other spouse.[47] Such interference with the right to hold property would generally seem to be consistent with the public interest in having a regime to divide property between spouses on divorce and fall within the category of relatively uncontroversial "conditions provided for by law". It is

---

[42] See ss. 1–5, which bestow occupancy rights and related remedies on all spouses, male or female and ss. 14 and 15 relating to matrimonial interdicts.

[43] See the Scottish Law Commission's Consultation Memo. "Occupancy Rights in the Matrimonial Home and Domestic Violence" (Cons Memo No. 41, 1978) and subsequent Report (Scot Law Comm No. 60,1980)

[44] Applications by men may be far less common and may be based more on the ancillary remedies than exclusion orders and interdicts, but, when made, they are no less likely to be successful. See, *e.g. Murphy v. Murphy*, 1992 S.C.L.R. 62; *O'Neill v. O'Neill*, 1987 S.L.T. (Sh.Ct.) 26.

[45] *Marckx v. Belgium*, 2 E.H.R.R. 330.

[46] s.8(1)(aa) Family Law (Scotland) Act 1985.

[47] s.8 (1)(baa) 1985 Act, as amended by s.20 of the Welfare Reform and Pensions Act 1999.

difficult to see at present that the law of financial provision on divorce in Scotland will be the subject of successful challenges on the basis of disproportionate violation of the right not to be deprived of property.

The method of determination of property disputes in divorce proceedings may be subject to greater scrutiny. Claims for financial provision on divorce involve the determination of civil rights and obligations in terms of Article 6(1) of the Convention. A party whose property interests will be affected by such claims is thus entitled to a "fair and public hearing within a reasonable time". Disputes of this type are determined both in the sheriff court and in the Court of Session using particular procedural rules that generally meet the requirements of Article 6(1).[48] There are one or two areas of concern, however, which may give rise to challenges.

First, in terms of section 14 of the Family Law (Scotland) Act 1985, certain far reaching orders, which are final in nature, can be made "before on or after" decree of divorce.[49] In particular, the court has power to order that a party's property be sold during the progress of the proceedings. The effect of the applicable rules is that a family home can be the subject of such an order for sale following the making of *ex parte* statements by each side at an early stage in the proceedings, well before to a full hearing.[50] Whether that constitutes fair procedure in the circumstances may be open to question in an appropriate case. Secondly, a more general criticism may relate to the length of time involved in the determination of a financial dispute on divorce, particularly where appeal procedures are invoked. In *Cuniff v. Cuniff*,[51] a reclaiming motion against the decision of a Lord Ordinary to grant a transfer of property order to a wife was heard some five years after the proof. While the inordinate delay would appear to have been caused by a number of factors, there were specific periods of inactivity in the court administration of the case that might well, were the situation to arise again, result in a claim of failure to comply with Article 6(1). The European Court found there had been such a failure in *Bunkate v. Netherlands*,[52] where the State Court of Appeal had taken over 15 months to remit a casefile to the supreme court of the Netherlands for consideration. While delays in proceedings are not a problem peculiar to family law, they are of particular interest to practitioners who deal with families whose private lives are to a large extent held in limbo pending resolution of disputes involving their status, family homes and children.

5.28   Questions of compliance with Convention requirements may arise in non-financial disputes in family breakdown. A feature of

---

[48] O.C.R. 1993, Chapter 33 and R.C.S., Chapter 49.
[49] s.14(1), read with s.14(2)(a),(b),(c),(h) and (k).
[50] R.C.S. r.49.47; O.C.R. r.33.49.
[51] 1999 S.C. 537.
[52] 19 E.H.R.R. 477.

the matrimonial interdicts that can be granted under the Matrimonial Homes (Family Protection)(Scotland) Act 1981 is that a power of arrest will be attached to them unless it can be shown to be unnecessary.[53] Such powers of arrest are often attached to *interim* orders made on the basis of *ex parte* statements. While the spouse against whom the power is to be granted must be given the opportunity to be heard on the matter or represented before the court prior to it being made, no independent investigation of the facts takes place before the power is attached to an *interim* order. In these circumstances there may be a question about whether the Article 6(1) "fair hearing" requirement has been adhered to.

Further, the duration of both exclusion orders and powers of arrest attached to matrimonial interdicts is essentially open-ended. Unless recalled by the court, they last as long as the marriage subsists, notwithstanding that divorce proceedings might not be in contemplation for some years after such orders are made.[54] This may give rise to concerns that the remedy is disproportionate to the aim it seeks to achieve. Exclusion orders and interdicts to which powers of arrest are attached are invasive of family life and interfere with a party's peaceful possession of his property. Powers of arrest also have more serious implications for the deprivation of liberty.[55] Arguments that the legislation as presently framed does not fulfil the "necessity" test in Article 8 or does not constitute an interference with property rights that is justified by the public interest may be anticipated. The Scottish Executive has already acknowledged the problem to some extent and has proposed that a power of arrest should lapse after three years, whether or not there is a divorce.[56]

(c) Parenthood

As discussed in the context of care proceedings and adoption,[57] the central objective of Article 8 is to protect the individual against arbitrary or unnecessary interference into his family life by public authorities. However, the Court has expressed the view that in order to afford respect for family life the state may be obliged to adopt positive measures, including a framework of general

5.29

---

[53] s.15(1)(b) 1981 Act. Powers of arrest are also attached to matrimonial interdicts ancillary to an exclusion order, simply on request—s.15(1)(a). However, the fairly rigorous test for an exclusion order (s.4(2)) will already have been met before the request can be made.

[54] s.5 1981 Act, which makes provision for the cessation of the effect of exclusion orders also anticipates that they may come to an end if the occupancy rights in the home themselves end, s.15(2) confirms that a power of arrest ceases to have effect upon termination of the marriage.

[55] The particular protection of the right to liberty in Article 5 is fully discussed in Chapter X

[56] Scottish Executive White Paper "Parents and Children" September 2000, Chapter 3 (Proposal 5).

[57] See pages 180-184.

protection of individuals' Article 8 rights.[58] Thus the effectiveness or otherwise of domestic legislation in providing that protection has come under scrutiny.

In both Scotland and England the treatment of "unmarried fathers" in domestic law has caused controversy for some years. The Children (Scotland) Act 1995[59] preserves the distinction made in previous legislation between mothers, who automatically have parental rights (and corresponding responsibilities) in relation to their children and fathers, who have such rights automatically only if married to the mother at the time of conception or subsequently.[60] While fathers who are not married can of course acquire parental rights by agreement with the mother or by order of court,[61] the distinction is highlighted in situations of parental conflict, when the mother is less likely to agree to share rights and responsibilities in relation to the child. On the basis of present authorities, however, the clear discrimination appears to be justified in terms of Article 8(2).

In *McMichael v. United Kingdom*,[62] where both parents had complained of failures in the children's hearing system, the father also separately claimed that the legislation denying him, as an unmarried father, the right to be present at the hearing amounted to Article 14 discrimination. The less favourable treatment on the grounds of his sex, he argued, deprived him of equal exercise of his Article 8 rights. His argument was rejected on the basis that the aim of the legislation in force at the time was to provide a mechanism for identifying "meritorious" fathers, who should have the same rights as the mother and distinguishing those who may fall into the other "unmeritorious" category. This was found to be a legitimate and proportionate aim in terms of Article 8(2). Therefore, there was no violation of Article 8. In the arena of private disputes between parents, the present English legislation came under challenge in the case of *B v. United Kingdom*.[63] There, the complaint of a natural, unmarried father was that the legislation, in failing to bestow automatic parental rights on him, amounted to an unjustified interference with his Article 8 rights in a discriminatory way. The lack of automatic rights had resulted in his having no remedy against the child's mother after she abducted his child to Italy. His application was rejected but the Court, which held that the English law disclosed

"an objective and reasonable justification for the difference in

---

[58] *X and Y v. The Netherlands,* 8 E.H.R.R. 235; *Osman v. U.K.* 29 E.H.R.R. 245.
[59] s.3(1)
[60] There are almost identical provisions in the Children Act 1989, which governs the position in England and Wales.
[61] see s.4 (agreements) and s.11(orders of court) of the 1995 Act
[62] 20 E.H.R.R. 205.
[63] [2000] 1 F.L.R. 1

treatment between married and unmarried fathers with regard to the automatic acquisition of parental rights."

Any improvement in the position of the unmarried father is unlikely, therefore, to emanate from the incorporation of the Convention into domestic law. Domestic reform is anticipated, however, by a proposal of the Scottish Executive that unmarried fathers should have automatic and full parental rights where they have taken the step of registering the child's birth together with the mother.[64]

5.30

Issues of discrimination aside, challenges to the law relating to parental rights and responsibilities have been made on the basis that the "welfare test" enshrined in domestic law, placing as it does an onus on the party seeking an order for parental rights, itself amounts to unjustified interference with the right to respect for family life. It is the parental right to enjoy ongoing relations with his or her child by exercising direct contact, that has engendered most debate.

In *Sanderson v. McManus* the House of Lords opined that any parent applying to a court in Scotland for an order relating to parental rights, such as a contact order, has the burden, of showing, "on a balance of probabilities that the welfare of the child requires that the order be made in the child's best interests".[65] That decision was made under the previous legislation on custody and access and concerned an application by an unmarried father for parental rights. In the more recent case of *White v. White*,[66] a divorced father sought a contact order in respect of the younger of his two children. He argued that, as he retained general parental rights and responsibilities, a presumption in favour of his being awarded contact applied, unless the mother could show that an award of contact would be contrary to the child's interests. The sheriff at first instance agreed, but his decision was overturned on appeal. In allowing the mother's appeal, the sheriff principal found that the Children (Scotland) Act 1995, far from elevating parental rights into something to which effect must be given unless their exercise could be shown to be detrimental to the child, expressly limited them. In particular, the responsibility to maintain direct contact with a child which formed the basis of the right asserted was, in terms of the statute, to be complied with only where "practicable and in the interests of the child."[67] Further, he opined, "the 1995 Act has not changed the nature of the test as interpreted in

---

[64] Scottish Executive White Paper, "Parents and Children", September 2000, Chapter 2 (Proposal 1).
[65] 1997 S.C. (H.L.) 55, per Lord Hope at p.62.
[66] 1999 S.L.T. (Sh.Ct.) 106.
[67] *Ibid*, at p.111, where reference is made to s.1(1) of the 1995 Act.

Sanderson, insofar as it requires the parent seeking the order to illustrate that the contact sought will benefit the child".[68]

The father appealed to the Inner House and during that appeal stage the Convention has been incorporated into Scots Law. He was successful, primarily on the basis that the Children (Scotland) Act 1995 alters the domestic position on onus.[69] Against that recent background, the question of whether the domestic "welfare test" is to any extent in conflict with the rights protected by Article 8 requires further consideration.[70]

5.31   The European Court has always recognised that a fair balance must be struck between the interests of the child and those of the parent. It has accepted that particular importance must be attached to the best interests of the child and that those interests may, in cases where there would otherwise be a risk to the child's health or development, override those of the parent.[71] But while the States have a fairly wide margin of appreciation in balancing those interests, they must, it is submitted, be careful to avoid elevating one over the other in the decision making process. In the recent case of *Elsholz v. Germany*[72] the Court again showed a willingness to scrutinise particularly carefully restrictions imposed on parental rights of access. There a father who had been denied contact with his child against a background of an acrimonious relationship with the child's mother complained that statements by his young child that he did not wish to see his father should have been independently assessed by a psychologist. He succeeded in arguing that the local court's reliance on the tensions between the parents was insufficient to justify a refusal to order that independent evidence and that, coupled with the appellate court's refusal to reinvestigate the merits of the application amounted to a violation of his Article 8 rights. Thus it was insufficient for the domestic court to conclude that contact between father and son would negatively affect the child where he had indicated he did not want it. In order to weigh in the balance the father's right to contact before reaching a decision, an available mechanism for evaluating the boy's views should have been utilised. While the interpretation of the welfare test by the Inner House in *White* may overcome the general criticism about the previous onus on the parent seeking parental rights, the *Elsholz* decision seems to provide some assistance with the more substantive issue of how the courts should approach what remains as a difficult balancing exercise.

---

[68]   *Ibid.*, at p.113

[69]   The appeal was heard on March 1, 2001 and the decision made available on March 6, 2001. The European authorities are referred to, but the matter was dealt with as an issue of domestic statutory interpretation. The decision has now been reported 2001 S.L.T. 485.

[70]   The issue is first considered in the context of care proceedings and adoption, *supra*, at p.182-184

[71]   *Olsson v. Sweden*, 11 E.H.R.R. 259 and *Johansen v. Norway*, 23 E.H.R.R. 33.

[72]   Appl. No.255735/94 [2000] 2 F.L.R. 486.

The approach taken by the domestic courts both in England and Scotland to contact between a father and his children and in particular the procedure and decisions involved in the enforcement of contact orders, came under scrutiny most recently in *Glaser v. United Kingdom*.[73] The background involved a married couple with three children who separated while living in England. A dispute over contact by the father to his children arose in English County Court proceedings. Ultimately, a contact order providing for weekly contact, overnight stays and holiday periods was made in 1993. The mother failed to comply with the order. She left the former family home and concealed her whereabouts. It subsequently transpired that she had moved to Scotland with the children. Between July 1993 and 1997 Mr Glaser attempted first to enforce the English order and later sought a fresh order for contact in Scotland. In 1996 he lodged an application against the United Kingdom, submitting that the authorities in England and Scotland failed effectively to enforce his right to contact with his children in terms of the court orders in his favour. Particular criticisms were made in relation to delays, and the lack of a coherent procedure for cross border enforcement of such orders.[74] The Court rejected Mr Glaser's claim that these amounted to violations of his Article 8 rights, finding that most of the difficulties flowed from the mother's determination to flout the court order rather than failures on the part of the authorities. In refusing to regard the domestic authorities' obligation to enforce contact rights as absolute, the Court answered the applicant's claim that they were, as follows,

"where other individuals are concerned, particularly children, the courts must ensure that steps taken do not infringe their rights. Their decision making process must inevitably involve a balancing of the respective interests, as coercive measures may in themselves present a risk of damage to the children concerned."

This dictum may be used, it is submitted, to rebut any future suggestions that the Convention elevates rights over welfare in dealing with the claims of parents under Article 8. Domestic legislation would thus appear to be compatible with the Convention in this area. Such challenges as are made are more likely to involve the court's care in implementing the law and available procedures, along the lines of the *Elsholz* application.

---

[73] Appl. No. 32346/96, (Judgment September 19, 2000, unreported)

[74] The framework for cross border enforcement of parental rights orders is contained in the Family Law Act 1986. Primary jurisdiction is retained by the court that dealt with the divorce, but there is provision for registration of that court's order in another jurisdiction. Once that is done the new jurisdiction has power to enforce the order as if it had made it. See ss.25–33. It was the implementation of these measures that concerned Mr Glaser.

This section has focused exclusively on heterosexual parenthood. Parenting issues are included in the matters that have been discussed in the law affecting homosexuality and transsexuality, to which consideration will now be given.

(d) Sexuality

5.32   The approach of Scots Law to the treatment of non-heterosexuals covers a range of issues, some of which involve the criminal law. The purpose of this section is to highlight only the areas of direct relevance to the family law practitioner, such as marriage, parenting and respect for family life generally. It is appropriate to address these areas insofar as they affect homosexuals and transsexuals separately, although the particular Convention rights under discussion are effectively the same.

(i) Homosexuality

5.33   In recent years, the courts in Scotland and south of the border have slowly come to accept that there is no reason to regard homosexuality as being generally inconsistent with acceptable forms of family life. The topic of lesbian and gay parenting has focused the argument. While decisions from the early part of the last decade continued to indicate disapproval of a gay lifestyle if it was to be coupled with the upbringing of children,[75] the only authoritative treatment of the relevance of homosexuality in decisions about parenting, by the Inner House in *T, Petitioner*,[76] firmly rejected such discriminatory treatment of homosexual parents. The case involved a Petition for adoption of a disabled boy made by a man who was involved in a stable homosexual relationship. The question that arose was whether the statutory process of adoption should be sanctioned by the court where the prospective adopter made clear the child would be brought up jointly by him and another man with whom he cohabited in a homosexual relationship. Citing English authority[77] to the effect that homosexuals could not be regarded as a class, but as people whose characteristics must be assessed individually, in child welfare matters, as with heterosexuals, the First Division took the view that the welfare test expressed in section 6 of the 1978 Act should be interpreted accordingly. There was nothing in the legislation to justify any objection being taken to adoption by a homosexual unless a concern about welfare of the child arose in the particular circumstances. It is interesting to read the court's treatment of the

---

[75] See, *e.g. Early v. Early*, 1990 S.L.T. 221 and the English Court of Appeal case, *C v. C* [1991] 1 F.L.R. 223.
[76] 1997 S.L.T. 724
[77] *Re D (Adoption: Parent's Consent)* [1977] A.C. 602, cited at p732 of "T"

possible application of the Convention to the issue, which it was accepted could be used, if necessary as an aid to construction of the Act.[78] The position of the Commission at that time, it was noted, was that the relationship of a homosexual couple did not fall within the scope of the right to respect for family life.[79] Restrictions on homosexual relationships had been justified by the Court as necessary to protect vulnerable individuals, in *Dudgeon v. United Kingdom*.[80] Thus the Inner House was seen to be more tolerant of homosexual parenting than it appeared the Convention would demand at that stage.

Since the decision in *T, Petitioner*, the European jurisprudence has developed to the point where the Court has now made a clear statement that distinctions in parental rights decisions based on sexual orientation cannot be tolerated under the Convention. The case of *Salgueiro da Silva Mouta v. Portugal*[81] involved an application by a man who had married, fathered a daughter, and then separated from his wife to pursue a long term homosexual relationship with another man. His wife raised divorce proceedings in the course of which an agreement was entered into by the parties. In terms of that agreement, the mother was attributed parental responsibility over the child, with the father being granted visiting or contact rights. The mother failed to comply with the agreement, by refusing contact and by sending the child to stay with her maternal grandparents. The father then raised further proceedings in an attempt to gain full parental responsibility over his daughter, in the course of which the mother claimed that his partner had abused the child sexually. These allegations were rejected by the first instance Court for Family Matters in Lisbon, which granted the father's application for full parental responsibility. On appeal the decision was reversed, largely on the basis that the father's domestic arrangements were "abnormal" and the antithesis of the Portuguese traditional family that the child should be part of. The father complained under the Convention that his Article 8 rights had been violated, both in isolation and in conjunction with Article 14. His application was upheld by the Court, which found that the Portuguese Court of Appeal's introduction of a new element of consideration, namely the husband's homosexuality, amounted to a difference in treatment based on sexual orientation. That difference in treatment could not be justified, being disproportionate to the objective of protecting the health and rights of the child. Accordingly, there had been a breach of the applicant's Article 8 rights read in conjunction with Article 14.

On the issue of parenting, then, it seems that Scots Law had

---

[78] see 1997 S.L.T. at pp.733–734.
[79] Reference was made to the cases of *Kerkhoven, Hinke and Hinke v. The Netherlands; X and Y v. U.K.* and *S v. U.K.* cited at page 734 of "T".
[80] 4 E.H.R.R. 149.
[81] 2001 Fam. L.R. 2

already adopted an approach that accords with the more recent interpretation of Articles 8 and 14 by the Court.

5.34   The more general issue of whether a homosexual relationship now falls within the scope of the right to respect for family life was not addressed in *da Silva Mouta*. It was considered, however, in the well-publicised applications of *Lustig-Praen and Becket v. United Kingdom* and *Smith and Grady v. United Kingdom*.[82] Four serving members of the British Armed Forces were discharged from duty solely on the basis of their sexual orientation. They challenged that decision by judicial review proceedings in the English courts. The matter came before the Court of Appeal,[83] which dismissed their appeals, albeit while recognising a discernible trend towards greater tolerance of homosexual relationships. The applicants took their case to Strasbourg,[84] arguing that the decisions to discharge them from duty on the basis of their homosexuality amounted to a violation of their Article 8 right to respect for private life. The Court agreed that their rights had been unjustifiably breached, making clear that such relationships must now be regarded as falling within the ambit of Article 8.

There remain aspects of homosexual personal and family life where different treatment has been considered appropriate in domestic law. However, even prior to the implementation of the Convention by the 1998 Act, the House of Lords broadened the interpretation of "family life" as including a stable homosexual partnership, at least for the purpose of a specific statutory provision relative to succession of tenancies. In *Fitzpatrick v. Sterling Housing Association*,[85] questions arose as to whether Mr Fitzpatrick could be regarded as the spouse of his deceased partner, having lived with him "as husband and wife", in order to succeed to the deceased's statutory tenancy, which failing whether he could be regarded as a member of the deceased's family for the purpose of succeeding at least to an assured tenancy in respect of the property where they had lived together. Their Lordships decided that the first question had to be answered in the negative, but that, in relation to the second, Mr Fitzpatrick and the deceased, who had lived together in a stable, close and loving homosexual partnership for about 18 years, fell within the definition of "family" in the relevant legislation.[86] This overturned the previous Court of Appeal ruling and was a majority decision, two out of the five judges dissenting. Lord Clyde, in supporting the majority decision to allow the appeal, expressed the view that the decision he had reached did not conflict

---

[82] 29 E.H.R.R. 493 (*Smith and Grady*) and 548 (*Lustig-Praen and Becket*).
[83] [1996] 1 All E.R. 257.
[84] The Court of Appeal having been refused them leave to appeal to the House of Lords. *Ibid.*, at 273.
[85] [1999] 4 All E.R. 705; [1999] 3 W.L.R. 1113.
[86] The statutory provisions under discussion were para. 2(2) of Sched. 1 to the Rent Act 1977 and para. 3 of Sched. 1 to that Act.

with, *inter alia*, the jurisprudence of the European Court of Human Rights. While accepting that homosexual relationships had not been regarded as falling within the right to respect for family life to date,[87] he referred to the Court's more recent recognition that family life is not confined to marriage and can encompass de facto relationships.[88] M da Silva Mouta's application against Portugal, which was not yet before the Court, was also mentioned. Lord Clyde was careful to distinguish the statute under consideration from those which specifically define the family members who might qualify for the benefits the legislation intends to impose.[89]

The majority decision in *Fitzpatrick* illustrates a willingness, at the highest domestic level, to recognise non-heterosexual relationships and to grant equal treatment to them, at least where this can be achieved within existing legislation. It leaves open important questions for the future, however, such as whether there are any circumstances in which homosexuals can be regarded as living together "as husband and wife". Given the extension of various statutory provisions to cohabitants living as spouses,[90] an interpretation that excludes their application to stable, homosexual partnerships, may, in time be seen as falling foul of the requirement to apply the Convention without distinction on the basis of sexual orientation. This would be a consistent and reasonable extension of the dicta in *da Silva Mouta*.

The domestic legislation governing one of the fundamental rights protected for heterosexuals, the right to marry expressed in Article 12, specifically excludes marriage between same sex partners.[91] The justification for that ongoing difference in treatment has been discussed judicially more in the particular context of relationships involving transsexuals, where the denial of the rights to marry and found a family are perhaps even more acutely focused.

5.35

(ii) Transsexuality

Transsexuality, sometimes referred to as gender dysphoria syndrome, usually involves an intense desire to be a member of the opposite sex.[92] It is thought that most transsexuals are heterosexual to the extent that, if what they perceive as an error of nature is rectified, they will form relationships with the other sex (the one

5.36

---

[87] [1999] 4 All E.R. 705, at p728-729, citing *S v. U.K.* (1986) 47 D.R. 274

[88] *X, Y and Z v. U.K.* cited in the Assisted Reproduction section at no.21 and discussed further in the section on transsexuality, below.

[89] See p 729-730 of the *Fitzpatrick* decision, where the wording of the Housing Act 1985 and the Rent Act 1977 is contrasted.

[90] See the examples given in the section on Marriage and Cohabitation, at pp. 194-195.

[91] s.5(4)(e), Marriage (Scotland) Act 1977

[92] for a useful summary of what attributing a particular "sex" to an individual means in this context, see Mason & McCall Smith at pp.38-39.

that they were previously thought to belong to). Transsexuals in this country are able to undergo gender re-assignment treatment, usually including surgery. After treatment, their classification in law as male or female may become an issue. However, an early Scottish case, *X, Petitioner*,[93] concerned an application to alter the recorded sex in a birth certificate without the petitioner having had such treatment. The application was refused on the basis that, in terms of the relevant legislation, birth registration details could only be amended if an error came to light. A change of sex, if it had taken place, did not render the original entry in the register erroneous. The present legislation, the Registration of Births, Deaths and Marriages (Scotland) Act 1965 (as amended) permits alterations to birth registration details only in specified circumstances, such as adoption.

The notion that one's sex is determined at birth and cannot change was challenged directly in the English case of *Corrbett v. Corbett otherwise Ashley*.[94] A man who had undergone a marriage ceremony with a post operative male to female transsexual, April Ashley, raised a petition seeking decree of nullity of marriage on the basis that the respondent was, in all relevant respects, a man. The court determined that the respondent was male, expressing the view that the relevant factors were the biological criteria—chromosomal, gonadal and genital. It was recognised that the respondent was now treated as a female socially and by the state for the purposes of National Insurance. However, Justice Omrod concluded that "Marriage is a relationship which depends on sex and not on gender."

The issue of alteration of the birth certificate, raised in *X, Petitioner*, was first considered in the European Human Rights context in the application of *Van Oosterwijck v. Belgium*,[95] where a Belgian female to male transsexual who had undergone gender altering surgery had failed to persuade state authorities that his birth certificate should be altered to accord with that change. He complained of breaches of Articles 8 and 12. The Commission was of the view that both Articles had been violated, confirming that the national laws must not restrict or reduce these rights to such an extent that their very essence was impaired.[96] The merits of the application were not ultimately considered by the Court, however, due to a failure to exhaust domestic remedies.

Both issues, that of the inability to alter a birth certificate and the consequent denial of the right to marry were subsequently addressed by the Court in the case of *Rees v. United Kingdom*[97] where the English position as outlined in *Corbett* was claimed to

---

[93] 1957 S.L.T.(Sh.Ct.) 61
[94] 1970 2 All E.R. 33
[95] 3 E.H.R.R. 557
[96] *ibid*, at para.56
[97] 9 E.H.R.R. 56

breach Article 12. That claim was firmly rejected by the Court, which opined that the right to marry guaranteed by Article 12 referred to traditional marriage between people of the opposite sex. The Article 8 complaint also failed, largely because the ability in the United Kingdom to alter nearly all other paperwork relative to identity with ease rendered any problems encountered by the applicant as minor, in comparison with the alternative of a requirement on the state to alter its whole system of birth registration.

As has been seen with attitudes towards de facto family life generally, however, the interpretation of the Convention can adapt to social change. In the later British application of *Cossey v. United Kingdom*,[98] another attempt was made to argue both the Article 8 and Article 12 issues, in light of changing scientific advances and societal attitudes towards transsexuals. The applicant had undergone male to female gender re-assignment surgery at the age of 20, after which she lived successfully as a woman. In her late 20's she wanted to marry, but was advised that any purported marriage would be void, an application to alter her birth certificate having been refused. She went ahead with the marriage anyway. When it broke down, the English court declared that it had been null and void. When Ms Cossey then complained of violations of Articles 8 and 12, the Court made clear that it was not bound by its previous findings, such as the decision in *Rees*. It would depart from an earlier decision if that was necessary to ensure that societal changes were taken into account in interpreting the Convention. Nonetheless, the application failed as there had been insufficient changes to justify a departure from the reasoning in *Rees* on identical issues. Two years later the Court refused to depart from the position taken in *Rees* and *Cossey* in relation to the restriction of Article 12 to traditional marriage, but felt able to distinguish those British applications on the birth certificate issue, in *B v. France*.[99] There, a French male to female transsexual succeeded in arguing that French Law, which seemed to require her to use her previous male identity on all official documents and even for items such as telephone bills, constituted an unjustified interference with her right to respect for her privacy. As birth certificates could, and often were, ordered to be amended on changes taking place in a person's life, the refusal to alter the applicant's certificate, coupled with the daily inconvenience of requiring her to disclose her original identity on other documents, was incompatible with due respect.

The statement of the Court in *Cossey*, indicating a willingness to alter its approach to these issues, if and when appropriate, has now been tested in two further British applications. The first, *X, Y and Z v. United Kingdom*[1] concerned a couple, a female to male

5.37

---

[98]   13 E.H.R.R. 622
[99]   16 E.H.R.R. 1
[1]   20 E.H.R.R. 143

transsexual (X) and his female cohabitant (Y), who had undergone artificial insemination by a donor to conceive a child (Z). The complaint related to the authorities' refusal to permit X to be registered as the father, which the relevant legislation would have permitted had he always been male.[2] The application was classified by both the Commission and the Court as one pertaining to family life, rather than private life as in *Rees* and *Cossey*. The de facto family ties between X, Y and Z were sufficient to bring them within the ambit of Article 8 protection. However, given the ongoing lack of consensus between states on these matters, it was decided that a wide margin of appreciation should be allowed. The state, it was held, could not be **obliged** to recognise someone as the father of a child where he was not the biological father. In the circumstances, the absence of legal recognition of the relationship between X and Z did not amount to a failure to respect their family life. Importantly, the view was expressed that transsexuality continued to raise complex scientific, legal, moral and social issues on which there was no common approach. Thus, the time for a radical departure from previous statements had not yet arrived.

5.38   The lack of consensus on the scientific and social issues relative to transsexuality was again relied on in 1998 when the Court rejected the most recent British application, *Sheffield and Horsham v. United Kingdom*.[3] The two applicants were both male to female transsexuals. They made complaints under Articles 8 and 12 in relation to the documentation and marriage issues and also claimed that they had been subject to discrimination in terms of Article 14, a point which had been raised but rejected in *X, Y and Z*. The Commission accepted that Sheffield and Horsham's right to respect for their privacy had been violated, but refused to recognise that any separate issues under Articles 12 or 14 arose. However, the Court concluded that no positive obligation on the state to give legal recognition to the applicants' altered gender had been established, in the absence of a common European approach to the issue. There was a reiteration of the need to keep the matter under review in light of the increased social acceptance of transsexualism.[4]

Despite that last statement, the domestic courts, in applying the now implemented Convention, are not likely to have any difficulty finding that Scots law on marriage and birth registration is compatible with the Convention as interpreted in each of the above European cases. Furthermore, the ability of any person with a legitimate interest to apply for parental rights in relation to children

[2]   see s.28(1) and (2), s.29(1) and s.49(3) of the Human Fertilisation and Embryology Act 1990 also referred to in the section on Assisted Reproduction, at p.172.

[3]   27 E.H.R.R. 163

[4]   *Ibid*, at para. 60

probably enables transsexual parents to participate as fully in family life as the unmarried father or the homosexual parent.[5]

There may well be scope, it is hoped, for further development of the argument that differential treatment of transsexuals under Article 12 amounts to clear discrimination on the ground of sex and therefore violates the prohibition against discrimination, just as homosexuals have now succeeded in claiming that some types of differential treatment on grounds of sexual orientation are not to be tolerated. The hope is tempered, however by the most recent English decision reiterating that a chromosomal test is the one that must be used to determine a party's sex for the purpose of entering marriage.[6] Whether a Scottish Court would now consider that the time has arrived to consider a different approach based on existing gender rather than sex remains to be seen.

5.39

---

[5] Discussed above under parenthood at pp.200-202 and homosexuality at pp204-205.
[6] *Bellinger v. Bellinger, The Times Law Reports*, November 22, 2000.

CHAPTER 6

NEGLIGENCE AND THE CONVENTION

The extent to which the incorporation of the European Convention   6.01
will impact on negligence actions is unlikely to be clear for some
years. During that period there is a danger that commentaries on
the topic may be unduly speculative. Uncertainty will be caused not
only by the difficulties of deciding when acts and omissions breach
the Convention but also by deciding what amounts to an effective
remedy. Nevertheless I would like to suggest in this chapter that
incorporation may encourage a higher priority being given to
negligence's traditional role of deterring dangerous behaviour. By
virtue of section 8 of the 1998 Act where a public authority is found
to have breached a Convention right, the court concerned will be
able to make such an order, or grant such relief or remedy as it
considers just and appropriate within its powers.[1] A narrow
approach to the role of a section dealing expressly with remedies
might mean that successful complaints of infringements of the Act
would simply lead to damages (or some other remedy) being
awarded under section eight. This might give rise to the possibility
that the common law of negligence would not evolve as a result of
the 1998 Act. A complaint of negligence in respect of a Convention
right might lead only to the statutory remedy contained in section 8.
However, if for no other reason than judicial desire to promote
law's internal coherence, it seems likely that the Convention will
stimulate change to the common law. A useful comparison may be
made with the way in which the statutory background can influence
the determination of whether or not a duty of care exists. In
litigation against public bodies pursuers will often seek a remedy in
negligence and, in seeking to establish that a duty of care was owed,
will point to relevant Convention rights. Such arguments will be
encouraged by section 6(1) of the 1998 Act which provides that it is
unlawful for a public authority to act in a way which is
incompatible with a Convention right. Section 6(3) provides that
a public authority includes a court. It will undoubtedly be argued
that to comply with section 6 a court will have to hand down

---

[1]   s. 8(1).

judgments which comply with Convention rights.[2] At the end of the day some provisions of the Convention are more likely to be relevant to negligence actions against public bodies than others. It is proposed to examine these and to consider how domestic law might evolve as a result.

Article 2

6.02 In *Osman v. United Kingdom* it was alleged that the United Kingdom was in breach of a number of articles of the Convention.[3] Article 2 was said to have been infringed by the failure to take adequate and appropriate steps to protect the lives of the applicants from real and known danger. The United Kingdom Government accepted that the article "may imply a positive obligation on the authorities of a Contracting State to take preventive measures to protect the life of an individual from the danger posed by another individual". However, they went on to argue that the scope of any such obligation was subject to three, highly restrictive, limitations. First, an obligation would only arise where there was a known risk of a real, direct and immediate threat to that individual's life. Second, the authorities would have to have assumed responsibility for the individual's safety. Third, the failure to take preventive action would have to amount to gross dereliction or wilful disregard of their duty to protect life.[4] In giving judgment the court took the view that the Article could give rise to "a positive obligation on the authorities to take preventive operational measures to protect an individual whose life is at risk from the criminal acts of another individual".[5] Where such a risk existed the scope of the duty derived from Article 2 was described as follows,

> "where there is an allegation that the authorities have violated their positive obligation to protect the right to life in the context of their above-mentioned duty to prevent and suppress offences against the person...it must be established to its satisfaction that the authorities knew or ought to have known at the time of the existence of a real and immediate risk to the life of an identified individual or individuals from the criminal acts of a third party and that they failed to take measures within the scope of their powers which, judged reasonably, might have been expected to avoid that risk."[6]

---

[2] Wade, "Horizons of Horizontality" (2000) 116 L.Q.R. 217 at 217–8 argues that the effect of s.6 is that "if a Convention right is relevant, a court deciding a case must decide in accordance with it, no less in a case between private parties than in a case against a public authority". For a view to the contrary see Sir Richard Buxton, "The Human Rights Act and Private Law" (2000) 116 L.Q.R. 48.

[3] (2000) 29 E.H.R.R. 245 and see Hoyano, "Policing Flawed Investigations" (1999) 62 M.L.R. 912.

[4] *Osman* at para. 107

[5] *ibid.* at para. 115.

[6] *ibid.* at para. 116.

Thus only the first of the limitations suggested by the United Kingdom was accepted. Moreover, any requirement that a breach of Article 2 would only arise where "gross negligence" existed was seen as incompatible with the obligation to secure the practical and effective protection of the rights and freedoms laid down in the Convention. Nevertheless the court has defined the obligation restrictively. One notes, in particular, that the risk should be to life rather than merely being of personal injury.

Article 2 may well be influential in future cases of negligence against the police where they have failed to prevent harm being done to the pursuer's person by a third party. Indeed already in *Gibson v. Strathclyde Police,* Lord Hamilton regarded the ECHR ruling as pointing towards a finding that a duty of care was owed by the defender.[7] It is important to emphasise that *Gibson* did not involve the police in their role in the investigation and suppression of crime. A more radical consequence is that there may well be a narrowing of the immunity set out in *Hill v. Chief Constable*[8] where it was held that a duty of care does not arise in the exercise of the police function "in the investigation and suppression of crime".[9] Were that immunity to be narrowed this might result in the police owing a duty of care along the lines of the obligation set out by the ECHR in *Osman*. It is perhaps debatable whether a duty would only be owed where there was a risk to life. It would be somewhat unusual to find that the scope of a duty of care embraced that risk only. One should note that a reformulation of the police immunity along the lines suggested by *Osman* would not mean that the result in a case like *Hill* would be any different. There the complaint was that the police failed to identify or apprehend a dangerous criminal who remained at large and committed further crimes. However, in an "*Osman* situation" matters might be very different. After all the applicants in *Osman v. United Kingdom* only failed in their Article 2 complaint on the facts.

What will be the consequences if the duty of care owed by the 6.03 police is reformulated in the way suggested? In terms of adjudication the practical result may well be that attention will move to the question of breach of duty. This is unlikely to present undue difficulties for the courts and may be, particularly in Scotland, viewed as a welcome development. For illustrative purposes it is helpful to examine how the United Kingdom courts would have dealt with a case like *Osman* had it involved assessing whether there had been a breach of duty.[10] It will be recalled that in the Court of Appeal in *Osman* it was alleged that there had been negligence by virtue of failing to apprehend Paget: "no further investigation was needed. All the police had to do was arrest him

---

[7] *Gibson v. Strathclyde Police,* 1999 S.C.L.R. 661.
[8] *Hill v. Chief Constable* [1989] A.C. 53.
[9] *ibid.* at 63, per Lord Keith.
[10] See D.Brodie, "Pursuing the Police" 1995 J.R. 292.

and keep him in custody and thereby suppress the crime that he in fact went on to commit."[11] In essence, in such a situation, the pursuer asserts that there was sufficient evidence to arrest and detain and weighing up this assertion should not be problematic since the courts are used to deciding the related question of whether there is enough evidence to convict. What other considerations would enter the calculus of risk in this sort of case? The burden of taking the precaution of arresting the suspect might be the risk that an early arrest would impede investigations into that crime or related crimes. Furthermore, there may be argument as to when time can be afforded to make the arrest or if the suspect evades capture what resources should be devoted to locating him. Again it may be suggested that the most efficient course of action is not to arrest the suspect but instead simply to cite him to appear before a criminal court. These factors would have to be taken into account in any particular case and given whatever degree of weight was appropriate in the circumstances. There is, however, nothing to suggest that the courts would find adjudicating on such matters problematic.

There is already some evidence to suggest that the Scottish courts may well be more than comfortable in taking on board factors peculiar to public authority liability in negligence at the stage of standard of care rather than at the stage of duty. In *Duff v. Highland and Islands Fire Board* the view was expressed that,

> "it is no doubt right that in operational matters much must be left to the professional judgement of the fire-fighters, but that can be achieved by applying a test analogous to the professional negligence test in determining what amounts to negligence. It is going too far...to suggest that operational judgement should be immune from challenge."[12]

Such an approach can, for instance, make allowance for the fact that members of the emergency services will often have very little time to reflect before making very important decisions. In *McCafferty v. Secretary of State,* Lord Johnston took such concerns on board in arriving at the view that,

> "the level and standard of care should be regulated to reflect the degree of stress involved in the decision and the circumstances in which it was made. The longer there is time for the decision maker to reflect, the easier it will be to criticise the decision under reference to negligence."[13]

In *Gibson* Lord Hamilton indicated that the police would be treated

---

[11] *Osman v. Ferguson* [1993] 4 All E.R. 344 at 353.
[12] *Duff v. Highland and Islands Fire Board,* 1995 S.L.T. 1362 at 1363.
[13] 1998 S.C.L.R. 379 (N) at 382.

in line with the foregoing cases when the question of standard of care was considered. Scholars of comparative law will be aware that the Canadian courts regard the concept of standard of care as a useful device through which one can balance the interests of a pursuer against the interests of a defender who is a public body. In *Just v. British Columbia,* the Supreme Court of Canada explained how the concept of standard of care might be applied where an action was brought against a public body:

> "Let us assume a case where a duty of care is clearly owed by a governmental agency to an individual that is not exempted either by a statutory provision or because it was a true policy decision. In those circumstances the duty of care owed by the government agency would be the same as that owed by one person to another. Nevertheless the standard of care imposed upon the Crown may not be the same as that owed by an individual. An individual is expected to maintain his or her sidewalk or driveway reasonably, while a government agency such as the respondent may be responsible for the maintenance of hundreds of miles of highway. The frequency and the nature of inspection required of the individual may well be different from that required of the Crown. In each case the frequency and method must be reasonable in light of all the surrounding circumstances. The governmental agency should be entitled to demonstrate that balanced against the nature and quantity of the risk involved, its system of inspection was reasonable in light of all the circumstances including budgetary limits, the personnel and equipment available to it and that it had met the standard duty of care imposed upon it."[14]

The judgment of the ECHR in *Osman* is confined to the criminal context but the reasoning in the case can be readily extended to public bodies other than the police such as other branches of the emergency services. The NHS may also be found to be the subject of litigation centring on the scope of Article 2. It is arguable, however, that Article 2 would have no impact when a doctor was treating a private patient.[15] However, if Article 2 is relevant to claims against NHS trusts it seems more likely that it would bring about a more fundamental change to the law of medical negligence. In weighing up the potential burden on public bodies one notes that it is clear from *Osman* that the police would not be in breach of Article 2 where they had taken reasonable steps to prevent the risk materialising. It is a matter of speculation what standards of behaviour might be imposed on the NHS though it may be that

---

[14] (1989) 64 D.L.R. 689.
[15] Owen in *An Introduction to Human Rights and the Common Law* (English and Havers eds) at 137

Article 2 would be used as a basis of challenge to the Bolam test.[16] Leaving the emergency services aside, a breach of Article 2 may arise where an injury is found to have been caused by the failure of a public body to exercise statutory functions. In the case of *Guerra v. Italy* the applicants complained that the authorities had not taken appropriate action to reduce the risk of pollution by a factory and to prevent the risk of accident.[17] This was said to infringe their rights to life and physical integrity. The Court found that whilst there had been an infringement of Article 8 it was unnecessary to consider the case under Article 2. However, Judge Jambrek in concurring said that,

"an analogy may be made with the Court's case law on Article 3 concerning the existence of 'foreseeable consequences'; where—mutatis mutandis—substantial grounds can be shown for believing that the person(s) concerned face a real risk of being subjected to circumstances which endanger their health and physical integrity, and thereby put at serious risk their right to life, protected by law. If information is withheld by government about circumstances which foreseeably, and on substantial grounds, present a real risk of danger to health and physical integrity, then such a situation may also be protected by Article 2."[18]

6.04   In the United Kingdom the current approach of the House of Lords, set out in the leading case of *Stovin v. Wise,* is highly restrictive where a duty of care is said to be owed in respect of a failure to exercise powers under statute.[19] Up until now one might have assumed that the Scottish courts would follow *Stovin.*[20] One wonders whether this might change in a situation where Article 2 is relevant. The distinction between acts and "pure" omissions may be of limited relevance where there is a claim that the latter Article has been infringed. The Canadian case of *Swanson v. The Queen*[21] may provide an example of the sort of situation where Article 2 could assist a pursuer. There the plaintiff recovered from a government agency on the basis that they had been negligent in not taking action against an airline that they knew to be indulging in unsafe practices.

Article 2 may be seen as supporting the stance of the Court of Appeal in *Perrett v. Collins* which has seemed somewhat out of line

---

[16]   *ibid.* at 140.
[17]   (1998) 26 E.H.R.R. 357. See also *L.C.B. v. U.K.* (1999) 27 E.H.R.R. 212.
[18]   *ibid.* at 387
[19]   *Stovin v. Wise* [1996] A.C. 923.
[20]   For instance, *Stovin* is referred to in *McKnight v. Clydeside Buses* (1999) S.C.L.R. 272 and *Forbes v. Dundee D.C.,* 1997 S.L.T. 1330 without any suggestion that it does not represent Scots law.
[21]   80 D.L.R. (4th) 741.

with the general approach in the United Kingdom to public authority liability.[22] There the plaintiff suffered personal injuries when the plane in which he was flying crashed. There were a number of defendants to the action including the Popular Flying Association (PFA). It is the involvement of the latter that gives rise to interest since the PFA performs delegated statutory functions on behalf of the Civil Aviation Authority (CAA). Under the framework of the Civil Aviation Act 1992 the plane could not have taken off without a certificate of airworthiness issued by a PFA inspector. The plaintiff alleged that had the PFA exercised reasonable care in carrying out their inspection functions they would have refused to issue a certificate of airworthiness. The PFA is not a public authority but a limited company. Nevertheless, since the PFA exercised statutory powers on behalf of the CAA the decision is important from the perspective of public authority liability. The decision in *Perrett* is based upon the view that the fundamental concern of the law of negligence is with unreasonable behaviour that entails the risk of personal injury. However, the court also had a clear view as to the nature of the relationship between the individual citizen and bodies who act "for the collective welfare". In holding that a duty was owed, mention was made of the (general) reliance placed upon regulatory bodies by the general public,

"any reasonably well informed member of the public, although not in possession of the detailed framework, would expect there to be such a regulatory scheme in force to ensure his safety when flying and would rely upon it. Furthermore, a member of the public would expect that a person who is appointed to carry out these functions of inspecting aircraft and issuing permits would exercise reasonable care in doing so.'[23]

Such reasoning is resonant of duty of care decisions of the 1970's such as *Dutton v. Bognor Regis U.D.C.* which adopted a collectivist stance.[24] It must be said that such reasoning did not appeal to the House of Lords in *Stovin v. Wise*. Lord Hoffmann thought that the application of the concept of general reliance would require "some very careful analysis of the role which the expected exercise of the statutory power plays in community behaviour."[25] However, the outlook of the law may be about to change; at least where Convention rights are at stake. The foregoing also provokes consideration of what would have happened in *Murphy v. Brent-*

---

[22] [1998] 2 LR. 255.
[23] *ibid.* at 272, per Buxton, L.J.
[24] [1972] 1 Q.B. 373.
[25] [1996] A.C. 923 at 955.

wood [26] if the plaintiff had suffered personal injury or damage to his property. The question was left open by the Law Lords in that case. [27]

Article 3

6.05   In *X v. Bedfordshire* the plaintiffs alleged that they had suffered parental abuse and neglect. [28] They brought negligence actions against the council alleging that, despite being aware of the situation, it had failed to investigate the matter adequately or protect the plaintiffs from further harm. It was held that no duty of care was owed. Apart from anything else it would not have been just and reasonable to have imposed one. This was because "a common law duty of care would cut across the whole statutory system set up for the protection of children at risk". [29] Other reasons included the belief that if a duty of care was imposed local authorities would adopt a more defensive approach to their duties. Again

> "the plaintiffs are seeking to erect a common law duty of care in relation to the administration of a statutory social welfare scheme. Such a scheme is designed to protect weaker members of society (children) from harm done to them by others. The scheme involves the administrators in exercising discretions and powers which could not exist in the private sector and which in many cases bring them into conflict with those who, under the general law, are responsible for the child's welfare." [30]

The claim in the *Bedfordshire* case is proceeding to the ECHR. However, the Commission has already deliberated on the application (*Z v. United Kingdom*) and expressed the view that there is a positive obligation on the State to take those steps that could be reasonably expected of them to avoid a real and immediate risk of ill-treatment contrary to Article 3 of which they knew or ought to have had knowledge. [31] The view also being taken that the protection of children who by reason of their age and vulnerability are not capable of protecting themselves requires not only the protection of the criminal law. The ECHR had previously held that children in particular were entitled to effective protection, in the form of effective deterrence, against serious breaches of personal

---

[26] [1991] 1 A.C. 398.
[27] See the speeches of Lord MacKay at 457, Lord Keith at 463 and Lord Jauncey at 492.
[28] [1995] 2 A.C. 633.
[29] *ibid.* at 749, per Lord Browne-Wilkinson.
[30] *ibid.* at 751, per Lord Browne-Wilkinson.
[31] Appl. No. 29392/95 (Sept 10, 1999).

integrity.[32]   There is a threshold level of severity of ill treatment before the obligation is engaged. That threshold is a flexible one,

> "it depends on all the circumstances of the case, such as the nature and context of the treatment, its duration, its physical and mental effects, and where relevant, the sex, age and state of health of the victim".[33]

However, in the view of the Commission, the denial of a duty of care in *X v. Bedfordshire* infringed Article 3.

The impact of *Z v. United Kingdom* is likely to be that, in the field of child welfare, a public body with appropriate powers under statute is more likely to be held to be under a duty of care (however defined) to exercise them to protect vulnerable children. This may not alter significantly the development of United Kingdom law as, of late, the courts have been somewhat less   inclined to protect public bodies from the impact of negligence actions. This is the case even where the public body is operating within a statutory framework in the realm of education/welfare. Thus in *Barrett v. Enfield* the common law duty of care was said to include a duty to act in *loco parentis* and to provide the appellant with the standard of care which could be expected of a reasonable parent, including a duty to provide a home and education, to take reasonable steps to protect him from physical, emotional, psychiatric or psychological injury and to promote his development.[34] The House of Lords refused to strike this out. In *X (Minors) v. Bedfordshire* Lord Browne-Wilkinson had concluded that an education authority owes no common law duty of care in the exercise of powers and discretions relating to children with special educational needs specifically conferred on it by the Act of 1981. In *Phelps v. Hillingdon L.B.C.* the House of Lords was invited by counsel to depart from this view of the law despite *X v. Bedfordshire* being a decision of very recent vintage.[35] Lord Nicholls certainly did not exclude that possibility but felt that such a change could wait for another day,

> "I prefer to leave this question open for decision in a case where the facts make a decision necessary. The existence of such facts will enable attention to be focused more effectively on the practical implications of the arguments for and against the existence of direct liability."[36]

More robustly, Lord Slynn did not accept Lord Browne-Wilkinson's "absolute statement" as to the absence of a duty.

It is also possible that Article 3 could be relevant to claims

---

[32]   *A v. U.K.* (1998) 5 B.H.R.C. 137.
[33]   *Costello- Roberts v. U.K.* (1993) 19 E.H.R.R. 112 (para. 30).
[34]   [1999] 3 All E.R. 193.
[35]   [2000] 3 WLR 776.
[36]   *ibid.* at 805.

against the NHS. In *Tanko v. Finland* the Commission expressed the view that a lack of proper care in a case where someone is suffering from a serious illness could in certain circumstances amount to treatment contrary to article three.[37]

Article 8

6.06   The *Newham* case, heard by the Lords along with *X v. Bedfordshire*,[38] illustrates one situation where Article 8 might be relevant.[39] There the local authority had removed M from her mother, placed her in foster care and restricted the mother's access to her. It was alleged that the authority had failed to investigate the situation with proper care. The claim was brought on the basis of vicarious liability for the alleged negligence of the professional staff involved who were a social worker and a psychiatrist. However, it was held that the behaviour of the professionals involved did not give rise to a duty of care. Yet, even if, *prima facie*, a duty had been owed it would not have been imposed for the policy reasons discussed above in relation to *X v. Bedfordshire*. The absence of a duty of care may well amount to a breach of Article 8. It is important to emphasise that

> "although the essential object of Article 8 is to protect the individual against arbitrary interference by the public authorities, there may in addition be positive obligations inherent in an effective 'respect' for family life."[40]

A second and very different example of where Article 8 may be relevant is furnished by the case of *Lopez Ostra v. Spain*.[41] There the court accepted that,

> "severe environmental pollution may affect individuals' well-being and prevent them from enjoying their homes in such a way as to affect their private and family life adversely, without, however, seriously endangering their health." [42]

---

[37] D.R. 77- A 133. And see *D v. U.K.* 24 E.H.R.R. 423.
[38] Wright, "Local Authorities, the Duty of Care and the European Convention on Human Rights" 1998 O.J.L.S. 1
[39] In *Osman* the applicants contended that the failure of the police to bring an end to the campaign of harassment, vandalism and victimisation which Paget-Lewis waged against their property and family constituted a breach of Article 8. The Commission found that the applicants' complaints concerning the failure of the authorities to protect their home and property against the attacks allegedly perpetrated by Paget-Lewis did not give rise to a breach of Article 8 since in its view it would have been open to the applicants to seek an injunction against Paget-Lewis. Given the facts the court agreed that there had been no breach of article eight but did not deal with the question of whether an injunction would have been an effective remedy.
[40] *Abdulaziz v. U.K.* (1987) 7 E.H.R.R. 471, para. 67.
[41] 1995 20 E.H.R.R. 277.
[42] *ibid.* at para. 51

In determining whether any obligation was owed by the State

> "regard must be had to the fair balance that has to be struck
> between the competing interests of the individual and of the
> community as a whole, and in any case the State enjoys a
> certain margin of appreciation".[43]

The applicant argued that by virtue of its general supervisory
powers the municipality had a duty to act. In finding for the
applicant the court noted that,

> "the State did not succeed in striking a fair balance between the
> interests of the town's economic well-being—that of having a
> waste treatment plant—and the plaintiff's effective enjoyment
> of her right to respect for her home and her private and family
> life."[44]

Similarly such a balancing of interests will frequently be involved in
determining whether a duty of care is owed,

> "whether it is fair, just and reasonable to impose a liability in
> negligence on a particular class of would-be defendants
> depends on weighing in the balance the total detriment to the
> public interest in all cases from holding such class liable in
> negligence as against the total loss to all would-be plaintiffs if
> they are not to have a cause of action in respect of the loss they
> have individually suffered".[45]

Again in *Guerra* the State breached Article 8 through its failure to
provide information about the risk of pollution. Had such
information been provided it would

> "have enabled them to assess the risks they and their families
> might run if they continued to live at Manfredonia, a town
> particularly exposed to danger in the event of an accident at
> the factory".

The stance in the foregoing environmental cases contrasts with the
approach taken in United Kingdom cases. In *R v. Lam* the plaintiffs
claimed over damage to their property and personal injury.[46] The
losses were said to have been caused by nuisances committed by a
factory. They sued the local authority alleging negligence in

---

[43] *ibid.* It should be noted that "The margin of appreciation, as it has been developed
by Strasbourg, will necessarily be inapt to the administration of the Convention in
the domestic courts for the very reason that they are domestic".
[44] *ibid.* at para. 58.
[45] *Barrett* op cit at 199 , per Lord Browne-Wilkinson.
[46] [1997] 3 P.L.R. 22.

granting planning permission and in failing to take later enforcement proceedings (either at all or sufficiently promptly to ensure that the plaintiffs did not suffer damage). There was held to be no duty of care in respect of the granting of planning permission. The planning system in the United Kingdom being a regulatory one for the benefit of the public at large and involving general administrative functions imposed on public bodies involving the exercise of administrative discretion. The Court of Appeal also declined to impose a duty of care with regard to the enforcement functions of the local authority. They also noted the possibility of a property owner raising a nuisance action.[47] By way of discouragement to future actions the court observed that:

> "Where an allegation of 'assumption of responsibility' is made against a person or body carrying out a statutory function, there must be something more than the performance (negligent or otherwise) of the statutory function to establish such assumption of responsibility".[48]

Article 6

6.07   In *Osman* the applicants succeeded under Article 6.[49] They alleged that the dismissal by the Court of Appeal of their negligence action against the police on grounds of public policy amounted to a restriction on their right of access to a court. Again in *Z v. United Kingdom* the Commission took the view that the denial of the existence of a duty in *X v. Bedfordshire* amounted to a breach of Article 6. The reasoning in *Z* and *Osman* is interesting. If there was no duty of care owed to the applicant one might have thought that no right existed which required to be determined in accordance with Article 6. Lord Browne-Wilkinson's reasoning on this issue in the later case of *Barrett* seems convincing:

---

[47] In *Osman v. U.K.* the commission were of view that the possibility of such an action meant that there was no breach of Article 8.

[48] *Harris v. Evans* [1998] 3 All E.R. 522 dealt with the actions of a health and safety inspector who, in the course of his duties, gave advice to certain local authorities about the safety of a mobile crane used by the plaintiff for the purpose of bungee jumping. This resulted in the business being shut down for a period of time with consequent loss of profit. The plaintiff failed to establish that a duty of care was owed but it was recognised, at 538, that there might come a point when a public authority came under a duty, "it could be that a particular requirement imposed by an inspector, whether expressed in an improvement notice or prohibition notice...might introduce a new risk or danger not present in the business activity as previously conducted. The new risk or danger might materialise and result in economic damage to the business itself as well as physical damage to the person or property. We do not need to decide the point but I would not be prepared to rule out the possibility that damage thus caused could be recover by means of a negligence action."

[49] The ECHR awarded each of the applicants £10,000 since they had been denied "the opportunity to obtain a ruling on the merits of their claim for damages against the police".

"At first sight this would seem to require that the applicant has, under the local law, a right (right A) enforceable in the local court. Under Article 6 he is given as a separate right (right B) a right of access to the local courts to assert right A being a separate, free standing right. Thus one would assume that right A would consist of, for example, a contractual right or a tortuous right not to be negligently injured. If a person is prevented from enforcing those rights that is not an infringement of right A but an infringement of right B, i.e. the right of access to the court. However, that is apparently not how the European Court of Human Rights construes Article 6."[50]

Again there was much to be said for the submission of the United Kingdom Government in *Osman* on this issue,

"since the applicants had failed to establish an essential ingredient of the duty of care under domestic law they did not have any substantive right for the purposes of the applicability of Article 6.1. Any other conclusion would result in the impermissible creation by the Convention institutions of a substantive right where none in fact existed in the domestic law of the respondent State."[51]

The response of the Court was to say that

"the common law of the respondent State has long accorded a plaintiff the right to submit to a court a claim in negligence against a defendant and to request that court to find that the facts of the case disclose a breach of a duty of care owed by the defendant to the plaintiff which has caused harm to the latter. The domestic court's enquiry is directed at determining whether the constituent elements of a duty of care have been satisfied, namely: whether the damage is foreseeable; whether there exists a relationship of proximity between the parties; and whether it is fair, just and reasonable to impose a duty of care in the circumstances."[52]

The crux of the problem is the reference to a right to "request that court to find that the facts of the case disclose a breach of a duty of care". On one reading, the foregoing would appear to be at odds with the Scottish law of relevancy.[53] It would also appear to

---

[50] *Barrett* at 198. But see Markesinis et al, *Tortious Liability of Statutory Bodies*, pp 100–104.

[51] *Osman* at para. 133

[52] *ibid.* at para. 137

[53] The case of *Crooks v. Haddow* (IH), March 1, 3000, which was not brought against a public authority, may suggest otherwise. There the pursuer's complaint in respect of article six met with the following rebuttal, "If it is suggested that

contradict what the court says in *Osman* about proximity (see below).

6.08   Nevertheless, it might mean that a duty of care case against a public authority could never be dismissed at the stage of relevancy.

From *Osman* it appears that, if it was clear from the pleadings that there was an absence of proximity between the parties, that would justify a refusal to allow a negligence claim to proceed:

> "It is to be noted that in the instant case Lord Justice McCowan...appeared to be satisfied that the applicants, unlike the plaintiff Hill, had complied with the proximity test, a threshold requirement which is in itself sufficiently rigid to narrow considerably the number of negligence cases against the police which can proceed to trial".[54]

Differentiating in this way between elements of the three stage test for duty of care seems unsatisfactory. Lord Oliver once remarking that

> "it is difficult to resist a conclusion that what have been treated as three separate requirements are, at least in most cases, in fact merely facets of the same thing, for in some cases the degree of foreseeability is such that it is from that alone that the requisite proximity can be deduced, whilst in others the absence of that essential relationship can most rationally be attributed simply to the court's view that it would not be fair and reasonable to hold the defendant responsible."[55]

However, in *Osman* the denial of the existence of a duty on the basis of the fair, just and reasonableness test was viewed by the ECHR as the conferral of an immunity. It was that conferral which led to the finding that Article 6 had been breached. Again valid criticism of the reasoning of the ECHR is furnished by Lord Browne-Wilkinson:

> "The public policy element in the duty of care formula is singled out for differential treatment. This may be because of a misunderstanding over the use of the word immunity. Although the word "immunity" is sometimes incorrectly used, a holding that it is not fair, just and reasonable to hold liable a particular class of defendants whether generally or in relation to a particular type of activity is not to give immunity from a

---

dismissal of his action deprived him of the opportunity of presenting evidence in support of his case, that is a consequence of the irrelevance of his pleadings. The dismissal of an action on the ground of the irrelevance of the pleadings does not constitute, in our view, a breach of either of the provisions to which he referred."

[54] *Osman* at para. 151.
[55] *Caparo v. Dickman* [1990] 1 All E.R. 568 at 585.

liability to which the rest of the world is subject. It is a prerequisite to there being any liability in negligence at all that as a matter of policy it is fair, just and reasonable in those circumstances to impose liability in negligence."[56]

It must be stressed that the ECHR in *Osman* did not view it as illegitimate to deny a negligence claim upon the basis of public policy grounds. The problem with the approach of the domestic courts in *Osman* was that the application of the rule emanating from *Hill* "provided a watertight defence to the police and that it was impossible to prise open an immunity which the police enjoy from civil suit in respect of their acts and omissions in the investigation and suppression of crime".[57] The blanket immunity conferred amounted "to an unjustifiable restriction on an applicant's right to have a determination on the merits of his or her claim against the police in deserving cases".[58] A decision on public policy grounds would have been wholly legitimate in *Osman* had it been

> "open to a domestic court to have regard to the presence of other public-interest considerations which pull in the opposite direction to the application of the rule. Failing this, there will be no distinction made between degrees of negligence or of harm suffered or any consideration of the justice of a particular case."[59]

In a similar vein in *Z* the commission accepted the denial of a duty

> "pursued a legitimate aim, namely to preserve the efficiency of a vital sector of public service....However, it is not satisfied that it was proportionate to that aim. It notes that the exclusionary rule gave no consideration to the seriousness or otherwise of the damage or the nature or degree of the negligence alleged or the fundamental rights of the applicants' which were involved. As regards the multi-disciplinary aspects of child protection work, this may provide a factual complexity to cases but cannot by itself provide a justification for excluding liability from a body found to have acted negligently."[60]

The decision in *Osman* may have implications for the approach to negligence claims in situations where statute has conferred a discretion on a public body. In *X v. Bedfordshire* Lord Browne-Wilkinson said that,

---

[56] *Barrett* op cit at 199.
[57] *Osman* at para. 150.
[58] *Osman* at para. 151.
[59] *ibid.*
[60] *Z* at para. 114.

"a local authority cannot be liable in damages for doing that which Parliament has authorised. Therefore if the decisions complained of fall within the ambit of such statutory discretion they cannot be actionable at common law. However, if the decision complained of is so unreasonable that it falls outside the ambit of the discretion conferred upon the local authority, there is no a priori reason for excluding all common law liability."[61]

In that case the House of Lords refined the law derived from *Anns* so that it became the case that

"if the factors relevant to the exercise of the discretion include matters of policy, the court cannot adjudicate on such policy matters and therefore cannot reach the conclusion that the decision was outside the ambit of the statutory discretion. Therefore a common law duty of care in relation to the taking of decisions involving policy matters cannot exist."[62]

In so doing the area of public authority activity which is non justiciable through the medium of a negligence action was increased a little. According to *Anns* a policy decision which was *ultra vires* might be the subject of a negligence action. The approach to discretion in *X v. Bedfordshire* might be thought to prevent a court from examining the merits of a pursuer's claim and, as a consequence, infringe Article 6. Admittedly the House of Lords has, of late, adopted a more relaxed position from that stated in *X v. Bedfordshire*.[63] *Osman* may encourage further dismantling of the "public law hurdle".

Responding to *Osman*

6.09   In some ways the case law on Article 6 is the most significant. Cases on other articles may well lead to changes in specific areas of law; such as a local authority's duty to children who are the victims of parental neglect. However, the *Osman* decision on Article 6 has the potential to have a much wider impact on the law of negligence. One possibility is that it will be less likely that negligence actions against public bodies will be excluded at the stage of relevancy. In *Barrett* the House of Lords was unwilling to strike out the claim of the plaintiff out lest it deprive

"the plaintiff of his right to have the balance struck between the hardship suffered by him and the damage to be done to the public interest in the present case if an order were to be made

---

[61]   *X v. Bedfordshire* op cit at
[62]   *X v. Bedfordshire* op cit at 173.
[63]   *Barrett* op cit.

against the defendant council".[64]

Nevertheless it may still be possible to resolve a case on the pleadings alone:

> "There may be cases, as exemplified by the case of *Swinney*, where the material required for carrying out this exercise is not provided by the pleadings. In such a case, the exercise falls to be performed by the trial judge after hearing the evidence. In other cases, such as the present, sufficient material is available on the pleadings so as to enable a decision to be taken at pretrial proceedings. In my opinion, that is the position here. I have the material to enable me to carry out the balancing exercise. Having regard to the nature of the functions which the police were carrying out and the importance of those functions in the context of this case, the extent of the acts complained of, the amount claimed by way of damages and the nature and extent of the injuries allegedly suffered by the plaintiff, I reach the firm conclusion that there is nothing in the present case, certainly nothing sufficient, which is capable of giving rise to such countervailing considerations as would outweigh the general public policy of preserving the well-established rule of immunity for police forces against suits of negligence."[65]

Cases which throw up no new questions of public policy may well be resolved in this way. After all

> "the question whether it is fair and reasonable to impose liability in negligence are decided as questions of law. Once the decision is taken that, say, company auditors though liable to shareholders for negligent auditing are not liable to those proposing to invest in the company (see *Caparo*), that decision will apply to all future cases of the same kind. The decision does not depend on weighing the balance between the extent of the damage to the plaintiff and the damage to the public in each particular case."[66]

What though if the new factor is "gross negligence"?

The analysis of negligence is immensely flexible. Lord Denning once famously remarking that "[i]n all these cases you will find that the three questions, duty, causation and remoteness, run continually into one another. It seems to me that they are simply three different ways of looking at one and the same problem."[67] One

---

[64] *Barrett* op cit at 199/200.
[65] *Kinsella v. Chief Constable of Nottinghamshire*, The Times, May 5, 1999.
[66] *Barrett* op cit at 199.
[67] *Roe v. Minister of Health* [1954] 2 Q.B. 66 at 85, *per* Denning, L.J..

possible result of *Osman* in the ECHR is that cases will simply be held to be irrelevant on the basis that a pursuer would be unable to demonstrate that sufficient proximity existed between the parties. Questions of competing public policy considerations will be neither here nor there. It is important to emphasise that often considerations of a type that might be dealt with at the third stage of the present approach to duty of care might equally well be considered at the second stage. By way of reaction to *Osman* public policy factors may become more influential at that earlier stage. Such a possibility is facilitated by the fact that it may well be unclear which matters are relevant to stage two and which to stage three. In *Yeun Kun Yeu v. Att.-Gen.*,[68] for example, were the factors which were used to deny proximity qualitatively different to those dealt with under stage three? It is difficult to see that they were. Thus concern over the affect that holding for the plaintiffs would have on depositors went against proximity whilst the belief that

"the prospect of claims would have a seriously inhibiting effect on the work of his department' was relevant to considerations of policy. Both factors are surely in the realm of wider considerations of policy. The problem of obfuscation does not arise simply in the context of allocating factors to stage two or to stage three. More fundamentally there is a reticence to indicate the nature of the considerations that are relevant to the stage of proximity. The late John Fleming wrote that proximity serves as 'a convenient excuse for not disclosing any specific reasons behind a decision for or against a finding of 'duty'.' This pervasive failure to give reasons, rather than postulating unsubstantiated conclusions, has its roots in the embarrassment which the British conservative tradition has generally treated the role of policy in judicial decision making."[69]

The Court of Appeal decision in *Palmer v. Tees H.A.* suggests that proximity may indeed take on a greater role;

"The Strasbourg jurisprudence permits an English court to treat proximity as a threshold requirement, however, and an English court may strike out an action if, applying its judgment to the facts presented by the plaintiff, it concludes that the necessary relationship between the parties is not established".[70]

Impact on negligence actions outwith the public sphere

6.10   More fundamentally, what of instances where a private

---

[68] [1988] A.C. 175.
[69] Fleming, *The Law of Torts* (8th ed) p 138.
[70] [1999] Ll Rep.Med. 352 at 362, per Thorpe, L.J..

individual is immune from a negligence action? What of *Caparo v. Dickman?*[71] Admittedly, the plaintiffs failed in that case because of lack of proximity but, the reasoning in *Osman* on proximity apart, one might argue that, in substance, the decision confers an immunity on auditors. An investor could not raise an action against an auditor directly for breach of the Convention. However, what if an action was held to be irrelevant on the basis of *Caparo?* An appeal might be possible upon the basis that Article 6 had been breached. The reasoning in *Osman* in respect of Article 6 might well be applicable if *Caparo* were to be regarded as conferring an immunity. The latter decision may amount "to an unjustifiable restriction on an applicant's right to have a determination on the merits of his or her claim". It is not inconceivable that modifying the approach in *Caparo* may be attractive to the domestic courts. In *Hall v. Simons* Lord Hope observed that,

> "although the common law and the human rights law tests are expressed in different language, they are both directed to the same essential point of principle that an immunity from suit is a derogation from a fundamental right which requires to be justified."[72]

Again in the latter case Lord Steyn, in the course of delivering an opinion supporting the removal of barristers' immunity, stated that

> "there would be benefits to be gained from the ending of immunity. First, and most importantly, it will bring to an end an anomalous exception to the basic premise that there should be a remedy for a wrong."[73]

It is interesting to note that the Commission have commented adversely on the lack of empirical evidence to support a number of policy arguments. In *Z* they observed that "The risk that liability would open a floodgate of litigation from discontented parents or relatives is a speculative factor which is only of limited weight". It may be that, in the absence of empirical supporting evidence, such arguments will lose a good deal of potency in future. There have been some indications that the domestic courts are moving in a similar direction. In *Hall* Lord Steyn said that:

> "The only argument that remains is that the fear of unfounded actions might have a negative effect on the conduct of advocates. This is a most flimsy foundation, unsupported by empirical evidence, for the immunity."[74]

---

[71] [1990] 1 All E.R. 568.
[72] [2000] 3 All E.R. 673 at 711.
[73] *ibid.* at 683.
[74] *ibid.*

In *Perrett* counsel for the defendant had argued that a decision against him would raise

> "the possibility of the PFA being charged greater insurance schemes, which cost would be spread generally over aircraft operators or the public; and the danger of 'defensive surveying' by the PFA".

Such arguments were treated as having little weight in the absence of supporting evidence,

> "the court should be very cautious before reaching or acting on any conclusions that are not argued before it in the way in which technical issues are usually approached, with the assistance of expert evidence".[75]

Somewhat inconsistently no evidence was sought to substantiate the notion of "general reliance" which was seen as supporting the plaintiff's case in *Perrett*.

Conclusions

6.11   The impact of the Human Rights Act on negligence actions is not easy to predict. It may be that it will give a boost to negligence's traditional role in deterring dangerous behaviour; especially where there is a risk of personal injury. The court has indicated that Article 2 "ranks as one of the most fundamental provisions in the Convention" and "together with Article 3, it enshrines one of the basic values".[76] To some extent domestic law may have lost sight of such fundamentals. In *Perrett*, Lord Justice Hobhouse clearly regarded the decision in favour of the plaintiff as a reassertion of traditional values. The defendant's stance was viewed as representing

> "a fundamental attack upon the principle of tortuous liability for negligent conduct which had caused foreseeable personal injury to others. That such a point should be considered even arguable shows how far some of the fundamental principles of the law of negligence have come to be eroded."[77]

Indeed, the *prima facie* case for the plaintiff was overwhelming:

> "The denial of a duty of care owed by such a person in relation to the safety of the aircraft towards those who may suffer personal injuries, whereas as passengers in the aircraft or upon

---

[75] *Perrett* op cit at 277, per Buxton, L.J.
[76] *McCann v. U.K.* (1996) 21 E.H.R.R. 97, para. 147.
[77] *Perrett* op cit at 257/8.

the ground, would leave a gap in the law of tort notwithstanding that a plaintiff had suffered foreseeable personal injury as a result of the unsafety of the aircraft and the unreasonable and careless conduct of the defendant. It would be remarkable if that were the law."[78]

At this juncture it is worth recalling the Scottish case of *Forbes v. Dundee D.C.*[79] where the pursuer suffered physical injury when she fell down a stairway leading to a supermarket. She alleged that the accident was caused by the fact that the local authority had exercised its statutory powers of inspection carelessly. The Lord Ordinary denied that a duty of care was owed. Such a denial results in a negating of the two core aims of the law of negligence: compensation and deterrence. The jurisprudence of the European Court of Human Rights also seems to place less emphasis on the distinction between positive acts and pure omissions This may have a significant impact on public bodies who possess regulatory functions.

Where obligations are owed by a public body on the basis of a particular Article it does not follow that there will be a breach of that Article in the absence of a duty of care. For instance, effective remedies may exist by virtue of provisions of the criminal law.[80] Alternatively a delictual remedy outwith the law of negligence may suffice.[81] However, it seems likely that the private law remedy of a negligence action will regain a much more primary role as a means of deterring dangerous behaviour. In *Z* the Commission found

> "that the possibility of applying for criminal injuries compensation or for an investigation by the ombudsman does not provide the applicants with adequate, alternative means of obtaining redress in respect of their claims. The former does not concern their complaint that the local authority failed in their duty to protect them from foreseeable and preventable harm and the latter does not provide any enforceable right to compensation in respect of the damage suffered, the ombudsman having only recommendatory powers."[82]

In *Hall* Lord Steyn reminds us that "one of the functions of tort law   6.12 is to set external standards of behaviour for the benefit of the public". Similarly in *Osman* the court held that "the applicants were

---

[78] *Perrett* op cit at 259/260, per Hobhouse L.J..
[79] 1997 S.L.T. 1330.
[80] And note *X and Y v. The Netherlands* where the Dutch government was held to be in violation of Article eight because Dutch law did not permit the victim of sexual assault or her father to bring an effective criminal prosecution against the assailant. This was so even although civil remedies were available.
[81] *Osman* and Article 8.
[82] *Z* at para. 115.

entitled to have the local authority account for their acts and omissions in adversarial proceedings".[83] Whereas the trend of United Kingdom authorities "has been to discourage the assumptions that anyone who suffers loss is prima facie entitled to compensation from a person...whose act or omission can be said to have caused it. The default position is that he is not."[84]

One likely consequence of all this is that the courts will hold that public bodies will owe a duty of care in a wider range of situations. In this incremental process argument by analogy will play a significant part in extending the obligations owed by public bodies. This process will mirror the way by which, hitherto, judicial denial of the existence a duty of care in respect of a specific situation may well have been justified, in part, by analogy. So in *X v. Bedfordshire* we find Lord Browne-Wilkinson observing that

> "the nearest analogies are the cases where a common law duty of care has been sought to be imposed upon the police (in seeking to protect vulnerable members of society from wrongs done to them by others) or statutory regulators of financial dealings who are seeking to protect investors from dishonesty. In neither of those cases has it been thought appropriate to superimpose on the statutory regime a common law duty of care giving rise to a claim in damages for failure to protect the weak against the wrongdoer."[85]

---

[83] Para. 153
[84] *Stovin* op cit at 949, per Lord Hoffmann.
[85] *X v. Bedfordshire* op cit 750.

CHAPTER 7

PROPERTY LAW

INTRODUCTION

It may seem a little odd to find a chapter on property in a textbook   7.01
devoted to analysis of a Convention which protects fundamental
rights and freedoms.[1] This uncertainty about the status of property
rights is perhaps reflected in the fact that the only provision relating
specifically to property does not form part of the Convention itself,
but is found in an additional Protocol, ratification of which was
optional. Whatever the reason for the initial hesitation, protection
of property is now firmly embedded in the Convention system.

That protection has been achieved not only through reliance on
the First Protocol but also, as will be seen, on other Convention
provisions. In the first part of this chapter, the various articles of
the Convention which have featured in property law cases before
the Court or the Commission will be analysed. The second part will
then consider how the Convention, as given effect to in the Human
Rights Act 1998, might impact on various aspects of Scots property
law.

THE CONVENTION JURISPRUDENCE ON PROPERTY LAW

There is a relatively extensive jurisprudence from decisions of the   7.02
Court and the Commission relating to the protection of property
rights under the Convention. Of most significance is the jurisprudence relating to Article 1, Protocol 1 but something must also be
said about a number of other articles, namely, Articles 6, 8, 14 and
41.

Article 1, Protocol 1,

The text of the article is as follows—
"Every natural or legal person is entitled to the peaceful   7.03

---

[1]   On the question of property as a fundamental right, see Schermers, "The
international protection of the right of property" in *Protecting Human Rights:
The European Dimension*, and Kingston, "Rich People have rights too? The status
of property as a fundamental right" in *Human rights: a European Perspective*.

enjoyment of his possessions. No one shall be deprived of his possessions except in the public interest and subject to the conditions provided for by law and by the general principles of international law.

The preceding provisions shall not, however, in any way impair the right of a State to enforce such laws as it deems necessary to control the use of property in accordance with the general interest or to secure the payment of taxes or other contributions or penalties."

In considering the scope and meaning of the article, it may be helpful to examine separately the following matters[2]—

(a) the meaning of "possessions"
(b) the "three rules"
(c) the Court's approach
(d) compensation

(a) The meaning of "possessions"

7.04   In accordance with the autonomous nature of Convention terms, "possessions" must be understood in its Convention sense which may in some instances be wider than that of domestic law. It is not limited to ownership of physical goods, but applies to moveable and heritable property, corporeal and incorporeal property. To give some idea of the width of the notion, the following have been considered by the Strasbourg authorities to be "possessions" within the meaning of Protocol 1, Article 1—

• Licences to serve liquor or extract gravel[3]
• The right to enforce an arbitration award[4]
• Claims for compensation[5]
• Shares and patents[6]
• Planning consents[7]

There will usually be no difficulty in identifying whether "possessions" are involved. There have, however, been some creative (although unsuccessful) attempts to widen the concept. Where the House of Lords ruled that licences to occupy could not defeat the operation of the Rent Acts, a complaint that there had been a

[2]   What follows is a brief outline of the jurisprudence in this area for the purpose of examining the effect of the Convention on Scots law in this area. More comprehensive analysis of Art. 1 of Protocol 1 can be found in the numerous text books relating to the Convention.
[3]   *Tre Traktorer Aktiebolag v. Sweden*, A159, 13 E.H.R.R. 309; *Fredin v. Sweden*, A192, 13 E.H.R.R. 142.
[4]   *Stran Greek Refineries v. Greece*, A301-B, 19 E.H.R.R. 293.
[5]   *Pressos Compania Naviera S.A. v. Belgium*, A332, 21 E.H.R.R. 301.
[6]   *Bramelid and Malmström v. Sweden*, Appl. Nos. 8588/79 and 8589/79, 29 D.R. 64; *Smith Kline and French Laboratories v. Netherlands*, Appl. No. 12633/87, 66 D.R. 70.
[7]   *Pine Valley Developments Ltd v. Ireland*, A222, 13 E.H.R.R. 784.

deprivation of possessions was found to be manifestly unfounded, partly on the basis that the applicant's rights did not constitute "individual rights enjoying in their own right, the protection awarded to possessions".[8] Somewhat easier to understand is the finding that the occupation of property without legal title cannot constitute a possession for the purposes of the Convention.[9] It should be noted that the right to acquire property is not protected.[10]

(b) The three rules

Since the case of *Sporrong and Lönnroth v. Sweden* in 1982[11], the Court has consistently observed that Article 1, Protocol 1 contains three distinct rules. The first rule, which is set out in the first sentence of the first paragraph, is of a general nature and states the principle of the peaceful enjoyment of property. The second rule, in the second sentence of the first paragraph, relates to deprivation of possessions which is subject to certain conditions. The third rule, found in the second paragraph, permits States to control the use of property in accordance with the general interest.[12]

7.05

Although the rules are described as "distinct", they are not unconnected. Indeed, the second and third rules are regarded as specific instances of an interference with the peaceful enjoyment of one's property and are therefore construed in light of the general principle enunciated in the first rule. The Court will consider whether the last two rules are applicable before considering whether the first rule has been complied with.

The *Sporrong and Lönnroth* case illustrates the distinction between the three rules. In that case, the applicants' properties had been affected by expropriation permits. Although the permits had not been implemented, they prevented the applicants from building on the sites, which were subject to planning blight. The Court held that there had been no *de facto* expropriation in terms of Rule 2. The prohibitions on construction, but not the expropriation permits, were within Rule 3 since the former controlled the use of the property. The latter were considered to fall within Rule 1. The Court then went on to find that there had been a violation of Article 1, Protocol 1.

Although the Court will carry out an analysis of the rule in terms of which the case is to be considered, the approach which it then takes to the case may not be significantly affected. As will be evident from the following, having attributed the factual circumstances to one of the rules in the Article, in general terms the Court's analysis will follow the same path no matter which rule is being considered.

---

[8] *Antoniades v. U.K.*, App. No. 15434/89, 64 D.R. 232.
[9] *Simpson v. U.K.* Appl. No. 11716/85, 47 D.R. 274.
[10] *Marckx v. Belgium*, A31, 2 E.H.R.R. 330.
[11] A52, (1983) 5 E.H.R.R. 35.
[12] The three rules are conveniently referred to as Rules 1, 2 and 3.

The question of compensation may, however, have greater or lesser significance depending on which rule is being applied.

(c) The Court's approach

7.06 Having determined under which rule there has been an interference in the applicant's property rights, the Court then applies a three stage test. First, it considers whether there was a legal basis for the interference. Secondly, it must be satisfied that the interference was in the "public interest" (Rule 2) or the "general interest" (Rule 3). Thirdly, the issue of proportionality will be examined.

So far as the first aspect is concerned, it will generally not pose any real problem.[13] It should be relatively easy to determine whether the interference has been in accordance with the law. In order to comply with this requirement, the law must in addition protect against arbitrariness.[14]

Turning to the second aspect, it should be noted that no distinction is drawn by the Court between the two different terms, *i.e.* between "general" and "public" interest. A wide margin of appreciation is allowed to States in determining what those interests require, and the Court will not interfere with that assessment unless it is considered by the Court to be "manifestly without reasonable foundation".[15]

The third and final aspect is that of proportionality, a concept which pervades the Convention. Thus there must be a fair balance between the interests of the individual and that of the general or public interest. There must also be a reasonable relationship of proportionality between the means employed and the aim pursued. The Court sometimes talks of whether the applicant is bearing a "disproportionate burden"[16] or an "individual and excessive burden".[17] Whether or not the State has compensated the applicant for the interference in his property rights may be of significance in determining whether a fair balance has been struck. The question of compensation is considered next.

(d) Compensation[18]

7.07 Although Article 1 contains no express provision requiring that there be compensation, it is established that

> "the taking of property without payment of an amount

[13] For an example of a breach of this requirement see *Iatridis v. Greece*, March 25, 2000.
[14] *Hentrich v. France*, A296-A, 18 E.H.R.R. 440.
[15] This phrase features in a number of the Court's judgments. See, for example, *Mellacher v. Austria*, A169 (para.47), 12 E.H.R.R. 391 (rent control measures); *James v. U.K.*, A98 (para. 49), 8 E.H.R.R. 123 (reform of leasehold tenure).
[16] See *Mellacher* (above) at para. 56.
[17] See *James* (above) at para. 50.
[18] On this aspect, see the detailed analysis by D. Anderson Q.C. "Compensation for Interference with Property" [1999] E.H.R.L.R. 543.

reasonably related to its value will normally constitute a disproportionate interference and a total lack of compensation can be considered justifiable under Article 1 only in exceptional circumstances."[19]

As yet, no such exceptional circumstances have arisen in any case before the Court.

In contrast to the situation where there has been a deprivation of property, there is no presumption in favour of compensation under Rules 1 and 3 of Article 1. Thus, where there is a control on the use of property or an interference with the substance of ownership, the question of compensation will simply be one aspect of the overall consideration of whether a fair balance has been struck.

As to the level of compensation, as can be seen from the above quotation the compensation, if such is required, need only be *reasonably* related to the property's value. Full compensation is not necessary, it being recognised that the interests of social or economic reform may require less than reimbursement of the full market value.[20]

Article 6

Article 6 has featured in more cases before the Strasbourg authorities than any other, and there is therefore an extensive jurisprudence. It is beyond the scope of this section to consider all the ramifications of Article 6. Rather, attention will be given to those areas where, in the context of property rights, the effect of Article 6 is likely to be felt most. In brief, Article 6 guarantees the right to have one's civil rights and obligations determined by an independent and impartial tribunal.   7.08

Meaning of "civil rights"

It is fundamental to Article 6 that the circumstances under consideration must involve the determination of "civil rights and obligations". A number of cases establish that property rights involve civil rights. The following are examples—   7.09

Lithgow v. United Kingdom[21]—the right to compensation following nationalisation of the aircraft and shipbuilding industries was a "civil right".

Tre Traktörer Aktiebolag v. Sweden[22]—Article 6(1) applied where a licence to serve alcohol was revoked.

Fredin v. Sweden[23]—the right to develop one's property in

---

[19] *Holy Monasteries v. Greece*, A301-A (para. 71), 20 E.H.R.R. 1.
[20] See in particular *Lithgow v. U.K.*, A102 (para 121), 8 E.H.R.R. 329.
[21] A102, para. 191 ff, 8 E.H.R.R. 329.
[22] A159,13 E.H.R.R. 309.
[23] A192, 13 E.H.R.R. 784.

accordance with the applicable laws and regulations was found to be a civil right. In that case, the applicants' licence to exploit gravel pits was revoked. Since there was no means by which they could challenge the decision in the courts, there was a breach of the article.

Oerlemans v. Netherlands[24]—environmental measures taken to protect particular areas which affect the use of an individual's property may also involve civil rights. Thus, where the applicant's land was subject to a designation order which prohibited any use of the land which might erode or damage the soil or the use of herbicides, Article 6(1) was engaged. The applicant was, however, able to raise before the domestic courts all the relevant points of law and fact that he wished to raise. There was therefore no breach of the article.

Recognition of right in domestic law

7.10   "Civil rights" has an autonomous meaning so far as the Convention is concerned. However, the Strasbourg court has made it plain that Article 6(1) only applies where there are "rights and obligations" which can be said, at least on arguable grounds, to be recognised under domestic law; it (Article 6) does not in itself guarantee any particular content for (civil) "rights and obligations" in the substantive law of the Contracting States".[25]

In *Powell and Rayner v. United Kingdom*[26], the applicants complained that they had no domestic remedy in relation to nuisance they suffered due to noise from Heathrow airport. The Commission rejected the claim under Article 6(1) as manifestly ill-founded on the ground that the applicants had no "civil right" under English law to compensation for unreasonable noise nuisance caused by aircraft. Accordingly, they could not claim to have a substantive right under English law which required to be adjudicated in accordance with Article 6(1).

The requirement of an arguable claim means that there must be a tenable argument. It does not mean that the applicant would have been bound to win. In *Allan Jacobsson v. Sweden,*[27] the applicant's property was subject to protracted building prohibitions. He complained that he did not have access to a court to challenge the decisions maintaining the prohibitions in force. The Court considered that the applicant could arguably have claimed before the domestic courts to have a right to a permit to build, albeit that the issue of such a permit would have involved the exercise of

---

[24] A219, 15 E.H.R.R. 561.
[25] See, for example, *Lithgow* (above), para.192.
[26] A172, 12 E.H.R.R. 355.
[27] A163, 12 E.H.R.R. 56.

administrative discretion. Since the dispute in question was determined by the Government in the final instance and its decisions were not open to review by any body which could be considered to be a "tribunal" for the purposes of Article 6(1), there was a violation of that article.

Review of decisions by administrative bodies

There are many circumstances where civil rights and obligations are determined not by the courts but by administrative bodies. This is also so in relation to property rights. In such circumstances, if the decision-making body at first instance does not provide the guarantees required by Article 6(1), there must be a right of access to a court or tribunal which does meet those standards.[28] The question which then arises is the scope of any review—is a review of the merits of the decision as well as its legal basis required? 7.11

In the *Albert Le Compte* case, the applicants wished to challenge on the merits disciplinary measures, which had been imposed by a professional association. The review by the Court of Cassation did not meet the requirements of Article 6(1) since it could only consider points of law.[29]

However, not every administrative decision will require a review of the merits by a court in order to comply with Article 6(1). Although the line is somewhat difficult to draw, it seems that where matters of policy are involved a limited review in the nature of judicial review may suffice. In *ISKCON v. United Kingdom*[30] the only available judicial remedy was on a point of law where the applicant wished to challenge an enforcement notice served on him under the planning legislation. The Commission considered that there had been no violation of article 6(1).

The issue was explored by the Court in *Bryan v. United Kingdom*,[31] where again the limited judicial review in the area of planning satisfied the requirements of Article 6(1). The Court indicated that even although the domestic court could not substitute its own findings in fact, it was able to satisfy itself that the findings were neither perverse nor irrational. Such an approach in specialised areas of law was to be expected especially where the facts had already been established in a quasi-judicial procedure. Accordingly, the scope of review was sufficient to comply with Article 6(1).

Bryan has now been considered by the Scottish courts in *County*

---

[28] *Albert and Le Compte v. Belgium*, A58, 5 E.H.R.R. 533.
[29] A similar result was arrived at in *W v. U.K.*, A121, 10 E.H.R.R. 29, relating to challenge to a local authority's decision restricting access to a child in care.
[30] Appl. No. 20490/92, 76A D.R. 90.
[31] A 335-A, 21 E.H.R.R.. This case is considered in more detail in the section dealing with planning law.

Properties Ltd v. The Scottish Ministers,[32] where it was distinguished on its facts. The case is considered in the section dealing with planning law below.

Content of Article 6(1) rights

7.12   The case law on the rights which are implicit in the notion of a fair hearing before an independent and impartial tribunal is extensive. Of that case law, there are four aspects which are particularly relevant in the field of property.

First, in general there must be a right of access to an independent and impartial tribunal. In *Lithgow v. United Kingdom* (above), one of the applicants complained that he did not have the right of access to an independent tribunal in the determination of his rights to compensation. The scheme laid down by the Act nationalising the industries in which the applicants held shares provided for a collective system for the settlement of disputes. The Court noted that

> "the right of access to the courts secured by Article 6 para. 1 is not absolute since the right of access by its very nature calls for regulation by the State, regulation which may vary in time and in place according to the needs and resources of the community and of individuals".[33]

Further, States enjoyed a margin of appreciation in laying down such regulations. However, the limitations must not restrict or reduce the access to the extent that the very essence of the right is impaired.

Following on from that, the right of access must be an effective one. This was not so in *De Geouffre de la Pradelle v. France*,[34] where the French administrative system of notifying decisions on the designations of areas of outstanding beauty was described by the Court as being of "extreme complexity". As such the system was not sufficiently coherent and clear, and there was accordingly a breach of Article 6(1).

The third aspect of Article 6(1) which merits some attention is the right to have one's civil rights and obligations determined within a reasonable time. What is reasonable will depend on the particular circumstances of the case, the complexity of the case, and the conduct of the parties and the authorities dealing with the case. Fourteen years—to review the constitutionality of rent control legislation—was excessive in *Pammel v. Germany*,[35] as was almost

---

[32]   2000 S.L.T. 965.
[33]   Para. 194.
[34]   A253-B.
[35]   RJD 1997-IV, 26 E.H.R.R. 100.

12 years—to secure eviction of a tenant—in *Scollo v. Italy*.[36] The "reasonable time" referred to in Article 6(1) normally begins to run from the moment action is instituted before the tribunal in question. It can, however, begin to run earlier. In *Erkner and Hofauer v. Austria*,[37] the dispute was determined to have arisen as at the date when the applicants objected to the authorities about the provisional transfer of their land. That was some two and a half years before proceedings before a tribunal were commenced.

Finally, Article 6(1) requires that reasons be given for the decision determining the rights in question. However, it does not require that the court give a detailed answer to every argument raised before it.[38]

Article 8

Article 8 of the Convention provides in short that individuals are   7.13
entitled to respect for their private and family life and their home. Those rights are not absolute, the second paragraph of Article 8 stipulating the circumstances in which the rights protected may be interfered with, for example where it is in the interests of the economic well-being of the country. For the purposes of considering property rights and the Convention, the following points arising out of Article 8 are of most significance.

First, and fundamental to Article 8, is the question of what constitutes a "home". Like many other concepts within the Convention, it has an autonomous meaning and therefore the classification which national law gives to the circumstances will not be determinative. What is of significance is the nature of the occupation and the connection which the individual has with the property in question. It has been suggested that only a legally established "home" can attract the protection of Article 8. The approach of the Commission initially varied,[39] but it is now well settled that the concept of home may extend to residences which are not legally established.[40]

Indeed, a property may qualify as a "home" even where there is no occupation of it. In *Gillow v. United Kingdom*[41] the applicants had established the property in question as their home (in Guernsey), had retained ownership of it intending to return there and had relinquished their other home (on the mainland). The refusal of the Guernsey authorities to grant a new residence permit

---

[36] A315-C, 22 E.H.R.R. 514.
[37] A117, 9 E.H.R.R. 464.
[38] *Van de Hurk v. Netherlands*, A288 at para. 61, 18 E.H.R.R. 481.
[39] See *Wiggins v. U.K.*, Appl. No. 7456/76, 13 D.R. 40 (applicant owned home but had no legal permission to occupy it—Article 8 applied) c.f. *Simpson v. U.K.*, Appl. No. 11716/85, 47 D.R. 274 (applicant no right to occupy after death of tenant partner—Article 8 not applicable).
[40] *Buckley v. U.K.*, RJD 1996-IV, 23 E.H.R.R. 101.
[41] A119, 11 EHRR 335.

was an interference with their right to respect for their home. There was therefore recognised a right to re-establish their home. There are, however, limits to the concept. It does not comprise property on which it is simply planned to build a house for residential purposes. Nor does it cover an area where the individual concerned has grown up and where his family has its roots but where he no longer lives.[42] The Court has indicated that it would "strain the meaning" of the notion "home" to extend it to cover such circumstances.[43]

Once it has been determined that a right protected by Article 8 is in issue, the Court will then assess whether there has been an interference with that right by a public authority. It should be noted in this context that Article 8 may impose positive duties on the authorities. The Court has frequently said that whether the question is analysed in terms of a positive duty or in terms of an interference, the applicable principles are broadly similar. What must be considered is whether a fair balance has been struck between the competing interest of the individual and of the community as a whole, bearing in mind the State's margin of appreciation.[44]

Having considered the question of interference in the right protected, the Court must satisfy itself that the interference is "in accordance with the law", pursues a legitimate aim and is necessary in a democratic society. It is outwith the scope of this section to analyse these aspects.[45] Their application in the field of property rights is, however, considered where relevant in the following sections.

Finally, it should be noted that the interests protected by Article 8, at least so far as "home" is concerned, include the right of access to and occupation of one's home.[46] It also protects the right to peaceful enjoyment of one's home.[47] The precise extent of the protection offered in the context of property rights is examined in more detail below.

Article 14

7.14   It is fundamental to any human rights instrument that there be a prohibition against discrimination. That aim is sought to be realised by Article 14, the provision which seeks to ensure that the Convention's rights and freedoms are secured to everyone without discrimination. Although the jurisprudence relating to this article is relatively under-developed, there may be circumstances where a complaint under this Article will succeed whereas that under other

---

[42] *Loizidou v. Turkey*, A310, 23 E.H.R.R. 513
[43] Para. 66 above.
[44] See for example *López Ostra v. Spain*, A303-C, 20 E.H.R.R. 277 at para. 51.
[45] Harris, O'Boyle, Warbrick, *Law of the European Convention on Human Rights*, devote a chapter to these issues, see pp. 283 ff.
[46] *Cyprus v. Turkey*, Appl. Nos 6780/74 and 6950/75, 2 D.R. 125, 4 E.H.R.R. 482.
[47] *Arrondelle v. U.K.*, Appl. No. 7889/77, 26 D.R. 5.

articles may fail.

The article has been described as a "parasitic provision" in that it is restricted to protecting against discrimination only in relation to the Convention rights.[48] It is not a "stand alone" provision protecting against discrimination in whatever sphere it occurs. Rather, the individual must be able to show that the facts of the case fall within the ambit of one or more of the Convention's provisions. There need not even be an allegation of a violation of one of the other Convention provisions,[49] although often there is.

Article 14 lists various grounds on which discrimination is prohibited, such as race, sex and religion. The list is not, however, exhaustive, nor does the discrimination complained of require to be of the same kind as those listed. In *James v. United Kingdom*, the Court accepted that there had been discrimination as the leasehold reform legislation entailed differences of treatment in regard to different categories of property owners in the enjoyment of the right guaranteed by Article 1, Protocol 1.[50] Whether this could be categorised as discrimination on the ground of "property" as referred to in Article 14 mattered not according to the Court.

In order to establish that there has been discrimination, the complainant must show that he has been subject to a difference of treatment, and that his position is analogous to those who have received more favourable treatment. It was this latter aspect which proved problematic for the applicants in *Fredin v. Sweden*.[51] Their complaint that they had been treated differently in relation to the revocation of a gravel exploitation permit appears to have been accepted. There was therefore a difference of treatment. However, the applicants were unable to show that they were in a similar situation to those companies whose permits were not revoked, i.e. those who had been treated more favourably.[52]

Even where the individual has been treated less favourably than others in a similar position, that may be capable of justification. What the Convention prohibits is a difference of treatment which "has no objective and reasonable justification", that is, if it does not pursue a "legitimate aim" or if there is not a "reasonable relationship of proportionality between the means employed and the aim sought to be realised".[53] The authorities are allowed a margin of appreciation "in assessing whether and to what extent differences in otherwise similar situations justify a different treatment in law; the scope of this margin will vary according to

---

[48] Harris, O'Boyle, Warbrick, *Law of the European Convention on Human Rights*, p.463.

[49] *Inze v. Austria*, A126, 10 E.H.R.R. 394.

[50] A98 at para.74, 8 E.H.R.R. 123.

[51] A192, 13 E.H.R.R. 142.

[52] Para. 57ff. The Court commented that the onus was on the applicants to establish this rather than for the State to explain the difference in treatment.

[53] See, for example, *Lithgow v. U.K.* A102 at para. 177, 8 E.H.R.R. 329.

the circumstances, the subject matter and its background".[54] That margin is particularly limited where there is discrimination on the ground of race or sex.[55]

Although frequently invoked, a violation of this article in property rights cases has rarely been found. This is due in part to the inherent limitations in the article, but is also a result of the Court's reluctance to examine any violation of Article 14 if a violation of another article has already been established.

Article 41

7.15   By virtue of this provision (formerly Article 50), an award of compensation may be made where there is a finding of a violation of the Convention. The approach which the Strasbourg authorities take to what is termed in the text of Article 41 as "just satisfaction" is somewhat different to our courts' normal approach to damages. That an understanding of the difference is important is evident from the Human Rights Act 1998. Section 8 in effect stipulates that an award of damages is only to be made where necessary to afford just satisfaction, and that in determining this the court is to take account of the principles applied by the Strasbourg Court.

Those principles are relatively few. The starting point is that there is no entitlement to damages by the mere finding of a violation. There may be circumstances where the Court considers that a finding on its own may constitute "just satisfaction". This, it is suggested, is likely to be relatively rare in cases involving property rights since by their very nature economic interests are at issue.

The heads of claim which the Court will consider include pecuniary and non–pecuniary damage.[56] In relation to the former, it is not surprising that the Court insists that there be a causal connection between the violation and the losses claimed. The Court has often stated that it will not be prepared to speculate as to what the result may have been if there had been no violation. This is particularly so where the breach is in respect of Article 6(1).[57] The Court is also prepared to recognise claims for loss of opportunity.[58]

Some of the most substantial awards made by the Court relate to cases involving property. In *Sporrong and Lönnroth v. Sweden*, the applicants were awarded approximately £100,000 where planning restrictions prevented development for 20 years.[59] In *Pine Valley Developments Ltd v. Ireland*,[60] £1,200,000 IR was awarded. The highest award so far is in the case of *Stran Greek Refineries v.*

---

[54]   Above at para.177.
[55]   See *Abdulaziz, Cabales and Balkandali v. U.K.*, A92, 7 E.H.R.R. 471.
[56]   See the tables of awards in Reid, *A Practitioner's Guide to the European Convention on Human Rights*, at pp. 399 ff.
[57]   *Fredin v. Sweden*, A192 at para. 65, 13 E.H.R.R. 142.
[58]   See, for example, *Inze v. Austria*, A126, 10 E.H.R.R. 394.
[59]   A52, 5 E.H.R.R. 35.
[60]   A246-B, 16 E.H.R.R. 379.

Greece, the award totalling an equivalent of approximately £15 million plus interest of £9 million.[61]

Awards have also been made in cases relating to property for non-pecuniary damages. Examples are *Gillow v. United Kingdom*[62] (£10,000 for stress and anxiety when refused a permit to live in their house), and *López Ostra v. Spain*[63] (£16,000 for nuisance, distress and anxiety relating to the building of a waste-treatment plant next to the applicant's home). The Court accepts in such claims that precise quantification is not possible and that compensation will accordingly be awarded on an equitable basis.

ASPECTS OF SCOTS LAW RELATING TO PROPERTY

1. Planning Law

The application of planning laws can often result in a clash between individuals and the relevant planning authorities. Although the Convention does not mention planning anywhere in the text, there have been a significant number of cases decided in Strasbourg involving planning issues, some of which have concerned the United Kingdom. Before considering how the Convention may affect planning in Scots law, it may be instructive to examine briefly some of the more notable cases in which the United Kingdom have featured.   7.16

Relevant U.K. cases

The case of *ISKCON v. United Kingdom* is of some interest in demonstrating how complaints under various articles may be combined (albeit unsuccessfully in this case).[64] The applicants, a registered religious charity, invoked a combination of Article 9 and Article 1, Protocol 1 along with Article 14. The substance of their complaint concerned service of an enforcement notice on them alleging a material change of use of their premises to a religious community. The Commission noted that a wide discretion was granted to States in planning control legislation, but that the enforcement notices interfered with the applicants' freedom of religion. Consequently, the question arose as to whether that interference was necessary in a democratic society. The legitimate aims of planning legislation were accepted (to protect the rights of others and to prevent uncontrolled development). There was no breach of Article 9 (or indeed any other article) since the   7.17

---

[61] A301-B, 19 E.H.R.R. 293.
[62] A109, 11 E.H.R.R. 335.
[63] A303-C, 20 E.H.R.R. 277.
[64] Appl. No. 20490/92, 18 E.H.R.R. CD 133.

enforcement notices were proportionate to these aims, and the decision of the authorities was based on proper planning considerations. The application was therefore inadmissible. Of significance in this area is the decision in *Bryan v. United Kingdom*.[65] The applicant contended that the proceedings which he had been able to bring under English law, firstly before a Planning Inspector and then before the High Court, to challenge a planning enforcement notice did not comply with Article 6(1). It was not contested that these proceedings involved a determination of the applicant's "civil rights" for the purposes of Article 6(1). So far as the proceedings before the inspector were concerned, the Court found that the very existence of the Secretary of State's power to issue a direction to revoke the power of an inspector to decide an appeal deprived the inspector of the requisite appearance of independence. The hearing before him therefore did not satisfy the requirements of an "independent and impartial" tribunal.

However, notwithstanding the limited nature of the review by the High Court, which had no power to disturb the findings in fact made by the inspector, the Court considered that the scope of the review available before the High Court was sufficient to comply with Article 6(1). The Court noted that there was no dispute as to the primary facts, but pointed out that even if there had been the High Court had the power to satisfy itself that the inspector's findings of fact or the inferences based on them were neither perverse nor irrational. It went on to say:

"Such an approach by an appeal tribunal on questions of fact can reasonably be expected in specialised areas of the law such as the one at issue, particularly where the facts have been established in the course of a quasi-judicial procedure governed by many of the safeguards required by Article 6 para. 1".[66]

Whether the limited review available in appeals or in judicial reviews in planning matters meets the requirements of the Convention in Scotland has been considered in *County Properties Ltd v. The Scottish Ministers*.[67] The petitioners sought to judicially review the decision of the respondents to call in an application for listed building consent and to appoint a Reporter to hear a public inquiry. They complained that the decision to call in the application was made as a result of an objection by Historic Scotland, an executive agency of the respondents. They also complained that the

---

[65] A335-A, 21 E.H.R.R. 342. See also *McGonnell v. U.K.*, The Times, February 22, 2000.

[66] Para. 47.

[67] 2000 S.L.T. 965. The decision has been reclaimed. See also *R v. Secretary of State for the Environment, Transport and the regions, ex p. Holding and Barnes plc*, Divisional Court, December 12, 2000.

Reporter was a part time reporter employed by the respondents on an *ad hoc* basis. Accordingly, the respondents' decision had deprived the petitioners of their entitlement to have their civil rights determined by an independent and impartial tribunal, and had subjected them to a tribunal which was (as conceded by the respondents) not independent and impartial.

The Court did not uphold the petitioners' contention that the first instance hearing before the Reporter and the respondents required to comply with Article 6(1). Instead the Court followed the European Court's jurisprudence to the effect that

> "in the case of an administrative decision-maker compliance with article 6(1) may be secured by the availability of review of the decision before a judicial body that has full jurisdiction and does provide the guarantees of the article".[68]

So far as the appeal to a court under section 58 of the Planning (Listed Buildings and Conservation Areas)(Scotland) Act 1997 was concerned, the petitioners argued that the circumstances of their case were materially different from those in *Bryan*. They relied on firstly, the circumstances which rendered the respondents not an independent and impartial tribunal, and secondly the nature of the issues which would fall to be determined. The Court found those submissions persuasive, and therefore held that the decision to call in the application was incompatible with the petitioners' Convention rights and accordingly *ultra vires* of the respondents in terms of section 57(2) of the Scotland Act 1998. The decision accordingly fell to be reduced.

7.18

Whether this decision will be upheld by the Inner House remains to be seen and is clearly not free from doubt. It is questionable whether the distinction sought to be drawn by the judge at first instance between the case before him and that of *Bryan* was in fact so significant as to be determinative.

An example of the application of article 8 in planning-type matters is provided by *Gillow v. United Kingdom*.[69] In that case, the Court held that the decision of the local authority (in Guernsey) to refuse the applicants a license to occupy their house was disproportionate, and that there had been a breach of Article 8. Although the legal control on occupation was a legitimate aim, there were other factors in favour of the applicants, such as the fact they had no other home, there were no other prospective tenants of the property and the island's population was no longer increasing.

Finally, although not involving the United Kingdom, some attention should be given to *Pine Valley Developments Ltd v. Ireland*.[70] The main interest of the case lies in the fact that although

---

[68] Para. 24.
[69] A109, 13 E.H.R.R. 593.
[70] A222, 14 E.H.R.R. 319.

the case under Article 1, Protocol 1 failed, it was held that there was a violation of Article 1, Protocol 1 in conjunction with Article 14. The facts were that the applicants had purchased property with the benefit of outline planning permission. The grant of outline planning permission was subsequently declared *ultra vires* and therefore a nullity by the Supreme Court. Legislation was then passed to validate retrospectively other planning permissions which were *ultra vires* on the same grounds, but in respect of which no court decision had been taken. However, the legislation did not affect the applicants' position. The case under Article 1, Protocol 1 did not succeed because although there had been an interference with the applicants' property, the annulment of the permission without any remedial action was not considered a disproportionate measure.

However, since the remedial action taken by the legislature benefited all the holders of permissions in the relevant category other than the applicants, and the Government did not advance any justification for the difference of treatment, there had been a difference of treatment which had not been justified. Accordingly, the Court found that there had been a violation of Article 14 taken together with Article 1 of Protocol 1.

The above cases give some indication of the way in which the articles of the Convention may be relevant in planning matters. In the next section, the question of whether specific areas of planning law and practice comply with the Convention is considered.

Planning issues

7.19   From the vast subject of planning, consideration is given to three specific areas in order to examine their compatibility with the Convention. First, the preparation of structure plans and local plans. Secondly, the determination of applications for planning permission. Thirdly, the enforcement process.

(1) Structure plans and local plans

7.20   In terms of the Town and Country Planning (Scotland) Act 1997, each local authority must prepare a local plan for its area. There are also 17 structure plan areas, the relevant local authorities contributing in the preparation of a structure plan to cover their area. The process of adopting local plans and structure plans differs, but both permit objections to be made.[71] Structure plans are approved by the Secretary of State, whereas local plans are adopted by the local authority preparing the plan.[72] In considering whether to approve a particular plan, the relevant authority may require for

[71] For a description of the process, see N. Collar, *Planning* (1999, 2nd ed).
[72] Ss 10 and 17 respectively of the 1997 Act.

the purposes of the Convention to consider whether a fair balance has been struck between the demands of the general interest and the requirements of the protection of the individuals' fundamental rights.[73]

A decision in a local plan may be a determination of a "civil right" within the meaning of Article 6(1), if it affects the use to which the property may be put. Accordingly, the procedure by which an authority's decision may be challenged will require to meet the exigencies of Article 6 if not at first instance at least on further challenge in the courts. The failure to comply with Article 6 is particularly evident in the local plan process. The plan is of course prepared by the local authority and adopted by it.[74] Although an objector to the final plan may require the authority to hold a local plan inquiry, the reporter's recommendations following that inquiry need not be accepted by the authority. The authority need only provide reasons as to why the recommendations are not being followed. If those reasons are briefly stated, it may present an obstacle to any challenge being made in the courts.[75] In those circumstances, the reasoning in *Bryan* may not necessarily apply in all respects. Consideration must also be given to the *County Properties* decision.

(2) Determining planning applications

Planning legislation removes from property owners the right to do as they wish with their own land. Instead, they must apply to the State for permission to develop their land. The determination of the application will affect not only the applicant, but also those with property in the neighbourhood. It can therefore be seen that decisions in these matters can interfere with the right to peaceful enjoyment of one's possessions.[76]

It may be considered that a certain imbalance exists between the Convention and current planning policies. In the planning context, individual circumstances are only relevant in exceptional circumstances.[77] Thus, National Planning Policy Guideline 1 at paragraph 52 states "The planning system does not exist to protect the commercial interest of one person or business against another, although in some cases private interests may coincide with the public interest." In contrast, the Convention puts individual rights first, insofar as it requires the interfering authority to justify the reason for its actions.

7.21

---

[73] See *Katte Klitsche de la Grange v. Italy*, A293-B, 19 E.H.R.R. 368.
[74] The Secretary of State has the right to intervene, but will only do so in exceptional circumstances. See ss 18 and 19 of the 1997 Act.
[75] *i.e* to challenges made in terms of s.238 of the 1997 Act.
[76] See, for example, the decision in *Allan Jacobsson v. Sweden*, A163, 12 E.H.R.R. 56.
[77] See *Westminster C.C. v. Great Portland Estates PLC* [1985] 1 A.C. 661, particularly Lord Scarman at p. 669.

It would therefore appear that planning authorities will require to take into account Convention rights in reaching their decisions on planning applications. It may be prudent for the reports of planning officers to make specific reference to Convention rights, and for the committee deciding the application to indicate in its decision what effect if any they have given to such rights.

(3) Enforcement

7.22   Part VI of the 1997 Act sets out the powers of planning authorities to take steps to secure compliance with planning controls. Since enforcement action may restrict the owner's rights in relation to his land, the authority taking action ought to be in a position to justify their actions. From a Convention point of view, this will entail demonstrating that the enforcement action pursues a legitimate aim (which should not prove difficult) and that the means adopted are proportionate to that aim. A fair balance must, of course, be struck between the effect of the action on the individual and on the public interest.

Before taking enforcement action, a planning authority is entitled to require information as to the activities being carried out on the land in question and various other matters from the owner or occupier, or any person carrying out operations on the land. This may be achieved by serving a planning contravention notice under section 125 or by using the more general powers under section 272. In either case, failure to comply with the notice is an offence.[78] The use in criminal proceedings against an individual of information supplied by that individual on pain of criminal sanctions might be considered to violate Article 6, in particular the right to silence and the right not to incriminate oneself.[79] The question has been considered in *R v. Hertfordshire County Council ex p. Green Environmental Industries Ltd* by the House of Lords in the context of the Environmental Protection Act 1990.[80] In terms of section 71(2) of that Act, the County Council were entitled to require information to be provided to it. Green Environmental Industries Limited ("Green") refused to provide the information which the Council required, and the Council proceeded to serve a summons on Green charging the offence of non-compliance with the request under section 71(2). At the same time, Green sought leave to apply for judicial review. The House of Lords dismissed Green's appeal, pointing out that the Council's requests were for factual information only. Further, had Green produced the required information it would have been open to them to challenge the use of it in any

---

[78] s. 126 and s.272(4) provide for offences respectively.

[79] See *Saunders v. U.K.* RJD 1996-VI, 23 E.H.R.R. 313. These rights have been considered in the context of the Road Traffic Act 1988 by the Scottish courts in *Brown v. Stott*, 2000 J.C. 328, and now also by the Privy Council in their decision of December 5, 2000 .

[80] [2000] 2 W.L.R. 373.

subsequent criminal proceedings.

It may, accordingly, be considered that firstly, it is not contrary to Article 6(1) to require owners and occupiers to supply information, provided the information sought is factual and does not require an admission of the existence of an infringement of the relevant legislation. Secondly, it may breach Article 6(1) if that information is used for the purposes of prosecuting the provider of the information.[81]

2. Compulsory Acquisition of Property

The compulsory acquisition of property is a large and complicated area of law.[82] Accordingly, what follows is not intended to be an exhaustive treatment of the impact of the Convention on this area, but rather as an overview of the most important issues .

7.23

Convention rights may be relevant at two stages. First, at the point where a decision is being made as to whether land should be compulsorily purchased, and secondly, at the point where compensation is being awarded. Compulsory purchase powers are contained in many Acts of Parliament, the most important being the Town and Country Planning (Scotland) Act 1997 (sections 188–201), and the Local Government (Scotland) Act 1973, (section 71).

In relation to compulsory purchase legislation, it is important to bear in mind two points. First, in general where there is an interference with an individuals' property rights the statute conferring the power will be interpreted restrictively.[83] Secondly, although there is no constitutional provision specifying that there must be compensation where an individual is deprived of his property, such a presumption applies in interpreting any statutory provision.[84]

For the purposes of this section, the terms of the Town and Country Planning (Scotland) Act 1997 ("the Act") will be examined in light of the requirements of the Convention. However, the comments may also be relevant to other legislation conferring compulsory purchase powers.

---

[81] See, in particular, Lord Cooke of Thorndon at page 384. See also Beloff and Brown, "Planning Contravention Notices and the Right to Silence: The Impact of the Human Rights Act 1998" 1999 J.P.L. 1069.

[82] For which see, Stair Encyclopaedia, Vol. 5; Rowan-Robinson, *Compulsory Purchase and Compensation—The Law in Scotland* (W. Green & Son Ltd, 1990).

[83] Langan, *Maxwell on the Interpretation of Statutes*, (12 ed., Sweet and Maxwell), p.252.

[84] See *Burmah Oil Co (Burmah Trading) Ltd v. Lord Advocate*, 1965 S.C. (H.L.) 117.

Town and Country Planning (Scotland) Act 1997

The basis for the decision to compulsorily acquire

7.24   As already indicated, the relevant sections are to be found at Part VIII of the Act (sections 188–201). In particular, section 189 sets out the basis on which a local authority, on being authorised by the Scottish Ministers, has power to purchase land for planning purposes. These are where the land

(a) is suitable for and is required in order to secure the carrying out of development, redevelopment or improvement; or

(b) is required for the proper planning of the area in which the land is situated.

In respect of (a), the local authority and the Scottish Ministers are directed to consider certain matters in determining whether land is suitable, namely the development plan, any existing planning permission for development and any other considerations which would be material in determining an application for planning permission for development on the land.

It is to be noted that the local authority and the Scottish Ministers are not specifically directed to take into account the interests of the individual whose land it is proposed be acquired. There is no requirement that they balance the interests of the public against those of the owner. That compulsory purchase of one's property amounts to an interference with the peaceful enjoyment of property in terms of Article 1, Protocol 1 is established beyond doubt.[85] Where the compulsory purchase relates to an individual's home, there may also be an interference in the exercise of the rights guaranteed by Article 8.[86] Such interferences can, of course, be justified provided that they pursue a legitimate aim, are in the public interest and are proportionate.

It would therefore appear that henceforth in order to comply with the Convention, local authorities in using such powers, and the Scottish Ministers in authorising the use of such powers, ought to carry out the exercise contained in Protocol 1, Article 1. Thus, they will require, first, to consider the aim which the compulsory purchase order seeks to achieve. Secondly, they should assess whether the measure is proportionate to that aim. Only when it is satisfied that the compulsory purchase order is the appropriate means to achieve the desired goal, and that the individuals whose property is to be acquired are not being unfairly burdened, would it be safe to proceed with the order.

---

[85] *Erkner and Hofauer v. Austria*, A117 at para. 72, 9 E.H.R.R. 464.

[86] *X v. U.K.*, Appl. No. 9261/81, 28 D.R. 177 and *R. & W. Howard v. U.K.*, Appl. No. 10825/84, 52 D.R. 198.

Objections to the compulsory purchase order

In terms of the Acquisition of Land (Authorisation Procedure)   7.25
(Scotland) Act 1947, objection may be made to the compulsory
purchase order. Although anyone may object, it should be noted
that there are certain differences between what are termed
"statutory objectors"[87] and "third party objectors".[88] Thus, the
confirming authority need not hold an inquiry where objection is
made by a third party objector, but must do so in the case of
statutory objectors.[89] Further, a third party objector has no
automatic right to be heard at any inquiry, although in practice
the reporter will usually allow anyone who wishes to be heard to
make submissions.[90] There is also no need for the Minister
confirming the order to notify third party objectors if he disagrees
with any of the reporter's findings in fact or receives new evidence
or wishes to take into account new facts.[91]

Such treatment of third party objectors may in particular
circumstances breach one of the Convention provisions relevant
in this area, possibly in conjunction with Article 14.[92] It may, of
course, be possible to justify such treatment, but it is an aspect
which those involved in the process of compulsory purchase ought
to consider.

Turning to the grounds for objection, there are no specific
grounds laid down by statute. Accordingly, it would seem that it
will be open to objectors to advance any ground of objection
including those based on Convention rights. However, as a matter
of reality certain objections will undoubtedly fail. Thus, if the
principle underlying the order has already been established, for
example, the area has already been designated as a housing action
area, it will be difficult if not impossible to challenge the order.
Likewise, if the order involves a matter of Government Policy, the
confirming authority will apply the policy regardless of any
objections. Further, the Secretary of State may disregard an
objection which is in effect an objection to the development plan.[93]
The relevance of these restrictions on the apparently unrestricted
right of objection becomes apparent when one considers the rights
of challenge which exist in the courts.

Before considering what challenge may be made in the courts,

---

[87] *i.e.* those on whom notice of the making of the order requires to be served,
namely, the owner, lessee and occupier of the land.
[88] Upon whom notice does not require to be served.
[89] 1947 Act, s. 5(1). The confirming authority *may* however hold an inquiry where
there are objections by third party objectors.
[90] Compulsory Purchase by Public Authorities (Inquiries Procedure)(Scotland)
Rules 1998, S.I. 1998 No. 2313, r.17(2) leaves the matter to the reporter's
discretion ("the 1998 Rules").
[91] 1998 Rules, r.21.
[92] Such as, Art. 6(1), Art. 8 or Art. 1, Protocol 1.
[93] Town and Country Planning (Scotland) Act 1997, s. 200.

there are two points which are worth noting so far as the inquiry itself is concerned. First, the merits of Government Policy cannot be examined at the inquiry.[94] Secondly, notwithstanding the reporter's recommendations, the confirming authority may approve the order or not in its discretion, as the decision involves questions of policy, and the reporter's recommendations are but one of the factors to be taken into account in coming to a decision.[95]

Turning to the grounds for challenging a compulsory purchase order, the Acquisition of Land (Authorisation Procedure)(Scotland) Act 1947 provides in Schedule 1, paragraphs 15 and 16, in short, that—

(1) there was no power to make the order, or
(2) that the 1947 Act or regulations made thereunder or the Tribunals and Inquiries Act 1992 had not been complied with, i.e. that there had been procedural defects which substantially prejudiced the applicant.

Although the grounds of challenge are expressed narrowly, they have been interpreted by the courts to include judicial review type grounds. Accordingly, in reviewing the Minister's decision, the courts can consider whether he has

"acted on no evidence; or if he has come to a conclusion to which, on the evidence, he could not reasonably come; or if he has given a wrong interpretation to the words of the statute; or if he has taken into consideration matters which he ought not to have taken into account or vice versa; or has otherwise gone wrong in law".[96]

7.26 Since the Minister will be obliged to act in a way which is compatible with the Convention, he will be required to take Convention rights into account in reaching his decision, and where he does not do so his decision may be open to challenge.[97]

The courts have also overturned orders on the grounds of breach of the principles of natural justice.[98] Accordingly, it may be that the rights conferred by Article 6(1) will not in fact greatly extend the existing protection. Until the *County Properties* decision, it would have seemed unlikely that a review of the decision would require to include a review of the merits in order to be compatible with the Convention. As can be seen from the earlier discussion of this

---

[94] 1998 Rules, r.18(4).
[95] See *General Poster and Publicity Co Ltd v. Secretary of State,* 1960 S.C. 266.
[96] *Ashbridge Investments Ltd v. Minister of Housing and Local Government,* [1965] 1 W.L.R. 132 at 135 .
[97] For an (unsuccessful) example of a pre-HumanRights Act challenge, see *Miles v. Secretary of State for the Environment* [2000] J.P.L. 192
[98] *Fairmount Investments Ltd v. Secretary of State for the Environment,* [1976] 2 All E.R. 865.

case,[99] the whole issue of what is required by way of appeal in administrative decision-making areas is uncertain.

Compensation

The provisions for calculating compensation for loss of land compulsorily acquired are complex and detailed. As noted previously, the Convention does not require that there be full compensation, but only that the compensation be reasonably related to the value of the land. It might be argued that disregarding the effects of the compulsory purchase scheme in measuring the level of compensation does not achieve a fair balance as required by the Convention. Such an argument, it is submitted, would be difficult to sustain in light of the Convention jurisprudence. Accordingly, it is considered that Convention compliant compensation should be capable of being obtained by virtue of compensation regime in place under the Land Compensation (Scotland) Act 1963.[1]

Where disputes do arise as to the measure of compensation, they are to be determined by the Lands Tribunal for Scotland. The attributes of the Tribunal, its procedure and powers would not suggest that a hearing before it would comprise anything other than a fair hearing for the purposes of Article 6 of the Convention.

There may, however, be difficulties in relation to differences in treatment, which may not be capable of justification in terms of Article 14 of the Convention. Thus, if a distinction is drawn between the level of compensation given to those who have had some land taken and those who have not, in relation to "injurious affection" resulting from construction works,[2] such difference in treatment will require to be justified.

3. Environment/Nuisance Issues

In this section, the likely impact of the Convention on the law of nuisance and environmental concerns will be considered. Although the Convention does not mention such issues in its text, creative use of the rights which it does protect has led in recent years to applications, some successful, relating to these areas. There are, however, limitations to the protection which the Convention can offer.

7.27

---

[99] At page 248 (above.)

[1] As amended by the Land Compensation (Scotland) Act 1973 and the Local Government, Planning and Land Act 1980.

[2] *i.e.* compensation for the injurious effects of the works resulting from the compulsory purchase scheme. See the Lands Clauses Consolidation (Scotland) Act 1845, s.61

Nuisance

7.28   The common law of nuisance seeks to some extent to regulate the use which private parties may make of their property. That use may be restricted in circumstances where it causes serious disturbance or substantial inconvenience to a neighbour or material damage to a neighbour's property.[3] It can immediately be seen that Article 1 of Protocol 1, and Article 8 may be relevant.

Further, in light of the court's obligation to act compatibly with the Convention in terms of the Human Rights Act 1998,[4] the requirements of the Convention may be given effect to notwithstanding that the litigation is between private parties. Thus, in considering whether to grant a remedy to the complainer, the court may require to take into account not only the interference to the complainer's enjoyment of his property, but also the interference caused to the defender in the enjoyment of his property. Similarly, where the complaint relates to the nuisance caused to an individual's home, the rights under Article 8 may need to be considered. The analysis which is required under each of these articles may become part of the court's reasoning in considering nuisance issues.

The (English) law of nuisance was considered by the Commission in the case of *Khatun v. United Kingdom*,[5] where the applicants complained of the effects of construction work carried out in the London Docklands enterprise zone. For two and a half years their homes were subject to dust from the construction work. Proceedings were taken in the English courts culminating in a decision in the House of Lords.[6] It was there established that those applicants who had no right to the land affected by the nuisance had no right of action. The damages to which those with proprietary interests might be entitled were restricted to a minimal amount for diminution in value. Further, dust nuisance of the type suffered by the applicants was not a statutory nuisance within the meaning of the Environmental Protection Act 1990.

The complaint under Article 8 was considered by the Commission. It was first of all noted that the distinction drawn in the domestic proceedings between applicants with a proprietary interest and those without such an interest was not appropriate. Article 8 applied to all the applicants provided the house was their "home" according to the Convention jurisprudence. The Commission accepted that the applicants' right to enjoy their homes and private or family lives had been severely impaired. However, the construction works pursued a legitimate aim, namely urban regeneration.

---

[3]   See for example *Watt v. Jamieson*, 1954 S.C. 56.
[4]   By virtue of s.6.
[5]   Appl. No. 38387/97, 26 E.H.R.R. CD 212.
[6]   Reported as *Hunter v. Canary Wharf Ltd*, and *Hunter v. London Docklands Development Corp.* [1997] A.C. 655 .

Further, the public interest in that aim together with the limited extent to which the applicants suffered resulted in the conclusion that the complaint under Article 8 was manifestly unfounded.

The same result was thus reached by the Commission as had been reached in the domestic proceedings, but the reasoning was significantly different. In other factual circumstances application of their reasoning might lead to a different result.

The Commission's opinion in relation to the distinction drawn in the House of Lords between those having, or not having, title to sue may be of some relevance in Scottish proceedings. Although in Scots law the owner and any tenant may sue, the right of other persons to sue is not entirely clear.[7] At least so far as those seeking to claim rights under Article 8 are concerned, recognition of their title to sue in Scots law may be necessary to comply with the Convention.

Environmental issues

Measures seeking to protect the environment have proliferated in recent times. Many powers are vested in the Scottish Environmental Protection Agency ("SEPA") by virtue of the Environment Act 1995, although local authorities continue to have a role in certain matters.[8] SEPA and local authorities will, of course, be "public authorities" for the purposes of the Human Rights Act 1998.

7.29

It should be noted that much environmental legislation is intended to implement European Community law, under which respect for fundamental rights is guaranteed. In such a situation a challenge might be based on European Community law as well as on the Scotland Act 1998 and the Human Rights Act.[9]

The 1998 Act is likely to have some impact where discretionary decisions of authorities are concerned. It may be that in those situations an individual will be able to rely on Convention rights to force a public authority to take action. In that connection, the case of *López Ostra v. Spain* is of some interest.[10] In that case, a waste treatment plant was constructed 12 metres from the applicant's home. The operators had not obtained the necessary licence from the relevant authorities. The plant caused health problems and nuisance to many local people including the applicant. Limited action was taken by the authorities, but the nuisance continued.

---

[7] See Stair Encyclopaedia, Vol. 14, para. 2134.

[8] For example in planning and environmental impact; investigation of nuisances as defined in the Environmental Protection Act 1995, ss.79–80; the right to serve adverse amenity land notices under the Town and Country Planning (Scotland) Act 1997, s.179.

[9] See, for example, *Booker Aquaculture Ltd v. Secretary of State for Scotland*, 2000 S.C. 9 discussed in the section headed "Destruction of property".

[10] A303-C, 20 E.H.R.R. 277.

7.30   In concluding that there had been a violation of Article 8, the Court stated that "severe environmental pollution may affect individuals' well-being and prevent them from enjoying their homes in such a way as to affect their private life adversely, without, however, seriously endangering their health." As the Court has often pointed out since, it did not matter whether the question was analysed in terms of a State's positive duty (to take reasonable and appropriate measures to secure the Article 8 rights) or as an interference by a public authority since the applicable principles are broadly similar. In both analyses regard must be had to the fair balance that has to be struck between the competing interests of the individual and the community as a whole. In the case of Mrs López Ostra that balance had not been struck and Article 8 had therefore been violated.

The case has been seen to some extent as championing the right of individuals to challenge State action which affects the environment, but some caution is required. The Court in *López Ostra*, it should be noted, spoke of "severe environmental pollution" and the case certainly concerned fairly extreme circumstances.[11] Further, at the European level, the doctrine of margin of appreciation allows States a measure of discretion to assess what is in the public interest and how that can best be reconciled with individual interests taking into account national conditions. Whilst that doctrine in itself is not applicable in national courts, it is nonetheless likely that our courts will defer to some extent to the assessment made by public authorities in these areas, an assessment which the courts will not be prepared to interfere with lightly.[12]

It also must be recognised that there are many more cases that have failed in this area than have met with success. For example, there was no breach where aircraft using Heathrow airport generated substantial amounts of noise, even although it was accepted that this adversely affected the applicant's private and home life.[13] Likewise there was no breach when a nuclear power station was erected 300 metres from the applicant's home

---

[11] See also *Balmer-Schafroth v. Switzerland*, 1997 R.J.D.-IV, 25 E.H.R.R. 598 where the Court spoke of the applicants failing to show that the operation of a nuclear power station exposed them "to a danger that was not only serious but also specific and, above all, imminent" (para. 40).

[12] As an example in the Scottish courts of "due deference" being given to the legislature's assessment see *Anderson v. the Scottish Ministers*, 2000 S.L.T. 873 at paras 48-53, quoting Lord Hope of Craighead's speech in *R. v. D.P.P. ex p. Kebilene* [1999] 3 W.L.R. 972. Amongst the many articles on this subject, see Singh, Hunt and Demetriou, "Is there a role for the 'margin of appreciation' in national law after the Human Rights Act?" 1999 E.H.R.L.R. 15.

[13] *Powell and Rayner v. U.K.* A172 (complaint examined under Art. 13). See also *Glass v. U.K.*, Appl. No. 28485/95, December 3, 1997, where the complaint was examined under Art.6, the applicant relying on the Commission decision in *Osman v. U.K.* (Appl. No. 23452/94) which was at that time pending before the Court (the Court's decision is reported at 1998 R.J.D. VIII).

transforming the rural surroundings.[14] In an early case, an application complaining that nuclear tests and dumping radioactive waste in the sea breached the right to life under Article 2 was found to be manifestly ill-founded.[15]

The Convention may, however, be of some assistance where information on environmental matters is sought by individuals. There may be circumstances where respect for private and family life requires the State to take positive action to provide information on environmental risks. The Court so found in *Guerra v. Italy*, where the applicants had complained that the authorities had taken no steps to ensure that the public were informed of the risks and of what was to be done in the event of an accident at an agricultural chemical factory, whose operations had already hospitalised 150 people.[16] 7.31

Interestingly, the complaint under Article 10 (freedom to receive information) failed since that article "basically prohibits a government from restricting a person from receiving information that others wish or may be willing to impart to him". [17] Accordingly, there was no positive obligation on the State under Article 10 to collect and disseminate information. Relying on the same facts, however, the complaint under Article 8 succeeded, since the authorities by not providing information had not taken the necessary steps to ensure effective protection of the applicants' Article 8 rights.[18]

It is of some interest that two judges, Judges Walsh and Jambrek, the Irish and Slovenian judges, considered that there may also have been a violation of Article 2 (right to life). Indeed, Judge Jambrek in his concurring opinion advocated developing the Court's case law on Article 2. Whether such a development will take place and what that development might be remains to be seen.

There is, however, no doubt that currently the protection of environmental rights under the Convention is not particularly extensive. This is due in part to the fact that complaints have to be fitted into articles which were not specifically designed to deal with such matters. It is also due, it seems, to reluctance on the part of the Strasbourg authorities to interfere in the decisions of national authorities in difficult areas where economic interests are involved. Whether the United Kingdom courts will be prepared to be more interventionist is open to doubt.[19]

---

[14] *S v. France*, Appl. No. 1372/88, May 1990 (presented under Art. 8).

[15] *Dr S v. Federal Republic of Germany*, Appl. No. 715/60, August 5, 1960. See also *LM and R v. Switzerland*, 1996 E.H.R.R. CD 130 concerning the transport of nuclear waste by rail (manifestly ill-founded).

[16] R.J.D. 1998-I, 26 E.H.R.R. 357

[17] At para. 53, quoting from *Leander v. Sweden*, A116, 9 E.H.R.R. 433.

[18] See also *McGinley and Egan v. U.K.* 1998 R.J.D.- 111, 27 E.H.R.R. 1.

[19] Articles of interest in this area include, Thornton and Tromans, "Human Rights and Environmental Wrongs" (1999) 11 J.E.L . 35; Hart, "The Impact of the European Convention on Human Rights on Planning and Environmental Law" [2000] J.P.L. 117.

4. Irritancy

7.32   The remedy of irritancy is one which has applied in the field of feudal contracts and leases. With the passing of the Abolition of Feudal Tenure etc. (Scotland) Act 2000, irritancy of the feu has been abolished.[20] In this section, consideration of irritancy is therefore restricted to its application to leases, in particular to commercial leases.[21]

Legal irritancies, that is irritancies which are implied by law, are not of particular significance and it is not proposed to examine them here. Rather, attention will be focussed on conventional irritancies, which are those irritancies provided for by the terms of the lease. Such irritancies are distinguished according to whether they relate to monetary or non-monetary provisions.

Prior to the Law Reform (Miscellaneous Provisions) (Scotland) Act 1985, conventional irritancies were not capable of being purged.[22] The 1985 Act, however, in light of adverse comments made by the House of Lords[23] and a Scottish Law Commission Report,[24] reformed the common law. In brief, section 4 provides in relation to monetary breaches that a landlord is not entitled to rely on a failure to pay, unless the tenant has not responded to a notice requiring payment within a period of not less than 14 days. As far as non-monetary breaches are concerned, a landlord may not rely on such a breach to terminate the lease if a fair and reasonable landlord would not do so. Whether the tenant has been given a reasonable opportunity to remedy the breach is relevant in considering if the "fair and reasonable" test has been met.[25]

The relevance of the Human Rights Act is likely to be at the point where the landlord seeks to enforce his remedy by an action of declarator of irritancy and removing. There may be instances where the landlord seeking to enforce an irritancy clause is itself a public authority and thus bound by the Human Rights Act 1998. However, more often the relevance of the Act will arise from the fact that the courts are also defined in the 1998 Act as public authorities. Thus, where two private parties are involved in an action of declarator of irritancy, by virtue of the possible horizontal application of the Convention, the Court in order to comply with its duties under the Act may require to reinterpret the existing common law in light of the Convention. It should also be borne in mind that section 3 of the 1998 Act requires that primary legislation (whenever enacted) must be read and given effect to in a

---

[20] Section 53. The Act received Royal Assent on June 9, 2000.
[21] Issues may arise under domestic leases and Art. 8, but these are not considered in this section.
[22] Unless the conventional irritancy was identical to the legal irritancy.
[23] In *Dorchester Studios (Glasgow) Ltd v. Stone*, 1975 S.C. (H.L.) 56.
[24] Scot Law Com No. 75 – Irritancies in Leases.
[25] See s.5 of the 1985 Act. For an application of the test see *Aubrey Investments Ltd v. DSC (Realisations) Ltd (in receivership)* 2000 S.L.T. 183.

way which is compatible with Convention rights.

The Convention provision which is most likely to be relevant in 7.33
this area is that of Article 1, Protocol 1. It is suggested that the
Court in considering the human rights dimension of an action of
irritancy may approach matters in the following way. First, the
question arises of whether there has been an interference in the
tenant's right of property and if so under which of the Rules
contained in Article 1, Protocol 1. It is well established in the
jurisprudence that the rights contained in a lease are "possessions"
for the purposes of the article.[26] Were the court to grant decree in
an action of irritancy, there would clearly be an interference with
the tenant's property as he would be deprived of the benefit of the
lease. Such would be a case arising under Rule 2 of Article 1. It is
acknowledged that not to grant decree may constitute an
interference with the landlord's right of property, but that is a
matter to be considered in the balancing exercise which is to be
carried out at a later stage.

The next step is to assess whether the interference pursues a
legitimate aim. In the case of irritancy, the aim is "to ensure that the
land was restored to (the owner's) possession in circumstances
where a tenant had become unable... to perform his obligations as
possessor".[27] There is also the general policy consideration of
respect for contractual terms whilst recognising the distinction
between "lubricating the working of a contract and altering its
terms".[28] That these aims would be considered legitimate seems
probable.

The final stage is for the court to consider whether the aim
pursued is proportionate to the means used, and whether the
individual can be said to be bearing an excessive burden. It is at this
stage that it is suggested that the effect of the Act may be felt most.
It has been recognised that the operation of the law of irritancy
even after the reforms implemented in the 1985 Act may result in an
unfair advantage to the landlord. In *C.I.N. Properties Ltd v. Dollar
Land (Cumbernauld) Ltd,*[29] the House of Lords expressed some
disquiet about whether the common law as modified by the 1985
Act "fairly reflected social policy in the case of long-investment
leases".[30] Lord Keith of Kinkel went so far as suggesting that where
the irritancy would confer a substantial benefit to the landlord at
the expense of the tenant, it may be appropriate to require the
landlord to compensate the tenant for the value of the improve-

---

[26] See, for example, *Velosa Bareto v. Portugal,* A334 and *S v. U.K.* (1984) 41 D.R.
226.
[27] Scot Law Com No. 75, para. 3.3.
[28] C. Thomson L.J., in *McDouall's Trustees v. MacLeod,* 1949 S.C. 593 at p.602,
quoted in Scot Law Com No. 75 at para. 3.2.
[29] 1992 S.L.T. 669.
[30] Lord Jauncey of Tullichettle in the leading speech at p. 676.

ments to the subjects carried out by the tenant or his predecessors.[31] Compensation where an individual has been deprived of his possessions is, as previously noted, presumed to be necessary according to the jurisprudence of the Strasbourg Court. In light of that and the comments made in the *C.I.N.* case, it might be argued that compensation would be required in certain circumstances if the proportionality test under the Convention is to be met.

Two other issues arise in this context. First, where a court is considering whether a fair and reasonable landlord would have served the notice of irritancy, the test which it applies may require to be modified to take into account the balancing exercise required by the Convention.[32] That would entail interpreting the 1985 Act so as to render it compatible with the Convention.[33] Alternatively, if the court considered it could not do so it might make a declaration of incompatibility.[34]

The second point relates to the position of sub-tenants and creditors. The position of both was considered by the Scottish Law Commission, but it was concluded that its proposed reforms need not extend any protection to them. Protecting sub-tenants might have the effect of discouraging permitted sub-tenancies, which was not considered desirable.[35] Likewise, the devising of a statutory scheme to protect the tenant's creditors was thought to be difficult, and could best be left to parties to deal with when negotiating the terms of the lease.[36] It therefore seems unlikely that the Convention will offer any better protection to such groups than is currently obtainable, that is, by negotiation.

5. Division and Sale

7.34 It is by no means unusual for property to be held in common even outwith the matrimonial sphere. In Scots law where a co-owner wishes to sell his share, he has the right to insist upon division and sale. This is an absolute right which admits of few exceptions, namely if parties have contracted not to do so, or possibly where there is personal bar.[37] Special rules apply in relation to matrimonial property and in sequestrations—these are considered below.

The issue of division and sale provides an interesting example of

---

[31] p. 672.

[32] See *Aubrey Investments Ltd* (above) and *Blythswood Investments (Scotland) Ltd v. Clydesdale Electrical Stores Ltd (in receivership)* 1995 S.L.T. 150.

[33] As the courts are obliged to do in terms of s.3(1). For an example, albeit in the criminal context, see *Brown v. Stott*, 2000 J.C. 328.

[34] In terms of s.4 of the Human Rights Act 1998.

[35] See Scot Law Com No. 75, paras 5.5–5.8.

[36] *supra*, paras 5.9–5.14.

[37] See *Burrows v. Burrows*, 1996 S.L.T. 1313 as an example of a contractual agreement not to insist on division and sale for a limited period. On personal bar, see *Upper Crathes Fishings Ltd v. Bailey's Executors*, 1991 S.L.T. 747 at p. 749 (per Lord President Hope).

the possible horizontal application of the Human Rights Act 1998, *i.e.* its application between private parties who, unlike public authorities, are not bound to act in a way which is compatible with the Convention. Rather the question is whether the courts, which *are* defined in the Act as public authorities,[38] will be required to re-interpret the existing law in this area in order to fulfil their obligation of acting compatibly with the Convention. It may be that a court in considering whether to grant decree in an action of division of sale ought to consider the terms of the Convention, on the basis that to grant such a decree might involve an interference with Convention rights, such as property rights and the right to respect for one's home.

If that is correct, what ought the court to do to comply with the Act? As indicated above, in what may be referred to as the general case, there is no defence to an action of division and sale (other than the limited matters referred to above). Equitable considerations are irrelevant as a defence to the action, although they may be relevant at the stage of deciding what remedy should be granted.[39] Thus the court may grant decree allowing the pursuer to purchase the co-owner's share at a price to be fixed by a court-appointed reporter,[40] or may conclude that a sale by private treaty would best serve both parties' interests.[41]

With the coming into force of the Act, the issue of the rights guaranteed by Article 1, Protocol 1 arise. Thus, it may be argued that to grant decree would interfere with the defender's right to property, in that the defender may not be in a position to purchase the pursuer's share or to compete in the open market. Not to grant decree would also involve, it could be argued, an interference with the pursuer's right of property, namely the right to dispose of that property.   **7.35**

It is suggested that the court should firstly consider what the nature of the interference is and its extent, including its implications for the co-owners. Next, the court must be satisfied that the interference is in the public or general interest. What is being considered here, it would seem, is not whether *this* interference in this particular person's property is justified in the public interest (which would seem unlikely). Rather, it is suggested, the issue is whether as a matter of public policy the interference which is represented in any action of division and sale is justified.

The reason for the absolute right of one owner to insist on division and sale was considered by the institutional writers,[42] and in the older cases[43] to be based on public policy, it being thought

---

[38] s.6(3)(a).
[39] *Upper Crathes Fishings Ltd* (supra).
[40] *Scrimgeour v. Scrimgeour*, 1988 S.L.T. 590, and *Gray v. Kerner*, 1996 S.C.L.R. 331.
[41] As in *Berry v. Berry (No. 2)* 1989 S.L.T. 292.
[42] Stair *Institutions* I, 7,15; Bankton *Institute* I, 8,36.
[43] *Brock v. Hamilton* (1852) 19 D. 701; *Banff Magistrates v. Ruthin Castle Ltd*, 1944 S.C. 36.

that ownership in common ought not to be encouraged, and once entered into should be capable of being ended. That the remedy should on public policy grounds be available was recognised more recently by the First Division in the *Upper Crathes Fishings Ltd* case. There Lord President Hope (as he then was) referred to the older authorities and, in rejecting considerations of equity as a defence, acknowledged that considerations of public policy justified the availability of the remedy.[44]

If the court is satisfied that the interference is in the public interest, it must then consider whether there is a fair balance between the demands of the interest of the public and the rights of the individual (it being remembered that the rights of at least two individuals are involved). An aspect of this balance is the question of compensation which, of course, will feature in every division and sale case.

Thus, while the Convention may require our courts to re-assess the remedy of division and sale, it is likely that in the general case a co-owner will still obtain a decree for division and sale, albeit the decision-making process may be affected, particularly at the stage of deciding what remedy should be granted.

7.36   So far, no mention has been made of the rights under Article 8 to respect for one's home. In many actions of division and sale, the defender's home may be at risk. Leaving aside matrimonial homes, which are specifically protected under the Matrimonial Homes (Family Protection)(Scotland) Act 1981, there may be situations where the property involved is the home of the co-owners. Were the court to grant decree for division and sale in those circumstances, they would also require to take into account the defender's Article 8 rights. How that may or may not affect the outcome will depend on the individual circumstances, but it appears that the approach to be taken in considering such actions may now require to be modified.

Reference has already been made to the special rules which apply in relation to matrimonial homes and in sequestrations. These can be found in the Matrimonial Homes (Family Protection)(Scotland) Act 1981 and the Bankruptcy (Scotland) Act 1985. The 1981 Act requires the court in considering any action of division and sale to have regard to all the circumstances of the case and sets out a number of matters to which the court is required to direct its attention.[45] These are likely to cover the matters which might be relevant under Article 8.[46]

---

[44]   See pp. 750–751, and Lord Mayfield at pp. 754–755.

[45]   s.19. The matters are the conduct of the spouses, their needs and financial resources, the needs of their children, whether the home is used for business purposes and whether the spouse bringing the action has offered alternative accommodation.

[46]   See, for example, the decision of Sheriff Principal Risk in *Milne v. Milne*, 1994 S.L.T. (Sh.Ct.) 15.

Under section 40 of the Bankruptcy (Scotland) Act 1985, the permanent trustee may apply to the court for authority to sell the debtor's share of the family home, where he has been unable to obtain the necessary consent to do so.[47] The court in deciding the application is directed to have regard to all the circumstances of the case and certain specific matters.[48] Again, it is likely that these factors are similar if not identical to the considerations which arise under Article 8. However, as with any action of division and sale after October 2000, the decision making process may require to be adapted to allow Convention rights to be considered.

6. Destruction of Property

There may be circumstances where a public authority wishes to take steps to have the property of an individual destroyed. Such circumstances will normally arise where the property concerned presents some danger to the public. Thus, for example, under the Food Safety Act 1990, food considered unsafe may be seized, and the matter brought before a sheriff or magistrate, who may order destruction of the food.[49] Similarly, animals suffering from certain diseases may be ordered to be slaughtered.[50] The legislation may or may not provide for compensation. Section 32 of the Animal Health Act 1981 does provide for compensation, whereas the Food Safety Act 1990 does not.

7.37

The application of the Convention to circumstances such as these has arisen in a number of cases in the United Kingdom courts as well as in Strasbourg. In *Booker Aquaculture Ltd v. Secretary of State for Scotland,*[51] the question at issue was the lack of compensation where fish stocks were ordered to be destroyed in terms of the Diseases of Fish (Control) Regulations 1994. These Regulations were made in implementation of a Council Directive. Accordingly, the issue that arose was whether, the right to property being recognised as a fundamental right under Community law, compensation for fish killed or destroyed was required. More specifically, the court had to determine whether Community law or national law governed the matter of compensation. The Inner House concluded that it was appropriate to make a reference to the

---

[47] A recent example is the decision of Lord Philip in *Ritchie v. Burns*, unreported, June 14, 2000.

[48] Namely, the needs and financial resources of the debtor's spouse and any children, the interests of the creditors, and the length of time the property was used as the family home.

[49] See s.9. Interestingly, in the case of *Errington v. Wilson*, 1995 S.C. 550 there was some discussion by the First Division of the rights of the individual as set against the public interest—see Lord President Hope at p. 558—which echoes the approach which might have been taken under the Convention.

[50] See, for example, the Animal Health Act 1981.

[51] The decision in the Outer House (Lord Cameron) is reported at [1999] EuLR 54; the two opinions of the First Division are reported at 2000 S.C. 9, and 1999 G.W.D. 36-1770.

European Court of Justice on this issue.[52]

There are a number of points of interest that arise. First, the respondents accepted that were Community law to apply compensation would normally be required, but argued that the circumstances of the case were sufficiently exceptional to justify ordering the destruction of the fish without compensation. Since the reference to the E.C.J. is to include a question dealing with the situation if Community law does apply, there may be some guidance as to what is meant by "exceptional circumstances", as has been referred to in the jurisprudence of the Strasbourg Court.

Secondly, the case is an interesting example of how the transitional period in respect of human rights may impact on a particular case. As has been pointed out, since the case was first determined in the Outer House (in May 1998), the Scotland Act 1998 has been brought into force and, in particular, the Scottish Executive is now obliged to act compatibly with the Convention.[53] Accordingly, the case might be argued as a "devolution issue" rather than relying on incorporation of the Convention through European Community law. Indeed, by the time the case returns to the Scottish courts, the Human Rights Act 1998 will be in force, in which case there might be direct reliance on its provisions.

7.38   The effect of Article 1 of Protocol 1 in this area was also considered in the case of *R. v. Secretary of State ex parte Eastside Cheese Company*[54] which concerned the making of an emergency control order under section 13 of the Food Safety Act 1990. The order prohibited the carrying out of any commercial operation relating to cheese originating from a certain manufacturer of cheese. The result was that the respondents were not entitled to compensation for cheese which was detained, even if the cheese was not unfit for human consumption. In challenging the making of the order, the respondents argued that the Secretary of State could not rely on Article 36 of the E.C. Treaty to justify the breach of Article 34 since the making of the section 13 order violated the rights guaranteed by Article 1, Protocol 1.[55]

The Court of Appeal considered that the effect of the order was to interfere with the respondents' peaceful enjoyment of their property, but that they had not been deprived of their property. The rule that compensation would be payable where there was a deprivation of property save in exceptional circumstances was noted. The Court then indicated that it had doubts as to whether

---

[52] See also the similar case of *Hydro Seafood GSP Ltd v. The Scottish Ministers*, Lord Hamilton, February 7, 2000.

[53] See Aidan O'Neill, Q.C., "The Protection of Fundamental Rights in Scotland as a General Principle of Community Law —the case of Booker Aquaculture" [2000] E.H.R.L.R. 18 at p. 32.

[54] [1999] 3 C.M.L.R. 123; [1999] Eu.L.R. 968.

[55] Arts 34 and 36 now Arts 29 and 30 following renumbering by the Treaty of Amsterdam.

that rule applied in these circumstances, but that if it did it considered the circumstances were sufficiently exceptional to displace it.[56] Further, if the position was more properly to be analysed as a control of the use of property, a fair balance as required by the Convention had been struck between the interests of the public and the private individual.[57]

In a similar vein is the European Commission of Human Rights' decision in the case of *Pinnacle Meat Processors Company v. United Kingdom*.[58] The circumstances of the case arose out of the BSE crisis, in particular regulations which made it an offence to sell or use in the preparation of food for human or animal consumption the heads of cattle. The business of the applicants involved buying cattle heads from abattoirs and processing head meat, which was then sold on to manufacturers of food products. Their businesses were consequently rendered illegal. Some compensation was payable in respect of unsold stock which was unsaleable by virtue of the Regulations. In fact, six of the nine applicants received payments totalling £430,000.

The applicants complained that they had been deprived of the peaceful enjoyment of their property and of their livelihood, and that in the absence of compensation the regulations placed upon them an excessive burden. The Commission considered that there had been no formal expropriation of assets, and that the interference was a control on the use of assets, namely, specified bovine material. Consequently the question was whether there had been a fair balance struck. In concluding that there had, the Commission pointed out that some of the applicants' assets could be put to other uses or sold, that the goodwill in their businesses was a possession whose value fluctuated, and that some compensation had been paid to some of the applicants in respect of eligible beef stocks. Accordingly, the application was manifestly ill-founded. The complaint under Article 14, that there was discrimination as against comparable sectors of the industry, was also rejected.

7.39

The cases illustrate a reluctance on the part of courts to interfere in matters of public health, it being considered that decisions in this sphere are best left to the authorities charged with enforcing legislation. Nonetheless, the Convention does provide a means by which those decisions can be reviewed. It remains to be seen whether any guidance, and if so what, is given by the European Court of Justice on the right to compensation where property has been destroyed in the public interest. That guidance, of course, might not necessarily be the same as that which would be given by the European Court of Human Rights. It should also not be forgotten that the provisions of Article 6 may be relevant, since the

---

[56] See paras 76–77.
[57] paras 78–80.
[58] Appl. No. 33298/96, 27 E.H.R.R. CD 217.

owner of the property affected will be entitled to have the matter determined in accordance with the requirements of that article.

7. Abolition of Feudal Tenure

7.40   The Abolition of Feudal Tenure etc (Scotland) Act 2000 received Royal Assent on June 9, 2000. It makes major changes to the system of land tenure in Scotland. A detailed analysis of those provisions is not appropriate here, but there are certain aspects which merit consideration from the point of view of their compatibility with the Convention.

It should be noted at the outset that the competency of the Scottish Parliament is limited and in particular it is obliged to act in a way which is compatible with the Convention.[59] Thus, any incompatibility between the terms of the Abolition of Feudal Tenure etc (Scotland) Act 2000 and the Convention would be open to challenge under the Scotland Act, notwithstanding any challenge which might be made under the Human Rights Act 1998.

The aspects referred to above which will be examined are first, the extinction of feuduties, and secondly, the extinction of other real burdens. Looking at the extinction of feuduties, sections 7–12 of the Act provide for these to be extinguished on the "appointed day" (which is expected to be approximately two years after the passing of the Act). However, a superior will be entitled to compensation provided he serves the required notice within two years after the appointed day.[60]

The amount of compensation is regulated by section 9. It is calculated by reference to

> "the sum of money which would, if invested in two and a half per cent. Consolidated Stock at the middle market price at the close of business last preceding the appointed day, produce an annual sum equal to the feuduty".[61]

It can be seen that the system is one whereby compensation to superiors will be due only where it is claimed by them, and that if they do not do so within the two year period following the appointed day their right to any compensation will be extinguished. The fairness of such a scheme was considered in the Scottish Law Commission's Report on Abolition of the Feudal System.[62] It was concluded that, although superiors may not know who the vassals are for the purpose of serving the required notice, the means of finding out are straightforward, as the vassal's title will be registered

---

[59] Scotland Act 1998, s.29.
[60] s.8(1).
[61] *i.e.* the same formula as applies under the Land Tenure Reform (Scotland) Act 1974.
[62] Scot Law Com No. 168, at para. 3.14 ff.

in the Register of Sasines or the Land Register.

Whilst the abolition of real burdens, and feuduty in particular, undoubtedly amounts to a deprivation of property within the meaning of the Convention, the system for compensating superiors for the loss of their right to feuduty does appear to strike a balance between the general interest and the rights of individuals. At least so far as abolition of feuduty is concerned, superiors do not appear to be suffering an "excessive burden".[63] It is not quite so apparent that the same can be said in relation to the abolition of other real burdens, which is the second aspect of the Act to be examined.

Although section 16 of the Act states that a superior's right to enforce a real burden shall be extinguished on the appointed day, that is subject to a number of exceptions. Thus, in certain circumstances, a superior may reallocate the right to enforce a feudal real burden to neighbouring land which he owns.[64] It is also possible for the superior to enter into an agreement with the vassal to maintain a burden in favour of land nominated in the agreement, or if agreement cannot be reached for the superior to apply to the Lands Tribunal.[65] In the latter case, the superior would require to show a genuine and practical interest in enforcing the burden.

Apart from compensation for the extinction of feuduties noted above, the only other provision regulating compensation for the extinction of feudal real burdens is where land has been feued subject to a reservation to the superior of the benefit of any development value of the land.[66] In such circumstances, a property may have been feued for a heavily discounted consideration, or for no consideration, on the understanding that if the land were later freed for some use prohibited by the burden, some financial return would be due to the superior. In these circumstances, the superior may before the appointed day register a notice as prescribed in the Act.[67] The superior will then be entitled to compensation if there is a breach of the burden (which after the appointed day is, of course, extinguished) in the five years before the appointed day or during the 20 years following the appointed day.[68]

7.41

The measure of compensation is stipulated in section 36. The amount payable is the amount of development value which would have accrued to the owner of the land if the burden had been modified so as to free the land for the development which has actually occurred. This is, however, subject to a limit, namely that the compensation should not exceed an amount which reflects the effect the burden had on reducing the consideration for the feu

---

[63] See *James v. U.K.*, A98 (para. 50), 8 E.H.R.R. 123.
[64] s.17.
[65] ss.18 and 19.
[66] ss.32–38.
[67] s.32.
[68] s.34(2).

grant at the time it was imposed.[69] As Professor Rennie points out,[70] the effect on price may be fairly obvious where a feu charter has been granted relatively recently. That may not be the case where the feu was created many years ago. Add to this the provision that the burden of proving any disputed fact will lie on the person relying on the notice or making the claim for compensation,[71] and the difficulties for superiors in making claims for compensation for development value are obvious.

How are these provisions to be analysed in terms of the Convention? Where there is a development value real burden, it may be that the interference in the superior's right of property should be categorised as a control of the use of his property rather than as a deprivation of property. If that is the case, there is not necessarily a right to *any* compensation. The availability of compensation would simply be one of the factors to be taken into account in deciding whether there has been a fair balance between the rights of the individual and the public interest. Since the Act provides for some compensation in certain situations, it might be thought that this would satisfy the balance, particularly since the rules are derived from existing formula.[72] Even if the interference were to be classified as a deprivation of property, it does not necessarily follow that the compensation obtainable would fall foul of the Convention, since full compensation is not required.

7.42   The final aspect of the Act which merits some consideration as to its compatibility with the Convention is the abolition of all other feudal real burdens (apart from the exceptions referred to above). In these circumstances, the Act provides for no compensation. Indeed, the Law Commission was quite clear that there should be no compensation for the loss of the right to enforce feudal restrictions or to exact fees for waivers of feudal restrictions, a practice which they described as an abuse of the feudal system and likened to some extent to blackmail.[73] Nonetheless the rights of superiors to obtain payment from their vassals where there has been a breach of a real burden or where the vassal wishes to do something which would breach a burden in the title, does have a value.

In light of the jurisprudence on the meaning of "possessions" in terms of the Convention, the extinction of superiorities and all that accompanies them is almost certainly a deprivation of property for the purposes of the Convention. In those circumstances, there would normally be a right to compensation. An absence of any compensation will be justifiable under the Convention only in

---

[69]   The justification for this approach is set out in the Law Commission's report at paras 5.41–5.46.

[70]   See "Abolition of the Feudal System", 1999 S.L.T. 85 at p.90.

[71]   See s.42.

[72]   Under the Conveyancing and Feudal Reform (Scotland) Act 1970, s.1(4)(ii).

[73]   See para. 5.60 of their Report.

exceptional circumstances,[74] although what will constitute "exceptional circumstances" has as yet not been defined. It has been suggested that it may apply to seizures of property in times of war.[75] Clearly, that is somewhat removed from the circumstances currently under consideration. It must therefore be concluded that the absence of any compensation for such superiors, albeit for understandable reasons, must raise some doubts about the compatibility of this aspect of the Act with the Convention. It might, however, be argued that some compensation has been payable since in many cases the superior will be compensated for the abolition of feuduty.[76]

8. Land Reform — the Community Right to Buy

It is anticipated that the Scottish Parliament will legislate to provide a so-called "community right to buy" in the near future. A White Paper "Land Reform: Proposals for Legislation"[77] was published in July 1999, it being intended at that time to publish a draft Bill in the Autumn. Such a Bill was expected to be published before the end of 2000.

7.43

The White Paper was preceded by a report by the Land Reform Policy Group "Recommendations for Action" which was published in January 1999. The proposals contained in the two documents are markedly different. Before considering the difficulties in legislating in this area from the point of view of the Convention, it is necessary to consider briefly the different approaches in the two documents.

So far as the Land Reform Policy Group's report is concerned, there were broadly three elements. First, in respect of land in certain areas (which were not clearly defined), landowners would be required to give notice of any forthcoming sale. There would be a minimum period imposed between the notice to sell and the date when the sale could proceed. A further period of delay could be imposed by the relevant Minister if this was considered to be in the public interest.

Secondly, community bodies were to be given a right to buy land in the areas controlled by the proposals when the land was being sold. The community group would require to satisfy the Minister that purchase by them would "be in the public interest". The price to be paid would then be fixed by a Valuer appointed by the Government, with disputes about valuation being referred to the Lands Tribunal for Scotland.

Thirdly, the Minister would be able to exercise a power of compulsory purchase where it appeared to him to be "in the public

---

[74] *Holy Monasteries v. Greece*, A301-A (para. 71), 20 E.H.R.R. 1.
[75] Harris, O'Boyle and Warbrick, *Law of the European Convention on Human Rights*, p. 532.
[76] The sort of reasoning applied in a quite different context in *Pinnacle Meat Processors Company v. U.K.*, Appl. No. 33298/96.
[77] "Land Reform: Proposals for Legislation", July 1999, SE/1999/1.

interest".

Turning to the terms of the White Paper, there are four main aspects which should be noted. The first is the establishment of a register of community interests. Thus, properly constituted community bodies will be able to register their interest in land such that the land in question cannot be sold without that interest being taken into account.[78] Before registering an interest, the Minister must be satisfied that most of the members of the community body live and/or work on the land, and that the community body is representative of the local community.[79]

The second aspect of the proposals is that once an interest in land has been registered, the land may not be sold without notice of the proposed sale being given by the landowner to the Minister. The minimum period between the notice to sell and the closing date will be 30 days. During that period the community body will decide whether to maintain its interest or not in the land. If it decides to exercise its right to buy, it must give notice to that effect during the 30-day period to the landowner and the Minister. A Government-appointed Valuer will then assess the price, being his best estimate of what the property would achieve on the open market.

The next step is for the community to be balloted on the proposed purchase.[80] If the ballot is in favour of purchasing, the community will then have up to six months to obtain funding for the purchase. It does not appear that the Minister approving the purchase has any discretion to exercise in giving his approval.

7.44 Fourthly, and finally, the White Paper proposed that the Minister be given a power to purchase land compulsorily where it appears to be in the public interest to do so.[81]

A contrast can be drawn between the White Paper's proposals and the Land Reform Policy Group's proposals. The latter concentrated on whether a particular community sale was in the public interest and required the Minister to make certain decisions based on what was in the public interest. The former, on the other hand, make no mention of what is in the public interest. Accordingly, if the legislation were to follow the White Paper, there would be no requirement on the Minister to be satisfied that the land in question should be subject to the legislation, that the community should have the right to register their interest in the

---

[78] The White Paper proposed that all rural land be included, rural being defined on a population density basis or by excluding built up areas. (para. 2.2)

[79] This will satisfied if there is evidence that at least 10 per cent of those aged over 18 who live and/or work on the land in question support the bid to register the interest in land. (para.2.9)

[80] The percentage of those entitled to vote who must vote in favour of purchase was not defined in the White Paper. (para. 4.7)

[81] It was anticipated that this power would be exercised where the beneficial ownership of property was being transferred without triggering the community right to buy provisions, *e.g.* where shares in a company holding land were being traded. (para. 5.2)

land or that the land should by bought by the community. Rather the White Paper proceeds on the unstated assumption that it is in the public interest for all rural land to be subject to the legislation, and that all community purchases are in the public interest.

In advance of publication of the Bill, it is possible only to comment in general terms on the issues which may arise under the Convention. It the legislation adopts the same premise as the White Paper, there may be room for argument as to whether such wide-ranging legislation could be justified as being "in the public interest" in terms of Protocol 1, Article 1. On one view, Protocol 1, Article 1 would require the Minister in any particular situation to establish why it was in the public interest either for all rural land or that particular land to be subject to the legislation. If no inquiry were made at the stage of registering an interest as to whether it was in the public interest to register the land, it might be difficult to justify why the particular land had been registered.

If there was also no requirement in the legislation for the Minister to be satisfied that it was in the public interest for a community body to purchase land in which it had registered an interest before the Minster approves the sale, then on one view the Minister might have some difficulty in justifying his approval of the sale as being in the public interest

As noted above, it is proposed that landowners will be compensated for land in respect of which the community right to buy proposals operate, compensation being assessed along the lines of that used in compulsory purchases. It is likely that such compensation would meet the Convention criteria since, as previously noted, these simply require that compensation be reasonably related to the value of the property.[82]

Further, since any disputes as to compensation are to be determined by the Lands Tribunal for Scotland, the landowner should have an opportunity to have his "civil rights" determined fairly in terms of Article 6 of the Convention. Other challenges to the exercise of the community right to buy powers would presumably be by judicial review of the Minister's decision. It is not entirely certain whether any such proceedings would comply with the requirements of article 6(1) in view of the limited scope of such review. In *W v. United Kingdom*[83] the court had no jurisdiction to review the merits of a decision restricting the applicant's access to his child. In those circumstances, there was a breach of Article 6(1). In contrast, in *Bryan v. United Kingdom,*[84] the limited scope of review in an appeal against a planning inspector's decision did not breach Article 6(1). It is likely that where matters of policy are involved that the Convention will only require a relatively limited

7.45

---

[82] See *Lithgow v. U.K.* A102, 8 E.H.R.R. 329.
[83] A121, 10 E.H.R.R. 329.
[84] A335-A, 21 E.H.R.R. 342. See also *County Properties Ltd v. The Scottish Ministers* discussed above.

review in order for the requirements of Article 6(1) to be met. The case of *James v. United Kingdom*[85] provides an interesting example of wholesale land reform which was found by the Court not to have breached the Convention. The circumstances related to the compulsory transfer of property under the Leasehold Reform Act 1967. The Court found that although the applicants had been deprived of their possessions, the compulsory transfer of property from one individual to another for the latter's private benefit may be "in the public interest". It then carried out an analysis of the aim of the legislation, eventually concluding that the system chosen could not be categorised as irrational or inappropriate and therefore fell within the State's margin of appreciation. This decision will no doubt prove of some comfort to those legislating in this difficult area. Nonetheless, some questions remain if the proposals contained in the White Paper are to form the basis of legislation.

---

[85] A98, 8 E.H.R.R. 123.

CHAPTER 8

HUMAN RIGHTS AND EMPLOYMENT LAW

INTRODUCTION

The position to date

Individual Rights

The impact of the ECHR on employment law within the United 8.01
Kingdom before the advent of the Human Rights Act 1998 was
modest. Although the articles of the Convention held great
potential for both individual and collective labour law, the
European Court of Human Rights'[1] generally conservative interpretation of them disappointed those who hoped to see the
Convention bring radical change to the law.[2] More recently there
have been signs of a more interventionist approach by the Court,
particularly in relation to the protection of Article 8 rights in the
workplace. Privacy of communication and the right to follow a
sexual orientation of choice have been upheld in important
decisions. In *Halford v. United Kingdom* [3] the ECHR held that
telephone tapping carried out surreptitiously by an employer at
work was in breach of Article 8 and unlawful. This ruling
incidentally provided confirmation that behaviour taking place
within the working environment could fall within the scope of
"private life".[4] In *Smith and Grady v. United Kingdom*[5] the
behaviour of the Royal Air Force in investigating suspected
homosexuality amongst serving airmen and airwomen (and the
subsequent discharge of those investigated) was found to amount to
an infringement of Article 8.

These and a few other decisions apart, the general observation
that "[t]he civil liberties of individuals tend to cease when when they
enter the private sphere of the labour market, regulated by the

---

[1]   Hereinafter referred to as ECtHR.
[2]   K.D. Ewing, "The Human Rights Act and Labour Law" (1998) 27 I.L.J. 27; S.
      Palmer, "Human Rights: Implications for Labour Law" [2000] C.L.J. 168; Bob
      Hepple, "The Impact on Labour Law" in *The Impact of the Human Rights Bill on
      English Law* (B. Markesinis ed., 1998); Grosz, Beatson, and Duffy, *Human Rights.
      The 1998 Act and the European Convention* (2000), p.313.
[3]   1997] I.R.L.R. 471, ECHR
[4]   *Alison Halford v. U.K.* (1997) 25 E.H.R.R. 523.
[5]   [1999] I.R.L.R. 734, ECtHR.

contract of employment"[6] remains a fair comment on the practical impact of the ECHR. The jurisprudence of the Court and Commission shows that, when freedom of contract conflicts with fundamental rights, the former tends to prevail. Thus a Muslim teacher has been held unable to rely on the Convention right (Article 9) protecting freedom of religion so as to insist upon a right to attend Friday prayers when that conflicted with his contractual hours of work.[7] And Article 9, it has been held, gives no right to an individual refusing for religious reasons to sign a contract to work on Sundays.[8] In the words of the Commission's decision in *Ahmad*, the freedom guaranteed by Article 9 may "be influenced by the situation of the person claiming that freedom". The cases show that the person's situation is to be assessed having regard to the contractual obligations he has freely undertaken, as well as to the nature of the job itself.[9] In effect, the interpretation of the Convention to date has recognised a substantial possibility of "contracting-out" of Convention rights.[10] It will always be important to know if the party complaining of infringement has ever agreed to or was aware of the employer's conduct. The issue of consent is always controversial but perhaps particularly significant in an employment law context, given the well-known contention that the main object of the law here is to counteract the inequality of bargaining power inherent in the employment relationship.[11]

Another problem in the application of the Convention to employment law has been the conceptual difficulties the Strasbourg institutions have had with public employment. Those who work in the public sector have, in the past, faced additional difficulty in relying upon the Convention to guarantee their fundamental rights in the workplace. In particular, the guarantees of a fair and expeditious determination of civil rights under Article 6 have, in the past, been held not to apply to civil servants and other public sector

---

[6] Bob Hepple, "The Impact on Labour Law" in *The Impact of the Human Rights Bill on English Law* (B. Markesinis ed., 1998), p.63.

[7] *Ahmad v. U.K.* (1981) 4 E.H.R.R. 125.

[8] *Stedman v. U.K.* (1997) 23 E.H.R.R. 168 CD. (It may be noted that the European Commission of Human Rights (hereinafter referred to as ECmHR) accepted that a dismissal on the part of private employer that amounted to an interference with rights under Art. 9 would engage the responsibility of the state.)

[9] K. Starmer, *European Human Rights Law* (1999), p.678, makes the important point that according to the ECmHR some employment by its very nature involves a degree of restriction on free speech. This is particularly so where the employment is in the civil service. cf. *Morissens v. Belgium* (1988) 56 D.R. 127.

[10] See, in particular, *Vereniging Rechtwinkel Utrecht v. The Netherlands* (1986) 46 D.R. 200 (contractual agreement); *Deweer* (1979-1980) 2 E.H.R.R. 439 (waiver of right of access to court in favour of arbitration). The President of the EAT (Mr Justice Lindsay) has (extra-judicially) apparently accepted that Convention rights can be waived: The Hon. Mr Justice Lindsay, "The Implied Duty of Trust and Confidence" [2001] I.L.J. 1, 10.

[11] Kahn-Freund, *Labour and the Law* (2nd ed., 1977), p.6. G. Morris, "Fundamental Rights: Exclusion by Agreement?" [2001] I.L.J. 49.

workers. Under the civilian legal tradition such workers are usually differentiated from private sector workers employed under contract. According to one view, where public employment was seen as governed by the exercise of discretion, it was seen by the ECtHR as not subject to Article 6, but where it was classed as falling under the performance of a statutory obligation, the Article did apply.[12] Persons who worked as state schoolteachers, judges, and as members of the police have all been found ineligible for the protection of Article 6 in disputes occurring with their employer,[13] and attempts by civil servants to challenge delays in dealing with employment disputes have also been blocked.[14] The special rules applicable to employment in the civil service were applied by the European Commission of Human Rights[15] to declare inadmissible a claim made by a British civil servant who had argued that the rules restricting discovery of documents for use before an industrial tribunal in connection with his unfair dismissal claim were in infringement of Article 6.[16]

Here again, however, the position appears to have changed somewhat in recent years, with the Court now taking a wider view of the scope of the Article.[17] It has now been held by the ECtHR that

8.02

"the only disputes excluded from the scope of Article 6.1 of the Convention are those raised by public servants whose duties typify the specific activities of the public service in so far as the latter is acting as the depositary of public authority responsible for protecting the general interests of the State or other public authorities. A manifest example of such activities is provided by the armed forces and the police."[18]

The ECtHR has come to accept that Article 6 affords equal treatment to public servants, irrespective of the domestic system of employment and in particular whether or not the employment relationship is seen as governed by contract.[19] Although doubt remains as to precisely which types of civil service employment falls within the exception relating to the protection of the general interests of the State, the *Pelegrin* and *Frydlender* decisions have established a new line of jurisdprudence, and generally extended the valuable protections offered by Article 6 to public sector employment.

---

[12] D.J. Harris, M. O'Boyle and C. Warbrick, *Law of the European Convention on Human Rights* (1995), p.182.
[13] *supra*, no. 4.
[14] *Neigel v. France* (1997) *Reports* 1997-II, p. 410.
[15] Hereinafter referred to as ECmHR.
[16] *Balfour v. U.K.*, Appl. No. 30976/96 [1997] E.H.R.L.R. 665.
[17] *Pellegrin v. France* [GC], no. 28541/95, ECHR 1999; *Frydlender v. France*, no. 30979/96, ECHR 2000.
[18] *Frydlender v. France* at para.33.
[19] *ibid.*, para. 31.

The ECtHR has also in the past expressed the view that the right of access to the civil service is an area falling outwith the scope of protection under the Convention.[20] That much remains so, there being no right of access to private sector employment either. In this respect the public sector employee (strictly, would-be employee) is no worse placed than his private sector counterpart.[21]

Again, Article 10, protecting freedom of expression, has in the past given little support to employees who speak out contrary to the instructions of their employer. As one commentator[22] notes, "Where contractually a person is bound by reasonable terms of confidentiality or loyalty, measures to suspend or dismiss for breach have generally been compatible [with Art 10]". The decision of the Court in *Vogt v. Germany*[23] is seen as a movement away from the narrowness of its earlier position, but this shows no more than a majority view of the ECtHR that the dismissal of a civil servant for taking part in Communist Party activities infringed rights protected under Article 10. It did so because it was a sanction disproportionately severe. The Court did not go so far as to say that the imposition of a disciplinary sanction in these circumstances was in itself objectionable.

Collective matters

8.03   So far as the United Kingdom is concerned, the record of the decision-taking bodies in collective matters is no more encouraging than it is in relation to the protection of individual rights.[24] The ECtHR (and also the European Commission of Human Rights, in its decisions on the admissibility of complaints lodged) has been reluctant to endorse effective rights to enforce collective bargaining as falling within the scope of Article 10 and Article 11 (which guarantees freedom of association). Indeed, there is no right to participate in collective bargaining as such.[25] There is no right for a union to refuse to disclose information which would allow an

---

[20] *Glasenapp v. Germany,* judgment of August 28, 1986 (1987) 9 E.H.R.R. 25; *Kosiek v. Germany* Judgement of 28 August 1986, (1987) 9 EHRR 328. See G. Morris, "The European Convention on Human Rights and Employmet: To Which Acts Does it Apply?" [1999] EHRLR, Issue 5, 496, at 497-9.

[21] Given the size and functions of the civil service, it is hard to see why, if access to such an employer is held not to be protected, access to a post offered by any employer in the private sector should be treated differently.

[22] K. Reid, *A Practioner's Guide to the European Convention of Human Rights* (1998) p.243.

[23] (1995) 21 E.H.R.R. 205.

[24] For a useful discussion of the general approach, with particular reference to freedom of association, see *Harvey on Industrial Relations,* paras N[1624]–[1638].

[25] *National Union of Belgian Police v. Belgium* A/9, Decision April 12, 1975, Judgment October 27, 1975 (1979–80) 1 E.H.R.R. 578; *Swedish Engine Drivers' Union v. Sweden* (1976) 1 E.H.R.R. 617.

employer to identify trade union members in advance of a strike.[26] Control of the political activities of certain categories of local government officials has been held not to infringe the right to freedom of expression protected under art 10.[27] The Court (in a jurisprudence which has been characterised as "minimalist"[28] has refused to read into the right of freedom of association right to union recognition, and has said that the essential right guaranteed by Article 11 to unions is no more than the right to be heard (in some unspecified way) by employers. Whether the right to strike in some form is indeed guaranteed by Article 11 remains a moot point, but, to the extent that this is so, the State may limit the exercise of this right to specified circumstances.[29] The Court of Appeal has said, with reference to Article 11(1) and *National Union of Belgian Police*,[30] that "Contracting States must permit and make it possible for a trade union to take action for the protection of its members' interests. That is as far as the authorities go in recognising a right to strike."[31] Probably the most famous incursion of the ECtHR into the realm of industrial relations has, for United Kingdom observers, been the decision in *Young, James and Webster v. United Kingdom*,[32] where a divided Court awarded substantial compensation to workers who lost their jobs with British Rail because of their refusal to accept a closed shop that had been introduced by their employer after they had been engaged. More recently, workers employed at GCHQ, who were deprived of their right to union membership by government order found that their complaints under Article 11 (in respect of denial of freedom of association) were declared inadmissible because of the nature of the work they did.[33] Attempts to challenge the strike balloting provisions of Trade Union and Labour Relations (Consolidation) Act 1992 have also failed at the stage of admissibility.[34]

Fairness in dispute handling

The use of Article 6(1) to guarantee fairness in disciplinary procedures between worker and employer is not straightforward.   8.04

---

[26] *NATFHE v. U.K.* (1998) 25 E.H.R.R. CD 122. (unsuccessful challenge made to the requirements of Trade Union and Labour Relations (Consolidation) Act 1992, s.22A).

[27] *Ahmed v. U.K.* [1999] I.R.L.R. 188, ECHR.

[28] see J. Hendy, "The Human Rights Act, Article 11, and the Right to Strike" (1998) E.H.R.L.R. 582 at 584.

[29] *Schmidt and Dahlstrom v. Sweden* (1976) 1 E.H.R.R. 632 at 644, para.36.

[30] *supra,* no. 23.

[31] *National Union of Rail, Maritime and Transport Workers v. London Underground Ltd,* February 16, 2001, C.A., *per* Robert Walker L.J. at para.61.

[32] [1982] 4 E.H.R.R. 38.

[33] *Council for Civil Service Unions v. U.K.* (1988) 10 E.H.R.R. 269.

[34] *National Association of Teachers in Further and Higher Education v. U.K.,* admissibility decision of April 16, 1998, noted [1998] E.H.R.R. 773.

On the one hand, the ECtHR has said that a dispute relating to the suspension of an employer from his job with a private sector employer is a dispute about private law relations between employer and employee. Thus it is a "civil" dispute which brings it within the scope of Article 6(1).[35] But this does not mean that an individual will be able to challenge the conduct of internal disciplinary procedures operated by his employer. For Article 6 to be engaged, there has to be a process which constitutes "the determination of ... civil rights and obligations" and internal procedures, even if they can result in the termination of the employment relationship, do not have such an effect. Where Article 6 has been successfully invoked before the ECtHR or ECmHR it has been to challenge dismissals which have subsequently been pursued in the courts. It is at that second stage that a "determination" of civil rights takes place. If the court (or tribunal) procedures do not themselves satisfy Article 6, the individual must have the right to challenge any sanction imposed by recourse to a court (or tribunal) which in its proceedings *does* satisfy the requirements of Article 6. It is not enough to have a right to appeal against a determination internally, or to a body which is not itself independent or otherwise functioning in accordance with Article 6.[36] Thus in *Obermeier* an appeal to a court which could only decide whether a disciplinary discretion had been exercised properly was held not enough to satisfy Article 6(1). Unreasonable delay in the conduct of proceedings will be enough to constitute breach of Article 6(1), and this may occur in an employment context. Nine years delay in issuing a final decision was held to constitute a breach in *Obermeier*, and a similar delay resulted in the same decision in *Darnell v. United Kingdom*.[37]

THE APPROACH OF THE UNITED KINGDOM COURTS

8.05　　The restraint shown by the Strasbourg institutions in applying the Convention to employment matters has until recently been evident also in the United Kingdom. Lord Denning M.R. famously expressed the view that Article 11(1), guaranteeing freedom of association, was part of law of England or at any rate the same as the law of England.[38] But these remarks were quite unrepresentative of any general endorsement by the superior courts. Other attempts to rely on the ECHR as a standard governing the exercise of judicial discretion in employment matters have generally been

[35] *Obermeier v. Austria* (1991) 13 E.H.R.R. 290.
[36] For these points, see, generally, *Tehrani (Petitioner)* January 25, 2001, (OH), *per* Lord Mackay of Drumadoon.
[37] (1993) 18 E.H.R.R. 205.
[38] *Cheall v. Association of Professional, Executive, Clerical and Computer Staff* [1982] I.R.L.R. 362, C.A., at para. 24; *UKAPE v. ACAS* [1979] I.R.L.R. 68 at p.72.

unsuccessful. Indeed, a somewhat oblique acceptance by Neill L.J. of the relevance of Article 10 in the exercise of judicial discretion in relation to the granting of injunctive relief against unlawful picketing[39] represents virtually the high water mark of judicial recognition of the relevance of the Convention in this area.[40] Nevertheless, the significance of the ECHR as an important aid in the interpretation of statute has become markedly more acknowledged in recent years.[41] In the week preceding the coming into force of the Human Rights Act the Strasbourg jurisprudence was used as the basis for a decision of fundamental importance in discrimination law. In a case dealing with the non-acceptance of homosexuals within the armed forces, the Employment Appeal Tribunal[42] in Scotland relied on the ECHR as the basis for extending the scope of the Sex Discrimination Act 1975 to cover discrimination on the ground of sexual orientation.[43] Lord Johnston was of the view that, having regard to the decisions of the ECtHR,[44] there was an ambiguity in that Act with regard to the meaning of "sex" and that this was to be resolved having regard to the acceptance by the ECtHR that, for the purposes of Article 8 and Article 14, "sex" extended to "sexual orientation". Thus the EAT held that discrimination on grounds of sexual orientation was, on a proper reading of the statute, prohibited alongside discrimination on the grounds of gender.[45] The Inner House has, however, held on appeal[45a] that the ECHR does not require the Sex Discrimination Act to be read in this way.

The new law

It is against this somewhat checkered background that one comes   8.06
to the task of assessing what the Human Rights Act 1998 may mean for employment law. Questions and doubts abound after the first few months of seeing the practical impact of the Act. Many issues of general importance remain undecided (such as the identification of what is a "public authority" for the purposes of the Act, and the extent to which the doctrine of "horizontal effect" will allow the application of Convention rights within the private sector). These impact on all aspects of the legal system, including those areas falling within the scope of employment law. Additionally, there is

---

[39] *Transport and General Workers' Union v. Middlebrook Mushrooms Ltd* [1993] I.R.L.R. 232, C.A.
[40] Though see also *R v. Ministry of Defence, ex p. Smith* [1996] 1 All E.R. 257.
[41] See, *e.g.* Lord Hope, *T, Petitioner* (1997) S.L.T. 724 at 733–4. *R v. DPP ex parte Kebeline* [1994] 4 All E.R. 801 at 838–9.
[42] Hereinafter referred to as EAT.
[43] *MacDonald v. Ministry of Defence*, EAT/121/00, September 25, 2000.
[44] In particular, *Smith and Grady v. U.K.* [1999] I.R.L.R. 734 and *Salguieiro da Silva Mouta v. Portugal* (Appl. No. 33290/96) December 29, 1999 (unreported to date).
[45] Another division of the EAT has since taken a different view: see *Gibson v. British Gas Energy Centres Ltd*, EAT, February 20, 2001.
[45a] *Advocate-General v. MacDonald*, June 1, 2001, unreported.

no shortage of employment-specific problems. For example, how and to what extent is the employment tribunal's task of assessing "reasonableness" in unfair dismissal law affected? Will an employment tribunal be concerned with whether an individual applicant who complains of infringement of Convention rights is acting out of step with his fellow employees?[46] How will damages under HRA section 8(3) be assessed when awarded to the employee or job applicant who is the victim of an unlawful act and brings proceedings under section 7? The wording of the section makes it clear that damages are to be regarded as an exceptional remedy, and the awarding court or tribunal is required to take into account a wide range of circumstances in reaching its assessment. Will the implied duty of mutual trust and confidence within the contract of employment be developed by the courts so as to encompass respect for the rights guaranteed by the Convention?[47] Perhaps most importantly of all, will the general obligation arising under HRA section 3 to interpret (so far as is possible) domestic law so as to bring it into conformity with the Convention mean that the Convention will become "pivotal"[48] in all employment cases where courts or tribunals are called upon to interpret statute or exercise a discretion?

Speaking in March 2001, the Lord Chancellor has stated that since the coming into force of the HRA, "There has been no significant impact on the length or complexity of hearings and no significant increase in outstanding cases at any level of the system".[49] That statement, made on the basis of Home Office statistics, is perhaps less convincing when looking at the Scottish experience of human rights to date. But whether the statement will in any event continue to be true for employment law cases is also debatable, especially in the light of developments which suggest that the constitution and functioning of employment tribunals may, by reference to Article 6, render them incompetent to deal with complaints which involve proceedings against the Crown.[50] In

---

[46] *Catamaran Cruisers Ltd v. Williams* [1994] I.R.L.R. 386, EAT.

[47] A question posed by B. Hepple, "Human Rights and Employment Law", *Amicus Curiae* (8 June 1998) 19 at 22.

[48] J. Wadham and H. Mountfield, *Blackstone's Guide to the Human Rights Act 1998* (1999), p.28. The principle contained in s.3 applies to an appeal heard on or after October 2, 2000, even though the appeal is against a court order made before the HRA came into force. See *J.A. Rye(Oxford) Ltd v. Graham*, February 6, 2001, Court of Appeal, approved and followed by the Inner House in *Advocate-General McDonald*, June 1, 2001, unreported.

[49] Evidence to the Joint Parliamentary Committee on Human Rights, March 19, 2001.

[50] See *Scanfuture U.K. Ltd v. Secretary of State for Department of Trade and Industry*, EAT, March 23, 2001. Applying the test of whether the "fairminded and informed observer" would on objective grounds conclude that there was a real possibility or a real danger that the Tribunal was biased, the Employment Tribunal could not be said to be independent and impartial in proceedings brought against the DTI by employees whose employer was insolvent.

Scotland, under the direct influence of the Convention, legal aid has now been selectively introduced to assist applicants before employment tribunals.[51] It is difficult to see why this change should not be generalised to cover proceedings in England and Wales as well.

The above list gives no more than a glimpse of the range of questions that may arise. Given the perceived significance of the HRA for constitutional law and civil liberties[52], it would certainly be surprising if employment law, which deals with the citizen in his or her capacity within the labour market, were to remain unaffected by a development of such importance.[53] There is no reason why the "permeating influence" of Convention rights[54] should not extend to employment law, in both its procedural and substantive aspects. Any debate as to the significance of the HRA within employment law will, of course, have to be located within the larger discussion as to the proper role of the HRA in the legal regulation of private law relationships.[55]

The duty to act in accordance with Convention rights

Under the new legislation there is an express duty on public authorities not to act in a way which is incompatible with Convention rights,[56] subject only to the qualification that they must if required to do so by primary legislation, or by the necessary interpretation of primary or secondary legislation.[57] This complements the general obligation imposed by HRA, section 3 to interpret and give effect to legislation in a way that is compatible with Convention rights. Failure by a public authority to act in compliance with the section 6 duty gives an individual "victim" a right of action.[58] Public sector employers, like the civil service and

8.07

---

[51] With effect from January 2001, publicly funded legal representation before Employment Tribunals in difficult and complex cases has been available to give assistance by way of representation. This is a category of advice and assistance under the Legal Aid (Scotland) Act 1986. The extension came in the light of claims that the failure to make legal assistance available for tribunal proceedings amounts to a violation of the right to a fair hearing under Art. 6(1) of the ECHR. See Advice and Assistance (Assistance by Way of Representation) (Scotland) Regulations 2001.

[52] Nothing less than "a new legal order". In the words of Lord Steyn, [1999] P.L. 55.

[53] As to the all-pervasiveness of Convention rights, see the remarks of the Lord Justice General in *H.M. Advocate v. David Shields Montgomery*, 2000 J.C. 111, HCJ at 117B.

[54] *H.M. Advocate v. David Shields Montgomery*, 2000 J.C. 111, HCJ *per* Lord Justice General Rodger at 117.

[55] But this cannot be explored here. See, for a concise summary of the different positions adopted and a conservative view of the likely impact of the new law Sir Richard Buxton, "The Human Rights Act and Private Law" (2000) 116 L.Q.R. 48. A. Bowen, "Fundamental Rights in Private Law" (2000) S.L.T. 157.

[56] HRA, s.6(1).

[57] HRA, s.6(2).

[58] HRA, s.7.

local authorities, falling within this description will thus have a particular concern with what is a new area of direct liability. For employers not in this category (or for quasi-public employers carrying out functions which are not deemed "public") the HRA will operate only indirectly. It will not provide a new cause of action for disappointed employees and prospective employees, or any new jurisdiction for employment tribunals, but it may allow tribunals and courts to rely on Convention rights in actions and claims (*e.g.* wrongful and unfair dismissal) which already exist.[59]

A number of bodies operating within the public sector may be unsure of their status under section 6 and the likely consequences if they are found to be subject to a section 6 duty. In particular, disciplinary committees concerned with the conduct of members within regulated professions (such as nursing or medicine) have the power to stop individuals found guilty of misconduct from practising as qualified members of that particular profession. The HRA has the highest importance for the disciplinary functions carried out by such bodies, for the sanction of removal form a register will very likely amount to a determination of civil rights and obligations, within the meaning of ECHR, Article 6(1). Does this therefore mean that such bodies must comply with the standards requiring impartiality and independence required by Article 6? The decision of Lord Mackay of Drumadoon in *Tehrani (Petitioner)*[60] offers both concern and comfort to disciplinary bodies faced with such a question. In the course of determining a petition for judicial review, Lord Mackay held that the activities of the UKCCN professional conduct committee (a disciplinary body exercising statutory powers giving it control over the conduct of registered nurses) did, by reason of its power to strike off nurses found guilty of misconduct from the register, give rise to an obligation to respect the requirements of independence and impartiality found in ECHR, Article 6(2). On the other hand, this did not mean that the committee had to show compliance with Article 6 requirements in everything it did at every stage of its proceedings. The argument that this was so because of the effect of HRA section 6 was rejected. It was enough, held Lord Mackay, if there was a right of appeal from a decision of the professional conduct committee to a court which itself was impartial and independent. The right of appeal that existed under section 12 of the Nurses, Midwives and Health Visitors Act 1997—which gave access to the Court of Session—was sufficient to show that the Article 6 requirement was met, even if individual aspects of the disciplinary process might be seen as falling short of what Article 6 required.

---

[59] For a useful general discussion see J. Cooper, "Horizontality: The Application of Human Rights Standards in Private Disputes" in *An Introduction to Human Rights and the Common Law* (English and Havers Q.C. ed., Hart Publishing, 2000), p.53.

[60] January 25, 2001, (OH).

The section 6 obligation also impacts substantially on the system of justice administered through the State, the courts (and employment tribunals) being themselves public authorities. There is an obligation to provide a system for the adjudication of complaints for civil disputes which, in particular, meets the procedural and substantive requirements of ECHR Article 6(1), and, as has been mentioned above, the system of employment tribunals and the EAT is vulnerable to attack by reason of the operational control exercised by the Department of Trade and Industry.[61]

Freedom of association

ECHR Article 11 protects "the right to freedom of peaceful assembly and to freedom of others, including the right to form and to join trade unions for the protection of his interests." By Article 11(2) any restrictions placed on the exercise of these rights must be prescribed by law and be necessary in a democratic society in the interests of national security or public safety, for the prevention of disorder or crime, for the protection of health or morals or for the protection of the rights and freedoms of others. There may be lawful restrictions on the exercise of these rights by members of the armed forces, of the police or of the administration of the State. The State is obliged to protect the exercise of Article 11 rights when these are placed in jeopardy by the acts of private individuals.[62]

8.08

From the comments already made, it will be appreciated that the protection of freedom of association under Article 11 is unlikely to be productive of any major changes in the law of collective labour relations, including the right to strike. Even apart from the specific qualifications relating to those working in the armed forces, police and administration of the State, Article 11 has been held to be fairly limited in scope, not applying to the freedom to participate in a profession.[63] Unlike the parallel protection given to freedom of association under Convention 98 of the International Labour Organisation, there is only a weak analysis of Article 11 to be found in the case law.

---

[61] *supra*, no. 44. See *Director General of Fair Trading v. Proprietary Association of Great Britain* December 21, 2000 the Court of Appeal stated that in the absence of actual bias, the test under Art. 6 of the Convention was whether the "fairminded and informed observer" would on objective grounds conclude that there was a real possibility or a real danger that a tribunal was biased. See now, for the application of Art. 6 to employment tribunals, *Scanfuture U.K. Ltd v. Secretary of State for the Department of Trade and Industry*, E.A.T., March 23, 2001, E.A.T./ 1353/99.

[62] *Young James and Webster*, ECHR Series A 44, para. 49.

[63] J.E.S. Fawcett, *The Application of the European Convention on Human Rights* (1987), p.284.

"Freedom of association is a general capacity for the citizen to join without interference by the State in associations in order to attain various ends. However, a right to the successful attainment of such ends is not guaranteed by Art 11."[64]

Not only does Article 11 stop short of guaranteeing a "right to strike" as such, but neither can it be used a basis for claiming the right to participate in collective bargaining.[65] As demonstrated in *Young James and Webster* (above) the Court has been as much concerned to protect the right to dissociate, (*i.e.* not to belong to a union) as the positive right to belong, although arguably there is no true equation between a right which guarantees a personal freedom and which is an essential underpinning of collective action.[66] That said, the Court has not always endorsed the position of the principled non-unionist. Mr Sibson, who, having left the union, had to move his place of employment because his fellow workers would no longer work with him had no right of complaint under Article 11.[67] Even is if expelled from his union a worker has little prospect of challenging that act by reference to Article 11, except where on the facts he can show the action causes him "exceptional hardship" or otherwise amounts to abuse of a dominant position.[68]

As a matter of principle, the act of an individual employee in taking part on strike action, whether in the form of an all-out stoppage or some lesser form of defective performance, such as a work to rule, is likely (absent any contrary provision in the contract of employment) to be held to be in breach of contract.[69] While it has been argued that the operation of that rule might itself be seen to an infringement of Article 11[70] there is no basis for such a radical interpretation to be found in the ECHR jurisprudence to date. Indeed the contrary is true; attempts to use Article 11 to establish the lawfulness of strike action have, as seen above, proved largely unsuccessful in Strasbourg. Since the strike is essentially a collective act, usually carried out at the behest of unions seeking to represent collectively the professional interests of their members, the extension of Article 11 in a way that would specifically legitimise action taken by employees *qua* individuals is, in many ways, much harder to justify. In any event, the recent introduction of new

---

[64] 6094/73 *Association X v. Sweden*, (Dec.), July 6, 1977, 9 D.R. 5, para.52.
[65] For a summary, see K.W.W. Wedderburn, "Freedom of Association or Right to Organise? The Common Law and International Sources" in *Selected Papers in Labour Law* (1991), pp 143–5.
[66] The ECtHR has expressly declined to say whether there is equality between the positive and negative rights under Art. 11—see *Gustaffson* (below), at para.45.
[67] *Sibson v. U.K.*, ECHR Series A 258-A (1993).
[68] *Cheall v. U.K.* [1985] 42 D.R. 178.
[69] *Secretary of State v. ASLEF (No.2)* [1972] 2 Q.B. 455, C.A.
[70] Hendy, op.cit., p.608. There is faint authority for the view that strikes lead to a suspension of contract rather than breach: *Simmons v. Hoover Ltd* [1977] I.C.R. 2, C.A.

protections (under the law of unfair dismissal) for employees who face disciplinary action because of taking part in industrial action[71] makes any challenge under this heading less likely to succeed.

Important new provisions on union recognition have been introduced by the Employment Relations Act 1999, following the White Paper *Fairness at Work* published in May 1998. These make provision for a statutory procedure to be used where voluntary negotiations fail, and give to workers protections against dismissal in connection with these procedures.[72] A possible outcome of the new procedures is not only that a request for recognition is rejected, but also that union recognition is awarded to one union in preference to another. If history is any guide,[73] those whose are disappointed, one way or the other, by the decisions of the Central Arbitration Committee under the new statutory procedures may well look to Art 11 as a means of challenge.[74] Employers too, of course, have rights, and it is to be expected that they will complain of infringement of their *negative* right to dissociate under Article 11 in circumstances where they are disadvantaged. In *Gustaffson v. Sweden*[75] such a complaint—in circumstances where an employer faced industrial action because of his refusal to participate directly or indirectly in collective bargaining—was held to be admissible. His case was that, on grounds of political and philosophical conviction, he chose not to subject himself and his employees to union corporatism, but elected to retain the personal character of the relationship between himself as employer and his employees. When it came before the Court, however, these arguments were rejected, mainly on the grounds that the union, by seeking to extend collective bargaining, was pursuing a legitimate objective. Where, however, a employer opposed to collective bargaining is subjected to industrial action motivated by concerns that are not legitimate, *e.g.* a wish to exact revenge on an employer because of previous differences or rivalry,[76] then there is no reason why *Gustoffson* could not be seen as distinguishable.

Whether, under United Kingdom law, allowing the linking of favourable terms and conditions of employment with the relinquishing of union membership is in breach of Article 11 is an issue which has been held admissible by the Commission in *Wilson, Palmer and Doolan v. United Kingdom.*[77] That application under the

---

71 Employment Rights Act 1999 s.16 and Sched. 5.
72 The protections for individual workers complement those already found in legislation —see Trade Union and Labour Relations (Consolidation) Act 1992, ss 146 and 15.
73 *cf. UKAPE v. ACAS* [1979] I.C.R. 303.
74 Additionally, of course, attempts may be made to rely on other provisions of the Convention, *e.g.* the procedural and substantive safeguards imposed with regard to the process of adjudication under Art. 6.
75 (1996) 22 E.H.R.R. 409.
76 *cf. Torquay Hotels v. Cousins* [1969] 1 All E.R. 522, C.A.
77 Applications 30668/96; 30671/96; 30678/96.

Convention arose out of the House of Lords judgment[78] ruling that no breach of the law occurred when the individuals were rewarded for agreeing to sign a "personal" contract and renounce collective bargaining. The United Kingdom Government, however, chose to make no observations when the matter came to the ECmHR on admissibility, so it would be wrong to infer eventual success from the fact that the applications succeeded in clearing the first hurdle in their paths. The Commission's view was only that the application raised complex issues of law and fact and were "not manifestly ill-founded." The decision of the Court is awaited.

Picketing and demonstrations

8.09   Whether other manifestations of collective action will be held protected by Articles 10 and 11 is also uncertain. It has been argued, for example, that the limitations imposed on peaceful picketing by such cases as *Piddington v. Bates*[79] are not compatible with Article 11.[80] While police intervention on the right to protest may be justified under Article 11(2), on the ground that it is necessary to protect the rights and freedoms of orders, it cannot be enough to show that the acts done to stop conduct which was seen, in the eyes of the policeman responsible, as a possible source of a breach of the peace. The test required under Scots law for breach of the peace is relatively easy to meet—there need only be conduct which "may reasonably be expected to cause any person to be alarmed, upset or annoyed or to provoke a disturbance of the peace".[81] It is suggested that the wide discretion which the present law gives to the police may have to be reviewed in the light of the incorporation of Article 11. In *Steel v. United Kingdom*[82] the ECtHR accepted (albeit in a non-industrial context) that the right to express opinion in the form of a peaceful public demonstration was protected under Article 10 and that control by the State in accordance with what was "necessary in a democractic society" should be by means which were proportionate to the end to be achieved. Such an approach does not fit easily with the view that the police have *carte blanche* to restrict conduct which they think may possibly give rise to some disturbance. Neither can the threat of trouble by counter-demonstrators justify suppression of the right of peaceful assembly. The State has an obligation to allow demonstrators to express their views free from the threat of physical violence by opponents. "In a democracy, the right to counter-

---

[78]   *Associated Newspapers Ltd v. Wilson; Associated British Ports v. Palmer* [1995] I.R.L.R. 258, H.L.
[79]   [1961] 1 W.L.R. 162.
[80]   O'Higgins, op.cit., p.582.
[81]   *Wilson v. Brown*, 1982 S.C.C.R. 49, *per* Lord Dunpark.
[82]   (1998) 28 E.H.R.R. 603.

demonstrate cannot extend to inhibiting the exercise of the right to demonstrate."[83] There is obviously a close link between the act of demonstrating and the purpose behind it. Picketing, whether or not in pursuance of industrial objectives, can also be seen as conduct protected within the scope of Article 10 (freedom of expression). This was implicitly acknowledged by Neill L.J. in *Middlebrook Mushrooms* (above). It may be that the link with Article 10 will be acknowledged as relevant to the considerations relevant when it comes to the granting or refusal of interim interdict to restrain picketing that is allegedly unlawful.[84] In connection with the freedom of the press, the link between the Convention and the granting of interim relief has already been identified: *Attorney-General v. Guardian Newspapers Ltd*.[85] Any future development of delictual liabilities by the judges must, it is submitted, take cognisance of Convention rights. It also follows that such rights could be used to limit the extension of liabilities already established in areas (such as picketing) where Convention rights are placed in issue. In some circumstances (*e.g.* the use of confidential information) the present law relating to the granting of interim interdict may even be affected, under reference to the right to freedom of expression.

Private life of employees— monitoring the workforce

It is probably in relation to the protection of privacy in employment that there are the highest expectations of the HRA, and this stems from the recent high-profile decisions of the ECtHR mentioned at the beginning of this chapter. The new law coincides with developments in technology which make it easier than ever before to know what others are thinking, doing, have done or are likely to do in the future. Issues such as remote monitoring of computer use, the use of closed-circuit television cameras, the taking of unauthorised photographs and the recording of telephone conversations (the list is not exhaustive) are all a familiar, if regrettable,   8.10

---

[83] *Plattform 'Artze fur des Lieben' v. Austria,* Series A 139 (1988), para. 32.
[84] Whether this should properly fall under the heading of 'balance of convenience' or otherwise is probably not important; cf. dicta of Lord Fraser in *(1) NWL Ltd v. Nelson and Laughton (2) NWL Ltd (plaintiffs/appellants) v. Woods* [1979] I.R.L.R. 478, H.L. at para. 40.
[85] [1987] 3 All E.R. 316, *per* Lord Bridge at 346. Note also that there is a specific requirement imposed on the granting of interim relief to restrain publication in the context of defamation. The HRA s.12(2) provides that such relief is not be granted before trial unless the court is satisfied that the applicant is likely to establish that publication should not be allowed. In other words, that the invocation of an Art. 10 right by the defender is unlikely to succeed. No such restriction on the grant of interim relief applies in the context of the labour injunction/interdict; logically, this must make it easier for a court to contemplate the granting of such a remedy on this basis.

part of ordinary life.[86] These phenomena cumulatively reduce the part of the citizen's life which can be called "private" and, importantly in this context, they can affect what goes on in the workplace as well as in the home, or on the streets. The principal Convention right (Article 8) gives to everyone "a right to respect for his private and family life, his home and his correspondence"[87] but other rights, particularly the rights of freedom of expression protected under Article 10, may also be engaged when there is intrusion on an individual's freedom of choice.

The right to enjoyment of a private life protected under Article 8 is not absolute in its nature. The other side to the protection of privacy is an unwarranted restriction on activities which may be in the general interest of society, *e.g.* investigative journalism, and it has been recognised by the ECtHR that balance between these competing objectives is inherent in the Convention.[88] An apparent breach of Article 8 will be justified if it can be shown (Article 8(2)) that it that it was done by a public authority in accordance with the law and is necessary in a democratic society in the interests of national, security, public safety or the economic well-being of the country, for the prevention of disorder or crime, for the protection of health or morals, or for the protection of the rights and freedoms of others.[89] The scope of that qualification is likely to be hotly contested as attempts to invoke the main protection in relation to workplace activities proliferate. It follows that not every instance of secret or unwanted surveillance of an employee will lead to a finding of an infringement of Article 8. The possibility of justification will always have to be considered alongside the infringing act itself, and courts and tribunals will have a wide discretion to hold that in individual circumstances what is allegedly an unlawful interference with privacy is not in breach of Article 8. Under this heading, a court or tribunal is likely to have to make judgements as to the adequacy (judged from the standpoint of "proportionality") of any reasons put forward by the employer by way of excusing intrusive conduct. Obviously, the more searching and intrusive the behaviour complained of, the more difficult it will be for the employer to

---

[86] It is reported (The Times, May 12, 1999) that the Data Protection Registrar plans to introduce a Code of Practice to limit workforce surveillance and genetic testing which cannot be justified on public or employee health and safety grounds. A draft Code of Practice has already been issued by her on the use of CCTV surveillance in public places.

[87] This Article entails, in some circumstances, a duty on the State not just to abstain from action but also to take positive action: see C. Warbrick, "The Structure of Article 8" [1998] E.H.R.L.R. 32; *X and Y v. The Netherlands* (1986) 26 E.H.R.R. 235.

[88] *Soering v. U.K.* (1989) 11 E.H.R.R. 439, para. 89.

[89] Particularly important is the phrase "necessary in a democratic society". The ECtHR has said that this "implies the existence of a 'pressing social need' " and has been prepared to apply a proportionality test to condemn a police search that was justified under domestic legal provisions: see *Niemitz v. Germany* (1993) 16 E.H.R.R. 97, at paras 69–78.

defend his actions, although there will be some situations where extensive background information on an employee or prospective employee is appropriate. An instance might be when a worker is being recruited to provide services to children or vulnerable persons, and it is essential that his or her background is fully investigated. Where it is claimed that an act is governed by national law and thus within the Article 8(2) exception, the Court will have to look at the detail of that law and to judge whether any exceptions or qualifications to it are such that regulation cannot be said to be "in accordance with the law" as Article 8(2) requires it must be.[90] The *Alison Halford* case, already mentioned, made clear the ECtHR's view that in some circumstances telephone calls made from business premises may be covered by the notions of "private life" and "correspondence" found within Article 8 and, in the light of this and earlier authority[91] some surveillance of employees at work is likely to be seen as an infringement of Article 8. This is most likely if no warning has been given or if the surveillance is carried out in secret. The prudent employer who is concerned with deterrence rather than detection will want to make sure he has informed his workforce in advance of any controls he undertakes, and, if possible, obtained their agreement to what he is doing.

While the types of behaviour that may be subject to control by reference to Article 8 have been the subject of considerable discussion, rather less attention has been paid to assessing the practical implications of breach. Suppose a situation in which a breach of Article 8 occurred, say as a result of a monitoring exercise by an employer, and that the breach was not excused under Article 8(2). To take a practical example, this might occur where a computer used by an employee at work was found, as a result of covert surveillance by the employer, to have been used to download material from the internet judged to be inappropriate or offensive. If dismissal resulted, it is not difficult to imagine a court or employment tribunal being called upon to take a view as to the relevance of Article 8 on the proceedings. If dismissal was summary and the employee sought damages for wrongful dismissal, then a question might be whether the misconduct should be categorised as gross misconduct. If the employer was a public authority and had acted in breach of Article 8 in obtaining the material to which objection was taken, should that factor affect how breach was classified? The argument that, in the example given, the employee's conduct should not be seen as "gross misconduct" is at its strongest

8.11

---

[90] *Kopp v. Switzerland*, 23224/94, March 25, 1998. In looking at the issue of justification in the jurisprudence of the ECtHR and the ECmHR, the doctrine of the 'margin of appreciation' is important. This is a recognition of the discretion accorded, at international level, to national courts.
[91] *Malone v. U.K.* (1985) 7 E.H.R.R. 14.

if the employee was in ignorance of what his employer was doing.[92] If the dismissal was challenged by the bringing of a complaint of unfair dismissal somewhat different considerations would arise. Would the employee's conduct be properly classed as a fair reason for dismissal?[93] or "some other substantial reason".[94] If neither, then the dismissal would automatically be unfair. It will be open to an applicant in such a situation to argue that the obligation on courts and tribunals to interpret (where they can) primary legislation in a way that is compatible with Convention rights[95] requires the Employment Rights Act 1996 to be read in this way. Even if that is not so and the behaviour could count as "conduct", so that dismissal is potentially fair, the test of reasonableness[96] would require the tribunal to look at the sanction of dismissal against all the circumstances of the case and to decide whether the employer acted reasonably or unreasonably in treating the conduct as a sufficient reason for dismissal. How, it will no doubt be argued, can it ever be "reasonable" for an employer to dismiss when he has acted in a way which infringes the Article 8 rights of his employee? A possible answer to this is that, if the employer in the disputed dismissal is not a "public authority",[97] then to make the concept of "reasonableness" under section 98(4) subject to Convention rights is to extend the horizontal effect of the HRA in a way that is unjustified. If however that is a good argument, we face the prospect of two significantly different standards of "reasonableness" being applied by the tribunals in unfair dismissals, depending on the status of the employer. It is difficult to see tribunals operating in such a schizophrenic manner, and certainly doubtful whether such a stance would win much public support.[98]

8.12   Additionally, it may be that the way in which investigations into an individual worker's private life is carried out constitutes breach of Article 8. In *Smith and Grady v. United Kingdom,*[99] for example, it was held by the Court that the way in which homosexuality in the armed forces was investigated by the service authorities constituted a breach of Article 8 rights. Thus it is not just a matter of looking to see whether the reason relied on by the employer breaches Article 8.

---

[92] Where it can be shown there is knowing consent, it may be argued there is little scope for Art. 8. cf. R. Booth, "General Common Law Claims and the Human Rights Act" in *An Introduction to Human Rights and the Common Law*, (R. English and P. Havers Q.C. eds., 2000), p.89 at 94.

[93] Employment Rights Act 1996, s.96(2)(b).

[94] s.98(1)(b)

[95] HRA, s.3(1).

[96] Employment Rights Act 1996, s.98(4).

[97] *i.e.* so that s.6(1) does not apply.

[98] Another argument which could be made against construing "reasonableness" as subject to Convention rights is that the new ACAS code on Disciplinary and Grievance Procedures (May 2000) makes no reference to the HRA or the ECHR. If there were to be major change in the content of the concept of reasonableness it might be expected that mention would be made of this here.

[99] [1999] I.R.L.R. 734, ECHR.

Also relevant is how any investigation into such matters is carried out. An example might be where an employer penalises staff who enter into a sexual relationship with each other. *Prima facie*, the imposing of sanctions for this type of conduct falls under the provision protecting the right to private life found in Article 8, and it is not lawful to impose sanctions because of this. It would thus appear to be unlawful for an employer to dismiss because of such considerations. But, separately, it could also be a breach of Article 8 if a (public authority) employer, in the course of and as part of his investigations, interrogated the persons involved in an oppressive or threatening way—and this would be so whether or not the actual outcome was dismissal.

There may also be occasions when it is necessary to evaluate the blameworthiness of the employee's conduct in relation to other parts of unfair dismissal law. For example, statute allows a reduction in the making of a compensatory award to the extent that is just and equitable "where the tribunal finds that the dismissal was to any extent caused or contributed to by any action of the complainant".[1] It would not be right to penalise under this provision someone who had done no more than exercise a protected right, however provocative or unacceptable this may have been to his employer.

Another potential breach of Article 8 exists when an employer seeks to gather health information about his employees without their agreement.[2] Given current concerns about genetic testing this is a matter of growing significance. In circumstances where such acts preceded the creation of an employment relationship, and led to a refusal of employment there is no obvious remedy. Where the act in question was that of a public authority, however, there would in principle be the possibility of bringing proceedings under HRA s.edition 7, before whichever court or tribunal is designated under Regulations as the appropriate forum for employment-related claims.

Security checks on employees may also amount to an interference with Article 8 rights, in circumstances where this involved the collection of excessive information about a person's private life.[3] By the same token there could be infringement of Article 8 if an employer were to use surveillance techniques and equipment (such as telephoto lenses) to test by reference to perceived activity whether or not alleged sickness absences are, in fact, genuine. It is difficult to know if this would be accepted by the courts, and, if so, where the dividing line between legitimate and illegitimate behaviour would be drawn. But, at the very least, it would appear

---

[1]   Employment Rights Act 1996, s.123(6).
[2]   *cf. Chare v. France,* No. 14461/88; 71 D.R. 141 at 155.
[3]   *cf. Leander v. Sweden* (1987) 9 E.H.R.R. 433 (police vetting of applicants for posts which are important for national security was a breach of Art. 8, but justified under the exception provided for acts "necessary in a democratic society").

to be competent for reference to the scope of Article 8 to be brought before a tribunal when the fairness of a dismissal in which reliance had been placed on such technology by an employer. As mentioned previously it is more difficult to envisage the control of such behaviour when it is used to deny access to employment, at least in circumstances when the body responsible cannot be categorised as a "public authority". In the special situation where employment is refused because the individual's name appears on a "blacklist" that refers to trade union membership or activities, a remedy is (prospectively) provided under section 3 of the Employment Relations Act 1999.[4] Where the "blacklist" is not union-related but refers instead to some other activity or quality judged undesirable, it may be that there will be no remedy for those who seek to work in the private sector.

Procedural implications for tribunals

8.13   Lastly, there is also a possible procedural implication for tribunals. Employment tribunals are not bound by the ordinary rules of evidence.[5] Would a tribunal be open to persuasion that evidence gathered by conduct amounting to an infringement of a Convention right should not be admissible in proceedings before it? Such an argument, if successful, could be the most effective deterrent to employers tempted to engage in surveillance techniques which subject employees and others behaviour that infringes their protected rights to privacy.[6] If the guidance given by the ECtHR on this point in relation to criminal trials is followed, then it would be appropriate, at the least, for the tribunal to consider whether the use of such evidence would go to substantive unfairness.[7] Thus, while breach of a Convention right would not automatically render evidence inadmissible, it could do so in an appropriate case.

Dismissal

8.14   The law of dismissal conventionally covers both unfair dismissal (Part 10 of the Employment Rights Act 1996) and the law of wrongful dismissal, *i.e.* dismissal which amounts to breach of contractual obligations (usually the obligation to give notice or pay in lieu) attendant upon an employer who unilaterally terminates an employment contract. The law of wrongful dismissal is primarily governed by the contract between the parties and its application in any given case is largely dictated by what the contract terms are and

---

4   Power is given to the Secretary of State to make regulations proscribing such behaviour; no regulations have to date been made.
5   W. Leslie, *Employment Tribunal Practice in Scotland*, (1998) para. 8.03.
6   Such an argument arose in the English criminal case of *Sultan Khan v. U.K.*
7   See, most recently, *Khan v. U.K.* (Appl. No. 35394/97), The Times, May 23, 2000, ECtHR.

how they should be construed.[8] In unfair dismissal, questions of contractual content and construction do not have the same pre-eminence. While the nature of the job and the scope of obligations voluntarily undertaken are important, they exist alongside standards which are objective and external to what the parties have themselves agreed. Dismissal is fair, according to Employment Rights Act, section 98(4) only if, being for a "fair" reason, it is in accordance with what is "just and equitable in all the circumstances".

The potential impact of Convention law on all this is controversial. Although it is most likely that questions will arise in relation to unfair dismissal, an impact on wrongful dismissal cannot be ruled out.

Wrongful dismissal

The question has already been put as to the extent, if any, to 8.15 which contractual provisions designed, or having the effect, of limiting specific rights guaranteed under the Convention may be open to attack. There is of course scope for judges holding unlawful agreements which are contrary to public policy. But does the Convention provide for any such argument? To take a hypothetical example, suppose the terms of an individual contract forbid, on pain of summary dismissal, any discussion of religious beliefs in the workplace. *Prima facie*, such a term would be a clear contravention of Articles 9 and 10 of the Convention, and could not (absent very special and unusual circumstances) be justified under Article 9(2) or Article 10(2). Would the provision be enforceable according to its terms, so that someone in breach might lawfully be summarily dismissed for gross misconduct?

There is scant backing in the authorities for any generalised attack on the doctrine of freedom of contract under the guise of protecting Convention rights. Indeed, as discussed earlier, it is the contrary view which finds greater support in the ECHR jurisprudence. In the *Sibson* decision, mentioned above, one of the reasons why the disaffected employee was unable successfully to invoke breach of Article 11 was because his employers, in seeking to move him to another depot, were doing no more than they were entitled to do under a mobility clause found in his contract. The ECtHR took the view that he had not been subjected to a compulsion that struck "at the very substance of the freedom of association guaranteed by Article 11"[9] and partly this was because his employers had the contractual right to require him to move. In *Ahmad v. United Kingdom*[10] (the case of the teacher who left his job because he was not permitted time off to attend a mosque) the fact

---

[8] See, *e.g. T and K Home Improvements Ltd v. Skilton* [2000] I.R.L.R. 595 CA.
[9] ECHR, Series A, 258-A, (1993), para.29.
[10] Appl. No. 8160/78, (1982) 4 E.H.R.R. 126.

that the employee had accepted, as part of his contract, an obligation to work certain hours was part of the reason why the Commission found no breach of his rights under Article 9(1) (right to freedom of thought, conscience and religion). And in *Morrissens v. Belgium*[11] a teacher was held, by entering the civil service, to have accepted that certain restrictions on freedom of expression were inherent in her duties. If this kind of analysis is applied to the right to freedom of expression under Article 10, one would expect that the employee who has agreed to limit or relinquish his freedom to express views would be bound by the terms of that agreement. Support for such a stand is to be found in the (non-employment) ruling of the Commission in *Vereniging Rechtswinkels Utrecht v. The Netherlands*.[12] But arguably there must be some limits to a doctrine potentially so destructive of fundamental rights. It seems that any such restriction must not go too far. It must not amount to compulsion which would strike at the very substance of the freedom of expression—see *Rommelfanger v. Federal Republic of Germany*.[13] There may therefore be scope for an adventurous court to distinguish between different instances of contractual provisions limiting behaviour otherwise protected under Article 10—and perhaps other Articles of the Convention as well. One basis for so doing would be to consider the content of the contractual restrictions against the nature of the job. A restriction which is linked to the type of job being done[14] is more likely to be upheld than one where no such link can be shown. Another factor might be the relative economic vulnerability of the individual concerned. Where the choice is in effect "accept this limitation or be unemployed" it is difficult to see in what meaningful sense a free choice by the employee has been made. Thus a restriction incorporated in the rules of profession and potentially restrictive of an individual's "right to work" would be more harshly judged than a restriction affecting work with a single employer. So also it would be relevant to know whether the nature of the employment itself imposed a duty not to discuss such matters, though it is surely hard to imagine a factual situation where simple discussion within the workplace (as opposed to vituperative comment expressed in public) could be so categorised.

---

[11] (1988) D.R. 56.

[12] Appl. No. 11308/84. (1986) 46 D.R. 200. Discussed by G. Morris, op. cit., pp. 501-2.

[13] Appl. No. 12242/86, (1989) 62 D.R. 151.

[14] *i.e.* as in *Rommelfanger*—doctor employed in a Catholic hospital—dismissed for speaking out in favour of abortion—no admissible case for infringement of Art. 10.

Contractual construction

Even though the presence of Convention rights may not entitle any   8.16
general overruling of contrary contractual terms, there is, before
reaching this stage, a need to ascertain the proper scope of such
terms. The use of the Convention as a guide towards contractual
construction raises different questions. The explicit duty placed on
courts by the HRA to give interpretations compatible with
Convention rights is limited to legislation,[15] but a similar issues
could arise with regard to the construction of a contractual
document. Suppose a situation arises where an employer's
contractual procedures could be read either as authorising or not
authorising acts which potentially intrude on private life, such as
extensive monitoring of performance. The provision is, in other
words, ambiguous.[16] A court which is called upon to interpret the
contract is in so doing obliged to act in a way which is compatible
with Convention rights, and it may take the view that it should
therefore favour the interpretation which least damages that right.
Arguably, a court should be reluctant to construe any contract so as
to bring about the denial to an employee of a protected right such
as the right to privacy or freedom of conscience. To say this is no
more than to recognise that "[t]he common law will be developed in
cases between private employers and employees so as to give effect
to Convention rights".[17] This view of the impact of the Convention
in dealings between private citizens is controversial, and runs
against the line taken in Parliament by the Lord Chancellor,
according to which the Convention has its origins in a desire to
protect people from the misuse of power by the State, rather than
from the actions of private individuals.[18] Whether the obligation
under section 3 would enable a court or tribunal to go even further,
and find a basis for a term implied by law within a contract of
employment by which the employee had the right to treatment in
accordance with Convention rights is a point that remains to be
debated.

Unfair dismissal

In relation to unfair dismissal, however, there may be greater   8.17
scope for arguing that the law should significantly change in

---

[15] HRA s.3(2).
[16] A common enough situation might be whether an individual previously involved
      in investigating an issue should, on a proper interpretation of the disciplinary
      rules, participate in the later adjudication.
[17] B. Hepple, op.cit., p.82. See also, as to the potential scope of the HRA on the
      common law, M. Hunt, "The 'Horizontal Effect' of the Human Rights Act"
      [1998] P.L. 423 at 439–440. and G. Morris, "The Human Rights Act and the
      Public/Private Divide in Employment Law" (1998) 27 I.L.J. 293 at 294.
[18] HL Deb., November 13 1997, cols. 1231-2.; see also the important reservations on
      the doctrine of indirect effect expressed by Lord Clyde and D. Edwards, *Judicial
      Review* (2000), para. 6.60.

response to the incorporation of Convention rights. In the first place, as mentioned earlier, dismissal law requires an employer, faced with a claim from an employee qualified to present a complaint to an employment tribunal, to show that the reason for dismissal is either one specifically classed as "fair" or "some other substantial reason of a kind such as to justify the dismissal of an employee holding the position which the employee held."[19] Whether the reason was a substantial one is for the tribunal to answer, using its common sense and experience, and its decision can only be attacked if it so obviously wrong that it must have misdirected itself.[20] But, were a tribunal to hold as "some other substantial reason" a reason which it saw as contravening a Convention-protected right, it is difficult to see how its decision could stand.

However pressing the circumstances, an employer could not, it is submitted, fairly dismiss on the ground, say, that his employee held particular religious or moral beliefs, any more than he could rely on a reason which constituted an act of sex, race or disability discrimination. The HRA is likely to render even more difficult the dilemma faced by schools, universities and like institutions when faced with staff who publicly disseminate ideas and policies abhorrent to sections of the community. On the other hand, a dismissal because of the way in which the employee chose to give effect to his religious or moral beliefs would not necessarily be protected in the same way. Dismissal for such a reason might be classed as not because of the rights protected under Article 9 or Article 10, but because of "conduct", "lack of judgment" or some other non-protected reason. What is likely to be crucial is how issues are categorised by the tribunal when they are confronted with a contested dismissal.[21] Those who wish to argue for an extensive scope for Convention-protected rights will no doubt seek to draw comfort from discrimination law decisions which show the courts prepared to take a broad view of what is protected behaviour.[22] But it is far from clear that the European case law supports, let alone requires, the same approach.[23] So one answer to the argument that a dismissal must be unfair because it infringes a Convention right is

---

[19] Employment Rights Act 1996, s.98(1)(b).

[20] *Priddle v. Dibble* [1978] I.C.R. 148.

[21] cf. *Obershlick v. Austria (No.2)*, judgment of the Court, July 1, 1997 (unreported). Discussed by Hepple, op.cit., p.91. Prosecution of a journalist who had insulted a politician was prosecution for what was categorised as a polemical critique (and so protected by Art. 10). It did not fall into the category of personal abuse. In *Stedman v. U.K.* (1997) 23 E.H.R.R. 168CD, the ECmHR referred to its earlier unpublished (Appl. No.24949/94, December 3, 1996) in which it held that a dismissal of State employee who refused to work after sunset on a Friday for religious reasons was not a dismissal for religious reasons but a dismissal because of refusal to respect his working hours.

[22] See, *e.g. O'Neill v. (1) Governors of St Thomas More RCVA Upper School (2) Bedfordshire County Council (Respondents)* [1996] I.R.L.R. 372, E.A.T.

[23] *Stedman* (above); *Konttinen v. Finland*, Appl. No. 24949/94, (1996) 87 D.R. 68.

likely to be that, on a proper consideration of the facts, it simply does not amount to infringement. Another answer may be to point to the fact that the principal rights (with the exception of the right to freedom of thought under Article 9(1)) are not unqualified under the terms of the Convention itself. So even though a dismissal may be for a reason which infringes the right to privacy, say, it is possible to maintain that the breach is justified because the special requirements set by Article 8(2) can be shown to have been met in the circumstances of the case.[24] An old illustration of the principle here is to be found in the analysis found in *Panesar v. The Nestle Co Ltd.*[25] Sikhs who challenged a rule forbidding the wearing of beards at work in a chocolate factory were unable to invoke Article 9(1), because the rule against beards, being for the protection of public health, fell within the exception allowed by Article 9(2). It must be open to a domestic court (or to the employment tribunal) to conclude, on sufficient evidence, that the circumstances for limiting the operation of the right in question are met, and thereby to excuse any apparent breach of the principal Convention right.

Section 98(4) and "reasonableness"

When it comes to a consideration of "reasonableness" under Employment Rights Act 1996 section 98(4), the same kind of questions may arise. It will again be necessary to identify a course of conduct as raising a Convention right, and for the tribunal to be satisfied that relevant, any limitation allowed for under that Article does not apply. That said, however, to what extent will a tribunal's discretion be curtailed by the Convention? As a tribunal is obliged to act in conformity with the requirements of the Convention, does this mean that the very concept of "reasonableness" itself will always have to be reconsidered in the light of the ECHR authorities? The question goes to the very root of unfair dismissal law, for reasonableness is the concept which underpins all dismissals outside the special category of those declared automatically unfair under statute. Traditionally, the concept of reasonableness, as developed through the cases, has[26] provided no more than a "derisory" protection for civil liberties. Rights (*e.g.* to freedom of speech, freedom conscious) which are accorded fundamental status under the ECHR are, in the pre-incorporation unfair dismissal law, no more than factors of indeterminate weight to be taken into account by a tribunal engaged in the balancing process between competing a variety interests which is the essence of reaching a decision under section 98(4). An early case, much

8.18

---

[24] *cf.*, with regard to Article 8 where a similar qualification exists: *R v. Chief Constable of North Wales Police ex p. AB* [1997] 4 All E.R. 691, C.A.

[25] [1980] I.R.L.R. 64, C.A.

[26] H. Collins, *Justice in Dismissal* (1992), p.185.

criticised but never formally overruled,[27] suggests that a failure by a tribunal even to refer to an individual's rights to personal privacy and choice of sexual orientation does not give grounds for appeal, should that person be dismissed on grounds of homosexuality. That, at least, must change.

While it is going too far to say that a tribunal will always have to find a dismissal unfair when it appears to contravene a Convention-protected right, it is very difficult how a failure to give proper consideration to the significance and proper scope of such a right can be excused. Thus, whether or not an applicant's case for unfair dismissal based on infringement of a Convention right succeeds or not, it will always be relevant for a tribunal to hear argument on the matter.

Dismissal and disciplinary acts by public authorities

8.19   The discussion so far has treated dismissal from an essentially private law point of view, and has suggested that the effect of the HRA should be to incline courts and tribunals in the exercise of their powers towards particular interpretations of either statutory provisions or terms within the contract of employment. There is, however, a further dimension to dismissal law, when what is in issue is dismissal from a body which is itself characterised as a public authority. Here it is not just a matter of interpretation of statute. An individual will have the specific right (under section 6(3)) not to have such a public authority act in a way that is incompatible with his Convention rights. If dismissed or disciplined in breach of such a right, he will be entitled to claim damages for the unlawful act in terms of sections 7 and 8, HRA. While the precise scope of "public authority" awaits clarification, it is clear that many public bodies, such as the civil service and local government will qualify. If such a body treats an employee in a way which is incompatible with a Convention right, the individual may seek a remedy in the court, so long as he can show he is a "victim".[28] This goes much further than the protection currently offered by judicial review, although there is certainly scope for overlap. It may be, for example, that an employee who is dismissed by a public body for misconduct for having expressed opinions in a way that his employer does not approve could successfully complain that the sanction is disproportionately severe (and therefore in breach of Article 10).[29] It does not follow that he could have the same success if, without reference to the HRA, he simply sought judicial review. The imposition of a disciplinary sanction which is held disproportionate by reference to

---

[27] *Saunders v. Scottish National Camps Association* [1981] I.R.L.R. 277, (IH).
[28] HRA, s.7(1).
[29] cf. A. Hooper, "Current Topic: The Impact of the Human Rights Act on Judicial Decision-Making" [1998] E.H.R.L.R. 676, at 684.

ECHR standards may not be so excessive as to be struck down as unlawful by reference to the *Wednesbury* standard.[30]

Dress and grooming codes

It has been held by the ECmHR that uniform requirements may, in some circumstances, constitute an infringement of an individual's rights under Article 8 and Article 10.[31] A negative uniform rule, where particular items of clothing or styles are not permitted, must be subject to the same scrutiny, and it is difficult to see why grooming codes, relating to personal appearance, should not also be in the same category. So an employer who insists that his female staff wear skirts, or that male staff do not wear beards, is potentially open to challenge. Where the employer is a public authority that challenge could be by way of a free-standing complaint brought by reference to section 6(1) of the HRA. In the case of private employer any challenge is likely to arise indirectly by reference to the principles of interpretation and the exercise of judicial discretion, as mentioned above.

8.20

In all cases, there is likely to be a justification defence put forward by the employer and in considering this a court will have regard to the degree of interference caused by the rule to which objection is taken, as well as to the reasons behind it; both will be relevant to any decision as to whether the proportionality requirement inherent in both Article 8(2) and Article 10(2) has been met. It may also be relevant that a restriction on an individual's chosen mode of appearance is of relatively minor importance, compared with, for example, a restriction on someone's entitlements or opportunities imposed by reason of their sexual preferences. In *Smith and Grady v. United Kingdom*,[32] for example, the Court emphasised the need for particularly serious reasons by way of justification in terms of Article 8(2) in a case where restrictions concerned a most intimate part of an individual's private life. It would appear to follow from that observation that a dress limitation would not attract a similar ranking, and should accordingly be easier to justify.

The standards imposed by pre-HRA employment law are somewhat less exacting. So far as sex discrimination law is concerned, it will not be easy to show that a rule which differentiated between standards required of the sexes actually amounts to discrimination between men and women on the ground of sex. Thus, *e.g.* in *Smith v. Safeway plc*[33] the Court of Appeal, dealing with a rule against long hair that applied only to men,

---

[30] See J. Wadham and H. Mountfield, *Blackstone's Guide to the Human Rights Act 1998* (1999), p.14.

[31] *Stevens v. U.K.* (1986) 46 D.R. 245 (school uniform rule held not unlawful).

[32] [1999] I.R.L.R. 734, ECHR.

[33] [1996] I.R.L.R. 456, C.A.

observed that a dress or grooming code which aims to achieve a conventional appearance will not be discriminatory, even although it requires different standards of men and women. One way of putting this to say that there is, in fact, no difference of substance, only of appearance. If there is no sex (or racial) discrimination in the standard imposed, then an individual who is refused employment will have no remedy. In *Burrett v. West Birmingham Health Authority*[34] it was held there was no sex discrimination when a nurse was disciplined for refusing to wear a cap—this was part of a uniform, and male nurses had also to comply with uniform requirements, albeit different. If non-compliance with the disputed standard is a relied on by the employer as the basis for dismissal, then the fairness of that dismissal must be judged by the usual tests. In the leading case of *Boychuck v. H J Symons Holdings Ltd*[35] it was said that a tribunal should take account of such factors as the reasons for the requirement, whether the requirements are spelled out in the contract, why the employee objected and how the employer enforces the standards on which he insists. Arguably, in the light of the protection offered by Articles 8 and 10, the employer who relies on justification will have to show more than would be enough to satisfy the test of reasonableness under ERA section 98(4) if the dismissal is to be held fair.

Interesting questions may be expected arise as to the extent to which individuals with unusual or eccentric dress preferences may be able to find protection under the HRA. Could, for example, a transvestite or fetishist argue that he has a right to wear particular clothes at work by reference to Articles 8 and/or 10? It is thought unlikely that any such argument would succeed. While those who wear clothes of the opposite sex as part of the process of undergoing a sex change enjoy protection against discrimination[36] there is no authority to support the argument that a requirement to wear the clothes conventional to one's sex while at work would infringe either the right to a private life or the right to freedom of expression. A prohibition on body piercing and visible tattoos is more questionable. Since a tattoo cannot be removed or changed in the way that clothes can be, a restriction on the wearing of one is much more of an intrusion into an individual's private life than the banning of the wearing of a particular item of clothing during working hours.[37]

---

[34] [1994] I.R.L.R. 7, EAT
[35] [1977] I.R.L.R. 395, EAT
[36] See the changes to the Sex Discrimination Act 1975 (as amended) made by the Sex Discrimination (Gender Reassignment) Regulations 1999, S.I. 1999 No. 1102.
[37] *cf.* the school uniform case (*Stevens v. U.K.* (1986) 46 D.R. 245) where a relevant factor in the ECmHR holding a complaint about a requirement to wear school uniform inadmissible under Art. 10 was the fact that children required to wear uniform were free to express themselves as they liked outside school hours.

Discrimination

The protection offered against discrimination by Article 14 is highly   8.21
qualified. There is no right to protection against discrimination as
such. What is protected is the right to enjoy the rights and freedoms
set forth in the Convention "without discrimination on any ground
such as sex, race, colour, language, religion, political or other
opinion, national or social origin, association with a national
minority, property, birth or other status." This is a right to non-
discrimination in relation to rights which fall within the ambit of
the Convention; in other words it protects individuals only in their
enjoyment of their Convention rights. Persons and bodies (such as
unions) within the employment field may thus only invoke Article
14 in circumstances where they can show differential treatment,
without justification, in relation to such rights. The chilling effect of
this limitation built into the scope of Article 14 is to some extent
mitigated by the open-ended nature of the grounds on which
discrimination is prohibited ("or other status") and by the
jurisprudence of the Court which indicates that indirect as well as
direct discrimination is proscribed.[38]

In relation to employment matters, one may therefore ask if there
are situations in which an individual (or body) is treated less
favourably in relation to the enjoyment of a relevant right, in
circumstances where there is no objective and rational justification
for such treatment. The test of justification requires both that there
is a legitimate reason for the treatment, and that there is
proportionality between the end sought and the means employed.
A primary concern, however, will be to establish that the cases
compared are in fact cases where like is being compared with
like—if this is not so, then no need to show justification arises for
the party against whom complaint is made.[39]

Article 14 is capable of applying even where there is no actual
breach of the Convention right in respect of which discrimination is
alleged, and it may be that in some circumstances the Article could
be used to widen the protections available to those who organise
and participate in certain forms of industrial action. Whilst strikes,
as such, have no obvious counterpart outside employment law,
industrial picketing does have a comparator in the form of peaceful
demonstration intended to show public protest in connection with
non-work issues.[40] To the extent that picketing, by imposing
controls on the number of pickets deemed appropriate and where
they may demonstrate, is subject to special limitations in the form
of Trade Union and Labour Relations (Consolidation) Act 1992
s.220 and the statutory Code of Practice on Picketing, it may be

---

[38] *Belgian Linguistics Case (No.2)* (1979-80) 1 E.H.R.R. 252, para.9.
[39] *Lindsay v. U.K.* (1986) 49 D.R. 181; *Nelson v. U.K.* (1986) 49 D.R. 170.
[40] See above, p.283.

possible to argue that there is unlawful discrimination.[41] The comparison would be with the lack of such controls on persons who protest in similar manner about, for example, environmental issues. Another possible use for Article 14 might be to extend or reinforce the present reach of the Sex Discrimination Act 1975. A number of possible examples of arguable cases can be given. In the first place, it has been noted that different dress or grooming codes for men and women are, under the existing case law, unlikely to be seen as amounting to unlawful discrimination under the SDA.[42] But could it be argued that their existence is separately unlawful under Article 14? If so then there would be a need to reinterpret the case law to bring domestic law into conformity with the Convention jurisprudence. Again, the imposition of different standards for male and female homosexuals in relation to job-seeking or terms of employment is likely to be contrary to Article 14, as well as contrary to the Sex Discrimination Act 1975. Though it would appear that the HRA does not require the Sex Discrimination Act 1995 itself in a way that renders unlawful discrimination on the ground of sexual orientation rather than gender.[42a]

The operation of courts, tribunals and other adjudicatory bodies

8.22   All courts and tribunals are public authorities within the meaning of section 6(1) HRA. Thus there is a general obligation on them to act in a way that is compatible with Convention rights, at first instance as well as at appeal. Particularly important is the right to a fair trial, as guaranteed by ECHR Article 6(1). Employment tribunals, the EAT, and all higher courts are subject to the section 6 and Article 6 duties. That means not only must their procedures be fair but also that the judges and members who sit in them must not, by reason of their system of appointment, be open to a reasonable suspicion of bias.[43] Other publicly-funded and appointed bodies charged with delivering reasoned decisions (such as the Central Arbitration Committee) are subject to the same fundamental duties. Bodies which operate under statutory powers to safeguard the public interest by regulating the right to enter or remain in a profession must probably also comply with Convention rights.[44] The disciplinary determinations of both the General Medical Council and the General Teaching Council (to take but two

---

[41] Compare, *e.g.* the arguments raised in *Christians against Racism and Fascism v. U.K.* (1980) 21 D.R. 138. Persons protesting against a ban on a proposed march maintained that other marches had not been regulated in similar fashion, and that consequently a violation of Art. 14 had occurred, having regard to the right of freedom of association protected under Art. 11.

[42] *Smith v. Safeway plc* [1996] I.R.L.R. 456, CA.

[42a] *Advocate-General v. MacDonald*, (IH) June 1, 2001; above, p.284 no.48.

[43] *Scanfuture U.K. Ltd v. Secretary of State for Department of Trade and Industry*, EAT, March 23, 2001. Above, note 61.

[44] *Konig v. Germany* (1978) 2 E.H.R.R. 170; *Wickramsinghe v. U.K.* [1998] E.H.R.L.R. 338.

examples) are properly seen as within the scope ECHR Article 6, at least when imposing penalties which remove the right of an individual to practise or work within the particular profession.[45]

When adjudication takes place not before a court of law or professional body, but within the framework of a public employer's own disciplinary procedures, then such a process may fall within the scope of at least some of the protections required by Article 6. However, it is unlikely that Article 6(1), which gives guarantees of impartiality and a fair trial, applies to what takes place at this first stage of proceedings. The requirement that there be a "determination of … civil rights and obligations" is not met when all that is being decided is the employer's own response to particular conduct. Even where the employer is a public body—and so subject to the general duty to act in accordance with Convention rights by reason of HRA, section 6—it is thought there is no requirement to meet the standards set by Article 6(1) in the operation of its internal disciplinary procedures.[46]

While in many cases persons who are dismissed will have the right to complain to an employment tribunal of unfair dismissal, this will not usually be so if they have less than a year's service with their employer. It is to be expected that the limitation on the right to complain will be attacked as contrary to ECHR Article 6. The argument will be that those who lack the service qualification are denied their right of access to an independent and impartial tribunal. But even if such an argument is accepted, it is unlikely to bring satisfaction to an individual applicant. Since the service requirement is set by primary legislation[47] it will not be open to tribunals (or any appellate court) to disregard it in a particular case. The most that could be achieved would be the making of a declaration of incompatibility under HRA section 4; whether this would result in legislative reform, and what content such reform might have, is a political rather than legal question.

A different point relates to the standard that will be applied by employment tribunals in hearing complaints of unfair dismissal. In the area of misconduct the relevance of the "band of reasonable responses" approach in the interpretation of Employment Rights Act 1996, section 98(4) has recently been reaffirmed by the Court of

---

[45] Whether Art. 6(1) applies may depend on the outcome of any disciplinary penalty imposed. In *X v. U.K.* (1984) 6 E.H.R.R. 583, the ECmHR held inadmissible a complaint by an English barrister who sought to challenge a reprimand imposed on him by the disciplinary tribunal of the Senate of the Inns of Court and the Bar for professional misconduct. In *Stefan v. U.K.* (1998) 25 E.H.R.R. CD 130, ECmHR was of the view that the Health Committee of the General Medical Council, in deciding whether or not a doctor was fit to practise, gave rise to a determination of civil rights and thus fell within Art. 6(1).

[46] *Terhani (Petitioner)* January 25, 2001. *C v. U.K.* (1987) 54 D.R. 162.

[47] Employment Rights Act 1996, s.108(1).

Appeal.[48] This means, broadly, that a tribunal faced with the task of assessing the fairness of a dismissal will look to see whether the employer has acted within a range of conduct seen as permissible, defined by reference to the standards expected of the 'reasonable' employer. It is definitely not for the tribunal to second-guess the decision that has been taken by the employer by substituting its judgement for that of the employer. Whether that standard of scrutiny will satisfy any requirement that there has to be a right of access to a body that is itself acting in full compliance with what is required in exercising its functions satisfies Article 6 is open to argument.[49] The decision of the employment tribunal is itself appealable to the Employment Appeal Tribunal on a point of law, and that further stage in the litigation must also be taken into account in considering compliance with Article 6.

Interesting questions may arise when a case which has been decided prior to the October 2, 2000 is heard on appeal after the implementation date of the HRA. It has been held[49a] that the appeal court by reason of section 3 should take account of arguments based on Convention rights even though these were not—and could not—have been advanced at the court or tribunal below. A related question is whether an appeal court should treat the operation of Convention rights in such a situation as *pars iudicis, i.e.* irrespective of any arguments to this effect being raised by the parties themselves.

The main elements required by Article 6(1) are well established The determination of civil rights and obligations must be achieved by a system which incorporates (a) an independent and fair tribunal; (b) a fair and public hearing; and (c) a hearing within a reasonable time.

Independent and fair tribunal

8.23   The need for an independent and fair tribunal calls into question the appointment and terms and service of those who sit as adjudicators in employment tribunals. While the use of temporary chairmen (and members) is not an issue,[50] the use of part-time appointments may be. The Inner House has taken the view that the use of part-time judges is not, *per se*, objectionable[51] and it is to be expected that following changes in the terms of appointment a

---

[48]   *Beedell v. West Ferry Printers Ltd* [2000] I.R.L.R. 650, EAT; *Foley v. Post Office; HSBC Bank plc (formerly Midland Bank plc) v. Madden,* The Times, August 17, 2000, C.A.

[49]   See, in particular, *Stefan v. U.K.* (1998) 25 E.H.R.R. CD 130.

[49a]   *J.A. Pye (Oxford) Ltd v. Graham,* CA, February, 6, 2001.

[50]   *cf. Starrs v. Ruxton,* 2000 S.L.T. 42.

[51]   *Clancy v. Caird,* 2000 S.L.T. 546.

similar view will be taken of part-time tribunal chairmen and lay members.[52]

Fair and public hearing

The concept of "fairness" in relation to a hearing raises a multitude of issues. In particular, the exclusion of evidence on security grounds may give rise to challenge. In *Balfour v. United Kingdom*[53] an attempt to challenge by reference to Article 6 a refusal to disclose information backed by public interest immunity certificates failed, but on grounds which are no longer apparently accepted by the ECtHR after *Pelegrin v. France*.[54] It is likely that the general discretion which tribunals have to decide on questions of procedure and the admissibility of evidence will have to be exercised in a way which respects Convention rights. This means that when disclosure is resisted, reference to ECHR rulings are likely to be relevant.

8.24

Should a tribunal otherwise decline to make available necessary services (such as a translator) to a party appearing before it, the requirement of fairness may well be found to be lacking.

The requirement found in Article 6(1) that there should be a "public hearing" and that "judgment shall be pronounced publicly" clearly militates against attempts to restrict the openness of proceedings when this is contrary to the wishes of the party who is entitled to seek and does seek the protection of the Article.[55] Sometimes, however, the contrary will be the case. A party may be actively discouraged from pursuing a complaint because of the fear of publicity that will attend a court hearing. This is particularly likely to happen in instances where an individual's right to privacy or to sexual orientation is directly or indirectly placed in issue. In the analogous situation that has arisen under the sex discrimination legislation, the EAT has held that, by reference to European law, it has a residual discretion to restrict the reporting of proceedings where to decline to do so would effectively deter an individual from pursuing an otherwise enforceable right.[56] A similar argument could certainly be made with reference to ECHR Article 6, although this provision does not have the same legal weight or

---

[52] The practice of appointing part-time chairmen for a period of one year has been changed in favour of three year appointments. See *Scanfuture U.K. Ltd v. Secretary of State for the Department of Trade and Industry*, March 23, 2001, E.A.T./1353/99.

[53] [1997] EHRLR 665

[54] *supra*, no. 17.

[55] There are only a limited number of grounds on which the press and public may be excluded from a trail—see Art. 6(1).

[56] *Chief Constable of the West Yorkshire Police v. A* [2000] I.R.L.R. 465, EAT. (EAT had a residual jurisdiction derived from the Equal Treatment Directive to make a restricted reporting order to cover proceedings before it).

effect as Article 6 of the Equal Treatment Directive, which is "directly effective" in proceedings against emanations of the State.

Delays in judgment

8.25 The point has already been made that lengthy delays in the determination of an issue falling within the scope of Article 6 may give rise to a breach of that article. In measuring the duration of proceedings it appears it is correct to look at the time span from the initiation of proceedings to the appeal decision which finally disposes of the matter.[57] Where a matter is referred from an appeal court back to the tribunal of first instance for rehearing, the scope for delay is greatly increased.

Legal aid

8.26 As mentioned earlier, in circumstances where applicants face particular difficulties in bringing claims to court, Article 6 may require legal aid to be available. This applies to employment law as much as to any other area of the law. The argument has been recognised as valid, in Scotland, to the extent that legal aid is now available, in complex cases and to a limited extent, to persons who complain to employment tribunals.[58]

CONCLUSION

8.27 The first few months of the Human Rights Act's operation has seen the beginnings of keen debate on implications for employment law. The foregoing discussion gives some indication of the potential for that debate continuing. But is all this change for the better? Whether the Human Rights Act 1998 will in time produce a "better" system of employment law depends on the values and judgments used in assessing the achievements of this branch of the law. Certainly it seems set to make employment law even more complex and, because of that, it will add to the expense of going to law. It is also likely to make even further inroads into "managerial prerogative", *i.e.* the doctrine by employers have employer the right to decide the conditions under which employment is to take place. In so doing it will take further a tendency which has been a feature of employment law over the last 30 years—a movement away from the crude certainties of the common law to a more balanced distribution of rights and responsibilities between the parties to the

---

[57] *Darnell v. U.K.* (1993) 18 E.H.R.R. 205.
[58] *supra*, p.284 no. 51.

employment relationship. One thing is certain; in a subject which has increasingly become governed by rules derived from legislation, the incorporation of the Convention places a new importance on interpretation. As such it places new responsibilities on judges at all levels, in employment tribunals as well as in courts, who have the task of identifying issues of Convention law when they arise and in deciding what the outcome of the new law should be.

CHAPTER 9

PUBLIC LAW

INTRODUCTION

The impact of Convention rights in the field of public law is not   9.01
easy to predict. This is partly because the term public law has no
defined meaning in Scots law. On one level it might be suggested
that Convention rights inevitably *always* raise issues of public law
as Convention law is, by its very nature, concerned primarily with
the relationship between the individual and the State.

Generations of Scots lawyers have however been taught that a
distinction can be drawn within the broad ambit of public law
between constitutional law and administrative law. As Professor
Mitchell observed whilst

> "it is impossible, with us, to divide administrative law from
> constitutional law...the only satisfactory division is to include
> within constitutional law major rules and broad principles, and
> to leave the detailed application of these rules to administrative
> law."[1]

It is not possible within the constraints of this chapter to give a
detailed account of the broad impact on constitutional law of
Convention rights even at the level of abstraction identified by
Professor Mitchell. The focus will be on that aspect of constitutional law which relates to the relationship between the citizen, the
courts and the state in light of Convention rights. To a great extent
some of these issues were examined in chapter 1, such as the
interpretative obligations on our courts under section 3 of the
Human Rights Act or section 101 of the Scotland Act[2] or the scope
of the declaration of incompatibility under section 4.The emphasis
in this chapter will be on this relationship in light of the *special
constitutional* dimension of Convention rights and judicial control
under the Scotland Act, although the position of the United
Kingdom Parliament as a public authority under the Human Rights
Act is also considered.

Administrative law might be defined as the law relating to the

---

[1]   J.D.B. Mitchell, *Constitutional Law*, (2nd ed., W. Green & Son Ltd, Edinburgh,
      1968), p.4.
[2]   See para.

administration of government, but that is in itself too wide, at least for the purposes of this chapter, as it could cover all the many and diverse substantive functions of government. If it is possible to isolate what is *pure* administrative law then the following might be a useful working definition:

> "Administrative law is the study of the rules and procedures that on the one hand serve to promote good administrative practices in governmental agencies, and on the other hand provide mechanisms of redress, judicial or otherwise, when grievances have arisen as a result of decisions or actions of government."[3]

Additional problems with definition

9.02   Even the foregoing definition might be too broad for the purposes of this chapter. The focus is on that part of administrative law which relates to *judicial control of administrative action* and the impact which Convention rights will have on this. Whilst the emphasis will be on the Human Rights Act (HRA), much of what is said will apply to judicial control under the Scotland Act (SA).

Whilst this inevitably emphasises the role of the courts in controlling administrative action on Convention grounds, the substance of what is to be understood by good administrative practice will also be affected by Convention rights whether by the impact of court rulings or perhaps just as significantly through internal methods of control and human rights auditing. We have already examined the general scope of sections 3 and 6 of the HRA and section 101 of the SA in Chapter 1.[4] In a very real sense these provisions are aimed just as much at administrators as well as the courts and tribunals who assess the legality of the decisions made by those administrators.[5] Equally, section 6 of the HRA is just as much about *prevention* of incompatible decisions through *proper* administrative practice as it is about *cure* for bad decisions when they reach the courts.

The Council of Europe has identified the link between good administrative practice and Convention rights. The link between these, and their relationship with the grounds of judicial control, is discussed above.[6]

Convention rights and other means of redress

9.03   Whilst the focus is on judicial resolution of grievances, other

---

[3] Jones and Thompson, Garner's *Administrative Law* (8th ed., 1996), p.4.
[4] See paras 1.10–1.14 and para.1.16.
[5] See para.9.25.
[6] At para.9.25.

administrative law mechanisms will also have to adapt to take account of Convention rights when addressing grievances. Some of these are informal such as internal mechanisms in both local and central government.[7]

More formal, are the Ombudsmen, the most significant being the new Scottish Parliamentary Commissioner for Administration.[8] Parliamentary Commissioner for Administration (Parliamentary Commissioner Act 1967) and the Commissioner for Local Administration in Scotland (Local Government (Scotland) Act 1975, Pt II). These will be public authorities for the purposes of section 6 of the HRA. It follows that these officials will require to construe their jurisdiction and powers in line with the Convention rights. Such bodies have already been subject to judicial review and review on Convention grounds would now seem open.[9]

There are other Ombudsmen and whilst some of these are likely to be obviously public, the nature of others and therefore their relationship with Convention rights is less certain.[10]

Finally other more formal means of control of administrative

---

[7] On the former, see, N. Lewis and P. Birkinshaw, "Taking Rights Seriously: A Study in Local Government Practice" in *Welfare Law and Policy* (1979); and on the latter, C. Harlow, "The MP's Complaints Service" (1990) 53 M.L.R. 22 and 149. For a survey of the issues in the wider public sector, see, M. Seneviratane and S. Cracknell, "Consumer Complaints in Public Sector Services" (1988) Public Administration 181. The system of review found in relation to Social Fund decision making is an example of *formal* internal review. See, Social Security Administration Act 1992 ss.12, 64–66, 78, 167–168 and see now Social Security Act 1998 ss.36–38. Insofar as Convention rights might be relevant to any decisions made, judicial review of decision making could have Convention content. Decisions are subject to judicial review: *Murray v. Social Fund Inspector*, 1996 S.L.T.38. Whether judicial review is always an adequate means of control raises other concerns—see para.9.31.)

[8] See SA s.91 and Scotland Act 1998 (Transitory and Transitional Provisions)(Complaints of Maladministration) Order 1999 (S.I.1999 No.1351) and for an account of jurisdiction and powers see S. Blair, *Scots Administrative Law Cases and Materials*, (1999, W.Green & Son Ltd, Edinburgh), paras 16–13 to 16–15, the (U.K.)

[9] On the Parliamentary Commissioner, *R v. Parliamentary Commissioner for Administration, ex parte Dyer* [1994] 1 All E.R. 375; *R v. Parliamentary Commissioner for Administration, ex parte Balchin* [1996] E.G.C.S. 166. The Scottish Parliamentary Commissioner would also be subject to judicial review. On local government *see R v. Local Commissioner for Administration for South, ex parte Eastleigh B.C.* [1988] 3 All E.R 151, *R v. Commissioner for Local Administration, ex parte Croydon LBC* [1989] 1 All E.R. 1033; *R v. Commissioner for Local Administration, ex parte H,* The Times, January 8, 1999; *R v. Local Commissioner for Administration, ex parte Liverpool C.C.*, The Times, March 3 2000.

[10] For an example of the former, see, Health Service Commissioner for Scotland - National Health Service (Scotland) Act 1972; Scottish Legal Services Ombudsman—Scottish Legal Services Ombudsman and Commissioner for Local Administration in Scotland Act 1997 and for the latter, see, *e.g.* the Banking Ombudsman and the Insurance Ombudsman which both rest on voluntary agreement and compare the Building Societies Ombudsman, partly based upon the Building Societies Act 1986. For a discussion of what is a public authority under the HRA see paras. 9.06–9.10.

action exist in the shape of tribunals and inquiries. They will require to consider Convention rights when dealing with the decisions of administrators which come before them *and* in how they go about their *own* decision making.[11]

Judicial Review and Convention Rights—General Issues

9.04   The effect of the HRA on administrative law and remedies is not easy to predict. This is a consequence of the scheme of the HRA which does not create any new means of litigating Convention rights, but which rather seeks to build upon pre-existing methods of asserting rights and challenging administrative decisions. Judicial review is therefore likely to emerge as a significant means of securing compliance with Convention rights.

The provisions of the Act, will however, change the judicial review process. Contrasting the traditional "legality based" approach with the new rights based approach, the Lord Chancellor observed:

> "The courts' decisions will be based on a more overtly principled, and perhaps moral basis. The court will look at the positive right. It will only accept an interference with that right where a justification, allowed under the Convention, is made out. The scrutiny will not be limited to seeing if the words of an exception can be satisfied. The court will need to be satisfied that the spirit of this exception is made out. It will need to be satisfied that the interference with the protected right is justified in the public interests in a free democratic society. Moreover, the courts will in this area have to apply the Convention principle of proportionality. This means the court will be looking substantively at that question. It will not be limited to a secondary review of the decision making process but at the primary question of the merits of the decision itself."[12]

The emphasis on judicial review as a significant means of ensuring compliance is not surprising. Convention rights help define the relationship between the individual and the State. The HRA (and the SA in relation to the Parliament and Executive) regulates how public authorities interact with those rights and will be particularly relevant as to how administrative discretion is exercised. Judicial review as it has been developed in the Scottish courts is similarly concerned with how the powers and discretion vested in our administrators are exercised[13] and has as its central feature the

---

[11] For discussion of the impact of Convention rights see para.9.29.

[12] (1998) P.L. 229.

[13] Although as we shall see it is not necessarily concerned with whether the administrator was a public body: see para.9.08.

judicial control of the wrongs committed by those administrators.

The growing scope of judicial review

Judicial review as a technical *term* connotes a particular form of procedure which is competent in the Court of Session only and which has as its aim the control of administrative action by ensuring that decision makers stay within the powers conferred upon them. 9.05

Whilst it is anticipated that many of the most significant challenges to administrative power on Convention grounds will be brought by that procedure and in that forum, judicial review in its *wider* sense as a distinct judicial *technique* involving particular *methods* of assessing the legality of administrative action may now have the potential of crossing over into *all forms* of judicial control of administrative action. This is because neither the HRA nor the SA provide any *special* mechanisms for resolving Convention based disputes arising in an administrative law context, nor is there any attempt to legislate for which parties and in which proceedings a Convention rights issue under the HRA or a devolution issue under the SA might arise. Whilst it is conceivable that the forum will often be judicial review in the Court of Session, that will not always be the case. The potential for judicial review as having this *broader* meaning has already been identified.[14] Convention issues and the legality of an act or omission of a public authority under the HRA or of the Scottish Executive or of legislation of the Scottish Parliament could be raised in the sheriff court in the course of a statutory appeal or as a defence to the enforcement of an administrative decision. Convention rights issues could arise in the course of the proceedings of administrative tribunals. Whether as a matter of practice such challenges will be taken outwith judicial review in the Court of Session is as we shall see, a different matter and it should not be forgotten that the monopoly of the Court of Session on the remedy of reduction has been expressly maintained.[15]

In substance what is being done in such a case is to rely upon breach of a Convention right as a new form of breach of a statutory duty which is implied into each and every exercise of administrative power, regardless of the form of that power. As a new form of "illegality" such a breach will have significance as a ground of review proper in formal judicial review proceedings[16] and as a basis for assessing the legality of administrative action in proceedings outwith that forum.

---

[14] See The Rt Hon. Lord Clyde and Denis J. Edwards, *Judicial Review*, (W. Green & Son Ltd, Edinburgh, 1999. Hereafter Clyde and Edwards at paras 1.14 and 7.03.
[15] See para.9.18.
[16] Although Convention rights may have impact on the other general grounds of review-see paras 9.29 to 9.54.

What is a public authority under the Human Rights Act?

9.06   Section 6(1) of the Act provides that "It is unlawful for a public authority to act in a way which is incompatible with a Convention right." An "act" includes "failure to act". This does *not* include a failure to propose legislation by the United Kingdom Parliament or a failure to make primary legislation.[17] Section 7(1) effectively extends the definition of "act" to include a proposed act. There is of course a defence where the authority is compelled to act in breach of Convention rights as a result of primary legislation or certain subordinate legislation.[18]

What is embraced in the idea of a public authority will be a key issue in determining the scope of judicial control. Public authority includes courts and tribunals[19] and "any person certain of whose functions are functions of a public nature."[20] Acts or failures to act by such an authority which are "private" are however excluded.[21] The cumulative effect of these provisions is to render unlawful the acts of obviously public bodies whether or not the "act" is private, but in the case of bodies which are only deemed public in terms of subsection (3)(b), private acts will not be subject to challenge.

It also follows for the purposes of this definition that the Scottish Parliament and Executive are public authorities,[22] but both Houses of the Westminster Parliament as well as persons "exercising functions in connection with proceedings" in that Parliament are excluded.[23]

A number of issues flow from this. These now fall to be examined.

The United Kingdom Parliament as a public authority

9.07   Whilst section 6(6) appears to exempt Parliamentary activity from the ambit of the Act, closer consideration of its terms suggests that there is scope for residual impact:

- The House of Lords in its judicial capacity is a public authority. This might extend to cover quasi-judicial functions such as the work of the Committee for Privileges.
- Much will depend on what is a "proceeding" in Parliament. It is for the courts to decide where the boundaries of Parliamentary

---

[17] s.6(6).
[18] See ss.6(2)(a), (b).
[19] s.6(3)(a).
[20] s.6(3)(b).
[21] s.6(5).
[22] See para.9.73.
[23] s.6(6).

privilege lie.[24] It is arguable that the absolute protection afforded to activities within the ambit of privilege might not be compatible with Convention rights where injury is caused to those outside Parliament.[25]

- Arguably the exclusion is confined to what happens in Parliament itself and would not impact on its relationships with its employees or with third parties outside of Parliament such as demonstrators.[26]
- The exclusion of the Houses of Parliament from the definition of public authority is limited to section 6. Whilst the legislative process is exempt from a Convention rights challenge, the Act has the potential to affect other activities.
- The provisions of section 10[27] may be subject to judicial review as may the obligation contained in section 19[28] to issue a statement of compatibility.[29]

Public authorities and judicial review—General Issues

Given the significant role of judicial review in protecting Convention rights it is perhaps appropriate to examine the scope of section 6 in light of our current understanding of the scope of judicial review. The emphasis is on review in the Court of Session, but much of the discussion will have relevance to other forms of judicial control. Specific procedural issues are dealt with later.[30]   9.08

Section 6 assumes that there are many *obvious* public authorities and that it should be relatively easy to determine if a body falls within that definition. Such bodies would include the Crown, central government, executive agencies, local government, prisons and the police.[31]

---

[24] *Stockdale v. Hansard* (1839) 9 A. & E. 1; *Clarke v. Bradlaugh* (1884) 12 Q.B.D. 271. For more recent definition of what is a "proceeding in Parliament", see *Rost v. Edwards* [1990] 2 Q.B. 460 and see *Prebble v. Television New Zealand Ltd* [1995] 1 A.C. 321; *Egan v. Willis* (1998) 73 A.L.J.R. 75 (HCA). For the position of the Scottish Parliament see para. 9.61.

[25] In *Prebble* it was held that a defence to a defamation claim fell to be dismissed as what was said in Parliament was absolutely privileged. It might be suggested that such a blanket exclusion is contrary to the right of access to the court secured by Art. 6(1). Such blanket rules have already fallen foul of the Convention: *Osman v. U.K.* (2000) 29 E.H.R.R.245. For defamation and the Scottish Parliament see para.9.61. In *Demicolo v. Malta* (1991) 14 E.H.R.R. 47, the Court rejected a claim that parliamentary privilege could be used to avoid the application of Art. 6 to proceedings for contempt of parliament.

[26] See *New Zealand Police v. Beggs,* 8 B.H.R.C.116.

[27] See para.1.14.

[28] See para.1.14.

[29] For discussion see *Clyde and Edwards* at paras 6.39 and 6.46.

[30] At paras 9.14–9.24.

[31] See generally the White Paper, *Rights Brought Home*, Cm 3782 (HMSO, 1997), para. 2.2. For the position of the Scottish Parliament and Executive see paras 9.59–9.72.

It will not always be such a simple task, but the effect of section 6(5) is that it that it becomes a necessary one. Whereas obvious public authorities will be subject to control in relation to all of their acts, whether "public" or "private" in nature, the same cannot be said for those bodies caught by section 6(3)(b). That is because as certain of their functions are of a public nature, their acts will be unlawful under section 6(1) *only* where the act is not private under section 6(5). The nature of the activity becomes crucial once the authority is concluded to be public, at least for some of its purposes.[32]

This test is similar to the test for competency in judicial review proceedings found in English case law starting with *O'Reilly v. Mackman*[33] where it was held that an element of public law was needed for judicial review to be competent. During debate the Home Secretary, Jack Straw, referring to English case law observed that "the most valuable asset we had to hand was jurisprudence relating to judicial review."[34]

The emphasis on the need for a public law element has been one that has not troubled Scots law of late. It has generally had less difficulty than English law with subjecting bodies which perform public functions to judicial review.[35] Apart from a brief period starting with *Tehrani v. Argyll and Clyde Health Board (No 2)*[36] the competence of judicial review being based on a public-private distinction has, arguably, never been Scots law. In that case a petition for judicial review of the decision of the Health Board to dismiss a surgeon was held to be incompetent as it disclosed no element of public law.[37]

The need for an element of public law as necessary to the competence of judicial review was rejected by the Inner House in

---

[32] For the explanation of the Lord Chancellor see *Hansard*, H.L. Vol. 583, col.811 (Nov 24 1997).

[33] [1983] 2 A.C. 237.

[34] See 314 HC Official Report (6th series) col. 409. In de Smith, Woolf and Jowell, *Judicial Review of Administrative Action*, (5th ed., 1995) the test was expressed in the following terms. There is a public law element where a body "seeks to achieve some collective benefit for the public or a section of the public and is accepted by the public or that section of the public as having authority to do so" p.167, at para. 3-024. See generally their survey of the case law at pp. 167–191, paras 3-024 to 3-066.

[35] But for a contrary view on the scope of judicial review in England see Lord Woolf, "Droit Public English Style" [1995] P.L. 57 at 63 *et seq*.

[36] 1989 S.C.302.

[37] For discussion of *Tehrani* and its progeny see Clyde and Edwards at para 8.27 to 8.36; Lord Clyde, "The nature of the Supervisory Jurisdiction and the Public/ Private Distinction in Scots Administrative Law" in *Edinburgh Essays in Public Law* (W. Finnie, C.M.G. Himsworth and N.Walker, ed., E.U.P, Edinburgh, 1991); D. Edwards, "Administrative Law in Scotland: The Public /Private Law Distinction revisited" in *Constitutional Adjudication on EC and National Law: Essays for the Hon. Mr Justice T.F.O'Higgins* (Cuffin, D and O'Keefe, D., eds., Butterworths, 1992).

West v. Scottish Prison Service.[38] Here the well known tripartite test was stated as the basis of the exercise of supervisory jurisdiction. It was held that for a decision or act or omission to be amenable to judicial review there must be a conferment of a jurisdiction-a power to determine rights and obligations-by statute, agreement or other instrument by one person to another and which is to be exercised in relation to another. The status of the parties as public or private is not relevant. The decision or other measure which is to be reviewed must involve the *exercise* of a jurisdiction. It follows that as all decisions do not involve the exercise of a jurisdiction then not all decisions of a body, public or otherwise are reviewable. Any remedy must lie elsewhere. It follows that matters of pure contract are not amenable to judicial review.[39] The challenge by the petitioner to a decision of his employers not to meet removal costs was held not to involve the exercise of a jurisdiction, but was a matter of contract.[40]

At the same time there has continued to be a degree of scepticism as to whether *West* is the sole or true basis of judicial review and it has been suggested that the public or administrative nature of the body or of its functions are till important in deciding if judicial review is competent.[41]

Aidan O'Neill Q.C. summarises the position,

"in English law it might be said that it is the acts of public bodies using or abusing public law powers which can be subject to judicial review, in Scots law the question to be asked is not whose acts are subject to judicial review, but rather what kinds of acts are subject to judicial review".[42]

So whilst English law would prevent judicial review of a significant regulatory sporting body on the basis that its jurisdiction was based on contract, the same result would not necessarily follow in

---

[38] 1992 S.C. 385.

[39] See the Lord President (Hope) at 413.

[40] See also, *e.g .Blair v. Lochaber D.C.*, 1995 S.L.T. 407—decision of a local authority to suspend chief executive not reviewable as contractual matter only; *McIntosh v. Aberdeenshire Council*, 1998 S.C.L.R. 435—agreement between planning authority and developer; *Fraser v. Professional Golfers Association*, 1999 S.C.L.R. 1132—decision to refuse admission to PGA. *Tehrani* was treated in *West* as a contractual dispute.

[41] See for example *Blair*, above, where absence of an "administrative" element may have been a significant factor for the court. For a survey of the debate see C.M.G. Himsworth, "Public Employment, the Supervisory Jurisdiction and Points West" 1992 S.L.T.(News) 257; W. Wolffe, "The Scope of Judicial Review in Scots Law" [1992] P.L. 625; W. Finnie, "Triangles as Touchstones of Review" 1993 S.L.T. (News) 51; C.M.G. Himsworth, "Further West? More Geometry of Judicial Review" 1995 S.L.T. (News) 127; C.M.G. Himsworth, "Judicial Review in Scotland" in *Judicial Review: A Thematic Approach* (B. Hadfield, ed., 1995); Clyde and Edwards at paras 8.27 to 8.36; Stair Memorial Encyclopaedia, Vol 1, *Administatrative Law* (hereafter SME Vol 1), para. 115.

[42] A. O'Neill Q.C., *Judicial Review: A Practitioners Guide* (Butterworths, 1999) (hereafter O'Neill), at para. 1.29

Scotland.[43] Similarly the non-established churches are subject to judicial review.[44] This has not been found to be the case in England.[45] Bodies and persons as diverse as the Scottish Labour Party, The St Andrews Ambulance Association, a housing association, the Chief Constable, public trusts and arbiters have all been held amenable to judicial review. Provided the body or person was exercising an inferior or subordinate jurisdiction then the public or private character of the body *or* act was not relevant as to whether review was competent.[46]

Public authorities and judicial review—specific impact

9.09   One implication of the statutory test is that it might now be argued that to bring a judicial review on Convention grounds it will be necessary to show that the body or person whose decision is being challenged is public in the sense of section 6 *and* that it falls within *West*. This would be as a result of the Act not changing the scope of existing jurisdictions or remedies, but seeking to integrate challenges into existing procedure.[47] If *West* is not met then the remedy must lie elsewhere, such as in an appeal. Often there will be overlap as the exercise of a jurisdiction and the act or omission of a public authority will often be co-extensive. The public acts of public authorities will remain reviewable. However it does not follow that there will be no conflicts or that undesirable anomalies might not arise.

On this basis insofar as judicial review of an act, decision or measure of a public authority is sought on the basis of a Convention ground it will be necessary to demonstrate as a matter of *competency* that the authority is public. If it is not possible to show this then insofar as the petition is a Convention challenge, it will fall to be dismissed. If any non-Convention grounds remained,

---

[43]   See *R v. Disciplinary Committee of the Jockey Club, ex parte Aga Khan* [1993] 1 W.L.R. 909—review incompetent as powers were not "governmental" in nature and compare *St Johnstone F.C. Ltd v. Scottish Football Association*, 1965 S.L.T. 171.

[44]   See *MacDonald v. Burns* 1940 S.C. 376 (Scottish Catholic Church), *Brentnall v. Free Presbyterian Church*, 1986 S.L.T. 471.

[45]   *R v. Chief Rabbi of the United Hebrew Congregations of Great Britain and the Commonwealth, ex parte Wachmann* [1992] 1 W.L.R. 1036; *Ali v. Imam of Bury Park Jame Masjid, Luton*, May 12, 1993, unreported, CA,

[46]   See respectively *Brown v. Executive Committee of Edinburgh Labour Party*, 1995 S.L.T. 985; *McDonald v. Council of St Andrews Ambulance Association*, below; *Boyle v. Castlemilk East Housing Association*, 1998 S.L.T. 56; *Rooney v. Chief Constable Strathclyde Police*, 1997 S.C.L.R. 367; *D. & J. Nicol v. Dundee Harbour Trustees*, 1915 S.C. (H.L.) 7; *Forbes v. Underwood* (1886) 13 R. 465.

[47]   See s.7(1), (3) and (5) and s.9(1)(b) of the HRA which refer to judicial review as a legal proceeding in which Convention rights can be relied upon but which do not alter the substantive basis of the scope of judicial review. For discussion see paras 9.13–9.18.

the petition could proceed, provided that the body is *otherwise* subject to judicial review. Such an approach would however have the effect of fragmenting the operation of the grounds of control. It must be open to doubt whether such an effect was intended. This approach would introduce further complications into this area. It would be necessary to determine if *West* was met. It would then be necessary to go on to consider three further questions. The first is whether it is an obvious public authority. If it is, then all of its acts are subject to the Act. The second is if it is not such an authority, are the nature of certain of its functions public so as to make it a public authority in relation to those functions? Finally, if the authority is of the second kind, is the act in question private? If the answer to the last question is yes then the Act does not apply.

One approach might be that where judicial review is sought on Convention grounds it will be *sufficient* that the authority is public and it will not then be necessary to also consider if the *West* criteria are present. Whilst some might argue that this could only be the case in relation to the issue of the nature of the acts of some "public" bodies it may be difficult to resist the public-private distinction from re-emerging as the basis for judicial review in Convention cases where the character of the body in issue.[48]

Even without the potential for impact on the scope of judicial review in this sense, there will remain a number of implications in judicial review proceedings:

- Arbiters have been treated as subject to judicial review. However, arguably under section 6 they will not be treated as obviously public and may not be subject to Convention grounds in judicial review *unless* they are caught by section 6(3)(b) *and* the act is not otherwise private under section 6(5). The same might possibly be said of bodies such as the SFA, the non-established churches, significant voluntary associations such as the St Andrews Ambulance Association or political parties.

- Under *West* not all decisions of a body caught by the supervisory jurisdiction are amenable to judicial review. Employment decisions are not reviewable. What section 6 does by creating a distinction between obvious public authorities and others is to set up a regime in which *all* decisions of obvious public authorities are subject to Convention rights.

- This also means that where the body is public *only* by virtue of section 6(3)(b) the same activity, *e.g.* employment would not be subject to review on Convention grounds as the nature of the act may be classed as private under section 6(5).

- Conversely where there has been difficulty in "fitting" a decision maker into a *West* triangle, its public nature should now ensure that it is subject to review and dispel any doubts as to the competency of review. It follows that decisions made under the

---

[48] For further discussion of the possible impact on *West* see para. 9.12.

prerogative power will be subject to the Act.[49]
- It will be necessary to develop a test to determine if a body is obviously public. It follows that issues such as who set it up, who finances it, to whom it is accountable, and so on might be helpful but not conclusive .Such an approach has an objective quality but it could be both over and under inclusive. The smallest connection with government might make it public. Focussing on the function of the body might avoid form masking reality but may involve an assessment which is unduly subjective for ready judicial approval. Can it be readily maintained in Scotland today that the provision of health care or education is *always* a matter in the public realm?[50]
- Where the body is not obviously public, it will be necessary to determine if carries out "functions of a public nature". The further problem is that the acts of such a body are private then control on Convention grounds is not open. There is no easy way of making this assessment.[51]

Public authorities and judicial review—guidance from case law

9.10   Clearly given the terms of section 2 of the HRA[52] the Convention approach to what might be termed "public" will be significant. However the European Court of Human Rights has not generally approached issues in terms of a public/private distinction. This is because the starting point of its analysis is whether a breach can be linked to the State. This is because the combined effect of Articles 1 and 13 of the ECHR is to engage the State's responsibility, even if a "public" body is independent of government.[53] The distinction between public bodies, public functions and private acts is not central to the approach of the ECtHR.

The European Court of Justice and national courts have had to consider in community law context whether a body was "an

---

[49] Whilst it is arguable that prerogative power was reviewable as an exception to *West*, there should now be little doubt that review is competent. That is of course a different issue from whether the courts will continue to accord a wide degree of deference to certain prerogative powers. See for example the speech of Lord Fraser of Tullybelton in *CCSU v. Minister for the Civil Service* [1985] A.C. 374 at 3984–4000 and see Clyde and Edwards at paras 4.12 to 4.15 and 9.14. Convention rights must have the potential to limit such deference, but much may depend on whether the exercise of such powers will fall within any discretionary area of judgment on which see paras 9.55–9.58.
[50] See further Clyde and Edwards at para. 8.48 and see the discussion at para. 9.10 on the Strasbourg approach to what is public.
[51] See Clyde and Edwards at para. 6.49.
[52] See para.1.04.
[53] See, *e.g. Young, James and Webster v. U.K.* (1981) 4 E.H.R.R. 38 (Trade Union); *X v. Ireland* (1971) 14 Yearbook of ECHR 198; *Costello-Roberts v. U.K.* (1995) 19 E.H.R.R. 112 (independent school); *Osman v. U.K.* (2000) 29 E.H.R.R 245 (police).

emanation of the State". In *Foster v. British Gas*[54] the ECJ held that a nationalised industry was an emanation as was a police Chief Constable.[55] The governing body of a voluntary aided school has also been held to be an emanation of the State.[56]

In general terms a body will be an emanation if it has been made responsible by the State for providing a public service and for which it has special powers beyond those which would arise between individuals.[57] This is a working definition and is not exhaustive.[58]

Whilst under section 6 of the HRA the main difficulties will arise under section 6(3)(b), the wider scope for challenge to obvious public authorities might mean that the issue of proximity of the State as understood in EC law will have relevance.

We have already touched upon the use of an "element" of public law being the test in English law. One case is worth noting here which stresses the need to look at substance, not form. This is *R v. Panel on Takeovers and Mergers, ex parte Datafin*.[59] The issue was whether the Panel was sufficiently public to make it subject to judicial review. A number of factors were relevant in reaching the conclusion that it was. It was part of the governments' regulatory framework although not created by it, its decisions could impact on the rights of citizens, it was obliged to act judicially, and its powers were ultimately backed by the DTI. That its powers did not derive from statute or prerogative power could not be the sole test as to whether it was subject to judicial review.[60]

Commonwealth case law might be relevant. The Canadian Supreme Court has emphasised that in determining if a body is public of particular relevance are the extent to which it is controlled by government, whether it implements government policies, or is responsible for the exercise of statutory powers.[61] All of these will be relevant in considering the scope of sections 6(1) and 6(3)(b). New Zealand law is similar. American law might be of some use although the very different constitutional context should be borne in mind.[62]

---

[54] [1990]E.C.R. I-3133.
[55] *Johnston v. Chief Constable of the RUC* [1986] E.C.R. 1651.
[56] *NUT v .Governing body of St. Marys School* [1997] I.R.L.R. 242.
[57] *Foster* at para. 20.
[58] See Schiemann L.J. in *St Marys School* at 247-249.
[59] [1987] Q.B. 815.
[60] See in particular Lord Donaldson M.R. at 838 ;Lloyd L.J. at 847 and Nicholls L.J. at 852.
[61] See *Eldridge v. Att.-Gen. of British Columbia* [1997] 3 S.C.R. 624, especially La Forest J. at 659-662.
[62] For analysis of the position in New Zealand and America, see Clyde and Edwards at para.6.55.

Horizontal effect in judicial review

9.11   As Aidan O'Neill explained in chapter 1, the inclusion of courts and tribunals as public authorities has the potential to generate difficult issues, particularly as to the extent to which private acts may result in a violation of Convention rights. In the context of judicial review the concern would focus around the extent to which authorities other than obvious public authorities are subject to Convention rights in relation to their private acts. This will be relevant in judicial review insofar as any attempt is made to review such private acts on the basis of a breach of Convention rights. It remains to be seen whether and to what extent such effect is possible .

Convention rights and the decline of West?

9.12   Perhaps the one consequence that will have the most profound effect on the development of administrative law generally is the extent to which *West* will continue to be regarded as the basis for judicial review in Scots law. A number of commentators have expressed doubt as to whether it will be able to withstand the pressure of Convention rights. One,[63] has argued that the doubts first expressed in *Naik v. University of Stirling*[64] as to whether *West* requires the presence of a tripartite relationship in *all* applications to the supervisory jurisdiction will require to be re-evaluated in light of Convention rights.

The very wide definition of public authorities provided by the HRA does not sit easily with the tripartite test. Equally it might be argued that the need for our courts to make a public/private distinction once again when considering Convention rights issues may lead to a revival of the *Tehrani* test, even although the issue of competence (*West/Tehrani*) is logically and legally distinct from whether there are grounds of review.

Aidan O'Neill has observed that the courts in Scotland may require to adopt a functionalist approach and provided that there is a public body exercising a public function judicial review will be competent and in particular that:

> "It may be that the courts in Scotland will then adopt a more functionalist approach to questions of the limits of judicial review such that decisions of public bodies or bodies exercising a public function vis-à-vis the individual as a member of the general public will be accepted as amenable to judicial review, whether or not any tri-partite relationship can be discovered,

---

[63] K.J. Campbell, "Judicial Review: Time to go further 'West'?", 2000 Sc.Con & Admin Law and Practice 9.

[64] 1994 S.L.T. 449 at pp.451L-452A per Lord MacLean and developed by that judge in *McIntosh v. Aberdeenshire Council*, 1999 S.L.T. 93 at 97J

invented or imposed. The tri-partite test might be retained in the case of a body contracting with an individual, not as a member of the general public but rather as an equal contracting party, whether as an employee or as a commercial contractor. without the suitable tri-partite relationship in the contractual case, judicial review should not be found to be competent".[65]

Finally the view has been expressed that the new constitutional order of a Scottish Parliament and Executive subject to, amongst other things, Convention rights will

"significantly increase the calls upon the Court of Session to exercise its supervisory jurisdiction in relation to the proceedings, acts and omissions of that body (*the Parliament*) -it will be straining the tri-partite test if the only basis for the courts reviewing the activities of the Scottish Parliament is *qua* delegated parish council of the Westminster legislature."[66]

Additionally the development of a body of *European* administrative law, particularly, but not exclusively through the medium of the Strasbourg court will have a deepening effect on the development of individual rights as against public administration in national jurisdictions which might promote a "European" basis for judicial review.[67]

Convention rights and judicial control

Procedure and remedies

Under both the HRA and the SA there are a range of provisions which define the means by which Convention rights can be enforced in terms of both procedure and remedies. Whilst the primary focus is on the HRA, where particular provisions of the SA can usefully be considered alongside these then this has been done. Other, more distinctive aspects of the SA are dealt with separately.[68]

The provisions have been grouped as follows:

9.13

---

[65] O'Neill at para. 1.41.
[66] O'Neill, para. 1.40 and see Campbell at p.10; Lord Hope of Craighead, "Helping each other to make law" 1997 S.L.P.Q. 93 at 102. See also *Whaley v. Lord Watson of Invergowrie* 2000 S.C. 125.
[67] See Council of Europe, *The Administration and you: principles of administrative law concerning the relations between administrative authorities and private persons*, Strasbourg 1996; and O'Neill at para. 1.40. See generally, J. Schwarze, "Developing Principles of European administrative law" [1993] P.L. 229; "Towards a Common European Public Law" (1995)1 E.P.L 227. On one view the decision in *Osman* might be viewed as being in the vanguard of such a movement. However, the recent decision in *Z v. U.K.*, May 10, 2001, suggests that a more cautious approach than that in *Osman* will be followed in the future.
[68] See para. 9.74.

- The procedural route
- The timing of challenge
- The victim test
- Remedies
- Expenses

The Procedural Route: General Scope

9.14   Section 7(1)of the HRA is the main procedural provision. It is important to understand that this section does not seek to create new procedures .It builds upon existing means of judicial control. Section 11 makes this clear by providing that the HRA does not affect the right of a person to make a claim or to bring any proceedings which could be brought apart from its provisions. The section goes on to provide that a person can rely on a Convention right without prejudice to any right or freedom conferred on him or under any law having effect in any part of the United Kingdom. This will include any human rights recognised at common law[69] insofar as they are not now contained in a Convention right.

Equally where the right is found in international human rights treaties ratified by the United Kingdom but not transposed into domestic law,[70] these remain relevant in the interpretation of statute or possibly as a means of assessing the disproportionality of administrative action. Moreover insofar as the Scottish Executive and Parliament is concerned where the Secretary of State has reasonable grounds to believe that either of these bodies proposes to act in a way which is incompatible with international obligations then he may by order prevent such action.[71]

Additionally international human rights instruments have been used as guides to the interpretation of the provisions of the Convention.

One must therefore have regard to those existing forms of control to fully understand the impact of the Act. In Chapter 1 Aidan O'Neill sketched the broad framework. It is intended to develop that discussion in the context of public law.

---

[69] See, *e.g. McColl v. Strathcyde R.C.,* 1983 S.L.T. 616 at 623; *Leech v. Secretary of State for Scotland,* 1993 S.L.T. 365 and see generally W.I.R. Fraser, *Constitutional law* (2nd ed., Edinburgh, 1948), Pt VI; Mitchell, Chap.18.

[70] Such as the United Nations International Covenant on Civil and Political Rights 1966; the United Nations International Covenant on Economic, Social and Cultural Rights 1966, the United Nations Convention on the Elimination of all Forms of Discrimination against Women 1979, and the United Nations Convention on the Rights of the Child 1989. For an example of the use of such international sources see *H.M.Advocate v. DP and SM,* 2001 G.W.D. 7–255.

[71] SA s. 35(1)(a) (proposed bill in Parliament); s.58(1) (action by the Executive).

Existing Scope of Judicial Control of Administrative Action

In Scots law the formal position is of course that we do not have a   9.15
separate system of judicial control in public law matters. We do not
have special public law remedies like the English prerogative writs.
Whilst we have a special procedure for judicial review, the
supervisory jurisdiction which it circumscribes is, as we have seen,
not peculiarly concerned with "public law" issues.

In reality Scots law does provide a body of evidence which points
towards the existence of, if not a system, at least an array of courts,
tribunals and procedures and remedies all of which are, in varying
degrees concerned with the relationship of the citizen and the state
and of resolving the claims and disputes which can be the
consequence of that relationship.

There are many tribunals from which there is often an appeal,
typically on a point of law ,to the courts.[72] The sheriff has a
significant role and is often called upon to exercise an adjudicative
role in matters of local authority administration such as in
licensing, education and building legislation appeals.[73]

Equally the peculiar nature of certain issues arising from land use
has led to the growth in specialised forms of procedure, such as
statutory applications to quash in the Court of Session.[74] Another
basis for judicial control is the *nobile officium*. This has continuing
relevance in administrative law.[75]

Finally whilst our system of judicial review is not exclusively
concerned with disputes involving the citizen and state, the bulk of
cases dealt with under this procedure do have this relationship at
their core. Moreover even if the number of cases dealt with by the
Court of Session in the exercise of its supervisory jurisdiction is
small compared with those dealt with in other fora, its status as a
Supreme Court in *settling* the standards by which the legality of
administrative acts are to be measured ensures that it occupies a
dominant position.

---

[72] See s.11 Tribunals and Inquiries Act 1992.

[73] See Licensing (Scotland) Act 1976 s.39; Civic Government (Scotland) Act 1982
ss.76, 84, 106, 116; Education (Scotland) Act 1980 ss. 28F, 38, 65; Building
(Scotland) Act 1959 s.16. For other examples of the shrieval administrative law
jurisdiction see SME Vol 1 para.154. For general accounts of the role of the
sheriff in administrative law see C.M.G. Himsworth, "Scottish Local Authorities
and the Sheriff" 1984 J.R. 63 and G. Little, "Local Administration in Scotland:
the Role of the Sheriff" in *Edinburgh Essays in Public Law*.

[74] See ss. 238 and 239 of the Town and Country Planning (Scotland) Act 1997 and in
the context of compulsory purchase Acquisition of Land (Authorisation
Procedure)(Scotland) Act 1947, Sched. 1, paras 15, 16.

[75] See SME Vol 1 para. 148 and Clyde and Edwards at paras 3-01 to 3.17.

The Effect of Section 7

9.16   Section 7 is not peculiarly concerned with public law. It is a general
provision. To that extent it reflects what has been said about the
general means of judicial control already available. Even so it has a
number of features which are of particular significance to this area,
not least because of the potential for use in judicial review
proceedings. It is on judicial review in the Court of Session that
the discussion will have its primary focus. It must, however, be
borne in mind that much of what is said will apply with equal force
to tribunals, the sheriff court and specialised forms of appeal and
review.

From its terms it is apparent that there are two routes of
challenge. It can be done in the "appropriate court or tribunal" in
terms of subsection (1)(a) or a person may rely on Convention
rights in any legal proceedings.[76] Judicial review is included in
"proceedings".[77] Convention points can be raised on appeal even if
not raised at first instance, where the initial decision is said to be
incompatible with Convention rights.

In substantive terms it follows that Convention rights can be used
both in *attack* in pursuit of a claim and in *defence* by their use to
provide collateral challenge to the validity and therefore enforcement of administrative decisions and measures.

In relation to *attack* it is not possible to bring a claim in respect
of a breach of Convention rights arising from unlawful acts which
occurred before the Act came into force.[78] In relation to defence it
will be possible to rely on such acts where a person relies on a
Convention right in proceedings which are "brought by or at the
instigation of a public authority". The Convention right may be
relied upon by way of defence whenever the act of the public
authority took place.[79] This is the *only* time that the rights secured
by section 6(1) have retroactive effect.[80]

The appropriate court or tribunal will be determined in

---

[76] s.7(1)(b).
[77] Counterclaims, proceedings brought by or at the instigation of a public authority,
and appeals against the decision of a court or tribunal. ss.7(3), (4), (6) are also
included.
[78] s.22(4). Note however that in Scotland the rights have been in effect as against the
Scottish Executive and Parliament since May 20, 1999 and July 1, 1999
respectively. This suggests that any remedy in respect of their acts will require
to be sought in terms of the SA .See para.9.73.
[79] s.22(4)
[80] It may not always be easy to determine whether one is dealing with attack or
defence. For example is an appeal part of the same proceedings as those which
lead to the decision which is the subject of the appeal? For discussion of some of
the difficulties see *R v. Director of Public Prosecutions, ex p Kebilene* [1999] 4 All
E.R. 801at 850-859 *per* Lord Hobhouse of Woodborough. The indications so far
are that the courts will take an expansive view: *J.A. Pye (Oxford) Ltd v. Graham*,
February 13, 2001, Court of Appeal.

accordance with rules to be made by the Secretary of State.[81] Rules have already been made which confirm that it will be the courts and tribunals with pre-HRA jurisdiction in the subject matter of the dispute which will determine Convention points.[82]

Under section 7(11) the minister who has power to make rules in relation to a particular tribunal may, to the extent he considers it necessary to ensure that the tribunal can provide an appropriate remedy, by order add to the relief or remedy which the tribunal may grant, or the grounds on which it may grant them. This power is necessary as there are some tribunals (such as special adjudicators under the Asylum and Immigration Appeals Act 1993) which have a limited jurisdiction which would otherwise prevent them from considering Convention rights. The order making power is a short term measure until primary legislation can be amended.[83] Any order will be by way of statutory instrument and be subject to affirmative resolution procedure.[84]

Where a claim is brought under section 7(1)(a) it must be brought against the responsible authority. So if a claim is made that subordinate legislation made by the United Kingdom Government is unlawful on Convention grounds any action would need to be brought against the United Kingdom Government and not against any Scottish public authority which acts to "give effect or to enforce" the provisions.[85] It has been suggested that new forms of remedies might be developed to deal with such situations, including vicarious liability on the part of the Crown.[86] It may be that such liability would have to be resolved in a challenge under section 7(1)(b).

Where reliance is placed on section 7(1)(b) the proceedings can be proceedings brought by or at the instigation of a public authority or they may be an appeal against any decision of a court or tribunal. Challenge is not confined to these examples. Whilst it is conceivable that judicial review proceedings might included here, the inherent nature of judicial review as a *sword* rather than a *shield* makes it more likely that insofar as judicial review is used, it is likely to rest on section 7(1)(a).

---

[81] s.7(9)(b) and in relation to courts and tribunals in devolved areas, the Scottish Ministers.

[82] See The Human Rights Act 1998 (Jurisdiction)(Scotland) Rules (S.S.I.2000 No.301). The Court of Session retains its exclusive jurisdiction in relation to reduction: r.3.

[83] See 584 HL Official Report (5th series) cols 1360-1362 ; 314 HC Official Report (6th series) cols 1109-1111.

[84] s.20(1), (4).By way of comparison and as an argument to bridge any gap in remedial protection the Canadian Supreme Court has held that all statutory tribunals have *inherent* jurisdiction to determine challenges based upon their Charter of Rights and Freedoms: *Cuddy Chicks Ltd v. Ontario Labour Relations Board* [1991] 2 S.C.R. 5; *Tetreault-Gadoury v. Canada Employment and Immigration Commission* [1991] 2 S.C.R. 22.

[85] s.6(2)(b).

[86] See Clyde and Edwards at para. 6.66 and see *Simpson v. Att.-Gen. of New Zealand* [1994] 3 N.Z.L.R. 667. See para.9.22.

Specific Procedural Route: Judicial Review in the Court of Session

9.17   Judicial review in the Court of Session is of course not the only form of procedure where it will be possible to raise Convention rights in attack or defence. However it is not always easy to determine if the proper procedure is judicial review or some other route. This is further compounded due to the potential for collateral challenge in proceedings outwith judicial review.

Where a case is brought which *requires* the exercise of the supervisory jurisdiction it will be *necessary* to proceed by way of a petition for judicial review.[87] When judicial review is *required* is a difficult question. In the absence of special public law remedies, our remedies only give limited guidance.[88] Whilst breach of a Convention right will often suggest the use of the remedies of declarator and reduction these are not exclusive to judicial review and their use does not imply the exercise of the supervisory jurisdiction.[89] Conversely if the remedy touches on a matter which is truly involves the exercise of the supervisory jurisdiction then the proceedings are incompetent if not brought as by way of judicial review.[90]

Specialised forms of review cannot be brought by judicial review. One form of procedure which could conceivably involve Convention rights and which is specifically excluded from Chapter 58 procedure is the statutory form of review of the application to quash.[91] It will now be competent to raise Convention points in the course of such an application.

Similarly although it is generally accepted that petitions to the *nobile officium* are in substance an application to the supervisory jurisdiction, judicial review is not the correct procedure.[92] Where such a petition is made which involves Convention rights the procedure contained in the Rules of Court should be followed.[93]

The problem of whether and indeed if judicial review is necessary may be particularly relevant where the remedy sought is damages for breach of a Convention right. Rule 58.4 permits damages in judicial review and section 8 of the HRA allows damages to be awarded for breach of a Convention right.[94] On one view all claims for damages alleging breach of a Convention right by a public authority rests on an act or omission being *ultra vires* and so suggest

---

[87]   Under RCS 1994 Chapter 58. See generally *Clyde and Edwards* at paras 8.14–8.16; *SME* Vol 1 para. 116; *McDonald v. Secretary of State for Scotland*, 1996 S.C. 113; 1996 S.L.T. 575; *cf Tait v. Central Radio Taxis (Tollcross) Ltd*, 1989 S.C. 4; 1989 S.L.T. 217.

[88]   Remedies are discussed at paras 9.22–9.23.

[89]   See *Bell v. Fiddes*, 1996 S.L.T. 51.

[90]   *Sleigh v. Edinburgh D.C.*, 1988 S.L.T. 253 (petition for interdict).

[91]   The procedure is governed by RCS 1994, r.41.18.

[92]   See, *e.g H, Petrs*, 1997 S.L.T. 3; *Sloan, Petr* 1991 S.L.T. 527.

[93]   RCS 1994, r. 14.3 (d).

[94]   For s. 8 see para.1.27.

that judicial review be used. It is suggested that such a position is extreme and that the following propositions will assist in determining if judicial review is *necessary* where damages for breach of a Convention right are sought:

- If the *substantive essence* of the action is a claim for damages, any incidental need to determine an issue of *vires* does not mean that judicial review is appropriate or indeed competent.[95]
- Where the primary aim of the action is the *jurisdictional control* of the decision maker and damages are an incident of that process judicial review should be sought.[96]
- Where the only or principal remedy is damages then an ordinary action, not judicial review should be sought.[97]

Judicial Review in the Court of Session and collateral challenge

There is considerable scope for collateral challenge given the terms of section 7(1)(b). Scots law has always permitted the validity of acts and decisions to be resolved outwith judicial review. Statutory appeals under the provisions of the Town and Country Planning (Scotland) Act 1997 are an example of this.[98] Issues of *vires* may arise incidentally in the course of tribunal proceedings.[99]

9.18

Even in a statutory appeal from a tribunal the issue of whether a provision in regulations was *ultra vires* was held to be a ground of appeal as it raised an issue as to whether the decision was "erroneous in point of law".[1] Section 7(1)(b) is the statutory endorsement for reliance upon Convention rights in such administrative law proceedings. Similar issues could also arise in the following situations:

- Proceedings for the confirmation of a byelaw before the sheriff may require resolution of Convention issues as well as more usual issues of *vires*.[2]
- Proceedings to enforce an obligation arising from the exercise of statutory powers may be resisted on the ground that the act or decision giving rise to the obligation is *ultra vires* as being in breach of Convention rights.[3]

---

[95] *Tait v. Central Radio Taxis (Tollcross) Ltd*, 1989 S.L.T. 217.
[96] *Joobeen v. University of Stirling*, 1995 S.L.T. 120.
[97] *Shetland (1994) Ltd v. Secretary of State for Scotland*, 1996 S.L.T. 653 at 658.
[98] ss.238–239
[99] *Carr v. U.K. Central Council for Nursing Midwifery*, 1989 S.L.T.580—whether reasons required and whether adequate.
[1] *Chief Adjudication Officer v. Foster* [1993] A.C. 754 and for an earlier Scottish example, *Scottish Milk Marketing Board v. Ferrier*, 1936 S.C. (H.L.) 39. For further analysis of the relationship between statutory appeals and judicial review see *SME*, paras 337–344.
[2] See for example *Western Isles Islands Council v. Caledonian MacBrayne Ltd*,1990 S.L.T. (Sh.Ct.) 97.
[3] This can be done in the sheriff court or any other inferior court or tribunal and is not dependent on any appeal to the Court of Session provided it is raised in the

There may be an issue over the extent to which collateral challenge will in fact be discouraged and direct challenge by judicial review in the Court of Session required. The difficulty lies in the fact that it is not entirely clear if section 7 is to be taken to over-ride any existing limitations on the scope of collateral challenge and to prevent the development of new ones. It is clear that the routes provided by subsections (1)(a) and (1)(b) are alternatives, but where an attempt is made to rely on (1)(b) when there was an *opportunity* to mount a direct challenge under (1)(a), should those proceedings be sisted to allow such a challenge to be determined by judicial review? Even if not required a practice may develop of encouraging judicial review. Is it desirable for such a practice to develop? Similar problems might arise under the SA, particularly where an Act of the Parliament is challenged.

It is arguable that there are strong policy reasons why human rights should not be constrained by procedural considerations even if resting on practice rather than strict law. It might also be argued that the section does not preclude judicial review as it can be a relevant legal proceeding under subsection (1)(b). However the extent to which judicial review is likely to be the legal proceeding in a collateral situation is likely to be limited. It might also be argued that the whole tenor of recent English House of Lords decisions is against the need for separate judicial review proceedings where an issue of *vires* is raised as a defence.[4]

However, it is arguable that where there are reasons of administrative convenience, legal uncertainty and reliance by others on the impugned decision then judicial review should be sought with the decision maker being called as respondent. This will be particularly so where the measure is in form or substance, "legislative".[5]

It may be some time before clear guidance emerges from the Courts as to how this problem will be resolved. Perhaps the key lies with a proper understanding of the *remedial* scope of judicial review.

Arguably on analogy with the position in ordinary pre-Convention judicial review, the underlying rationale for the use of

pleadings: *Malloch v. Aberdeen Corporation,* 1971 S.C. (H.L.); *SSEB v. Elder,* 1978 S.C. 132. Where however the challenge is a *direct* one to the *vires* of the act or decision, whether in form or substance, then judicial review must be sought. See Clyde and Edwards at paras 1.07. and 8.15 and consider *Brown v. Hamilton D.C.,* 1983 S.C.(H.L.) 1; *McDonald v. Secretary of State for Scotland (No.2),* 1996 S.L.T. 575.

4   For a review of these see Clyde and Edwards at para. 8.16 and see in particular *Boddington v. British Transport Police* [1999] 2 A.C. 143.

5   See Clyde and Edwards at para. 1.07 and *Stornoway Town Council v. MacDonald* 1971 S.C. 78 *per* Lord Kissen at pp.84–85 and compare *Magistrates and Town Council of the City of Edinburgh v. Paterson* (1880) 8 R. 197. For the position in criminal law see Clyde and Edwards at para 1.08.

judicial review is based upon the inability of courts other than the Court of Session to instruct a public authority as to what the law of the Convention requires, quash or reduce decisions which are in breach of Convention rights or stop it from taking action beyond the powers allowed by the Convention. If those elements are in substance absent from a collateral challenge then judicial review in the Court of Session will not be necessary.

Judicial review in the Court of Session—residual issues

There may be a number of further consequences which flow from the fact that in exercising the supervisory jurisdiction the Court of Session is itself a public authority for the purposes of the HRA:

- The question as to whether a petition for judicial review should be refused because of a failure to exhaust an alternative remedy may require consideration as to whether that remedy of itself meets Convention rights, *e.g.* is an alternative tribunal "independent and impartial "in terms of Article 6.[6] Reliance on affidavit evidence and the pleadings may have to be reconsidered where the petitioner disputes the underlying facts of a judicial review which involves "civil rights and obligations" or a "criminal charge".[7]
- Arguably the necessity for there to be a decision which is dispositive of legal rights or expectations as a pre-requisite of competency may require to be re-assessed.[8]
- Although there is no requirement for leave, it is possible for the Court to dismiss a petition at first order stage.[9] In principle such an approach is consistent with the Convention.

The timing of challenge

Proceedings under section 7(1)(a) must be brought before the end of one year from the date on which the act complained of took place. The period may be extended to such longer period as the court or tribunal considers equitable having regard to all the circumstances. This is a general time limit. It extends to judicial review proceedings which is to be contrasted with the lack of a fixed time-limit in "non-

9.19

---

[6] See RCS, r.58.3(2); Clyde and Edwards Chapter 12; O.Neill at paras 6.12–6.20. On Art. 6 see paras 9.48–9.51.

[7] On current practice see generally Clyde and Edwards at para. 23.24; O'Neill at 6.54–6.55 and see in particular the views of Lord Morison in *Walker v. Strathclyde Regional Council (No. 2)* 1987 S.L.T. 81.

[8] See, *e.g. Hands v. Kyle and Carrick D.C.*, 1989 S.L.T. 124; Clyde and Edwards at para. 13.03.

[9] See RCS, r.58.7 and *Butt v. Secretary of State for the Home Department*, March 15, 1995, Lord Gill.

Convention" cases. If a stricter time-limit exists then this is preserved.[10] Notwithstanding the statutory time limit the common law plea of mora, taciturnity and acquiescence would appear to be competent in relation to claims brought *within* the year. This plea is often relied upon in judicial review proceedings although it is not confined to them. Whether the plea could be made out would be a matter of circumstances in each case. The period of taciturnity and apparent acquiescence of the claimant in relation to the act or decision would clearly be one consideration, but the reliance of the other party and indeed others on the decision and the prejudice to them if it were set aside are of greater importance.[11] Any common law plea will itself have to be compatible with Convention rights both in content and in its application.

The situation of the claimant will be relevant, perhaps more so in Convention rights cases. If the person, whilst silent, is one of a large group of people who have clearly not acquiesced in the decision in issue or is perhaps inexperienced or unsophisticated and "a private individual of modest means" rather than a "company or an individual with resources, experience and ready access to legal advice" a plea is less likely to be successful.[12] Arguably this is more likely to be the case where the law in question is new or uncertain in scope. Uncertainty as to the position in European law has been held a sufficient basis for defeating a plea of mora, tacitunity and acquiescence.[13]

It is possible that a plea of waiver might be taken in appropriate circumstances. In two cases under the Scotland Act which alleged that temporary sheriffs[14] and that temporary Court of Session judges,[15] did not constitute a fair and impartial tribunal under Article 6, the plea of waiver was successful. In a planning case, *County Properties Ltd v. Scottish Ministers*[16] it was not.

The period can be extended if the court or tribunal considers it equitable in all of the circumstances.

No guidance is given as to the factors to be taken into account. The burden of showing why the period should be extended would

---

[10] s.7(5)(b). See for example the "6 week" rule in relation to, *inter alia*, statutory applications to quash under ss. 238-239 of the Town and Country Planning (Scotland) Act 1997. Whether such a limit complies with Art. 6(1) may be open to challenge—see para.9.53. See D. Nicol, "Limitation Periods under the Human Rights Act 1998 and Judicial Review" (1999) 115 L.Q.R. 216.

[11] See *Conway v.Secretary of State for Scotland,*1996 S.L.T. 689 at 690. For a survey of the case law see Clyde and Edwards at paras 13.20–13.26; O'Neill at para. 6.25-6.28 ; *SME Vol 1* at para.121.

[12] See *King v. East Ayrshire Council*, 1998 S.C. 182 at 188.

[13] See *Swan v. Secretary of State for Scotland,*1998 S.C.L.R. 763. Here the uncertainty as to extent of legal rights derived from an allegedly incomplete implementation of an EC Directive was held to be sufficient.

[14] *Millar v. Dickson,* 2000 S.C.C.R 793

[15] *Clancy v. Caird,* 2000 S.L.T. 546

[16] 2000 S.L.T. 973.

appear to lie with the party seeking it. It would seem relevant to consider the conduct of the claimant and prejudice to both them, their opponent and third parties. Prejudice to the wider public interest, including the need for certainty in administrative decision making, might be relevant.[17] Conversely the factors in *King* might be prayed in aid of an extension.

Some guidance might also be derived from the case law under the powers given to Employment Tribunals under the Sex Discrimination Act 1975 s.76(5) and the Race Relations Act 1976 s.68(6) to extend the time limit allowed for claims. In *Mills and CPS v. Marshall*[18] this power was exercised where a claim for sex discrimination by a transsexual was lodged late.

Any time limit and any decision to extend it must of course be consistent with Convention rights. So a time limit which operated as a restriction of the right to access to a court might breach Article 6(1).[19] Any limit to its application must not be discriminatory.[20]

Where the allegation is a breach of a Convention right under the SA the one year limit does not apply.[21] This is anomalous as it could mean that an Act of the Parliament is subject to less protection than a local authority byelaw!

Title and interest: the victim test

In relation to Convention challenges under both the HRA and the SA the petitioner is taken to have title and interest to sue in relation to the allegedly unlawful act only if he is, or would be (in the case of a proposed act), a victim of the act.[22] Though a general test it is specifically extended to judicial review.[23]

At common law both title and interest were required to constitute standing. Title connotes a legal relationship.[24] Interest will often be pecuniary or involve status, but these categories are not exhaustive.[25] It must be material or sufficient. The interest must not be hypothetical or academic.[26]

The requirement of title and interest has meant that representa-

9.20

---

[17] See *Kwik Save Stores Ltd v. Secretary of State for Scotland*, 1999 S.L.T. 193 at 196.

[18] [1998] I.R.L.R. 494, EAT.

[19] See para.9.53 in relation to "six-week rules".

[20] *Stubbings v. U.K.* (1996) 23 E.H.R.R. 213 at para.54.

[21] See para.9.74.

[22] HRA s.7(3) and SA s.100.For an example of the scope of a *proposed act*, see *A v. Scottish Ministers*, 2000 S.L.T.873.

[23] s.7(4).

[24] *D and J Nicol v. Dundee Harbour Trustees*, 1915 S.C. (H.L.) 7 at 12, 13.

[25] *Scottish Old Peoples Welfare Council, Petrs.*, 1987 S.L.T. 179 at 186.

[26] *Kincardine and Deeside D.C. v. Forestry Commissioners*, 1992 S.L.T. 1180. For discussion of the position at common law and the victim test see Clyde and Edwards at Chapter 10 and SME vol. 1.paras 122 to 139.

tive interests such as pressure or campaign groups have had difficulty in accessing judicial review.[27] Although Scots law recognises the *actio popularis* its scope is restricted to certain public rights. It does not provide a basis for representative groups to seek judicial review.[28] There have been some liberal decisions such as *EIS Petrs., v. Robert Gordon University*.[29] Sometimes no challenge has been taken to allow the merits of a significant issue to be explored.[30] Associations have title and interest.[31] A community council was held to have a close relationship with the local authority for its area so as to confer title and interest.[32] It is however difficult to discern any coherent move way from the position exemplified by *Scottish Old Peoples Welfare Council*. More recently the scope of public interest intervention in judicial review proceedings has been given a boost by new Rules of Court.[33]

The application of the victim test will often lead to a similar conclusion on standing as the existing law, although it has the potential to be more restrictive. It may have peculiar impact in those situations in administrative law, where for reasons of cost or practicality representative action is considered or where the decision in question is not yet implemented or challenge to a policy is made. Those who had hoped for a more liberal test, possibly along the English test of *sufficient interest* were left disappointed.[34]

The following principles can be derived from the jurisprudence of the Convention:

9.21   •   The victim test does not provide a human rights *actio popularis*.

---

[27] *Scottish Old Peoples Welfare Council, Petrs*—charitable pressure group had title but no interest to challenge *vires* of regulations on cold weather payments as they did not include anyone entitled to a payment; *PTOA Ltd v. Renfrew D.C.*, 1997 S.L.T. 1112—no title to sue where business organisation sought to challenge taxi licensing policy; *Glasgow Rape Crisis Centre, Petrs.*, 2001 S.L.T. 389.

[28] See C. Munro, "Standing in Judicial Review" 1995 S.L.T.(News) 279 in relation to *Wilson v. Independent Broadcasting Authority*, 1979 S.C. 351.

[29] May 29, 1996, unreported—trade union has a strong claim to represent its members

[30] *The Royal Society for the Protection of Birds v. Secretary of State for Scotland*, 2000 S.L.T. 22.

[31] *Glasgow and District Restaurateurs and Hotelkeepers Association v. Dollan*, 1941 S.C. 93; *Association of Optical Practitioners Ltd v. Secretary of State for Scotland*, December 10, 1985.

[32] *Cockenzie and Port Seton Community Council v. East Lothian D.C.*, 1997 S.L.T. 81.

[33] See Act of Sederunt (Rules of the Court of Session Amendment (No.5) Public Interest Intervention in Judicial Review) 2000 (S.S.I.2000 No.317)

[34] For a discussion of English law, particularly with reference to the sufficient interest test being held to cover representative or public interest groups see Munro, below; I. Cram "The Reform of Standing in Scots Public Law" (1995) J.R.332. An amendment to substitute a "sufficient interest" test in judicial review proceedings was rejected during the House of Lords Committee stage: 585 HL Official Report (5th Series) cols 805-812.

There must be a concrete dispute and it is not sufficient to claim that a law in the abstract is in breach of the Convention.[35] Although there requires to be a concrete or real issue a victim does not stop having that status because the measure in question has caused no prejudice.[36]

- To show victim status it is however unnecessary to show that their rights have been violated by an "individual measure of implementation". It is enough that they run the risk of being directly affected by the measure of which they are complaining. So in *Norris v. Ireland*[37] the existence of a criminal law which prohibited homosexual acts was sufficient. Even although the policy was not to enforce the law, that policy could be changed at any time.[38]
- It is possible to be an indirect victim. So where for example he or she is a close relative of the affected person.[39]
- An organisation or trade union cannot claim to be a victim where it claims to be representing its members.[40]
- A corporate body can be a victim and has been held to be so in relation to rights to freedom of expression.[41] A company cannot act as a representative of its members nor can the share-holders claim to be a victim unless there are unusual circumstances, such as the company being unable to make the complaint.[42]
- A governmental organisation cannot claim to be a victim as it does not fall within the definition "any person, non-governmental organisation or group of individuals claiming to be a victim".[43]
- A person cannot be a victim where he has not previously asserted the right on which he relies.[44]
- Where an applicant is exposed to an imminent act which might be a violation such as extradition or deportation then he might be a victim.[45]

There may remain scope for circumventing the test in appropriate circumstances. One situation might be where a trade union wishes

---

[35] *Hakansson and Sturesson v. Sweden* (1990) 13 E.H.R.R. 1 at 11-12, para. 46.
[36] *Eckle v. Federal Republic of Germany* (1982) 5 E.H.R.R. 1 at 24, para. 66; *Ludi v. Switzerland* (1992) 15 E.H.R.R. 173 at 197, para 34
[37] (1984) 44 D.R. 132.
[38] See also *A v. Scottish Ministers*, 2000 S.L.T.873.
[39] See *McCann v. U.K.* (1995) 21 E.H.R.R. 97, and *Campbell and Cosans v. U.K.* (1980) 3 E.H.R.R .531 at 545, para. 112.
[40] *Purcell v. Ireland*, 70 D.R. 262 (1991) at 272–273 and compare with *EIS Petrs.* A trade union can be a victim in its own right if it claims that it has suffered a breach of its own rights under the Convention: *CCSU v. U.K.* (1987) 50 D.R. 228.
[41] *Observer Ltd and Guardian Newspapers Ltd v. U.K.* (1991) 14 E.H.R.R. 153 and in more obvious areas such as property rights on which see Chapter 7.
[42] *Agrotexim v. Greece* (1995) 21 E.H.R.R. 250 at 284, para. 66.
[43] *Rothenthurm Commune v. Switzerland*, 59 D.R. 251 (1988) and *Ayuntamiento de M v. Spain*, 68 D.R. 209 (1991).
[44] Appl. No. 13562/88 *Guenoun v. France* 66 D.R. 181 (1990).
[45] *Soering v. U.K.* (1989) 11 E.H.R.R. 439.

to take action. There is now arguably a difficulty under the new test. It may be that an associational petitioner might suffer similar problems. Representative groups may still experience difficulties. The new rules on public interest intervention permit intervention in *existing* judicial review proceedings and are *not* a general basis for *initiating* judicial review. Such circumstances might include:

- It is arguable that the victim test does not affect the ability of parties to rely on the Convention in the same circumstances and for the same purposes, as they could do *prior* to the HRA or SA. They could argue that the Convention can be used as a means of assessing the rationality of a measure or decision,[46] or as an interpretative tool.[47]

- Other means by which fundamental rights can be enforced at common law or under European Community law may give a level of protection which is at least equal to Convention rights.

- It is arguable that the duty of the courts under section 3 of the HRA and section 101 of the SA to interpret legislation in a manner which is compatible with Convention rights is a free-standing duty which applies *regardless* of whether the person who benefits is a victim or not. To do otherwise would mean that the meaning of a provision would change according to the status of the party relying on it.

Remedies

9.22   We have already noted that the HRA makes provision for a new form of declaratory remedy, the declarator of incompatibility.[48] It would be competent for the court to award this remedy in a petition for judicial review.[49]

Apart from this the HRA does not introduce any new remedies and so the remedies which are available, whether in judicial review in the Court of Session or in other administrative law proceedings, are those which are within the existing jurisdiction of the court or tribunal. It was this belief in the adequacy of existing remedies that led the government to exclude Article 13 of the Convention from the Convention Rights in Schedule 1 of the Act.[50]

There has also been speculation that the Act might lead to the development of a new form of remedy through judicial innovation. This would be a form of *public law liability* of the state. It is accepted that the law of the E.C. allows individuals to claim

---

[46] See para.9.31.
[47] See *AMT, Petr*, 1996 S.C.L.R.897.
[48] Paras 1.14–1.16.
[49] For remedies under the SA see paras 9.66–9.67.
[50] See for example Jack Straw M.P. 312 HC Official Report (6th series); Lord Irvine of Lairg 583 HL Official Report (5th series).

damages for breach of E.C. law.[51] The experience of a number of Commonwealth jurisdictions suggests that there is scope for such a remedy. In *Maharaj v. Attorney-General of Trinidad and Tobago (No.2)*[52] the Privy Council held that Article 6(1) of the Islands' Constitution which provided that any person alleging a violation of a constitutional right may "without prejudice to any other action with respect to the same matter which is available...apply to the High Court for redress", created a "liability in public law of the state". More recently the New Zealand Court of Appeal held in *Simpson v. Attorney-General*[53] that their 1990 Bill of Rights Act created a new remedy of damages against the Crown for violation of rights by its officers. Clyde and Edwards argue that "the similarity between the New Zealand Bill and the 1998 Act is that both are ordinary enactments which do not have the formal status of higher constitutional law".[54]

They argue that *Simpson* might be viewed as an argument for the HRA to create a new public law liability of the Crown for violations which are not otherwise remediable.[55]

Section 8 of the Human Rights Act provides the general basis upon which remedies can be awarded for a breach of a Convention right. Its terms are summarised in chapter 1[56] and it is only proposed to touch upon a number of features peculiar to public law.[57]

Section 8 does not create any new remedies. Instead the court or tribunal hearing a case which results in a finding of a violation of a Convention right will require to apply the remedies within its existing powers and only then to the extent necessary to afford just satisfaction. So in judicial review proceedings the remedies available under RCS Rule 58.4 could be sought.

In other areas of administrative law it would not be possible for the sheriff hearing an appeal against refusal of a liquor licence to

---

[51] See *Francovich v. Italy* [1991] E.C.R. I-5357 and generally M.Upton, "Crown Liability for Damages in E.C. Law" 1996 (News) S.L.T. 175 and 211; C. Boch and R. Lane, "A New Remedy in Scots Law:Damages from the Crown for Breach of Community Law" 1992 S.L.T. (News) 145.

[52] [1979] A.C. 385.

[53] [1994] 3 N.Z.L.R.667.

[54] At para.6.70.

[55] Not all constitutional systems have reached the same conclusion about this form of liability for example see *Kruger v. Commonwealth* (1997) 109 C.L.R. 1 (High Court of Australia); *Nilabati Bahera v. State of Orissa AIR*, 1993 S.C. (Supreme Court of India); and compare *Bivens v. Unknown Named Agents of Federal Bureaux of Narcotics*,403 U.S. 388 (U.S Supreme Court). For the position of the Scottish Parliament and Executive see para.9.66.

[56] Para.1.27.

[57] For detailed discussion see M. Amos, "Damages for breach of the Human Rights Act 1998" [1999] 2 E.H.R.L.R.178 and S. Blair "Just Satisfaction?—Damages under the Human Rights Act 1998" (2000) 1 S.H.R.J. 3 and (2000) 2 S.H.R.J. 2. Damages under the HRA has also been considered in the joint report of the Law Commission's *Damages under the Human Rights Act 1998* (SLC No.180, 2000).

award damages as part of any disposal as it is not competent to do so under this procedure.[58] It will continue to be incompetent to seek interdict and specific performance against the Crown.[59] Interim interdict is also excluded.[60] In England, in judicial review proceedings, injunction is competent.[61] It is unclear whether the availability of a declarator under section 23(a) will be a sufficient remedy where a breach of a Convention right is established.[62] In European Community law the rule has had to give way to the need to provide a meaningful remedy to protect E.C. rights.[63] The competence of seeking an order for enforcement of a statutory duty against the Crown has been left open.[64] As Article 13 is not a Convention right it is unclear whether the difficulties in securing certain remedies against the Crown defects can be remedied by judicial action alone.[65]

In the case of administrative tribunals, available remedies are defined by the statute creating the tribunal. Common law remedies are not open to them. It follows that where existing remedies are insufficient to protect Convention rights there will require to be an extension to their jurisdiction to permit *additional* remedies. Provision is made for this in the Act.[66]

9.23   The use of damages as a remedy is potentially the single most significant development in this field. As with any other remedy the tests set out in section 8 have to be met in considering whether to make an award and its amount. Where the act is the making of legislation or any other act or failure to act, of a member of the Scottish Executive then the extent to which damages are available is

---

[58]   See Sir Crispin Agnew of Lochnaw Q.C. "The Human Rights Dimension" (2000) 6 S.L.L.P. 20.

[59]   Crown Proceedings Act 1947 s.21(1)(a).

[60]   *McDonald v. Secretary of State for Scotland*, 1994 S.C. 234. See Clyde and Edwards para. 23.36; SME Vol. 1, para.144.

[61]   *M v. Home Office* [1994] 1 A.C. 377. It was held in that case that the 1947 Act did not prevent an injunction being awarded against a Minister in his personal capacity (or any other officer of the Crown) who personally committed a wrongful act.

[62]   Where an interim remedy is required, declarator is not competent: *Ayr Town Council v. Secretary of State for Scotland*, 1965 S.C. 394.

[63]   *R v. Secretary of State for Transport, ex parte Factortame Ltd (No. 2)* [1991] 1 A.C. 603 and see also *Millar & Bryce Ltd v. Keeper of the Registers of Scotland*, 1997 S.L.T. 1000.

[64]   See Court of Session Act 1988 s.45(b); Clyde and Edwards para. 22.37; SME Vol. 1 para.151.

[65]   Arguably courts and tribunals are bound to take judicial notice of Convention jurisprudence on remedies in terms of both ss. 2 and 8 and there is therefore scope for argument that the HRA is intended of itself to implement the Art. 13 guarantee. This may provide scope for reassessment of (a) the inclusion of judicial review as a proceeding in which these remedies are not competent and (b) whether interim interdict at least should be permitted. As both of these might be said to rest upon judicial interpretation rather than express provision, there may be scope for re-interpretation. However standing the express terms of s.21(1)(a), legislative reform may be required in that regard.

[66]   See ss.7(11)(a),(b).

also regulated by section 8.[67] Damages for breach of a Convention right are competent in judicial review proceedings although it will not always be necessary to seek judicial review to obtain an award.[68]

In judicial review proceedings damages have been rarely awarded, although in the wider field of public law are relatively common[69] To date there appears to have been only one decision in which damages have been awarded.[70] This reluctance to award damages undoubtedly derives from the view that judicial review is concerned with jurisdictional control rather than for compensation for wrong suffered. Doubt has been expressed about the use of the remedy in judicial review proceedings of any complexity—a different procedure may be preferable at least to resolve that aspect of a dispute.[71] Finally, where the decision (or omission) involved the exercise of discretion, then liability could only arise where it could be shown that there was a failure to keep within the terms of the statute or that there was a lack of good faith or that there was an irrational failure.[72] Where the decision involved policy bad faith must be averred.[73] Even where the allegation involved intentional misuse of powers it was necessary to aver malice or bad faith.[74] These are high hurdles to surmount. It view of the decisions in *Osman v. United Kingdom*[75] and *Z v. United Kingdom* and *TP and KM v. United Kingdom*[76] it may be that that we will begin to see the erosion of the protection available to public authorities and a consequent increase in the number of claims for damages in judicial review petitions.

Expenses

In rights litigation there may be scope for argument that the usual rules on expenses should be applied with the regard being paid to the potential for inhibitory effect on other persons considering the pursuit of a claim based on breach of rights. An unduly rigid application of the usual rules on expenses against

9.24

---

[67] SA s.100(3)–(4) and see para. 9.66.
[68] See para.9.17.
[69] see Clyde and Edwards at paras 26.27–26.37 for a survey of recent case law; SME Vol. 1, para.149.
[70] *Mallon (sub. nom Kelly) v. Monklands D.C.*, 1986 S.L.T. 169 a case involving breach of statutory duty under the homeless persons legislation.
[71] See *Shetland Line (1984) Ltd v. Secretary of State for Scotland* 1996, S.L.T. 653.
[72] *Hallett v. Nicholson*, 1979 S.C. 1 at 9 and on irrational failures see *X (Minors) v. Bedfordshire C.C.* [1995] 2 A.C. 633 and *Stovin v. Wise* [1996] A.C. 923 at 953 *per* Lord Hoffmann. For a possible softening of the position see *Barrett v. Enfield LBC* [1999] 3 All E.R. 193; *Kent v. Griffiths* [2000] 2 All E.R. 474; *S v. Gloucestershire C.C.* [2000] 3 All E.R. 346.
[73] *Ross v. Secretary of State for Scotland*, 1990 S.L.T. 13.
[74] *Micosta SA v. Shetland Islands Council*, 1986 S.L.T. 193 at 198.
[75] Chapter 6.
[76] September 10, 1999, Commission. However, the extent to which this process will occur may have to be reassessed in light of *Z v. U.K.*, May 10, 2001, ECtHR.

unsuccessful litigants might itself amount to a breach of the right to access the courts secured by Article 6. Issues might arise under both the HRA and the SA.

This concern has been recognised in other jurisdictions. In *Motsepe v. IRC*[77] Justice Ackermann for the Constitutional Court of South Africa observed,

> "one should be cautious in awarding costs against litigants who seek to enforce their constitutional rights against the state, particularly where the constitutionality of a statutory provision is attacked, lest such orders have an unduly inhibiting or "chilling effect" on other potential litigants in this category. This cautious approach cannot, however, be allowed to develop into an inflexible rule so that litigants are induced into believing that they are free to challenge the constitutionality of statutory provisions in this court, no matter how spurious the grounds for doing so may be or how remote the possibility that this court will grant them access. This can neither be in the interests of the administration of justice nor fair to those who are forced to oppose such attacks."

Convention Rights and the Grounds of Legal Control

9.25　　The classic statement of the grounds for judicial review is that of Lord Greene, M.R. in *Associated Provincial Picture Houses Ltd v. Wednesbury Corporation*[78]:

> "The court is entitled to investigate the action of the local authority with a view to seeing whether they have taken into account matters which they ought not to have taken into account, or, conversely, have refused to take into account or neglected to take into account matters which they ought to take into account. Once that question is answered in favour of the local authority, it may still be possible to say that although the local authority have kept within the four corners of the matters which they ought to consider, they have nevertheless come to a conclusion so unreasonable that no reasonable authority could ever have come to it."

In *Council of Civil Service Unions v. Minister of State for the Civil Service*[79] Lord Diplock reformulated the grounds under three heads—illegality, irrationality and procedural impropriety. This formulation was accepted as representing Scots law in *City of Edinburgh District Council v. Secretary of State for Scotland.*[80]

---

[77] (1997) (6) BCLR 692 at 705, para. 30
[78] [1948] 1 K.B. 223 at 233-234.
[79] [1985] A.C. 374.
[80] 1985 S.C. 261

Where the basis of control rests upon appeal rather than review, appeal is often restricted to a point of law, an aspect of illegality. Appeal on the basis of a point of law is the general basis of appeal from many statutory tribunals.[81] Similarly some appeals permit challenge on grounds of reasonableness or procedural error such as a breach of natural justice, which clearly have parallels to the grounds of review.[82] Even where the appellate court has the ability to consider the merits of an administrative decision, the case law does not always suggest a willingness to do so.[83]

Convention rights will allow for a more substantive approach to the issues before the reviewing or appellate court, rather than simply approaching matters in terms of the propriety and legality of the decision-making process, subject to an over-riding requirement of reasonableness. The reviewing or appellate court will require to modify its approach to how it deals with the grounds of review or appeal. What may become clearer is that Convention rights may possibly have a number of different applications in judicial control of administrative action.

This is likely to arise both by direct application of Convention rights in the short term but in the longer term, more subtle changes might occur as our courts begin to take on board the *philosophy* of the requirements of good administration. It is possible to distil from Convention jurisprudence general principles of good administration .These were recently summarised as follows:

"In procedural terms—access to public services; the right to be heard ;a right to representation and assistance; the right to due notification of a decision with explanatory reasons; and an indication of the remedies available to challenge the decision; and the performance of administrative acts within a reasonable time.

In substantive terms—lawfulness; conformity with statutory purpose; objectivity and impartiality equality of treatment; proportionality; openness; the fair protection of legitimately held trust and existing rights."[84]

One can see immediate parallels with some of the existing grounds of review but there are also differences.

---

[81] s.11 of the Tribunals and Inquiries Act 1992.
[82] See Licensing (Scotland) Act 1976, s.39(4) and Civic Government (Scotland) Act 1982 s.4, Sched. 1, para. 18(7).
[83] See *Glasgow Corporation v. Glasgow Churches Council*, 1944 S.C. 97 for a broad interpretation of the powers of the sheriff and I.D. MacPhail, *Sheriff Court Practice*,(2nd ed., W.Green & Son Ltd, Edinburgh, 1998.) chaps 25 and 26 for discussion of the more restrictive case law.
[84] See Council of Europe, *The Administration and You: Principles of administrative law concerning the relations between administrative authorities and private persons—a handbook* (Strasbourg, 1996)

9.26   In *Salah Abadou v. Secretary of State for the Home Department*[85] Lord Eassie drew a link between the Convention and the traditional approach to control of administrative action:

> "In the present state of the law it is, I think, clear that direct reference to the European Human Rights Convention as a means of judicially controlling or reviewing the exercise of administrative discretion is not permissible...In light of the speeches in *Brind* I do not consider that merely averring a breach of the Convention would be relevant to invalidate an exercise of administrative discretion...In judging whether a decision is unreasonable, in the sense of being outwith the range open to a reasonable decision taker, the human rights context is important and the more substantial interference with human rights the more a court will require by way of justification, in the sense of it's being within that range. However, while the fact that a decision is in breach of the Convention may assist in the contention that it is unreasonable in the *Wednesbury* sense, the ultimate test must be whether the decision falls outwith the range or span of decision open to a reasonable decision taker."[86]

Brind is discussed later.[87] His Lordship concluded that it was both a disproportionate interference with family life under Article 8 and a *Wednesbury* unreasonable decision to deport an Algerian national and illegal immigrant married to a British national, to Algeria during a period when that country was in the grip of a violent civil war.

Whilst it was accepted it was appropriate to have regard to the Convention in determining whether a decision was *Wednesbury* unreasonable his Lordship did not feel bound to have regard to the wide margin of appreciation accorded by Strasbourg to States in the exercise of their discretion in dealing with entry to the State of non-nationals. It follows from this approach that the national court may feel itself able to offer greater protection than a strict application of Convention jurisprudence would entail.[88]

What is significant about *Salah Abadou* is that on one view this treatment of human rights protection is echoed by section 2(1) of the HRA. In terms of section 2(1)(a) courts and tribunals are obliged to take into account any judgment, decision, declaration, or advisory opinion of the Court and a number of other Convention institutions. There is no obligation to follow as a matter of precedent such decisions and, provided the national court or tribunal meets its obligations under the section, it is free to develop

---

[85]   1998 S.C. 504.
[86]   At 518.
[87]   Para.9.35.
[88]   For margin of appreciation see paras 9.55–9.52.

its own approach to human rights protection. In this sense the Convention sets the *minimum* standards for administrative decision-making.

It follows from this that our existing grounds of judicial control, both substantive and procedural fall to be assessed against Convention criteria, but compliance with those criteria should not be taken to de-limit development. Domestic grounds may be found wanting and may require to be re-cast. Conversely it may be that in some areas the Convention will have nothing to add to these grounds, except perhaps additional legitimacy. The Convention may lead to the development of additional grounds. In the following treatment *possible* grounds of control such as proportionality, legal certainty, and substantive fairness have been given separate treatment to reflect this.

Under section 6 of the Act it is unlawful for a public authority to act in away which is incompatible with any of the rights and fundamental freedoms which are Convention rights. Whilst this embraces judicial control on the basis of the simple illegality,[89] illegality in its *widest* sense as embracing all forms of *ultra vires* can arise in a number of guises. These grounds will also be relevant in considering the legality of Acts of the Scottish Parliament and acts and decisions of the Scottish Executive under the SA. They will be relevant to both the grounds of judicial review *and* similar grounds of appeal.

9.27

We shall examine the following as either existing or potential grounds of control—

- Illegality
- Rationality
- Proportionality.
- Legal certainty
- Procedural Impropriety
- Substantive fairness

Illegality

Error of law

A decision maker must understand the law governing his decision making power correctly and must apply it correctly. If the law has been misunderstood or has been misapplied then a decision will be unlawful.

9.28

Often this will involve questions of statutory interpretation.[90]

---

[89] For an account of Convention rights in this sense see Clyde and Edwards at chapter 16.

[90] See, *e.g.* *Ferguson v. Secretary of State for Social Services,* 1989 S.L.T. 117; *Gordon v. Kirkcaldy D.C.,* 1989 S.L.T. 507 and 1990 S.L.T. 644 and for a general account of this ground of control see Clyde and Edwards chap. 22; SME Vol. 1 at paras 47-51; R.J.Reed, "Judicial Review of Errors of Law" 1979 S.L.T. (News) 241.

Where error of law is alleged the Scottish courts have been reluctant to interfere unless the error was material and going to the jurisdiction of the decision maker.[91] In English law all errors of law are deemed material and are amenable to review.[92] What is a material error cannot be stated with certainty. The distinction has the potential to restrict the powers of the court. This may be difficult to justify in a case involving Convention rights. Whatever the future of the distinction it is arguable that the role it played-that of ensuring decision makers had a margin within which they could operate free from judicial intervention-may now have a counterpart in the concept of the discretionary area of judgment.[93]

The interpretative obligations imposed by section 3 of the HRA and section 101 of the SA[94] mean that where a decision maker is construing legislation, whether primary or subordinate, they must give it a meaning which is compatible with the Convention unless it is not possible to do so. Whilst these obligations enjoin courts and tribunals to act in this manner, there is every reason to suppose that the obligation is to be extended to all decision makers who require to construe the scope and nature of their statutory powers. The impact on review for error of law is clear. Challenge on this basis would be possible even if the decision itself did not go so far as to open up challenge under section 6.[95] Where such an interpretation is not possible then the remedy would be a declarator of incompatibility under section 4 of the HRA[96] or in the case of Scottish legislation appropriate action under the SA.[97]

It also follows that decision makers and courts can no longer feel themselves bound by previous decisions on the interpretation of legislation. Moreover as the demands of the Convention change over time[98] so interpretation must continually evolve.

When it is realised that a basic ground of judicial control in Convention rights cases is *illegality* it becomes apparent that it is not only the traditional grounds of judicial review that stand to be affected. Many administrative appeals are based on a point of law and appeal from many tribunals to the court is restricted to on a point of law. If the relevant law now has Convention content then error as to Convention law and its application will found a basis for an appeal.

---

[91] *Watt v. Lord Advocate,* 1979 S.L.T. 137 following *Anisminic Ltd v. Foreign Compensation Commission* [1969] 2 A.C. 147.
[92] *R v. Lord President of the Privy Council, ex parte Page* [1993] 1 All E.R. 97.
[93] See paras 9.55–9.58.
[94] see para.9.65.
[95] Or ss.29, 54, 57 of the SA.
[96] See paras 1.14–1.16.
[97] See paras 9.67–9.71.
[98] See para.1.04.

Relevant considerations

In judicial control of administrative action a decision-maker must   9.29
only act on the basis of relevant considerations and leave out of
account irrelevant considerations.[99] What is or is not relevant is a
matter of statutory construction and it is not always east to
determine relevance
Even the broadest regulatory power has its limits.[1]
When the relevant considerations are determined it is a matter for
the decision maker as to the *weight* to be accorded to each
consideration.[2] Provided that the weight accorded to the consideration was not unreasonable in the *Wednesbury* sense, the court will
not intervene.[3]
Convention rights will have an impact here. Whilst latterly the
courts were more receptive to argument that a failure to act in
accordance with the Convention was evidence of irrationality,[4] it
would be stretching that approach to convert it into a *positive*
obligation to take it into account as a *pre-requisite* of legality.
Again separately from the obligation to act compatibly with
Convention rights under section 6 (or under the provisions of the
SA), as a matter of general administrative law, it could become the
case that public authorities will be required to *positively* show that
they have paid proper regard to Convention rights for their conduct
or decisions to be *intra vires*, even if there is no allegation or evidence
that the conduct was unlawful under the relevant provisions. It
follows that the range of potentially relevant factors will be
broadened and the *weight* to be attached to them will also have
Convention content. The issue of weight is considered further below.[5]

Lawful Purpose

A decision maker must act to promote the objects or policy of the   9.30
Act or other measure which gave that person the power to make
decisions.[6] So a decision cannot be motivated by malice or bad
faith, which must always be contrary to the purpose of legislation.[7]

---

[99] *Wordie Property Co Ltd v. Secretary of State for Scotland*, 1984 S.L.T 345
[1]   See, *e.g. R v. Somerset C.C., ex p. Fewings* [1995] 1 W.L.R. 1037—general power
      to manage land to improve area did not include power to ban deer-hunting on the
      land on ethical grounds.
[2]   See *Harvey v. Strathclyde R.C.*, 1989 S.L.T 612 and *London and Midland
      Developments v. Secretary of State for Scotland*, 1996 S.C.L.R. 465.
[3]   See *Bromley LBC v. Greater London Council* [1983] A.C.768—unreasonable for
      local authority to give greater weight to election pledges to subsidise public
      transport over fiduciary duty owed to ratepayers—*cf Harvey*—not unreasonable
      for Secretary of State to differ from parental wishes as to closure of a school
      provided he took those wishes in to account
[4]   See para.**.
[5]   See para.**.
[6]   *Padfield v. Minister of Agriculture, Fisheries and Food* [1968] A.C. 998.
[7]   *Pollok School Ltd v. Glasgow Town Clerk* 1946 S.C. 373; *Demetriades v. Glasgow
      Corporation* [1951] 1 All E.R. 457, H.L.

There is considerable overlap between this ground and that of relevant considerations.

This ground will be considerably reinforced as a result of both obligations to act in accordance with Convention rights and to interpret purpose in light of Convention rights.

There can be difficulties in establishing as a matter of evidence that an improper purpose exists.[8] The courts have been prepared to infer such from the nature and content of the decision in question. It may be that in a Convention context that inference will be more readily drawn so passing the onus to the decision maker to show compliance with Convention rights such as in the case of the restrictions on rights found in Articles 8 to 12.

Where a single decision leads to various results, some authorised by the legislation and some not, the court has developed a number of tests to determine legality. Where the dominant purpose is within powers, the fact that some other purpose is not, will not invalidate the decision.[9] It might be open to question whether, if the subsidiary purpose violates Convention rights whether directly or incidentally the same result should obtain. To hold otherwise might entail no sanction for a breach of Convention rights and may conflict with the basic obligation to act in manner which is compatible with Convention rights. Where, however, two or more purposes exist, one of which is unlawful and cannot be separated from the valid purpose and can be shown to have had a demonstrable influence on the decision, then the whole decision falls.[10] Again this will be relevant where the bad purpose infringes a Convention right.

It has been held that in some situations, purposes not expressly authorised by statute, may be taken into account in the public interest.[11] In Convention terms this might give some scope to argue that the public interest in securing Convention objectives could be taken into account in assessing the legality of a purpose not expressly authorised.

Irrationality

9.31   Unreasonableness or irrationality is a familiar ground in judicial review. Where power or discretion has been conferred on a decision maker it must be exercised reasonably.[12] Because of its potential in judicial review to stray into the forbidden area of the substance or

---

[8]   *Commission for Local Authority Accounts in Scotland v. Grampian R.C.*, 1994 S.L.T. 1120.

[9]   *R v. ILEA, ex p. Westminster C.C.* [1986] 1 All E.R. 19

[10] *R v. Lewisham LBC, ex p. Shell U.K. Ltd* [1988] 1 All E.R. 938.

[11] *Michael v. Edinbugh Magistrates* (1895) 3 S.L.T. 109; *Fleming v. Liddesdale District Committee* (1897) 5 S.L.T.191 although *cf R v. Secretary of State for Foreign and Commonwealth Affairs, ex p. World Development Movement Ltd* [1995] 1 All E.R. 611.

[12] *Donaldson's Hospital v. Educational Endowments Commissioner*, 1932 S.C.585

merits of a decision the level of review is pitched at a high level. Reasonableness is also a ground in a number of statutory appeals. Even so the court has been unwilling to enter upon a general assessment of the merits.[13]

The classic formulation is found in the judgment of Lord Greene M.R. in *Associated Provincial Picture Houses Ltd v. Wednesbury Corporation*.[14] More recently the expression irrationality has been used. In the course of delivering his speech in *Council of Civil Service Unions v. Minister for the Civil Service*[15] Lord Diplock stated that the ground, "applies to a decision which is so outrageous in its defiance of logic or of accepted moral standards that no sensible person who had applied his mind to the question to be decided could have arrived at it". This formulation was adopted in Scotland by the Inner House in *McTear v. Scottish Legal Aid Board*.[16] This is a high test and as a consequence successful review on the basis of irrationality is rare.[17]

In the context of human rights irrationality has been used as a ground of challenge. We have seen this already in *Abadou*. The most significant discussion of the applicability of the test prior to the HRA was in *R v. Ministry of Defence, ex parte Smith*.[18] Here three men and a woman were administratively discharged due to their homosexuality. There was no suggestion that their sexuality had interfered with how they discharged their duties. They sought judicial review on the grounds, *inter alia*, that the blanket ban nature of the policy requiring discharge purely on the basis of their sexuality was irrational having regard to Article 8 of the Convention. The Court of Appeal rejected this submission, primarily because having regard to the basis of the policy, its support by Parliament, and the lack of sufficiently cogent evidence from other states as to how the lifting of similar bans had worked in practice, it could not be said to be irrational. A number of important observations on rationality were made by Sir Thomas Bingham M.R.[19]:

> "The court may not interfere with the exercise of an administrative discretion on substantive grounds save where the court is satisfied that the decision is unreasonable in the sense that it is beyond the range of responses open to a reasonable decision-maker. But in judging whether the decision-maker has exceeded this margin of appreciation the

---

[13] See *Loosefoot Entertainments Ltd v. City of Glasgow District Licensing Board*, 1990 S.C.L.R. 584 and on appeal 1991 S.L.T. 843
[14] [1948] 1 K.B. 223 at 233-234
[15] [1985] A.C. 374 at 410
[16] 1995 S.C.L.R. 611.
[17] For examples see Clyde and Edwards paras.21.19-21.20
[18] [1996] 1 All E.R 257, C.A.
[19] at 263d.

human rights context is important. The more substantial the interference with human rights, the more the court will require by way of justification before it is satisfied that the decision is reasonable in the sense outlined above."

So heightened rationality scrutiny has been applied in a number of contexts such as access to the courts[20]; immigration and family life[21]; and curtailment of freedom of expression under Article 10.[22]

Where matters of policy are involved the irrationality test requires further modification:

"The greater the policy content of a decision, and the more remote the subject matter of a decision from ordinary judicial experience, the more hesitant the court must necessarily be in holding a decision to be irrational. That is good law and. like most good law, common sense. Where decisions of a policy-laden, esoteric or security-based nature are in issue, even greater caution than normal must be shown in applying the test, but the test is sufficiently flexible to cover all situations."[23]

In the present case his Lordship was not prepared to hold that the policy in question fell within this area, but even applying a stricter approach to rationality, the policy, despite its blanket nature, could not be described as irrational. When the case was taken to Strasbourg it was held that the rationality test threshold was still pitched:

"So high that it effectively excluded any consideration by the domestic courts of the question of whether the interference with the applicants' rights answered a pressing social need or was proportionate to the national security and public order aims pursued, principles which lie at the heart of the Court's analysis of complaints under Article 8 of the Convention."[24]

---

[20] *R v. Lord Chancellor, ex p. Witham* [1997] 2 All E.R. 777 at 788 per Laws J .and see *Leech v. Secretary of State for Scotland*, 1993 S.L.T. 365

[21] *Kriba v. Secretary of State for the Home Department*, 1998 S.L.T. 1113 at 1116; *Salah Abadou*; *Singh,Petr* (1988) G.W.D 32–1377; *R v. Lord Saville of Newdigate, ex p. A* [1999] 4 All E.R. 860

[22] *R v. Secretary of State for Health, ex parte Wagstaff*, The Times, August 31, 2000 (refusal to hold inquiry into the Dr Harold Shipman case in public). See generally C.R. Munro, "Fundamental Rights in National Law" 1997 S.L.T. (News) 221; Sir J. Laws, "The Limitations of Human Rights" [1998] P.L. 254

[23] At p.264g–j. So for example where matters of macro-economic importance are concerned a less demanding or minimal form of rationality has been applied, see, e.g. *City of Edinburgh D.C. v. Secretary of State for Scotland*, 1985 S.L.T. 551 and see also *Nottinghamshire C.C. v. Secretary of State for the Environment* [1986] A.C. 240.

[24] *Smith and Grady v. U.K.* (2000) 29 E.H.R.R. 493 at para.138 and see also *Lustig-Prean and Beckett v. U.K.* (2000) 29 E.H.R.R. 548.

This does not mean the rationality cannot be a sufficient basis for 9.32
judicial control. *Wednesbury* rationality has been held to be a
sufficient safeguard in other contexts.[25] Rather the traditional
model, even in its heightened form, could not address the issue of
the balancing of the basic right as against the forms of interference
permitted by Article 8. It could not address the merits of a blanket
ban as it applied to the individuals in question. The proportionality
of the ban required to be considered as it applied to individual cases
and this could not be done.

Smith and Grady should be understood as deciding that in certain
cases involving measures of general application and rights which
are particularly valuable and which can only be interfered with on
recognised grounds,[26] the application of heightened rationality
scrutiny *alone* is unlikely to be a sufficient safeguard of the right
unless the court is, in addition, able to assess proportionality as
well.

Salah Abadou must be seen as an important decision in the
development of rationality as basis of control. The case may pave
the way for the development of a rationality test that is closer to
that found in other human rights jurisdictions, where the value of
the right in question will be a factor in the assessment of the
rationality of a decision impacting on that right. This may lead to
different levels of rationality being developed, depending on
whether the right is fundamental—clearly Convention rights are
in this category—demanding the most searching inquiry as to
rationality, or less so and requiring a lower standard. So there
might be argument that a lower standard might be appropriate in
relation to the assessment of the rationality (or more accurately the
disproportionality) of decisions taken in areas covered by international human rights treaties of which the United Kingdom is a
signatory.[27]

What is all the more surprising is that *Salah Abadou* appears to
cast doubt over the approach of the House of Lords in *Brind* where
a sliding scale approach to rationality was rejected. Lord Irvine of
Lairg[28] summarised the position with specific reference to the dicta
of Sir Thomas Bingham in *Smith*:

---

[25] *Vilvarajah v. U.K.* (1992) 14 E.H.R.R. 248—asylum application—whether
effective remedy under Art. 13; *Air Canada v. U.K.* (1995) 20 E.H.R.R.
150—judicial review of reasonableness of decision to levy statutory penalty
sufficient to protect rights under Art. 1 of the First Protocol and see too, *Bryan v.
U.K.* (1995) 21 E.H.R.R. 342; *TI v. U.K.* Appl. No. 43844/98, March 6, 2000,
admissibility decision—deportation and extradition and Art. 3. Heightened
Wednesbury rationality was described as the "touchstone" of judicial control for
alleged breaches of Art. 8 in immigration cases in one of the first HRA challenges:
R. v. Secretary of State for the Home Department, ex p Mahmood, December 12,
2000, Court of Appeal.
[26] Such as, *e.g.* Art. 8(2) or Art. 10(2).
[27] See para.9.59.
[28] "Judges and Decision-Makers: The Theory and Practice of Wednesbury Review"
[1996] P.L. 59 at 65

"This is to stray far beyond the limits laid down in *Brind*, and to lead the judges into dangerous territory. In practice, few cases which touch upon the protection of fundamental rights reflect the beguiling simplicity of the legal slogan. The political and legal choices which import consideration of fundamental rights protection are among the most difficult and the most subjective, and offer immense scope for political and philosophical disagreement. It cannot be right that such questions should be regarded as more rather than less suitable to judicial determination. The approach adopted in *Brind*, which states conclusively that the *Wednesbury* threshold of unreasonableness is not lowered in fundamental rights cases, must prevail."

9.33   Clearly this approach can no longer be regarded as reflecting the new realities. It may be some time before we are in a position to truly assess whether the courts embraced the full implications of substantive review. Much will also depend on the extent to which the courts develop a domestic discretionary area of judgement.[29] The presence of policy considerations may continue to be significant in determining the strictness of the test and the scope of any such area. Will more deference be accorded to interference with certain rights or certain forms of interference? Are certain rights found in the Act more amenable to judicial scrutiny?

One should also not lose sight of the fact that the caution found in Lord Irvine's views may still have relevance in relation to rights not within the scope of Convention rights. An alleged " social" right to housing or to a particular standard of education or an "economic" right to work might be regarded by many as of fundamental importance along with freedom of expression or the right to privacy, perhaps more so. Yet it is conceivable that such rights might be treated as touching upon social and economic issues of the kind where *at most*, the basic level of rationality scrutiny is appropriate.

It should not be assumed that even within the classic "liberal" rights of the Convention that there is contained an exhaustive statement of those rights. The values and concerns of society are continually changing. The Convention has yet to recognise a right to homosexual marriage. The content of the Convention itself has changed with protocols being added to reflect such pressures. Unless and until such new rights are either "found" in the Convention or are incorporated by protocol, then it is arguable that they will be subject to a lower level of rationality scrutiny. *Wednesbury* scrutiny and it's relationship with human rights in their widest sense may not yet be dead. That is not to imply that the lowest level of *Wednesbury* review would be taken to apply. In such cases a heightened form of rationality might be used, albeit, it might

---

[29] See paras 9.55–9.58.

operate at a lower level of intensity of scrutiny than would be accorded to Convention rights.

The potential for *tiers* of rationality has been recently acknowledged by Lord Clyde and Denis Edwards in their work on judicial review. They suggest that the existing doctrine of rationality already allows the court to vary the intensity of review depending on the subject matter. They state that:

"A balancing process may be required under which the importance of the right or interest affected must be balanced against the nature of the decision-making process. As the right or interest becomes more important, the court's review becomes more stringent."

As authority for this they refer to the decision in *Smith*. They continue[30]:

"Such an approach clearly merges with the concept of proportionality and it is no accident that in human rights cases that the courts have suggested that a more searching or " anxious " scrutiny is appropriate in review on grounds of irrationality. Indeed, in such cases, it may be that a decision violating fundamental human rights can only be supported where there are rational reasons for it, which is a qualitatively different inquiry from that involved in deciding if the decision is irrational."

Proportionality

Proportionality is likely to be the single most significant development in the grounds upon which administrative action can be controlled. Its significance lies not just in its potential as a new ground of review but in the way its operation will, over time, redefine the relationship between the courts and decision makers. 9.34

The doctrine is well recognised in the law of major continental jurisdictions such as France and Germany as well as in European Community law.[31] It is and is a central principle by which the legality of a restriction on a Convention right or the scope of a positive obligation to respect that right, can be measured. It is recognised in the human rights jurisprudence of the Commonwealth countries.[32] It follows that where a decision or measure impacts on a Convention right it will be necessary to assess the extent to which it meets the criteria of proportionality.

---

[30] At para. 21.09
[31] For an account of its role in these systems see O'Neill paras 2.08 and 2.99-2.106., and for its impact in judicial review, paras 2.114-2.125; Clyde and Edwards paras.21.21-21.26
[32] See, *e.g. Ming Pao Newspapers Ltd v. Att.-Gen. of Hong Kong* [1996] A.C. 907.

The use of proportionality requires flexibility. Its use requires regard to be paid to any discretionary area of judgement. The latter acts as a check on the unduly rigid application of the principle and might be seen as a way of ensuring that the focus of the test is as a basis for review with substantive content, rather than as a basis for a general appeal on the merits of a decision.[33] As with rationality, proportionality may therefore be applied with varying degrees of strictness according to the circumstances. In those cases which involve the most significant of rights, the difference between heightened rationality scrutiny and proportionality might be more a matter of form than of substance.[34]

Where a decision maker wishes to restrict a right or freedom guaranteed by the Convention he must act in a way which is "proportionate to the legitimate aim pursued".[35]

To meet the test a measure must comply with the following:

- the legislative or other objective must be important enough to justify the restriction of the right;
- there must be a rational connection to the objective of the measure and so cannot be arbitrary in form, unfair in operation or based upon any consideration which is not relevant or irrational;
- the means used to limit the right or freedom can be no more than is necessary to achieve the objective. It follows that the greater the effect of the restriction the more important the objective must be if it can be justified in a democratic society. It also follows that the judge is required to consider if there are other less restrictive means open.[36]

Whilst this analytical approach is useful in distilling the elements of the test it does not follow that it should be applied in a mechanistic manner. It is to be "applied broadly and flexibly with an eye to the basic principle of fairness".[37] Rationality is but one part of the

---

[33] For discussion the discretionary area of judgement and the general issue of a balanced approach to rights see paras 9.55–9.58.

[34] This flexible approach to proportionality and its relationship with rationality has been recognised in the context of E.C. law in *R v. Chief Constable of Sussex, ex parte International Traders Ferry Ltd* [1999] 1 All.E.R. 129, HL.See especially Lord Slynn at 145H and Lord Cook of Thorndon at 157A-E. For comment see O'Neill paras .2.121-2.125 ; Lord Hoffmann, "A Sense of Proportion" in Andenas and Jacobs (eds), *European Law in the English Courts*. See also J.Jowell and A.Lester, "Proportionality : Neither Novel nor Dangerous" in Jowell and Oliver (eds), *New Directions in Judicial Review* (Stevens, London, 1988).

[35] See *Handyside v. U.K.* (1976) 1 E.H.R.R. 737 at 754, para. 49.

[36] See also: Smith and Grady, Lustig-Prean and Beckett, below; *De Freitas v. Permanent Secretary of Agriculture, Fisheries, Land and Housing* [1998] 3 W.L.R. 675, PC per Lord Clyde at 684A-F; *Germany v. Council of the European Union* [1995] E.C.R. I-3723 at 3755-3756; Halsbury's Laws of England (4th Ed.) para. 2.296; Jurgen Schwarze, *European Administrative Law*, chapter 5.

[37] Clyde and Edwards at para. 21.25 and see for an example of this flexible approach, *Thomson Newspapers v. Canada* (1998) 1 S.C.C.R. 877.

overall legal calculus. In particular even if a measure passes threshold rationality it will still be unlawful if it cannot meet the third test It is this additional degree of scrutiny which makes proportionality a *qualitatively* different test from rationality, even the more rigorous form of that test. It follows that the judiciary will be called on to assess objective of the measure or decision is in itself one which justifies the restriction. The combination of tests means that it is no longer sufficient to say that a measure is reasonable and that the fact that the judge might have reached a different decision is irrelevant to its legality. The test requires the judiciary to make decisions about substantive choices, an approach which is very different from the traditional unwillingness in judicial review for the judge to take a different view of the merits of a decision from that taken by the decision maker. The court is still fixing a band of lawful choices open to the decision maker, save that its limits are (usually) narrower than under *Wednesbury*.

The contrast between the two approaches was put in this way by Laws J.:

"The difference between *Wednesbury* and European review is that in the former case the legal limits lie further back. I think there are two factors. First the limits of domestic review are not, as the law presently stands, constrained by the doctrine of proportionality. Secondly, at least as regards a requirement such as that of objective justification in an equal treatment case, the European rule requires that the decision maker to provide a fully reasoned case. It is not enough merely to set out the problem, and assert that within his jurisdiction the minister choose this or that solution, constrained only by the requirement that his decision must have been the one which a reasonable minister might make. Rather the court will test the solution arrived at, and pass it only if substantial factual considerations are put forward in its justification: considerations which are relevant, reasonable and proportionate to the aim in view. But as I the jurisprudence the court is not concerned to agree or disagree with the decision: that would be to travel beyond the boundaries of proper judicial review, and usurp the decision maker's function. Thus *Wednesbury* and European review are different models—one looser, one tighter —of the same judicial concept, which is the imposition of compulsory standards on decision-makers so as to secure the repudiation of arbitrary power".[38]

9.35

It was the implications of this fundamental shift in the relationship between the judiciary and the administration which led the House

---

[38] *R v. Ministry of Agriculture, Fisheries and Food, ex p First City Trading Ltd* [1997] 1 C.M.L.R. 250 at para 69; [1997] EuLR 195 at 219D-F.

of Lords to reject the use of proportionality as a ground of review in areas outwith European Community Law in *R v. Secretary of State for the Home Department ex p Brind*.[39] Here it was alleged that the ban on broadcasting the voices of members of certain political organisations, including Sinn Fein, was disproportionate to the stated objective of "starving the terrorist of the oxygen of publicity". Lord Ackner said[40]:

> "Unless and until Parliament incorporates the [European] Convention [on Human Rights and Fundamental Freedoms] into domestic law ... there appears to me to be at present no basis on which the proportionality doctrine applied by the European Court [of Human rights] can be followed by the courts of this country".[41]

In view of the new status of Convention rights, in light of the interpretative obligations imposed on the courts by the Human Rights Act and the Scotland Act[42], and in view of the obligation on the part of the courts to have regard to, inter alia, the case law of the European Court of Human rights (HRA s.2), the approach in *Brind* must be departed from, at least in Convention rights cases. It is of course not correct to say that the Human Rights Act has *incorporated* proportionality wholesale into our law. Rather it will be for the courts through their approach to interpretation-which will also include the obligation placed upon them under to interpret a measure as narrowly as possible to ensure compliance with Convention rights -and their use of Convention case law to develop the doctrine in a domestic context.

Where the proceedings are ordinary judicial review there would appear to be an acceptance that the grounds of review are not fixed and continue to evolve.[43] There is considerable scope for proportionality to evolve into a free-standing ground of review in Convention rights cases. This might also extend to cases involving other human rights such as those protected at common law.[44] As *Salah Abadou* has shown there is potential for the development of this ground in the context of decisions involving the Crown or Scottish Executive when bound by other International Human Rights Treaties.[45]

---

[39] [1991] A.C. 696
[40] at 763A.
[41] See also Lord Lowry at 750G and Lord Templeman at 751G.
[42] s.3 of the HRA and s.101 of the SA.
[43] *West v. Secretary of State for Scotland*, 1992 S.C. 385.
[44] See para.9.59. For early examples of the use of proportionality brought in relation to challenges under Art. 1 of the First Protocol and Art. 6 see *Westerhall Farms v. Scottish Ministers*, April 25, 2001; *Shepherd v. Scottish Ministers*, 2001 G.W.D. 15–570.
[45] See para. 9.59.

Proportionality and other forms of review and appeal

Where the grounds of control are fixed by statute then there may be   9.36
potential for conflict between the needs of proportionality and these
limited grounds. For example where one seeks to judicially
challenge a planning decision it is necessary to invoke the provisions
of the Town and Country Planning (Scotland) Act 1997[46] and
Wordie Property Co. Ltd v. Secretary of State for Scotland.[47]

Given this interpretation there is very little scope for the court to
engage in the assessment of matters impinging on the merits and so
the scope for the use of proportionality would seem limited. The
extent to which difficulties will arise are unclear, and there is already
case law from the Outer House which is arguably at variance with
the existing Strasbourg case law which suggests that limited
Wednesbury review is sufficient protection, at least in cases
involving interference with possessions.[48]

There maybe similar problems in other statutory appeals such as
in relation to licensing under the provisions of the Licensing
(Scotland) Act 1976 and the Civic Government (Scotland) Act
1982.[49] Even where an appeal is taken under the provisions of the
1976 or 1982 Acts, it would be wrong to regard these as appeals at
large on the merits. Many appeals turn on the reasonableness of
decisions and so *Wednesbury* limitations are present. So long as this
is the case, assessment of proportionality is not open. Even where
an appeal is taken on the basis of error of material fact,[50] this does
not permit review of the merits of a decision. This ground of appeal
is concerned with whether there were facts before the Board or

---

[46] s.238 challenge to structure or local plan or s.239, challenge to a planning order,
decision or direction. There are similar provisions for CPO's contained in the
Acquisition of Land (Authorisation Procedure) (Scotland) Act 1947, Sched. 1
para 15(1)).To date the scope for judicial challenge to decisions in these fields has
been couched in the modified *Wednesbury* formula found in *Ashbridge
Investments Ltd v. Minister of Housing and Local Government* [1965] 3 All E.R.
371, C.A.

[47] 1984 S.L.T. 345

[48] See *County Properties Ltd v. Scottish Ministers,* 2000 S.L.T. 973 and compare
Bryan, below. For detailed discussion see Chap 7. See also A. Ferguson, "Human
Rights and Planning Law Collide" 2000 S.L.T. (News) 211 and A. O'Neill Q.C.,
"Developers have human rights too" 2000 45 (9) J.L.S.S. 16. The decision in
County Properties Ltd was relied upon by the Divisional Court to issue a
declaration of incompatibility in relation to planning and other land use inquiry
procedures where the Secretary of State was both the maker of relevant policy and
the decision-maker in relation to the applications in question. The Court found
this to be a breach of Art. 6 as judicial review of any decision reached did not offer
sufficient protection: *R. v. Secretary of State for Transport, Environment and the
Regions, ex p Holding and Barnes plc* [2001] 5 E.G. 170. That conclusion has now
been disapproved by the House of Lords in their decision of May 9, 2001.

[49] See for the 1976 Act, s.39(4) and for the 1982 Act, s.4, Sched. 1, para. 18(7).

[50] 1976 Act, s.39(4)(d) and 1982 Act s.4, Sched. 1 para. 18(7).

committee to engage its jurisdiction to make a decision, not whether the merits of any factual decision can be challenged.[51] The extent to which limitations on the availability of proportionality might violate Convention rights is unclear. The extent to which there are other safeguards in place might determine whether or not such appeals are "fair", at least as seems likely where challenge is made under Art 6.[52] Equally the extent to proportionality is required may depend on the extent of any discretionary area of judgment accorded to the decision maker.[53] If proportionality is required there may be scope for argument as to whether the courts can re-interpret the statutory grounds, particularly the ground of reasonableness, to embrace it. It is not immediately clear that such a result is precluded by statute.

A *General* Test of Proportionality ?

9.37   The extent to which these developments will lead to the use of proportionality in the protection of rights outwith the Convention or as general ground of judicial control of administrative action is less clear. With anything other than a full reception of proportionality a diluted or piecemeal approach is likely to lead to anomalies. If *Brind* is now treated as authority for the view that outside of Convention and Community law the standard of reasonableness still applies, then this is likely to lead to the difficult question of why some rights are less deserving than others. This concern might be alleviated by the development of the type of tiered rationality review discussed below.[54]

Legal Certainty

9.38   The concern that administrative and executive decisions should rest upon the law and not upon arbitrary power has long been a concern for public lawyers.

Over the years this concern has manifested itself in relation to the growth of state regulation of activity in a number of ways. It was this basic concern that led to the development of our present grounds of judicial control so that even apparently unfettered discretion could be subjected to judicial control. Concern has been expressed about the accessibility and intelligibility of administrative rule-making. The courts have been keen to ensure that where administrators act in accordance with policy, that they do so in a

---

[51] For a helpful discussion of the issues see Sir Crispin Agnew of Lochnaw Q.C., "Human Rights and Licensing Law" (2000) 6 S.L.L.P. 20.

[52] See para. 9.42.

[53] See paras 9.55–9.58.

[54] At para.9.33 and for a useful analysis of the problems of other than a full reception as a general ground of control of administrative action see O'Neill, paras 2.111-2.116.

manner which is consistent with certainty and not based on considerations which are unknown to those whose lives are affected by their actions.[55]

It would be accurate to describe this concern as one of the *unspoken assumptions* of our system which underpins and informs existing grounds of control, although it has never figured greatly as a *distinct* ground of control.[56]

The requirement of legal certainty is made explicit under the Convention. Where a decision is made which seeks to interfere with or limit a right or freedom, the decision must meet the over-riding requirement of legality that it must have been "in accordance with the law" or in manner "prescribed by law". Typically we are here concerned with the qualified rights contained in Articles 8–11 although the concern of legal certainty is wider. Law can be statute or common law. The expression does not just mean that it is enough for there to be *some* law in support of the decision. The law must also pass a *qualitative* test, requiring it to be compatible with the *rule of law*.[57] This is especially so where, as often is the case, in administrative law, "the law bestows on the executive wide discretionary powers".[58]

To ensure that the legal basis of a decision is sufficiently certain the law has to be:-

- Adequately accessible by ensuring that the citizen must be able to have an indication that it is adequate in the circumstances of the legal rules applicable to the case.
- Sufficiently precise to enable the citizen to regulate his conduct by being able to foresee to a degree that is reasonable in the circumstances, the consequences which a given action may entail.

The requirement of precision does not mean there must be absolute certainty. It is recognised that many laws are couched in terms which are vague and whose meaning and scope are questions of practice. In assessing foreseeability the use of legal advice is relevant.[59]

---

[55] For discussion of this with particular regard to the requirements of Art. 6 on "informal" decision making see **.

[56] See O'Neill at para.2.54. It has arisen where administrative action has purported to have had retrospective effect : *Burmah Oil Co. v. Lord Advocate* [1965] A.C. 75.Consider also the impact of s.102 of the SA at para.**.

[57] *Malone v. U.K.* (1984) 7 E.H.R.R. 14 at 40, para. 67

[58] *Silver v. U.K.* (1983) 5 E.H.R.R. 347 at 373, para. 90 and also *De Freitas v. Permanent Secretary of Ministry of Agriculture, Fisheries, Lands and Housing* [1998] 3 W.L.R. 675, PC per Lord Clyde at 682C-H.

[59] See generally *Sunday Times v. U.K.* (1979) 2 E.H.R.R. 245 at 271, para. 49; *Muller v. Switzerland* (1988) 13 E.H.R.R. 212 at 226,para. 29.

Procedural Impropriety

9.39   Challenge on the ground of procedural impropriety falls into two broad categories. There can be a failure to comply with an express statutory provision or with the implied obligations derived from the common law rules of natural justice or fairness. Although the two are legally distinct, express procedural provisions are often supplemented with common law requirements.[60] Equally statute can require that a decision maker acts in accordance with natural justice.[61]

The Convention will have its impact here. In particular Article 6(1) which secures the right to a fair hearing in certain defined circumstances will be of particular relevance. Existing protections and Article 6(1) have as their focus *procedural* fairness. The text of the Article is produced in the Appendix and reference should be made to it in the discussion which follows.

It is important to understand that other rights might be relevant to issues of *substantive* fairness and these should not be over-looked.[62]

The general scope of Article 6(1) is considered in the next section. For present purposes it is however convenient to retain the traditional distinction between statutory and common law requirements. One should not lose sight however of the fact that the content of Article 6(1) is general and it applies with equal force to the interpretation of statutory requirements as well as to the development of our common law of procedural fairness.

Article 6, Natural Justice and Procedural Fairness: General Scope

9.40   To understand the potential relationship between natural justice and fairness and Article 6(1) there is merit in examining the existing general approach. Lawyers are familiar with the two main rules of natural justice, *nemo iudex in sua causa* (the rule against bias) and *audi alteram partem* (the right to a hearing and to know the case to be met) which are long rooted in our law.[63] Alongside these traditional notions there has been a growing awareness that administrative powers must be used fairly. Whether this idea of fairness is distinct from natural justice is not clear as the terms are often used inter-changeably. It has been suggested that the older rules are themselves derived from a general doctrine of fairness the content of which will vary according to circumstances.[64]

Control on grounds of natural justice or fairness is not limited to

---

[60] See, *e.g. Malloch v. Aberdeen Corporation*, 1971 S.C. (H.L.) 85
[61] See, *e.g.* Licensing (Scotland) Act 1976, s.39(4); Civic Government (Scotland) Act 1982, s.4, Sched. 1, para 18 (7).
[62] See for example Art. 8 and see para.9.54.
[63] See SME Vol. 1, paras 56.-57 and Clyde and Edwards at paras 18.12–18.24 and 18.25–18.57.
[64] See SME Vol. 1, para. 67

judicial review proceedings in particular. Failure to comply with natural justice is a common ground of appeal in a range of statutory appeals whether expressly[65] or impliedly[66] or as the basis for an appeal arising from error of law.[67]

Many of the Article 6(1) protections exist as requirements of natural justice. Moreover, whilst the concepts of procedural fairness provided by Article 6(1) are drafted in absolute terms, the Court has construed them in a flexible manner much in the same way as natural justice and procedural fairness have been applied in a flexible manner.[68] For example the court has interpreted the requirement to have judgement in public flexibly.[69] The duty to give reasons has also been interpreted as requiring broad, but not detailed compliance.[70] The content under Article 6(1) of what is fair, like the common law ,cannot be reduced to a code.[71]

Overall Article 6(1) may not greatly extend the existing scope of natural justice or procedural fairness, particularly as its primary focus is on the courts or tribunals who determine administrative disputes as opposed to first instance administrative decision makers. Nevertheless it will be important in a number of areas such as the extension of a general duty to give reasons to administrative tribunals, the imposition of a reasonable time requirement on the overall time taken to determine a case, and as providing a test to measure the adequacy of existing judicial means of control as securing fairness in the determination of administrative law disputes.

To determine the scope of protection under Article 6 is necessary to break it down into its component parts.

The General Scope of Protection: The determination of Civil rights and obligations

The distinction between matters of public law and private law has   9.41
peculiar importance in this context. Civil rights and obligations are matters of private law. This would seem to exclude public law claims which rest upon broad powers and duties and are often determined by the exercise of administrative discretion. "Civil Right" should not be limited the private law conception of what is constituted by a right. It has its own meaning independent of domestic definitions.[72]

---

[65] See Licensing (Scotland)1976 s.39(4); Civic Government (Scotland) Act 1982, s.4, Sched. 1, para. 18(7).

[66] See *Lithgow v. Secretary of State for Scotland* 1973 S.C. 1;-statutory applications to quash planning decisions.

[67] *Crake v. Supplementary Benefits Commission* [1982] 1 All E.R. 498-failure to give adequate reasons; *City of Glasgow D.C. v. Doyle*, 1995 S.L.T. 327-failure to give notice of criteria to be relied on in issuing licences.

[68] See Clyde and Edwards at paras 18-01 to 18.04

[69] See para.9.46.

[70] See para.9.45.

[71] See para.9.44.

[72] *Konig v. Federal Republic of Germany* (1978) 2 E.H.R.R. 170, para. 88

In assessing the nature of the right regard must be had to the national system to determine how the right falls to be treated in domestic law. That classification does not mean that the same definition should applies in the Convention context as in *Feldbrugge v. Netherlands.*[73]

Here the Netherlands treated a claim to social security benefits as a matter of public law. The Strasbourg Court held it to be a civil right. Domestic law is directly relevant in that it determines the *scope* of the right. So in *Konig* it was held that the right to practice medicine in West Germany was a civil right and in reaching this conclusion the court took into account that in domestic law the medical profession did not provide a public service.

Of some significance to Scots lawyers given the scope of our supervisory jurisdiction is that the nature of the right falls to be determined according to its *substance* rather than the *nature* of the parties (whether private or public) or the relevant legislation or the court or tribunal with power to determine the dispute.[74]

Amongst civil rights of significance in administrative law:

- A claim for sickness benefit is a relevant civil right[75] as is industrial injury pension.[76]
- The right to engage in commercial activity such as a liquor licence.[77]
- A claim arising from a compulsory purchase order.[78]
- State compensation for an *ultra vires* act.[79]
- The right to practise a liberal profession.[80]
- The fairness of planning inquiry procedure.[81]
- Criminal injuries compensation claims if not purely *ex gratia* and discretionary.[82]

In the field of social security there was some doubt as to whether Art 6 could cover benefit claims. Initially the court approached the matter by comparing the public law elements of a claim with any private law features of the relevant scheme. The issue of whether it was contributory or non-contributory was significant. In *Feldbrugge* it was contributory. More recently the court has extended protection to the general field of social insurance, even where the

---

[73] (1986) 8 E.H.R.R. 425.
[74] *Stran Greek Refineries and Stratis Andreadis v. Greece* (1994) 19 E.H.R.R. 293, at para. 39
[75] *Feldbrugge*
[76] *Deumeland v. Germany* (1986) 8 E.H.R.R. 448.
[77] *Tre Traktorer Aktielbolag v. Sweden* (1991) 13 E.H.R.R. 309.
[78] *Sporrong and Lonnroth v. Sweden* (1983) 5 E.H.R.R. 35.
[79] *National and Provincial Building Society v. U.K.* (1997) 25 E.H.R.R. 127, paras 97-98 and *Editions Periscope v. France* (1992) 14 E.H.R.R. 597, paras 35-40
[80] *Konig; Diennet v.France* (1995) 21 E.H.R.R. 554
[81] *Bryan v. U.K.* (1995) 21 E.H.R.R. 342, para. 31 and see para.9.43.
[82] *Gustafson v. Sweden* (1998) 25 E.H.R.R. 623 and compare *B v. Netherlands* (1985) 43 D.R. 198.

benefit is wholly borne by the state. In domestic law income support would be such a benefit.[83]

Some matters have never been held to involve a civil right. These include taxation,[84] fines,[85] educational rights such as a claim for special needs schooling,[86] and disputes arising from civil service employment.[87]   9.42

The application of Article 6(1) to immigration and nationality cases had been uncertain. Commission case law suggested that it does not apply.[88] This is so even where the decision clearly affects the exercise of other civil rights and obligations.[89]

The concept embraces the supervisory jurisdiction of the Court of Session itself. This raises the question of the adequacy of judicial review as a procedure which fulfils Article 6(1). It can no longer be readily assumed that judicial review as traditionally understood is a sufficient protection in the absence of a right of appeal nor that a right of appeal is sufficient when restricted to a point of law alone.[90]

Article 6 does *not* create a new form of "super" natural justice which applies to *all* forms of decision making. It requires a trigger for the protection of civil rights and obligations and this is a dispute or in the French text a "contestation". It is only when the stage of a dispute arrives in the decision making process can the specific protections be invoked.[91]

A dispute can relate to the existence of a right or its scope or the manner of its exercise. It can involve both matters of fact or law. Provided that the dispute is "genuine and of a serious nature" it will be subject to Article 6[92]. It is *only* if there is such a dispute that there is triggered the obligation to resolve it by the provision of a court or tribunal whose characteristics must in turn comply with the terms of the Article.

Accordingly the *initial* determination of an administrative decision *will not* attract protection. So the initial determination of a benefits decision would not be a dispute. Where the applicant

---

[83] *Salesi v. Italy* (1993) 26 E.H.R.R. 187.
[84] *Schouten and Meldrum v. Netherlands* (1994) 19 E.H.R.R. 432, para. 50 although compare *National and Provincial Building Society*
[85] *Procola v. Luxembourg* (1995) 22 E.H.R.R. 193.
[86] *Simpson v. U.K.* (1989) 64 D.R. 188
[87] *Huber v. France* (1998) 26 E.H.R.R. 457, although that may require to be re-assessed by a future court: *Maillard v. France* (1998) 27 E.H.R.R. 232.
[88] *Agee v. U.K.* (1976) 7 D.R. 164, deportation on security grounds; *Omkaranda v. Switzerland* (1981) 25 D.R. 105, expulsion; *P v. U.K.* (1987) 54 D.R. 256 -asylum; *S v. Switzerland* (1988) 59 D.R. 256 (nationality proceedings.
[89] *Agee* at para.28.)
[90] See para.9.42.
[91] *H v. Belgium* (1987) 10 E.H.R.R. 339, para. 40; *Georgiadis v. Greece* (1997) 24 E.H.R.R. 606, para. 30. For a useful survey of the issues see Meechan, "When is a dispute not a 'dispute'?" (2001) S.L.T. (News) 95.
[92] *Benthem v.Netherlands* (1985) 8 E.H.R.R. 1, para. 32- refusal of a petrol licence; *Le Compte v. Belgium* (1981) 4 E.H.R.R. 1, para. 49—fairness of disciplinary proceedings of a professional body

contests that decision, a dispute would arise. Article 6(1) is therefore concerned with the *tribunal* which determines the civil right or obligation in question as opposed to fairness before the initial decision maker. As such Art 6(1) has potential for considerable impact on the operation of the many administrative tribunals in operation in Scotland as well as courts which determine administrative law cases.

That is not to say that Article 6(1) has no application to decision making where civil rights and obligations are determined *other* than by a court or tribunal. Local authority care decisions are not made by a "tribunal" nor would a housing benefit review board qualify as such. Such bodies will be unable to meet all of the obligations of Article 6(1). However if there is a right of review or appeal to a tribunal or court, then the decision making process as a *whole* must meet Article 6(1). As many administrative decision makers will not comply with Article 6(1), the scope of review or appeal will be significant in determining *overall* compliance.

There may also in time be *indirect* pressure for first instance decision makers to comply with Article 6. If a decision maker can fulfil the obligations, then it will be less likely to be subject to review or appeal.

It should be understood that this flexible approach to the fairness of the proceedings as a whole applies *only* where the initial decision is taken by a body other than a court or tribunal. It does not apply where the courts or tribunals are "integrated within the standard judicial machinery of the country".[93] In the case of such courts and tribunals, Article 6(1) must be complied with at the *initial* hearing *and* on any appeal.

The Specific Protections

Right of access to a court

9.43   In the area of administrative law it has been held that in relation to a decision of the executive or an adjudicative authority which is in breach of Article 6(1), that the state has to provide a right to seek a judicial challenge to such a decision and that the body hearing the challenge must itself comply with Article 6.[94] The right must be *effective* and so may require the state to provide legal aid.[95] The right includes the right to personal and reasonable notice of an administrative decision so that there is afforded a proper opportunity to challenge it in court.[96]

In this area a margin of appreciation is afforded as to how the

[93] See *De Cubber v. Belgium* (1984) 7 E.H.R.R. 236.
[94] *Albert Le Compte v. Belgium* (1983) 5 E.H.R.R. 533, para. 29.
[95] See *Airey v. Ireland* (1979) 2 E.H.R.R. 305.
[96] *De La Pradelle v. France* (1992) A 253-B, para. 34.

right is respected.[97] However the terms and nature of access must not impair the essence of the right and they must be proportionate to a legitimate aim and be legally certain.[98]

It does not follow that where the remedy provided is judicial review rather than a full appeal on the facts and merits would be a breach. In *Kaplan v. United Kingdom*[99] the Commission held that the unqualified right to such a full appeal would be inconsistent with the well-recognised and lawful distinction between appeal and review found in the bulk of Convention states.

In certain areas of administrative law which involve the determination of matters of fact, the exercise of discretion or the application of policy then Article 6(1) *may* be held satisfied by an appeal on a point of law *alone* to a judicial body .Appeal on a point of law alone is familiar in our law. Many tribunals are subject to appeal on this basis.[1] The Franks Committee, Report on Administrative Tribunals and Inquiries examined but rejected appeals to the courts on matters of fact or the merits as this would mean allowing appeals from an expert first instance tribunal to an inexpert court.[2]

Much will depend on the issues which are in dispute and the extent to which the court can supervise the resolution of those issues, so no general assumption can be made that appeal on a point of law alone or judicial review will always suffice. In *Bryan* v. *United Kingdom*.[3] The applicant appealed against a planning enforcement notice, first to an inspector appointed under the relevant Act[4] and then sought judicial review in the High Court. The inspector held an inquiry. The ECtHR held that the inquiry was fair, save for the inspector lacking independence as he was appointed by and subject to direction of the Secretary of State. This raised the issue of whether the availability of judicial review cured this by rendering the process as a whole "fair". It was argued that judicial review was inadequate as it could not review the inspectors' factual findings.

[97] *Golder v. U.K.* (1975) 1 E.H.R.R. 524 at para. 38.
[98] *Ashingdane v. U.K.* (1985) 7 E.H.R.R. 528. *Societe Levage Prestations v. France* (1996) 24 E.H.R.R. 351 paras 40-50.
[99] (1980) 4 E.H.R.R. 64, para. 161. An argument that the terms of s.6 of the HRA meant that *full* compliance with Art.6 was necessary before a professional disciplinary body and that the approach in *Kaplan* should not be followed was rejected in *Tehrani v. U.K. Central Council for Nursing, Midwifery and Health Visiting*, 2001 G.W.D. 1–161.
[1] See for example appeals from employment tribunal to the EAT, Employment Act 1996, s.21; from an immigration adjudicator to the IAT, Immigration Act 1971, s.20; from an appeal tribunal to a Social Security Commissioner, Social Security Act 1998, s.14 and for the general basis of such appeals to the Court of Session see Tribunals and Inquiries Act 1992, s.11 and generally see SME Vol. 1, para. 155 and Blair, Chapter 12.
[2] Cmnd. 218 (1957). See paras 105–107.
[3] (1996) 21 E.H.R.R. 342
[4] Town and Country Planning Act 1990. The Inspector is the equivalent of the Scottish Reporter.

However that factor was not conclusive. To determine the sufficiency of review it was necessary to have regard to the subject matter of the decision, the procedure by which the decision was reached, the nature of the dispute and the claimed and existing grounds of appeal were all treated as relevant factors. Also important was the fact that the proceedings were quasi-judicial, that the appeal to the High Court did not challenge the findings in fact, and that the matters that were raised were dealt with by that court.[5]

Where the kind of special administrative or technical considerations of the type in *Bryan* are absent it would appear there is greater scope for challenge. So in *Albert Le Compte* the absence of an appeal on the merits was held to be a breach in the context of the disciplinary decision of a professional body. In *Obermeier v. Austria*[6] the lack of an appeal on the merits on dismissal from a government body was a breach. In *W v. United Kingdom*[7] judicial review was held to be an inadequate protection in the context of a local authority decision to put children into care where parents wished to challenge the merits of that decision. Where in reality the absence of a means of challenge has not prejudiced the position as where a decision is challenged on the law alone then the lack of an ability to challenge the factual basis of a decision will not be fatal where no criticism was made of the factual basis of the decision.[8] It follows that any dispute about the adequacy of any review or appeal must have practical consequences.[9]

A fair and public hearing

9.44   The concept of fairness is an integral feature of procedural

---

[5]   See generally Lester and Pannick at para. 4.6.25 and compare *County Properties Ltd v. Scottish Ministers*, 2000 S.L.T. 973. But see now *R. v. Secretary of State for the Environment, Transport and the Regions, ex p Holding and Barnes plc*, May 9, 2001, (HL). In *X v. U.K.* (1998) 25 E.H.R.R. C.D. 88, the Commission followed *Bryan* in deciding that an application which alleged a breach of Article 6 due to the limited scope of review of the Court of Session of the merits of a decision to make a statutory disqualification order on the chairman of an insurance company from holding office was "manifestly ill-founded". Given the technical context in which the decision was made, it was appropriate that the decision of the Secretary of State, should only be subject to judicial review.

[6]   (1995) 21 E.H.R.R. 511, para. 36. In *Tehrani* it was held that as the available statutory appeal to the Court of Session was expressed in unqualified terms it should be construed as permitting a right of appeal to permit a complete rehearing of the case. In *Carr v. U.K.C.C.*, 1989 S.L.T. 580, the Inner House had held that the right of appeal did not embrace such a full hearing. However, the Lord Ordinary held that in view of the interpretative obligation found in s.3 of the HRA he was no longer obliged to follow *Carr*.

[7]   (1987) 10 E.H.R.R. 29, para. 29

[8]   *Fischer v. Austria* (1995) 20 E.H.R.R. 349, paras 33-34

[9]   For further discussion of the adequacy of judicial review as a remedy see para.9.31.

protection under Article 6(1). At common law where a right to a fair hearing arises the precise obligations which flow from that right do not form a precise or general code. In any case the obligations "depend on the circumstances of the case, the nature of the inquiry, the rules under which the tribunal is acting, the subject matter that is being dealt with and so forth".[10] The scope of Article 6(1) is equally flexible.

Under Article fairness has been held to include:

- That there be equality of arms, which requires a reasonable opportunity of presenting ones case and in a way which does not place oneself in a position which is at a substantial disadvantage vis-a-vis one's opponent.[11]
- In some cases fairness may require free legal advice or indeed legal representation.[12]
- As well as having time to prepare, each party must have the opportunity to have knowledge of and to comment on the arguments and evidence put by the other party.[13]
- Fairness may also require that there is in place a remedy by which documents held by another party can be recovered or disclosed.[14]

A reasoned decision

The pre-HRA position is that there is no *general* rule which requires tribunal decisions to contain reasons.[15] Statute can sometimes impose a duty.[16]

9.45

---

[10] *Russell v. Duke of Norfolk* [1949] 1 All E.R. 109 at 118, CA per Tucker L.J.

[11] *Dombo Beheer BV v. The Netherlands* (1994)18 E.H.R.R. 213, para.33.

[12] See *Airey v. Ireland* (1979) 2 E.H.R.R. 305. Compare *R v. Secretary of State for the Environment, Transport and the Regions, ex p. Challenger, The Times,* July 11, 2000, CA. Article 6(1) considered in deciding no right to legal aid for resident at planning inquiry to oppose development, although it could not be said that legal aid should never be available in such cases.

[13] *Ruiz-Mateos v. Spain* (1993) 16 E.H.R.R. 505, para .63; *Unterpertinger v. Austria* (1991) 13 E.H.R.R. 175 (lack of cross-examination of evidence in witness statements a breach); *Kotovski v. Netherlands* (1990) 12 E.H.R.R. 434—anonymous witnesses.

[14] *Lamy v. Belgium* (1989) 11 E. R.R.R 529 and see the discussion in *McLeod, Petr,* 1998 S.L.T. 233; *McMichael v. U.K.* (1995) 20 E.H.R.R. 205, paras 80, 83 on failure to disclose vital documents in childrens' panel proceedings and compare *McGinley and Egan v. U.K.* (1998) 27 E.H.R.R. 1, para. 86.

[15] See *R v. Higher Education Funding Council, ex p. Institute of Dental Surgery* [1994] 1 All E.R. 651 for a full survey of the current rule and the exceptions to it and generally see Clyde and Edwards paras 18.52 to 18.67.

[16] See, *e.g.* Licensing (Scotland) Act 1976, s.18; Civic Government (Scotland) Act 1982, Sch 1, para.17 ; Town and Country Planning (Scotland) Act 1997, ss. 8(9), 90(1)(c) and Town and Country (Planning)(General Development Procedure)(Scotland) Order 1992, (SI 1992/224), Art. 22 (reasons to be given for refusal or conditional grant of permission); Social Security Administration Act 1992, Pt II ss. 17-70.

Notwithstanding this, where a body exercising *judicial* functions does not give reasons for its decision then it runs the risk of having being held to have acted irrationally.[17] This has sometimes been extended to administrative functions.[18] Fairness may, in certain circumstances, require reasons as where basic rights are in issue such as personal liberty.[19] Unless one can argue that the instant case falls within these categories then it is unlikely that a claim based on lack of reasons will succeed. Protection is piecemeal and the basic legal principles underpinning any duty unclear.

Even where there is a statutory duty to provide reasons it does not always follow that the standard by which the adequacy of reasons falls to be assessed is satisfactory. Where there is such a duty the failure to provide adequate reasons will be treated as an error of law, but a decision will be struck down only if the error is material.[20] One further criticism that is often made is that statutory formulae often fail to draw out the real reasons and so a decision maker can pass the statutory test but does not reveal the factual basis of the decision or if certain findings were made.[21]

Article 6(1) provides scope for a wider duty to give reasons independent of irrationality or fairness. It is a free-standing right. Whilst its concern is about the reasons provided by the court or tribunal determining the civil right or obligation, it is arguable that this requirement will in turn filter down to first-instance decision makers as well. It is arguable that any hearing before a court or tribunal can only be "fair" if that body can address the reasons given for the decision it is being asked to consider.[22] The Privy Council has suggested that there is now scope for "possible reappraisal of the *whole* position [in relation to the duty to give reasons which the passing of the Human Rights Act 1998 may bring about" and went on to say that Article 6 will "require closer attention to be paid to the duty to give reasons at least in relation to

---

17 *R v. Civil Service Appeal Board, ex p. Cunningham* [1991] 4 All E.R. 310
18 *R v. Secretary of State for Trade and Industry, ex p. Lonhro plc* [1989] 2 All E.R. 609 at 620 *per* Lord Keith of Kinkel
19 see *R v. Secretary of State for the Home Department, ex p. Doody* [1994] 1 A.C. 531 and *Ritchie v. Secretary of State for Scotland*, 1999 S.L.T 55 and see also *R v. City of London Corpn, ex p Matson* [1997] 1 W.L.R 765
20 See for example *Crake v. Supplementary Benefits Commission* [1982] 1 All E.R 498 and *Glasgow D.C. v. Secretary of State for Scotland* 1980 S.C. 150 and in the context of immigration, *Dillon* v. *Secretary of State* for *the Home Department*, 1997 S.L.T. 842
21 See JUSTICE-All Souls, *Report of the JUSTICE-All Souls Review of Administrative Law, Administrative Justice: Some Necessary Reforms* (1988) at paras.3.58-3.59 and for an example of the standard of acceptable reasoning see *Wordie Property Co. Ltd v. Secretary of State for Scotland*, 1984 S.L.T. 345 at 348 *per* the Lord President (Emslie).
22 See, *e.g. Hadjianastassiou v. Greece* (1993) 16 E.H.R.R. 219

those cases where a person's civil rights and obligations are being determined".[23]

It may be harder to resist the extension of the duty to *all* forms of administrative decision making, not just those covered by Article 6, once the walls of this particular dam are breached. Equally Art 6 may shape the duty where it is already recognised at common law or under statute.

A number of principles can be derived from the case law:-

- The content of the right is a matter for the circumstances of each case.[24]
- Every point made in argument before the decision-maker need not be mentioned in the reasons.[25]
- Argument which might be decisive should be dealt with.[26]
- Where sparse reasoning is given a fair procedure requires that the *essential* issues for determination be the subject of *proper* reasons.[27]

The last point could well have significance in relation to those who consider existing provisions on the duty to give reasons to be inadequate.[28] The relative brevity of a traditional statement of reasons in a licensing case or a decision letter in a planning case, is arguably a consequence of the lower level of judicial "*Wednesbury*" scrutiny afforded in these areas to date. With the coming of Convention rights which require to be respected there may be scope for argument that traditional formulae are inadequate as a means of *assessing the extent* to which those rights have been respected.

The court will also require to assess if an appeal or review system is able to make good any deficiency in the reasoning of the body whose decision is being considered by the reviewing or appellate body.

If that conclusion can be reached then notwithstanding any defect in reasoning, the overall proceedings will be found to be fair.[29]

---

[23] *Stefan v. General Medical Council* [1999] 1 W.L.R. 1293 In that case however the availability of a "fair" appeal was sufficient to off-set the "unfairness" of a lack of reasons

[24] see *Van der Hurk v. Netherlands* (1994) 18 E.H.R.R. 481; *Ruiz Torija v. Spain* (1994)19 E.H.R.R. 606, para. 29; *Georgiadis v. Greece* (1997) 24 E.H.R.R. 606, paras 42-43.

[25] *Van der Hurk.*

[26] *Hiro Balani v. Spain* (1995) 19 E.H.R.R. 566

[27] *Helle v. Finland* (1997) 26 E.H.R.R. 159.

[28] See *supra* no.21.

[29] As in *Bryan v. United Kingdom* above; *Wickramsinghe v. U.K.*, Appl. No. 31503/96 December 9, 1997, unreported, where an appeal to the Privy Council from a medical professional committee ensured overall fairness.

Does Article 6(1) require an oral hearing?

9.46   Where a right to a hearing is recognised at common law it does not
follow that the right will be to an oral hearing. Much depends on
the context and will often turn on whether there are matters of fact
in dispute. In *Young v. CICB*[30] it was held that the right to a hearing
did not include the right to an oral hearing to challenge the
conclusions drawn from the previous convictions of the applicant.
The convictions themselves were not disputed so there was no
factual dispute which might require an oral hearing. Written
representations were enough.[31]

Under Article 6(1) there would appear to be extensive scope to
claim that a hearing be oral, the purpose being to protect the citizen
from "the administration of justice in secret with no public
scrutiny".[32] The right to such a hearing would appear to be
divorced from the contextual issues raised at common law and
would arise provided that the other qualifying conditions of Article
6(1) are met. Again we are of course concerned with the hearing
before the relevant tribunal. This may have implications for those
situations where no oral hearing. For example appeals to the Social
Security Commissioner are dealt with without an oral hearing. The
relevant regulations require an oral hearing if a request is made
unless the Commissioner is satisfied that in all the circumstances of
the case that the appeal can be determined without one.[33] The
standard reasons for refusal often just repeat the statutory formula.
There may be scope for argument that in practice the onus has been
placed upon the applicant that an oral hearing is needed, despite the
wording of the regulations.

It is possible to have a practice of no oral hearings unless one of
the parties expressly requests it to do so. If no such request is made
then the right to an oral hearing will be waived.[34] Whether the
hearing is a public one is a related consideration. If the right to an
oral hearing has been waived, public interest might still require a
public hearing.[35] Failure to have a public hearing before an

---

[30]   1997 S.L.T. 297
[31]   Compare *Malloch v. Aberdeen Corporation*, 1971 S.C. (H.L.) 85 and *McIndoe v.
Glasgow District Licensing Board*, 1989 S.C.L.R. 325. See also *Lloyd v. McMahon*
[1987] A.C. 625 (no right to oral hearing for councillors before District Auditor
imposed a surcharge); *R v. Army Board of the Defence Council, ex p. Anderson*
[1992] 1 Q.B. 169 (soldier complaining of racial abuse entitled to oral hearing into
his complaint), see in particular Taylor L.J. at 187; *R v. Secretary of State for
Wales ,ex p Emery* [1996] 4 All E.R. 19—obliged to have oral hearing by of public
inquiry into status of footpath although no statutory obligation under Wildlife
and Countryside Act 1981
[32]   *Pretto v. Italy* (1983) 6 E.H.R.R. 182, ECtHR, para 21; see too *Diemont v. France*
(1995) 21 E.H.R.R. 554, ECtHR, para. 33
[33]   See the *Social Security Commissioner Procedure Regulations 1987* ,(S.I.1987/214)
[34]   *Zumtobel v. Austria* (1993) 17 E.H.R.R. 116, para 34
[35]   *Hakansson* v. *Sweden* (1990) 13 E.H.R.R. 1 and see also *Pauger v. Austria* (1997)
25 E.H.R.R. 105.

administrative body or tribunal may not be a breach of if there is an appeal to a court sitting in public.[36]

The right to a hearing within a reasonable time

The idea that a decision on civil rights or obligations should be produced within a reasonable time is arguably a new basis for challenge to administrative decision making. This ground could potentially embrace both the initial administrative decision making process and any remedial process such as appeal or review. The case of *Sporrong and Lonroth*[37] is an example of delay at both levels. First of all there was delay at the level of the initial decision. Thereafter that delay was compounded by the lack of a domestic structure to remedy this. The lesson for administrative lawyers is clear. The administrative system has to be capable of delivering a decision and remedies in relation thereto within a reasonable time. This is an innovation in our administrative law. There are already signs of its use. In *Lafarge Redland Aggregates Ltd v. The Scottish Ministers*,[38] a seven year overall delay between application for planning permission, an inquiry, and determination by Scottish Ministers was both unreasonable and a breach of Article 6(1). 9.47

Whether a delay is lawful depends on establishing the length of the delay and thereafter all of the circumstances.[39] Complexity, the conduct of the party and authorities, and the background are all relevant.[40] Lack of resources is not an excuse for delay where that is an inherent problem such that the state must take steps to resolve it[41] but not if it is exceptional see.[42] Special considerations (including the political and social significance of certain cases) apply in relation to "constitutional courts".[43]

The right to an independent and impartial tribunal established by law

Whilst the word "tribunal" does not carry with it the distinction between courts and administrative tribunals familiar to the Scots lawyer the primary focus in the following discussion will be on the issues that are most likely to be of significance in determining whether any administrative tribunal complies with Article 6(1). Informal tribunals are not subject to Article 6(1).Tribunals are, 9.48

---

[36] *Schuler-Zgraggen v. Switzerland* (1993)16 E.H.R.R. 405.
[37] See para.9.42.
[38] 2000 S.L.T. 1361.
[39] *Silva Pontes v Portugal* (1994) 18 E.H.R.R. 156
[40] See Clyde and Edwards at para.16.34
[41] *Zimmerman and Steiner v.Switzerland* (1984) 6 E.H.R.R. 17
[42] *Bucholz v. Federal Republic of Germany* (1981) 3 E.H.R.R. 597, para. 51.
[43] *Submann v. Germany* (1996) 25 E.H.R.R. 64.

along with courts, obliged to act in manner which is compatible with Convention rights,[44] the term tribunal is defined in section 21(1) as any tribunal in which legal proceedings may be brought. Where a tribunal is of the former kind, whether Article 6 is met depends on whether any appeal or review from its decisions ensures overall compliance. Where a tribunal is part of the general adjudicative apparatus of the state then it must of itself comply with Article 6(1).[45]

The role of the ordinary courts should not be overlooked. They are tribunals too. Whilst more obviously judicial in function, it does not follow that they will always operate a wide enough jurisdiction to ensure that the decision making as a *whole* from the administrative tribunal of first instance, any appellate tribunal and the court will ensure compliance with Article 6(1).We have already looked at this problem in relation to the adequacy of the right of access to a court, but it arises in this context as well.

The determination of administrative law *disputes* by tribunals is a major feature of our system. To a great extent such tribunals were established to take these disputes away from the courts. Generally their decisions are subject to appeal to the courts, typically, although not always on a point of law only.

Where appeal is not available, then judicial review is the traditional means by which their decisions are policed. Most tribunals make decisions intended to resolve disputes. Some also have an advisory role. Some are composed of persons with extensive legal training and are highly judicial in character. Others have significant lay content. The methods of appointment vary. The procedures vary from the court like to the very informal. Almost all tribunals are meant to reflect the values of openness, fairness and impartiality.[46]

Article 6 of the Convention will impose new demands upon our tribunal system. The public lawyer will now have to assess whether any tribunal meets the criteria demanded by it in respect of its judicial nature, its independence and its impartiality.[47]

Tribunal

9.49   What is a tribunal is determined by the nature of its judicial function. A tribunal which is administrative can still be a judicial

---

[44] s.6(3).

[45] See para 9.42.

[46] Report of the Committee on Administrative Tribunals and Inquiries Cmnd. 218 (1957), (the Franks Report).

[47] The tribunal system is currently the subject of a consultation paper issued by the Lord Chancellor. The Scottish Committee of the Council of Tribunals is undertaking its own review. Convention issues are a key aspect of the review. See http://www.tribunals-review.org.uk.

tribunal for the purposes of the test.[48] An inquiry can be a tribunal.[49] A tribunal can be imposed entirely of persons who are not legally qualified professional judges.[50] It must have full jurisdiction to examine all issues of fact and law relevant to the dispute.[51] Relevancy is the key here and there is no right to a tribunal which acts as an appellate court at large. This may mean that whilst the availability judicial review may not always meet the test, that result does not always follow.[52] In all circumstances its decisions must be based on rules of law and its decisions must be legally binding, not merely advisory.[53]

In the domestic context there could be scope for challenge in a number of areas:

- Will the informal nature of some tribunals be sufficiently "judicial"?[54]
- Tribunal procedure is often informal and to a great extent self-regulated. Does such an approach have a sufficient basis in law for decisions of a procedural nature?
- Tribunals generally have no power to cite witnesses or order documents to be produced. Can they properly determine a dispute without these powers?[55]
- Can an *advisory* tribunal comply?[56]
- Policy oriented tribunals are often subject to a real degree of ministerial control. To what extent does this detract from their ability to enforce their decisions?[57]
- The Unified Appeals Tribunal or the Social Security Commissioners may not be a tribunal under Article 6 as their decisions can be superseded by the Secretary of State.[58]

---

[48] *Campbell and Fell v. U.K.* (1984) 7 E.H.R.R. 165, para. 8—Prison Board of Visitors
[49] See *Bryan v. U.K.* below at para.9.43 and see *Redland Lafarge Aggregates Ltd v. Scottish Ministers,* below at para.9.47.
[50] *Ettl v. Austria* (1987) 10 E.H.R.R. 255, para.38.
[51] *Terra Woningen v. Netherlands* (1996) 24 E.H.R.R. 456, para 52.
[52] See para.9.43.
[53] See *Belilos v. Switzerland* (1988) 10 E.H.R.R. 466, para. 64; *Benthem v. Netherlands* (1985) 8 E.H.R.R. 1, para 40; *Van der Hurk v. Netherlands* (1994) 18 E.H.R.R. 481, para. 52 power to disregard tribunal decision a breach, although power never in fact exercised.
[54] Franks Report para. 64 "Informality without rules of procedure may be positively inimical to right adjudication."
[55] The Franks Committee recommended that all should and some do, such as Employment Tribunals, the CAA and the Lands Tribunal for Scotland.
[56] See, in the context of deportation the previous system of Special Security Advisory Committee ,and the decision in *Chahal v. U.K.* (1996) 23 E.H.R.R. 413.
[57] See for example s. 3(2) of the Civil Aviation Act 1971 and consider the role of the CAA in *Laker v. Department of Trade* [1977] Q.B. 643, C.A.
[58] s.10(1) Social Security Act 1998.

Independent and impartial

9.50   In order to determine if a tribunal can be considered "independent", "regard must be had, *inter alia*, to the manner of appointment of its members and to their term of office, to the existence of guarantees against outside pressures and to the question whether the body presents an appearance of independence".[59]

Independence includes independence from the parties, the executive and the legislature. It does not follow that appointment by the executive or the legislature is prohibited.[60] If it can be shown that appointment was done with a view to securing a particular outcome that would be different.[61] The term of office might be relevant to assessing independence, although short terms have been upheld.[62]

In relation to guarantees from outside pressure, instructions from the executive could constitute a breach. Breaches have been established where a tribunal treated itself as bound by government advice on the meaning of a treaty,[63] or where a tribunal member was dealing with a case where his superior was acting for the government.[64]

Like the common law position "justice must also be seen to be done".[65] So the appearance of independence is also important. This has had consequences in a number of cases. In *Bryan* a planning inspector was not independent in view of the power of the Secretary of State to call in and determine planning appeals.[66] In *McGonnell v. United Kingdom*,[67] the Bailiff of Guernsey who was a senior member of the judiciary, legislature and executive was not independent for the purposes of his determination as a judge that planning enforcement action should be permitted in relation to an application which he, as a member of the executive, had refused.[68] In *Campbell and Fell* there was no breach as prisoners were not reasonably entitled to believe that the Board of Visitors was not independent of the executive.[69]

There may be potential challenges in the following areas:-

- Section 26 of the Social Security Act 1998 permits the Secretary

---

[59] See *Bryan v. U.K.* at para 37 and see para.9.43.

[60] *Campbell and Fell v. U.K.*, below, (prison visitors).

[61] *Zand v. Austria* (1978) 15 D.R. 70 at 81.

[62] Three years in *Campbell and Fell*. See also *Starrs v. Ruxton* 2000 J.C. 208 and compare *Clancy v. Caird*, 2000 S.L.T. 546.

[63] *Beaumartin v. France* (1994) 19 E.H.R.R. 485.

[64] *Sramek v. Austria* (1984) 7 E.H.R.R. 351.See also *Starrs*, below.

[65] See for example *Barrs v. British Wool Marketing Board* 1957 S.C. 72 at 82.

[66] See now *County Properties Ltd v Scottish Ministers*, 2000 S.L.T. 965.

[67] 30 E.H.R.R. 289.

[68] See also *Incal v. Turkey*, June 9, 1998, ECtHR.

[69] At para.81

of State as a party to a dispute to direct the appeals tribunal on the determination of an appeal.

- The appointment of the Reporter in a Local Plan Inquiry by the local planning authority may be challengeable.[70]
- Prior involvement in support for an objection by constituents to an application for planning consent as an MP has not prevented the MP from later determining an appeal on the application as Minister. That approach may no longer be sustainable.[71]

Impartiality requires that there be an absence of prejudice or bias. As such it is essentially concerned with the same issues as the scope of the existing common law rule of *nemo iudex in sua causa*. Its substance is not materially different from that rule.[72] There is both a subjective element of the personal views of the judge in given case and an objective test as to whether the judge offered sufficient guarantees to exclude legitimate doubt.[73] In substance this is the familiar distinction between cases of actual partiality and those where there is concern in the absence of actual partiality that justice has not been seen to be done.[74]

A judge is presumed impartial until the contrary is proved. The views of the party who alleges partiality are important, but not conclusive. The test is whether there is objective justification for that allegation.[75]

In the context of administrative tribunals the following have been held to constitute breaches:

- Financial or personal interest in the case.[76]
- Where tribunal members act as advisers and judges.[77]

---

[70] See Town and Country Planning (Scotland) Act 1997 s.15(3).

[71] See *London and Clydeside Estates Ltd v. Secretary of State for Scotland*, 1987 S.C.L.R. 195–provided "intransigence" not apparent on his part, he was not disbarred from determining an appeal. However, the decision of the House of Lords in *R. v. Secretary of State for Transport, Environment and the Regions, ex p Holding and Barnes plc*, May 9, 2001, would suggest that the traditional approach may in fact be sustainable.

[72] For the scope of the common law see *Wildridge v.Anderson*,(1897) 25 R. (J) 27 at 34, per Lord Moncrieff and generally SME vol. 1. Paras 58–65; Clyde and Edwards at paras 18-12 to 18-24.

[73] See *Piersack v. Belgium* (1982) 5 E.H.R.R. 169; *Bulut v. Austria* (1996) 24 E.H.R.R. 84; *Thomann v. Switzerland* (1997) 24 E.H.R.R. 553.

[74] For an example of the former see *Bradford v. Mcleod*, 1986 S.L.T. 244 and for the latter see *Barrs v. British Wool Marketing Board*, below.

[75] See *Ferrantelli and Santangelo v. Italy* (1996) 23 E.H.R.R. 288; *Hauschildt v. Denmark* (1989) 12 E.H.R.R. 266.

[76] *Langborger v. Sweden* (1989) 12 E.H.R.R. 416—lay tribunal members adjudicating on deletion of clause in a lease were members of a body who wished the type of clause to be retained.

[77] *Procola v. Switzerland* (1995) 22 E.H.R.R. 193.

- Where a tribunal member has already expressed a view on the case.[78]
- Although necessarily speculative at this stage a number of potential challenges to features of our
- administrative system might be suggested:-
- Will the right to an impartial tribunal be infringed where the local authority from whom a Licensing Board's members are drawn is also an objector[79] or the complainer in a suspension hearing?[80]
- Is a housing benefit review board composed of councillors from the housing authority an impartial tribunal in relation to a decision to refuse benefit.[81]

Established by law

9.51   It follows from this requirement that the particular court or tribunal which is provided must have a basis in law as opposed to being for example a body whose existence, decisions and powers depend upon administrative discretion.[82] It follows that such "informal" means of resolving disputes will not meet the requirements of Article 6(1). Such bodies are common in administrative practice. Patrick Birkinshaw[83] argues that government departments often adopt informal mechanisms for dealing with complaints to avoid "a more rigorous and formal statutory process of hearing grievances or complaints". The Council on Tribunals has also criticised reliance on internal review mechanisms instead of a formal right of appeal to a tribunal.[84] Nor is this a phenomenon confined to central government.[85]

It is suggested that those criticisms may now have a greater degree of force. Moreover as we have already seen the availability of judicial review will not always be the answer to problems which emerge at an earlier stage in the decision making process, informal or otherwise.

---

[78] *De Haan v. Netherlands* (1998) 26 E.H.R.R. 417—President of social security appeal tribunal heard appeal in a case in which he had already made a determination against the applicant.

[79] Licensing (Scotland) Act 1976 s.16 (1)(f)

[80] s.31(1) of the 1976 Act and para. 11, Sched. 1 ,of the Civic Government (Scotland) Act 1982.

[81] If not can the availability of judicial review ensure overall compliance? See para. 9.42.

[82] *Zand v. Austria* 15 D.R. 70 at 80 (1978)

[83] "Decision-making and its Control in Administrative Process—An Overview" in *Law, Legitimacy and the Constitution* (McAuslan and McEldowney ed., 1985), at pp.164–165.

[84] Annual Reports for 1989-90 (1990-91 H.C. 64), paras 1.6-1.10 and 1990-91 (1991-92 H.C. 97, paras.3.25 -3.28)

[85] For discussion in the context of local authority decision making see N. Lewis and P. Birkinshaw, "Taking Complaints Seriously: A Study in Local Government Practice" in *Welfare Law and Policy* (M. Partington and J. Jowell eds., 1979).

It does not follow that every detail of the operation must be laid
down in law. Provided that judicial review is available then the
executive or other public body can, in the exercise of its discretion,
deal with many of the aspects of the operation of such "tribunals".
Exercise of this ability through delegated legislation or more
informal rulemaking is therefore legitimate.[86] Where the legitimacy
of setting out the rules by which prison visitors operated in
delegated legislation was not disputed. Equally, informal rules do
not escape the ambit of judicial review.[87]

Gaps in protection?

There is no right in civil proceedings to legal representation. Whilst   9.52
the extent to which such a right exists at common law is a matter of
dispute there is some authority at common law that failure to allow
legal representation might amount to abuse of discretion.[88] Under
the Convention fairness may require such assistance, but in the
absence of a right the onus will be on the party alleging the need for
it to show unfairness.

There is no right to an appeal .This reflects the position at
common law.[89] Where an appeal exists Article 6 will be apply to
it.[90]

Procedural Impropriety

Failure to meet statutory requirements

The Convention will be relevant to this ground of challenge.   9.53
Where procedure is contained in legislation to (whether primary
United Kingdom legislation or subordinate legislation, whether
Acts of the Scottish Parliament or ordinary subordinate legislation)
it will fall to be construed in light of Convention rights under
section 3 of the HRA and section 101 of the SA.

Where subordinate legislation cannot be construed as compatible
with Convention rights it is unlawful.[91] This could have a
significant impact on many areas of administrative law, particularly
where, as is often the case, the detailed procedure is contained in

---

[86] *Campbell and Fell v. U.K.* (1984) 7 E.H.R.R. 165
[87] *R v. Secretary of State for the Home Department, ex p. Khan* [1985] 1 All E.R. 40;
      Rooney v. Chief Constable, Strathclyde Police, 1997 S.L.T. 1261; *Scottish Old
      Peoples Welfare Council, Petrs,* 1987 S.L.T. 179
[88] See *Abbas v. Secretary of State for the Home Department,* 1993 S.L.T. 502 at 504;
      Tait v. Central Radio Taxis (Tollcross) Ltd 1987, S.L.T. 506 and compare *Pett v.
      Greyhound Racing Association* [1970] 1 Q.B. 46 with *Maynard v. Osmond* [1977]
      Q.B. 240 at 252
[89] *Ward v.Bradford Corporation* (1971) 70 L.G.R. 27.
[90] *Delcourt v. Belgium* 1 E.H.R.R. 355
[91] Subject to the defence in s.6(2) of the HRA.

subordinate legislation.[92]

Historically the courts have been particularly concerned to ensure the statutory requirements are followed in the case of action which has an adverse affect on property rights or on a person's ability to practise a trade or occupation, even to the extent of intervening where the statute *prima facie* excludes review on procedural grounds.[93]

Convention rights will heighten this scrutiny both as regards the interpretation of the relevant provisions and by providing an additional requirement by which the lawfulness of such provisions can be assessed. One further consequence is likely to be that insofar as there is a distinction between failures to observe requirements which lead to a finding of *ultra vires* and those which do not,[94] it is arguable that where the failure involves a breach of a Convention right then that should *always* lead to a finding of *ultra vires*.

Where Article 6 is relevant to the determination of a dispute it will be necessary to construe and ultimately test procedural provisions in light of its requirements. This could for example call into question whether a tribunal created by statute is independent if its members are selected by one of the parties to an administrative dispute.

It could have consequences in a number of areas where statute seeks to exclude access to the courts.

One area might be where reliance is put upon a certificate that a certain state of affairs exists and which is conclusive in effect such as a certificate that an act was done for the purpose of national security.[95]

Another example might be statutory "ouster clauses". These have generally been interpreted as not excluding judicial review on the basis that a purported (*ultra vires*) decision is not a decision for the purposes of such a clause.[96]

Article 6(1) will strengthen any such challenge. In other cases ouster clauses which limit the *time* during which challenge can be

---

[92] See for example Town and Country Planning (Inquiries Procedure)(Scotland) Rules 1997 (S.I. 1997 No. 796).

[93] *Moss' Empires Ltd v. Glasgow Assessor,* 1917 S.C. (HL) 1; *McDaid v. Clydebank D.C.,* 1984 S.L.T. 162.

[94] On which see *Ryrie (Blingery) Wick v. Secretary of State for Scotland,* 1988 S.L.T. 806; *Wang v. Commissioner of Inland Revenue* [1995] 1 All E.R. 367, PC; *R v. Immigration Appeal Tribunal, ex p. Jeyeathan* [1999] 3 All E.R. 231, CA and see Lord Hailsham of St Marylebone L.C. in *London and Clydeside Estates Ltd v. Aberdeen D.C.,* 1980 S.C. (H.L.) 1 at 30 and Lord Keith of Kinkel at 42-43.

[95] Such certificates have violated both E.C. law and Art.6(1): *Johnston v. Chief Constable of the RUC* Case 222/84 [1986] E.C.R. 1651; *Tinnelly and Sons Ltd and McElduff v. U.K.* (1999) 27 E.H.R.R. 249.

[96] See *Anisminic v. Foreign Compensation Commission* [1969] 2 A.C. 147.

made—such as a "6 week rule"—have been upheld.[97] It may be that this approach to the interpretation of time limit clauses will have to be reconsidered in light of Article 6(1).[98]

Substantive Fairness

Every public authority in the exercise of their powers must act fairly. This requires respect for the two rules of natural justice as well as a duty to act fairly in other procedural respects.[99] Fairness in the sense of the substance of the decisions being fair is no part of the grounds of review in our law.[1]

9.54

Insofar as fairness requires that legitimate expectations be protected the scope of that protection has generally been confined to ensuring procedural fairness in requiring a hearing in relation to a decision affecting the substance of the expectation—*R v. Secretary of State for the Home Department, ex parte Hargreaves.*[2] Although some cases do seem to acknowledge some form of substantive protection[3] that was generally confined to cases where there was an "irrational" deprivation of the expectation. Any form of protection beyond that has however been treated as straying beyond the bounds of *Wednesbury* review and into the realms of interference with the merits of a decision.[4]

The idea that fairness in this sense is essentially a procedural matter and that at most protection for the underlying expectation is confined to *Wednesbury* review requires to be revised in light of Convention rights.

In *R v. North and East Devon Area Health Authority, ex parte Coughlan,*[5] the Court of Appeal held that the failure to honour a

---

[97] See *Martin v. Bearsden and Milngavie D.C.,* 1987 S.L.T. 300; *Hamilton v. Secretary of State for Scotland,* 1972 S.C. 72. Such clauses have been held to be effective even where bad faith or fraud are alleged *R v. Secretary of State for the Environment, ex p. Ostler* [1977] Q.B. 122 and *Smith v. East Elloe Rural D.C.* [1956] A.C. 736; and even where there has been a failure to notify a planning application *and* an inquiry as required by statute to the party seeking review : *Pollock v. Secretary of State for Scotland,* 1993 S.L.T. 1173.

[98] In E.C. law such clauses must not be interpreted in such a way as to make access to the courts "virtually impossible" in practice: Case 199/82 *San Giorgio v. Amministazione delle Finanze dello Stato* [1983] E.C.R. 3595.

[99] *Errington v. Wilson,* 1995 S.C. 550 at 554, 560-561 *per* the Lord President (Hope) and Lord Clyde: "It is not a matter of discretion, as the duty to act fairly does not leave it to the discretion of the decision maker to decide what is and what is not fair" at 555, *per* the Lord President

[1] *Lakin Ltd v. Secretary of State for Scotland,* 1988 S.L.T 780 at 787 *per* Lord Justice-Clerk; *Shetland Line (1984) Ltd v. Secretary of State for Scotland,* 1996 S.L.T. 653 at 658 *per* Lord Johnston

[2] [1997] 1 All E.R. 397, CA

[3] *e.g. Walsh v. Secretary of State for Scotland,* 1990 S.L.T. 526; *R v. Secretary of State for the Home Department, ex p. Ruddock* [1987] 2 All E.R. 518; *R v. Ministry of Agriculture, Food and Fisheries, ex p. Hamble (Offshore) Fisheries Ltd* [1995] 2 All E.R. 714

[4] See in particular *Hargreaves* at 921 *per* Hirst L.J.

[5] [2000] W.L.R. 621.

promise to let a person stay in a care home was an *irrational* breach of a *substantive* legitimate expectation. The local authority who operated the care home argued that they were not bound by that promise and that in any event there was no scope for the operation of a substantive legitimate expectation. What is of particular interest in this pre-HRA case is the extent to which the court was prepared to use Article 8 as a check upon the rationality of the authorities decision *both* as the basic right of respect for the home found in Article 8(1) and whether the decision could be justified in terms of Article 8(2). If taken now not only would the decision be open to rationality scrutiny, it would be subject to proportionality as well.

In light of this approach a decision such as *McPhee v. North Lanarkshire Council*,[6] where it was held that a local authority was not bound by an earlier promise to allow a traveller to return to her pitch after she left it to allow for its upgrading, might now be subject to Convention challenge along similar grounds. The case turned on the extent to which departure from any promise was irrational and whether if it was, whether the petitioner could be afforded the benefits flowing from this substantive legitimate expectation. It was held not to be irrational on the basis that the protection of substantive as opposed to procedural legitimate expectations beyond *Wednesbury* review was not open in our law.

The development of greater protection for substantive legitimate expectations in human rights cases has been acknowledged in the context of (as yet unincorporated) International Treaties. This could be significant in the context of rights protection *outwith* the Convention rights contained in Schedule 1 of the HRA.[7] This is in view of a recent decision of the High Court of Australia that ratification of a Treaty not incorporated into national law may create a legitimate expectation that executive decisions will conform to the treaty.[8] There are already signs that the United Kingdom courts will be prepared to accept the principle in *Teoh*.[9]

Intensity of scrutiny: balance, the margin of appreciation and the discretionary area of judgement

9.55   As we have seen the various grounds of review can be applied with varying degrees of intensity. We have seen that where the matter is one of error of law the court will only intervene if any

---

[6]   1998 S.L.T 1317.

[7]   See, *e.g.* para.9.59.

[8]   *Minister of State for Immigration v. Teoh* (1995) 128 A.L.R. 353 and for comment see R. Piotrowicz [1996] P.L. 190

[9]   See *R v. Secretary of State for the Home Department,ex parte Ahmed* [1998] INLR 570, CA; *Thomas v. Baptiste* [1999] 3 W.L.R. 249, PC; *R v. Uxbridge Magistrates' Courts, ex p. Adimi* [1999] 4 All E.R. 520. See further *R v. Director of Public Prosecutions, ex p. Kebeline* [1999] 4 All E. R.801, H.L.—commencement provisions of HRA excluded legitimate expectation of compliance before commencement of Act.

error of law was material.[10] Where the matter is related to the *weight* given to a relevant consideration then generally the court would not interfere. We have seen that the intensity of review on grounds of rationality and proportionality varies and that the scope of procedural protection is flexible.

All of these are, in substance, a form of a margin of appreciation in which the decision maker is left with a degree of flexibility in how decisions are reached.[11]

It is clear is that Convention rights will have an impact on this approach. It is a necessary consequence of Convention rights that decision makers will have to take into account Convention rights, both in the *manner* in which decisions are reached and the substantive *effect* on those rights that the decision will have. It is now implied into the exercise of all forms of power, that decisions must be made in accordance with Convention rights. There is then potential for argument as to the *weight* to be accorded to these rights and therefore to the *intensity of scrutiny*.

The idea of there being a permitted balance in the determination of the scope of a right and the limitations that might be placed upon it has found expression in Commonwealth human rights cases. Whilst accepting that a "generous or purposive" approach to the right under scrutiny is appropriate,[12] provisions which limit rights must be narrowly construed in light of the reason for limit and its weight. The parallel with proportionality is clear. However, the courts have also gone on to stress that claims under human rights guarantees must *themselves* have a "sense of proportion" or balance.[13]

This idea of balance has a parallel with the concept of margin of appreciation. In the jurisprudence of the European Court of Human Rights this is also sometimes called the discretionary area of judgment. This doctrine reflects the assumption that national state authorities are in a better position than the Strasbourg Court to assess the needs of the particular state and affords a degree of latitude or deference in recognition of this advantage. The margin applies both to identifying the meaning of a right and to the permissibility of any limit placed upon it.

The doctrine has been justified as "the machinery of protection established by the Convention is subsidiary to the national systems

---

[10] See para. 9.28.

[11] See Kennedy L.J. in *R v. Chief Constable of Sussex, ex p. ITF* [1997] 2 All E.R. 65 at 80–81.

[12] See, *e.g. Minister of Home Affairs v. Fisher* [1980] A.C. 319 per Lord Wilberforce at 329 and see also *Att.-Gen. of the Gambia v. Jobe* [1984] A.C. 689. The Canadian courts have a similar approach: *Hunter v. Southam* [1984] 2 S.C.R. 145 as do the New Zealand Courts: *Ministry of Transport v. Noort* [1992] 3 N.Z.L.R. 260,

[13] See *Att.-Gen. for Hong Kong v. Lee Kwong Kut* [1993] A.C. 951 per Lord Woolf at 965 and see too *R v. Grayson and Taylor* [1997] 1 N.Z.L.R. 399, especially at 409 and see now *A v. Scottish Ministers*, 2000 S.L.T. 885 G-H *per* the Lord Justice General. On *A* see para.9.58.

of safeguarding human rights".[14] National authorities are in principle better placed than an international court to evaluate local needs and conditions".[15]

The objection to the extension of a similar doctrine to the domestic context is that it is rooted in the peculiar relationship between an international court and national states and that the peculiar features of that relationship do not have a domestic parallel. It has been observed in another context that the Convention is not

> "concerned directly with the validity of domestic legislation but whether, in relation to a particular complaint, a state has in its domestic jurisdiction infringed the rights of a complainant under the European Convention."[16]

9.56　Moreover on one view *Salah Abadou* suggests an approach which if followed in cases involving Convention rights, could give greater protection to those rights if the domestic court decides not to see the Convention as simply the *minimum* standard of protection. Equally one might say that that is one justification but not necessarily the sole or main one. *Buckley* suggests that the underlying concern is to ensure that the most *appropriate* body for the circumstances in hand is given the task of protecting Convention rights, and that is not always the judiciary.

One other way of understanding the concept is to consider its relationship with proportionality. Where strict proportionality applies then the scope of any margin is correspondingly reduced. Where a more flexible use of proportionality occurs that would suggest in turn that any margin is more broadly defined. To that extent the margin of appreciation is a means of determining the strictness with which proportionality will be applied and serves as a way of ensuring that concerns over the legitimacy of judicial power in the control of governmental acts are addressed. Understood in that light the parallel with tiered scrutiny becomes clear.[17] A similar approach can be found within a number of *national* human rights jurisdictions.[18]

---

[14]　*Handyside v. U.K.* (1976) 1 E.H.R.R. 737 at 753 para. 48.
[15]　*Buckley v. U.K.* (1997) 23 E.H.R.R. 101 at 129, para. 75. On the margin generally see Clyde and Edwards para 6.19.
[16]　*Att.-Gen. of Hong Kong v. Lee Kwong-Kut* at 966H–967A *per* Lord Woolf. For criticism of the use of a margin of appreciation in a domestic context see Sir John Laws, "Wednesbury" in *The Golden Metwand and the Crooked Cord* (Forsyth and Hare ed., OUP, Oxford, 1998), at p.201. See too Singh, Hunt and Demetriou, "Is there a role for the 'Margin of Appreciation' in National Law after the Human Rights Act?" [1999] E.H.R.L.R. 15.
[17]　See para.9.33.
[18]　See generally Clyde and Edwards at para. 6.20 and for the position in Canadian law see *R v. Oakes* [1986] 1 S.C.R. 103 and *R v. Edwards Books and Art* [1986] 2 S.C.R. 713.

Insofar as experience with judicial review of the legality of Acts of the Scottish Parliament is concerned it would seem that a domestic margin in that context at least will have scope for development.[19] The potential for any development beyond that is unclear but models have already been suggested. The following model has—in broad terms—been commented on with approval in the House of Lords.[20]

David Pannick Q.C. suggests that there may well be scope for the development of such a doctrine in the domestic context. He argues that:

> "Just as there are circumstances in which an international court will recognise that national institutions are better placed to assess the needs of society, and to make difficult choices between competing considerations, so national courts will accept that there are circumstances in which the legislature and the executive are better placed to perform those functions."[21]

He goes on to suggest a tentative list of factors which the court might take into account in assessing the extent of this discretionary area as follows:

> "(1) The nature of the Convention right. Many of the rights protected by the Convention (for example Articles 8–11 and Article 1 of Protocol No. 1) require a balance to be struck between competing considerations. [For example, Article 8(2) permits interference by a public authority in accordance with law provided the interference is necessary in a democratic society in the interests of national security, public safety or the economic well-being of the country, for the protection of health or morals or for the protection of the rights and freedoms of others.] Other rights (such as Article 3) are absolute.

9.57

---

[19] See *A v. Scottish Ministers*, 2000 S.L.T. 873 discussed at para.9.58.

[20] See *R v. Director of Public Prosecutions, ex p. Kebeline* [1999] 4 All E.R. 801 at p844–845 *per* Lord Hope of Craighead and see also *A v. Scottish Ministers* at p885 D–F per the Lord Justice-General. The statement of principle is beginning to find practical application in classic areas of administrative law. The Court of Appeal has emphasised the need to ensure that there remains a principled distance between the decision making of the minister in immigration matters and the courts review of his compliance with Art. 8 and in particular his assessment on whether any interference with that right can be justified under Art. 8(2): *R. v. Secretary of State for the Home Department, ex p Mahmood*, December 12, 2000 and *R. v. Secretary of State for the Home Department ex p Isiko*, December 20, 2000. The scope of such a distance will be founded upon any existing judicial deference but taking into account relevant Strasbourg case law and the gravity of the interference. *Mahmood* has been followed in the Outer House: *Ahmed v. Secretary of State for the Home Department*, 2001 G.W.D. 10–365.

[21] "Principles of interpretation of Convention rights under the Human Rights Act and the discretionary area of judgement" [1998] P.L. 545 at 549.

(2) The extent to which the issues require consideration of social, economic or political factors. [In this connection he goes on to note that the Supreme Court of Canada in interpreting its Canadian Charter of Rights and Freedoms has observed that:] courts are not specialists in the realm of policy-making, nor should they be. This is a role properly assigned to the elected representatives of the people, who have at their disposal the necessary institutional resources to enable them to compile and assess social science evidence, to mediate between competing social interests and to reach out and protect vulnerable groups.

(3) The extent to which the court has special expertise, for example in relation to criminal matters.

(4) Where the rights claimed are of special importance, "a high degree of constitutional protection" will be appropriate [*Libman v. Attorney-General of Quebec* (1998) 3 B.H.R.C.269 at 289–290, para.60 (Supreme Court of Canada). The European Court of Human Rights has recognised as being of especial importance rights to freedom of expression (especially in relation to political speech), access to the courts, and protection of intimate aspects of private life. In such contexts, judicial deference is far less appropriate, and the courts will carry out particularly strict scrutiny of state conduct."

In relation to the last point sections 12 and 13 of the HRA require the court to have *particular* regard to the importance of the Convention right to freedom of expression,[22] and any question arising under the Act which might affect the exercise by a religious organisation, the Convention right to freedom of thought, conscience and religion.[23]

One issue that will require to be resolved is to whom will any discretionary area of judgement apply? Whilst there are particular concerns deriving from questions of democratic accountability in difficult areas of policy which might suggest a role for the margin at the higher levels of administration, the extent to which a margin can be extended to lower level decision makers is less clear. It might be argued that to do this would accord a double layer of protection by extending the margin to *both* the initial legislative or executive decision *and* to its implementation. Conversely it might be said that difficult issues do not become easier in the lower levels of administration faced, in addition, with practical problems of implementation. Given that in our administrative law tradition we already accord a degree of deference to decision makers at this level, it is a perhaps likely that something similar will develop in the Convention context.

---

[22] s.12(4).
[23] s.13(1).

Margin of appreciation and the Scottish courts

The Scottish courts will require to be particularly careful in the   9.58
manner in which they apply any discretionary area of judgement in
view of the nature of the Scottish Executive and Parliament as
devolved bodies. Ultimately the Judicial Committee of the Privy
Council will shape any margin, but it is legitimate to consider
whether all Scottish courts have the ability to apply such a margin
as a consequence of the distinctive power of all Scottish courts to
declare an Act of the Parliament as not being law.[24]

Guidance from the Commonwealth in cases involving devolved
government might assist. In *Ming Pao Newspapers Ltd v. Attorney -
General of Hong Kong*,[25] the Judicial Committee of the Privy
Council held that the Hong Kong legislature enjoyed a margin of
appreciation in determining the scope of any limits to their Bill of
Rights in view of the nature of the *international* jurisdiction of the
Committee.

It might be argued that such an approach is relevant only in the
context of a international court such as the Judicial Committee and
that it has no application when considering local conditions
throughout the United Kingdom. Yet, arguably, it is a consequence
of devolution itself that more than before it can be argued that such
conditions do now prevail. There would therefore seem to be
considerable scope for the distinctive powers of the Scottish courts
and the Scottish Parliament to justify the use of a discretionary area
of judgement.

There is already scope for the development of such an approach
in light of the decision in *A v. Scottish Ministers*.[26] Here the Mental
Health (Public Safety and Appeals)(Scotland) Act 1999 was
challenged as being contrary to Article 5(1)(e) of the Convention
as being an unlawful deprivation of liberty and therefore was "not
law" in terms of section 29(2)(d) of the SA. In simple terms the Act,
which had retrospective effect was passed to prevent the release of
persons with untreatable personality disorders from the State
Hospital, a result which would follow under the previous
legislation.[27] The new Act was retrospective in effect and three
men who were affected by it challenged it.

In reaching the conclusion that the Act was lawful the court had
regard to a number of factors;

- it was accepted that a balance required to be struck between
individual rights and the interests of the community. In doing

---

[24] See paras 9.64–9.71.
[25] [1996] A.C. 907.
[26] 2000 S.L.T 873.
[27] See Mental Health (Scotland) Act 1984 ss.17 and 64, and *Reid v. Secretary of State for Scotland*, 1999 S.C.L.R. 74.

this the court expressly adopted the approach to the discretionary area of judgment outlined in *Kebilene*.[28]

- The right was *itself* subject to a sense of proportion or balance as described by Lord Woolf in *Lee Kwong-kut*.

- Finally it was clear from an examination of how the Parliament had gone about legislating that in considering difficult policy issues it had been mindful of the need to respect rights under the Convention and that due deference should be afforded to the decision made.[29]

SCOTLAND ACT 1998 AND CONVENTION RIGHTS

Public Law, Convention Rights and the Scotland Act

General

9.59   As we have seen in Chapter 1 in defining the scope of the powers of the Scottish Parliament and the Executive and their relationship with Convention rights, the Scottish courts will have a significant role. In view of the scheme of devolution and the powers open to them it would perhaps be quite realistic to say that our courts will operate the power of *constitutional judicial review* .It is this added dimension which gives Convention rights a special status in challenges to the activities of the Scottish Parliament and Executive.

The term constitutional judicial review has no technical meaning but serves to highlight this new dimension to an ancient jurisdiction. One should not take it from the use of the expression "judicial review" that it will only be the Court of Session in the exercise of its supervisory jurisdiction that will have a role to play. As we have seen in relation to the HRA many of the techniques of judicial review will spill over into "ordinary" proceedings which hitherto would not have been concerned with matters of *vires*. Under the SA where Acts of the Scottish Parliament are reviewed for compliance with Convention rights, this is as much judicial review in substance, even if the form of determination of the issue is a forum other than the supervisory jurisdiction of the Court of Session. To that extent the discussion of the impact on the grounds of review of Convention rights in relation to the HRA has as much bearing here.[30]

One matter should not be overlooked and this is the potential for human rights other than Convention rights to impact on the new government. Although the most immediate and effective source of human rights control will be via Convention rights, the new rights culture may have further legal consequences. First, at common law

---

[28] See para.9.56.
[29] See in particular the Opinion of the Lord Justice-General at pp.885-886.
[30] See Clyde and Edwards para.7.03 for further analysis of the distinction.

reference was sometimes made to basic rights as requiring legal protection. It may be that these may now be reclassified as human rights, which is arguably a more emotive and perhaps more—legally?—value laden term.[31]

Secondly, once conditioned to think in terms of human rights it might be easier to argue that these rights are deserving of greater protection than "ordinary rights".[32]

Thirdly, the new political and constitutional climate may engender legally enforceable respect for other human rights documents. Just as there was a creeping acceptance that the ECHR could be used as an interpretative aid prior to the HRA and SA,[33] and as a indicator of the rationality[34] of decisions, there may come to be an acceptance of the use of the rights contained in these documents. For example the United Nations Covenant on Civil and Political Rights[35] requires to be observed by the Scottish Parliament and Executive.[36] What observance might mean is open to debate but it is at least arguable that it may impose a form of interpretative obligation. There are already signs of this happening.[37] In addition democratic political process rights might be more readily implied, a phenomenon that has arisen in a number of Commonwealth jurisdictions.[38]

Convention rights and the Parliament

Under section 29(1) "An Act of the Scottish Parliament is not law so far as any provision of the Act is outside the legislative competence of the Parliament". Within that simple statement there lies a new legal principle with profound implications for the relationship between the citizen, the courts and government. Subsection 2 goes on to list the five areas into which the Parliament cannot stray without exceeding its powers and one of these is compliance with Convention rights.[39]

Whilst this is the most obvious means by which Convention rights will impact upon it, Convention rights have significance in relation to a number of other areas of its activities.

9.60

---

[31] See para.9.14.

[32] For discussion see para. 9.33.

[33] *AMT, Petr.*,1996 S.L.T.724 and compare *Kaur v. Lord Advocate*, 1980 S.C. 319 for the rejection of the use of the ECHR in this role.

[34] disproportionality, see para.9.26.

[35] Cmnd 6702

[36] See SA Sched. 5, Pt I, para.7(2)

[37] *R v. Secretary of State for the Home Department, ex p. Venables and Thompson* [1997] 3 W.L.R. 23 at 49 F-H-UN Convention on the Rights of the Child. For the use of relevant international Human rights documents in interpreting Convention Rights see: *H.M.Advocate v. DP and SM*, 2001 G.W.D. 7–255.

[38] See for example, *Nationwide News Party Pty Ltd v. Wills* (1992) 177 C.L.R. 1 and see Clyde and Edwards, para 7.33

[39] s.29(2)(d).

Convention Rights and Proceedings in Parliament

9.61　To what extent can Convention rights be used as a basis for challenge to a Parliamentary proceedings? Proceedings might be of two kinds. Proceedings leading to the enactment of legislation and the general proceedings of the Parliament itself, including the activities of its officers and members.

Unlike the Westminster Parliament, the Scottish Parliament, its officials and members do not enjoy the same degree of protection from Convention rights which is conferred by the HRA.[40] Moreover it would appear that the Parliament is itself a public authority for the purposes of the HRA and logically this would seem to extend to the Parliamentary Corporate Body.[41] Questions might arise as to whether the Presiding Officer[42] or the Clerk of the Parliament[43] or other officials are public authorities subject to Convention rights.[44]

Where the proceedings relate to the enactment of legislation there is specific provision in the Act. Where the validity of an Act is impugned on the basis of procedural flaws there is an apparently clear answer. Section 28(5) provides that the validity of an Act of the Scottish Parliament "is not affected by any invalidity of the proceedings leading to its enactment".

This is a statutory restatement of the enrolled Act rule which prevented similar challenges to Acts of the Westminster Parliament.[45]

Proceedings in Parliament includes "proceedings of any committee or sub-committee"[46] but beyond that is not defined, but is broad enough to cover failure to comply with standing orders and arguably any failures under section 31.[47] On the face of it the scope for Convention based challenge seems limited. There may be scope for challenge on Convention grounds where it is alleged that the proceedings are simply "purported proceedings". Section 28(5) might be viewed as an exclusion or ouster clause. Historically the courts have construed such clauses

---

[40]　See s.6(6) of the HRA and see discussion at para.9.07.

[41]　See para.9.73. The Body was set up under s.21 of the SA. Its functions include the bringing or defence to legal proceedings by or against the Parliament under s.40.

[42]　s.19

[43]　s.20

[44]　See for example *New Zealand Police v. Beggs,* 8 B.H.R.C.116, High Court of New Zealand-Speaker of N.Z. Parliament a public authority under their Bill of Rights in relation to a decision to remove protesters from land outside the Parliament.

[45]　*British Railways Board v. Pickin* [1974] A.C. 765 and see *Edinburgh and Dalkeith Railway Co. v. Wauchope* (1842) 1 Bell App.Cas. 252 and generally see Clyde and Edwards paras 4.32 and 9.10. For a statement of the older Scots position which was not necessarily to the same effect see Mitchell, pp.82-87 and see *Queensberry v. Officers of State* (1807) Mor.App.Juris.19.

[46]　s.126(1).

[47]　On which see para.9.62.

narrowly so as to ensure that a body acts within its jurisdiction.[48] It might be argued that as the SA itself must be construed in a manner which is compatible with Convention rights under section 3 of the HRA, and so an absolute bar on judicial challenge might, in certain circumstances, be an unlawful denial of the right of access to the courts under Article 6(1).[49]

Set against this is the argument that this is a special exclusion clause and that the whole scheme of pre-enactment scrutiny suggests that it is for the Parliament, its officers and the Executive to ensure compliance with Convention rights at that stage and interference from the court at pre-enactment stage is excluded.[50]

One should not overlook that section 28(5) only applies to proceedings leading to an Act. No special legal privilege is accorded to other proceedings in Parliament. In *Whaley v. Lord Watson of Invergowrie*[51] the Inner House gave short shrift to the argument that deference to the right of the Parliament to regulate it affairs precluded judicial scrutiny of such proceedings.[52]

What then of the proceedings of a Parliamentary Committee or inquiry which infringes Convention rights, such as the right afforded to respect for private life and correspondence under Article 8 or the right against self-incrimination under Article 6(1)? The powers contained in sections 23 to 27 to compel attendance of persons to give evidence or produce documents might engage Convention protection and, if so, would require to be construed and exercised in a way which was compatible with Convention rights.

Another example could be the operation of standing orders. Provision is made in the Act for the regulation of the Parliament's proceedings by standing orders.[53] Again it is arguable that these will require to be construed and operated subject to Convention rights. For example Schedule 3 permits standing orders to allow for the withdrawal of a member's rights and privileges.[54] There may be an argument as to whether these are civil rights and obligations for the purposes of Article 6(1), although there may be doubt as to whether these are matters of civil right.[55] *Whaley* suggests that the courts will be prepared to police internal proceedings. There is

---

[48] See most famously *Anisminic Ltd v. Foreign Compensation Commission* [1969] 2 A.C. 147 and generally Clyde and Edwards para. 7.08

[49] See also para.9.43.

[50] See further below in relation to Bills at para.9.62. In addition in giving his opinion in *Whaley* the Lord Justice General expressed the view, albeit obiter, that s.28(5) excluded challenge.

[51] 2000 S.C. 125.

[52] For comment see C.Munro, "Privilege at Holyrood" 2000 P.L.43.

[53] s.22 and Sched. 3.

[54] See Sched. 3, 2.

[55] See discussion at para.9.41. In *Pierre-Bloch v. France* (1997) 26 E.H.R.R. 202 the office of MP was held not to be a civil right for the purposes of Art. 6 in relation to disqualification proceedings.

perhaps an even greater argument for so doing or for applying heightened scrutiny to those activities where there is Convention content. Subject to what is said below about the limits on available remedy it is submitted that there is scope for challenge.

Finally under section 41 for the purposes of the law of defamation any statement made in proceedings in Parliament or any publication under the authority of the Parliament are absolutely privileged.[56] The extent to which absolute privilege is justified in light of Convention rights is unclear. It may operate as a bar on access to the courts under Article 6(1) or in some cases be a violation of Article 8 if privilege is used to violate respect for private and family life. Section 41 reflects the position at Westminster.[57] The *operation* of Parliamentary privilege has been held to be subject to judicial review in South Africa on the basis that as the Constitution binds Parliament no privilege could be inconsistent with it.[58]

Convention Rights and Bills of the Parliament

9.62   Under the Act there are a number of mechanisms for ensuring pre-enactment scrutiny which includes scrutiny on Convention grounds.

* Section 31 of the Act requires member of the Scottish Executive[59] and the Presiding Officer[60] to affirm that Bills introduced into the Parliament are within its legislative competence.

* Section 33 allows the Advocate General for Scotland, Lord Advocate and the Attorney-General to refer to a Bill or a provision therein to the Judicial Committee of the Privy Council to determine its competence.[61]

---

[56] ss.41.(1)(a), (b).
[57] See para.9.07.
[58] See *De Lille v. Speaker of the National Assembly*, 1998 S.A. 430. See also Appl. No. 35373/97, *McNeill v. U.K.*—complaint to the Commission that absolute privilege was a violation where defamatory statements made in bad faith by M.P. but still absolutely privileged. Should (could?) s.41 be read as allowing claims where privilege is abused? In *Demicoli v. Malta* (1991) 4 E.H.R.R. 47 contempt of Parliament proceedings were held to be criminal for the purposes of Art. 6, privilege could not be used so as to permit Parliament to prosecute and try a journalist said to have published material in contempt of Parliament.
[59] subs (1)
[60] subs.(2)
[61] s.35 permits the Secretary of State to make an order prohibiting the submission of a Bill for the Royal Assent where he has reasonable grounds to believe that it would be incompatible with any international obligations or the interests of defence or national security, or which modifies the law on a reserved matter in an adverse manner. International obligations does not include the ECHR: s.126(1), but clearly this power could impact on Bills which involve other international rights obligations on which see para.9.59 or any rights located in a reserved area. Similar provisions in relation to the acts of the Scottish Executive are found in s.58.

A number of points can be made here. It is not apparent what remedy if any is open to a citizen who alleges that there has been a breach of section 31 where there has been a failure to secure such a statement or where the statement was based on some fundamental error which relates to Convention rights.

Secondly, to what extent can it be said that a reference to the Judicial Committee of the Privy Council precludes a later challenge to the *vires* of an Act on Convention grounds? Section 103 provides that its decisions "shall be binding in all legal proceedings (other than proceedings before the Committee." On one view this suggests that a decision on the compliance of a Bill with Convention rights is determinative of questions of *vires* raised in post-enactment proceedings. However it is submitted that such a reference does not prevent such a challenge. Any reference must of necessity be based on hypotheses which are at that point, untested. Secondly, the content of the Convention is constantly evolving and the standards that might apply at the point of challenge may well differ from those considered by the Committee at the point of reference.[62]

The greatest difficulty in the way of a challenge to legislation at the stage of its passage through Parliament is the question of title. First, a person seeking to challenge an such a proposed Act would have to show that they were a victim. This is not an easy test to satisfy and would appear not to be satisfied in the context of pressure groups, perhaps the most likely source of such a challenge.[63] There may be particular difficulty in persuading the court that a person can claim to be a victim before the legislation has been enacted. Such a challenge may fail on that basis.

Challenges to failure to legislate?

There might be an argument that a failure to introduce a Bill might 9.63 be a breach of a Convention right. This raises the difficult question of whether there is a positive obligation to promote legislation to protect Convention rights as opposed to the simple obligation to ensure that legislation does not conflict with them. To date the Courts have been unwilling to attach enforceable rights to ensure a particular legislative outcome.[64]

Section 100(4) of the SA defines failure to act for the purposes of section 100 as "making any legislation" and "any other act or failure to act, if it is the act or failure of a member of the Scottish Executive." This suggests that there can, in some circumstances, be a positive obligation on the Executive to act and this would seem to include an obligation to introduce legislation. Equally it may be that a failure which is attributable to the Parliament itself will

---

[62] See further Clyde and Edwards at para.7.52-7.53.
[63] See para.9.21.
[64] See, *e.g. Bates v. Lord Hailsham* [1972] 1 W.L.R. 1373.

violate Convention rights, such as a failure to repeal legislation if certain provisions of the HRA are held to apply.[65]

Unlike the Westminster Parliament[66] there may be a positive obligation to act. Where that obligation is breached this may lead to liability in damages. This is not such a novel argument. In the context of European Community law there is already argument as to the extent to which a court can compel enactment of legislation or to make a finding of Parliamentary liability to ensure compliance with E.C. law.[67]

There may also be scope for an argument to be constructed upon there being a legitimate expectation of a particular legislative provision being enacted. That might arise where there was some form of promise of legislative action which is then departed from. Could there be an argument that failure to have regard to such an expectation was sufficiently irrational as to attract judicial review? To date the courts have been unwilling to afford such substantive protection to legitimate expectations although that may have to be re-assessed in light of the Convention.[68] The withdrawal of the promise to legislate upon which it was based might now be subject to proportionality. This test would seem to afford substantive protection. Even if such protection were available there may be difficulty in securing an enforceable remedy against the executive to compel them to act.[69] There may be a defence based on prematurity of challenge.[70]

There may be technical objections. First, it is not clear if the provisions of section 31 and 33 are designed to preclude challenge by third parties to the passage of legislation, such as against the member of the Scottish Executive who makes the statement under section 31(2); or against the law officers as to the exercise of their discretion under section 33(1); or indeed against the Parliament itself as to how it deals with the legislation. Could a third party prevent a proposed amendment on the grounds of alleged incompatibility with Convention rights? Or prevent a decision to pass a Bill? In principle all of these persons can be the subject of legal proceedings.[71] There is also the presumption of interpretation that in enacting the SA, Parliament did not intend to deny access to the courts.[72] There may still be other difficulties.

Challenge may be premature. Parliament may not pass the Bill or

---

[65] See s.6(1), (6)of the HRA.
[66] See para.9.07.
[67] See Upton, "Crown Liability in Damages under Community Law" 1996 S.L.T. (News) 211 and Clyde and Edwards paras.5.51 and 6.45 and see para.9.22.
[68] See para.9.54.
[69] Crown Proceedings Act 1947, s.21 and see also SA, ss.52(2), (7) and 126(1). See also para.9.22.
[70] See, *e.g.* 592 HL Official Report (5th Series) cols 2019-2020 (28 October 1998).
[71] s.40
[72] See, *e.g. Raymond v. Honey* [1983] 1 A.C. 1; *Leech v. Secretary of State for Scotland*, 1991 S.L.T. 910.

it may do so in a form which meets any difficulty. There may be a concern that the separation of powers would be infringed. Finally it may be that the most effective remedy would be post-enactment challenge as that would at least afford the certainty of having a final statement of the content and therefore legality of a measure.[73]

Even if these difficulties can be overcome there remains the difficulty of whether issues touching upon the legislative competence of the Parliament can be raised other than as a devolution issue. Such a challenge would not fall within the scope of what constitutes a devolution issue[74] and might circumvent the protections afforded by that procedure. Challenge under the HRA might still be open.[75]

It is arguable that some of the sensitivity that surrounds pre-enactment challenge on Convention grounds is not as relevant to the exercise or non-exercise of powers contained in sections 31 or 33. Decisions made in the exercise of these powers are complete in themselves. The problems associated with prematurity of challenge may not be present. Standing may still be problematic.[76]

Convention rights and Acts of the Parliament

Once a Bill is enacted it can be challenged on the basis that it is "not law" in that it fails to comply with Convention rights.[77] Such challenges raise complex issues both procedurally and substantively.[78]   9.64

In substantive terms the first task of the court in determining such a challenge is to apply section 101. This imposes an interpretative obligation on the court. In carrying out this interpretative exercise the court may have to consider whether to apply any discretionary area of judgement.[79] Even if it does hold that the Act or any provision in it is not law, difficult issues as to the remedy to be awarded arise. We shall examine these in turn.

Section 101 and Convention rights

Under this provision the consequences of interpretative difficulties   9.65

---

[73]   *cf. Rediffusion (Hong Kong) Ltd v. Att.-Gen. of Hong Kong* [1970] A.C. 1136 and *McDonald v. Cain* [1953] V.L.R. 411; *Cormack v. Cope* (1974) 131 C.L.R. 432; *Victoria v. Commonwealth* (1975) 134 C.L.R. 81.

[74]   See para.9.74.

[75]   See para.9.73.

[76]   See in another context, *Whaley v. Lord Watson of Invergowrie* at para.9.61—members of the public had no standing to challenge operation of rules on members interests.

[77]   s.29(1), (2)(d).Convention rights is given the same meaning as in the HRA.

[78]   The procedural aspects are dealt with at para.9.62.

[79]   See para.9.58.

have the potential for greater impact than under section 3 of the HRA. This is because under the SA such difficulty might lead the court to hold that the Act is not law. The most that the court can do under the HRA is to make a declaration of incompatibility.[80]

One issue that may require to be clarified is whether there is any substantive difference between the interpretative obligations contained in the HRA and the SA. Section 101 of the SA provides that an Act of the Scottish Parliament or a Bill or any subordinate legislation made or confirmed or approved (or purporting to be so) "which could be read in such a way as to be outside competence is to be read as narrowly as is required for it to be within competence, if such a reading is possible, and is to have effect accordingly". Competence means the "legislative competence of the Parliament" and in relation to subordinate legislation, "the powers conferred by virtue of this Act".[81]

However section 3(1) of the HRA provides "So far as it is possible to do so, primary legislation and subordinate legislation must be read and given effect in a way which is compatible with the Convention rights". Is there a substantive distinction here? The answer at this stage has to be "possibly". Section 101 requires a narrow reading to be given. It is conceivable that there could be a provision which is *prima facie* incompatible with Convention rights on the basis of the section 3 approach but which is saved by a narrow reading. A narrow reading may be a strained reading and may not properly reflect the *intention* behind the provision. Moreover according a narrower reading to one part of an Act may have unintended consequences for another provision. There is on one view potential for some of the difficulties associated with severance[82] to be generated in a different guise as a problem in interpretation.

On the other hand it might be argued that Parliament could not have intended a substantive difference as it could mean that different levels of Convention rights protection would prevail in different parts of the United Kingdom. Equally it might be said that a justification for a difference might lie in the structural differences between the two Parliaments. It may be that the devolved Parliament with limited competence and with the potential for having its Acts set aside[83] requires a different degree of protection than the sovereign United Kingdom Parliament. It might also be said that since section 21(1) of the HRA includes Acts of the Scottish Parliament in its definition of subordinate legislation and that in turn must apply section 3. If that is so then why have the differently framed obligation in section 101? On that basis it would follow that if an Act of the Parliament is challenged under section 3

---

[80] See s.4.
[81] s.101(3)(a),(b).
[82] See para.9.70.
[83] Para.9.58.

a different obligation would apply than if it were challenged as a Devolution Issue under section 98 of the SA.

Remedies and the Scotland Act

The remedial provisions of the Scotland Act must be considered from a Convention rights standpoint. Where judicial review is sought against the Scottish Executive the remedies which can be obtained are the remedies that have always been competent in judicial review, and will be subject to the same limitations, such as the inability to obtain interdict against the Crown.[84]

9.66

One possible development is in the context of possible public law liability in damages for wrongful legislation or indeed failure to legislate .We have examined the scope of this argument in relation to the HRA.[85] In the context of the Scottish Executive and Parliament there might be a stronger argument for such liability given the higher *constitutional* status of Convention rights under the SA. Could this raise the spectre of damages for wrongful legislation or of wrongful failure to legislate to protect Convention rights? It should not go unnoticed that the courts' power to award damages for an act of these bodies is in turn constrained by the limits placed upon it by section 100(3) of the SA which imports the provisions of sections 8(3) and (4) of the HRA into such an award. That *may* limit the scope for such an award.[86]

Arguably the main problems will arise in relation to Acts of the Parliament and subordinate legislation made by the Executive found to breach of Convention rights. It is to this area we turn.

Available Remedies

Any challenge to the *vires* of an Act or subordinate legislation on Convention grounds would be a devolution issue.[87] and would engage the procedure set out in Schedule 6 of the Act. Whilst it is anticipated that the bulk of such challenges would take the obvious route of judicial review in the Court of Session of the *vires* such a measure, there remains considerable scope for challenge to arise in the course of other proceedings, such as in the defence to a criminal charge. Schedule 6 is however a purely procedural provision and does not assist in determining the nature of any remedy that should be sought where it is alleged that an Act or piece of subordinate legislation is *ultra vires*.

9.67

Section 40 provides that proceedings against the Parliament are

---

[84] See para.9.22.
[85] See para.9.22.
[86] For consideration of this kind of argument in the context of Westminster in the context of E.C. law, see para.9.22.
[87] See para.9.74.

to be brought against the Parliamentary corporation on behalf of the Parliament. Under section 40(3) it is provided that "in any proceedings against the Parliament, the court shall not make an order for suspension, interdict, reduction, or specific performance (or other like order) but may instead make a declarator". Whilst this would seem to ensure that the business of the Parliament is to proceed unhindered by positive judicial intervention it would appear to be wide enough to cover proceedings aimed at challenging the *vires* of an Act as being outwith the powers conferred upon it by falling within the prohibited areas of legislative activity found in section 29(2) of the Act. There is similar provision in section 40(4) in relation to proceedings against any member of the Parliament and its officers or the Parliamentary corporation, if the effect of any of the remedies other than a declarator would be to give relief against the Parliament which could not have been given in proceedings against the Parliament.

So far the only challenge to an Act has arisen indirectly by way of reference by the Sheriff to the Court of Session in *A v. Scottish Ministers*.[88] Although the circumstances were somewhat unusual the Parliament was not joined as a party and its absence did not provoke comment from the Bench. However as the interests of the Parliament are not necessarily co-extensive with those of the Executive there may be sound reasons why it is *constitutionally* desirable for the Parliament to be a party to proceedings which touch on its role in any event.[89]

Even if constitutional propriety dictates such a course, the extent to which challenges to the *vires* of Acts *require*, as a matter of law, to be brought against the Parliament remains uncertain. If that were the case then the remedy would be limited to a declarator although there would appear to be nothing to prevent damages being sought as well as it would not appear to be in the class of remedy excluded by section 40(3).

Until the position is clarified it must remain conceivable that a challenge to an Act could be brought against the Executive. In view of the limited remedies in section 40(3) and the exclusion of the Executive from the effect of section 40(4) there may be advantage in doing this. There is, however, something anomalous in being able to seek reduction if the party called is the Executive, but not the Parliament. Such an "indirect" challenge would appear to deny the protection afforded to an Act which is arguably intended by section 40(3).

Whether in substance this matters is perhaps less of an issue than it would otherwise have been. This is because of the provisions of section 102 which can be used to modify the effect of traditional judicial remedies. This is discussed below.[90]

---

[88] For the facts see para.9.58.
[89] See *Whaley v. Lord Watson of Invergowrie,* 1999 G.W.D. 39–1882, *per* Lord Johnston at p.2 of the transcript.
[90] See para.9.69.

The effect of a finding of ultra vires

One of the issues which will require resolution in the context of   9.68
remedies is the extent to which a finding that an Act of the
Parliament breaches Convention rights renders it invalid, if at all.
This is because section 29(1) provides that "an Act of the Scottish
Parliament is not law so far as any provision is outside the
legislative competence of the Parliament." What does the expression "not law" mean? Does this mean invalid or simply ineffectual?
Does such a finding have retrospective effect? Similar difficulties
might also arise in the context of the Scottish Executive in the
making of subordinate legislation.

This is not a new problem. It is a general problem in
administrative law. In many judicial review proceedings the
consequences of a finding of *ultra vires* have had to be worked
out. There has been particular difficulty in relation to whether a
decision or measure found to be ultra vires should be held as void
or null from the start.[91]

The main difficulty with legislation is the *general* nature of such a
measure. Many persons beyond the scope of the litigation may have
relied on the terms of the legislation. Such reliance could have
arisen in relation to past and completed acts or decisions. The
continuing validity of the legislation may have consequences for
ongoing and future acts and decisions. How then can the court act
to resolve the potentially conflicting demands of legality, certainty
and fairness to the wider interest? Should the decision have wholly
retrospective effect? Should it have limited retrospective effect?
Should the effect of a decision be prospective only?

One way to approach this problem is to examine the approaches
in the jurisprudence of other countries with a longer tradition of
constitutional judicial review of legislation.

- In America it has been stated that retroactive effect must be
  given to such a decision.[92] Equally the Supreme Court has stated
  that a a general principle of retroactive effect cannot be
  justified.[93] Prospective effect might be an option,[94] although
  this approach may now have fallen out of favour.[95]
- The High Court of Australia has held that an inconsistent law
  "remains valid though it is rendered inoperative to the extent of
  that inconsistency".[96] Some acts done under such a law are

---

[91] See *London and Clydeside Estates Ltd v. Aberdeen D.C.,* 1980 S.C. (H.L.) 1
   especially Lord Hailsham of St Marylebone L.C. at 30 and Lord Keith of Kinkel
   at 43 and more recently *Boddington v. British Transport Police* [1999] 2 A.C. 143 ;
   Clyde and Edwards at para.14.16.
[92] *Norton v. Shelby County,* 118 U.S. 425 (1886).
[93] *Chicot County Drainage District v. Baxter State Bank* 308 U.S. 371 (1940) *per*
   Chief Justice Hughes.
[94] see *Linkletter v. Walker,* 381 U.S. 618 (1965)
[95] *Griffith v. Kentucky,* 497 U.S. 314 (1987).
[96] *Western Australia v. Commonwealth* (1995) 183 C.L.R. 373 at 465.

invalid and can lead to liability in relation thereto,[97] whereas others do not.[98]

- Canadian law is similar to the Australian position. Unconstitutional law will be declared invalid with retrospective effect.[99] As with Australia, acts done under a law found to be invalid can have valid effects and sometimes the Supreme Court has exercised a discretion to enforce an unconstitutional law, albeit for a fixed period of time.[1]

- European Community law suggests that a strict rule of absolute invalidity might be impractical. Under Article 231 of the Treaty of Rome, where a challenge under Article 230 is successful the European Court of Justice will declare the measure "void". However this is tempered by Article 231(2) which confers a discretion on the Court as to the extent of retrospective effect of a decision. Moreover as a matter of general jurisprudence measures are assumed valid until declared otherwise unless the breach is so serious that the measure is in effect deemed to be non-existent.[2]

It may be that there can be no universal solution to this problem and that the court will require to "tailor" the remedy to suit the case in hand. Clyde and Edwards suggest that restitution might afford assistance in some cases.[3] However that will not always be the case. In criminal cases it is possible to conceive of a situation where a conviction based on an invalid law, remains a valid conviction if the courts' decision is not wholly retrospective.[4]

Section 102

9.69   Although it may not offer a complete answer, Section 102 of the SA might afford some guidance. It is a general provision and its operation is not confined to Convention rights cases. It gives power to courts and tribunals where they decide that a provision in an Act of the Scottish Parliament is not within legislative competence or a member of the Scottish Executive does not have the power to make, confirm or approve a provision of subordinate legislation. After intimation to the Lord Advocate and where relevant to the appropriate law officer,[5] the court or tribunal may make an order "(a) removing or limiting any retrospective effect of the decision, or (b) suspending the effect of the decision for any period and on any

---

[97]   *James v. Commonwealth* (1939) 62 C.L.R. 339
[98]   *Clayton v. Heffron* (1960) 105 C.L.R. 214 at 246-248.
[99]   *Central Canada Potash Co. v. Government of Saskatchewan* [1979] 1 S.C.R. 42
[1]   *Re Manitoba Language Rights* [1985] 1 S.C. R. 721
[2]   *Commission v. BASF AG* [1994] E.C.R. I-2555.
[3]   See for example *Kleinwort Benson Ltd v. Lincoln C.C.* [1998] 4 All E.R. 513.
[4]   *Bilodeau v. Att.-Gen. of Manitoba* [1986] 1 S.C.R. 449
[5]   As defined by s.102(7).

conditions to allow the defect to be corrected".[6]

This power is available in *any* court or tribunal where the issue arises and not just in judicial review proceedings although where it arises in such proceedings it must be presumed to be without prejudice to any existing discretion as to remedy. The court is directed to a number of considerations in the exercise of this power. Section 102(3) provides:

> "In deciding whether to make an order under this section, the court or tribunal shall (among other things) have regard to the extent to which persons who are not parties to the proceedings would otherwise be adversely affected."

Apart from this specific consideration regard must be had to "other things". Presumably these must include the benefits which would accrue to parties and non-parties if no order were made. Also included must be the practical consequences and conceivably political issues might be relevant. Although in judicial review proceedings the court already has a discretion as to whether the remedy or remedies sought should be granted[7] there is little authority on the factors which might be relevant to the refusal of a remedy. Moreover any existing discretion would not appear to extend to "tailoring" a remedy in the manner envisaged by this provision. Regard might now have to be given to English law on the factors relevant to refusal of a remedy such as, but not limited to, the needs of good administration.[8]

There may be particular considerations in the context of challenge based upon Convention rights. Where the court exercises its power it would have to do so in such a way that in protecting innocent third parties who have relied on the measure that it does not afford disproportionate protection at the cost of others. It will require to ensure that such difference in treatment does not fall foul of the provisions of Article 14 which prohibits discrimination in the way in which Convention rights are secured.

On one view there does not appear to be a requirement to consider the retrospective impact of a decision which confirms that a provision is *ultra vires*. It is therefore possible that where the court is not considering the making of an order under either sections 102(2)(a) or (b), there is no requirement to intimate nor to take into account the interests of third parties. A decision in those circumstances would have the same effect as any other judicial decision which has retrospective effect. It remains to be seen whether this interpretation is open.

---

[6]   s.102(2).
[7]   See *Grahame v. Magistrates of Kirkcaldy* (1882) 9 R. (HL) 91 and see Clyde and Edwards at para.23.32.
[8]   *R v. Monopolies and Mergers Commission, ex p. Argyll Group plc* [1986] 1 W.L.R. 763 at 774 per Sir John Donaldson M.R.

Finally it should not be overlooked that under section 107 the United Kingdom government can make subordinate legislation to "cure" any matter of *vires* of such an Act or any consequence flowing therefrom, such as rights purportedly accrued or any liabilities incurred.[9] Similar provision is made in relation to functions of the Executive.[10] Such a provision could have retrospective effect, putting parties in the position they were in before the flaw in the Scottish legislation was discovered.[11] The use of this power does not depend on there being a preceding judicial decision. There may be a certain attractiveness about this as a remedy to those prepared to lobby government for action. It might be easier to "tailor" a remedy this way than through the judicial route. Moreover, as it does not require a judicial decision it can be used proactively by government to remove *perceived* problems of *vires*.

Severance

9.70   Another aspect of the issue of remedy related to, but distinct from the issue of retroactive effect, is the extent to which part of a measure which is *ultra vires* can be severed from the rest of the measure. In our administrative law the courts have been prepared to exercise this power in a number of contexts provided that it was possible to sever the unlawful part from the rest and that the part severed was not essential to the measure or decision.[12] The power has been exercised in relation to delegated legislation.[13]

How might this apply in relation to a provision contained in an Act of the Parliament or in subordinate legislation? Normally this power would be exercised by way of reduction to the extent needed to sever the unlawful part. However reduction is not a competent remedy insofar as an action directed against the Parliament is concerned. As we have seen no such restriction would seem to apply to action concerning the validity of an Act directed against the Executive—or to subordinate legislation made by the Executive. It may be that the same net practical effect could be achieved by the use of a declarator which specifies the extent of the severed part.

Whilst such a declarator would have the effect of specifying the extent to which the provision is not law there may be difficulty in extending the scope of severance to Acts due to concern that in so

---

[9] See s.107(a).

[10] See s.107 (b).

[11] For examples see *Hansard*, H.L. Vol.593, cols. 592-594 and see also (1997-98) H.L. 124.

[12] See *Cox Bros v. Binning* (1867) 6M 161; *Ashley v. Rothesay Magistrates* (1873) 11M 708; *Bain v. Lady Seafield* (1887) 14 R 939; *Islay Estates Ltd v. McCormick* 1937 S.N. 28.

[13] *DPP v. Hutchinson*[1990] 2 All. E.R. 836 and see also *R v. Inland Revenue Commissioners, ex p. Woolwich Equitable Building Society* [1990] 1 W.L.R. 1400

doing the courts are in effect "re-legislating". This concern has already been voiced here in the context of delegated legislation—see the speech of Lord Lowry in *Hutchinson*—and has found expression in a number of other constitutional jurisdictions.[14] When to apply severance and when to leave it to the legislature to make changes will inevitably raise delicate constitutional issues. here the issues involved relate to Convention rights these may be acute.

"Reading in"

One solution which might avoid some of these difficulties is to   9.71
permit the "reading in" of words to remove the element which leads to a finding of *ultra vires* and so avoid the problems associated with severance. Reading in is an accepted solution in a number of jurisdictions and has been deployed with particular effect in cases involving fundamental human rights.[15] Reading in may be an attractive solution where severance of the unlawful part might reduce the beneficial effect of the legislation as a whole or where severance is not possible, here a finding that part of the measure containing the offending provision not being law might have the same negative effect. Although not restricted to cases involving fundamental rights it may have particular relevance in that context.

Reading in might be of particular significance in cases in view of the requirement placed upon courts and tribunals in section 101 of the Act to read an Act of the Parliament as narrowly as possible to ensure it remains within legislative competence. On one view this suggests that whilst reading down might be possible, reading in may not. Whilst concern has been expressed that in the case of Convention rights at least, this is a different interpretative test than that found in section 3 of the HRA[16]—it does seem arguable that in *substance* the tests are the same and that the twin objectives of upholding legislation wherever possible and protecting Convention rights can be met be permitting reading in when appropriate.

The issue was examined recently by South African Constitutional Court in *National Coalition for Gay and Lesbian Equality v. Minister of Home Affairs*.[16a] The issue was whether the omission of same sex couples from certain benefits under South African immigration law which were afforded to "spouses" was unconstitutional. Such a couple could not claim that a partner who was not resident in South

---

[14] *Schacter v. Canada* [1992] 2 S.C.R. 679 and *Wenn v. A-G of Victoria* (1948) 77 C.L.R. 84 at 122, *per* Dixon J. where severance was denied as it would change the *overall effect* of the measure.

[15] *Vriend v. Alberta* [1998] 1 S.C.R. 493 and generally Childs, "Constitutional Review and Underinclusive Legislation"[1998] P.L. 647.

[16] In relation to United Kingdom legislation that so far as it is possible to do so legislation is to be read in such a way as to be compatible with Convention rights-see C.M.G. Himsworth and C.R. Munro, *The Scotland Act 1998*, pp.125-126.

[16a] South African Constitutional Court, December 2, 1999.

Africa had a right to settle there with his or her South African partner. In deciding to read into the statute the words "or partner in a permanent same-sex life partnership" the Court set out the following principles:

• Reading words into a statute should be consistent with the Constitution and its fundamental values.
• The result of so doing should interfere with the laws adopted by the legislature as little as possible.
• The Court must be able to define with sufficient precision how the statute ought to be extended to comply with the Constitution.
• A Court should try to give effect to what the legislature intended within the constraints of the Constitution.
• Even where the remedy of reading in words into a provision is otherwise justified, it ought not to be done where it would compel the State to meet excessive additional expenditure.
• Where reading in would, by expanding the group of persons protected, sustain a policy of long-standing or one that is constitutionally encouraged, it should be preferred to one of removing that protection completely.

In relation to the last point it was of significance in this case that to have struck down the provision would also have invalidated it to the extent that spouses would have been deprived of the protection given by the statute, and with no *gain* to homosexual couples. It remains to be seen whether reading in will be adopted by our courts as a way of resolving some of the difficulties which our new system of judicial review of legislation might entail.

Convention rights and the Scottish Administration

9.72   The Scottish Administration is comprised of a number of persons. There are the Scottish Ministers also known as the Executive,[17] junior ministers,[18] and the (Scottish) civil service. The First Minister, the Lord Advocate and the Solicitor-General for Scotland are members of Executive as are ministers appointed by the First Minister under section 47. It does not include the Scottish judiciary.[19]

At the level of devolution of executive power the SA[20] provides for the transfer of existing Ministerial functions within devolved competence to the Scottish Ministers. These cover three categories of function which mirror the functions of a Minister of the Crown. The only exception are the "retained functions" of the Lord

---

[17] SA 1998 s.44(2).
[18] SA 1998 s.49.
[19] *H.M.Advocate. v. Dickson,* 1997 S.C.C.R. 859.
[20] s.53(1).

Advocate.[21] Those functions "shall, so far as they are exercisable within devolved competence be exercisable by the Scottish Ministers".

Devolved competence has the same meaning as it does in relation to the Parliament and so it follows that the Administration is subject to Convention rights.[22] This means that any provision contained in subordinate legislation made by the Executive or the approval or confirmation of such a provision which would be outside devolved competence if it were included in an Act of the Parliament would be outside its own devolved competence.[23] Similarly in relation to any other function other than the making, confirming, or approving subordinate legislation it is outside devolved competence to exercise that function or to exercise it in a way so far as a provision of an Act of the Scottish Parliament conferring the function or conferring it so as to be exercisable in that way, would be outside the legislative competence of the Parliament.[24]

It also follows that if the exercise of a function by a United Kingdom Minister of the Crown is incompatible with Convention rights, then that function cannot be transferred to the Scottish Ministers. Where such a function was retained by the Lord Advocate before he ceased being a Minister of the Crown then it is transferred.

There is further provision in section 57(2) of the Act to the effect that no member of the Scottish Executive has power to make any subordinate legislation, or to do any act, so far as the legislation or act is incompatible with any of the Convention rights. Act in this context includes failure to act.[25] Special provision is made for certain acts of the Lord Advocate.[26]

Finally, in addition to the Scottish Executive and Administration there are a range of public authorities who will, or continue to exercise authority in or as regards Scotland. Some of these will be created by the Scottish Parliament. Others predate devolution. Some will have authority in Scotland and the rest of the United Kingdom and are known as cross-border public authorities. The acts and omissions of such bodies are subject to challenge under the HRA, not the SA.[27]

---

[21] s.53(2).
[22] s.54(1).
[23] s.54(2)(a),(b).
[24] s.54(3).
[25] See s.100(4).
[26] s.57(3) and see HRA ss.6(1)and (2).
[27] See generally SA Sched. 5, Pt III, para. 1; R.Reed Q.C., "Devolution and Regulatory Authorities ", in *Devolution to Scotland: the Legal Aspects* (Bates ed., Edinburgh, 1997)

The Scotland Act and the Human Rights Act

9.73   The relationship between these two pieces of legislation requires to be examined for the full implications of Convention rights protection to be understood.

- The Scottish Parliament and Executive would appear to be public authorities under the HRA and are therefore subject to control under the human rights regime imposed by that Act in addition to the Scotland Act.
- The Scotland Act is itself subject to the interpretative obligation contained in section 3 of the HRA.
- Under the HRA, section 21(1), legislation of the Scottish Parliament is to be defined as subordinate legislation for the purposes of that Act.

There is scope for considerable overlap between the two regimes and this may have practical implications. Should a challenge be brought under the HRA directly or should reliance be placed on the Scotland Act and the Devolution Issue procedure? At this stage any answer has to be tinged with a high degree of speculation, but it might be argued that to allow a challenge to proceed under the HRA would undermine the Devolution Issue procedure with all of its detailed provisions, which are arguably required to ensure that the Convention rights issues are examined from the *constitutional* perspective of *devolved* government and not simply as a matter of *pure* Human Rights. Even if one were to argue that nothing meaningful turns upon such a distinction there is also the argument that it could not have been the intention of Parliament to elide the devolution issue procedure.[28] It is unfortunate that such a fundamental question has been left in doubt.

Convention rights, Devolution Issues and Judicial Review

9.74   Unlike the HRA the SA does create a special set of procedural provisions for dealing with Convention rights challenges. This is the Devolution Issue procedure.[29] The procedure is not confined to Convention rights challenges. A detailed discussion of devolution issue procedure is beyond the scope of this chapter.[30]

The role of judicial review and devolution issues has been left

---

[28] See Clyde and Edwards who note at para.7.38 that the SA postdates the HRA by 10 days and so might be viewed as the latest expression of Parliament's will. For further discussion of the issues see A. Stewart Q.C., "Devolution Issues and Human Rights" 2000 S.L.T. 239; A. O'Neill Q.C., "The Scotland Act and the Government of Judges" 1999 S.L.T.(News) 65; Lord Hope of Craighead, "Devolution and Human Rights" [1998] E.H.R.L.R. 367; S. Tierney, "Devolution Issues and S.2(1) of the Human Rights Act 1998" [2000] E.H.R.L.R. 345.

[29] s.98 and Sched. 6.

[30] See chapter 1 for an outline and see Clyde and Edwards, paras 7.47–7.53; O'Neill, paras 5.21–5.29 and 5.48–5.66.

undefined. As with challenges under the provisions of the HRA,[31] challenge involving a devolution issue could arise in a wide range of proceedings either as a direct challenge or collaterally.[32] However it is anticipated most devolution issues in non-criminal matters whether relating to Acts of the Parliament or actings of the Executive are likely to be raised by way of judicial review in the Court of Session.[33] It follows that many Convention challenges are likely to be brought in this way. It may be that collateral challenge in the course of other proceedings will create a number of difficulties which would be better resolved by judicial review in the Court of Session.[34]

However other administrative or "public" law proceedings should not be discounted. Convention rights raising devolution issues could arise in tribunal hearings, in the course of statutory forms of review, in statutory appeals or of course in the course of proceedings under section 33 of the SA.

There are parallels with a number of provisions of the HRA. Whether in judicial review or in other proceedings the SA adopts the victim test as the basis for standing to bring proceedings and the meaning given to that test under the HRA.[35] In addition the SA does not allow a court or tribunal to award damages for an act which is incompatible with Convention rights which it could not award if sections 8(3) and (4) of the HRA applied.[36]

There are differences. The one year time limit in the HRA to bring proceedings does not apply to the SA, although common law pleas of *mora* and waiver appear to be competent.[37] The court structure is different under the two Acts.[38]

---

[31] See s.7 and para.9.14.

[32] For the distinction see para.9.18. For examples of direct challenge see: *County Properties Ltd v. Scottish Ministers*, 2000 S.L.T. 973; *Varey v. Scottish Ministers*, 2000 G.W.D. 27–1065; *Redland Lefarge Aggregates v. Scottish Ministers*, 2000 S.L.T. 1361; *Westerhall Farms v. Scottish Ministers*, April 25, 2001, unreported; *Shepherd v. Scottish Ministers*, 2001 G.W.D. 15–570.

[33] See the views of the Lord Advocate—Nov 2, 1998 Hansard, H.L. Vol. 594, col.79.

[34] See para.9.18.

[35] See SA, s.100 (1), s.7.(1) and see para.9.21.

[36] See s.100(3).

[37] See para.9.19.

[38] See para.1.33.

INDEX

Abortion, 5.05–5.08
Absconding, 3.19
Abuse. *See* **Sexual abuse**
Access to courts
appeals, 9.43
disciplinary hearings, 9.43
independent and impartial tribunal,
7.12
judicial review, 9.43
negligence, 6.07
planning, 9.43
police, 6.07
public law, 9.43
tribunals, 9.43
Access to legal advice
fair hearings, 3.09
foreseeability, 2.12
judicial review, 9.52
public law, 9.52
questioning of suspects, 3.09
Accessibility principle
correspondence, 2.11
criminal law, 2.10, 2.11, 2.15–2.16
European Convention on Human
Rights, 2.10, 2.11
institutional writers, 2.16
legality, 2.10, 2.11, 2.15–2.16
Scots law, in, 2.15–2.16
Acts of Parliament, 9.64, 9.68–9.72
Administrative action, judicial control of,
9.02, 9.05, 9.13–9.38
Administrative decision-making
delay, 9.47
illegality, 9.28–9.30
independent and impartial tribunals,
9.48
judicial review, 7.11, 9.27
procedural impropriety, 9.40, 9.42
public law, 9.03, 9.28–9.30, 9.38
reasons, 9.45
Administrative law, 9.01–9.02
Adoption, 5.13–5.16, 5.17, 5.33
Advice. *See* **Access to legal advice**
Age
consent, of, 2.28
criminal responsibility, of, 2.24
custodial sentences, 4.16, 4.18
marriage, 5.24

AIDS/HIV, 4.28
Aircraft accidents, 6.04
Alimentary obligations, 5.24–5.25
Ancillary orders, 4.30–4.32
Appeals
access to courts, 9.43
bail, 3.19
Convention rights, 1.23
criminal proceedings, 1.31, 1.53
education, 5.23
employment tribunals, 8.22
exhaustion of local remedies, 1.28
fair trials, 3.27
House of Lords, 1.33
irrationality, 9.28
judicial review, 9.18, 9.25
planning, 7.17
Privy Council, 1.32, 1.33
procedural impropriety, 9.40
proportionality, 9.36
tribunals, 9.18
Armed forces
criminal law, 2.05
discrimination, 1.13
employment, 8.01, 8.05, 8.12
homicide, 2.05
irrationality, 9.31
nuclear tests, 1.28
public authorities, 2.05
self-defence, 2.05
sexual orientation, 1.13, 5.34, 8.01,
8.05, 8.12, 9.31
statutory interpretation, 1.13
use of force, 2.05
Arrest, 3.03–3.08
compensation, 4.06
competent legal authority, bringing
before, 3.07
divorce, 5.28
exclusion orders, 5.28
liberty,
deprivation of, 3.05, 3.07–3.08
right to, 3.04
rights of persons deprived of, 3.08
preventative,. 3.07
private life, right to respect for, 3.07
procedure prescribed by law, 3.06
proportionality, 3.07

Arrest—*cont.*
reasonable suspicion, 3.07
reasons for, informed promptly of,
    3.08
Artificial insemination, 5.02
Assembly, freedom of, 4.12
Assisted reproduction, 5.02–5.04
Association. *See* **Freedom of association**
Australia, 9.68

Bail, 3.18–3.20
appeals, 3.19
committal, 3.19, 3.20
course of justice, interference with,
    3.19
crime prevention, 3.19
detention, 3.20
European Convention on Human
    Rights, 3.19
financial guarantees, 3.19
flight, danger of, 3.19
public interest, 3.19
remand, 3.19
time limits, 3.19
Barristers' immunity, 6.10
Beijing Rules, 2.24
Bias, 9.40. *See also* **Independent and
    impartial tribunals**
Bills of Parliament, 9.62–9.63
Blasphemy, 2.13–2.14
Breach of Convention rights
damages, 1.27, 1.40, 1.42–1.44
devolution, 1.39–1.47
Human Rights Act 1998, 1.27
justified, 1.18, 1.41–1.44
Lord Advocate, 1.18, 1.42
Northern Ireland, 1.41
procedure, 1.22–1.26
public authorities, 1.18
remedies, 1.45–1.47
Scottish Executive, 1.42
Scottish Parliament, 1.42
time limits, 1.51
victim test, 1.39
Welsh Assembly, 1.41
Breach of the peace, 2.13, 2.17–2.18,
    8.09
Breach of statutory duty, 9.05
Breakdown of the family, 5.26–5.28
BSE crisis, 7.38–7.39
Building permits, 7.10
Burden of proof
intoxication, 2.27
presumption of innocence, 2.26
reverse, 2.26
Business leases, 7.32–7.33
Buy, right to, 7.43–7.45

Caesarean sections, 5.08

Canada
discrimination, 1.47
procedural impropriety, 9.57
retrospectivity, 9.68
sexual orientation, 1.47
Capital punishment, 4.15
Care proceedings, 5.13–5.16, 5.18
Censorship, 4.44
Charges. *See* **Criminal charges**
Children and young people
adoption, 5.13–5.16, 5.17, 5.33
age of criminal responsibility, 2.24
assisted reproduction, 5.02–5.04
Beijing Rules, 2.24
Caesarean sections, 5.08
care proceedings, 5.13–5.16
Children's Hearings system, 5.16,
    5.17, 5.29
corporal punishment, 5.19–5.20
criminal trials, 3.29
cross-border enforcement of orders
    relating to, 5.31
custodial sentences, 4.23
disclosure, 5.17–5.18
divorce, 5.26
education, 5.21–5.23
fair trials, 5.17–5.18
Her Majesty's Pleasure, detention at,
    4.23
legal representation, 5.18
litigation, in, 5.17–5.18
inhuman or degrading treatment,
    2.25
negligence, 6.05
parenthood, 5.29–5.31, 5.33
prisoners' rights, 4.42
public hearings, 3.29
rights of, 5.01, 5.12
UN Convention on the Rights of the
    Child, 2.24, 5.17, 5.20
unmarried fathers, 5.29–5.30
views of, 5.18
Churches, 1.25
Civil rights and obligations
administrative bodies, reviews of
    decisions by, 7.11
building permits, 7.10
Community right to buy, 7.45
criminal trials, 3.26
delay, 7.12
development of property, 7.09
divorce, 5.27
employment, 8.04
environment, 7.09
fair trials, 7.09–7.12
licences, revocation of, 7.09
meaning, 7.10, 9.41–9.42
nationalisation, 7.09
nuisance, 7.10

Civil rights and obligations—*cont.*
planning, 7.20
procedural impropriety, 9.41
property, 7.09–7.12
social security, 9.41
Civil service, 8.01–8.02
Class actions, 1.26
Clinical negligence, 6.03
Cohabitation, 5.24–5.25
Collective rights, 8.03, 8.08
Commercial leases, 7.32–7.33
Committal, 3.19, 3.20
Committee proceedings, 9.61
Community right to buy, 7.43–7.45
Community service, 4.29
Compensation. *See also* **Damages**
arrest, 4.06
Community right to buy, 7.45
compulsory acquisition, 7.23, 7.26
destruction of property, 7.37, 7.39
detention, 4.06
feudal tenure, abolition of, 7.40–7.42
fish stocks, destruction of, 7.37
irritancy, 7.33
just satisfaction, 7.15
nationalisation, 7.12
peaceful enjoyment of possessions,
7.07, 7.33
property, 7.15
Compulsory acquisition of property,
7.23–7.26
Community right to buy, 7.43–7.44
compensation, 7.23, 7.26
Convention rights, 7.23, 7.26
home, right to respect for the, 7.24
natural justice, 7.26
planning permission, 7.24
proportionality, 7.24
public interest, 7.24
statutory interpretation, 7.23
**Compulsory powers to question of
suspects**, 3.09
Confiscation orders, 1.33, 4.30–4.31
Conjoined twins, 5.09–5.11
Conscience, freedom of, 4.10
Consent, age of, 2.28
Constitutional court, 1.33
Constitutional judicial review, 9.59
Constitutional law, 9.01
Construction. *See* **Statutory
interpretation**
Contracts of employment, 8.14–8.16
Convention rights. *See also* **Breach of
Convention rights, Particular
Convention rights (eg Fair
trials)**
Acts of Parliament, 9.64, 9.68
appeals, 1.23
balancing, 1.08–1.09

Convention rights—*cont.*
Bills of Parliament, 9.62
Children's Hearings system, 5.16
compulsory acquisition, 7.23, 7.26
contracting out of, 8.01
criminal law, 2.02–2.03
criminal proceedings, 1.28, 3.01
custodial sentences, 4.18–4.26
defensive use of, 1.22
deportation, 4.32
devolution issues, 1.51
dismissal, 8.17
effective remedy, right to, 1.03
employment, 8.01, 8.07
environment, 7.29
future use in criminal trials of, 2.03
hierarchy of, 1.08
horizontal effect of, 2.02, 2.04–2.05
Human Rights Act 1998, 1.02–1.03,
1.52
indirect effect, 1.10–1.13
intensity of review, 1.07–1.09
illegality, 9.29–9.30
independent and impartial tribunals,
9.48
indirect effect of, 1.10–1.13
individuals, 1.17
judicial review, 1.23, 9.04–9.12, 9.16–
9.17, 9.19/1, 9.25–9.28
judiciary, 1.42
legal control, grounds of, 9.25–9.28
list of, 1.02–1.03
Lord Advocate, 1.01
negligence, 6.01
Northern Ireland, 1.01
planning, 7.18, 7.22
procedural impropriety, 9.53–9.57
proportionality, 9.35, 9.36
public authorities, 1.50, 9.72
public law, 9.01–9.03, 9.13–9.38,
9.59–9.74
remedies, 9.66, 9.68–9.69
retrospectivity, 1.44
review of, intensity of, 1.07–1.09
Scotland Act 1998, 1.42, 1.46, 1.53,
9.59–9.74
Scottish Administration, 9.72
Scottish Executive, 1.43, 9.59
Scottish Ministers, 9.72
Scottish Parliament, 1.42–1.43, 9.59–
9.65
statutory interpretation, 1.10–1.13,
1.31
vertical effect of, 2.02
Welsh Assembly, 1.01
Convictions, detention following, 4.17
Co-ownership, 7.34–7.36
Corporal punishment, 5.19–5.20
Corporate bodies, 1.25

Correspondence, right to respect for
accessibility test, 3.11
censorship, 4.44
European Convention on Human
Rights, 4.46
interference with, 4.43–4.46
legal advisors, with, 4.45
prisoners' rights, 4.43–4.46
private life, right to respect for, 4.44
public authorities, 4.44
searches, 3.11
surveillance, right to respect for, 3.11
Costs, 1.27
Courts. *See* **Access to courts, European
Court of Human Rights, National
courts**
Criminal charges, 3.21–3.25
accusation, nature and cause of, 3.22
criminal trials, 3.26
information, 3.21–3.24
detailed, 3.24
prompt giving of , 3.23
interpreters, 3.25
language, 3.25
Criminal law. *See also* **Criminal
proceedings, Particular crimes (eg
Breach of the peace)**
accessibility, 2.10, 2.11, 2.15–2.16
age of criminal responsibility. 2.24
armed forces, 2.05
burden of proof, 2.26
common law, 2.03
consent, 2.28
Convention rights,
future use of, 2.03
horizontal effect of, 2.02, 2.04–2.05
impact of, 2.02
vertical effect of, 2.02
defences, positive, 2.26–2.27
discrimination, 2.28
European Court of Human Rights,
guidelines from, 2.21
extension of responsibility,
unreasonable or unforeseeable,
2.19–2.23
Scots law, in, 2.21–2.23
fair trials, 2.26–2.27
foreseeability, 2.12, 2.21–2.22
Human Rights Act 1998, 2.02–2.03
inhuman or degrading treatment,
2.04, 2.24
institutional writers, 2.16
intoxication, 2.26
judicial development of, 2.19–2.21
legality principle, 2.06–2.23
liability, general principles of
criminal, 2.06–2.28
margin of appreciation, 2.03
mental element, 2.25

Criminal law—*cont.*
police, 2.05
precision, 2.10, 2.12–2.15, 2.17–2.18
presumption of innocence, 2.26
privacy, 2.28
private life, right to respect for, 2.04
public authorities, 2.02, 2.04–2.05
retrospectivity, 2.08–2.09
self-defence, 2.06
sexual orientation, 2.28
sources of, 2.16
South Africa, 2.03
statutory crimes, 2.21
strict liability, 2.26
substantive, 2.01–2.28
use of force, 2.05
Criminal proceedings, 3.01–3.41. *See
also* **Criminal trials**
appeals, 1.31, 1.53
arrest, 3.03–3.08
bail, 3.18–3.20
Convention rights, 1.28, 3.01
criminal charges, 3.21–3.26
detention, 3.03–3.08
European Commission on Human
Rights, 3.01
European Convention on Human
Rights, 3.01
evidence, 3.01, 3.11, 3.17
exhaustion of domestic remedies, 1.28
fair trials, 1.31
Human Rights Act 1998, 3.01
investigation of crime, 3.02–3.17
Lord Advocate, 1.30
questioning of suspects, 3.09–3.10
retrospectivity, 1.36
Scotland Act 1998, 3.01
searches, 3.11–3.17
surveillance, 3.11–3.17
Criminal trials, 3.26–3.41
children and young persons, 3.29
civil rights and obligations, 3.26
criminal charges, 3.26
delay, 3.30–3.33
disclosure, 3.37–3.38
fair, 3.26–3.41
independent and impartial tribunals,
3.26, 3.34
hearsay, 3.40–3.41
legal assistance, right to, 3.39
preparations for, 3.37–3.38
presumption of innocence, 3.35
presumptions, 3.36
public hearings, 3.29
reasonable time, within, 3.30–3.33
time limits, 3.30–3.33
Custodial sentences, 4.16–4.28. *See also*
Detention, Prisoners' rights
age, 4.16, 4.18

Custodial sentences—*cont.*
children and young persons, 4.23
conditions, 4.17
continuing detention, legality of, 4.24
Convention rights, compatibility
    with other, 4.18–4.26
convictions, following, 4.17
determinate sentences, length of,
    4.25–4.26
desert grounds, 4.19
designated life prisoners, 4.22–4.24
Designated Life Tribunal, 4.24
discretionary life sentences, 4.06,
    4.17–4.19, 4.22, 4.26
discrimination, 4.27–4.28
Her Majesty's Pleasure, detention at,
    4.23
hospital orders, 4.16
independent and impartial tribunals,
    4.24
indeterminate sentences, 4.18–4.24
    review of, 4.20–4.24
inhuman or degrading treatment,
    4.19, 4.25–4.26
legality of, 4.17
life sentences,
    discretionary, 4.06, 4.17–4.19,
        4.22, 4.26
    mandatory, 4.17–4.19, 4.21, 4.23
mandatory life sentences, 4.17–4.19,
    4.21, 4.23
mental disabilities, 4.17
murder, 4.19–4.21
Parole Board, independence and
    impartiality of, 4.24
proportionality, 4.19, 4.26
public, protection of, 4.19, 4.20
punitive grounds, 4.19
range of, 4.16
release on licence, 4.18

Damages. *See also* **Compensation**
breach of Convention rights, 1.27,
    1.40, 1.42–1.44
costs, 1.27
defamation, 1.19
devolution, 1.40, 1.42–1.44
EC law, 9.22
employment, 8.06
Human Rights Act 1998, 1.27, 7.15
judicial review, 9.17, 9.21–9.22
just satisfaction, 1.27, 1.40, 7.15
negligence, 6.01
New Zealand, 9.22
nuisance, 7.28
pecuniary, 1.27
public law, 9.66
Scotland Act 1974
time limits, 1.27

Death penalty, 4.15
Deaths in custody, 4.03
Declarations, 2.09. *See also*
    Declarations of incompatibility
Declarations of incompatibility
effect of, 1.14–1.16
devolution, 1.50
final, 1.16
Human Rights Act 1998, 1.14–1.16
intervention, Ministers by, 1.14–1.16
judicial review, 1.16
national courts, 1.14–1.16
parliamentary sovereignty, 1.14
primary legislation, 1.14–1.16
remedial orders, 1.16
retrospectivity, 1.51
statutory interpretation, 1.15
subordinate legislation, 1.16
Defamation, 1.19, 9.61
Defences, 2.26–2.27
Delay
administrative decision-making, 9.47
civil rights and obligations,
    determining, 7.12
criminal trials, 3.30–3.33
employment tribunals, 8.25
fair trials, 3.30–3.33, 8.25, 9.47
judicial review, 9.47
prejudice, causing, 3.30–3.33
priorities, 3.33
reasonableness, 3.30–3.33
Demonstrations, 8.09
Deportation
ancillary orders, 4.30, 4.32
Convention rights, risk of violation
    of, 4.32
death penalty, 4.15
Destruction of property, 7.37–7.39
Detention
bail, 3.19
compensation, 4.06
competent legal authority, bringing
    before, 3.07
conditions of, 4.17, 4.34–4.39
continuing, legality of, 4.24
Her Majesty's Pleasure, detention at,
    4.23
hospital orders, 4.16
investigation of crime, 3.03–3.08
liberty,
    deprivation of, 3.05, 3.07–3.08
    right to, 3.04
    rights of persons deprived of, 3.08
mental disabilities, 1.55–1.56, 4.06,
    4.17–4.18
prisoners' rights, 4.06
procedure prescribed by law, 3.06
reasons for, 3.08
time limits, 3.06

Development of property, 7.09
Devolution
  acts,
    definition of, 1.38
    review of, 1.38
  breach of Convention rights, 1.39–1.47
  constitutionality, 1.29
  Convention rights, 1.51
  damages, 1.40, 1.42–1.44
  declarations of incompatibility, 1.50
  destruction of property, 7.36
  fair trials, 1.31
  fish stocks, destruction of, 7.37
  Human Rights Act 1998, 1.37, 9.73
  issues, 1.29–1.36, 7.37, 9.74
  judges as legislators, 1.48–1.49
  judicial review, 9.74
  law officers, role of, 1.35
  Lord Advocate, 1.01, 1.32
  margin of appreciation, 9.58
  omissions, review of, 1.38
  Privy Council, 1.30–1.32, 1.34, 1.35, 1.51
  procedural exclusivity, 1.50–1.53
  prospective overruling, 1.36
  public law, 9.74
  retrospectivity, 1.36
  Scotland Act 1998, 1.29–1.36, 1.38, 1.52
  Scottish Executive, 1.38
  Scottish Ministers, 9.72
  Scottish Parliament, 1.29, 9.63
  Solicitor General for Scotland, 1.01
  victim test, 1.39
  Welsh Assembly, 1.01
  Westminster Parliament, 1.52
Direct effect, 1.13, 1.20
Disciplinary hearings, 8.07, 8.19, 8.22, 9.43
Disclosure
  adoption, 5.17
  care proceedings, 5.18
  children and young persons, 5.17–5.18
  criminal trials, 3.37–3.38
Discretionary life sentences, 4.06, 4.17–4.19, 4.22, 4.26
Discrimination. *See also* **Sex discrimination**
  AIDS/HIV, 4.28
  armed forces, 1.13
  Canada, 1.47
  cohabitation, 5.24–5.25
  criminal law, 2.28
  custodial sentences, 4.27–4.28
  dismissal, 8.17, 8.20, 8.21
  divorce, 5.26
  dress and grooming codes, 8.20, 8.21

Discrimination—*cont.*
  incest, 2.28
  justification for, 7.14, 8.21
  less favourable treatment, 7.14
  marriage, 5.24–5.25
  parenthood, 5.29–5.30
  picketing, 8.21
  property, 7.14
  sentencing, 4.27–4.28
  sexual orientation, 1.13, 1.47, 2.03, 2.28
  South Africa, 2.03
  statutory interpretation, 1.13
  transsexuals, 8.20
  unmarried fathers, 5.29–5.30
Dismissal, 8.14–8.21
  contracts of employment, 8.14–8.16
  Convention rights, 8.17
  disciplinary actions, 8.19
  discrimination, 8.17, 8.20, 8.21
  fair reasons for, 8.14, 8.17
  freedom of association, 8.15
  freedom of expression, 8.15, 8.20
  grooming codes, 8.20
  gross misconduct, 8.11, 8.15
  Human Rights Act 1998, 8.19
  private life, right to respect for, 8.20
  public authorities, 8.19, 8.20
  reasonable responses, range of, 8.22
  reasonableness, 8.18
  some other substantial reason, 8.17
  unfair, 8.12, 8.14, 8.17–8.18, 8.22
  wrongful, 8.14, 8.15
Division and sale of property, 7.34–7.36
Divorce, 5.26–5.28
  arrest, 5.28
  children, 5.26
  civil rights and obligations, 5.27
  discrimination, 5.26
  division and sale of property, 7.36
  equality, 5.26
  European Convention on Human Rights, 5.26–5.28
  exclusion orders, 5.28
  family home, 5.26
  pensions, 5.27
  possessions, 5.27
  property, 5.26–5.28
  recovery of , 1.28
Domestic courts. *See* **National courts**
Dress codes, 8.20, 8.21
Drug trafficking, 1.33, 4.31

EC law
  damages for breach of, 9.22
  destruction of property, 7.37–7.38
  direct effect, 1.13
  employment tribunals, 8.24
  environment, 7.29

EC law—*cont.*
fish stocks, destruction of, 7.37
food safety, 7.38
judicial review, 9.22
legislation and, 1.52
proportionality, 9.35
remedies, 9.22, 9.68
state liability, 9.22
validity of laws and, 9.68
Effective remedy, right to
Convention rights, exclusion from
HRA list of, 1.03
Human Rights Act 1998, 1.45
national courts, 1.19
Emergencies, 6.03
Employment, 8.01–8.27. *See also*
Dismissal
adjudicatory bodies, 8.22–8.26
appeals, 8.22
armed forces, 8.01, 8.05, 8.12
civil rights and obligations, 8.04
civil service, 8.01–8.02
collective rights, 8.03, 8.08
Convention rights, 8.22
contracting out of, 8.01
duty to act in accordance with,
8.07
damages, 8.06
delays in judgments, 8.25
demonstrations, 8.09
disciplinary hearings, 8.04, 8.07, 8.22
discrimination, 8.21
dress codes, 8.20, 8.21
EC law, 8.24
employment tribunals, 8.22–8.26
procedural implications for, 8.13
European Convention on Human
Rights, 8.01–8.02, 8.05
European Court of Human Rights,
8.01, 8.03–8.05, 8.08
fair trials, 8.01–8.02, 8.04, 8.06–8.07,
8.22–8.24
forced labour, 4.05, 4.29
freedom of association, 8.05, 8.08–
8.09
freedom of expression, 8.02, 8.03,
8.05, 8.10
genetic testing, 8.12
grooming codes, 8.20, 8.21
gross misconduct, 8.11
Human Rights Act 1998, 8.06, 8.27
independent and impartial tribunals,
8.22–8.23
individual rights, 8.01–8.02
judicial review, 9.09
legal aid, 8.26
monitoring employees, 8.10–8.11
national courts, 8.05–8.26
picketing, 8.09, 8.21

Employment—*cont.*
private life, right to respect for, 8.01,
8.10–8.12
professional conduct hearings, 8.07
public authorities, 8.01–8.02, 8.07,
8.10, 8.12, 8.22
public hearings, 8.24
public interest immunity hearings,
8.24
religion, 8.01
security checks, 8.12
sexual orientation, 8.01, 8.05, 8.12
strikes, 8.03, 8.08
surveillance, 8.01, 8.10, 8.13
trade unions, 8.03, 8.08
UK courts, 8.05–8.25
Employment tribunals, 8.22–8.26
appeals, 8.22
composition, 8.23
delays in judgments, 8.25
EC law, 8.24
evidence, 8.13
fair trials, 8.22–8.24
independent and impartial tribunals,
8.22, 8.23
legal aid, 8.26
procedural implications for, 8.13
public authorities, as, 8.22
public hearings, 8.24
surveillance, 8.13
unfair dismissal, 8.22
Enjoyment of possessions. *See* **Peaceful
enjoyment of possessions**
Environment
civil rights and obligations, 7.09
Convention rights, 7.29
EC law, 7.29
family life, right to respect for, 7.31
information, 7.22, 7.31
local authorities, 7.29
Human Rights Act 1998, 7.29
margin of appreciation, 7.30
negligence, 6.06
noise, 7.30
private life, right to respect for, 7.31
public authorities, 7.29–7.30
Scottish Environmental Protection
Agency, 7.29
**European Commission on Human
Rights**, 3.01
European Community. *See* **EC law**
European Convention on Human Rights.
See also **Convention rights**
accessibility, 2.10, 2.11
age of criminal responsibility, 2.24
bail, 3.19
common law, effect on, 1.19–1.21
constitutional status in Scotland,
1.01

European Convention on Human Rights—*cont.*
death penalty, 4.15
divorce, 5.26–5.28
employment, 8.01, 8.05, 8.07
extension of criminal liability, unreasonable or unforeseeable, 2.19–2.20
institutional writers, 2.16
legal certainty, 9.38
legality, 2.10
living instrument, as, 1.04
negligence, 6.01–6.12
precision, 2.10, 2.18
retrospectivity, 2.08
Scotland Act 1998, 1.01
victims, 1.25, 1.39
European Court of Human Rights
applications to, 1.28
correspondence, 4.46
criminal law, guidelines on development of, 2.21
criminal proceedings, 3.01
destruction of property, 7.39
employment, 8.01–8.05
exhaustion of local remedies, 1.28
fair trials, 3.27–3.28
Human Rights Act 1998, 1.04–1.09, 1.28
jurisprudence of, relevance of, 1.04–1.09
margin of appreciation, 1.06
marital rape, 2.21
non-binding nature of decisions of, 1.04–1.09
peaceful enjoyment of possession, 7.06
proportionality, 9.35
self-incrimination, 1.04, 1.05
time limits, 1.28
European Union. *See* **EC law**
Evidence
criminal proceedings, 3.01, 3.11, 3.17
employment tribunals, 8.13
exclusion of, 3.11
fair hearings, 3.11
improperly obtained, 3.11
incitement, 3.17
surveillance, 3.11
witnesses, 3.27
Exclusion orders, 5.28, 9.53, 9.61
Executive. *See* **Scottish Executive**
Exhaustion of local remedies, 1.28
Expenses, 9.24
Expression. *See* **Freedom of expression**
Expropriation, 7.05. *See also* **Compulsory purchase**
Extension of criminal liability, unreasonable or unforeseeable, 2.19–2.23

Extradition, 4.15

Failure to act
'act', meaning of, 1.45
public authorities, 1.45
Scottish Executive, 1.45
Scottish Parliament, 1.45, 9.63
Fair hearings. *See also* **Public hearings**
access to legal advice, 3.09
compulsory powers to require answers to questions, 3.09
evidence, 3.11
incitement, 3.17
judicial review, 9.44
procedural impropriety, 9.39, 9.53, 9.54
public law, 9.44
questioning of suspects, 3.09
searches, 3.17
substantive fairness, 9.54
surveillance, 3.17
Fair trials. *See also* **Fair hearings**
appeals, 3.27
children and young persons, 5.17–5.18
Children's Hearings system, 5.17
civil rights and obligations, 7.09–7.12
criminal proceedings, 1.31, 3.26–3.41
positive defences, in, 2.26–2.27
delay, 3.30–3.33, 8.25, 9.47
devolution, 1.31
documents, recovery of, 1.28
employment, 8.01–8.02, 8.04, 8.06–8.07, 8.22–8.24
tribunals, 8.22–8.24
European Court of Human Rights, 3.27–3.28
hearsay, 3.40–3.41
intoxication, 2.27
judicial review, 7.11
legal aid, 8.25
legal assistance, right to, 3.39
Lord Advocate, 1.32
negligence, 6.07
overriding fairness, 3.27–3.28
planning, 7.11
press, 3.28, 3.34
presumption of innocence, 3.35
prisoners' rights, 4.07
Privy Council, 1.30–1.31
property, 7.08–7.12
public authorities, 8.07
qualifications to rights of, 1.08
reasons, 7.12, 9.45
retrospectivity, 1.36
self-incrimination, 1.32
social security, 9.41
victims, 3.27
witnesses, 3.27

Family home, 5.26, 7.36
Family life, right to respect for, 5.01–
5.34. *See also* Children and young
persons, Marriage
abortion, 5.05–5.08
access to family members, 4.40–4.42
adoption, 5.13, 5.15
assisted reproduction, 5.02–5.04
care proceedings, 5.13–5.16
interference with, 5.13–5.14
margin of appreciation, 5.14
marriage, 5.24
negligence, 6.06
neonates, 5.09–5.11
parenthood, 5.29–5.31, 5.33
prisoners' rights, 4.09, 4.34, 4.40–
4.42
property, 7.13
proportionality, 5.14
same sex partners, 5.01
searches, 3.11
sexual orientation, 5.01, 5.32–5.35
surveillance, right to respect for, 3.11
transsexuals, 5.05, 5.36–5.39
unmarried fathers, 5.29–5.30
Fertility treatment, 5.02–5.04
Feudal tenure, abolition of, 7.40–7.42
Feuduties, 7.40–7.41
Financial measures, legality of, 4.07
First Minister, 9.72
Fisheries, 7.37
Foetuses, 5.05–5.09
Food safety, 7.38
Force, use of, 2.05
Forced labour, 4.03, 4.29
Forcible feeding, 4.38
Foreseeability, 2.12, 2.21–2.23
Freedom of assembly, 4.12
Freedom of association
breach of the peace, 8.09
demonstrations, 8.09
employment, 8.05, 8.08–8.09
prisoners' rights, 4.12
strikes, 8.08
trade unions, 8.08
Freedom of expression
defamation, 1.19
dismissal, 8.15, 8.20
dress and grooming codes, 8.20
employment, 8.02–8.03, 8.05, 8.10
injunctions, 1.19
interim measures, 1.23
judiciary, 1.49
local authorities, 8.03
national courts, 1.19
picketing, 8.09
prisoners' rights, 4.11
procedural impropriety, 9.57
remedies, 1.23

Freedom of thought, conscience and
religion, 4.10

GCHQ, 8.03
Gender reassignment. *See* Transsexuals
Genetic testing, 8.12
Government, standing of, 1.25
Grooming codes, 8.20, 8.21
Group actions, 1.26

Hearsay, 3.40–3.41
Her Majesty's Pleasure, detention at,
4.23
HIV. *See* AIDS/HIV
Home, right to respect for
compulsory acquisition, 7.24
environment, 7.31
interference with, 7.13
meaning of, 7.13
nuisance, 7.28
occupation, 7.13
property, 7.13
public authorities, 7.13
searches, 3.11
surveillance, right to respect for, 3.11
Homicide. *See also* Murder
armed forces, 2.05
police, 2.05
public authorities, 2.05
self-defence, 2.05
Homosexuality. *See* Sexual orientation
Hospital orders, 4.16
House of Lords
appeal, as final court of, 1.33
preliminary rulings, 1.34
Privy Council, 1.33, 1.34
public authority, as, 9.07
Human Fertilisation and Embryology
Authority, 5.02
Human Rights Act 1998, 1.02–1.28
Convention rights, 1.02–1.03, 1.52
indirect effect of, 1.10–1.13
intensity of review in cases on,
1.07–1.09
criminal law, 2.02, 2.03
criminal proceedings, 3.01
damages for breach of Convention
right, 1.27, 7.15
declarations of incompatibility, 1.14–
1.16
devolution, 1.37, 9.73
dismissal, 8.19
division and sale of property, 7.34
divorce, 5.26
effect of, 1.56
effective remedy, right to, 1.45
employment, 8.06, 8.07, 8.27
entry into force, 1.01
environment, 7.29

Human Rights Act 1998—*cont.*
European Court of Human Rights,
　applications to, 1.28
　relevance of jurisprudence of,
　　1.04–1.09
interpretation, 1.10–1.13
irrationality, 9.28
irritancy, 7.32
judicial review, 1.07, 9.04, 9.10, 9.12
judiciary, 1.48
Lord Advocate, 1.42
margin of appreciation, 1.06
national courts, 1.19–1.20
negligence, 6.11
Northern Ireland Act 1998, 1.52
precedent, 1.21
procedural impropriety, 9.53, 9.57
procedure for raising Convention
　points in domestic courts, 1.22–
　1.26
proportionality, 9.35
public authorities, 9.06, 9.12
public law, 9.02, 9.13–9.14, 9.73
public/private distinction, 1.17–1.21
remedies, 9.22
repeal, implied, 1.52
retrospectivity, 1.24
Scottish Parliament, 9.61, 9.65
Scotland Act 1998, 1.01, 1.52
statutory interpretation, 1.10–1.13,
　1.21
Humanity, crimes against, 2.08

Illegality
administrative decision-making,
　9.28–9.30
appeals, 9.28
Convention rights, 9.29–9.30
errors of law, 9.28
Human Rights Act 1998, 9.28
judicial review, 9.05, 9.25, 9.29–9.30
lawful purpose, 9.30
public authorities, 9.29
Immunities
barristers, 6.10
negligence, 6.02–6.03, 6.07–6.10
police, 6.02–6.03, 6.07–6.09
public interest immunity, 8.24
silence, right to, 3.09
Impartiality, 9.40. *See also* **Independent
　and impartial tribunals**
Imprisonment. *See* **Custodial sentences,
　Prisoners' rights**
Incest, 2.28
Incitement, 3.17
**Indecent manner, conducting oneself in a
　shamelessly,** 2.17–2.18
Independent and impartial tribunals
access to courts, 7.12

Independent and impartial tribunal—
　cont.
administrative decision-making, 9.48
appearance of, 9.50
Convention rights, 9.48
criminal trials, 3.26, 3.34
custodial sentences, 4.24
employment tribunals, 8.22, 8.23
'established by law', 9.51
executive, instructions from, 8.50
'impartial', meaning of, 9.50
'independent', meaning of, 9.50
judicial review, 9.48–9.51
judiciary, 1.48–1.49
　categories of, 3.34
juries, 3.34
nationalisation, 7.12
Parole Board, 4.24
planning, 7.17–7.18, 9.50
Privy Council, 1.53
property, 7.12
public law, 9.48–9.51
'tribunals', meaning of, 9.49
Industrial action, 8.03, 8.08, 8.09, 8.21
Information
criminal charges, 3.21–3.24
environment, 7.22, 7.31
planning, 7.22
Inhuman or degrading treatment
children and young persons, 2.24
corporal punishment, 5.19–5.20
criminal law, 2.04, 2.24
custodial sentences, 4.19, 4.25–4.26
investigation of crime, 3.02
negligence, 6.05, 6.11
prisoners' rights, 4.04, 4.34–4.35,
　4.38–4.39, 4.47
searches, 3.16
segregation, 4.35
Injunctions 1.19
Innocence. *See* **Presumption of
　innocence**
Inquiries, 9.03
Institutional writers, 2.16
Insults, 2.13
Interception of communications. *See*
　Surveillance
Interim measures, 1.23
**International Covenant on Civil and
　Political Rights,** 1.46, 9.59
**International Covenant on Economic,
　Social and Cultural Rights,** 1.46
International obligations
public law, 9.04
Scotland Act 1998, 1.46
Scottish Ministers, 1.47
Interpretation. *See* **Statutory
　interpretation**
Interpreters, 3.25

Intestacy, 5.24
Intoxication, 2.26–2.27
Investigation of crime
arrest, 3.03–3.08
detention, 3.03–3.08
inhuman or degrading treatment,
  3.02
life, right to, 3.02
negligence, 6.02–6.03
questioning of suspects, 3.09–3.10
searches, 3.11–3.17
surveillance, 3.11–3.17
torture, 3.02
victims, 3.02
Ireland, 5.08
Irrationality, 1.07, 9.31–9.34, 9.45, 9.54
Irritancy, remedy of, 7.32–7.33

Judges. *See* **Judiciary**
Judicial Committee. *See* **Privy Council**
Judicial review
access to courts, 9.43
access to legal advice, 9.52
administrative decision-making, 7.11,
  9.27
appeals, 9.18, 9.25
breach of statutory duty, 9.05
collateral challenges, 9.18
  timing of, 9.19/1
Community right to buy, 7.45
competency, 9.08–9.09
constitutional, 9.59
Convention rights, 1.23, 9.04–9.12,
  9.16–9.17, 9.19/1, 9.25–9.28
Court of Session, 9.18–9.19, 9.42,
  9.59, 9.74
damages, 9.17, 9.22–9.23
declarations of incompatibility, 1.16
delay, 9.47
devolution, 9.74
EC law, 9.10
emanations of the state, 9.10
employment, 9.09
expenses, 9.24
fair hearings, 9.44
fair trials, 7.11
horizontal effect in, 9.11
Human Rights Act 1998, 1.07, 9.04,
  9.10, 9.12
illegality, 9.05, 9.25, 9.29–9.30
independent and impartial tribunals,
  9.48–9.51
irrationality, 1.07, 9.31–9.34
legal control, grounds of, 9.25–9.28
margin of appreciation, 9.58
national courts, 9.11, 9.59
nobile officium, petitions to, 9.17
oral hearings, 9.46
planning, 1.33, 7.11, 7.17

Judicial review—*cont.*
procedural impropriety, 9.39–9.42,
  9.53–9.58
procedure, 9.17–9.33
proportionality, 1.07–1.09, 9.35–9.37
public authorities, 9.04–9.12, 9.27
public hearings, 9.44, 9.46
public/private distinction, 1.17, 9.08–
  9.10
reasonableness, 9.25
reasons, 9.45
refusal of, 9.19
remedial orders, 1.16
remedies, 9.04, 9.22–9.23, 9.66–9.67,
  9.69
scope of, growing, 9.05
Scottish Parliament, 9.59
standing, 9.20–9.21
time limits, 9.19/1
title to sue, 9.20–9.21
tribunals, 9.05, 9.11, 9.18
ultra vires, 9.18
victims, 1.26, 9.20–9.21
Wednesbury unreasonableness, 1.07,
  9.25, 9.27
Westminster Parliament, 9.07
Judiciary
administrative action, control of,
  9.02, 9.05, 9.13–9.38
categories of, 3.34
constitutional role of, 1.55
Convention rights, 1.43
criminal law, development of, 2.19–
  2.21
devolution, 1.48–1.49
freedom of expression, 1.49
Human Rights Act 1998, 1.49
independent and impartial tribunals,
  1.48–1.49, 3.34
legislators, as, 1.48–1.49
Pinochet decision, 1.49
Privy Council, 1.30, 1.32
public authority, as, 1.49
public law, 9.13–9.38
role of, 1.55
surveillance, 3.13
Juries, 3.34

Land reform, 7.43–7.45
Language, 3.25
Law officers, 1.35
Leases, 7.32–7.33
Legal advice. *See* **Access to legal advice**
Legal aid, 8.26
Legal assistance, right to, 3.39. *See also*
  Access to legal advice
Legal certainty, 9.38
Legal representation. *See also* **Access to
  legal advice, Legal assistance, right to**

Legal representation—*cont.*
  barristers' immunity, 6.10
  children and young persons, 5.18
  correspondence, 4.45
Legality principle
  accessibility, 2.10, 2.11, 2.15–2.16
  criminal law, 2.06–2.23
  European Convention on Human
    Rights, 2.10
  extension of law, unreasonable or
    unforeseeable, 2.19–2.23
  precision, 2.10, 2.12–2.15, 2.17–2.18
  retrospectivity, 2.08–2.09
Legislation. *See* **Declarations of
  incompatibility**
Legitimate expectations, 9.54, 9.63
Liberty, right to
  arrest, 3.04
  deprivation of, 3.05, 3.07–3.08
  detention, 3.04
  mental disabilities, 9.58
  prisoners' rights, 4.06
  procedure prescribed by law, 3.06
  proportionality, 3.07
  rights of persons deprived of liberty,
    3.08
Licences
  civil rights and obligations, 9.36
  proportionality, 9.36
  revocation of, 7.09
Life, right to
  abortion, 5.06–5.07
  conjoined twins, 5.10–5.11
  death penalty, 4.15
  investigation of crime, 3.02
  mothers, 5.07
  negligence, 6.02–6.04, 6.11
  neonates, 5.09
  prisoners' rights, 4.03
Life sentences
  discretionary, 4.06, 4.17–4.19, 4.22,
    4.26
  mandatory, 4.17–4.19, 4.21, 4.23
Limitation periods. *See* **Time limits**
Living instrument, Convention as, 1.04
Local authorities
  environment, 7.29
  freedom of expression, 8.03
  public authorities, 7.29
Locus standi. *See* **Standing**
Lord Advocate
  breach of Convention rights, 1.18, 1.42
  Convention rights and, 1.01
  criminal proceedings, 1.30
  devolution, 1.01, 1.32
  fair trials, 1.32
  Human Rights Act 1998, 1.42
  role of, 1.30–1.31, 9.72
  Scottish Administration, 9.72

Mandatory life sentences, 4.17–4.19,
    4.21, 4.23
Margin of appreciation
  care proceedings, 5.14
  criminal law, 2.03
  devolution, 9.58
  environment, 7.30
  European Court of Human Rights,
    1.06
  family life, right to respect for, 5.14
  Human Rights Act 1998, 1.06
  judicial review, 9.58
  meaning of, 1.06
  national courts, 9.58
  Privy Council, 9.58
  procedural impropriety, 9.55–9.57
  proportionality, 1.08
  transsexuals, 5.37
Marital rape, 2.19–2.21
Marriage, 5.24–5.28. *See also* **Divorce**
  age, 5.24
  alimentary obligations, 5.24–5.25
  breakdown of the family, 5.26–5.28
  cohabitation, 5.24–5.25
  discrimination, 5.24–5.25
  division and sale of property, 7.36
  family life, right to respect for, 5.24
  occupancy rights, 5.24–5.25
  prisoners' rights, 4.13
  private life, right to respect for, 5.24
  promotion of, 5.25
  proportionality, 5.24
  tenancies, 5.24–5.25
  transsexuals, 5.36–5.38
Matrimonial homes, 5.26, 7.36
Media. *See* **Press**
Medical negligence, 6.03, 6.05
Medical treatment
  conjoined twins, 5.09–5.11
  forcible, 4.37
  neonates, 5.09–5.11
  prisoners' rights, 4.36–4.37
Mental disabilities
  detention, 1.55–1.56, 4.06, 4.16–4.17
  hospital orders, 4.16
  liberty, right to, 9.58
  prisoners' rights, 4.06
Military service. *See* **Armed forces**
Multi-party organisations, 1.26
Murder
  custodial sentences, 4.19–4.21
  intoxication, 2.26

National courts
  Convention rights, acting in
    compatible manner with, 1.19
  declarations of incompatibility, 1.14–
    1.16
  defamation, 1.19

National courts—*cont.*
  direct effect,
    horizontal, 1.20
    vertical, 1.20
  division and sale of property, 7.34
  effective remedy, right to, 1.19
  European Court of Human Rights
    jurisprudence, relevance of,
    1.04–1.09,
  freedom of expression, interference
    with, 1.19
  Human Rights Act 1998, 1.19–1.20
  indirect effect,
    horizontal, 1.20
  judicial review, 9.11, 9.59
  margin of appreciation, 9.58
  precedent, 1.21
  public authorities, as, 1.19–1.21,
    1.44, 6.01, 8.22
  remedies, 1.47
  standing, 1.25
Nationalisation, 7.09, 7.12
Natural justice
  compulsory acquisition, 7.26
  procedural impropriety, 9.39, 9.40,
    9.42
Negligence
  access to courts, 6.07
  aircraft accidents, 6.04
  barristers, 6.10
  children, 6.05
  Convention rights, 6.01
  damages, 6.01
  dangerous behaviour, deterring,
    6.01–6.03, 6.11
  deterrence, 6.01
  emergency services, 6.03
  environment, 6.06
  European Convention on Human
    Rights, 6.01–6.12
  fair trials, 6.07
  family life, right to respect for, 6.06
  gross, 6.09
  Human Rights Act 1998, 6.11
  immunity, 6.02–6.03, 6.07–6.10
  inhuman or degrading treatment,
    6.05, 6.11
  investigation of crime, 6.02–6.03
  life, right to, 6.02–6.04, 6.11
  medical, 6.03, 6.05
  omissions, 6.04, 6.11
  planning permission, 6.06
  police immunity, 6.02–6.03, 6.07–6.09
  proximity, 6.07–6.10
  public authorities, 6.01–6.06, 6.08–
    6.12
  public policy, 6.09
  remedies, 6.11
  standard of care, 6.03

Neonates, 5.09–5.11
New Zealand, 9.22
Nobile officium, **petitions to,** 9.17
Noise, 7.10, 7.30
Northern Ireland. *See also* **Northern
    Ireland Act 1998**
  Convention rights, 1.01
    breach of, 1.41
  Human Rights Act 1998, implied
    repeal of, 1.52
  Northern Ireland Act 1998, 1.52
  public authority, as, 1.18
  subordinate legislation, acts of, 1.50
Nuclear tests, 1.28
Nuisance
  civil rights and obligations, 7.10
  damages, 7.28
  home, right to respect for, 7.28
  noise, 7.10
  property, interference with
    enjoyment of, 7.28

Occupancy rights, 5.24–5.25
Ombudsman, 9.03
Omissions, 1.38, 6.04, 6.11
Oral hearings, 9.46
Ouster clauses, 9.53, 9.61

Parenthood, 5.29–5.31, 5.33
Parliament. *See also* **Scottish
    Parliament, Westminster
    Parliament**
  declarations of incompatibility, 1.14
  limits on, 1.54
  privilege, 9.07, 9.61
  sovereignty, 1.14, 1.54
Parole Board, 4.24
Peaceful enjoyment of possessions, 7.03–
    7.07
  Community right to buy, 7.45
  compensation, 7.07, 7.33
  destruction of property, 7.38–7.39
  European Court of Human Rights,
    7.06
  expropriation, 7.05
  feudal tenure, abolition of, 7.42
  interference with, 7.06
  irritancy, 7.33
  leases, 7.33
  'possessions', meaning of, 7.04
  proportionality, 7.06
  public and general interest, 7.06
  three rules, 7.05
Pensions, 5.27
Picketing, 8.09, 8.21
***Pinochet* decision,** 1.49
Planning
  access to courts, 9.43
  appeals, 7.17

Planning—*cont.*
applications, determining, 7.21
civil rights and obligations, 7.20
compulsory acquisition, 7.24
Convention rights, 7.18, 7.21
enforcement, 7.22
notices, 7.17
environment, 7.22
fair trials, 7.11
independent and impartial tribunals,
7.17–7.18, 9.50
information, 7.22
judicial review, 1.33, 7.11, 7.17
licence to occupy houses, 7.18
local plans, 7.20
negligence, 6.06
proportionality, 7.17, 7.18, 7.22
public interest, 7.22
religion, 7.17
Scotland Act 1998, 7.18
Scots law on, 7.16–7.22
Scottish Executive, 1.42
Scottish Parliament, 1.42
structure plans and local plans, 7.20
UK cases, 7.17–7.18
Police
access to courts, 6.07
criminal law, 2.05
homicide, 2.05
incitement, 3.17
interviews, 3.09–3.10
negligence, 6.02–6.03, 6.07–6.09
public authorities, 2.05
self-defence, 2.05
undercover agents, 3.17
use of force, 2.05
Possessions, 5.27. *See also* **Peaceful
enjoyment of possessions**
Precedent, 1.21
Precision principle
breach of the peace, 2.13, 2.17–2.18
criminal law, 2.10, 2.12–2.15, 2.17–
2.18
European Convention on Human
Rights, 2.10, 2.18
indecent manner, conducting oneself
in a shamelessly, 2.17–2.18
legality, 2.10, 2.12–2.15, 2.17–2.18
presumption against, 2.17
Scots law, in, 2.15, 2.17–2.18
Preliminary rulings
courts which may refer, 1.34
House of Lords, 1.34
Privy Council, 1.34, 1.35
Press, 3.28, 3.34
Presumption of innocence
burden of proof, 2.26
confiscation orders, 4.31
criminal trials, 3.35

Presumption of innocence—*cont.*
fair trials, 3.35
financial measures, legality of, 4.07
intoxication, 2.26
questioning of suspects, 3.09
silence, right to, 3.09
Prisoners' rights, 4.01–4.13, 4.33–4.46.
See also **Detention**
children, separation from, 4.42
conditions, 4.17, 4.34–4.39
correspondence, interference with,
4.43–4.46
death row, 4.34
deaths in custody, 4.03
discretionary life sentences, 4.06
fair trials, 4.07
family life, right to respect for, 4.09,
4.34, 4.40–4.42
family members, access to, 4.40–4.42
financial measures, imposition of,
4.07, 4.08
forced labour, 4.05, 4.29
forcible feeding, 4.38
freedom of assembly, 4.12
freedom of association, 4.12
freedom of expression, 4.11
inhuman or degrading treatment,
4.04, 4.34, 4.35, 4.38–4.39, 4.47
liberty, right to, 4.06
life, right to, 4.03
location of prisons, 4.34, 4.40–4-42
marry, right to, 4.13
medical treatment, 4.36–4.37
forcible, 4.37
mental disabilities, 4.06
private life, right to respect for, 4.09
religion, 4.10
remission, losing, 4.07
retrospectivity, 4.08
sanitary facilities, 4.34
security, right to, 4.06
segregation, 4.35
seizure of assets, 4.08
sentencing, 4.01
slavery, 4.05
solitary confinement, 4.35
thought, conscience and religion,
freedom of, 4.10
torture, 4.04
vagrants, 4.06
vulnerable prisoners, 4.39
Private life, right to respect for
abortion, 5.08
arrest, 3.07
criminal law, 2.04
correspondence, 4.44
dismissal, 8.20
dress and grooming codes, 8.20
employment, 8.01, 8.10–8.12

Private life, right to respect for—*cont.*
environment, 7.31
interference with, 3.11–3.15
  necessary, 3.15
investigation of crime, 3.02
marriage, 5.24
prisoners' rights, 4.09
property, 7.13
public authorities, 8.10
searches, 3.11–3.12, 3.14–3.15
sexual abuse, 2.04
sexual orientation, 2.28
surveillance, 3.11–3.15
Privilege against self-incrimination. *See*
  Self-incrimination
Privy Council
appeals, 1.32, 1.33
appointment, 1.53
binding nature of decisions of, 1.33
composition, 1.30, 1.32
constitutional court, as, 1.30–1.32
devolution issues, 1.30–1.32, 1.34,
  1.51
  judges who may sit on, 1.30
fair trials, 1.30–1.31
House of Lords, 1.33, 1.34
independent and impartial tribunal,
  1.53
judiciary, 1.30, 1.32
margin of appreciation, 9.58
preliminary references to, 1.34, 1.35
Scotland Act 1998, 1.30–1.32
Scottish and non-Scottish judges,
  1.32
Scottish Parliament, 9.62
uniformity of approach, 1.53
Procedural impropriety
administrative decision-making, 9.40,
  9.42
appeals, 9.40
bias, 9.40
Canada, 9.57
civil rights and obligations, 9.41
Convention rights, 9.53–9.57
fair hearings, 9.39, 9.53, 9.54
freedom of expression, 9.57
hearing the other side, right of, 9.40
Human Rights Act 1998, 9.53, 9.57
irrationality, 9.54
judicial review, 9.39–9.42, 9.53–9.58
legitimate expectations, 9.54
margin of appreciation, 9.55–9.57
natural justice, 9.39, 9.40, 9.42
ouster clauses, 9.53
proportionality, 9.56
public authorities, 9.54, 9.57
public law, 9.39–9.42, 9.52–9.58
public/private law distinction, 9.41
Scotland Act 1998, 9.53

Procedural impropriety—*cont.*
scrutiny, intensity of, 9.55–9.57
subordinate legislation, 9.53
substantive fairness, 9.54
tribunals, 9.42
Wednesbury unreasonableness, 9.54
Procedure. *See also* **Criminal**
  proceedings, Time limits
breach of Convention rights, 1.22–
  1.26
Convention rights, defensive use of,
  1.22
devolution, 1.50–1.53
exclusivity of, 1.50–1.53
Human Rights Act 1998, 1.22–1.26
national courts, raising Convention
  points in, 1.22–1.26
prospective overruling, 1.24
public authorities, 1.22–1.23
public law, 9.13–9.14
standing, 1.25–1.26
victims, 1.25–1.26
Professional conduct hearings, 8.07, 9.43
Property, 7.01–7.45
administrative bodies, review of
  decisions by, 7.11
building permits, 7.10
civil rights and obligations, 7.09–7.12
compensation, 7.15
compulsory acquisition, 7.23–7.26
destruction of, 7.37–7.39
development, 7.09
discrimination, 7.14
division and sale, 7.34–7.36
divorce, 5.26–5.28
environment, 7.29–7.31
European Convention on Human
  Rights, 7.01–7.45
fair trials, 7.08–7.12
family life, right to respect for, 7.13
feudal tenure, abolition of, 7.40–7.42
home, right to respect for, 7.13
Human Rights Act 1998, 7.01
independent and impartial tribunals,
  7.12
irritancy, remedy of, 7.32–7.33
land reform, 7.43–7.45
nuisance, 7.27
peaceful enjoyment of possessions,
  7.03–7.07
planning, 7.16–7.22
private life, right to respect for, 7.13
right to buy, 7.434-7.45
Proportionality
administrative action, judicial
  control of, 9.34–9.37
appeals, 9.36
arrest, 3.07
care proceedings, 5.14

Proportionality—*cont.*
compulsory acquisition, 7.24
compulsory powers, 3.09
Convention rights, 9.35–9.36
custodial sentences, 4.19, 4.26
EC law, 9.35
European Court of Human Rights, 9.35
family life, right to respect for, 5.14
general test for, 9.37
Human Rights Act 1998, 9.35
irrationality, 1.07, 9.32, 9.33, 9.34
irritancy, 7.33
judicial review, 1.07–1.09, 9.35–9.37
liberty, deprivation of, 3.07
licensing, 9.36
margin of appreciation, 1.08
marriage, 5.24
peaceful enjoyment of possessions, 7.06
planning, 7.17, 7.18, 7.22
procedural impropriety, 9.56
public law, 9.34–9.37
questioning of suspects, 3.09–3.10
Scotland Act 1998, 9.35
searches, 3.15
self-incrimination, 1.09, 1.32
strict liability, 2.26
Wednesbury unreasonableness, 9.35, 9.36
Proselytism, 2.14–2.15
Public authorities
armed forces, 2.05
breach, justified, 1.18
Convention rights, 1.50, 9.72
correspondence, 4.44
courts, as, 1.19–1.21, 1.44, 6.01, 8.22
criminal law, 2.02, 2.04, 2.05
definition, 1.17, 1.50, 9.08, 9.12
deportation, 4.32
destruction of property, 7.36
disciplinary hearings, 8.19
discretion, 6.08
dismissal, 8.19, 8.20
dress and grooming codes, 8.20
emanations of the state, 9.10
employment, 8.01–8.02, 8.07, 8.10, 8.12, 8.22
environment, 7.29–7.30
failure to act, 1.45
fair trials, 8.07
functions of a public nature, 1.17
home, right to respect for, 7.13
homicide, 2.05
House of Lords, 9.07
Human Rights Act 1998, 9.06, 9.12
illegality, 9.29
irritancy, 7.32
judicial review, 9.04–9.12, 9.27

Public authorities—*cont.*
judiciary, 1.49
local authorities, as, 7.29
negligence, 6.01–6.06, 6.08–6.12
Northern Ireland Assembly, 1.18
ombudsmen, 9.03
police, 2.05
procedural impropriety, 9.54, 9.57
procedure for claims against, 1.22–1.23
public/private distinction, 1.17, 9.08–9.10
Scottish Parliament and Executive, 1.18, 9.61, 9.73
self-defence, 2.02
standard of care, 6.03
tribunals, 1.19, 8.22
Welsh Assembly, 1.18
Westminster Parliament, as, 9.07
Public hearings
children and young persons, 3.29
criminal trials, 3.29
employment tribunals, 8.24
judicial review, 9.44, 9.46
oral hearings, 9.46
public law, 9.44–9.47
Public interest immunity, 8.24
Public law, 9.01–9.74. *See also* **Judicial review**
access to courts, 9.43
access to legal advice, 9.52
administrative action, judicial control of, 9.02, 9.13–9.38
administrative decision-making, 9.03, 9.28–9.30, 9.38
administrative law, 9.01–9.02
constitutional law, 9.01
Convention rights, 9.01–9.03, 9.13–9.38, 9.59–9.74
damages, 9.66
devolution, 9.74
fair hearings, 9.44
Human Rights Act 1998, 9.02, 9.13–9.14, 9.73
independent and impartial tribunals, 9.48–9.51
inquiries, 9.03
international obligations, compatibility with, 9.14
judicial control, 9.13–9.38
legal certainty, 9.38
ombudsmen, 9.03
procedural impropriety, 9.39–9.42, 9.52–9.58
procedure, 9.13–9.14
proportionality, 9.34–9.37
public hearings, 9.44–9.47
reasons for decisions, 9.45
remedies, 9.13–9.16, 9.66–9.71

Public law—*cont.*
Scotland Act 1998, 9.02, 9.13, 9.59–9.73
Scottish Administration, 9.72
Scottish Parliament, 9.60–9.65
statutory interpretation, 9.14
subordinate legislation, unlawfulness of, 9.16
tribunals, 9.03, 9.15–9.16
unlawful acts, 9.16
Public/private distinction
Human Rights Act 1998, 1.17–1.21
judicial review, 1.17, 9.08–9.10
procedural impropriety, 9.41
public authorities, 1.17–1.18

Questioning of suspects, 3.09–3.10

Rape, 1.43, 2.19–2.21
Reading in, 9.71
Reasonableness. *See* **Wednesbury unreasonableness**
Reasons
administrative decision-making, 9.45
arrest, 3.08
detention, 3.08
dismissal, 8.17
fair trials, 7.12, 9.45
irrationality, 9.45
judicial review, 9.45
public law, 9.45
Religion
blasphemy, 2.13–2.14
churches, 1.25
education, 5.22
employment, 8.01
freedom of thought, conscience and religion, 4.10
planning, 7.17
prisoners' rights, 4.10
proselytism, 2.14–2.15
standing, 1.25
Remand, 3.19
Remedies
breach of Convention rights, 1.45–1.47
Convention rights, 9.66, 9.68–9.69
declarations of incompatibility, 1.16
division and sale, 7.34–7.36
EC law, 9.22, 9.68
effective, right to, 1.03, 1.19, 1.45
exhaustion of local, 1.28
freedom of expression, 1.23
Human Rights Act 1998, 9.22
interim remedies, 1.23
irritancy, 7.32–7.33
judicial review, 9.04, 9.22–9.23, 9.66–9.67, 9.69
national courts, 1.47

Remedies—*cont.*
negligence, 6.11
public law, 9.13–9.16, 9.22, 9.66–9.71
reading in, 9.71
retroactivity, 9.68–9.69
Scotland Act 1998, 1.45, 9.66–9.71
Scottish Parliament, 1.44, 9.67
severance, 9.70
state liability, 9.22
tribunals, 9.22
ultra vires, 9.67, 9.68–9.71
Westminster Parliament, 1.44
Remission, 4.07
Representative actions, 1.26
Reproduce, right to, 5.02
Retrospectivity
Australia, 9.68
Canada, 9.68
Convention rights, 1.44
criminal law, 2.08–2.09
criminal proceedings, 1.36
declarations of incompatibility, 1.51
declaratory power of the High Court, 2.09
derogation, 2.08
devolution, 1.36
European Convention on Human Rights, 2.08
fair trials, 1.36
Human Rights Act 1998, 1.24
humanity, crimes against, 2.08
legality, 2.08–2.09
prisoners' rights, 4.08
remedies, 9.68–9.69
United States, 9.68
war crimes, 2.08
Right to buy, 7.43–7.45
Right to liberty. *See* **Liberty, right to**
Right to life. *See* **Life, right to**
Right to respect for correspondence. *See* **Correspondence, right to respect for**
Right to respect for family life. *See* **Family life, right to respect for**
Right to respect for the home. *See* **Home, right to respect for**
Right to respect for private life. *See* **Private life, right to respect for**
Right to security, 4.06
Right to silence, 3.09–3.10

Same sex relationships, 5.01, 5.34–5.35, 9.71
Scotland Act 1998, 1.29–1.36
Convention rights, 1.42, 1.46, 1.53, 9.59–9.74
criminal proceedings, 3.01
damages, 9.74
devolution, 1.29–1.36, 1.38, 1.52
effect of, 1.56

Scotland Act 1998—*cont.*
European Convention on Human
Rights, 1.01
feudal tenure, abolition of, 7.40
Human Rights Act 1998, 1.01
implied repeal of, 1.52
international obligations, 1.46
planning, 7.18
procedural impropriety, 9.53
proportionality, 9.35
public law, 9.02, 9.13, 9.59–9.73
remedies, 1.45, 9.66–9.71
Scottish Parliament, 9.63, 9.65
statutory interpretation, 1.16, 9.73
time limits, 9.74
victims, 9.74
Scottish Administration, 9.72
**Scottish Environmental Protection
Agency**, 7.29
Scottish Executive
Convention rights, 1.43, 1.46, 9.59
breach of, 1.42
devolution, 1.38
failure to act, 1.45
Parole Board, 4.24
planning, 1.42
public authority, as, 1.18, 9.73
UN Covenant on Civil and Political
Rights, 9.59
Scottish Ministers
Convention rights, 9.72
devolved competence, 9.72
First Minster, 9.72
functions, date of starting exercise of,
1.01
international obligations, complying
with, 1.47
Scottish Administration, 9.72
Scottish Parliament
Acts of Parliament, 9.64–9.65, 9.68
Bills, 9.62
failure to introduce, 9.63
committee proceedings, 9.61
competency of, 7.40
Convention rights, 1.42–1.43, 9.59–
9.65
breach of, 1.42
defamation, 9.61
devolution issues, 1.29, 9.63
European Social Charter, 1.46
exclusion clauses, 9.61
failure to act, 1.45, 9.63
Human Rights Act 1998, 9.61, 9.65
International Covenant on Civil and
Political Rights, 1.46
International Covenant on
Economic, Social and Cultural
Rights, 1.46
judicial review, 9.59

Scottish Parliament—*cont.*
legislative competence of, 1.43, 9.60,
9.62
legitimate expectations, 9.63
ouster clauses, 9.61
planning, 1.42
privilege, 9.61
Privy Council, 9.62
proceedings, in, 9.61
public authority, as, 1.18, 9.61, 9.73
public law, 9.60–9.65
remedies, 9.67
incompatibility, for, 1.44
Scotland Act 1998, 9.60, 9.63, 9.65
scrutiny, 9.62
standing orders, 9.61
statutory interpretation, 9.64–9.65
subordinate legislation, acts of, 1.50
UN Covenant on Civil and Political
Rights, 9.59
Searches
correspondence, right to respect for,
3.11
fair hearings, 3.17
family life, right to respect for, 3.11
home, right to respect for, 3.11
inhuman or degrading treatment,
3.16
investigation of crimes, 3.11–3.17
private life, right to respect for, 3.11–
3.12, 3.14–3.15
proportionality, 3.15
warrants, 3.13
Security checks, 8.12
Security, right to, 4.06
Segregation, 4.35
Seizure, 4.08, 4.31, 7.42
Self-defence, 2.02, 2.05
Self-incrimination
European Court of Human Rights,
1.04, 1.05
fair trials, 1.32
proportionality, 1.09, 1.32
Sentencing, 4.14–4.32. *See also*
Custodial sentences
AIDS/HIV, 4.28
ancillary orders, 4.30–4.32
community service, 4.29
confiscation orders, 4.30–4.31
death penalty, 4.15
deportation, 4.30, 4.32
discretionary life sentences, 4.06
discrimination, 4.27–4.28
financial measures, legality of, 4.08
forced labour, 4.29
non-custodial, 4.29
prisoners' rights, 4.01
seizure, 4.31
Severance, 9.70

Sex discrimination
alimentary obligations, 5.25
dress and grooming codes, 8.20, 8.21
time limits, 1.22
transsexuals, 1.22, 5.39
unmarried fathers, 5.29–5.30
Sexual abuse, 2.04
Sexual orientation
adoption, 5.33
age of consent, 2.28
armed forces, 1.13, 5.34, 8.01, 8.05,
8.12, 9.31
Canada, 1.47
criminal law, 2.28
discrimination, 1.13, 1.47, 2.03, 2.28
employment, 8.01, 8.05, 8.12
family life, right to respect for, 5.01,
5.32–5.35
irrationality, 9.31
parent rights, 5.33
private life, right to respect for, 2.28
same sex relationships, 5.01, 5.34–
5.35, 9.71
South Africa, 2.03
statutory interpretation, 1.13
tenancies, 5.34
victims, 1.26
Siamese twins, 5.09–5.11
Silence, right to
compulsory powers, 3.10
immunities, 3.09
presumption of innocence, 3.09
questioning of suspects, 3.09–3.10
Slavery, 4.03
Solicitor General for Scotland, 1.01,
9.72
Solitary confinement, 4.35
South Africa, 2.03, 9.71
Sovereignty. *See* **Parliamentary
sovereignty**
Standing
churches, 1.25
corporate bodies, 1.25
government bodies, 1.25
judicial review, 9.20–9.21
legal persons, 1.25
national courts, 1.25
procedure, 1.25–1.26
religious organisations, 1.25
representative actions, 1.26
unincorporated bodies, 1.25
victims, 1.25–1.26
Standing orders, 9.61
Statutory interpretation
ambiguity, 1.11–1.12
armed forces, 1.13
canons of, 1.12
compulsory acquisition, 7.23
Convention rights, 1.10–1.13, 1.31

Statutory interpretation—*cont.*
declarations of incompatibility, 1.15
direct effect, 1.13
discrimination, 1.13
Human Rights Act 1998, 1.10–1.13,
1.21
'obvious' construction, 1.12
precedent, 1.21
presumptions, 1.10
public law, 9.16
purposive, 1.10–1.11
Scotland Act 1998, 1.16, 9.73
Scottish Parliament, 9.64–9.65
sexual orientation, 1.13
sympathetic, 1.13
ultra vires, 1.16
Westminster Parliament, 1.44
Strasbourg court. *See* **European Court
of Human Rights**
Strict liability, 2.26
Strikes, 8.03, 8.08
Subordinate legislation, 1.16, 9.53, 9.65,
9.69–9.70, 9.72
Surrogacy, 5.03–5.04
Surveillance
correspondence, right to respect for,
3.11
directed, 3.13
employment, 8.01, 8.10
tribunals, 8.13
evidence, 3.11
fair hearings, 3.17
family life, right to respect for, 3.11
home, right to respect for, 3.11
intrusive, 3.13
investigation of crimes, 3.11–3.17
judiciary, 3.13
private life, right to respect for, 3.11–
3.15
serious crimes, 3.13
Surveillance Commissioners, 3.13

Telephone tapping. *See* **Surveillance**
Tenancies, 5.24–5.25, 5.34, 7.32–7.33
Textbooks, 2.16
Theft
foreseeability, 2.23
intention permanently to provide,
2.23
mens rea, 2.22–2.23
Thought, freedom of, 4.10
Time limits
bail, 3.19
breach of Convention rights, 1.51
criminal trials, 3.30–3.33
damages, 1.27
detention, 3.06
European Convention on Human
Rights, 1.28

Time limits—*cont.*
  extension of, 1.22
  judicial review, 9.19/1
  public authorities, claims against,
    1.22
  Scotland Act 1998, 9.74
  sex discrimination, 1.22
Title to sue. *See* **Standing**
Torture, 3.02, 4.04
Trade unions, 8.03, 8.08
Transsexuals
  assisted reproduction, 5.04
  birth certificates, 5.36–5.38
  discrimination, 8.20
  dress codes, 8.20
  family life, right to respect for, 5.04,
    5.36–5.38
  margin of appreciation, 5.37
  marriage, 5.36–5.38
  sex discrimination, 1.22, 5.39
  standing, 1.26
Trials. *See* **Criminal trials**
Tribunals. *See also* **Independent and
    impartial tribunals**
  access to courts, 9.43
  appeals, 9.18
  definition, 9.49
  employment, 8.13, 8.22–8.26
  judicial review, 9.05, 9.11, 9.18
  procedural impropriety, 9.42
  public authorities, as, 1.19, 8.22
  public law, 9.03, 9.15–9.16
  remedies, 9.22

Ultra vires
  remedies, 9.67, 9.68–9.71
  Scotland Act 1998, 1.16
  severance, 9.70
  subordinate legislation, 1.16
**UN Convention on the Rights of the
    Child**, 2.24, 5.17, 5.20
**UN Covenant on Civil and Political
    Rights**, 1.46, 9.59
Unborn children, 5.05–5.09
Undercover agents, 3.17
Unfair dismissal, 8.12, 8.14, 8.17–8.18,
    8.22
Unincorporated bodies, 1.25
United States, 9.68
Unmarried fathers, 5.29–5.30
Unreasonableness. *See* **Wednesbury
    unreasonableness**

Use of force
  armed forces, 2.05
  criminal law, 2.05
  police, 2.05

Vagrants, detention of, 4.06
Victims
  breach of Convention rights, 1.39
  devolution, 1.39
  European Convention on Human
    Rights, 1.25, 1.39
  fair trials, 3.27
  investigation of crime, 3.02
  judicial review, 1.26, 9.20–9.21
  meaning, 1.26
  procedure, 1.25–1.26
  public interest, 9.21
  Scotland Act 1998, 9.74
  sexual orientation, 1.26
  standing, 1.25–1.26
  test, 9.21
  transsexuals, 1.26

War
  crimes, 2.08
  feudal tenure, abolition of, 7.40
    seizure, 7.42
Warrants, 3.13
***Wednesbury* unreasonableness**
  irrationality, 9.32–9.33
  judicial review, 1.07, 9.25, 9.27
  procedural impropriety, 9.54
  proportionality, 9.35, 9.36
Welsh Assembly
  Convention rights, 1.01
    breach of, 1.41
  devolution, 1.01
  public authority, as, 1.18
  subordinate legislation, acts of, 1.50
Westminster Parliament
  competence of, 1.44
  devolution, 1.52
  parliamentary privilege, 9.07
  public authority, as, 9.07
  remedies for incompatibility, 1.44
  statutory interpretation, 1.44
Witnesses, 3.27
Wrongful dismissal, 8.14, 8.15

Young persons. *See* **Children and young
    persons**